216

Istanbul City Centre

BEYOĞLU

Bosphorus

THE BAZAAR QUARTER

SERAGLIO POINT

SULTANAHMET

Sea of Marmara

The Black Sea
Pages 264–279

Sinop

0 kilometres 100

0 miles 50

Hopa

Samsun

Ordu

Trabzon

Amasya

THE BLACK SEA

Gümüşhane

Erzurum

Erzincan

Sivas

...CIA &
...ATOLIA

EASTERN ANATOLIA

Kayseri

Elazığ

Van

Malatya

Diyarbakır

Adana

Gaziantep

Antakya

Mediterranean Turkey
Pages 208–239

Cappadocia and Central Anatolia
Pages 280–303

Eastern Anatolia
Pages 304–323

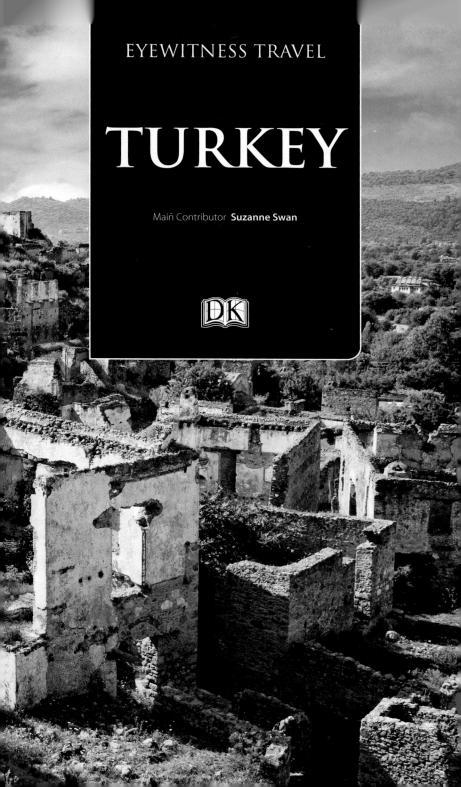

EYEWITNESS TRAVEL

TURKEY

Main Contributor **Suzanne Swan**

DK

LONDON, NEW YORK,
MELBOURNE, MUNICH AND DELHI
www.dk.com

Produced by
Struik New Holland Publishing (Pty) Ltd, Cape Town, South Africa

Managing Editors Alfred Lemaitre, Laura Milton
Managing Art Editor Steven Felmore
Editors Amichai Kapilevich, Anna Tanneberger
Editorial Assistant Christie Meyer
Designer Peter Bosman
Map Co-ordinator John Loubser
Cartographer Carl Germishuys
Picture Researchers Sandra Adomeit, Karla Kik
DTP Check Damian Gibbs
Production Manager Myrna Collins

Main Contributor
Suzanne Swan

Other Contributors
Rosie Ayliffe, Rose Baring, Barnaby Rogerson, Canan Silay, Dominic Whiting

Photographers
Kate Clow, Terry Richardson, Anthony Souter, Dominic Whiting,
Linda Whitwam, Francesca Yorke

Illustrators
Richard Bonson, Stephen Conlin, Gary Cross, Bruno De Robillard,
Richard Draper, Steven Felmore, Paul Guest, Ian Lusted, Maltings Partnership,
Chris Orr & Associates, David Pulvermacher, Paul Weston, John Woodcock

Printed and Bound In Malaysia By Vivar Printing Sdn. Bhd.

First published inthe UK in 2003
By Dorling Kindersley Limited
80 Strand, London, WC2R 0RL

14 15 16 17 10 9 8 7 6 5 4 3 2 1

Reprinted with Revisions 2006, 2008, 2010, 2012, 2014

Copyright 2003, 2014 © Dorling Kindersley Limited, London
A Penguin Random House Company

MIX
Paper from
responsible sources
FSC
www.fsc.org FSC™ C018179

Contents

Commagene stone head on Mount Nemrut
(Nemrut Daği)

Front cover main image: View of the New Mosque on the banks of the Golden Horn, Istanbul

◀ Kayaköy, an abandoned Greek village in Mediterranean Turkey that is now a UNESCO World Heritage site

The village of Üçağız, on the Mediterranean coast

Istanbul Area by Area

Turkey Region by Region

Vendor selling *boza*, a drink made from lightly fermented grain

Emblems of Istanbul, the Haghia Sophia and Blue Mosque

Travellers' Needs

Survival Guide

Sumela Monastery *(see p276)*

HOW TO USE THIS GUIDE

This guide helps you to get the most from your stay in Turkey. It provides expert recommendations and detailed practical advice. *Introducing Turkey* locates the country geographically, and sets it in context. *Istanbul Area by Area* and *Turkey Region by Region* are the main sightseeing sections, giving information on major sights, with photographs, maps and illustrations. Suggestions for restaurants, hotels, entertainment and shopping are found in *Travellers' Needs*, while the *Survival Guide* contains useful advice on everything from changing money to travelling by bus.

Istanbul Area by Area

Turkey's largest city has been divided into four sightseeing areas. Each has its own chapter opening with a list of the sights that are described. The *Further Afield* section covers many peripheral places of interest. All sights are numbered and plotted on an *Area Map*. Information on the sights is easy to locate as it follows the numerical order used on the map.

Sights at a Glance lists the chapter's sights by category, such as Museums and Galleries, Mosques, Parks and Gardens and Historic Buildings.

All pages relating to Istanbul have the same colour thumb tabs.

A locator map shows clearly where the area is in relation to other areas of the city.

1 Area Map For easy reference, sights are numbered and located on a map. City centre sights are also marked on the Istanbul Street Finder maps (*see pp139–44*).

Stars indicate the sights that no visitor should miss.

2 Street-by-Street Map This gives a bird's-eye view of the key areas in each sightseeing area.

Story boxes explore specific subjects in detail.

A suggested route for a walk covers the more interesting streets in the area.

3 Feature Each feature looks in detail at an important attraction, tracing its history or cultural context, and providing detailed information on what can be seen today.

1 Introduction
A general account
of the landscape,
history and character
of each region is
given here, explaining
both how the area
has developed over
the centuries and
what attractions
it has to offer
visitors today.

Turkey Region by Region

Apart from Istanbul, the rest of
the country is divided into seven
regions, each with a separate
chapter. The most interesting
towns and sights to visit are
numbered on a *Regional Map* at
the beginning of each chapter.

Each area of Turkey can be easily
identified by its colour coding,
shown on the inside front cover.

2 Regional Map This shows the
main road network and gives an
illustrated overview of the
whole region. All interesting places to
visit are numbered and there are
also useful tips on getting to,
and around, the region.

A town map shows the
locations of all the sights
described in the text.

3 Detailed information All
the important towns and
other places to visit are
described individually. They
are listed in order, following
the numbering on the
Regional Map. Within each
entry, there is further
detailed information on
important buildings and
other sights.

For all the top sights,
a Visitors' Checklist provides
the practical information you
will need to plan your visit.

4 Turkey's Top Sights The
historic buildings are dissected
to reveal their interiors; important
archaeological sites have maps
showing key sights and facilities.
The most interesting towns or
city centres have maps, with
sights picked out and described.

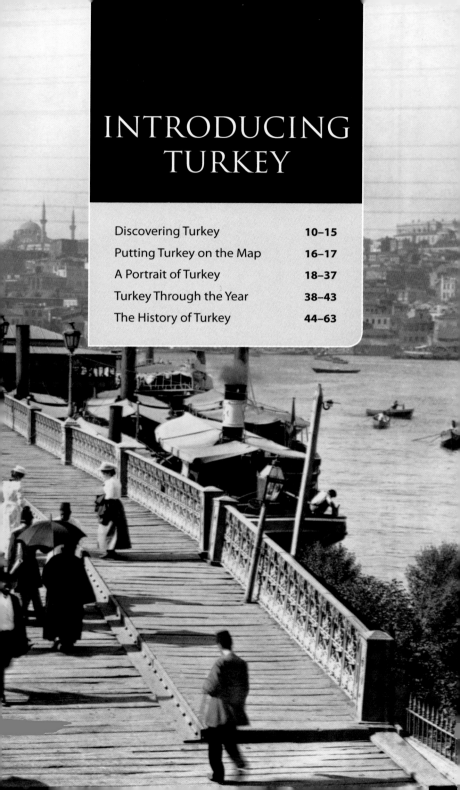

INTRODUCING
TURKEY

DISCOVERING TURKEY

Turkey is vast, the size of France and Germany put together, so attempting to visit the entire country in one trip would be a mammoth (though hugely rewarding) task. Consequently, the following tours concentrate on the most-visited western half of this beguiling land. To start with there is a two-day tour of one of the world's truly great cities, continent-straddling Istanbul, with its rich Byzantine

Christian and Muslim Turkish history. Next up are three week-long itineraries, which can be connected to form a three-week trip, taking visitors from the ancient Greek and Roman ruins of the Aegean to the sun-blessed beaches of the Mediterranean and, finally, inland across the rolling steppes of the Anatolian plateau to the geological wonderland of Cappadocia.

A Week on the Aegean Coast

- At legendary **Troy** and the World War I conflict zone of **Gallipoli** bloody battles were fought in beautiful locations.

- The pretty traditional village of **Behram Kale** and hill-top site of ancient **Assos** make for a memorable outing.

- Ascend the craggy acropolis of ancient **Bergama** to see its stone theatre and temples.

- The extensive ruins of ancient **Ephesus** are a truly world-class ancient site.

- Discover the captivating ancient sites of **Priene, Didyma** and **Miletus**.

- Tranquil **Lake Bafa** has plenty of bird life and remote Byzantine settlements.

- Bohemian **Bodrum** has buzzing nightlife, a Crusader castle and lots of beaches.

Key

— Turquoise coast
— Aegean coast
— Mediterranean and Anatolian Turkey

Gallipoli Peninsula
Çanakkale
Troy
Balıkesir
Behram Kale
Bergama and Pergamum
Usak
TURKEY
Dinar
Hierapolis
Selçuk
Kuşadası — Ephesus
Priene
Denizli
Miletus — Lake Bafa
Didyma
Euromos
Bodrum
Caunos — Lake Koyceğiz
Dalyan
Fethiye — Tlos
Kayaköy — Saklıkent Gorge — Olympos
Patara — Phaselis
Kalkan — Kaş — Finike
Üçağız and Simena

A Week on the Turquoise Coast

- Explore the turtle-nesting beach at **Iztuzu** from charming **Dalyan**.

- The haunting remains of the Greek ghost village of **Kayaköy** stand sentinel near **Fethiye**.

- One of the longest beaches in the Mediterranean, sandy **Patara**, is delightfully uncrowded.

- Venture into the cool depths of **Saklıkent** **Gorge** and explore the fascinating ruins of ancient Lycian **Tlos**.

- Mellow **Çıralı** has a long shingle beach, ancient riverside ruins and eternal flames burning deep in the pine forest.

- Ancient port **Phaselis** makes for an ideal combination of romantic ruins to visit and beaches to relax on.

Bodrum harbour, overlooked by the Castle of St Peter

◀ Pedestrians cross the Golden Horn via the Galata Bridge, with the Blue Mosque in the foreground (c. 1890s)

Saklıkent Gorge
Located around 40 minutes' drive from Fethiye, Saklıkent is Turkey's longest and deepest gorge. From April to September, energetic visitors can walk the 4 km (2 miles) along the bottom of the gorge.

A Week in Mediterranean and Anatolian Turkey

- Explore **Antalya's** quaint old walled quarter of **Kaleiçi** and swim from the attractive town beach of **Mermerli**.

- The Roman theatre at **Aspendos** is one of the best preserved in the world; a visit to the Roman ruins at **Side** can be combined with a swim from a lovely beach.

- **Eğirdir**, set high in Turkey's unspoilt Lake District, is a great town in which to relax and admire the scenery.

- Conservative **Konya** is famed for its **Mevlâna Museum**, once home to the whirling dervishes.

- The central Anatolian volcanic landscape of **Cappadocia** is bizarrely beautiful – all curiously capped rock pinnacles, rippling canyons and soaring table-top outcrops.

- Backed by the symmetrical cone of Mount Hasan, the dramatic **Ihlara Valley** with its rock-cut churches is a perfect location for hiking.

Lake Tuz

Avanos

Göreme Open-Air Museum

Uçhisar

Ürgüp

Derinkuyu

Ihlara Valley

Antiocheia-in-Pisidia

Lake Eğirdir

Lake Beyşehir

Konya

Çatalhöyük

Lake Suğla

Karaman

rge

Aspendos

ntalya

Side

Silifke

Mediterranean Sea

Anamur

0 kilometres   100

0 miles   100

The temples of Apollo and Athena, Side
Dating from the 2nd century BC, these partially reconstructed temples in Side frame stunning views of the Gulf of Antalya. The evening makes a particularly atmospheric time to visit the ruins.

For map symbols *see back flap*

2 Days in Istanbul

Vibrant Istanbul, standing astride Europe and Asia, boasts a wealth of remains from its time as fulcrum of both the Byzantine and Ottoman Turkish worlds, as well as a lively arts and nightlife scene.

- **Arriving** Istanbul has two major airports. Atatürk Airport on the city's European side is linked to the centre by metro, buses and taxis. Sabiha Gökçen Airport on the Asian side has buses to Taksim Square.

- **Moving on** Flights from both airports link Istanbul with many provincial cities, while ferries ply the Sea of Marmara. Buses and trains also offer good transport links.

Day 1

Morning Most of Istanbul's major attractions are clustered at the end of the peninsula on which the original city was founded back in the 7th century BC. An obvious place to begin is the **Archaeological Museum** *(pp76–7)*, which has an excellent exhibition detailing the origins and development of the city. Delve into the Byzantine past in the eerie yet compellingly beautiful **Basilica Cistern** *(p90)* before heading to the spiritual heart of the Byzantine Christian

The Blue Mosque with the Bosphorus River in the background

world, the **Haghia Sophia** *(pp86–9)*, a monumental church rightly famed for its mighty dome and glittering mosaics.

Afternoon Mirroring the Haghia Sophia from the far side of a small park is the 16th-century **Blue Mosque** *(pp92–3)*. Inside is the carapace of some 5,000 superb, predominantly blue Iznik tiles that give the mosque its name. Just west of the Blue Mosque, a long, paved square represents what is left of a chariot racing stadium, the **Hippodrome** *(p94)*, notable today for its hieroglyphic-carved Egyptian Obelisk and bronze Serpentine Column, originally from Delphi in Greece. For a change of scene either hop on the tram or walk to the vast **Grand Bazaar** *(pp108–9)* for some retail therapy in the 4,000 plus shops. A soak, scrub and massage in the nearby

Ottoman-era **Çemberlitaş Baths** *(p95)* makes for a relaxing end to a busy day.

Day 2

Morning An early start at the splendid **Topkapı Palace** complex *(pp72–5)* should help beat the queues. Once the nerve-centre of the Ottoman Turks, it is composed of a series of pavilions set amongst attractive courtyard gardens overlooking the Bosphorus. Highpoints include the exotic women's quarters, the Harem, the Divan council room, the Pavilion of the Holy Mantle, which contains many sacred Islamic treasures, and the Treasury, which holds the famous, jewel-encrusted Topkapı dagger.

Afternoon Catch the tram out to the line of the 5th-century **Theodosian Walls** *(p121)* and follow them north to the exquisite **Church of St Saviour in Chora** *(pp122–3)*. Here a dazzling collection of figurative mosaics tell biblical tales and frescoes rival those of the Renaissance. From the terminus of the Theodosian Walls at Ayvansaray catch a ferry down the historic **Golden Horn** *(p103)* to the people-thronged environs of Eminönü waterfront and the Galata Bridge. Walk across the angler-lined bridge and uphill to the Genoese-era **Galata Tower** *(p114)*, which affords fabulous views of the old city's skyline of domes and minarets, before grabbing a beer or glass of wine in one of buzzing Beyoğlu's many bars.

View over Istanbul and to the Princes' Islands beyond, as seen from the Galata Tower

A Week on the Aegean Coast

- **Getting there** From Istanbul's Yenikapı terminal take the fast car ferry or sea bus across the Sea of Marmara to Bandirma, then an inter-city coach to Çanakkale. The journey time is about 5 hours. Alternatively, take a coach from Istanbul's Esenler bus station (10 km/6 miles northwest of the city) or fly.

- **Transport** Inter-city coaches connect several of the major towns on this itinerary, including Çanakkale and Selçuk in around 6 hours. A hire car is a better option, however, as some sights are tricky and time-consuming to reach by public transport.

Day 1: Çanakkale

Enjoy views overlooking the narrow Dardanelles strait in **Çanakkale** *(p178)*, then head onwards to Gallipoli. Preserved as a national park, the battlefields of the **Gallipoli Peninsula** *(pp172–3)*, scene of one of the bloodiest campaigns of World War I, are hauntingly beautiful. South lays Homer's legendary **Troy** *(p178)*, a brilliantly interpreted ancient site where many millennia of human history have been uncovered and excavations are ongoing.

Day 2: Assos and Behram Kale

Enjoy breathtaking views across a deep blue sea to the Greek island of Lesbos from the atmospheric hill-top ruins of the Temple of Athena, the high point of ancient **Assos** *(p179)*. The attractive village of **Behram Kale** *(p179)*, home to legions of traditionally garbed women proffering handicrafts and Aegean herbs, guards the approach to Assos. Overnight in **Bergama** *(pp180–81)*, whose old Greek quarter clings to the base of the acropolis.

Day 3: Pergamum and Selçuk

Built on a series of terraces wrought from a towering outcrop above Bergama, the remains of ancient **Pergamum** *(pp180–81)* are remarkable. The Temple of Trajan dominates the hilltop; even more impressive is the spectacularly steep theatre. Stay in relaxed **Selçuk** *(p184)*, where storks nest on the columns of a Byzantine aqueduct. Must-sees are the massive 6th century Basilica of St John and the Temple of Artemis – a remnant of one of the Seven Wonders of the Ancient World.

> **To extend your trip...**
> Head inland to Pamukkale, where glistening white travertine formations have been deposited on a steep hillside beneath the ruins of the Roman spa town of **Hierapolis** *(pp190–91)*.

Day 4: Ephesus

Perhaps the best restored classical ruins in the Mediterranean world lie a couple of kilometres from Selçuk in **Ephesus** *(pp186–7)*; allow half a day or more to see the elegant Library of Celsus, the Colonnaded Street, monumental theatre, baths and much more, including intimate terraced houses. Spend the afternoon people watching, exploring the 14th-century Genoese castle, or swimming in the pretty port of **Kuşadası** *(p185)*. Stay overnight in either Selçuk or Kuşadası.

Day 5: Priene, Miletus and Didyma

South of Selçuk are three ancient sites worth visiting for their beautiful settings alone – **Priene**, **Miletus** and **Didyma** *(pp194–5)*. Priene's cobbled streets nestle beneath pines above the Meander river valley, dwarfed by a rocky spur behind. The oracular shrine at Didyma, reached by crossing the Meander river, is a vast Aegean Greek temple ruin. Miletus, marooned in marshland, sprawls around a magnificent stone theatre. Stay in either Selçuk or Kuşadası.

Day 6: Lake Bafa

Brackish yet beautiful, **Lake Bafa** *(p196)* is backed by Mount Latmos' distinctive five peaks. On its remote eastern shores, the little-visited ancient site of Heracleia-under-Latmos awaits, while Byzantine monasteries lay hidden in the mountains. There is an abundance of bird life too, including the endangered crested pelican. En route to Bodrum, the incredibly well preserved temple at **Euromos** *(p196)* is a must.

Day 7: Bodrum

Lively sea-front **Bodrum** *(pp198–9)* is noted for its open-air Halikarnas disco. More sedate attractions include harbour-front strolls, and the impressive Castle of St Peter complete with Bronze Age shipwrecks.

The stunning white travertine terraced pools at Pamukkale

The ancient ruins of Caunos on the western bank of the Dalyan River

A Week on the Turquoise Coast

- **Arriving** Arrive at Dalaman Airport and depart from Antalya Airport.
- **Transport** Minibuses and midi-buses link the towns, villages and resorts along this beautiful coast, but they can be time consuming and frustrating to use. Hiring a car allows you to travel at your leisure, head up remote mountain roads to isolated sights, and stop for a quick dip at a sandy cove.

Day 1: Dalyan
Strung-out along the attractively reed-fringed banks of a lazy river backed by a cliff riddled with mock-temple rock-cut tombs, **Dalyan** (pp214–15) makes a refreshing change from the standard resort town. Swim in the river or take a boat down to the fine sand of beautiful Iztuzu beach, home to nesting loggerhead turtles, and explore the ruins of ancient **Caunos** (p214) across the river.

> **To extend your trip…**
> Take the boat trip from Dalyan to the warm-water **mud baths** at Ilıca (p215) and onto the lake at **Köyceğiz** (p214).

Day 2: Kayaköy
On the way to the abandoned Greek village of Kayaköy is the market town cum yacht harbour of **Fethiye** (p216), with abundant eating places, rock-cut Lycian tombs, a fine archaeological museum and a lively Friday farmers' market. Made famous by Louis de Bernières' epic *Birds Without Wings*, **Kayaköy** (p216) is set in an idyllic valley, but is a haunting reminder of the 1923 population exchanges (see p62). Hotels and rental homes are available in the valley.

> **To extend your trip…**
> Follow the marked coastal walk from Kayaköy to swim in the blue lagoon at **Ölü Deniz** (pp216–17).

Day 3: Patara
En route to the well-known resort of Kalkan stop to visit **Patara** (p218), an old city which combines a stunning turtle-nesting beach (one of the longest in the Mediterranean) with the romantic, dune-engulfed ruins of Roman Patara. Stay in either the close-by, low-key village of Gelemiş or **Kalkan** (p218).

The beautiful lagoon and restaurant-fringed beach at Ölü Deniz

Day 4: Saklıkent Gorge and Tlos
Visit the hinterland of a region known in ancient times as Lycia by exploring **Saklıkent Gorge** (p217), formed by waters tumbling down from Mount Akdağ. Enjoy a trout lunch at its entrance before heading to **Tlos**, (p217) a well-preserved Lycian site. Finish with a dip off Patara beach before overnighting again in Gelemiş or Kalkan.

Day 5: Üçağız and Kale
Explore the lively resort of **Kaş** (p218), formerly a tranquil Greek fishing village. South westward on a magnificent stretch of heavily indented, islet-dotted coast sits the village of **Üçağız** (p220). Close-by, picturesque Kale (ancient **Simena**, p220) huddles beneath the ruins of Simena castle and is reachable only by boat or on foot. Simple accommodation is available in both places.

> **To extend your trip…**
> Head back to **Kaş** (p218) for a day's scuba diving, canyoning or paragliding. Alternatively, kayak or take a boat trip around **Kale/Kekova Island** (p220).

Day 6: Cıralı
Follow the beautiful coastal road from Üçağız to **Çıralı/Finike** (p221). Swamped in citrus groves fronting a shingle beach and backed by high, forested peaks, this low-rise, low-key resort is the ideal place to relax. In the evening visit the eternal flames issuing from vents in a pine-clad mountainside.

Day 7: Phaselis
A short drive brings you to the beachside ruins of ancient **Phaselis** (p221), where a skeletal Roman aqueduct rises above pines. Beyond it, the rest of the ruins adjoin three beaches, the middle one shelving gently into a lagoon. Behind Phaselis, a cable car takes visitors to the summit for superb views of Mount Olympos. Stay overnight in Cıralı or **Antalya** (pp222–3).

A Week in Mediterranean and Anatolian Turkey

- **Airports** Arrive at Antalya Airport; depart from either Nevşehir or Kayseri airports.
- **Transport** This itinerary is best done by a combination of public transport, hire car and/or organised excursions. A direct inter-city coach between Antalya and Cappadocia has a journey time of around 11 hours.

Day 1: Antalya

Perched on cliffs overlooking the Gulf of Antalya and Lycian mountains, **Antalya** *(pp222–3)* is a lively city. Its heart is the walled old quarter (Kaleiçi), a maze of narrow alleys lined with Ottoman-era houses. There are plenty of restaurants and nightlife, but spare a half day either for the **Archaeological Museum** *(p222)*, a drive northwest to clamber over the mountain-top ruins of **Termessos** *(p224)*, or a swim from Mermerli Beach.

Day 2: The Pamphylian Plain

The fertile plain east of Antalya, known in antiquity as Pamphylia, was home to several powerful cities whose ruins are now a major draw. Join a tour or hire a car to explore **Perge** *(p224)* and **Aspendos** *(p225)*, the latter famed for its superb Roman theatre. Alternatively, head east

to **Side** *(pp228–9)* for a day exploring its attractive old town, Roman ruins and gently-shelving sandy beaches,

Day 3: Lake Eğirdir

Turkey's second largest freshwater lake, **Eğirdir** *(p258)* sits at an altitude of 900 m (2,952 ft). Ringed by high peaks, it is best reached by inter-city coach from Antalya. Accommodation is either on a rocky peninsula or a tiny island linked to the mainland by a causeway. Look around the old Greek houses, church and castle, or swim from one of the small beaches.

> **To extend your trip…**
> Hire a car to tour around the lake, taking in **Antiocheia-in-Pisidia** *(p258)*.

Day 4: Konya

Trundle across the steppe lands of the Anatolian plateau on an inter-city coach to **Konya** *(pp254–5)*. The former capital of the Selçuk Turks is best known as the home of Mevlâna, founder of a mystic Islamic sect whose followers are known as "Whirling Dervishes". An afternoon at **Mevlâna Museum** *(pp256–7)* is time well spent.

> **To extend your trip…**
> For anyone with an interest in the prehistoric, the "world's first city" at **Çatalhöyük** *(p258)* is a must.

Day 5: Konya and Cappadocia

Konya set on and around Alaeddin's Hill has some fascinating medieval Islamic monuments left by the Selçuk Turks, including the **Alaeddin Mosque** *(p255)* and the **Karatay Museum** *(p255)*. The coach journey onto **Cappadocia** *(pp282–3)* takes in caravanserais that once serviced camel trains on the Silk Road. In Cappadocia, aim for a sunset view over the eerie valleys and rock formations from **Uçhisar** *(p282)*. Overnight in **Göreme** *(pp287)*, **Ürgüp** *(p287)* or Uçhisar.

Day 6: Cappadocia

Göreme Open-Air Museum *(pp288–9)*, with its weirdly eroded rock pinnacles carved from the soft volcanic rock, requires several hours to explore. Some of the best rock formations are in nearby Zelve *(p286)*. Then head to **Avanos** *(p287)*, which is known for its pottery workshops.

Day 7: Cappadocia

The landscape of southern Cappadocia is quite different so either hire a car or join a tour to the **Ihlara Valley** *(p296)*. Walk its beautiful gorge and explore its pretty rock-cut churches. En route visit the labyrinthine underground city of **Derinkuyu** *(p286)*.

> **To extend your trip…**
> Explore this region further on a mountain bike, horse, on foot with a guide, or even in a hot-air balloon.

Hot-air balloons glide over the spectacularly eroded landscape of the Cappadocia region

Putting Turkey on the Map

Lying between Europe, Asia and the Middle East, Turkey
is located midway between the equator and the North
Pole. It covers an area of 814,578 sq km (314,533 sq miles).
A small area (3 per cent) called Thrace forms part of the
European continent, while the larger section, Anatolia,
forms part of Asia. The city of Istanbul is situated at the
meeting point of Europe and Asia and is divided by
the Bosphorus, the strait linking the Black Sea and the
Sea of Marmara. Countries bordering Turkey are Greece
and Bulgaria on the European side, and Georgia, Armenia,
Iran, Iraq, Syria and Nakhichevan to the east and southeast.

Europe

Melitopol

Sea of Azov

North Sea
Atlantic Ocean

SWEDEN
DENMARK
ESTONIA
LATVIA
LITHUANIA
REP. OF IRELAND
UNITED KINGDOM
NETH.
BELGIUM
GERMANY
POLAND
BELARUS
RUSSIAN FEDERATION
CZECH REPUBLIC
SLOVAKIA
UKRAINE
FRANCE
SWITZ.
AUSTRIA
HUNGARY
MOLDOVA
SLOV.
CROATIA
ROMANIA
BOSNIA HERZ.
SERBIA
ITALY
MONTEN.
KOS.
MAC.
BULGARIA
Black Sea
ALBANIA
GREECE
Caspian Sea
GEORGIA
Ankara
ARMENIA
TURKEY
SPAIN
PORTUGAL
CYPRUS
SYRIA
IRAN
LEBANON
IRAQ
Mediterranean Sea
ISRAEL
MOROCCO
ALGERIA
TUNISIA

0 kilometres 1200
0 miles 600

Turkey's Coastal Borders
Turkey is bounded by the
Black Sea to the north, the
Aegean Sea to the west, and
the Mediterranean to the south.
Its coastline, including islands,
runs to 8,330 km (5,176 miles).

RUSSIAN FEDERATION

nop
Bafra
Samsun
795
Ordu
010
Giresun
Kutaisi
GEORGIA
Tbilisi
Hopa
Artvin
Trabzon
Rize
010
rum
Amasya
100
Tokat
Gümüşhane
050
Bayburt
950
Kars
Kumajri
ARMENIA
200
Sivas
200
Divriği
100
Erzincan
Horasan
Erzurum
957
Ağrı
100
Jerevan
Kızılırmak
Kangal
850
Keban Dam
Bingöl
Murat
300
965
Doğubeyazıt
Bünyan
300
Elazığ
Tatvan
Lake Van
290
Van
975
IRAN
Kayseri
825
Malatya
885
Diyarbakır
965
300
Kurtalan
360
Tigris
Mardin
Hakkâri
Kahramanmaraş
850
950
400
Nusaybin
Yüksekova
Adana
052
Gaziantep
Şanlıurfa
1
Mosul
Erbil
hurtalik
850
İskenderun
Akçakale
Al-Hasakah
Antakya (Antioch)
4
2
handagi
Aleppo
Ar Raqqah
Kirkuk
akia
4
SYRIA
Deir ez-Zur
Hamah
42
Al Qa'im
Homs
Palmyra
4
BANON
5
2
irut
Damascus
IRAQ

Key
✈ Airport
━━ Motorway
━━ Major road
┄┄ Secondary road
┈┈ Railway
━━ International boundary

A PORTRAIT OF TURKEY

The popular image many visitors have of Turkey is one of idyllic Mediterranean beaches lapped by an azure sea. Sun and sand, however, barely hint at the riches this country has to offer. A bridge between Asia and Europe, Turkey is one of the great cradles of civilization – a proud country whose cultural and historic treasures will delight and inspire even seasoned travellers.

Contrasts between old and new add greatly to the fascination that overwhelms visitors to Turkey. Istanbul, the metropolis of this fast-changing nation, displays all the hustle and bustle of a great world city, while only a few hours away rural people congregate around communal water supplies and collect wood to light their fires.

The superb scenery and landscape reflect a remarkable geographical diversity. Beguiling seascapes, soft beaches and brooding mountains along the Mediterranean coast yield to the tranquillity of Turkey's Lake District, while the deep forests and cool *yayla* (plateaux) of the Black Sea region leave visitors unprepared for the vast empty steppes of the eastern provinces. Pictures can only hint at the enchantment that awaits travellers in Cappadocia. Here, centuries of underground activity have resulted in entire cities carved deep into the porous tuff, while aeons of erosion have carved the landscape into fantastic fairytale-like mushroom formations.

Many of Turkey's national parks and wetland sanctuaries are a last refuge for species that are almost extinct elsewhere in Europe, and for botanists there is an amazing display of flora.

Add to this countless ancient ruins, and the friendliness and hospitality of the Turkish nation, and you are guaranteed an unforgettable holiday.

Looking out over the Bosphorus from Sultanahmet

◀ Turkish Muslims gather to break their first day of fasting during Ramadan, İstiklal Cad, Istanbul

The Library at Ephesus *(see pp186–7)*, one of the most famous Roman sites in Turkey

Historical Framework

Anatolia has seen the rise and fall of sophisticated civilizations, including that of the great Assyrians, Hittites, Phrygians and Urartians. Over the centuries, this land was populated almost continuously. The Hellenistic period produced some of the finest sites. Near Çanakkale, on the Aegean coast, lie the remains of ancient Troy *(see p178)*, and in the mountainous south-west are the ruined settlements of Lycia *(see p219)*, whose inhabitants left behind an assortment of unusual rock tombs.

In the early Christian era, St Paul travelled through Asia Minor, then part of the Roman empire, to preach the Gospel. Between the 3rd and 7th centuries, Christianity was a central force in the development of Anatolia. This was the period when the Byzantine empire attained the pinnacle of its glory. The Romans and Byzantines endowed Turkey with glorious architectural masterpieces, which can still be seen at places like Ephesus *(see pp186–7)*,

Aphrodisias *(see pp192–3)*, and in Istanbul, where the former church of Haghia Sophia has stood for more than 14 centuries *(see pp86–9)*.

The Seljuk Turks added their superb architectural legacy, as did the Ottomans, whose empire at one point stretched from Hungary to Iraq. Many other peoples, among them Jews, Russians, Armenians and Greeks, have played an important part in Turkey's complex history. The fruits of this diversity can be seen in superb mosaics and frescoes, colourful tilework, underground cities, interesting historic and biblical sights, city walls and fortresses.

Turks are proud of the modern nation Atatürk *(see p62)* forged out of the ruined Ottoman empire. *"Ne Mutlu Türküm Diyene"* is a common Turkish phrase that means "happy is the person who can say he is a Turk."

Ottoman tilework at the Topkapı Palace, Istanbul

Religion

Most of Turkey's population of 76 million people follow

the Sunni branch of Islam, but one quarter of the population are Alevis, Mevlevis *(see p229)* or other Muslim sects.

Because the Turkish Republic is founded on secular principles, religion does not seem to hold the significance that it does in other Muslim countries. The devout do attend prayer times in the mosque five times daily as laid down by the Koran, but some Turkish Muslims do not go to mosque at all.

A department of religious affairs exists and carries out the function of exercising control over family morals and to safeguard the principles of Islam. Mosque and state are not separated by statute, and so the boundaries between them can be unclear at times. Invariably, Atatürk's principles are invoked as sacred when religion appears to steer too close to politics. The issue of Islamic dress is emotionally charged and a subject of debate.

Approximately 130,000 non-Muslims, including Greek and Armenian Orthodox, are found in larger cities, and members are allowed to worship freely within their own communities.

A card game interrupted for a tray of *simit*

Byzantine mosaic, Haghia Sophia

Society

The Turkish language is of Central Asian origin but uses the Latin alphabet. It has a natural vowel harmony that makes it sound melodic and soft. Turkish terms such as *divan* and *ottoman* have entered the English vocabulary, while Turkish borrows words like *tren* and *randevu* from English and French.

Turks have an uninhibited body language that is as emphatic as speech. They are unrestrained about enjoying themselves, but traditional segregation of the sexes means that groups of men sitting around smoking, drinking endless cups of *çay* (tea) and playing dominoes, cards or *tavla* (backgammon) are a common sight. A pronounced family ethos cements the generations, and festivals unite the extended family. It is all bound together by hospitality, an age-old Turkish tradition, in which food and drink play a central role.

Children are regarded as national treasures, but many families blame the advent of television and the Internet for eroding the discipline and respect for elders that were once sacred.

The Blue Mosque *(see pp92–3)* in Istanbul

Turkey's gradual transition to a modern, Western society received a major boost in 1952 when it became a member of the North Atlantic Treaty Organization (NATO). This brought advances in communications, transport and its defence policy. New roads, highways and projects to improve the tourism infrastructure changed the face of the country.

Modernization is, more than ever, the hallmark of Turkish society. Today, remote villages can boast of high-speed, fibre-optic telephone connections, but may lack adequate water or reliable electricity supplies. The Internet and mobile telephones have become essential accessories, and new housing projects are quickly festooned with satellite TV dishes.

Traditional juice vendor

Modern Turkey

For most Turks, the modern version of their ancient country dates from the founding of the Turkish Republic in 1923. Its architect was Mustafa Kemal – better known as Atatürk – a decorated former army officer who became Turkey's first President.

Atatürk set Turkey on the road to becoming a modern state. His reforms, strictly enacted, steered Turkey towards becoming European rather than Asian, and his status in the eyes of the Turkish nation has scarcely dimmed since his death. His picture is everywhere and his statue adorns almost every village square. Few statesmen have matched his integrity and style, and the soldier-turned-politician model still appeals strongly to Turks.

Democracy has proved much more difficult to implement than Western theoretical models. Turkey's military leaders, who intervened in politics in 1960, 1971 and 1980, keep a close eye on political life. In 1997, democratically elected prime minister, Necmettin Erbakan, was ousted from office for his overt religious leanings, but few Turks challenge the idea of a secular safety net. In November 2002 an Islamic party scored a victory in national elections, sweeping aside a decade of coalition party alliances whose populist tendencies overshadowed democratic reforms.

Soldiers mounting guard at the Atatürk Mausoleum *(see p248)*, Ankara

Children hard at work in school

Many Turks consider themselves Europeans, despite income gaps and social inequalities.

Population Movement

In the 1960s, many Turks left for Germany to work under a government scheme offering remittances in foreign currency – an important source of export income. Many settled there, and 2.2 million Turks now call Germany their home. There are large Turkish communities in other EU states, too.

In Ottoman times, the state provided an all-encompassing social service to its citizens, who willingly complied with its ordered governance. Today, the role of the state is being redefined. Officials are elected and democracy is the goal of society. Many state-owned joint-stock companies and monopolies that put Turkey on its feet are scheduled for privatization. Several are well prepared for global competition but others view change as eroding a comfortable status quo.

Folk dancers from the Black Sea

Within Turkey, the trend has been for rural people to leave the land and seek a more stable life in urban areas. Few plan to return, even if city life is not what they hoped for. Some of Turkey's best-known films, such as *Sürü* (The Herd), and *Eşkıya* (The Bandit), highlight the common themes of identity, lifestyle and poverty. Turkey's indomitable spirit and vitality are best seen and appreciated in its proud people. Journeys invariably result in friendships. If a Turk declares himself your *arkadaş* (friend), he will be a steadfast soulmate long after your holiday memories have faded.

Maintaining a centralized state has placed a huge financial burden on Turks. Interest on international loans consumes a large chunk of public money, while the military budget exceeds that of health, social services and education. Since 2002, political and economic reforms have transformed Turkey. Inflation, running at 100 per cent in 2001, is now in single digits and the Turkish Lira has shed its awkward zeros *(see p385)*.

Fish sold on the quayside along Istanbul's Golden Horn *(see p103)*

Landscape and Geology

Mountain ranges are Turkey's most distinctive geographic feature, with the Taurus and Pontic ranges enclosing the high Anatolian Plateau. The mountains are geologically young, and the many faulting and folding areas indicate that mountain building is still active. In fact, 80 per cent of the country lies in an extremely active tectonic zone, and earthquakes are frequent. Turkey has eight main drainage basins but the most important ones are the Euphrates (Fırat) and the Tigris (Dicle). About one quarter of Turkey is covered with forest, with stands of pine, spruce and cedar, as well as deciduous trees. About 13 per cent of this area is productive; erosion, logging and fires have all depleted forested areas.

Saklıkent Gorge is typical of the Mediterranean coastal region, where steep valleys and gorges bisect elongated mountain ridges.

İzmit, east of Istanbul, was the epicentre of the 1999 earthquake that measured 7.4 on the Richter scale and claimed the lives of at least 25,000 people.

North Anatolian fault

Ankara

Istanbul

İzmit

Anatolian Plate

Eurasian Plate

Sea of Marmara

Aegean Sea

Mediterra

African Plate

Plate Movements

Continental plate   Continental plate

Strike-slip faulting is found along the North Anatolian Fault. When rocks suddenly shift or move along such fault lines, the tension is released as an earthquake.

Key

— Fault line

→ Direction of plate movement

New mountain range   Continental plate

Continental plate

Collisions between two continental plates result in crust being pushed upwards to form mountain ranges.

The Mediterranean and Aegean coasts are characterized by mountain soils which are clay-based and red, brown and grey in colour. Plains around Adana and Antalya support extensive food, crop and horticultural production.

Lake Van lies in a crater-like depression that became landlocked when lava flows from the adjacent Pleistocene-era volcano blocked the flow of water. Today, drainage from feeder streams fills the lake and only evaporation sustains a constant water level. It has a surface area of 3,713 sq km (1,440 sq miles) and a very high level of sodium carbonate.

Pontic Mountains

Black Sea

Erzurum

Erzincan

Lake Van

Arabian Plate

Adana

Antakya

Taurus Mountains

Geology and Earthquakes

Turkey lies between three converging continental plates – the Anatolian, Eurasian and Arabian plates. As the Arabian plate moves northward into the Eurasian plate, it pushes the Anatolian plate westward, causing earthquakes along the North Anatolian Fault. Further west, the African plate pushes beneath the Anatolian plate, stretching the crust under the Aegean Sea. Tectonic activity is prevalent throughout Turkey.

East of Adıyaman, the alluvial Mesopotamian plain lies between the Tigris and Euphrates rivers. This fertile area produces much of Turkey's wheat and cotton.

Isolated Mediterranean bays were, for centuries, havens for pirates. The Taurus Mountains made sections of the coast inaccessible, allowing peoples like the Lycians (1st and 2nd century BC) to resist Roman rule and retain their own language and culture. As harbours silted up, such civilizations declined.

Southeast Anatolian Project (GAP)

This showpiece project was conceived during the 1980s to produce hydroelectric power by harnessing the flow of the Tigris and Euphrates rivers. Plans involve the building of 22 dams and 19 power plants spread over more than 1.7 million hectares (4.2 million acres) of land. The project is intended to help develop Turkey's poor eastern provinces, but critics argue that flooding 300,000 sq km (115,800 sq miles) will submerge ancient cultural treasures and displace local people.

The massive Atatürk Dam

Flora and Fauna of Turkey

Turkey offers much for the naturalist, with rich marine ecosystems, abundant birdlife and elusive larger mammals. The rugged eastern provinces still harbour large mammals such as bear, jackal, and wolf. The country is also floristically rich, with more than 11,000 plant species recorded. The tulip is perhaps the most famous of these. The great diversity of plants stems from the variety of habitats – from arid plains to mountains and temperate woodland – but also from Turkey's position as a "biological watershed" at the crossroads of Europe and Asia. There are huge tracts of unspoiled countryside, some of which have been set aside as national parks.

The Anatolian lynx can still be found in upland areas, although its habitat is under threat.

The Mediterranean Coast

Large areas of the Mediterranean and Aegean coast are dominated by evergreen scrub, with Jerusalem sage, kermes oak, broom and sun roses among the common species. More open scrub areas contain orchids, bulbs and annuals. Tucked under bushes are hellebores and Comper's orchid with its distinctive trailing tassels. Arum lilies exude a fetid odour to entice pollinators. Late summer brings the spires of sea squill and sea daffodil. The carob tree sheds its pods in autumn while colchicum and sternbergias unfold.

Common sternbergia

Wetlands

Here, dragonflies hover over flowering rush, waterlilies and irises, while water meadows fill with buttercups, bellevalia, marsh orchids and pale blue asyneumas. Despite international recognition of their diversity, Turkish wetlands are under threat from dams, drainage, pollution and climatic change.
Surviving examples are Sultansazlığı near Niğde *(see p293)*, Kuşcenneti National Park near Bursa *(see p161)*, and the Göksu Delta *(see p233)*.

Marsh orchid

Woodlands

Coniferous forests harbour stands of peonies, orchids, foxgloves, fritillaries and golden peas. The western Taurus range has an endemic subspecies of cedar of Lebanon, and in the north are forests of Oriental beech and fir, with rhododendron, ferns, lilies, primulas and campanulas. In autumn cyclamen and edible mushrooms appear. There are giant cedar at Dokuz Göl near Elmalı, endemic oak species at Kasnak near Eğirdir *(see p258)*, and ancient mixed woodland, now threatened by a dam, in the Fırtına valley.

Peony

Steppe

Despite their sparse appearance, the broad expanses of the Anatolian Plateau support many flowering plants. Highlights include stately asphodelines, which reach 1.8 m (6 ft) in height, purple gladioli, flax in yellow, pink or blue, and the colourful parasite *Phelypaea coccinea*. On the eastern steppe are found the lovely white, purple or blue oncocyclus iris. Göreme National Park in Cappadocia and Nemrut Dağı National Park *(see p310)* are good places to see this flora. Deforestation and erosion have greatly altered the steppe, and intensive farming practices have accelerated this process.

Iberian oncocyclus

Mountains

Snowdrop

In spring, subalpine meadows are carpeted with buttercups. Above the treeline, snowdrops, winter aconite and crocus crowd together near the snowmelt. These are followed by star-of-Bethlehem, grape hyacinth, fritillaries, foxtail lilies, asphodelines and bright red tulips. Scree and rocky slopes are dotted with colourful alpine flowers like iris, rock jasmine and aubretia. Important mountain reserves include Kaçkar Mountains National Park near the Black Sea coast, Aladağlar National Park, Beyşehir Gölü National Park near Eğirdir *(see p258)* and the ski centres at Uludağ *(see p161)* and Erciyes *(see p292)*.

Birds of Anatolia

More than 440 species of bird have been recorded in Turkey, which offers a range of habitats from woodlands and mountains to wetlands and steppe. The country's position on the migratory flyways makes its a paradise for bird-watchers. Autumn offers the spectacle of vast flocks of migrating storks and raptors over the Bosphorus. In winter, lakes and wetlands hold thousands of wintering wildfowl.

Alpine chough can be seen in the mountains, where they nest on ledges, nooks and crevices. They store food in cracks, which they cover with stones.

Adult golden eagles are resident, but the young of northern Europe migrate south in winter to the mountainous areas of the Mediterranean.

Chukar partridge is one of many game birds in Turkey, where hunting is a popular pastime.

Serin live in woodlands and vineyards. Local populations are augmented by migratory birds in autumn.

Hans and Kervansarays

Dotted across Anatolia are many *hans* (storage depots) and *kervansarays* (hostelries) built in Seljuk and Ottoman times to protect merchants travelling the caravan routes that crossed Anatolia along the Roman-Byzantine road system. From the 13th century, the Seljuks built more than 100 *hans* to encourage trade. It was under the Ottomans, though, that *hans* and *kervansarays* became a part of the state-sponsored social welfare system and played a key role in expanding Ottoman territory and influence. Several of these facilities can be visited today, and some have been turned into hotels or restaurants.

Locator Map

← Major trade routes

Portal of the storage hall

A small mosque raised on arches stands in the centre of the courtyard.

Camel caravans laden with silks and spices from China made their way through Anatolia to the great commercial centre of Bursa *(see pp166–71)*. Slaves from the Black Sea hinterland were another important trading commodity.

A thick curtain wall surrounded the *kervansaray*.

The central gate provided the only entry to the fortified structure.

The central courtyard, surrounded by arcades, provided shelter from the hot sun and contained apartments and a *hamam* (Turkish bath) to revive weary travellers.

Corner turret for defence

The stone bridge over the Köprü River near Antalya was built by the Seljuks near the site of a Roman bridge. The structure has been restored.

A *kervansaray* at Mylasa, a bustling commercial centre in western Anatolia, is shown in this 19th-century oil painting by the English artist, Richard Dadd.

Barrel-vaulted ceiling

The octagonal lantern tower let light into the interior.

The Sultanhanı

The Sultanhanı, near the central Anatolian city of Aksaray (see pp296–7), is one of the best-preserved Seljuk kervansarays. Built between 1226 and 1229 for Sultan Alaeddin Keykubad (see p254), the complex consisted of a courtyard surrounded by various amenities – stables, mosque, Turkish bath and accommodation – for the use of travellers, and a covered hall in which trade goods could be safely stored.

Five-aisled storage hall

The Cinci Hanı *(see p272)* was an important fixture of the busy trading centre of Safranbolu, which lay on the key Black Sea caravan route.

Accommodation for travellers was provided in two tiers of rooms.

The Kızlarağası Hanı in İzmir *(see p182)* is an Ottoman *han* dating from 1744. *Hans* had the same amenities found at a *kervansaray*, together with storerooms, offices and rows of cell-like workshops, all grouped around a central courtyard. The restored Kızlarağası Hanı houses a variety of cafés, shops and craft workshops.

Customs and Traditions

Turkish customs have been passed down from generation to generation and are integrated into contemporary life. Climate, geography and ethnic background play a significant role, but many customs have their origins in Islam and have changed little over the years. An enduring faith is attached to the blue bead, or *mavi boncuk*, an amulet that protects the wearer from the evil eye. It may be seen dangling wherever good luck is needed.

Religious and social mores dictate separate lives for many men and women, so customs bring them together for celebrations such as weddings, births and rites of passage. Family life is pivotal to Turkish culture, and communities are strengthened by the social and economic ties of the extended family.

In Karagöz shadow puppet theatre, a cast of stock characters enact satiric themes. The puppets are three-dimensional cut-outs made from camel skin.

Circumcision

For the celebration of his *sünnet*, or circumcision ritual, a boy is dressed in the satin uniform of a sergeant major, and his parents throw as lavish a celebration as they can afford. Relatives and friends proffer money as gifts for the young man, and the whole event is often photographed for the family album.

Gold coins attached to ribbons

Offerings pinned to a pillow symbolize the gifts the young man will take into manhood.

In line with Islamic tradition, Turkish boys are circumcised between the ages of seven and 10. A lavish uniform is worn for this special occasion.

Village Weddings

Celebrations such as weddings may last for several days and involve a number of individual rituals. In the rural areas, families often approve and sanction wedding partners. The bride always has a *çeyiz* (trousseau) comprising lovely, handcrafted articles she and her mother have made for the new home.

Headscarves are worn by many rural women.

Village square *(meydan)*

Making flat bread for the marriage feast is the responsibility of the women of the family. The tradition of making *katmer* or *gözleme* (crepes) is being revived in some parts of Turkey.

Wedding festivities in the picturesque village of Midyat, near the Syrian border, bring a large and appreciative crowd out to watch dancers performing.

Handicrafts

Craft skills were handed down from the Ottoman guild system, and Turkey has many skilled craftspeople. One example is *oya*, or needle lace, which is noted for its intricate floral designs crocheted in silk. These were originally crafted for a bride's trousseau. As late as the 1920s, wives crocheted them as part of their husband's headdress. Quilt-making, on the other hand, was traditionally passed down from the father.

Weaving is a rural tradition and done mainly by women. Designs of carpets and *kilims (see pp366–7)* are handed down from one generation to the next.

Copper and brass ware, worked by hand, is an integral part of the Turkish household.

Local markets are the best places to look for traditional crafts. Shown here are handmade linens in Kalkan.

Hand-printed textiles, known as *yazma,* are a proud and venerable craft tradition in central Anatolian towns such as Tokat.

Woodworking skills were handed down from the Ottomans. Unique wooden walking sticks are made in Devrek, near the Black Sea. These wooden bowls were produced near Adana.

Traditional Dress

Traditionally, Turkish women wove their clothing according to individual designs, and dyed them using plant extracts. Today, each region has its own styles of *şalvar* (trousers worn by women) and head coverings such as *başörtüsü* (scarves).

A group of folk dancers wears the traditional costume of the Van region. Folk dancing is hugely popular, with regional costumes as much a part of the show as music and laughter.

Printed skirt

Full robe

Decorative headdress

National Service

All men over the age of 20 must serve compulsory military service of varying duration, and Turkish society still considers this to be a fundamental rite of passage to manhood. For rural youths, this may be their first time away from home, and *askerlik* (military service) fulfils a social role as a bridge to adulthood. The departing conscript may be required to visit friends and relatives to ask forgiveness for any wrongdoings and be presented with gifts and money before he reports for duty.

Young soldiers of the Turkish Army on duty

Islamic Art in Turkey

In Islamic art, the highest place is held by calligraphy, or the art of beautiful writing. This is because a calligrapher's prime task is writing the Holy Koran, believed by Muslims to be the word of God. In the purest forms of Islam, the use of animal forms in works of art is regarded as detracting from pious thoughts. Thus artists and craftsmen turned their talents to designs featuring geometric motifs and intricate foliage designs known as arabesques. As well as calligraphy, these highly disciplined forms included miniature paintings, jewellery, metal, tiles and ceramics, stone-carving and textiles. Under the Ottomans, the finest creations came from the Nakkaşhane, or sultan's design studio. Here, an apprentice system that lasted up to 10 years maintained the imperial traditions of excellence and innovation.

Ceramic tile panels contain messages taken from the Koran, executed in Arabic or Kufic script.

Calligraphic inscription in embossed metal

Floral decorations

The sultan's *tuğra* was his personal monogram, used in place of his signature. It would be drawn by a calligrapher or engraved on a wooden block as a stamp. This example shows the *tuğra* of Abdül Hamit I (1774–89).

Ornamental loops

Tile panel featuring plant motifs

Koranic texts provided templates for woodcarvers, metal-workers, weavers and ceramic painters. Although highly decorative, Islamic art is filled with meaning: the tulip (*lāle*), a much-used motif, is an anagram for Allah.

Floral tile motif

Sokollu Mehmet Paşa Mosque In Kadirga, Istanbul

Designed by Sinan (1577–8) for a distinguished grand vizier, the prayer hall features a beautiful qibla (wall of the mosque at right angles to the direction of Mecca). The calligraphic decoration includes exquisite tilework and stone-carving.

Inscription in metal

Tilework on squinches supporting the dome

The minaret of the Green Mosque (Yeşil Camii) in İznik *(see p164)* features complex patterns of coloured tiles. The mosque, which was completed in 1378, takes its name from the richly decorated minaret.

The Art of the Ottoman Miniature

Ottoman miniature painting was primarily a courtly art form, which reached a peak of development in the late 16th century during the rule of Süleyman the Magnificent *(see p59)*. Miniature painting was influenced by Persian art, with many of the finest Persian minaturists being brought to work at the court workshops of Topkapı Palace *(see pp72–5)*. As well as illustrations for manuscripts of Koranic texts and Persian epics – Persian was the language of the Ottoman court – a unique style was developed to record the history of the dynasty. This included battle scenes, palace rituals, major festivals and topographical scenes. By the 17th century, miniature painters had mastered three-dimensional representation, while the 18th century heralded a more naturalistic style and a broadening of subjects to include landscapes, still lifes and portraits. Although there were a number of celebrated miniature artists, these exquisite works were, for the most part, neither signed nor dated.

This tile panel is set into the the stone wall.

The conical roof of the *minbar (see p36)* features polychrome tiling.

Stained-glass windows

An Arabic inscription winds around a gravestone in the grounds of the Alanya Museum *(see p230)*.

A tile panel over the entrance to the Mausoleum of Selim II, in the precincts of Haghia Sophia in Istanbul, shows a masterful integration of calligraphy and organic motifs.

Early 17th-century miniature showing Hasan, grandson of Mohammed, on his deathbed

Ottoman Architecture

From Albania to Tripoli, and from Baghdad to Bosnia, the Ottomans left superb examples of their architectural skills. Nowhere is this more apparent than in Istanbul, where the sultans built beautiful mosques, palaces and *külliyes* (Islamic charitable institutions).

Ottoman architecture is marked by a strict hierarchy of forms, scales and materials, reflecting the rank of a building's patron. Mosques commissioned by members of the Ottoman family, for example, were the only ones entitled to two or more minarets. Another distinguishing feature is the influence of Byzantine architecture. Many architects, among them Mimar Sinan *(see p105)*, were of Greek or Armenian origin.

Ornamental fountains *(çeşme)* were built in busy central squares or markets. This example is in the bazaar in Kayseri *(see pp294–5)*.

The Early Ottoman Mosque

The earliest form of the Ottoman mosque consisted of a single large prayer hall covered by a hemispheric dome, with a covered porch and minaret outside. The Junior Hacı Özbek Mosque (1333) in İznik is considered the earliest example of this form. It was modified by adding bays (often covered by small domes) around the central dome, and by the addition of a covered portico and arcaded courtyard.

Rubble-filled masonry wall

A pier supports the central dome.

The pillared portico is covered by seven domes.

A ground plan of the Selimiye Mosque shows the domed bays surrounding the central hall.

The Selimiye Mosque, in Konya *(see pp254–5)*, was started in 1558 by Sultan Selim II when he was governor of Konya. It was finished in 1587. Clearly visible is the bulk of the central prayer hall, which is topped by a hemispheric dome. The mosque adjoins the Mevlâna Museum.

The Later Ottoman Mosque

The form of the Ottoman mosque underwent a dramatic evolution in the years following the conquest of Constantinople. The Ottomans frequently converted Orthodox churches, notably Haghia Sophia *(see pp86–9)*, into mosques. Under the influence of such models, architects began to create higher, single-domed mosques, and greatly open up the interior space.

The Şehzade Mosque (also called the Prince's Mosque) in Istanbul was the first imperial mosque built by the architect, Mimar Sinan *(see p105)*. It was commissioned in 1543 by Süleyman the Magnificent.

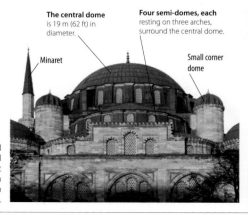

The central dome is 19 m (62 ft) in diameter.

Four semi-domes, each resting on three arches, surround the central dome.

Minaret

Small corner dome

Fountains (Şadirvan)

Based on the Koranic principle that water is the source of life, the provision of public water supplies was a civic duty. Every town had its *çeşme* (public fountain), and *külliyes* offered *sebil* (free distribution of water). The *şadırvan* was placed in a mosque courtyard for the performance of ritual ablutions.

Decorative cupola

Calligraphic panels feature verses from the Koran.

Basin

The Fountain of Sultan Ahmet III is one of the most famous sights of Istanbul. Built in 1728, the square structure has basins on all sides.

The Konak

Like many other Ottoman buildings, the *konak* (mansion house) consisted of a wooden structure built on a foundation of stone and brick to withstand the cold Anatolian winter. The ground floor contained granaries, stables and storage areas. The kitchens and public rooms were on the first floor, with the private quarters on the top floor.

Pitched roof

Wooden upper floor

Living areas had *sofas* (upholstered benches) along the walls. The nook shown here is in a konak that has been turned into a hotel in Safranbolu *(see pp272–3).*

Stone foundation

A rural konak in northern Turkey shows the typical three-storey form. Some had separate entrances for the *harem* (women's quarters) and *selamlık* (men's quarters).

Yali

The *yalı* (waterfront villa), is found along the Bosphorus. Most *yalıs* were built during the 18th and 19th centuries as grand summer residences for wealthy citizens of Ottoman Istanbul. Sited to make maximum use of the waterside location, they also incorporated boathouses or moorings.

Wood was the main building material.

Decorative pilasters

The waterside location provided easy access and maximum visibility.

Yalıs were built in a variety of forms and architectural styles, from simple wooden structures to this lavish Russian-style mansion.

Building Types

Bedesten Covered stone market

Çeşme Public water fountain

Daruşşifa Hospital

Hamam Bath house *(see p81)*

İmaret Soup kitchen

Külliye Educational/charitable complex surrounding a major mosque *(see pp36–7)*

Medrese Theological college *(see pp36–7)*

Mescit Small prayer hall

Tekke Dervish lodge

Tımarhane Lunatic asylum

Türbe Tomb

Exploring Mosques

Five times a day throughout Istanbul a chant is broadcast over loudspeakers set high in the city's minarets to call the faithful to prayer. Over 99 per cent of the population is Muslim, though the Turkish state is officially secular. Most belong to the Sunni branch of Islam, but there is also a small population of Shiites. Both follow the teachings of the Koran, the sacred book of Islam, and the Prophet Mohammed (c.570–632), but Shiites accept, in addition, the authority of a line of 12 imams directly descended from Mohammed. Islamic mystics are known as Sufis *(see p259).*

Overview of the impressive Süleymaniye Mosque complex

The ablutions fountain (şadırvan) was used by worshippers for ritual washing.

The *han or kervansaray* (see pp28–9) provided accommodation for travellers.

The kitchen (imaret) catered for mosque officials, students, the sick and the poor.

Hospital (darüşşifa)

Turkish baths (hamam)

Courtyard (avlu)

Prayer hall (cami)

A mausoleum (türbe) was built for the founder of the mosque.

Colleges (medreses) for general and theological education were built adjacent to the mosque. Most now serve other uses.

Plan of a Typical Mosque Complex (Kulliye)

The külliye was a charitable foundation as well as a place of worship. This example forms part of the Süleymaniye Mosque (see pp104–5) in Istanbul. A typical külliye had a school, hospital, Islamic study halls, kervansaray (lodgings for travellers), public soup kitchen and bath house.

Inside a Mosque

The prayer hall of a great mosque can offer visitors a soaring sense of space. Islam forbids images of living things (human or animal) inside a mosque, so there are never any statues or figurative paintings, but the geometric and abstract architectural details of the interior can be exquisite. Men and women pray separately. Women often use a screened-off area or a balcony.

The *müezzin mahfili* is a platform found in large mosques. The *muezzin* (mosque official) stands on this when chanting responses to the prayers of the *imam* (head of the mosque).

The *mihrab*, a niche in the wall, marks the direction of Mecca. The prayer hall is laid out so that most people can see the mihrab.

The *minbar* is a lofty pulpit to the right of the mihrab. This is used by the imam when he delivers the Friday sermon (khutba).

Muslim Beliefs and Practices

Muslims believe in God (Allah), and the Koran shares many prophets and stories with the Bible. However, whereas for Christians Jesus is the son of God, Muslims hold that he was just one in a line of prophets – the last being Mohammed, who brought the final revelation of God's truth to mankind. Muslims believe that Allah communicated the sacred texts of the Koran to Mohammed through the archangel Gabriel.

Muslims have five basic duties. The first of these is the profession of faith: "There is no God but Allah, and Mohammed is his Prophet". Muslims are also enjoined to pray five times a day, give alms to the poor, and fast during the month of Ramazan *(see p40)*. Once during their lifetime, if they can afford it, they should make the pilgrimage *(haj)* to Mecca (in Saudi Arabia), the site of the Kaaba, a sacred shrine built by Abraham, and also the birthplace of the Prophet.

The call to prayer used to be given by the muezzin from the balcony of the minaret. Nowadays loudspeakers broadcast the call. Only imperial mosques have more than one minaret.

(see p40)

Prayer Times

The five daily prayer times are calculated according to the times of sunrise and sunset, and thus change throughout the year. Exact times are posted on boards outside large mosques. Those given here are a guide.

Prayer	Summer	Winter
Sabah	5am	7am
Öğle	1pm	1pm
İkindi	6pm	4pm
Akşam	8pm	6pm
Yatsi	9:30pm	8pm

Ritual ablutions must be undertaken before prayer. Worshippers wash their head, hands and feet either at the fountain in the courtyard or at taps set in a wall of the mosque.

When praying, Muslims face the Kaaba in Mecca, even if they are not in a mosque, where the *mihrab* indicates the right direction. Kneeling and lowering the head to the ground are gestures of humility and respect for Allah.

The loge (hünkar mahfili) provided the sultan with a screened-off balcony where he could pray, safe from would-be assassins.

The kürsü, seen in some mosques, is a throne used by the imam while he reads extracts from the Koran.

Visiting a Mosque

Visitors are welcome at any mosque in Turkey, but non-Muslims should avoid visiting at prayer times, especially the main weekly congregation and sermon on Fridays. Take off your shoes before entering the prayer hall. Shoulders and knees should be covered. In remote areas women should cover their head with a scarf but main touristic mosques insist less on this. Do not eat, take photographs with a flash or stand very close to worshippers. A contribution to a donation box or mosque official is courteous.

Board outside a mosque giving times of prayers

TURKEY THROUGH THE YEAR

Turkey's national and regional holidays fall into three categories: religious feasts celebrated throughout the Islamic world, festivities associated with events or people in Turkish history, and traditional festivals, usually with a seasonal theme. The joyful spirit is tangible on public holidays and religious feast days when old and young, rich and poor unite and extended families gather. Regional events celebrate Turkey's diverse origins in terms of music, folklore, sport and the performing arts. Urban centres like İzmir and Istanbul host well-publicized festivals, but smaller towns also stage lively celebrations. *Luna park* (fun fairs) are wildly popular. The passage of the seasons is important, as many venues are outdoors. In the eastern provinces, harsh winters restrict the types of events that can be staged.

Spring

This is the best season for visiting Turkey. Temperatures are comfortable and the days longer and warmer. Many places receive a facelift after winter and restaurants arrange their tables outdoors. This is also the time to see Turkey's wild flower displays. Most tourist attractions, such as the historic sights, are far less crowded and thus more peaceful at this time of year.

Turkish children paying their respects to the memory of Atatürk

March
International Film Festival (late Mar–mid-Apr), Istanbul. Various cinemas in the city screen a selection of Turkish and foreign films.

April
Tulip Festival (Apr–May), Emirgan, Istanbul. A colourful celebration of the flower that originated in Turkey, held in a chic suburb north of the Fatih Bridge.

Tulips in Emirgan Park, scene of the Tulip Festival in spring

National Sovereignty and Children's Day (23 Apr). Anniversary of the first Grand National Assembly that convened in Ankara in 1920. Children from all around Turkey commemorate the life of the revered Atatürk. **ANZAC Day** (24–25 Apr), Çanakkale and Gallipoli Peninsula (see pp172–3). Representatives from Australia, New Zealand and Turkey commemorate the courage in battle displayed by both sides in World War I.

May
Yunus Emre Culture and Art Week (6–10 May), Eskişehir (see p261). A weeklong commemoration of the life and devotional love poetry of the 13th-century mystic, Yunus Emre.

Memorial at Gallipoli

Marmaris International Yachting Festival (2nd week in May), at Marmaris (see pp204–5). Mainly a convention for yacht owners, brokers and buyers, this event fills the marina with all kinds of vessels and is sure to appeal to anyone interested in yachting. **National Youth and Sports Day** (19 May). Celebrated all over the country to mark Atatürk's birthdate in 1881 and the anniversary of his arrival in the town of Samsun (see p269) in 1919 to plan the War of Independence. **Conquest of Istanbul** (29 May), Istanbul. The anniversary of Constantinople's capture by Sultan Mehmet the Conqueror in 1453. **Cirit Games** (May–Sep; see September p40).

Turkey's beaches, popular with locals and visitors in summer

Summer

Turks take their holidays seriously, and summer sees coastal areas of the Aegean and Mediterranean, in particular, crowded with university students and families on the move. Those city-dwellers lucky enough to own a summer house usually move to the coast to escape the oppressive heat when the school holidays begin in June.

Turkey's beaches offer opportunities for all kinds of activities, and resorts such as Bodrum and Marmaris are renowned for their active nightlife. Be on the look-out for impromptu festivals involving grease-wrestling or folk dancing, for example. Although local tourist offices have information on events in their area, these may not be well publicized and full details may be unavailable until just prior to the event.

June
Kafkasör Culture and Arts Festival *(second week Jun)*, Artvin *(see p279).* A festival in an alpine meadow that offers country handicrafts, folk dancing and singing, as well as bull wrestling.
Istanbul Festival of Arts and Culture *(mid-Jun–mid-Jul),* venues around the city. A prestigious event for opera, theatre and ballet performances. Both Turkish and Western classical music are

featured and the highlight is a one-night performance of Mozart's *Abduction from the Seraglio*, which is authentically staged at the Topkapı Palace.

Kırkpınar Festival and Grease Wrestling Championship *(last week Jun),* Edirne *(see pp156–7).* A popular event with men, in which the contenders, in *kıspet* (leather breeches) and smeared with olive oil, compete for the coveted honour in this traditional national sport.

Grease-wrestling tournament

International Opera and Ballet Festival *(Jun–mid-Jul),* Aspendos *(see p225).* The Roman amphitheatre is

International Opera and Ballet Festival poster, Aspendos

the venue for thrilling, open-air performances of opera, ballet and orchestral music. Visitors can also enjoy a picnic at the site before performances.

July
Navy Day *(1 Jul).* This holiday has some symbolism for Turks as it commemorates the anniversary of the end of the capitulations, or trade concessions, granted by the Ottoman sultans to a number of European powers from the mid-16th century onwards.
International Hittite Festival *(first week Jul),* Çorum *(see p298).* Students of Hittite art and culture and enthusiasts from around the globe gather for this annual event to attend lectures, debates and related outings.

Istanbul Jazz Festival *(first two weeks Jul),* Istanbul. An eclectic programme of jazz, world music, soul and R&B performances takes place at venues across the city.

August
Troy Festival *(10–15 Aug),* Çanakkale *(see p178).* Dance, theatre and art events that attract foreign performers.
Hacı Bektaş Commemorative Ceremony *(mid-Aug),* Avanos *(see p287).* Annual ceremony held in remembrance of Hacı Bektaş Veli, the mystic and philosopher who founded an Islamic sect based on the principles of unity and human tolerance.
International İzmir Festival *(last week Aug–early Sep),* İzmir *(see pp182–3).* An excellent programme for connoisseurs of music, ballet and theatre. Some performances also take place at Çeşme and Ephesus.
Victory Day *(30 Aug).* This day, known as Zafer Bayramı, is celebrated throughout Turkey. It celebrates the victory of the Turkish Republican army over the Greeks at the battle of Dumlupınar in 1922 during the War of Independence.

Racing yachts competing in Marmaris Race Week

Autumn

Autumn is an ideal time for visiting Turkey. The rural regions have grape or wine festivals and many villages celebrate their successful harvests of wheat, apricots, cotton or other crops. In coastal regions, the sea is still warm and watersports can continue well into October. Along the south coast, warm weather can last until quite late in November.

Watermelon cart, Diyarbakır

September

Cirit Games *(May–Sep)*, Erzurum *(see pp322–3)*. Cirit originated with nomads from Central Asia.

Horse and rider at the Cirit Games in Erzurum

It is a rough-and-tumble cross between polo and javelin-throwing in which horse and rider enjoy equal prestige. The games take place every Sunday.

Kaş-Lycia Culture and Art Festival *(first week Sep)*, Kaş. Renowned for its superb performances of contemporary dance and theatre, as well as painting exhibits.

Tango Festival *(second week in Sep)*, in Marmaris *(see pp204–5)*. A popular six-day event in which couples follow the lead of professional dance couples.

Watermelon Festival *(16–23 Sep)*, Diyarbakır *(see pp314–15)*. One of only a few festivals in eastern Turkey, this one focuses on the gigantic watermelons grown by the local farmers.

Cappadocia Grape Harvest Festival *(mid-Sep)*, Ürgüp *(see p287)*. Celebration of local food and wine in an area that has been called the birthplace of viticulture.

October

Golden Orange Film Festival *(first week Oct)*, Antalya *(see pp222–3)*. Turkish-language films and those with a local flavour now feature more prominently in this festival that has been going for over 20 years.

International Bodrum Cup Regatta *(third week of Oct)*, Bodrum *(see pp202–3)*. This regatta is open to several classes of wooden yachts only. Both Turkish and foreign yachtsmen compete.

Race Week *(last week Oct to first week Nov)*, Marmaris *(see pp204–5)*. In-and offshore races held in three divisions under authority of the Turkish Sailing Federation. There is also a fancy-dress night, and cocktail and dinner parties.

Republic Day *(29 Oct)*. This important national holiday commemorates the proclamation of the Turkish Republic in 1923.

November

Atatürk Commemoration Day *(10 Nov)*. Atatürk's death in 1938 is recalled each year with a poignant one-minute silence. This show of respect is observed throughout the country at 9:05am, the exact moment the revered leader passed away in Istanbul's Dolmabahçe Palace. Everything in the country grinds to a halt – people and even the traffic stops.

Muslim Holidays

The dates of the Muslim calendar and its holy days are governed by the phases of the moon and therefore change from year to year. In the holy month of **Ramadan**, Muslims do not eat or drink between dawn and dusk. Some restaurants are closed during the day and tourists should be discreet when eating in public. Straight after this follows the three-day **Şeker Bayramı** (Sugar Festival), when sweetmeats are prepared. Two months and 10 days later, a four-day celebration, **Kurban Bayramı** (Feast of the Sacrifice), commemorates the Koranic version of Abraham's sacrifice. This is the main annual public holiday in Turkey, and hotels, trains and roads are packed.

Whirling Dervishes at the Mevlevi Monastery in Istanbul

Winter

When the street vendors begin roasting chestnuts in Ankara and Istanbul, it is a sign that winter is near. Both cities can be damp and cold. Ankara frequently has temperatures below freezing and much snow. This is when coastal regions have their rainy season. Winter is a good time for visitors to explore Turkey's museums, as major sights are open and uncrowded. The ski centres *(see p388)* at Palandöken *(see p323)* and Uludağ *(see p161)* have their busiest season from December to April, and offer activities both on and off the slopes.

Turks do not celebrate Christmas, but most hotel chains offer a special menu on the day. New Year's Day, however, is an official holiday throughout Turkey.

It is celebrated heartily in restaurants and at home, and a lavish meal is served. Often

Christmas trees are decorated. Visitors are always welcome to join in these celebrations, but advance booking is advisable for popular places. Some establishments that close for the winter open again just for the New Year's Eve celebrations.

December

St Nicholas Symposium and Festival *(first week Dec)*, Demre *(see p220)*. Visitors who have an interest in the legend of Santa Claus will not want to miss this symposium and the discussions and ceremonies that accompany it. A host of related debates is organized, and pilgrimages are made to the 4th century church of St Nicholas in Demre, located near Antalya, and to the birthplace of Nicholas in Patara, near Kaş.

Mevlâna Festival *(10–17 Dec)*, Konya *(see pp254–5)*. A festival that commemorates Celaleddin Rumi *(see p259)*, the

mystic who founded the Mevlevi order. This is the only time that the whirling dervishes are in residence in their home city and offers one of the best performances anywhere in Turkey.

January

New Year's Day *(1 Jan)*. A national holiday.
Camel Wrestling *(mid-Jan)*, Selçuk *(see p184)*. Premier championship event held in the ruined Roman theatre at Ephesus *(see pp186–7)*.

February

Camel Wrestling *(through Feb)*, Aydın, İzmir and other Aegean towns. Impromptu camel wrestling bouts *(deve güreşi)* that coincide with the mating season (Dec–Feb), after which male camels become docile again.

A champion camel, adorned with tassels and rugs

National Holidays

New Year's Day (1 Jan)

National Sovereignty and Children's Day *Ulusal Egemenlik ve Çocuk Bayramı* (23 Apr)

Labour and Solidarity Day *Emek ve Dayanışma Günü* (1 May)

National Youth and Sports Day *Gençlik ve Spor Günü* (19 May)

Navy Day *Denizcilik Günü* (1 Jul)

Victory Day *Zafer Bayramı* (30 Aug)

Republic Day *Cumhuriyet Bayramı* (29 Oct)

Atatürk Commemoration Day (10 Nov)

New Year's celebrations in Istanbul

The Climate of Turkey

Turkey's mountainous terrain and maritime influence have created diverse climatic regions. The Aegean and Mediterranean coasts enjoy mean temperatures of 29°C (84°F) in July and 9°C (48°F) in January. Rain falls mainly in winter; Antalya receives an annual average of 991 mm (39 in). Along the Black Sea, rainfall is heavier, averaging 2,438 mm (96 in) a year. The rugged northeast has warm summers, but severe winters, with temperatures averaging -9°C (16°F). Precipitation is more evenly spread throughout the year, and snow lasts 120 days. The central plateau has hot, dry summers averaging 23°C (73°F) and cold, moist winters, when temperatures average below 0°C (32°F).

CAPPADOCIA AND CENTRAL ANATOLIA

°C

month	Apr	Jul	Oct	Jan
max	16	28	18	4
min	5	13	7	-4
hrs	13 hrs	3 hrs	6 hrs	3 hrs
mm	52 mm	9 mm	31 mm	42 mm

THE BLACK SEA

°C

month	Apr	Jul	Oct	Jan
max	15	26	20	11
min	8	19	13	4
hrs	4 hrs	5 hrs	4 hrs	2 hrs
mm	97 mm	147 mm	289 mm	219 mm

Samsun
Ordu
Amasya
Hopa
Trabzon
Gümüşhane
Erzurum
Sivas
Erzincan
Elazığ
Malatya
Van
Diyarbakır
Gaziantep
Antakya

EASTERN ANATOLIA

°C

month	Apr	Jul	Oct	Jan
max	20	38	25	7
min	7	22	10	-2
hrs	7 hrs	12 hrs	7 hrs	4 hrs
mm	69 mm	1 mm	35 mm	68 mm

MEDITERRANEAN TURKEY

°C

month	Apr	Jul	Oct	Jan
max	22	31	27	15
min	13	24	17	6
hrs	7 hrs	10 hrs	7 hrs	6 hrs
mm	36 mm	8 mm	39 mm	110 mm

Average monthly maximum temperature

Average monthly minimum temperature

Average daily hours of sunshine

Average monthly rainfall

0 kilometres 100

0 miles 50

The First Town

Together with Hacılar, Çatalhöyük *(see p258)* near Konya was possibly the world's first town. It had a population of around 5,000 people and is thought to have been the largest settlement at the time. Most of its inhabitants were farmers, but there was also brisk trade in obsidian (volcanic glass), brought into workshops from nearby volcanoes and used to fashion sharp cutting tools.

Archaeologists have been able to determine with certainty that Çatalhöyük's houses were sturdy structures built of brick and timber. The architectural designs also reflect the demands of an advanced culture that valued comfort. They typically feature separate living quarters and cooking areas, as well as several sheds and a number of store rooms.

Cattle seem to have played a rather important part in this ancient culture of Anatolia. This is evident from the fact that many of the rooms that were excavated at Çatalhöyük were decorated with elaborate wall paintings depicting cows, as well as clay heads with real horns moulded in relief onto the walls. Since Çatalhöyük's people had animistic beliefs, it has been suggested that the murals and bull's-head emblems could point to the practice of ritual or cult activities. Similarly, small terracotta figurines of a voluptuous female deity (the mother goddess) probably played a part in fertility rites, offerings or other religious ceremonies.

The Copper Age

By the Copper Age (from about 5500 to 3000 BC), farming had become a way of life

Flint dagger with bone handle

and people were raising crops and animals for a living. The increase in agricultural activity created a growing need for tools and implements. Methods for ore extraction and smelting were refined and passed on from father to son. Copper implements were widely used. Focal points of this period were Hacılar and Canhasan, both of which also manufactured fine pottery items, using advanced techniques. Their attractive clay vessels were decorated with distinctive multicoloured backgrounds.

The Bronze Age

Between 3000–1200 BC, the Anatolian metalworkers began to experiment with various techniques and developed new skills. Their workshops produced a surplus of goods and a brisk trade began to flourish. Among these items were gold jewellery, ornaments, belts, drinking vessels and statuettes of the mother goddess.

Artist's impression of Çatalhöyük, possibly the world's first town

8000 BC Start of the Neolithic period in Anatolia

Statuette of mother goddess, Çatalhöyük

5600 BC Fertility figurines made of terracotta at Hacılar and Çatalhöyük

| 8000 BC | 7000 BC | 6000 BC | 5000 B |

7250–7500 BC Community at Cayonu near Diyarbakır farms with sheep and goats

6800 BC Çatalhöyük develops into a farming town of 5,000 people

Terracotta jar from Canhasan

5000 BC Pottery begins to combine functionality with attractive design

The Assyrians

The empire of Assyria developed in northern Mesopotamia sometime in the 3rd millennium BC. It expanded and, by about 1900 BC, a network of Assyrian trading colonies had been established. Commerce between northern Mesopotamia and Anatolia began to take shape.

As trade goods circulated, the demand for them quickly grew and merchants found themselves catering to a rapidly expanding market.

The Assyrians grasped the importance of keeping track of their transactions, and developed a writing system using cuneiform symbols to represent words. Their trade agreements and accounts were imprinted on clay tablets, several of which have been preserved. The commercial records that were found at the Assyrian trading colony at Kanesh (modern Kültepe,

Assyrian clay 'letter' and envelope

see p295) are the earliest examples of writing to have been discovered in Anatolia.

Lively trade meant increased travel and demands on transport. Some areas saw the introduction of simple taxation systems. For the first time in history, money came to be regarded as the primary source of wealth, and envy, conflict and violence ensued as communities sought to protect territories, routes and resources from outsiders.

Not all inhabitants of the area presently occupied by Turkey gathered in central Anatolia. The city of Troy, immortalized by Homer and Virgil, stood at the strategic entrance to the Dardanelles Straits (see p172). Some scholars believe that the fall of Troy, as told in Homer's *Iliad*, coincides with the end of the Bronze Age, an era that had helped to establish an artistic and civilized culture in which the next civilization, the Hittites, would thrive and flourish.

Helen of Troy

According to Greek mythology Helen was the most beautiful woman of the ancient world. She was the daughter of King Tyndareus and Leda, who had been seduced by Zeus. In childhood, Helen was abducted by Theseus, who hoped to marry her when the time came. After having been rescued by her twin brothers Castor and Pollux, King Tyndareus decreed that Helen should marry the man of her choice. Helen chose Menelaus, king of Sparta, and lived happily at his side until she met Paris. Her elopement with the Trojan prince resulted in a heated battle between Greece and Troy as Menelaus fought to free his wife. After nine years of futile warfare Menelaus and Paris agreed to meet in single combat. Paris died as a result of his wounds; the victorious Menelaus reclaimed his Helen and returned with her to Sparta, where they lived happily to an old age.

Beautiful Helen of Troy with Paris

4000–3000 BC Settlement at Alacahöyük flourishes		3000 BC Beginning of Bronze Age in Anatolia; Troy, Ephesus and Smyrna become important cities		1900 BC Brisk trade by Assyrian trading colonies
4000 BC		**3000 BC**		**2000 BC**
	3900 BC Cities begin to emerge and a simple form of writing develops	**2500 BC** Hatti civilization establishes city kingdoms	**1900–2000 BC** Arrival of Hittites from the Caucasus; rise of Hittite empire	Assyrian cylinder seal made of serpentine

Gold cup, Alacahöyük

The Hittites

Historians are uncertain about the origins of the Hittites and how they got to Anatolia. It is clear that they arrived some time before the second millennium BC and were established at the time of the Assyrian trading colonies. Theirs was the first powerful empire to arise in Anatolia. Its capital was at Hattuşaş, present-day Boğazkale (see pp300–1).

The Hittite language, which was written in both cuneiform script and hieroglyphics, is believed to be the oldest of the Indo-European languages and was deciphered only in 1915. Large collections of Hittite writings were discovered at Hattuşaş. They contained cuneiform texts on various subjects, such as religious rituals, omens, myths and prayers, as well as royal annals, state treaties and diplomatic letters. Religion and appeasing the gods played an important role in Hittite life. They worshipped the "Thousand Gods of the Land of Hatti", an impressive pantheon of semitic deities, chief among whom were the Weather or Storm god, and his wife, the Sun goddess.

An advanced people, Hittites knew the art of forging iron, an advantage that made them a powerful military force.

Carved reliefs on the Sphinx Gate at Alacahöyük

Remains of Hittite relief, Boğazkale

Their cuneiform texts also revealed a complex legal system and their remarkably fair treatment of criminals and prisoners.

King Anitta conquered large parts of central Anatolia, including the Assyrian trading colony at Kanesh. His conquests increased the might of the kingdom, but also led to decentralization. The empire splintered into several city-states, until King Huzziya began to reunite the independent elements and fought to regain parts of Anatolia.

One of King Huzziya's successors, Labarna Hattushili I, is considered to be the founder of the Old Hittite Empire. He had his eye on wealthy Syria, then an important centre of trade, crafts and agriculture, and in an effort to annex its city-states he began to extend his campaigns into northern Syria. One of his grandsons finally managed to conquer Babylon around 1530 BC, but the constant wars made expansion difficult, and in general, Hittite rulers repeatedly gained, lost and regained territories throughout the duration of their empire.

Golden Age of the Hittites

The Hittite empire reached its peak around 1260 BC, when Hattushili III and Ramses II, the ruler of Egypt, signed an agreement of peace and friendship. As a result of this treaty, Hittite culture could flourish and the city of Hattuşaş grew rapidly. The Hittite empire entered its Golden Age. Hattuşaş grew into a large city. It was surrounded by sturdy walls and had an impressive temple and palace complex. The columns of the royal palace were supported on bases in

	1750 BC Pitkhana of Kushar and his son Anitta conquer large parts of central Anatolia		1530 BC Murshili I conquers Babylon		1400 BC Disputes lead to temporary loss of control over northern Syria	
2000 BC	**1800 BC**		**1600 BC**			**1400 BC**
Spouted jug, Kültepe	1700 BC King Anitta's empire dissolves into city-states	Hittite statuette		1550 BC Labarna Hattushili I establishes capital at Hattuşaş (present-day Boğazkale)		

Croesus, the wealthy king of the Lydians

the shape of bulls and lions, while the city gates were decorated with elaborate relief sculptures of fantastic sphinxes and armed gods.

Relative peace and stability saw a flowering of Hittite culture. Elegant pottery items, metal figures, animal-shaped vessels and stamp seals bearing royal symbols were produced. They also collected the documents in cuneiform script that now provide valuable information about their culture for archaeologists. According to records written at the time, Hittite kingdoms flourished throughout Anatolia.

Decline of the Hittites

In the early 12th century BC, an indistinct group of maritime marauders knowns as the "Sea Peoples" migrated to the eastern Mediterranean, and the collapse of the Hittites is attributed to their warring tactics. Around 1205 BC, Mediterranean pirates harried the boundaries of the empire, while the empire was suffering under a terrible famine. Many people died or fled, leaving only vestiges of the former empire in Syria and southern Anatolia. The Assyrians used the sufferings of the Hittites to their advantage and incorporated many of their kingdoms. The remaining pieces of the former Hittite empire were occupied by the Phrygians, a Balkan tribe, who had invaded from the northwest.

Lydian coin from 700 BC

Towards the Hellenistic Age

During the 7th century BC, Anatolia gradually became dominated by the Lydians, while the Lycian civilization flourished along the Mediterranean coastline. Their rock tombs *(see p219)* can still today be seen between Fethiye and Antalya *(see pp222–3)*.

The Lydians, a powerful Hittite-related tribe, settled in western Anatolia. Under the leadership of their king, Croesus, they conquered and annexed many Anatolian city-states around 700 BC. Renowned silversmiths, they are credited with the invention of coinage.

In the meanwhile, the Ionian Renaissance saw a flowering of Greek culture and economy along the Aegean coast. Pioneers from Miletus *(see pp194–5)* established colonies along the shores of the Mediterranean and Black Sea. City-states such as Knidos and Halicarnassus flourished, setting the stage for the next act in Anatolia's history.

1274 BC War between Syria and Egypt

1259 BC War with Egypt ends with the first written peace treaty signed by Ramses II and Hittite king Hattushili III

1200 BC

1000 BC Urartians establish a state near Lake Van

Urartian gold button

1000 BC

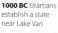
Assyrian-influenced statue of King Tarhunza

800 BC

800 BC Phrygians rise to power in central and southeastern Anatolia

700 BC Remaining Hittite kingdoms annexed by Assyria

The Hellenistic Age

Eastward expansion of Greek influence, roughly between 330 BC and 132 BC, was led by Alexander the Great (356–324 BC). After the assassination of his father, Philip II of Macedon, the young Alexander first consolidated his position in Europe and then took on the might of the Persian Empire, which had absorbed most of Anatolia during the 5th century BC. He first invaded Anatolia and Phoenicia, proceeding on to Egypt and India, setting up cities and leaving garrisons behind as he went. In Anatolia, the new colonists soon became the ruling class and imposed laws to promote Hellenization.

Alexander's Empire

◄— Alexander's campaigns

***Sarisses* (spears)** used by the Macedonian phalanx (battle formation) were 5.5 m (18 ft) long.

Pergamum
This artist's impression shows what the hilltop city would have looked like in 200 BC. It depicts the magnitude of Alexander's vision to create Pergamum as the perfect Greek city.

Alexander is on his stallion, Bucephalus.

Perge
The city of Perge, reputedly founded by two Greek seers after the Trojan War, welcomed Alexander the Great in 333 BC and gave him guides for his journey from Phaselis to Pamphylia.

The Battle at Issus

After campaigning in Asia Minor for just one year, Alexander won his first major battle. In November 333 BC, he and the Persian king, Darius III, clashed for the second time. At a mountain pass at Issus (near İskenderun), Macedonian troops managed to encircle the Persian cavalry. When Darius saw Alexander cut through his men and head straight for him, he fled the field leaving his troops in disarray and his mother, wife and children as hostages. Victorious Alexander pressed o n to Egypt and then across Persia to the Himalayas until a mutiny by his exhausted soldiers in 324 BC forced him to turn back. He died of a sudden fever in Babylon the following year, at the age of 32.

Alexander Sarcophagus
Dating from the late 4th century BC, this sarcophagus is named after Alexander because he is depicted in the battle scene friezes. The carvings are regarded as being among the most exquisite examples of Hellenistic art ever discovered.

Gold Octodrachma
This coin was minted by one of Alexander's successors, King Seleukos III of Syria, who ruled from 226–223 BC.

Darius III   Golden chariot

The Lycian Sarcophagus and Harpy Tomb at Xanthos
Xanthos was the chief city of ancient Lycia. Ravaged by the Persians around 540 BC, it was rebuilt and soon regained its former prominence. The Lycian sarcophagus and the Harpy Tomb shown here date from this period. Together with Pinara and many other Lycian cities, Xanthos surrendered to Alexander the Great in 334 BC.

Alexander and the Gordian knot

The Gordian Knot

Zeus, the father of the gods, had decreed that the people of Phrygia should choose as their king the first person to ride a wagon to his temple. The unlikely candidate, according to legend, was a peasant by the name of Gordius. Hardly able to believe his good fortune, the newly crowned king dedicated his wagon to Zeus, tying it to a pillar of the temple with an intricate knot. A subsequent oracle prophesied that the person who managed to untie it would become ruler of all Asia. That honour fell to Alexander the Great, who cheated the oracle by using his sword to cut the strands.

Rome Moves Eastward

The Roman Republic, established in central Italy around 500 BC, began a rapid expansion to the east during the 2nd century BC. After defeating their old enemies and rivals, the Carthaginians, the Roman armies defeated the Greeks at Corinth and Galatian forces in northern Anatolia. While the Romans were victorious in battle, the civilization of the Greeks in time exerted a great influence on Rome. This led the poet Horace to write

Marble head of a Greek youth

"Graecia capta ferum victorum cept" (Greece took her fierce conqueror captive). Greek art and culture dominated the Roman way of life. The Romans even adopted Greek as lingua franca in their newly acquired territories east of the Adriatic Sea.

Roman rule brought the benefits of Roman civilization, such as law, better hygiene and civil engineering. As they advanced, Roman armies built impressive military roads. These were of vital importance for trade. At the height of the Roman empire, it was possible to travel from the Adriatic coast to Syria on well-constructed, wide stone roads. The Stadiusmus (guidepost) monument at Patara (near Kalkan), possibly erected by Claudius, displays an inventory of roads and distances throughout Lycia.

Roman Expansion

The short-lived empire of Alexander the Great produced a number of successor states, including the Seleucid empire, which controlled much of Anatolia by the 2nd century BC. In two wars, known as the First and Second Macedonian Wars, Rome gained control of key city-states and kingdoms on the Mediterranean coast and in the Anatolian interior. Most submitted without resistance; others were simply handed over. King Atallus III of Pergamum, for example, simply left his kingdom to Rome in 133 BC when he realized that resistance was futile. Those who fought back, such as Mithridates VI of Pontus, were eventually defeated. But the wars against Mithridates marked the beginning of the turbulent Roman civil wars.

In 31 BC, Octavian, the nephew of Julius Caesar, emerged as victor of the civil wars. As a sign of its gratitude, the Roman Senate declared him emperor, and he was henceforth known as Augustus. Apart from extending the Roman territory and reorganizing the army, Octavian also established *colonia*, communal villages for retired soldiers. Examples of these can still be seen today, at Sagalassos and Antiocheia-in-Pisidia (near modern-day Eğirdir).

Roman Religion

The Romans worshipped an impressive array of gods. The greatest were Jupiter, his wife Juno, Minerva, the goddess of wisdom, and Mars, god of war. Apart from their own deities, the Romans also adopted those of the people they conquered, and allowed

19th-century depiction of Mithradates VI of Pontus

	546 BC Sardis, captial of the Lydian Empire, is overthrown by the Persians under Cyrus the Great	**130 BC** The Roman province of Asia is created	**AD 96–180** Five good emperors rule Rome
Cyrus the Great			Emperor Hadrian
600 BC	**400 BC**	**200 BC**	**AD 1**
560–546 BC King Croesus rules the Lydian empire	**334 BC** Alexander the Great claims Anatolian peninsula from the Persians	**68 BC** Pompey defeats the pirates St Paul's Well in Tarsus	**AD 1** St Paul (Saul of Tarsus) born in Cilicia

the local customs to continue. The people of Anatolia, therefore, continued to perform the fertility rites that were associated with the mother goddess, Cybele. Other, smaller sects and cults also flourished. Mithraism, originating with the Zoroastrian religion that was practised in Persia, was extremely influential, particularly among the soldiers of the Roman army. Many people, especially the poor, were drawn to the popular cult of the Egyptian god, Osiris

Statuette of the Mother Goddess, Cybele

numerous other towns erected elaborate, beautiful memorial arches to honour the emperor and commemorate his visit.

Christianity

St Paul, born Saul of Tarsus around AD 1, established the first churches in Asia Minor. Early Christian communities soon came into conflict with Roman authorities when they refused to make sacrifices to the emperor. However, all this changed in the 4th century AD, when Constantine, who ruled from AD 324 to 337, converted to Christianity. His conversion came about just before the Battle of the Milvian Bridge in AD 311, when he had a vision of a flaming cross inscribed with the words "in this sign, conquer".

Five Good Emperors

By the 2nd century AD, peace and order again prevailed in Rome's outlying provinces. At home, the empire prospered under the rule of the "five good emperors" (Nerva, Trajan, Hadrian, Antonius Pius, and Marcus Aurelius with Lucius Verus). During this period of relative peace and prosperity, the Romans endowed their far-flung territories with countless sophisticated aqueducts and *nymphaea* (reservoir systems) to distribute fresh water and remove waste products. Theatres and council chambers were built, as were *stadia* and *gymnasia* to host the popular sporting events. When emperor Hadrian (AD 117–138) toured the remote provinces, the delighted citizens of Attaleia (modern Antalya) *(see pp222–3)*, Termessos *(see p224)* and

In AD 324, Constantine founded the city of Constantinople (the site of modern-day Istanbul), and within six years had made it the capital and Christian centre of the empire. Massive walls enclosed its seven hills, and the emperor ordered the construction of a hippodrome, forum and public baths. Coastal cities were plundered for works of art to adorn the new capital, and new settlers were enticed by offers of bread and land. Constantine was succeeded by Theodosius, after whose death the empire was divided into two halves ruled by his sons, Arcadius and Honorius. The division sowed the seeds of Rome's eventual decline.

Hadrian, one of the "five good emperors"

284–305 Diocletian divides the Roman Empire into east and west	**324** Constantine becomes sole ruler of the Roman Empire	*Constantine and his wife, Helen*	**641** Constantine III, born Heraclonas in 626, becomes co-ruler at age 15

200 — **400** — **600** — **800**

| **141** Major earthquake in southern Asia Minor | **311** Edict of tolerance towards Christianity | **330** Constantinople is founded by emperor Constantine | *Justinian* | **518** Dynasty of Justinian begins with the rule of Justin (518–527) | **716** Treaty signed by Theodosius III and Bulgarian Khan Tervel establishes the border of Thrace |

The Byzantine Empire

The Byzantine empire reached its height under Justinian (AD 527–65), who reconquered much of North Africa, Italy and southern Spain and initiated major building programmes, including the construction of the Haghia Sophia *(see pp86–7)*. Under his rule, Constantinople was endowed with beautiful palaces, churches and public buildings. In the 8th century, the empire became wracked by the iconoclastic dispute, which centred on the role of images in religious life, and its territory steadily shrank under pressure from Arab expansion and the influx of the Seljuk Turks.

Byzantine Empire

  Extent in AD 565

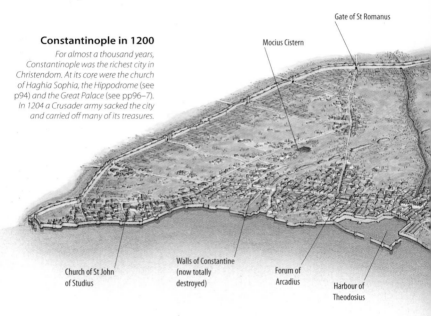

Constantinople in 1200

For almost a thousand years, Constantinople was the richest city in Christendom. At its core were the church of Haghia Sophia, the Hippodrome (see p94) and the Great Palace (see pp96–7). In 1204 a Crusader army sacked the city and carried off many of its treasures.

Gate of St Romanus

Mocius Cistern

Church of St John of Studius

Walls of Constantine (now totally destroyed)

Forum of Arcadius

Harbour of Theodosius

Byzantine Church Architecture

Early Byzantine churches were either basilical (such as St John of Studius, *see p120*) or built to a centralized plan (as in SS Sergius and Bacchus, *see p96*). From the 9th century, churches were built around four corner piers, or columns. Exteriors consisted mostly of unadorned brickwork, but the interiors were lavishly decorated with golden mosaics. Although the Ottoman sultans converted Constantinople's churches into mosques after their conquest of the city, many original features are still clearly discernible today.

Typical Late Byzantine Church

A central apse is flanked by two smaller side apses.

Four columns support the dome.

Brickwork may alternate with layers of stone.

The narthex, a covered porch, forms the entrance to the church.

Golden mosaics cover the ceilings and upper walls.

Walls of Theodosius
The land walls built by Theodosius II withstood many sieges until the Ottoman conquest in 1453.

"Greek Fire"
The Byzantines defended their shores using powerful ships called *dromons*, oared vessels from which "Greek fire" (an early form of napalm) could be directed at enemy vessels.

Blachernae
Palace

Forum of
Constantine
(see p95)

Aqueduct of Valens
Water from the Belgrade Forest and the mountains west of the city was brought into Constaninople on this double-tiered structure.

Basilica Cistern *(see p90)*

Church of SS
Sergius and
Bacchus

Hippodrome
(see p94)

Great Palace
(see pp96–7)

Haghia Sophia
The great church *(see pp86–7)* blazed with mosaics, including this example showing Christ flanked by the Emperor Constantine IX and Empress Zoe.

Justinian and Theodora, who ruled the Byzantine Empire at its height

Origins of the Turks

The Turkish people are descended from tribes of Central Asian nomads, known as the Turkmen. In the 10th century, some of these tribes moved into Russia, China and India, while others began raiding Byzantine-ruled Anatolia. The attacks increased as the century progressed, until one group, the Seljuks, broke away and gradually began to move eastward.

Seljuk manuscript depicting Aristotle and disciples

Around the middle of the 11th century, the Seljuk Turks crossed the Oxus River and invaded Persia. Baghdad fell in 1055, and it was here that Seljuk leader Tuğrul Bey, was crowned caliph – ruler of the Islamic world. Tuğrul Bey established the powerful Great Seljuk Sultanate, which ruled much of the Islamic world from 1055 until 1156.

The Seljuk Rum Sultanate

Alp Arslan, nephew of Tuğrul Bey, succeeded him as sultan in 1063, and went on to occupy Syria and Armenia, and to launch various raids into Anatolia. In 1071, the Byzantines tried to defeat the Seljuks, but their army was destroyed at the Battle of Manzikert (Malazgirt) on 26 August 1071, a disaster which saw the capture of the emperor, Romanus IV Diogenes.

Romanus IV Diogenes (left), vanquished at Manzikert

Although the victorious Seljuks did not actively seek to govern Anatolia, the vacuum left by the Byzantine defeat resulted in the formation of a series of Islamic-Turkish states. The most famous of these states was the Seljuk Sultanate of Rum (1077–1308), initially based in Nicaea

(modern-day İznik) *(see pp164–5)*. Other states established by the Seljuks were those of the Danışman at Sivas (1095–1175) and Saltuks (1080–1201) at Erzurum.

The period from the late 11th to late 12th century was one of turmoil in Anatolia. The arrival of the Crusaders, who seized Nicaea in 1097, and then Antioch (modern Antakya) the following year, altered the balance of power drastically. The Crusader influence was especially pronounced in southern Anatolia, where Crusader knights established the Principality of Antioch and the County of Edessa (centred on modern-day Şanlıurfa). The Seljuks moved their capital to Konya, and the Byzantines tried once more to repel the Seljuks, only to be soundly defeated at the Battle of Myriocephalon in 1176.

Under the rule of Kılıç Arslan II (1156–92), the Seljuk Sultanate of Rum became the most powerful state in Anatolia. The capture of Antalya *(see pp222–3)* in 1207 gave access to the Mediterranean, and Seljuk Anatolia prospered. The capture of Sinop

---

867 Macedonian dynasty comes to power under Basil I

843 Icons are permitted again after an era of destruction

800

886 Death of Basil I

900

913–959 Rule of Constantine VII Porphygenitus

1000 Asia Minor is invaded by the Seljuk Turks

1000

1018 Anatolia is invaded by the Seljuk Turks

1025 Death of Basil II

1071 Byzantine defeated at Battle Manzike

Seljuk stone bridge near Aspendos

in 1214 secured trade across the Black Sea, and the capture of Alanya (see p230) in 1221 provided an additional boost to maritime trade.

Wealth and Prosperity

To consolidate their power, the Seljuks forged trade relations with other states signing agreements with Byzantium, Cyprus, Provence, Pisa, Venice, Florence and Genoa between 1207 and 1253. They constructed bridges to facilitate overland trade and built hans and caravanserais (see pp28–9) to provide shelter for travelling merchants and their goods.

The Seljuk empire was at its height under Sultan Malik Şah (1072–92), who generously patronized the arts and sciences. Yet the hallmark of Seljuk civilization was their architecture, which reached a peak in the 13th century. The hospital complex at Divriği (see p323), harbour fortifications at Alanya, the Sultanhanı near Aksaray (see pp28–9) and the Karatay theological college in Konya (see pp254–5) were all built during this efflorescence. Under the Rum Seljuks, science and literature flourished, together with painting and sculpture. This cultural renaissance was partly caused by an influx of skilled and educated people fleeing the advance of the Mongols from the east.

Mongol Domination

In 1243 Mongol forces defeated the Seljuk army at Kösedağ, and until 1308 the Seljuk sultans were reduced to the status of vassals under the Mongols. During the 13th and 14th centuries, many Christians converted to Islam, because the Mongols offered reduced taxation for Muslims.

The Mongols ruled Anatolia until 1335, when the first Beylik states were set up by rebel Turkmen. These included the Karamanids in the Taurus highlands and the Danişman-dids in central Anatolia. However, it was the small emirate of Ertuğrul, based in Eskişehir, that triumphed. Ertuğrul's son, Osman, founded a dynasty known as the Ottomans, and created one of the greatest empires the world has known.

Mongol archers attacking Seljuk cavalry

Crusader	**1131** Sultan Mesut I establishes the Seljuk Rum sultanate with its capital at Konya	**1204** Constantinople is besieged, sacked and looted during the Fourth Crusade	**1326** Ottoman armies capture Bursa; Orhan Bey is the first Ottoman ruler to call himself sultan
1100		**1200**	**1300**
1100–1400 Start of the Crusades, undertaken to liberate the Holy Land	**1176** Defeat of Byzantines at Myriocephalon	**1243** Mongol invasion of Anatolia	**1299** Osman Bey establishes Ottoman principalities in Söğut and Domaniç

The Ottoman Empire

The expansion of the Ottoman lands accelerated during the late 13th century. A turning point was Mehmet II's capture of Constantinople in 1453. Constant wars advanced the imperial frontiers deep into the Balkans and the Middle East. Syria and Egypt fell in 1516–17, bringing the holy cities of Mecca and Medina under Ottoman control. By the mid-1500s the Ottoman sultan was the central figure of the (Sunni) Muslim world. The Ottoman Empire, though often associated with excessive opulence, was characterized also by its efficient administration, religious tolerance and immense military power.

Ottoman Empire

▨ Maximum Extent (1566)

The elite Janissaries *(see p60)* were professional soldiers.

Osman I
The founder of the Ottoman dynasty ruled a small emirate on the frontiers of the declining Byzantine empire. Expansion of the Ottoman lands began under his son, Orhan.

Foot soldiers were often poorly trained auxiliaries.

Cannons were used in large numbers by the Ottoman armies.

The Fall of Constantinople
Constantinople, the last remnant of Byzantium, fell to the army of Mehmet II on 29 May 1453. This view shows the Turkish camp, and the bridge of boats built to cross the Golden Horn.

Mehmet II (The Conqueror)
The sultan safeguarded freedom of worship and successfully repopulated Constantinople.

Barbarossa

Regarded as a glorious Ottoman hero, and in 1543 admiral of the navy, to adversaries Barbarossa was a fearless corsair. Ottoman naval power was less invincible after his death.

Ottoman Cartography

In 1521, the Ottoman admiral and cartographer, Piri Reis, drew on the accounts of Spanish and Portuguese explorers and captured sailors to compile a remarkable map of the world on gazelle hide.

Horses were held in high regard. The banner of the sultan's troops was a horse-tail.

Ottoman soldiers were known for their skilful archery.

Sipahis fought on horseback.

Süleyman the Magnificent

One of the most enlightened sultans, Süleyman (1520–66) was a poet, lawmaker and patron of the arts. Art and architecture flourished during his prosperous rule.

The Battle Of Mohacs

At Mohacs, on 28 August 1526, Süleyman the Magnificent led an army of 200,000 against the forces of Louis II, the 14-year-old king of Hungary. The Hungarian forces were outmanoeuvred by the Janissaries (see p60) and faltered under massed Ottoman artillery fire. Despite this great success, the expansion of the Ottoman empire into Europe came to an end after two unsuccessful sieges of Vienna in 1529 and 1532.

The Battle of Lepanto, 1571

Ottoman sea power was fatally weakened after the defeat by Don John of Austria, commanding the fleet of the Holy League in the waters of the Gulf of Patros.

The Empire of Suleyman

The Ottoman Empire reached its zenith under the leadership of Sultan Süleyman the Magnificent (1520–66). It stretched from the borderlands of southern Hungary to Yemen, and from the Crimea to Morocco.

This advance was aided by well-organized administration, as well as military organization. A key practice was *devşirme*, which required rural Christian subjects to give one son to the service of the sultan. The boys converted to Islam and were educated to become civil servants or Janissaries (soldiers).

Members of the Janissary corps

Janissaries were subject to strict discipline, including celibacy, but could gain high-ranking privileges that were previously reserved for bureaucrats. An ambitious *kul* (slave) could attain powerful status. In fact, many grand viziers (prime ministers) were products of the *devşirme* system.

By the 18th century, however, the former elite corps had become a corrupt political power and a serious threat to the sultanate. Whenever the Janissaries felt that their privileges were under threat, they rioted violently and no-one dared to intervene.

Dolmabahçe Palace, a lavish display of opulence

Displays of Wealth

After Süleyman's death, the empire was ruled by a succession of mediocre sultans who concentrated on enjoying their riches rather than ruling their vast territories. Selim II (Selim the Sot) was known more for his fondness for wine than his interest in the affairs of state. Thus the empire became easy prey for the plotting and intrigue of the Janissaries, as well as the expansionist ambitions of other powers.

At the signing of the Treaty of Karlowitz in 1699, the empire lost half its European possessions. This marked the beginning of the empire's decline and opened the way for Russian advances in the Black Sea region. Long years of war followed, forcing the state to reorganize its finances.

Families that could afford to buy state land began to accumulate great personal wealth. In imitation of Sultan Ahmed III (1703–30), the elite built palaces on the Bosphorus, sported the latest European fashions and lived in luxury. Corruption and nepotism affected the entire empire, while its borders were constantly threatened. In 1730, an uprising in Istanbul overthrew Ahmed III. In short wars with Russia, Venice, Austria and Persia, the empire continued to lose territory.

Revival and Decline

A period of peace, from 1739 to 1768, produced an economic upswing and a brief artistic renaissance that saw the

1335 Beginning of the Beylik Period	**1397** The first Ottoman siege of Constantinople	*Mehmet the Conqueror*	**1513** Piri Reis creates a map of the world	
1300	**1400**		**1500**	**1600**
1364 Sultan Orhan recaptures Edirne (Adrianople)	**1453** Constantinople falls to Mehmet II, the Conqueror, and is renamed Istanbul	**1533** Barbarossa becomes admiral of Ottoman fleet	**1569** Great fire of Istanbul destroys much of the city	

completion of the Nurosmaniye in 1755 – the first sultanic mosque complex built in Istanbul since that of Ahmed I in 1617. This interlude was shattered when Russian troops mobilized by Catherine the Great invaded the feeble Ottoman empire. In two periods of war (1768–74 and 1788–91), the Russians gained access to the Black Sea and managed to annex the Crimean region. This was the first Muslim territory lost by the Ottomans and they were also forced to pay reparations to Russia.

Portrait of the hero Sultan Abdül Hamit II

In 1826, Mahmud II suppressed the Janissaries in a massacre known as the "Auspicious Event" and reorganized the bureaucracy in an effort to modernize the empire. Russia, meanwhile, encouraged Greece, Serbia, Moldavia and the Ottoman vassal state of Wallachia (in modern Romania) to demand self-rule. Mahmud II hoped that by passing the Tanzimat Reforms (1839 and 1856) he could ensure good government, equality for all and a stronger state. However, the edict of 1856, written under pressure from European powers after the disastrous Crimean War (1853–1856) and based on Western-style, secular ideals, was greeted with indignation.

Times of War

In the 1870s, a reformist movement known as the Young Ottomans began to press for a constitutional monarchy. Sultan Abdül Hamit II enacted some liberal reforms, but dissolved the infant parliament in 1878 as the country entered a disastrous war with Russia.

During the next few years, further debilitating wars took place, gradually ensuring the independence of the Balkan provinces. In 1908, a rebellious group of officers formed the Committee of Union and Progress, dubbed the Young Turks. When Abdül Hamit II refused to accept a constitution, he was replaced by the weak Mehmet V, and the CUP took control.

In 1912 and 1913, the empire lost most of its remaining European possessions in the Balkan Wars. Greatly weakened, it slid into World War I a year later on the side of Germany and Austria-Hungary. The cost of the war in economic and human terms was immea- surable. By 1918, only the heartland of Anatolia remained of the Ottoman Empire. Foreign troops occupied Istanbul, İzmir, Antakya and Antalya. Turkish nationalists reacted by setting up an assembly in Ankara, but the ensuing war for independence set the seal on a Turkey that determined its own destiny.

Russian troops fighting Turkish forces in the Caucasus in 1914

Atatürk

648 Great earthquake Istanbul

1699 Treaty of Karlowitz

1807 Janissaries rebel against reforms to control their power

1881 Mustafa Kemal (later Atatürk) is born in Salonika

1700

1800

1900

86 Ottomans are forced to evacuate Hungary

1740 Stirrings of dissent in Egypt

1826 Mahmud II crushes the Janissaries in a brutal revolt

1840–1855 Tanzimat reforms attempt to modernize and revive the Ottoman Empire

1906 Early movement towards the Committee of Union and Progress (CUP)

The Treaty of Lausanne

The disastrous losses of World War I and the subsequent occupation of parts of Turkey by powers such as Britain, France and Italy, fuelled Turkish nationalism. When Greek troops occupied İzmir on 15 May 1919 and pushed eastwards to Ankara, the seeds for war were sown. Turkish efforts met with little success until Mustafa Kemal, an army officer respected for his heroism during the

Signatories at Lausanne, with Mussolini among them

Gallipoli campaign of 1915–16, assumed the leadership. At Nationalist congresses in Erzurum and Sivas in 1919, his ideas for the establishment of a Turkish republic aroused unanimous support.

Greek forces were routed by Nationalist forces in 1922 and Allied ambitions for power sharing in what remained of Ottoman territories faded. The Treaty of Lausanne (1923) recognized the borders and territories of the newly formed state and the Turkish Republic was proclaimed the same year, with Ankara as the new capital city.

As part of the peace settlement and to underpin the framework for a cohesive Turkish state, Greece and Turkey agreed to exchange their ethnic populations. Around 1.25 million Greeks returned to Greece, and 450,000 Muslims were repatriated to Turkey. The impact of resettling such considerable numbers delayed the recovery of both countries after the war.

Ataturk's Vision

Mustafa Kemal's election as leader of the new state came as no surprise and he was, thereafter, known as Atatürk, father of the Turks. He greatly admired European lifestyles

and culture and his forward-thinking ideas envisaged a modern, secular Turkish state. His aim was to establish a multi-party democracy with an opposition party.

He instituted radical reforms and borrowed legal and social codes from other European countries. Ottoman scripts were replaced by the Latin alphabet and the new Turkish language. Dress codes changed and surnames were adopted. Schools and courts based on religious laws were abolished and, in 1928, a secular state underwritten by a civil constitution was recognized. Most Turks embraced democratic reform but some minorities, notably Kurds, who had been guaranteed land by Allied countries in

Atatürk demonstrating the Latin alphabet

1900	1910	1920	1930	1940	1950

1915–16 Gallipoli campaign

1924 Caliphate abolished

1925–38 Atatürk introduces reforms destined to modernize Turkey

1950 Call to prayer returned to Arabic after 27 years in Turkish

1961 Second Constitution of the Republic

1923 First Constitution implemented with the formation of the Republic

Turkish flag

1938 Atatürk dies

Atatürk memorial

1952 Turkey becomes a member of NATO

1960 First military coup

World War I under the Treaty of Sèvres (1920), saw İslam and a chance for autonomy slipping away.

Building the State

Atatürk's founding doctrines gave Turks a distinct identity and set the seal on the indivisibility of the Turkish state. When Atatürk died in 1938, Turkey had an impressive infrastructure and state-run enterprises which satisfied basic needs. During World War II, Turkey pursued peaceful and friendly policies and remained neutral. The Truman Doctrine and Marshall Plan strengthened foreign policy and ties with the West. Turkey became a NATO member in 1952 and 5,500 Turkish troops fought in the Korean War (1950–54).

Veteran political leader
Bülent Ecevit

Growing Pains

Turkey's military services, defenders of secularism and Atatürk's principles, intervened in 1960, 1971 and 1980 to restore law and order, with remote regions of Turkey remaining under martial law until the mid-1990s. During this period, civilian leaders such as Bülent Ecevit grappled with the challenges of political instability and economic modernization. The invasion of Cyprus by Turkey in 1974 left the island partitioned into Turkish and Greek sides. A Kurdish challenge for more self-expression slid into armed conflict that lasted until the capture of the Kurdish Workers' Party leader Abdullah Öcalan in 1999.

Balancing political stability and the demands of a modern economic state often undermined democratic goals. However, when Turgut Özal became Prime Minister in 1983 he spurred businesses to realize their export potential. Many factories today display his photograph and recall the exhilarating days of the "Great Transformation". Taxes like VAT were introduced to bolster state revenues. Tourism potential also began to be realized.

Economic Miracle

By 2001, however, Turkey's economy had drifted off course, inflation was over 100 per cent and the banking system had collapsed. In 2002 a religious-leaning party called Justice and Development, or AK, was elected with a two-thirds majority. Prime Minister Recep Tayyip Erdoğan implemented unprecedented reforms with a commitment to steering Turkey into the European Union.

By 2004 inflation had reverted to single figures and sufficient reforms had been achieved for European leaders to agree to open membership talks with Turkey. Much has been achieved since then, although rapid change and high consumer prices have also brought financial burdens to many.

Folklore dancers in traditional dress

1970	1980	1990	2000	2010	2020

NATO emblem

1996 Turkey enters European customs union, bringing potential trade advantages

1980 Military coup; third Constitution (1982)

1999 Earthquake shatters İzmit

2009 Arrests made over the Ergenekon plot to bring down the government

2011 Earthquake shakes Ercis and Van in eastern Turkey

1971 Military coup

1978 Kurdish Workers' Party formed

1991 As NATO partner, Turkey provides support for the US during the Gulf War

2006 The new Turkish Lira (TL) becomes the country's official currency

2013 Gezi Park Protests

2010 A referendum aims to bring Turkish constitution in line with European Union standards

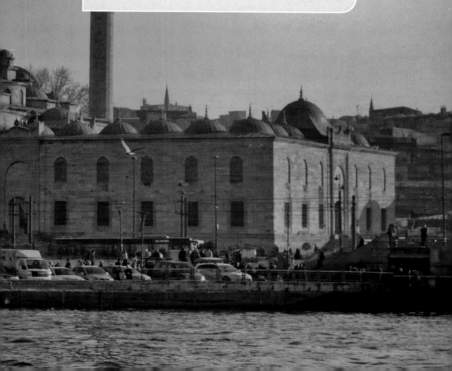

INTRODUCING ISTANBUL

Istanbul at a Glance

Numerous interesting places to visit in Istanbul are described in the *Area by Area* section of this book, which covers the sights of central Istanbul as well as those a short way out of the city centre. They range from mosques, churches, palaces and museums to bazaars, Turkish baths and parks. For a breathtaking view across the city, climb Galata Tower *(see pp114–15)* or take a ferry ride *(see p397)* to the city's Asian shore. If you are short of time, you will probably want to concentrate on only the most famous monuments, namely Topkapı Palace, Haghia Sophia and the Blue Mosque, which are located conveniently close to each other.

The Mevlevi Monastery *(see p114)* houses an interesting museum dedicated to classical Ottoman poetry. The Whirling Dervishes also perform here on the last Sunday of every month.

A boat trip along the Bosphorus *(see pp130–31)* is a wonderful way of viewing sights such as the 14th-century Genoese Castle (above the village of Anadolu Kavağı).

THE BAZAAR QUARTER *(see pp98–109)*

SULTANAHM *(see pp82–9)*

Süleymaniye Mosque *(see pp104–5)* was built by the great architect, Sinan, in honour of his patron, Süleyman the Magnificent *(see pp58–9)*.

The Grand Bazaar *(see pp108–9)* is a maze of shops under an intricately painted, vaulted roof. Shopkeepers are relentless, and bargaining *(see p134)* is a must.

◀ The New Mosque at sunset, Istanbul

❷ ★ Archaeological Museum

Classical statues, dazzling carved sarcophagi, Turkish ceramics and other treasures from all over the former Ottoman Empire make this one of the world's great collections of antiquities.

Locator Map
See Street Finder map 5

Çinili Pavilion (see p78)

The Executioner's Fountain is so named because the executioner washed his hands and sword here after a public beheading.

❶ ★ Topkapı Palace

For 400 years the Ottoman sultans ruled their empire from this vast palace. Its fine art collections, opulent rooms and leafy courtyards are among the highlights of a visit to Istanbul.

Entrance to Topkapı Palace

Topkapı Palace ticket office

❸ Imperial Mint

This museum houses exhibitions on the historical background to Istanbul.

❹ Haghia Eirene

The Byzantine church of Haghia Eirene dates from the 6th century. Unusually, it has never been converted into a mosque.

Imperial Gate

❺ Fountain of Ahmet III

Built in the early 18th century, the finest of Istanbul's Rococo fountains is inscribed with poetry likening it to the fountains of paradise.

For keys to symbols *see back flap*

❶ Topkapı Palace
Topkapı Sarayı

Between 1459 and 1465, shortly after his conquest of Constantinople *(see p58)*, Mehmet II built Topkapı Palace as his principal residence. Rather than a single building, it was conceived as a series of pavilions contained by four enormous courtyards, a stone version of the tented encampments from which the nomadic Ottomans had emerged. Initially, the palace served as the seat of government and contained a school in which civil servants and soldiers were trained. In the 16th century, however, the government was moved to the Sublime Porte *(see p77)*. Sultan Abdül Mecid I abandoned Topkapı in 1853 in favour of Dolmabahçe Palace *(see pp126–7)*. In 1924 it was opened to the public as a museum.

★ Harem
The labyrinth of exquisite rooms where the sultan's wives and concubines lived can be visited on a guided tour *(see p75)*.

Entrance to Harem

Gate of Salutations: entrance to the palace

Divan
The viziers of the imperial council met in this chamber, sometimes watched covertly by the sultan.

İftariye Pavilion
Standing between the Baghdad and Circumcision pavilions, this canopied balcony provides views down to the Golden Horn.

VISITORS' CHECKLIST

Practical Information
Babıhümayun Cad. **Map** 5 F3.
Tel (0212) 512 04 80.
🇼 **topkapisarayi.gov.tr**
Open 9am–4:30pm Wed–Mon.
📷 🚫 ♿ Harem: **Open**
9am–4pm Wed–Mon. 🎫

Transport
🚋 Sultanahmet.

Baghdad Pavilion
In 1639 Murat IV built this pavilion to celebrate his capture of Baghdad. It has exquisite blue-and-white tilework.

KEY

① **The kitchens** contain an exhibition of ceramics, glass and silverware (see p74).

② **The Gate of Felicity** is also called the Gate of the White Eunuchs.

③ **Second courtyard**

④ **Harem ticket office**

⑤ **Exhibition of arms and armour** (see p74).

⑥ **Audience Chamber**

⑦ **Library of Ahmet III**, erected in 1719, is an elegant marble building. This ornamental fountain is set into the wall below its main entrance.

⑧ **Privy Chamber** (see p75).

⑨ **Circumcision Pavilion**

⑩ **Konyalı Restaurant**

⑪ **The fourth courtyard** is a series of gardens dotted with pavilions.

⑫ **Third courtyard**

⑬ **Exhibition of Imperial costumes** (see p74).

★ **Treasury**
This 17th-century jewel-encrusted jug is one of the precious objects exhibited in the former treasury (see pp74–5).

Exploring the Palace's Collections

During their 470-year reign, the Ottoman sultans amassed a glittering collection of treasures. After the foundation of the Turkish Republic in 1923 (see p62), this was nationalized and the bulk of it put on display in Topkapı Palace. As well as diplomatic gifts and articles commissioned from the craftsmen of the palace workshops, many of the items in the collection were the booty from successful military campaigns. Many date from the massive expansion of the Ottoman Empire during the reign of Selim the Grim (1512–20), when Syria, Arabia and Egypt were conquered.

Ceramics, Glass and Silverware

The kitchens contain the palace's ceramics, glass and silverware collections. Turkish and European pieces are massively overshadowed by the vast display of Chinese (as well as Japanese) porcelain. This was brought to Turkey along the Silk Route, the overland trading link between the Far East and Europe. Topkapı's collection of Chinese porcelain is the world's second best, after China.

Japanese porcelain plate

The Chinese porcelain on display spans four dynasties: the Sung (10–13th centuries), followed by the Yüan (13–14th centuries), the Ming (14–17th centuries) and the Ching (17–20th centuries). Celadon, the earliest form of Chinese porcelain collected by the sultans, was made to look like jade, a stone believed by the Chinese to be lucky. The Ottomans prized it because it was said to neutralize poison in food. More delicate than these are a number of exquisite blue-and-white pieces, mostly of the Ming era.

Chinese aesthetics were an important influence on Ottoman craftsmen, particularly in the creation of designs for their fledgling ceramics industry at İznik (see p165). Although there are no İznik pieces in the Topkapı collection, many of the tiles on the palace walls originated there. These clearly show the influence of designs used for Chinese blue-and-white porcelain, such as stylized flowers and cloud scrolls. Much of the later porcelain, particularly the Japanese Imari ware, was made for the export market. The most obvious examples of this are some plates decorated with quotations from the Koran. A part of the kitchens, the old confectioners' pantry, has been preserved as it would have been when in use. On display are huge cauldrons and other utensils wielded by the palace's chefs as they prepared to feed its 12,000 residents and guests.

Arms and Armour

Taxes and tributes from all over the empire were once stored in this chamber, which was known as the Inner Treasury. Straight ahead as you enter are a series of horse-tail standards. Carried in processions or displayed outside tents, these proclaimed the rank of their owners. Viziers (see pp60–61), for example, merited three, and the grand vizier five, while the sultan's banner would flaunt nine.

The weaponry includes ornately embellished swords and several bows made by sultans themselves (Beyazıt II was a particularly fine craftsman). Seen next to these exquisite items, the huge iron swords used by European crusaders look crude by comparison. Also on view are pieces of 15th-century Ottoman chainmail and colourful shields. The shields have metal centres surrounded by closely woven straw that has been painted with flowers.

Imperial Costumes

A collection of imperial costumes is displayed in the Hall of the Campaign Pages, whose task was to look after the royal wardrobe. It was a palace tradition that on the death of a sultan his clothes were carefully folded and placed in sealed bags. As a result, it is possible to see a perfectly preserved kaftan once worn by Mehmet the Conqueror (see p58). The reforms of Sultan Mahmut II included a revolution in the dress code. The end of an era came as plain grey serge replaced the earlier luxurious silken textiles.

Sumptuous silk kaftan once worn by Mehmet the Conqueror

Treasury

Of all the exhibitions in the palace, the Treasury's collection is the easiest to appreciate, glittering as it does with thousands of precious and semi-precious stones. Possibly the only surprise is that there are so few women's jewels here. Whereas the treasures of the sultans and viziers were owned by the state, reverting to the palace on their deaths, those belonging to the women of the court did not.

In the first hall stands a diamond-encrusted suit of chainmail, designed for Mustafa III (1757–74) for ceremonial use. Diplomatic gifts include a fine pearl statuette of a prince seated beneath a canopy, which was sent to Sultan Abdül Aziz (1861–76) from India. The greatest pieces are to be seen in the second hall. Foremost among these is the Topkapı dagger (1741). This splendid object was commissioned by the sultan from his own jewellers. It was intended as a present for the Shah of Persia, but he died before it reached him. Among the exhibits are a selection of bejewelled *aigrettes* (plumes), which were used to add splendour to imperial turbans.

The Topkapı dagger

In the third hall is the 86-carat Spoonmaker's diamond, said to have been discovered in a rubbish heap in Istanbul in the 17th century, and bought from a scrap merchant for three spoons. The gold-plated Bayram throne was given to Murat III by the Governor of Egypt in 1574 and used for state ceremonies.

The throne in the fourth hall, a gift from the Shah of Persia, was acknowledged by the equally magnificent gift of the Topkapı dagger. In a cabinet near the throne is an unusual relic: a case containing bones said to be from the hand of St John the Baptist.

Miniatures and Manuscripts

It is possible to display only a fraction of Topkapı's total collection of over 13,000 miniatures and manuscripts at any one time. Highlights of it include a series of depictions of warriors and fearsome creatures known as *Demons and Monsters*

in the Life of Nomads, which was painted by Mohammed Siyah Qalem, possibly as early as the 12th century. It is from this Eastern tradition of miniature painting, which was also prevalent in Mogul India and Persia, that the Ottoman style of miniatures (see p33) arose.

Also on show are some fine examples of calligraphy (see pp32–3), including copies of the Koran, poetry and manuscripts in Turkish, Arabic, Persian, Latin, Hebrew and Greek, along with several *firmans*, or imperial decrees.

Clocks

European clocks given as diplomatic gifts to, or bought by, various sultans form the majority of this collection, despite the fact that there were makers of clocks and watches in Istanbul from the 17th century. The clocks range from simple, weight-driven 16th-century examples to an exquisite 18th-century English mechanism encased in mother-of-pearl and featuring a German organ which played tunes every hour, on the hour. The only male European eyewitness accounts of life in the Harem were written by mechanics who serviced the clocks.

17th-century watch made of gold, enamel and precious stones

Pavilion of the Holy Mantle

Some of the holiest relics of Islam are displayed in the Pavilion of the Holy Mantle, five domed rooms that are a place of pilgrimage for Muslims. Most of the relics found their way to Istanbul as a result of the conquest by Sultan Selim the Grim of Egypt and Arabia, and his assumption of the caliphate (the leadership of Islam) in 1517.

The most sacred treasure is the mantle once worn by the Prophet Mohammed. Visitors cannot actually enter the room in which it is stored; instead they look into it from an antechamber through an open doorway. Night and day, holy men chant passages from the Koran over the gold chest in which the mantle is stored. A stand in front of the chest holds two of Mohammed's swords. Behind a glass cabinet in the anteroom are hairs from the beard of the Prophet, a tooth, a letter written by him and an impression of his footprint.

In other rooms are some of the ornate locks and keys for the Kaaba (Muslim shrine in Mecca), which were sent to Mecca by successive sultans.

(see p33)
(see pp32–3)

Life in the Harem

Apart from the sultan's mother, the most powerful woman in the Harem, and the sultan's daughters, the women of the Harem were slaves, gathered from the furthest corners of the Ottoman Empire and beyond. Their dream was to become a favourite of the sultan and bear him a son, which, on some occasions, led to marriage. Competition was stiff, however, for at its height the Harem contained over 1,000 concubines, many of whom never rose beyond the service of their fellow captives. The last women eventually left the Harem in 1909.

A Western view of life in the Harem, from a 19th-century engraving

❷ Archaeological Museum
Arkeoloji Müzesi

Although this collection of antiquities was begun only in the mid-19th century, provincial governors were soon sending in objects from the length and breadth of the Ottoman Empire. Today the museum has one of the world's richest collections of classical artifacts, and also includes treasures from the pre-classical world. The main building was erected under the directorship of Osman Hamdi Bey (1881–1910), to house his finds. This archaeologist, painter and polymath discovered the exquisite sarcophagi in the royal necropolis at Sidon in present-day Lebanon. An additional wing, opened in 1991, contains a children's museum.

★ **Alexander Sarcophagus**
This fabulously carved marble tomb from the late 4th century BC is thought to have been built for King Abdalonymos of Sidon. It is called the Alexander Sarcophagus because Alexander the Great is depicted on it winning a victory over the Persians.

Sarcophagus of the Mourning Women

The porticoes of the museum take their design from the 4th-century BC Sarcophagus of the Mourning Women.

Key

- ☐ Classical Archaeology
- ☐ Children's Museum
- ☐ Thracian, Bithynian and Byzantine Collections
- ☐ Istanbul Through the Ages
- ☐ Anatolia and Troy
- ☐ Anatolia's Neighbouring Cultures
- ☐ Turkish Tiles and Ceramics
- ☐ Museum of the Ancient Orient
- ☐ Non-exhibition space

Çinili Pavilion

★ **Karaman Mihrab**
This blue, richly tiled mihrab *(see p36)* comes from the city of Karaman in southeast Turkey, which was the capital of the Karamanid state from 1256–1483. It is the most important artistic relic of that culture.

Gallery Guide
The 20 galleries of the main building house the museum's important collection of classical antiquities. The additional wing has displays on the archaeology of Istanbul and nearby regions, and includes the Children's Museum. There are two other buildings within the grounds: the Çinili Pavilion, which houses Turkish tiles and ceramics, and the Museum of the Ancient Orient.

Geometric Period Cypriot Jug
Stylized fish decorate this jug, in a design typical of the Geometric Period (1050–750 BC), when a vibrant ceramics culture flourished on Cyprus.

Stairs to main building

Third floor

Second floor

First floor

Indoor café

Ground floor of additional wing

Statue of Marsyas

Statue and bust of Alexander the Great

Outdoor café

Entrance

Mosaic Icon of the Presentation
Dating from the 6th–7th centuries AD, this battered panel from Kalenderhane Mosque *(see p103)* is the only religious figurative mosaic to have survived Byzantium's iconoclastic period.

Porphyry Sarcophagi
These monumental purple sarcophagi (4th–5th centuries AD) are thought to have held the bodies of some of the early Byzantine emperors.

★ Treaty of Kadesh
This tablet constitutes the world's earliest surviving peace treaty, agreed between the Egyptians and Hittites in 1269 BC. Among its many clauses are provisions for the return of political refugees.

❸ Imperial Mint
Darphane-i Amire

First courtyard of Topkapı Palace. **Map** 5 E4. 🚇 Gülhane or Sultanahmet.

The Ottoman Mint opened here in 1727, but most of what can be seen today dates from the reign of Mahmut II (1808–39), when the complex was extended. In 1967, the mint moved to a new location. The buildings now house laboratories for the state restoration and conservation department, but visitors can look around the outside of the building during office hours.

❹ Haghia Eirene
Aya İrini Kilisesi

First courtyard of Topkapı Palace. **Map** 5 E4. **Tel** (0212) 522 17 50. 🚇 Gülhane or Sultanahmet. **Open** for concerts.

Though the present church dates only from the 6th century, it is at least the third building to be erected on what is thought to be the oldest site of Christian worship in Istanbul. Within a decade of the Muslim conquest of the city in 1453 *(see p58)* it had been incorporated within the Topkapı Palace complex and pressed into use as an arsenal. Today the building, which has good acoustics, is the

One of the four elaborately decorated sides of the Fountain of Ahmet III

setting for concerts during the Istanbul Music Festival *(see p39)*.

Inside are three fascinating features that have not survived in any other Byzantine church in the city. The *synthronon*, the five rows of built-in seats hugging the apse, were occupied by clergy officiating during services. Above this looms a simple black mosaic cross on a gold background, dating from the iconoclastic period in the 8th century, when figurative images were forbidden. At the back of the church is a cloister-like courtyard where deceased Byzantine emperors once lay in their porphyry sarcophagi. Most have been moved to the Archaeological Museum.

❺ Fountain of Ahmet III
III Ahmet Çeşmesi

Junction of İshak Paşa Cad & Babıhümayun Cad. **Map** 5 E4. 🚇 Gülhane or Sultanahmet.

Built in 1729, the most beautiful of Istanbul's countless fountains survived the violent deposition of Sultan Ahmet III two years later. Many other monuments constructed by the sultan during his reign, which has become known as the Tulip Period, were destroyed. The fountain is in the delicate Turkish Rococo style, with five small domes, mihrab-shaped niches and dizzying floral reliefs.

Ottoman "fountains" do not spout jets of water, but are more like ornate public taps. They sometimes incorporated a counter, or *sebil*, from which refreshments would be served.

In this case, each of the fountain's four walls is equipped with a tap, or *çeşme*, above a carved marble basin. Over each tap is an elaborate calligraphic inscription by the 18th-century poet Seyit Vehbi Efendi. The inscription, in gold on a blue-green background, is in honour of the fountain and its founder. At each of the four corners there is a *sebil* backed by three windows covered by ornate marble grilles. Instead of the customary iced water, passers-by at this fountain would have been offered sherbets and flavoured waters in silver goblets.

The apse of Haghia Eirene, with its imposing black-on-gold cross

❻ Soğukçeşme Sokağı

Map 5 E4. 🚋 Gülhane.

Charming old wooden houses line this narrow, sloping cobbled lane ("the street of the cold fountain"), which squeezes between the outer walls of Topkapı Palace and the towering minarets of Haghia Sophia. Traditional houses like these were built in the city from the late 18th century onwards.

The buildings in the lane were renovated by the Turkish Touring and Automobile Club (TTOK, *see p395*) in the 1980s. Of these, nine buildings now form the Ayasofya Pansiyonları, a series of attractive pastel-painted guesthouses popular with tourists. Another building has been converted by the TTOK into a library of historical writings on Istanbul, and archive of engravings and photographs of the city.
A Roman cistern towards the bottom of the lane has been converted into the attractive Sarnıç restaurant.

Restored Ottoman house on Soğukçeşme Sokağı

Ottoman Houses

The typical, smart town house of 19th-century Istanbul had a stone ground floor above which were one or two wooden storeys. The building invariably sported a *çıkma*, a section projecting out over the street. This developed from the traditional Turkish balcony, which was enclosed in the northern part of the country because of the colder climate. Wooden lattice covers, or *kafesler*, over the windows on the upper storeys ensured that the women of the house were able to watch life on the street below without being seen themselves. Few wooden houses have survived. Those that remain usually owe their existence to tourism and many have been restored as hotels. While the law forbids their demolition, it is very expensive to obtain insurance for them in a city that has experienced so many fires.

Traditional calligraphy on sale in Caferağa Courtyard

❼ Caferağa Courtyard

Caferağa Medresesi

Caferiye Sok. **Map** 5 E3. 🚋 Gülhane. **Open** 8:30am–8pm daily.

This peaceful courtyard at the end of an alley was built in 1559 by the architect Sinan *(see p105)* for the chief black eunuch as a *medrese* (theological college, *see p36*). Sinan's bust presides over the café tables in the courtyard. The former students' lodgings are now used to display a variety of craft goods typically including jewellery, silk prints, ceramics and calligraphy.

❽ Gülhane Park

Gülhane Parkı

Alemdar Cad. **Map** 5 E3. 🚋 Gülhane. **Open** daily. 🎫

Gülhane Park occupies what were the lower grounds of Topkapı Palace. Today it has a neglected air but it is still a shady place to stroll that also includes a couple of interesting landmarks.

The History of Islamic Science and Technology Museum, housed in the stables, exhibits the discoveries and inventions of Islamic scientists through the history of Islam. At the far end of the park is the Goths' Column, a well-preserved 3rd-century victory monument, surrounded by a cluster of clapboard teahouses. Its name comes from the Latin inscription on it which reads: "Fortune is restored to us because of victory over the Goths".

Across Kennedy Caddesi, the main road running along the northeast side of the park, there is a viewpoint over the busy waters where the Golden Horn meets the Bosphorus.

❾ Sublime Porte

Bab-ı Ali

Alemdar Cad. **Map** 5 E3. 🚋 Gülhane.

Foreign ambassadors to Ottoman Turkey were known as Ambassadors to the Sublime Porte, after this monumental gateway which once led into the offices and palace of the grand vizier. The institution of the Sublime Porte filled an important role in Ottoman society because it could often provide an effective counterbalance to the whims of sultans.

The Rococo gateway you see today was built in the 1840s. Its guarded entrance now shields the offices of Istanbul's provincial government.

Rococo decoration on the roof of the Sublime Porte

⑩ Cağaloğlu Baths

Cağaloğlu Hamamı

Prof Kazım İsmail Gürkan Cad 34,
Cağaloğlu. **Map** 3 E4 (5 D3).
Tel (0212) 522 24 24. 🚇 Sultanahmet.
Open 8am–10pm daily.
🆆 cagalogluhamami.com.tr

Among the city's more
sumptuous Turkish baths, the
ones in Cağaloğlu were built
by Sultan Mahmut I in 1741.
The income from them was
designated for the maintenance
of Mahmut's library in Haghia
Sophia *(see pp86–7)*.

The city's smaller baths have
different times at which men
and women can use the same
facilities. But in larger baths,

Corridor leading into the Cağaloğlu Baths,
built by Mahmut I

such as this one, there are
entirely separate sections. In the
Cağaloğlu Baths the men's and
women's sections are at right
angles to one another and
entered from different streets.
Each consists of three parts: a
camekan, a *soğukluk* and the
main bath chamber or *hararet*,
which centres on a massive
octagonal massage slab.

The Cağaloğlu Baths are
popular with foreign visitors
because the staff are happy to
explain the procedure. Even if
you do not want to sweat it out,
you can still take a look inside
the entrance corridor and
camekan of the men's section.
Here you will find a small display
of Ottoman bathing regalia,
including precarious wooden
clogs once worn by women on
what would frequently be their
only outing from the confines of
the home. You can also sit and
have a drink by the fountain in
the peaceful *camekan*.

⑪ Sirkeci Station

Sirkeci Garı

Sirkeci İstasyon Cad, Sirkeci. **Map** 3 E3
(5 E1). **Tel** (0212) 520 65 75. 🚇 Sirkeci.
Open daily.

This magnificent railway station
was built to receive the long-
anticipated Orient Express from
Europe. It was officially opened
in 1890, even though the

Sirkeci Station, final destination of the
historic Orient Express

luxurious train had been
running into Istanbul for a year
by then. The design, by the
German architect Jasmund,
successfully incorporates
distinctive windows, arches and
stonework that mirror Istanbul's
diverse architectural traditions.

As part of a cultural enhance-
ment project in the area, some
of Topkapı Palace's entrepôt
treasures will be displayed in
the station concourse.

The station café is a good
place to escape the bustle
of the city for a while. Sirkeci
serves the European part of
Turkey and other Euro points
west. Istanbul's other mainline
railhead, Haydarpaşa *(see p133)*,
has lines to Asian Istanbul
and Anatolia.

The World-famous Orient Express

The Orient Express made its first run from Paris to Istanbul
in 1889, covering the 2,900-km (1,800-mile) journey in
three days. Both Sirkeci Station and the Pera Palas Hotel
(see p112, 114) in Istanbul were built especially to receive
its passengers. The wealthy and often distinguished
passengers of "The Train of Kings, the King of Trains"
did indeed include kings among the many presidents,
politicians, aristocrats and actresses. King Boris III of
Bulgaria even made a habit of taking over from the
driver of the train when he travelled on it through
his own country.

A byword for exoticism and romance, the train was
associated with the orientalist view of Istanbul as a
treacherous melting pot of diplomats and arms dealers.
It inspired no fewer than 19 books – *Murder on the Orient
Express* by Agatha Christie and *Stamboul Train* by Graham
Greene foremost among them – six films and one piece
of music. During the Cold War standards of luxury crashed,
though a service of sorts, without even a restaurant car,
continued twice weekly to Istanbul until 1977.

A 1920s poster for the Orient Express, showing a
romantic view of Istanbul

❷ ★ Basilica Cistern
This marble Medusa head is one of two classical column bases found in the Basilica Cistern. The cavernous cistern dates from the reign of Justinian I *(see p53)* in the 6th century.

Locator Map
See Street Finder map 5

A stone pilaster next to the remains of an Ottoman water tower is all that survives of the Milion, a triumphal gateway.

❶ ★ Haghia Sophia
The supreme church of Byzantium is over 1,400 years old but has survived in a remarkably good state. Inside it are several glorious figurative mosaics.

Yeşil Ev Hotel *(see p331)*

❹ Baths of Roxelana
Sinan *(see p105)* designed these beautiful baths in the mid-16th century. After housing a carpet shop for several years, the building reopened as a public bathhouse in 2011.

❸ Istanbul Crafts Centre
Visitors have a rare opportunity here to observe Turkish craftsmen practising a range of skills.

Cavalry Bazaar
Eager salesmen will call you over to peruse their wares – mainly carpets and handicrafts – in this bazaar. With two long rows of shops on either side of a lane, the bazaar was once a stable yard.

0 metres	75
0 yards	75

For keys to symbols *see back flap*

❶ Haghia Sophia

Ayasofya

The "church of holy wisdom", Haghia Sophia is among the world's greatest architectural achievements. More than 1,400 years old, it stands as a testament to the sophistication of the 6th-century Byzantine capital and had a great influence on architecture in the following centuries. The vast edifice was built over two earlier churches and inaugurated by Emperor Justinian in 537. In the 15th century the Ottomans converted it into a mosque: the minarets, tombs, and fountains date from this period. To help support the structure's great weight, the exterior has been buttressed on numerous occasions, which has partly obscured its original shape.

Print of Haghia Sophia from the mid-19th century

Byzantine Frieze
Among the ruins of the monumental entrance to the earlier Haghia Sophia (dedicated in AD 415) is this frieze of sheep.

Historical Plan of Haghia Sophia

Nothing remains of the first 4th-century church on this spot, but there are traces of the second one from the 5th century, which burned down in AD 532. Earthquakes have taken their toll on the third structure, strengthened and added to many times.

Entrance

Key

☐ 5th-century church

▨ 6th-century church

☐ Ottoman additions

★ Nave
Visitors cannot fail to be staggered by this vast space which is covered by a huge dome reaching to a height of 56 m (184 ft).

VISITORS' CHECKLIST

Practical Information
Ayasofya Sultanahmet Meydanı 1.
Map 5 E4.
Tel (0212) 522 17 50.
Open 9am–5pm Tue–Sun.
🎫 📷 ♿ ground floor only.

Transport
🚊 Sultanahmet.

★ The Mosaics
The church's splendid Byzantine mosaics include this one at the end of the south gallery. It depicts Christ flanked by Emperor Constantine IX and his wife, the Empress Zoe.

KEY

① **Buttress**

② **Outer narthex**

③ **Inner narthex**

④ **Imperial Gate**

⑤ **The galleries** were originally used by women during services.

⑥ **Kürsü** *(see p37).*

⑦ **Calligraphic roundel**

⑧ **Seraphims** adorn the pendentives at the base of the dome.

⑨ **Sultan's loge**

⑩ **Müezzin mahfili** *(see p36).*

⑪ **The Coronation Square** served for the crowning of emperors.

⑫ **Library of Sultan Mahmut I**

⑬ **The Baptistry**, part of the 6th-century church, now serves as the tomb of two sultans.

⑭ **The mausoleum of Murat III** was used for his burial in 1599. Murat had by that time sired 103 children.

⑮ **Mausoleum of Selim II**, the oldest of the three mausoleums, was completed in 1577 to the plans of Sinan *(see p105).* Its interior is entirely decorated with İznik tiles *(see p161).*

⑯ **Mausoleum of Mehmet III**

⑰ **Brick minaret**

Exit

★ Ablutions Fountain
Built around 1740, this fountain is an exquisite example of Turkish Rococo style. Its projecting roof is painted with floral reliefs.

Exploring Haghia Sophia

Designed as an earthly mirror of the heavens, the interior of Haghia Sophia succeeds in imparting a truly celestial feel. The artistic highlights are a number of glistening figurative mosaics – remains of the decoration that once covered the upper walls but which has otherwise mostly disappeared. The remarkable works of Byzantine art date from the 9th century or later, after the iconoclastic era. Some of the patterned mosaic ceilings, however, particularly those adorning the narthex and the neighbouring Vestibule of the Warriors, are part of the cathedral's original 6th-century decoration.

Interior as it looked after restoration in the 19th century

Ground Floor

The first of the surviving Byzantine mosaics can be seen over the Imperial Gate. This is now the public entrance into the church, although previously only the emperor and his entourage were allowed to pass through it. The mosaic shows **Christ on a throne with an emperor kneeling beside him** ① and has been dated to between 886 and 912. The emperor is thought to be Leo VI, the Wise.

The most conspicuous features at ground level in the nave are those added by the Ottoman sultans after the conquest of Istanbul in 1453,

when the church was converted into a mosque.

The **mihrab** ②, the niche indicating the direction of Mecca, was installed in the apse of the church directly opposite the entrance. The **sultan's loge** ③, on the left of the mihrab as you face it, was built by the Fossati brothers. These Italian-Swiss architects undertook a major restoration of Haghia Sophia for Sultan Abdül Mecit in 1847–9.

To the right of the mihrab is the *minber* ④, or pulpit, which was installed by Murat III (1574–95). He also erected four *müezzin mahfilis* ⑤, marble platforms for readers of the Koran (*see p36*). The largest of

these is adjacent to the *minber*. The patterned marble **coronation square** ⑥ next to it marks the supposed site of the Byzantine emperor's throne, or omphalos (centre of the world). Nearby, in the south aisle, is the **library of Mahmut I** ⑦, which was built in 1739 and is entered by a decorative bronze door.

Across the nave, between two columns, is the 17th-century marble **preacher's throne** ⑧, the contribution of Murat IV (1623–40). Behind it is one of several **maqsuras** ⑨. These low, fenced platforms were placed beside walls and pillars to provide places for elders to sit, listen and read the Koran.

In the northwestern and western corners of the church are two **marble urns** ⑩, thought to date from the Hellenistic or early Byzantine period. A rectangular pillar behind one of the urns, the **pillar of St Gregory the Miracle-Worker** ⑪, is believed to have healing powers. As you leave the church you pass through the Vestibule of the Warriors, so called because the emperor's bodyguards would wait here for him when he came to worship. Look behind you as you enter it at the wonderful mosaic of the **Virgin with Constantine and Justinian** ⑫ above the door. It shows Mary seated on a throne holding the infant

Floorplan of Haghia Sophia

Key

☐ Upper walls and domes
☐ Galleries
☐ Ground floor

Apse

North gallery

West gallery

Ramp to gallery

Upper walls and domes

South gallery

Apse

Nave

Vestibule of the Warriors

Entrance

Outer narthex

Narthex

Jesus and flanked by two of the greatest emperors of the city. Constantine, on her right, presents her with the city of Constantinople, while Justinian offers her Haghia Sophia. This was made long after either of these two emperors lived, probably in the 10th century, during the reign of Basil II (see p56). Visitors exit the church by the door that was once reserved for the emperor, due to its proximity to the Great Palace (see pp96–7).

Figure of Christ, detail from the Deësis Mosaic in the south gallery

Galleries

A ramp leads from the ground floor to the north gallery. Here, on the eastern side of the great northwest pier, you will find the 10th-century mosaic of **Emperor Alexander holding a skull** ⑬. On the west face of the same pier is a medieval drawing of a galleon in full sail. The only point of interest in the west gallery is a green marble disk

marking the location of the Byzantine **Empress's throne** ⑭.

There is much more to see in the south gallery. You begin by passing through the so-called **Gates of Heaven and Hell** ⑮, a marble doorway of which little is known except that it predates the Ottoman conquest.

Around the corner to the right after passing through this doorway is the **Deësis Mosaic** ⑯ showing the Virgin Mary and John the Baptist with Christ Pantocrator (the All-Powerful). Set into the floor opposite it is the tomb of Enrico Dandalo, the Doge of Venice responsible for the sacking of Constantinople in 1204 (see p57).

In the last bay of the south gallery there are two more mosaics. The right-hand one of these is of the **Virgin holding Christ, flanked by Emperor John II Comnenus and Empress Irene** ⑰. The other shows **Christ with Emperor Constantine IX Monomachus and Empress Zoe** ⑱. The faces of the emperor and empress have been altered.

Eight **wooden plaques** ⑲ bearing calligraphic inscriptions hang over the nave at the level of the gallery. An addition of the Fossati brothers, they bear the names of Allah, the Prophet Mohammed, the first four caliphs and Hasan and Hussein, two of the Prophet's grandsons who are revered as martyrs.

Mosaic depicting the archangel Gabriel, adorning the lower wall of the apse

Upper Walls and Domes

The apse is dominated by a large and striking mosaic showing the **Virgin with the infant Jesus on her lap** ⑳. Two other mosaics in the apse depict the archangels **Gabriel** ㉑ and, opposite him, Michael, but only fragments of the latter now remain. The unveiling of these mosaics on Easter Sunday 867 was a triumphal event celebrating victory over the iconoclasts.

Three mosaic portraits of **saints** ㉒ adorn niches in the north tympanum and are visible from the south gallery and the nave. From left to right they depict: St Ignatius the Younger, St John Chrysostom and St Ignatius Theophorus.

In the four pendentives (the triangular, concave areas at the base of the dome) are mosaics of six-winged **seraphim** ㉓. The ones in the east pendentives date from 1346–55, but may be copies of much older ones. Those on the west side are 19th-century imitations that were added by the Fossati brothers.

The great **dome** ㉔ itself is decorated with Koranic inscriptions. It was once covered in golden mosaic and the tinkling sound of pieces dropping to the ground was familiar to visitors until the building's 19th-century restoration.

Mosaic of the Virgin with Emperor John II Comnenus and Empress Irene

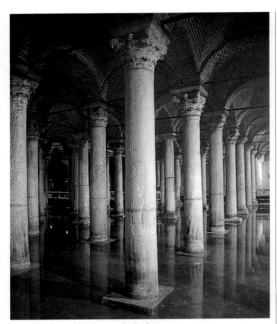

The cavernous interior of the Byzantine Basilica Cistern

❷ Basilica Cistern

Yerebatan Sarnıcı

13 Yerebatan Cad, Sultanahmet.
Map 5 E4. **Tel** (0212) 522 12 59.
Sultanahmet. **Open** 8:30am–5:30pm
daily (Oct–Apr 8:30am–4pm).

This vast underground water
cistern, a beautiful piece of
Byzantine engineering, is the
most unusual tourist attraction
in the city. Although there may
have been an earlier, smaller
cistern here, this cavernous vault
was laid out under Justinian in
532, mainly to satisfy the
growing demands of the Great
Palace *(see pp96–7)* on the other
side of the Hippodrome *(see p94)*.
For a century after the conquest
(see p58), the Ottomans did not
know of the cistern's existence.
It was rediscovered after people
were found to be collecting
water, and even fish, by
lowering buckets through holes
in their basements.

Visitors tread walkways, to the
mixed sounds of classical music
and dripping water. The cistern's
roof is held up by 336 columns,
each over 8 m (26 ft) high. Only
about two thirds of the original
structure is visible today, the

rest having been bricked up
in the 19th century.

In the far left-hand corner
two columns rest on Medusa
head bases. These bases are
evidence of plundering by the
Byzantines from earlier monuments. They are thought to
mark a *nymphaeum*, a shrine
to the water nymphs.

❸ Istanbul Crafts Centre

Istanbul El Sanatları Çarşısı

Kabasakal Cad 5, Sultanahmet.
Map 5 E4. **Tel** (0212) 517 67 84.
Adliye. **Open** 9am–5pm daily.

If you are interested in Turkish
craftwork, this former Koranic
college is worth a visit. You can
watch skilled artisans at work:
they may be binding a book,
executing an elegant piece of
calligraphy or painting glaze
onto ceramics. All the pieces
that are produced here are for
sale. Other good buys include
exquisite dolls, meerschaum
pipes and jewellery based on
Ottoman designs.

Next door is the Yeşil Ev Hotel
(see p331), a restored Ottoman
building with a pleasant café in
its courtyard.

❹ Baths of Roxelana

Haseki Hürrem Hamamı

Ayasofya Meydanı, Sultanahmet.
Map 5 E4. **Tel** (0212) 638 00 35.
Sultanahmet. **Open** 8:30am–
5:30pm daily (to 6:30pm summer).

These baths, also known as
Ayasofya Hürrem Sultan Hamam,
were built in 1556 for Süleyman
the Magnificent *(see pp58–9)* by
Sinan *(see p105)*, and are named
after Roxelana, the sultan's wife.
They were designated for the use

Roxelana

Süleyman the Magnificent's
power-hungry wife Roxelana
(1500–58, Haseki Hürrem in
Turkish), rose from being a
concubine in the imperial harem
to become his chief wife, or first
kadın (see p75). Thought to be
of Russian origin, she was also
the first consort permitted
to reside within the walls of
Topkapı Palace *(see pp72–5)*.
Roxelana would stop at
nothing to get her own
way. When Süleyman's grand
vizier and friend from youth,
İbrahim Paşa, became a threat to her position, she persuaded
the sultan to have him strangled. Much later, Roxelana
performed her *coup de grâce*. In 1553 she persuaded
Süleyman to have his handsome and popular heir, Mustafa,
murdered by deaf mutes to clear the way for her own son,
Selim, to inherit the throne.

The exterior of the 16th-century Baths of Roxelana

of the congregation of Haghia Sophia (see pp86–7) when it was used as a mosque. With the women's entrance at one end of the building and the men's at the other, their absolute symmetry makes them perhaps the most handsome baths in the city.

Each end of the baths starts with a *camekan*, a massive domed hall that would originally have been centred on a fountain. Next is a small *soğukluk*, or intermediate room, which opens into a *hararet*, or steam room. The hexagonal massage slab in each *hararet*, the *göbek taşı*, is inlaid with coloured marbles, indicating that the baths are of imperial origin.

The Baths of Roxelana functioned as a public bathhouse for more than 350 years, until 1910. After their closure, they continued to be used for various purposes, including as a coal and fuel store and as a government-run carpet shop. Following a programme of renovation to restore the baths to their original function, the building was reopened to the public as a bathhouse. The feel of the place is now like that of a high-end spa, combined with lovingly restored original features on which no expense has been spared.

❺ Mosaics Museum
Mozaik Müzesi

Arasta Çarşısı, Sultanahmet. **Map** 5 E5. **Tel** (0212) 518 12 05. ⊞ Sultanahmet. **Open** 9am–5pm Tue–Sun (to 6pm summer). 🖼

Located near Arasta Bazaar, among a warren of small shops, this museum was created simply by roofing over a part of the Great Palace of the Byzantine Emperors (see pp96–7), which was discovered in the 1930s. In its heyday the palace boasted hundreds of rooms, many of them glittering with gold mosaics.

The surviving mosaic has a surface area of 1,872 sq m (1,969 sq ft), making it one of the largest preserved mosaics in Europe. It is thought to have been created by an imperial workshop that employed the best craftsmen from across the Empire under the guidance of a master artist. In terms of imagery, the mosaic is particularly diverse, with many different landscapes depicted,

Detail of a 5th-century mosaic in the Mosaics Museum

including domestic and pastoral episodes, such as herdsmen with their grazing animals, as well as hunting and fighting scenes. It portrays more than 150 different human and animal figures, including both wild and domestic beasts. There are also scenes taken from mythology, with fantastical creatures featuring on the design.

The mosaic is thought to have adorned the colonnade leading from the royal apartments to the imperial enclosure beside the Hippodrome, and dates from the late 5th century AD.

❻ Blue Mosque
See pp92–3.

❼ Museum of Turkish and Islamic Arts
Türk ve İslam Eserleri Müzesi

Atmeydanı Sok, Sultanahmet. **Map** 5 D4. **Tel** (0212) 518 18 05/06. ⊞ Sultanahmet. **Open** 9am–5pm Tue–Sun (to 7pm summer). 🖼

Over 40,000 items are on display in the former palace of İbrahim Paşa (c.1493–1536), the most gifted of Süleyman's many grand viziers. Paşa married Süleyman's sister when the sultan came to the throne. The collection was begun in the 19th century and ranges from the earliest period of Islam, under the Omayyad caliphate (661–750), through to modern times.

Each room concentrates on a different chronological period or geographical area of the Islamic world, with detailed explanations in both Turkish and English. The museum is particularly renowned for its collection of rugs. These range from 13th-century Seljuk fragments to the palatial Persian silks that cover the walls from floor to ceiling in the palace's great hall.

On the ground floor, an ethnographic section focuses on the lifestyles of different Turkish peoples, particularly the nomads of central and eastern Anatolia. The exhibits include recreations of a round felt *yurt* (Turkic nomadic tent) and a traditional brown tent.

Recreated *yurt* interior, Museum of Turkish and Islamic Arts

❻ Blue Mosque

Sultan Ahmet Camii

The Blue Mosque, which takes its name from the mainly blue İznik tilework *(see p165)* decorating its interior, is one of the most famous religious buildings in the world. Serene at any time, it is at its most magical when floodlit at night, its minarets circled by keening seagulls. Sultan Ahmet I commissioned the mosque during a period of declining Ottoman fortunes, and it was built between 1609–16 by Mehmet Ağa, the imperial architect. The splendour of the plans provoked great hostility at the time, because a mosque with six minarets was considered a sacrilegious attempt to rival the architecture of Mecca.

A 19th-century engraving showing the Blue Mosque viewed from the Hippodrome *(see p94)*

KEY

① **Imperial Pavilion**

② **The loge** *(see p37)* accommodated the sultan and his entourage during mosque services.

③ **Mihrab**

④ **Prayer hall**

⑤ **The 17th-century Minbar** is intricately carved in white marble. It is used by the imam during prayers on Friday *(see p36)*.

⑥ **Thick piers** support the weight of the dome.

⑦ **Müezzin mahfili** *(see p36)*.

⑧ **Originally, over 250 windows** allowed light to flood into the mosque.

⑨ **The courtyard** covers an area the same size as the prayer hall, balancing the whole building.

⑩ **Each minaret** has two or three balconies.

Exit for tourists

Entrance to courtyard

★ **İznik Tiles**
No cost was spared in the decoration. The tiles were made at the peak of tile production in İznik *(see p165)*.

★ **Inside of the Dome**
Mesmeric designs employing flowing arabesques are painted onto the interior of the mosque's domes and semidomes. The windows which pierce the domes no longer have their original 17th-century stained glass.

★ **View of the Domes**
The graceful cascade of domes and semidomes makes a striking sight when viewed from the courtyard below.

Entrance

★ **Ablutions Fountain**
The hexagonal *şadırvan* is now purely ornamental since ritual ablutions are no longer carried out at this fountain.

Exit to Hippodrome

Washing the Feet
The Muslim's ritual ablutions conclude with the washing of the feet (*see p37*). Taps outside the mosque are used by the faithful for this purpose.

VISITORS' CHECKLIST

Practical Information
Meydanı 21. **Map** 5 E5.
Tel (0212) 518 13 19.
W sultanahmetcami.org
Open 9am–5pm daily.
Closed prayer times. Son et Lumière: May–Sep: daily after dusk.

Transport
Sultanahmet.

Egyptian Obelisk and the Column of Constantine Porphyrogenitus

Another obelisk still standing, but of unknown date, is usually referred to as the **Column of Constantine Porphyrogenitus**, after the emperor who restored it in the 10th century AD. Its dilapidated state owes much to the fact that young Janissaries *(see p60)* would routinely scale it as a test of their bravery.

The only other structure in the Hippodrome is a domed fountain, which commemorates the visit of Kaiser Wilhelm II to Istanbul in 1898.

The Hippodrome was the scene of one of the bloodiest events in Istanbul's history. In 532 a brawl between rival chariot-racing teams developed into the Nika Revolt, during which much of the city was destroyed. The end of the revolt came when an army of mercenaries, under the command of Justinian's general Belisarius, massacred an estimated 30,000 people trapped in the Hippodrome.

❽ Hippodrome
At Meydanı

Sultanahmet. **Map** 3 E4 (5 D4).
🚋 Sultanahmet.

Little is left of the gigantic stadium which once stood at the heart of the Byzantine city of Constantinople *(see pp54–5)*. It was originally laid out by Emperor Septimus Severus during his rebuilding of the city in the 3rd century AD. Emperor Constantine I *(see p53)* enlarged the Hippodrome and connected its *kathisma*, or royal box, to the nearby Great Palace *(see pp96–7)*. It is thought that the stadium held up to 100,000 people. The site is now an elongated public garden, At Meydanı, the Square of the Horses. There are, however, enough remains of the Hippodrome to get a sense of its scale and importance.

The road running around the square almost directly follows the line of the chariot racing track.

You can also make out some of the arches of the *sphendone* (the curved end of the Hippodrome) by walking a few steps down İbret Sokağı. Constantine adorned the *spina*, the central line of the stadium, with obelisks and columns from Ancient Egypt and Greece. Conspicuous by its absence is the column, which once stood on the spot where the tourist information office is located. This was topped by four bronze horses which were pillaged during the Fourth Crusade *(see p56)* and taken to St Mark's in Venice. Three ancient monuments remain, however. The

Relief carved on the base of the
Egyptian Obelisk

Egyptian Obelisk, which was built in 1500 BC, stood outside Luxor until Constantine had it brought to his city. This carved monument is probably only one third of its original height.

Next to it is the **Serpentine Column**, believed to date from 479 BC, which was shipped here from Delphi.

❾ Marmara University Museum of the Republic
Cumhuriyet Müzesi

Atmeydanı Sok 1, Sultanahmet.
Map 5 D4. **Tel** (0212) 518 16 00.
🚋 Sultanahmet. **Open** 10am–6pm Tue–Sun.

This fine art collection run by Marmara University includes works by more than 85 artists from Turkey and around the world. The museum started in 1973 as an etching exhibition held to celebrate 50 years of Turkey as a republic. Today, print, painting, calligraphy and other traditional Turkish art forms are part of the collection.

❿ Cistern of 1,001 Columns
Binbirdirek Sarnıcı

Klodfarer Cad, Sultanahmet.
Map 3 D4 (5 D4). 🚋 Çemberlitaş.

This cistern dates back to around the 4th century AD, and was second in size only to the nearby Basilica Cistern *(see p90)*. It was also known as the Cistern of Philoxenus and measured

Ceremonies in the Hippodrome

Beginning with the inauguration of Constantinople on 11th May 330 (see p53), the Hippodrome formed the stage for the city's greatest public events for the next 1,300 years. The Byzantines' most popular pastime was watching chariot racing in the stadium. Even after the Hippodrome fell into ruins following the Ottoman conquest of Istanbul (see p58), it continued to be used for great public occasions. This 16th-century illustration depicts Murat III watching the 52-day-long festivities staged for the circumcision of his son Mehmet. All the guilds of Istanbul paraded before the Sultan displaying their crafts.

Sultan Murat III

Palace of İbrahim Paşa (Museum of Turkish and Islamic Arts, see p167)

Column of Constantine Porphyrogenitus

Serpentine Column

Egyptian Obelisk

---

64 m (210 ft) by 56 m (184 ft). It could hold enough water to supply a population of 360,000 for about 10 days.

The herring-bone brick roof vaults are supported by 264 marble columns – the 1,001 columns of its name is poetic exaggeration. Interestingly, due to its dampness, the cistern building proved to provide the ideal atmosphere for the silk weaving process and, for many decades, it was thus used by Istanbul's silk weavers as a workplace.

⓫ Tomb of Sultan Mahmut II

Mahmut II Türbesi

Divanyolu Cad, Çemberlitaş.
Map 3 D4 (4 C3). 🚊 Çemberlitaş.
Open 9:30am–4:30pm daily.

This large octagonal mausoleum is in the Empire style (modelled on Roman architecture), made popular by Napoleon. It was built in 1838, the year before Sultan Mahmut II's death and is shared by sultans Mahmut II, Abdül Aziz and Abdül Hamit II (see p61). Within, Corinthian pilasters divide up walls which groan with symbols of prosperity and victory. The huge tomb dominates a cemetery that has beautiful headstones, a fountain and, at the far end, a good café.

⓬ Constantine's Column

Çemberlitaş

Yeniçeriler Cad, Çemberlitaş.
Map 3 D4 (4 C3). 🚊 Çemberlitaş.
Çemberlitaş Baths: Vezirhanı Cad 8.
Tel (0212) 522 79 74.
Open 6am–midnight daily.
🆆 cemberlitas hamami.com

This 35-m (115 ft) high column was constructed in AD 330 as part of the celebrations to inaugurate the new Byzantine capital (see p53). It once dominated the magnificent Forum of Constantine.

Made of porphyry brought from Heliopolis in Egypt, it was originally surmounted by a Corinthian capital bearing a statue of Emperor Constantine dressed as Apollo. This was brought down in a storm in 1106. Although what is left is relatively unimpressive, it has been carefully preserved. In the year 416 the 10 stone drums making up the column were reinforced with metal rings. These were renewed in 1701 by Sultan Mustafa III, and consequently the column is known as Çemberlitaş

(the Hooped Column) in Turkish. In English it is sometimes referred to as the Burnt Column because it was damaged by several fires, especially one in 1779 which decimated the Grand Bazaar (see pp108–9).

A variety of fantastical holy relics were supposedly entombed in the base of the column, which has since been encased in stone to strengthen it. These included the axe which Noah used to build the ark, Mary Magdalen's flask of anointing oil, and remains of the loaves of bread with which Christ fed the multitude. Next to Constantine's Column, on the corner of Divanyolu Caddesi, stand the Çemberlitaş Baths. This splendid *hamam* complex (see p83) was commissioned by Nur Banu, wife of Sultan Selim II, and built in 1584 to a plan by the great Sinan (see p105). The original women's section no longer survives, but the baths still have separate facilities for men and women. The staff are used to foreign visitors, so this is a good place for your first experience of a Turkish bath.

Constantine's Column

⓲ Sokollu Mehmet Paşa Mosque
Sokollu Mehmet Paşa Camii

Şehit Çeşmesi Sok, Sultanahmet. **Map** 5 D5. **Tel** (0212) 518 16 33. 🚇 Çemberlitaş or Sultanahmet. **Open** daily. 🏛 donation.

Built by the architect Sinan *(see p105)* in 1571–2, this mosque was commissioned by Sokollu Mehmet Paşa, grand vizier to Selim II. The simplicity of Sinan's design solution for the mosque's sloping site has been widely admired. A steep entrance stairway leads up to the mosque courtyard from the street, passing beneath the teaching hall of its *medrese (see p36)*. Only the tiled lunettes above the windows in the portico give a hint of the jewelled mosque interior to come.

Inside, the far wall around the carved mihrab is entirely covered in İznik tiles *(see p165)* of a sumptuous green-blue hue. This tile panel, designed specifically for the space, is complemented by six stained-glass windows. The "hat" of the *minbar* is covered with the same tiles. Most of the mosque's other walls are of plain stone, but they are enlivened by a few more tile panels. Set into the wall over the entrance there is a small piece of greenish stone, which is supposedly from the Kaaba, the holy stone at the centre of Mecca.

The Byzantine Church of SS Sergius and Bacchus, now a mosque

⓳ SS Sergius and Bacchus' Church
Küçük Ayasofya Camii

Küçük Ayasofya Cad. **Map** 5 D5. 🚇 Çemberlitaş or Sultanahmet. **Open** daily. ♿

Commonly referred to as "Little Haghia Sophia", this church was built in 527, a few years before its namesake *(see pp86–7)*. It too was founded by Emperor Justinian *(see p55)*, together with his empress, Theodora, at the beginning of his long reign. Ingenious and highly decorative, the church gives a somewhat higgledy-piggledy impression both inside and out and is one of the most charming of all the city's architectural treasures.

Inside, an irregular octagon of columns on two floors supports a broad central dome composed of 16 vaults. The mosaic decoration, which once

Reconstruction of the Great Palace

In Byzantine times, present-day Sultanahmet was the site of the Great Palace, which, in its heyday, had no equal in Europe and dazzled medieval visitors with its opulence. This great complex of buildings – including royal apartments, state rooms, churches, courtyards and gardens – extended over a sloping, terraced site from the Hippodrome to the imperial harbour on the shore of the Sea of Marmara. The palace was built in stages, beginning under Constantine in the 4th century. It was enlarged by Justinian following the fire caused by the Nika Revolt in 532. Later emperors, especially the 9th-century Basil I, extended it further. After several hundred years of occupation, it was finally abandoned in the second half of the 13th century in favour of Blachernae Palace.

The Mese was a colonnaded street lined with shops and statuary.

Hippodrome *(see p94)*

Hormisdas Palace

Church of SS Peter and Paul

Church of SS Sergius and Bacchus

Interior of the 16th-century Sokollu Mehmet Paşa Mosque

adorned some of the walls, has long since crumbled away. However, the green and red marble columns, the delicate tracery of the capitals and the carved frieze above the columns are original features of the church.

The inscription on this frieze, in boldly carved Greek script, mentions the founders of the church and St Sergius, but not St Bacchus. The two saints were Roman centurions who converted to Christianity and were martyred. Justinian credited them with saving his life when, as a young man, he was implicated in a plot to kill his uncle, Justin I. The saints supposedly appeared to Justin in a dream and told him to release his nephew.

The Church of SS Sergius and Bacchus was built between two important edifices to which it was connected, the Palace of Hormisdas and the Church of SS Peter and Paul, but has outlived them both. After the conquest of Istanbul in 1453 *(see p58)* it was converted into a mosque.

⓰ Bucoleon Palace
Bukoleon Sarayı

Kennedy Cad, Sultanahmet.
Map 5 E5. 🚋 Sultanahmet.

Finding the site of what remains of the Great Palace of the Byzantine emperors requires precision. It is not advisable to visit the ruins alone as they are usually inhabited by tramps.

Take the path under the railway from the Church of SS Sergius and Bacchus, turn left and walk beside Kennedy Caddesi, the main road along the shore of the Sea of Marmara, for about 400 m (450 yards). This will bring you to a stretch of the ancient sea walls, constructed to protect the city from a naval assault. Within these walls you will find a creeper-clad section of stonework pierced by three vast windows framed in marble. This is

all that now survives of the Bucoleon Palace, a maritime residence that formed part of the sprawling Great Palace. The waters of a small private harbour lapped right up to the palace and a private flight of steps led down into the water, allowing the emperor to board imperial *caïques*. The ruined tower just east of the palace was a lighthouse, called the Pharos, in Byzantine times.

Wall of Bucoleon Palace, the only part of the Byzantine Great Palace still standing

The Kathisma was the imperial box of the Hippodrome.

The Milion was the point from which road distances were measured.

Haghia Sophia *(see pp86–7)*

The Augusteum was a porticoed public square.

The Chalke Gate was the main entrance to the palace.

Daphne Palace

Hall of Gold (site of Mosaics Museum, *see p91*)

The Bucoleon Palace had a magnificent façade looking out over the sea.

The Nea Ekklesia, erected by Basil I, set the style for all subsequent Byzantine churches.

Lighthouse

Magnaura Palace

THE BAZAAR QUARTER

Trade has always been important in a city straddling the continents of Asia and Europe. Nowhere is this more evident than in the warren of streets lying between the Grand Bazaar and Galata Bridge. Everywhere, goods tumble out of shops onto the pavement. Look through any of the archways in between shops and you will discover courtyards or hans (see pp28–9) containing feverishly industrious workshops.

With its seemingly limitless range of goods, the labyrinthine Grand Bazaar is at the centre of all this commercial activity. The Egyptian Bazaar is equally colourful but smaller and more manageable.

Up on the hill, next to the university, is Süleymaniye Mosque, a glorious expression of 16th-century Ottoman culture. It is just one of numerous beautiful mosques in this area.

Sights at a Glance

Mosques and Churches
1. New Mosque
3. Rüstem Paşa Mosque
5. *Süleymaniye Mosque pp104–105*
6. Prince's Mosque
7. Kalenderhane Mosque
8. Tulip Mosque

Bazaars, Hans and Shops
2. Egyptian Bazaar
11. Book Bazaar
12. Valide Hanı
13. *Grand Bazaar pp108–109*

Museums and Monuments
9. Forum of Theodosius

Squares and Courtyards
10. Beyazıt Square
14. Çorlulu Ali Paşa Courtyard

Waterways
4. Golden Horn

See also Street Finder maps 4 and 5

◀ Colourful spices arranged on a stall at the Egyptian Bazaar

For keys to symbols *see back flap*

Street-by-Street: Around the Egyptian Bazaar

The narrow streets around the Egyptian Bazaar encapsulate the spirit of old Istanbul. From here, buses, taxis and trams head off across the Galata Bridge and into the interior of the city. The blast of ships' horns signals the departure of ferries from Eminönü to Asian Istanbul. It is the quarter's shops and markets, though, that are the focus of attention for the eager shoppers who crowd the Egyptian Bazaar and the streets around it, sometimes breaking for a leisurely tea beneath the trees in its courtyard. Across the way, and entirely aloof from the bustle, rise the domes of the New Mosque. On one of the commercial alleyways that radiate out from the mosque, an inconspicuous doorway leads up stairs to the terrace of the serene, tile-covered Rüstem Paşa Mosque.

❸ ★ Rüstem Paşa Mosque
The interior of this secluded mosque is a brilliant pattern-book made of Iznik tiles *(see p165)* of the finest quality.

The *pastırma* shop at 11 Hasırcılar Caddesi sells thin slices of dried beef, spiced with fenugreek – a Turkish delicacy.

Tahtakale Hamamı Çarşısı, now a bazaar, was formerly a Turkish bath.

Kurukahveci Mehmet Efendi is one of Istanbul's oldest and most popular coffee shops. You can drink your coffee on the premises or buy a packet to take away with you.

KUTUCULAR CAD

UZUNÇARŞI CAD

BALKAPANI SOK

HASIRCILAR CAD

TAHTAKALE CAD

SABUNCUHANI SOK

MARPUCCU

| 0 metres | 75 |
| 0 yards | 75 |

Stall holders and street traders, such as this man selling garlic, ply their wares in Sabuncuhanı Sokağı and the narrow streets around the Egyptian Bazaar.

Eminönü is the port from which ferries depart to many destinations and also for trips along the Bosphorus (see pp130–31). It bustles with activity as traders compete to sell drinks and snacks.

Locator Map
See Street Finder maps 4 and 5

The Royal Pavilion, a suite of beautifully tiled private rooms, is linked by a passage to the sultan's loge inside the New Mosque.

Galata Bridge

Eminönü sea bus boarding point

Eminönü tram stop

BEŞADIYE CAD

CAMI MEYDANI SOK

HMIŞ CAD

VENI CAMI CAD

IÇEK PAZARI SOK

Cafés

Mausoleum of Turhan Hatice Valide Sultan, mother of Mehmet IV

Pet market and garden centre

❶ ★ New Mosque
This mosque, which dominates the Eminönü waterfront, was completed in the 17th century by the mother of Sultan Mehmet IV.

❷ ★ Egyptian Bazaar
This market was built in 1660 as part of the New Mosque complex, and it has always been associated with the sale of spices, though today there is much more on offer.

Key

━ Suggested route

For keys to symbols *see back flap*

❶ New Mosque
Yeni Cami

Yeni Cami Meydanı, Eminönü.
Map 5 D2. 🚊 Eminönü. **Open** daily.

Situated at the southern end of Galata Bridge, the New Mosque is one of the most prominent mosques in the city. It dates from the time when a few women from the harem became powerful enough to dictate the policies of the Ottoman sultans.

The mosque was started in 1597 by Safiye, mother of Mehmet III, but building was suspended on the sultan's death as his mother then lost her position. It was not completed until 1663, after Turhan Hatice, mother of Mehmet IV, had taken up the project.

Though the mosque was built after the classical period of Ottoman architecture, it shares many traits with earlier imperial foundations, including a monumental courtyard. The mosque once had a hospital, school and public baths.

The turquoise, blue and white floral tiles decorating the interior are from İznik (*see p165*) and date from the mid-17th century, though by this time the quality of the tiles produced there was already in decline. More striking are the tiled lunettes and bold Koranic frieze decorating the porch between the courtyard and the prayer hall.

At the far left-hand corner of the upper gallery is the sultan's loge (*see p37*), which is linked to his personal suite of rooms.

A selection of nuts and seeds for sale in the Egyptian Bazaar

❷ Egyptian Bazaar
Mısır Çarşısı

Cami Meydanı Sok. **Map** 5 D2.
🚊 Eminönü. **Open** 8am–7pm Mon–Sat.

This cavernous, L-shaped market was built in the early 17th century as an extension of the New Mosque complex. Its revenues once helped maintain the mosque's philanthropic institutions.

In Turkish the market is named the Mısır Çarşısı – the Egyptian Bazaar – because it was built with money paid as duty on Egyptian imports. In English it is also known as the Spice Bazaar. From medieval times spices were a vital and expensive part of cooking and they became the market's main produce. The bazaar came to specialize in spices from the Orient, taking advantage of Istanbul's site on the trade route between the East (where most spices were grown) and Europe.

Stalls in the bazaar stock spices, herbs and other foods such as honey, nuts, sweetmeats and *pastırma* (dried beef). Today's expensive Eastern commodity, caviar, is also available, the best variety being Iranian. Nowadays an eclectic range of items

can be found in the Egyptian Bazaar, from household goods, toys and clothes to exotic aphrodisiacs. The square between the two arms of the bazaar is full of commercial activity, with cafés, and stalls selling plants and pets.

Floral İznik tiles adorning the interior of Rüstem Paşa Mosque

❸ Rüstem Paşa Mosque
Rüstem Paşa Camii

Hasırcılar Cad, Eminönü. **Map** 4 C2.
🚊 Eminönü. **Open** daily.

Raised above the busy shops and warehouses around the Egyptian Bazaar, this mosque was built in 1561 by the great architect Sinan (*see p105*) for Rüstem Paşa, son-in-law of and grand vizier to Süleyman I (*see p59*).

The staggering wealth of its decoration says something about the amount of money that the corrupt Rüstem managed to salt away. Most of the interior is covered in İznik tiles of the highest quality. The four piers are adorned with tiles of one design, but the rest of the prayer hall is a riot of different patterns, from abstract to floral. Some of the finest tiles can be found on the galleries, making it the most magnificently tiled mosque in the city.

The New Mosque, a prominent feature on the Eminönü waterfront

❹ Golden Horn

Haliç

Map 4 C1. 🚊 Eminönü. 🚌 55T, 99A.

Often described as the world's greatest natural harbour, the Golden Horn is a flooded river valley that flows southwest into the Bosphorus. The estuary attracted settlers to its shores in the 7th century BC and later enabled Constantinople to become a rich and powerful port. According to legend, the Byzantines threw so many valuables into it during the Ottoman conquest *(see p58)* that the waters glistened with gold. Today, numerous small boats can be seen plying the upper reaches of the estuary.

Spanning the mouth of the Horn is the Galata Bridge, which joins Eminönü to Galata. The bridge, built in 1992, opens in the middle to allow access for tall ships. It is a good place from which to appreciate the complex geography of the city and admire the minaret-filled skyline. Fishermen's boats selling mackerel sandwiches are usually moored at each end.

The present Galata Bridge replaced a pontoon bridge with a lower level of restaurants. The Old Galata Bridge has been reconstructed further up the Golden Horn, just south of the Rahmi Koç Museum.

❺ Süleymaniye Mosque

See pp104–5.

❻ Prince's Mosque

Şehzade Camii

70 Şehzade Başı Cad, Saraçhane.
Map 4 B3. 🚊 Laleli. **Open** daily.
Tombs: **Open** 9am–5pm Tue–Sun.

This mosque complex was erected by Süleyman the Magnificent *(see p59)* in memory of his eldest son by Roxelana, Şehzade (Prince) Mehmet, who died of smallpox at the age of 21. The building was Sinan's *(see p105)* first major imperial commission and was completed in 1548.

Dome of the Prince's Mosque, Sinan's first imperial mosque

The architect used a delightful decorative style in this mosque before abandoning it in favour of the classical austerity of his later work. The mosque is approached through an elegant porticoed inner courtyard, while the other institutions making up the mosque complex, including a *medrese (see p36)*, are enclosed within an outer courtyard. The mosque's interior is unusual and was something of an experiment: symmetrical, it has a semi-dome on all four sides.

The three tombs to the rear of the mosque, belonging to Şehzade Mehmet himself and grand viziers İbrahim Paşa and Rüstem Paşa, are the finest in the city. Each has beautiful İznik tiles *(see p165)* and original stained glass. That of Şehzade Mehmet also boasts the finest painted dome in Istanbul.

On Fridays you may notice a crowd of women flocking to another tomb within the complex, that of Helvacı Baba. This has been done traditionally for over 400 years. Helvacı Baba is said to miraculously cure crippled children, solve any fertility problems and find husbands or accommodation for those who beseech him.

❼ Kalenderhane Mosque

Kalenderhane Camii

16 Mart Şehitleri Cad, Saraçhane.
Map 4 B3. 🚊 Üniversite.
Open prayer times only.

Sitting in the lee of the Valens Aqueduct, on the site where a Roman bath once stood, is this Byzantine church with a chequered history. Built and rebuilt several times between the 6th and 12th centuries, it was converted into a mosque shortly after the conquest in 1453 *(see p59)*. The mosque is named after the Kalender brotherhood of dervishes, which used the church as its headquarters for some years after the conquest.

The building has the cruciform layout characteristic of Byzantine churches of the period. Some of the decoration remaining from its last incarnation, as the Church of Theotokos Kyriotissa (her Ladyship Mary, Mother of God), also survives in the prayer hall with its marble panelling and in the fragments of fresco in the narthex (entrance hall).

A shaft of light illuminates the interior of Kalenderhane Mosque

❺ Süleymaniye Mosque
Süleymaniye Camii

Istanbul's most important mosque is both a tribute to its architect, the great Sinan, and a fitting memorial to its founder, Süleyman the Magnificent *(see p59)*. It was built above the Golden Horn in the grounds of the old palace, Eski Saray, between 1550 and 1557. Like the city's other imperial mosques, the Süleymaniye Mosque was not only a place of worship, but also a charitable foundation, or *külliye* *(see p36)*. The mosque is surrounded by its former hospital, soup kitchen, schools, caravanserai and bath house. This complex provided a welfare system which fed over 1,000 of the city's poor – Muslims, Christians and Jews alike – every day.

Courtyard
The ancient columns that surround the courtyard are said to have come originally from the *kathisma*, the Byzantine royal box in the Hippodrome *(see p94)*.

Muvakkithane Gateway
The main courtyard entrance (now closed) contained the rooms of the mosque astronomer, who determined prayer times.

KEY

① **Café in a sunken garden**

② **The İmaret (kitchen)** – now a restaurant – fed the city's poor as well as the mosque staff and their families. The size of the millstone in its courtyard gives some idea of the amount of grain needed to feed everyone.

③ **İmaret Gate**

④ **The *kervansaray*** provided lodging and food for travellers and their animals.

⑤ **Tomb of Sinan**

⑥ **Minaret**

⑦ **The Tomb of Roxelana** contains Süleyman's beloved Russian-born wife.

⑧ **Graveyard**

⑨ **These marble benches** were used to support coffins before burial.

⑩ **"Addicts Alley"** is so called because the cafés here once sold opium and hashish as well as coffee and tea.

⑪ **The medreses** to the south of the mosque house a library containing 110,000 manuscripts.

⑫ **Former hospital and asylum**

★ Mosque Interior

A sense of soaring space and calm strikes you as you enter the mosque. The effect is enhanced by the fact that the height of the dome from the floor is exactly double its diameter, which is 26 m (85 ft).

★ Tomb of Süleyman

Ceramic stars said to be set with emeralds sparkle above the coffins of Süleyman, his daughter Mihrimah and two of his successors, Süleyman II and Ahmet II.

Entrance

Sinan, The Imperial Architect

Like many of his eminent contemporaries, Koca Mimar Sinan (c.1491–1588) was brought from Anatolia to Istanbul in the *devşirme*, the annual roundup of talented Christian youths, and educated at one of the elite palace schools. He became a military engineer but won the eye of Süleyman I, who made him chief imperial architect in 1538. With the far-sighted patronage of the sultan, Sinan – the closest Turkey gets to a Renaissance architect – created masterpieces which demonstrated his master's status as the most magnificent of monarchs. Sinan died aged 97, having built 131 mosques and 200 other buildings.

Bust of the great architect Sinan

❽ Tulip Mosque
Laleli Camii

Ordu Cad, Laleli. **Map** 4 B4. 🚇 Laleli.
Open prayer times only.

Built in 1759–63, this mosque complex is the city's best example of the Baroque style, of which its architect, Mehmet Tahir Ağa, was the greatest exponent. A variety of gaudy, coloured marble covers all of its surfaces. Underneath the body of the mosque is a great hall, supported on eight piers with a fountain in the middle, used as a market and packed with Eastern Europeans and Central Asians haggling over clothing.

The nearby Büyük Taş Hanı, or Big Stone Han, probably part of the mosque's original complex (*see pp36–7*), now houses shops and a restaurant. To get to it, turn left outside the mosque into Fethi Bey Caddesi, and take the second left into Çukur Çeşme Sokağı. The main courtyard of the han is at the end of a long passage off this lane.

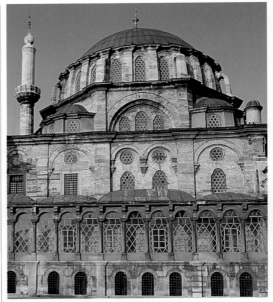
The Baroque Tulip Mosque, housing a marketplace in its basement

❾ Forum of Theodosius

Ordu Cad, Beyazıt. **Map** 4 C4.
🚇 Üniversite or Beyazıt.

The city of Constantinople (*see pp54–5*) was built around large public squares or forums, the largest of which stood on the site of Beyazıt Square. It was once known as the Forum Tauri (Forum of the Bull) because of the huge bronze bull in which sacrificial animals, and sometimes criminals, were

Peacock feather design on a column at the Forum of Theodosius

roasted. The huge columns, decorated with a motif reminiscent of a peacock's tail, are particularly striking. When the forum became derelict these columns were reused in the city, some in the Basilica Cistern (*see p90*), and fragments from the forum were built into Beyazıt Hamamı, a Turkish bath (*see p81*) further west down Ordu Caddesi, now a bazaar.

❿ Beyazıt Square
Beyazıt Meydanı

Ordu Cad, Beyazıt. **Map** 4 C4.
🚇 Beyazıt.

Always filled with crowds of people and huge flocks of pigeons, Beyazıt Square is the most vibrant space in the old part of the city. During the week the square hosts a flea market, with carpets (*see pp366–7*), silks and general bric-a-brac on sale and many cafés located beneath shady plane trees.

On the northern side of the square is the Moorish-style gateway leading into Istanbul University. Within the wooded grounds rises **Beyazıt Tower**, a fire look-out point built in 1828.

Two original timber towers were destroyed by fire. At one time you could climb to the top of the tower but it has been closed to the public since 1972.

On the square's eastern side is **Beyazıt Mosque**. Completed in 1506, it is the oldest surviving imperial mosque in the city. Behind the impressive outer portal is a harmonious courtyard with an elegant domed fountain at its centre. The layout of its interior is heavily inspired by the design of Haghia Sophia (*see pp86–7*).

Beyazıt Tower, within the wooded grounds of Istanbul University

⓫ Book Bazaar
Sahaflar Çarşısı

Sahaflar Çarşısı Sok, Beyazıt.
Map 4 C4. 🚇 Üniversite.
Open 8am–8pm daily. ♿

This charming booksellers'
courtyard, on the site of
the Byzantine book and
paper market, can be
entered either from Beyazıt
Square or from inside the
Grand Bazaar *(see pp108–9)*.
Early in the Ottoman
period *(see pp58–9)*, printed
books were seen as a
corrupting influence and were
banned in Turkey, so the bazaar
sold only manuscripts. On 31
January 1729 İbrahim
Müteferrika (1674–1745)
produced the first printed
Turkish book, an Arabic
dictionary, and today his bust
stands in the centre of the
market. Book prices are fixed
and cannot be haggled over.

Customers browsing in the Book Bazaar
(Sahaflar Çarşisi)

⓬ Valide Han
Valide Hanı

Junction of Çakmakçılar Yokuşu &
Tarakçılar Sok, Beyazıt. **Map** 4 C3.
🚇 Beyazıt, then 10 mins' walk.
Open 9:30am–5pm Mon–Sat.

If the grand bazaar *(see pp108–9)*
seems large, it is sobering to
realize that it is only the covered
part of a huge area of seething
commercial activity which
reaches all the way to the
Golden Horn. Most of the
manufacturing and trade takes
place in *hans (see pp28–9)*
hidden away from the street
behind shaded gateways.
  The largest han in Istanbul is
Valide Han, built in 1651 by
Kösem, the mother of Sultan
Mehmet IV. You enter it from
Çakmakçılar Yokuşu through a
massive portal, pass through an
irregularly shaped forecourt,
and come out into a large
courtyard centring on a Shiite
mosque. This was built when
the han became the centre of
Persian trade in the city. The han
now throbs to the rhythm of
hundreds of weaving looms.
  A short walk further down
Çakmakçılar Yokuşu is Büyük
Yeni Han, hidden behind

another impressive doorway.
This 1764 Baroque han has
three arcaded levels. In the
labyrinth of streets around the
hans, artisans are grouped
according to their wares.

⓭ Grand Bazaar
See pp108–9.

⓮ Çorlulu Ali Paşa Courtyard
Çorlulu Ali Paşa Külliyesi

Yeniçeriler Cad, Beyazıt. **Map** 4 C4.
🚇 Beyazıt. **Open** daily.

Like many others in the city,
the *medrese (see p36)* of this
mosque complex outside the
Grand Bazaar has become the
setting for a tranquil
outdoor café. It was built for
Çorlulu Ali Paşa, son-in-law of

Mustafa II, the grand vizier
under Ahmet III.
  The complex is entered from
Yeniçeriler Caddesi by two
alleyways. Several carpet shops
now inhabit the *medrese* and
rugs are spread all around for
prospective buyers. The carpet
shops share the *medrese* with
a *kahve*, a traditional café, which
is popular with locals and
university students. It advertises
itself irresistibly as the
"Traditional Mystic Water Pipe
and Erenler Tea Garden" where
you can sit, drink tea and
perhaps smoke a *nargile* (water
pipe), while deciding which
carpet to buy *(see pp366–7)*.
  Situated across Bileyciler
Sokak, an alleyway off Çorlulu
Ali Paşa Courtyard, is the Koca
Sinan Paşa tomb complex, the
courtyard of which is another
tea garden. The charming
medrese, mausoleum and *sebil*
(a fountain where water was
handed out to passers-by) were
built in 1593 by Davut Ağa, who
succeeded Sinan *(see p105)* as
chief architect of the empire.
The tomb of Koca Sinan Paşa,
grand vizier under Murat III
and Mehmet III, is a striking
16-sided structure.
  Just off the other side of
Yeniçeriler Caddesi is Gedik Paşa
Hamamı, probably the city's
oldest working Turkish baths *(see
p81)*, built around 1475 for Gedik
Ahmet Paşa, grand vizier under
Mehmet the Conqueror *(see p58)*.

Carpet shops in Çorlulu Ali Paşa Courtyard

⓫ The Grand Bazaar

Kapalı Çarşı

Nothing can prepare you for the Grand Bazaar. This labyrinth of streets covered by painted vaults is lined with thousands of booth-like shops, whose wares spill out to tempt you and whose shopkeepers are relentless in their quest for a sale. The bazaar was established by Mehmet II shortly after his conquest of the city in 1453 *(see p58)*. It can be entered by several gateways, two of the most useful being Çarşıkapı Gate (from Beyazıt tram stop) and Nuruosmaniye Gate (from Nuruosmaniye Mosque). It is easy to get lost in the bazaar in spite of the signposting. Many of the bazaar's goods are made behind the scenes in secluded ateliers.

Muhlis Günbattı is a well-known textile and carpet shop *(see p135)*.

The Rooftops of the Grand Bazaar
Cafés, restaurants, toilets, banks, a post office, a police station and a mosque serve those who work and shop inside the bazaar.

Egyptian Bazaar *(p102)*, Valide Han *(p107)*

Örücüler Gate

ASTARCI HANI

İÇ CEBECİ HAN

PERDAHÇILAR

YAĞLIKÇILAR SOK

KAVAFLAR S

TORGANCILAR CAD

HACI HASAN SOK

ZENNECİLER SOK

BODRUM HANI

FESÇİLER CAD

FERACECİLER SOK

KALPAKÇILAR

Beyazıt Gate

Çadırcılar Caddesi, Book Bazaar *(see p107)*

Havuzlu Lokanta is a popular restaurant in the bazaar.

Beyazıt tram stop

Çarşıkapı Gate

Şark Kahvesi
This traditional Turkish café is a popular choice with local bazaar traders.

Marble Fountain
Two copper and marble fountains once provided the bazaar with fresh water.

0 metres 40
0 yards 40

For additional map symbols *see back flap*

Zincirli Han
This is one of the prettiest hans in the bazaar. Here a piece of jewellery can be made to your own choice of design.

The İç Bedesten is the oldest part of the bazaar. Once a warehouse, it also served as a place where jewellers could make and sell their wares.

The Oriental Kiosk was built as a coffee house in the 17th century and is now a jewellery shop.

ZINCIRLI HAN

Mahmut Paşa Gate

AYNACILAR SOK

CILAR ÇARSISI CAD

Money traders

AĞA SOK

BEDESTEN

MUHAFAZACILAR SOK

ESECİLER CAD

TERZİ BAŞI SOK

SANDAL BEDESTEN SOK

SANDAL BEDESTEN

Rugs on Display
Carpets and *kilims* (see pp366–7) from all over Turkey and Central Asia are on sale in the bazaar.

Gateway to the İç Bedesten
Though the eagle was a symbol of the Byzantine emperors (see pp54–5), this eagle, like the bazaar itself, postdates the Byzantine era.

The Sandal Bedesteni dates from the 16th century and is covered by 20 brick domes supported on piers.

Nuruosmaniye Mosque, Çemberlitaş tram stop

Nuruosmaniye Gate

Souvenirs
Traditionally crafted items, such as this brass ewer, are for sale in the bazaar.

Kalpakçılar Başı Caddesi, the widest of the streets in the bazaar, is lined with the glittering windows of countless jewellery shops.

Key
— Suggested route
 Antiques and carpets
 Leather and denim
 Gold and silver
 Fabrics
 Souvenirs
 Household goods and workshops
 Boundary of the bazaar

BEYOĞLU

For centuries Beyoğlu, a steep hill north of the Golden Horn, was home to the city's foreign residents. First to arrive here were the Genoese. As a reward for aiding the reconquest of the city from the crusader-backed Latin Empire in 1261, they were given the Galata area, which is now dominated by the Galata Tower. During the Ottoman period, Jews from Spain, Arabs, Greeks and Armenians settled in communities here. From the 16th century the European powers established embassies in the area to further their interests within the lucrative territories of the Ottoman Empire. The district has not changed much in character over the centuries and is still a thriving commercial quarter today.

Sights at a Glance

Historic Buildings and Monuments
1. Pera Palas Hotel
3. Mevlevi Lodge
4. Galata Tower

Museums
2. Pera Museum
5. Ottoman Bank Museum
7. Istanbul Museum of Modern Art

Mosques and Churches
6. Nusretiye Mosque

Quarters
8. Çukurcuma
9. Taksim

0 metres   500
0 yards   500

See also Street Finder map 1

◀ A vintage tram on İstiklâl Caddesi in Taksim

For keys to symbols *see back flap*

Street-by-Street: İstiklâl Caddesi

The pedestrianized İstiklâl Caddesi is Beyoğlu's main street. Once known as the Grande Rue de Pera, it is lined by late 19th-century apartment blocks and European embassy buildings whose grandiose gates and façades belie their use as mere consulates since Ankara became the Turkish capital in 1923 (see p62). Hidden from view stand the churches, which used to serve the foreign communities of Pera (as this area was formerly called), some still buzzing with worshippers, others just quiet echoes of a bygone era. Today, the once seedy backstreets of Beyoğlu, off İstiklâl Caddesi, have taken on a new lease of life, with trendy jazz bars opening and shops selling hand-crafted jewellery, furniture and the like. Crowds are also drawn by the area's cinemas and numerous stylish restaurants.

❶ ★ Pera Palas Hotel
This hotel is an atmospheric period piece. Many famous guests, like Agatha Christie, have stayed here since it opened in 1892. The hotel has been extensively restored to its original splendour.

St Mary Draperis is a Franciscan church dating from 1789. This small statue of the Virgin stands above the entrance from the street. The vaulted interior of the church is colourfully decorated. An icon of the Virgin, said to perform miracles, hangs over the altar.

Tünel underground railway to Karaköy

Tünel Square

❸ ★ Mevlevi Lodge
A peaceful garden surrounds this small museum of the Mevlevi Sufi sect (see p259). On the last Sunday of every month visitors can see dervishes perform their famous swirling dance.

Key

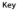 Suggested route

Swedish Consulate

Russian Consulate

For additional map symbols see back flap

Galatasaray Fish Market
(Balık Pazarı) mainly sells
fresh fish, but inside you
will also find delicatessens
offering everything from
meats and cheeses to
sweetmeats and pickles.

Locator Map
See Street Finder map 1

British
Consulate

HAMALBAŞI CAD

Armenian
church

İYENİ ÇARŞI CAD

İSTİKLAL CAD

Galatasaray Lisesi
(high school)

Çiçek Pasajı was originally
a flower market. Its stalls
have been replaced by
bars and restaurants,
which are particularly
lively in the evenings.

Dutch
Consulate

2 Pera Museum
Oriental paintings,
Anatolian weights and
measures and Kütahya
tiles and ceramics are
part of the collection.

| 0 metres | 75 |
| 0 yards | 75 |

The Church of the Panaghia
serves the now much-reduced
Greek Orthodox population of
Beyoğlu. Dedicated to the
Virgin Mary, it contains this
beautiful classical iconostasis.

The peaceful courtyard of the Mevlevi Lodge

❶ Pera Palas Hotel
Pera Palas Oteli

52 Meşrutiyet Cad, Tepebaşı. **Map** 1 D3. **Tel** (0212) 251 40 00. ⬛ Tünel. ♿ by arrangement. 🌐 **perapalace.com**

Throughout the world there are hotels that have attained a legendary status. One such hotel is the Pera Palas, which opened in 1892 to cater for travellers on the Orient Express (*see p80*).

After an extensive renovation, it still evokes images of uniformed porters and exotic destinations such as Baghdad. The Grand Orient bar serves cocktails beneath its original chandeliers, while the patisserie offers irresistible cakes and a genteel ambience. A room used by the thriller writer Agatha Christie can be visited on request.

❷ Pera Museum
Pera Müzesi

Merutiyet Cad 141, Tepebaı. **Map** 7 D4. **Tel** (0212) 334 99 00. ⬛ Tünel. 🚌 From Taksim Square down Tarlabaşı. **Open** 10am–7pm Tue– Sat, noon–6pm Sun. **Closed** 1 Jan, first day of Religious Holidays. ♿ 📷 (disabled visitors enter free). 📷 🅿 🌐 **peramuzesi.org.tr**

The Pera Museum was opened in 2005 by the Suna and İnan Kıraç Foundation.

Formerly the Hotel Bristol, it has been transformed into a fully equipped modern museum. Notable collections include Ottoman weights and measures, over 400 examples of 18th-century Kütahya tiles and ceramics, and the Suna and İnan

Kıraç Foundation's exhibition of Orientalist art. This collection brings together works by European artists inspired by the Ottoman world from the 17th century to the early 19th century and also covers the last two centuries of the Ottoman Empire.

❸ Mevlevi Lodge
Mevlevi Tekkesi

15 Galip Dede Cad, Beyoğlu. **Map** 1 D3. **Tel** (0212) 245 41 41. ⬛ Tünel. **Open** 8am–5pm Wed–Mon. 🅿

Although Sufism was banned by Atatürk in 1925, this Dervish lodge has survived as the Divan Edebiyatı Müzesi, a museum of *divan* literature (classical Ottoman poetry). The lodge belonged to the most famous Sufi sect, known as the Whirling Dervishes (*see p259*). The original dervishes were disciples of the mystical poet and great Sufi master

Čelaleddin Rumi, known as "Mevlâna" (Our Leader)."

Tucked away off Galip Dede, the focus of the 18th-century lodge is a beautiful octagonal wooden dance floor where the *sema* (ritual dance) is performed on the last Sunday of every month. There is also a small exhibition of artifacts.

❹ Galata Tower
Galata Kulesi

Büyük Hendek Sok, Şişhane. **Map** 5 D1. **Tel** (0212) 293 81 80. ⬛ Tünel. **Open** 8am–7pm daily. 🍴 Restaurant & Show **Open** 8pm–midnight daily. 🅦 **galatatower.net**

The most recognizable feature on the Golden Horn, the Galata Tower, is 60 m (196 ft) high and topped by a conical tower. Its origins date from the 6th century when it was used to monitor shipping. After the conquest of Istanbul in 1453, the Ottomans turned it into a prison and naval depot. Aviation pioneer, Hezarfen Ahmet Çelebi attached wings to his arms and "flew" from the tower to Üsküdar in the 1700s. The building was subsequently used as a fire watchtower.

It has been refurbished to blend with local improvement schemes and, in the evenings, the 9th floor is a noteworthy restaurant with authentic Turkish entertainment. The unmissable view from the top encompasses the Istanbul skyline and beyond to Princes' Islands (*see p162*).

The distinctive Galata Tower, as seen from across the Golden Horn

❺ Ottoman Bank Museum
Osmanlı Bankası Müzesi

Bankalar Cad 35–37, Karaköy.
Map 5 D1. **Tel** (0212) 292 76 05.
Tünel. 25E, 56.
Open 10am–6pm daily.

The Ottoman Bank Museum has the most interesting collection of state archives in Turkey. From the official Ottoman state bank in 1856 to its incorporation into Garanti Bank in 2001, no other records mirror Turkey's recent social, political and economic events so authentically. Exhibits include Ottoman bank notes, promissory notes, photos of the Empire's ornately crafted bank branches and outstanding photos of employees throughout the bank's history.

Nusretiye Mosque

❻ Nusretiye Mosque
Nusretiye Camii

Necatibey Cad, Tophane. **Map** 1 E3.
25E, 56. **Open** daily.

The Baroque "Mosque of Victory" was built in the 1820s by Kirkor Balian. A very ornate building, it is in fact more like a large palace pavilion than a typical mosque. It was commissioned by Mahmut II to commemorate his abolition of the Janissary corps in 1826 *(see p61)*. The marble panel of calligraphy around the interior of the mosque is particularly fine.

Colourful display at the museum shop, Istanbul Museum of Modern Art

❼ Istanbul Museum of Modern Art
İstanbul Modern Sanat Müzesi

Meclis-i Mebusan Cad, Liman İşletmeleri Sahası, Antrepo 4, Karaköy.
Map 1 B5. **Tel** (0212) 334 73 00.
Tophane. 56. **Open** 10am–6pm Tue–Sun (to 8pm Thu). free on Thu.
W istanbulmodern.org

Perched on the Golden Horn, this is the most upbeat and thoroughly European museum in Turkey. It houses both permanent collections and temporary exhibitions, providing a showcase for many of the eccentric and talented personalities who have shaped modern art in Turkey, and reflecting the main trends and themes of Turkish art from the early 20th century to the present day. Many of the paintings and drawings are from the private collection of the Ecacıbaşı family, who founded the museum.

The collection includes abstract art, landscapes, watercolours and the plastic arts as well as a sculpture garden and a stunning exhibition of black-and-white photography. Exhibitions by contemporary artists from abroad are held regularly, as the museum embraces "Modern Experiences".

❽ Çukurcuma
Map 1 E4. Taksim.

This charming old quarter of Beyoğlu, radiating from a neighbourhood mosque on Çukurcuma Caddesi, has become an important centre for the furnishings and antiques trades. Old warehouses and homes have been converted into shops and showrooms, where modern upholstery materials are piled up in marble basins and antique cabinets. Browsing can yield the likes of 19th-century Ottoman embroidery to 1950s biscuit boxes.

❾ Taksim
Map 1 E3. Taksim. Taksim Art Gallery: **Tel** (0212) 245 20 68.
Open 11am–7pm Mon–Sat.

Centring on the vast, open Taksim Square (Taksim Meydanı), the Taksim area is the hub of activity in modern Beyoğlu. Taksim means "water distribution centre", and from the early 18th century it was from this site that water from the Belgrade Forest was distributed throughout the modern city. The original stone reservoir, built in 1732 by Mahmut I, still stands at the top of İstiklal Caddesi.

On Cumhuriyet Caddesi is the modern building of the **Taksim Art Gallery**, which shows temporary exhibitions as well as permanent displays of Istanbul landscapes by some of Turkey's most important 20th-century painters.

An extensive redevelopment project of Taksim Square is ongoing. The resulting roadworks around the area may cause delays and disruption for cars and buses.

❶ Ahrida Synagogue
Ahrida Sinagogu

Gevgili Sok, Balat. 55T, 99A.
Open by appointment only.
Tel Karavan Travel, (0212) 523 47 29.

The name of the oldest and most beautiful synagogue in Istanbul is a corruption of Ohrid, the name of a town in the former Yugoslavia from which its congregation came.

Founded before the Muslim conquest of Istanbul in 1453, it has been in constant use ever since. The painted walls and ceilings, dating from the late 17th century, have been restored to their Baroque glory. Pride of place, however, goes to the central Holy Ark, which is covered in rich tapestries.

Visits are possible by prior arrangement with one of various specialist tour operators, such as Karavan Travel.

❷ Church of St Stephen of the Bulgars
Bulgar Kilisesi

85 Mürsel Paşa Cad, Balat. 55T, 99A. Balat. **Open** 9am–4pm daily.

Astonishingly, this entire church was cast in iron, even the internal columns and galleries. It was created in Vienna in 1871, shipped all the way to the Golden Horn *(see p103)* and assembled on its shore. The church was needed for

The Church of St Stephen of the Bulgars, wholly made of cast iron

the Bulgarian community who had broken away from the authority of the Greek Orthodox Patriarchate just up the hill. Today, it is still used by this community, who keep the marble tombs of the first Bulgarian patriarchs permanently decorated with flowers. The church stands in a pretty little park dotted with trees, and which runs down to the edge of the Golden Horn.

❸ Church of the Pammakaristos
Fethiye Camii

Fethiye Cad, Çarşamba-Fatih. 90, 90B. **Open** prayer times only. Museum: **Open** Tue–Thu. for museum.

This Byzantine church is one of the hidden secrets of Istanbul. It is rarely visited despite the important role it has played in the history of the city, and its

breathtaking series of mosaics. For over 100 years after the Ottoman conquest it housed the Greek Orthodox Patriarchate, but was converted into a mosque in the late 16th century by Sultan Murat III.

The charming exterior is obviously Byzantine, with its alternating stone and brick courses and finely carved marble details. The main body of the building is the working mosque, while the extraordinary mosaics and frescoes are in a side chapel. This now operates as a museum.

Dating from the 14th century, the great Byzantine renaissance, the mosaics show holy figures isolated in a sea of gold, a reflection of the heavens. On either side are portraits of the Virgin Mary and John the Baptist beseeching Christ. They are overlooked by the four archangels, while the side apses are filled with other saintly figures. In the centre of the main dome are images of Christ Pantocrator ("the All-Powerful") and the Old Testament prophets.

❹ Greek Orthodox Patriarchate
Ortodoks Patrikhanesi

35 Sadrazam Ali Paşa Cad, Fener.
Tel (0212) 521 19 21. 55T, 99A.
Open 9am–5pm daily.

This walled complex has been the seat of the patriarchan of the Greek Orthodox Church since the early 17th century. Though nominally head of the whole church, the patriarch is now shepherd to a diminishing Istanbul flock.

The main door to the Patriarchate has been welded shut in memory of Patriarch Gregory V, hanged here for treason in 1821 after encouraging the Greeks to throw off Ottoman rule at the start of the Greek War of Independence (1821–32). Turkish–Greek antagonism worsened with the Greek occupation of parts of Turkey in the 1920s *(see p62)*, anti-Greek riots in 1955, and the expulsion of Greek residents in the

Byzantine façade of the Church of the Pammakaristos

The ornate, gilded interior of the Church of St George in the Greek Orthodox Patriarchate

(see p165) made by the *cuerda seca* technique – each colour is separated during the firing process, affording the patterns greater definition. Similar tiles lend decorative effect to the simple prayer hall, with its fine mosque furniture *(see pp36–7)* and original, carefully painted woodwork.

mid-1960s. Today the clergy at the Patriarchate is protected by a metal detector at the entrance.

The Patriarchate centres on the basilica-style Church of St George, dating back to 1720, yet the church contains much older relics and furniture. The patriarch's throne is thought to be Byzantine, while the pulpit is adorned with fine wooden inlay and icons.

❺ Mosque of Selim I
I Selim Camii

Yavuz Selim Cad, Fener. 55T, 90, 90B, 99A. **Open** daily.

This much-admired mosque is also known locally as Yavuz Sultan Mosque: Yavuz, "the Grim", being the nickname the infamous Selim acquired. It is idyllic in a rather offbeat way, which does seem at odds with Selim's barbaric reputation.

The mosque, built between 1522 and 1529, sits alone on a hill beside what is now a vast sunken parking area, once the Byzantine Cistern of Aspar. Sadly, it is rarely visited and has an air of neglect, yet the mosque's intimate courtyard gives an insight into Islam's concept of paradise.

The windows set into the porticoes in the courtyard are capped by early İznik tiles

İznik tile panel in the Mosque of Selim I

❻ Fatih Mosque
Fatih Camii

Macar Kardeşler Cad, Fatih. **Map** 4 A2. 28, 87, 90, 91. **Open** daily.

A spacious outer courtyard surrounds this vast Baroque mosque, the third major structure on this site. The first was the Church of the Holy Apostles, the burial place of most of the Byzantine emperors. Most of what you see today was the work of Mehmet Tahir Ağa, the chief imperial architect under Mustafa III. Many of the buildings he constructed around the prayer hall, including eight Koranic colleges *(medreses)* and a hospice, still stand. The only surviving parts of Mehmet the Conqueror's mosque are the three porticoes of the courtyard, the ablutions fountain, the main gate into the prayer hall and, inside, the mihrab. Two exquisite forms of 15th-century decoration can be seen over the windows in the porticoes: İznik tiles and lunettes adorned with calligraphic marble inlay. Stencilled patterns decorate the domes of the prayer hall, and parts of the walls are revetted with beautiful tiles.

The tomb of Mehmet the Conqueror stands behind the prayer hall, near that of his consort, Gülbahar. His sarcophagus and the turban decorating it are both appropriately large. It is a place of enormous gravity, always busy with supplicants.

If you pay a visit to the mosque on a Wednesday, you will also see the weekly market, which turns the streets around it into a circus of commerce. From tables piled high with fruit and vegetables to trucks loaded with unspun wool, this is a real spectacle.

Church of the Pantocrator, built by Empress Irene in the 12th century

❼ Church of the Pantocrator
Zeyrek Camii

İbadethane Sok, Küçükpazar. **Map** 4 B2. 28, 61B, 87. **Open** prayer times daily.

Empress Irene, the wife of John II Comnenus, founded the Church of the Pantocrator ("Christ the Almighty") during the 12th century. This hulk of Byzantine masonry was once the centrepiece of one of Istanbul's most important religious foundations, the Monastery of the Pantocrator. The complex included an asylum, a hospice and a hospital. Now a mosque, it boasts a magnificent figurative marble floor and is composed of three interlinked chapels. A caretaker may let you in outside prayer times during the afternoon.

❽ Church of St John of Studius

İmrahor Camii

İmam Aşir Sok, Yedikule. 🚌 80, 80T. 🚃 Yedikule.

Istanbul's oldest surviving church, St John of Studius, is now merely a shell consisting of its outer walls, but you can still get an idea of the original beauty of what was once part of an important Byzantine institution.

The church was completed in AD 463 by Studius, a Roman patrician who served as consul during the reign of Emperor Marcian (450–57). Originally connected to the most powerful monastery in the Byzantine Empire and populated with ascetic monks, in the late 8th century it was a spiritual and intellectual centre under the rule of Abbot Theodore, who is now highly venerated in the Greek Orthodox Church as St Theodore. The most sacred relic housed in the church was the head of St John the Baptist, until its removal by the soldiers of the Fourth Crusade (*see pp54–5*). The reigning emperor would visit the church each year for the Beheading of the Baptist feast on 29 August.

In the 15th century the church housed a university and was converted into a mosque. The building was abandoned in 1894 after it was damaged by an earthquake. The church is a perfect basilica, with a single apse at the east end, preceded by a narthex and a courtyard. It has a magnificent entrance portal, with carved Corinthian capitals and a sculpted architrave and cornice, but it is empty inside.

Battlements at Yedikule, an Ottoman addition to the fortress

❾ Fortress of Seven Towers

Yedikule

Kale Medanı 4, Yedikule İmrahor Mahallesi. **Tel** (0212) 585 89 33. 🚌 31, 80, 93T. **Open** 9am–5pm daily.

Yedikule, the "Fortress of Seven Towers", was built in 1455 against the southern section of the Theodosian Walls. It displays both Byzantine and Ottoman features, being built in stages over a long period. Its seven towers are joined by thick walls to make a five-sided fortification. The two square marble towers built into the great land walls once flanked the Golden Gate (now blocked), which consisted of three magnificent golden portals. The gate was built by Emperor Theodosius I in AD 390 as the triumphal entrance into the thriving medieval city of Byzantium.

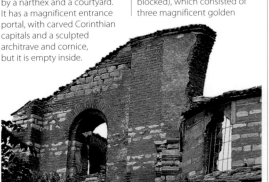

Carving of the Byzantine eagle over Yedikule Gate

In the 15th century, Sultan Mehmet II (the Conqueror) completed Yedikule by adding three round towers and connecting curtain walls. After viewing the castle from the outside, you can enter through a doorway in the northeastern wall. The tower to your left as you enter is the *yazılı kule*, "the tower with inscriptions". It was used as a prison for foreign envoys and others who fell out of favour with the sultan. Its name is derived from the names and epitaphs which many of these doomed individuals carved into the walls. Some of these morbid inscriptions are still visible.

The northern of the two towers flanking the Golden Gate was a place of execution. Among those who met their end here was the 17-year-old Sultan Osman II, who was dragged off to Yedikule by his own Janissaries in 1622, after four years of misrule. The walkway around the ramparts is accessible via a steep flight of stone steps and offers good views of the land walls, the southern marble tower and market garden allotments.

Ruins of the Church of St John of Studius

❿ Theodosian Walls
Teodos II Surları

From Yedikule to Ayvansaray.
Ⓜ Ulubatlı. 🚋 Topkapı.

With its 11 fortified gates and 192 towers, this great chain of double walls sealed Constantinople's landward side against invasion for more than a thousand years. Extending for a distance of 6.5 km (4 miles) from the Sea of Marmara to the Golden Horn, the walls are built in layers of red tile alternating with limestone blocks. They can be reached by metro, tram or train, but to see their whole length you will need to take a taxi or dolmuş *(see p396)* along the main road that runs outside them.

The walls were built by Theodosius II in AD 412–22. They endured many sieges, and were only breached by Mehmet the Conqueror in May 1453 *(see p58)*, when the Ottomans took Constantinople. Successive Ottoman sultans continued to maintain the walls until the end of the 17th century.

Many parts of the walls have been rebuilt, and the new sections give an idea of how the walls used to look. Some of the gateways are still in good repair, but a section of walls was demolished in the 1950s to make way for a road. The Charsius Gate (now called Edirnekapı), Silivrikapı, Yeni Mevlanakapı and other original gates still give access to the city. The Yedikule Gate (which stands beside the fortress of the same name) has an impressive imperial Byzantine eagle carved above its main archway.

⓫ Shrine of Zoodochus Pege
Balıklı Kilise

3 Seyit Nizam Cad, Silivrikapı.
Tel (0212) 582 30 81. 🚋 Seyitnizam.
🚌 93T. **Open** 8:30am–4pm daily.

The fountain of Zoodochus Pege ("Life-Giving Spring") is built over Istanbul's most famous sacred spring, which is believed to have miraculous powers. The fish in it are said

Silivrikapı, one of the gateways through the Theodosian Walls

to have arrived by miracle shortly before the fall of Constantinople *(see p58)*. They are believed to have leapt into the water from a monk's frying pan on hearing him declare that a Turkish invasion of the fortified town was as likely as fish coming back to life. The spring was probably the site of an ancient sanctuary of Artemis.

⓬ Gazi Ahmet Paşa Mosque
Gazi Ahmet Paşa Camii

Undeğirmeni Sok, Fatma Sultan.
Open Prayer times only. Ⓜ Ulubatlı.
🚋 Topkapı. 🚌 93T.

One of the most worthwhile detours along the city walls is the Gazi Ahmet Paşa Mosque. This lovely building, with its peaceful leafy courtyard and graceful proportions, is one of the imperial architect Sinan's *(see p105)* lesser known achievements, which he built in 1554 for Kara Ahmet Paşa,

a grand vizier of Süleyman the Magnificent *(see p59)*.

The courtyard is surrounded by the cells of a *medrese* and a *dershane*, or main classroom. Attractive apple-green and yellow İznik tiles *(see p165)* dating from the mid-1500s grace the porch, with blue-and-white tiles on the east wall of the prayer hall. Outside the city walls is tiny Takkeci İbrahim Ağa Mosque, which dates from 1592 and has some particularly fine İznik tile panels.

⓭ Palace of the Porphyrogenitus
Tekfur Sarayı

Şişehane Cad, Edirnekapı. **Tel** (0212) 522 175. 🚌 87, 90, 126. **Open** daily.

Only glimpses of the former grandeur of the Palace of the Porphyrogenitus (sovereign), during its years as an imperial residence, are discernible from the sketchy remains. Its one extant hall, now open to the elements, has an attractive three-storey façade in typically Byzantine style. It was most likely built in the late Byzantine era as an annexe of the Blachernae Palace. These palaces became the principal residences of the imperial sovereigns during the last two centuries before the fall of Constantinople to the Ottomans in 1453.

During the reign of Ahmet III (1703–30) the last remaining İznik potters *(see p165)* moved to the palace and it became a centre for tile production. Cezri Kasım Paşa Mosque in Eyüp has some very fine examples of these tiles.

Tilework over *medrese* doorway at Gazi Ahmet Paşa Mosque

⑭ Church of St Saviour in Chora

Kariye Camii

Some of the very finest Byzantine mosaics and frescoes can be found in the Church of St Saviour in Chora. Little is known of the early history of the church, although its name "in Chora", which means "in the country", suggests that the church originally stood in a rural setting. The present church dates from the 11th century. From 1315 to 1321 it was remodelled, and the mosaics and frescoes were added by Theodore Metochites, a theologian, philosopher and one of the elite Byzantine officials of his day.

View of St Saviour in Chora

The Genealogy of Christ

Theodore Metochites, who restored St Saviour, wrote that his mission was to relate how "the Lord himself became a mortal on our behalf". He takes the *Genealogy of Christ* as his starting point: the mosaics in the two domes of the inner narthex portray 66 of Christ's forebears.

The crown of the southern dome is occupied by a figure of Christ. In the dome's flutes are two rows of his ancestors: Adam to Jacob ranged above the 12 sons of Jacob. In the northern dome, there is a central image of the Virgin and Child with the kings of the House of David in the upper row and lesser ancestors of Christ in the lower row.

Mosaic showing Christ and his ancestors, in the southern dome of the inner narthex

The Life of the Virgin

All but one of the 20 mosaics in the inner narthex depicting the *Life of the Virgin* are well preserved. This cycle is based mainly on the apocryphal Gospel of St James, written in the 2nd century, which gives an account of the Virgin's life. This was popular in the Middle Ages and was a rich source of material for ecclesiastical artists.

Among the events shown are the first seven steps of the Virgin, the Virgin entrusted to Joseph and the Virgin receiving bread from an angel.

The Infancy of Christ

Scenes from the *Infancy of Christ*, based largely on the New Testament, occupy the semicircular panels of the outer narthex. They begin on the north wall of the outer narthex

Guide to the Mosaics and Frescoes

Outer narthex looking east

Outer narthex looking west

Key

- The Genealogy of Christ
- The Life of the Virgin
- The Infancy of Christ
- Christ's Ministry
- Other Mosaics
- The Frescoes

with a scene of Joseph being visited by an angel in a dream. Subsequent panels include Mary and Joseph's *Journey to Bethlehem for Taxation*, the *Nativity of Christ* and, finally, Herod ordering the *Massacre of the Innocents*.

The *Enrolment for Taxation*

Christ's Ministry

While many of the mosaics in this series are badly damaged, some beautiful panels remain. The cycle occupies the vaults of the seven bays of the outer narthex and some of the south bay of the inner narthex. The most striking mosaic is the portrayal of Christ's temptation in the wilderness, in the second bay of the outer narthex.

Theodore Metochites presents St Saviour in Chora to Christ

Other Mosaics

There are three panels in the nave of the church, one of which, above the main door from the inner narthex, illustrates the *Dormition of the Virgin*. This mosaic, protected by a marble frame, is the best preserved in the church. The Virgin is depicted laid out on a bier, watched over by the Apostles, with Christ seated behind. Other devotional panels in the two narthexes include one, on the east wall of the south bay of the inner narthex, of the *Deësis*, depicting Christ with the Virgin Mary and, unusually, without St John. Another, in the inner narthex over the door into the nave, is of Theodore Metochites himself, shown wearing a large turban, and humbly presenting the restored church as an offering to Christ.

The Frescoes

The frescoes in the parecclesion are thought to have been painted just after the mosaics were completed, probably in around 1320. The most engaging of the frescoes – which reflect the purpose of the parecclesion as a place of burial – is the *Anastasis*, in the semidome above the apse. In it, the central figure of Christ, the vanquisher of death, is shown dragging Adam and Eve out of their tombs. Under Christ's feet are the gates of hell, while Satan lies before him. The fresco in the vault overhead depicts *The Last Judgment*, with the souls of the saved on the right and those of the damned to the left.

Figure of Christ from the *Anastasis* fresco in the parecclesion

Inner narthex looking east

Parecclesion and outer narthex looking south

Inner narthex looking west

Parecclesion and outer narthex looking north

Visitors at the tomb of Eyüp Ensari, Mohammed's standard bearer

⓯ Eyüp Sultan Mosque

Eyüp Sultan Camii

Cami-i Kebir Sok. **Tel** (0212) 564 73 68. 39, 55T, 99A. **Open** daily.

Mehmet the Conqueror built the original mosque on this site in 1458, five years after his conquest of Istanbul, in honour of Eyüp Ensari. That building fell into ruins and the present mosque was completed in 1800, by Selim III.

The mosque's delightful inner courtyard features two huge plane trees on a platform. This was the setting for the Girding of the Sword of Osman, part of a sultan's inauguration in the days of Mehmet the Conqueror.

Opposite the mosque is the tomb of Eyüp Ensari himself, said to have been killed during the first Arab siege of Constantinople in the 7th century. The tomb dates from the same period as the mosque and its decoration is in the Ottoman Baroque style.

⓰ Complex of Valide Sultan Mihrişah

Mihrişah Valide Sultan Külliyesi

Seyit Reşat Cad. 39, 55T, 99A. **Open** 9:30am–4:30pm Tue–Sun.

Most of the northern side of the street leading from Eyüp Mosque's northern gate is occupied by the largest Baroque *külliye (see p36)* in Istanbul, although unusually it is not centred on a mosque. Built for Mihrişah, mother of Selim III, the *külliye* was completed in 1791.

The complex includes the ornate marble tomb of Mihrişah and a soup kitchen, which is still in use today. There is also a beautiful grilled fountain *(sebil)*, from which an attendant once served water and refreshing drinks of sweet sherbet to passersby.

⓱ Pierre Loti Café

Piyer Loti Kahvehanesi

Gümüşsuyu Cad, Balmumku Sok 5, Eyüp. **Tel** (0212) 616 23 44. 39, 55T, 99A. **Open** 8am–midnight daily.

This famous café stands at the top of the hill in Eyüp Cemetery, a 20-minute walk up Karyağdı Sokağı from Eyüp Mosque. A funicular will also take you up and down the steep hill leading to the café. It is named after the French novelist, Julien Viaud, a French naval officer, popularly known as Pierre Loti, who frequented the café during his stay here in 1876. Loti defiantly fell in love with a married Turkish woman and wrote an autobiographical novel, *Aziyade*, about their affair. The café is prettily decked out with 19th-century furniture and the waiters wear period outfits. No alcohol.

⓲ Military Museum

Askeri Müze

Vali Konağı Cad, Harbiye. **Map** 1 F1. **Tel** (0212) 233 27 20. 46H. **Open** 9am–5pm Wed–Sun. Mehter Band performances: 3–4pm Wed–Sun.

One of Istanbul's most impressive museums, the Military Museum traces the history of the country's conflicts from the conquest of Constantinople in 1453 *(see p58)* through to modern warfare. The building used to be the military academy where Atatürk studied from 1899 to 1905.

The museum is also the main location for performances by the Mehter Band *(see p371)*, formed in the 14th century during the reign of Osman I *(see p58)*. Until the 19th century the musicians were Janissaries, who accompanied the sultan into battle and performed songs about hero-ancestors and battle victories. The band had a wide influence and is thought to have provided some inspiration for Mozart and Beethoven.

Some of the most striking weapons on display on the ground floor are the curved daggers *(cembiyes)* carried at the waist by foot soldiers in the 15th century. These are ornamented with plant, flower and geometric motifs in relief and silver filigree. Other exhibits include 17th-century copper head armour for horses and Ottoman shields made from cane and willow covered in silk thread.

Period interior of the Pierre Loti Café

An Ottoman curved dagger *(cembiye)* displayed in the Military Museum

A moving portrayal of trench warfare is included in the section concerned with the ANZAC landings of 1915 at Chunuk Bair on the Gallipoli peninsula *(see pp172–3)*, and upstairs is a spectacular exhibit of the tents used by sultans on their campaigns.

From the nearby station on Taşkışla Caddesi you can take the cable car across Maçka Park to Abdi İpekçi Caddesi in Teşvikiye. Some of the best designer clothes, jewellery, furniture and art shops in the city are here *(see pp134–5)*.

🅳 Dolmabahçe Palace

See pp126–7.

🅴 Yıldız Park

Çırağan Cad, Beşiktaş. **Map** 3 D2.
25E, 40. **Open** dawn to dusk daily.
for vehicles.

Yildiz Park was originally laid out as the garden of the first Çırağan Palace. It later formed the grounds of **Yıldız Palace**, an assortment of buildings from different eras now enclosed behind a wall and entered separately from Ihlamur-Yıldız Caddesi. The palace is a collection of pavilions and villas built in the 19th and 20th centuries. Many of them are the work of the eccentric Sultan Abdül Hamit II (1876–1909, *see p61*), who made it his principal residence as he feared a seaborne attack on Dolmabahçe Palace *(see pp126–7)*. The main building in the entrance courtyard is the State Apartments (Büyük Mabeyn), dating from the reign of Sultan Selim III (1789–1807). Around the corner, the **City Museum** (Şehir Müzesi) has a display of Yıldız porcelain. The Italianate

building opposite is the former armoury, or Silahhane. Next door to the City Museum is the **Yıldız Palace Museum**, housed in what was the Marangozhane (Abdül Hamit's carpentry workshop), and containing a changing collection of the palace's art and objects.

Further on is Yıldız Palace Theatre (completed in 1889 by Abdül Hamit), now a museum. The theatre's restored interior is mainly blue and gold, and the stars on the domed ceiling refer to the palace's name: yıldız means "star" in Turkish. Backstage, the former dressing rooms contain theatre displays, including original costumes and playbills.

The lake in the grounds is shaped like Abdül Hamit's *tuğra* *(see p32)*. A menagerie was once kept on the lake's islands where some 30 keepers tended tigers, lions, giraffes and zebras.

Several other little pavilions dot Yıldız Park, which, with its many ancient trees and exotic shrubs, is a very popular spot for picnics. As the park is situated on a hill, and it is a fairly long climb to the top, you may prefer to take a taxi up to the Şale Köşkü (Chalet Villa) and walk back down past the other sights.

Şale Köşkü is one of the most impressive in the park and built by Abdül Hamit. Although its façade appears as a whole, it was in fact built in three stages.

The Malta and Çadır pavilions were built during the reign of Abdül Aziz who ruled from 1861–76. Both of them formerly

served as prisons but are open as cafés. Malta Pavilion, also a restaurant, is a favoured haunt of locals on Sundays.

Mitat Paşa, reformist and architect of the constitution, was among those imprisoned in Çadır Pavilion, for instigating the murder of Abdül Aziz. Meanwhile, Murat V and his mother were locked away in Malta Pavilion for 27 years after a brief incarceration in the Çırağan Palace.

In 1895 the Imperial Porcelain Factory began production here, to satisfy the demand of the upper classes for chic European-style ceramics. The unusual building was designed to look like a stylized medieval castle of Europe, complete with several turrets and portcullis windows. The original household items such as sugar bowls, vases and plates that were produced here usually depict idealized scenes of the Bosphorus and other local spots. Examples of these items can today be seen in various museums and palaces all over Istanbul.

🏛 **City Museum**
Tel (0212) 258 53 44.

🏛 **Yıldız Palace Museum**
Tel (0212) 258 30 80 (ext 280).

A bridge in the grounds of Yıldız Palace

❶ Dolmabahçe Palace
Dolmabahçe Sarayı

Sultan Abdülmecid built Dolmabahçe Palace in 1856. As its designers he employed Karabet Balyan and his son Nikoğos, members of the great family of Armenian architects who lined the Bosphorus *(see pp130–31)* with many of their creations during the 19th century. The extravagant opulence of the Dolmabahçe belies the fact that it was built at a time when the Ottoman Empire was in decline. The palace can be visited only on a guided tour, of which two are on offer. The best tour takes you through the Selamlık (or Mabeyn-i Hümayun), the part of the palace that was reserved for men and which contains the state rooms and the enormous Ceremonial Hall. The other tour goes through the Harem, the living quarters of the sultan and his entourage. If you want to go only on one tour, visit the Selamlık.

★ Crystal Staircase
The apparent fragility of this glass staircase stunned observers when it was built. In the shape of a double horseshoe, it is made from English crystal and brass, and has a polished mahogany rail.

Imperial Gate of the Palace
Once used only by the sultan and his ministers, this gate is now the main entrance to the palace. The Mehter, or Janissary, Band *(see pp371, 124)* performs in front of the gate every Tuesday afternoon throughout the summer.

Entrance

Swan Fountain
This fountain stands in the Imperial Garden. The original 16th-century garden here was created from recovered land, hence the palace's name, Dolmabahçe, meaning "Filled-in Garden".

★ **Ceremonial Hall**
This magnificent domed hall was designed to hold 2,500 people. Its chandelier, reputedly the heaviest in Europe, was bought in England.

VISITORS' CHECKLIST

Practical Information
Dolmabahçe Cad, Beşiktaş.
Map 2 B4. **Open** 9am–4pm (last adm) Tue, Wed & Fri–Sun (Oct–Feb: last adm 3pm).

Transport
🚌 25E, 40.

Blue Salon
On religious feast days the sultan's mother would receive his wives and favourites in the Harem's principal room.

KEY

① **The Red Room** was used by the sultan to receive ambassadors.

② **The Süfera Salon**, where ambassadors waited for an audience with the sultan, is one of the most luxurious rooms in the palace.

③ **Selamlık and Harem**

④ **The Zülvecheyn, or Panorama Room**

⑤ **Sultan Abdül Aziz's bedroom** had to accommodate a huge bed built especially for the 150 kg (330 lb) amateur wrestler.

⑥ **Harem**

⑦ **The Rose- coloured salon** was the assembly room of the Harem.

⑧ **Atatürk's Bedroom**, where Atatürk *(see p62)* died at 9:05am on 10 November 1938. Some of the clocks in the palace, such as the one near the crystal staircase, are stopped at this time.

⑨ **Reception room of the sultan's mother**

⑩ **Main shore gate**

★ **Main Bathroom**
The walls of this bathroom are revetted in finest Egyptian alabaster, while the taps are solid silver. The brass-framed bathroom windows afford stunning views across the Bosphorus.

Leander's Tower, on its own small island in the Bosphorus

㉑ Leander's Tower
Kız Kulesi

Üsküdar. **Map** 6 A3. 🚢 Üsküdar.
Tel (0216) 342 47 47.
🌐 **kizkulesi.com.tr**

Located on an islet offshore from Üsküdar, the tiny, white Leander's Tower is a well-known Bosphorus landmark, dating from the 18th century. The tower once served as a quarantine centre during a cholera outbreak, as a lighthouse, a customs control point and a maritime toll gate. The tower is now used as a restaurant and pricey offshore disco.

In Turkish the tower is known as the "Maiden's Tower" after a legendary princess, confined here after a prophet foretold that she would die of a snake-bite. The tower's English name derives from the Greek myth of Leander, who swam the Hellespont (the modern-day Dardanelles, *see pp172–3*) to see his lover, priestess Hero.

㉒ Şemsi Paşa Mosque
Şemsi Paşa Camii

Sahil Yolu, Üsküdar. **Map** 6 A2.
🚢 Üsküdar. **Open** daily.

This is one of the smallest mosques to be commis- sioned by a grand vizier (Ottoman prime minister). Its miniature dimensions combined with its picturesque waterfront location make it one of the most attractive little mosques in the city. It was built in 1580 by the architect Sinan (*see p105*),

at the request of Şemsi Ahmet Paşa, who succeeded Sokollu Mehmet Paşa.

The mosque's garden, overlooking the Bosphorus, is surrounded on two sides by the theological college or *medrese* (*see p36*), with the small mosque on the third side and the sea wall on the fourth. The mosque itself is also quite unusual in that the tomb of Şemsi Ahmet Paşa is joined to the main building, divided from the interior by a grille.

㉓ İskele Mosque
İskele Camii

Hakimiyeti Milliye Cad, Üsküdar.
Map 6 B2. 🚢 Üsküdar. **Open** daily.

One of Üsküdar's most prominent landmarks, the İskele Mosque (also known as Mihrimah Sultan Mosque), takes its name from the ferry landing where it stands. A massive

Fountain set into the platform below the İskele Mosque

structure on a raised platform, it was built by Sinan between 1547 and 1548 for Mihriman Sultan, favourite daughter of Süleyman the Magnificent. Without space to build a courtyard, Sinan constructed a large protruding roof which extends to cover the *şadırvan* (ablutions fountain) in front of the mosque.

㉔ Atik Valide Mosque
Atik Valide Camii

Çinili Camii Sok, Üsküdar. **Map** 6 C3.
🚌 12C (from Üsküdar).
Open prayer times only.

The Atik Valide mosque, set on the hill above Üsküdar, was one of the most extensive mosque complexes in the whole of Istanbul. The name translates as the Old Mosque of the Sultan's Mother, as the mosque was built for Nur Banu, the wife of Selim II ("the Sot") and the mother of Murat III. She was the first of the sultans' mothers to rule the Ottoman

Dome in the entrance to Atik Valide Mosque

Empire from the Harem (*see p75*). Sinan completed the mosque, which was his last major work, in 1583. It has a wide shallow dome which rests on five semidomes, with a flat arch over the entrance portal.

The interior is surrounded on three sides by galleries, the undersides of which retain the rich stencilling typical of the period. The mihrab apse is almost completely covered with panels of fine İznik tiles (*see p165*), while the mihrab itself and the *minbar* are both made of sculpted marble. Side aisles were added in the 17th century, while the grilles and architectural trompe l'oeil paintings on the royal loge in the western gallery date from the 18th century.

Outside, a door in the north wall of the courtyard leads down a flight of stairs to the *medrese* (theological college), where the *dershane* (classroom)

projects out over the street below, supported by an arch. The *şifahane* (hospital), built around a central courtyard just east of the mosque, is also worth a visit.

㉕ Selimiye Barracks
Selimiye Kışlası

Çeşmei Kebir Cad, Selimiye. **Map** 6 B5. 🚢 Harem. 🚌 12.

The Selimiye Barracks were originally made of wood and completed in 1799 under Selim III, who was sultan from 1789 to 1807. They were built to house the "New Army" that formed part of Selim's plan for reforming the Imperial command structure and replacing the powerful Janissaries (*see pp60–1*). The plan backfired and Selim was deposed but the barracks were, nevertheless, a striking symbol of Constantinople's military might, perhaps becoming even more so when they were rebuilt in stone in 1829 by Mahmut II. The building still houses Istanbul's First Army Division and is off limits to the public.

The Florence Nightingale Museum is found within the Selimiye Barracks. It still contains some of the original furniture and the famous lamp which

gave her the epitaph "Lady of the Lamp." Visits must be arranged in advance by faxing the Army Headquarters, (0216) 333 10 09.

Nearby are two other sites worth seeing – the Selimiye Mosque and the British War Cemetery (also known as the Crimean Memorial Cemetery). The mosque was built in 1804 and is set in a lovely courtyard. The Cemetery, south on Burhan Felek Caddesi, contains the graves of men who died in the Crimean War, World War I battles at Gallipoli (*see pp172–3*) and during World War II in the Middle East.

Haydarpaşa Station, former terminus for trains arriving from Anatolia

㉖ Haydarpaşa Station
Haydarpaşa Garı

Haydarpaşa İstasyon Cad. **Tel** (0216) 348 80 20. 🚢 Haydarpaşa or Kadıköy.

A fire in 2010 did not diminish the grandeur of Haydarpaşa Station, which, with its tiled jetty, was once the most impressive point of arrival or departure in Istanbul. Train services stopped for two years in June 2013, and the future of the station is unknown, but the building remains one of Istanbul's landmarks. Built on land reclaimed from the sea, the station is surrounded by water on three sides – a unique feature.

The first Anatolian railway line, which was built in 1873, ran from here to İznik (*see p164*). The extension of this railway was a major part of Abdül Hamit II's drive to modernize the Ottoman Empire. Lacking sufficient funds, he applied for help to his German ally, Kaiser Wilhelm II. The Deutsche Bank agreed to invest in the construction and operation of the railway. In 1898 German engineers were contracted to build the new railway lines running across Anatolia and beyond into the far reaches of the Ottoman Empire.

Construction on Haydarpaşa, the grandest of these, started in 1906. Its two German architects, Otto Ritter and Helmut Conu, chose to build on a grand scale, using a Neo-Classic German style. The station was completed in 1908.

Florence Nightingale

The British nurse Florence Nightingale (1820–1910) was a tireless campaigner for hospital, military and social reform. During the Crimean War, in which Britain and France fought on the Ottoman side against the Russian Empire, she organized a party of 38 British nurses. They took charge of medical services at the Selimiye Barracks in Scutari (Üsküdar) in 1854. By the time she returned to Britain in 1856, at the end of the war, the mortality rate in the barracks had decreased from 20 to 2 per cent, and the fundamental principles of modern nursing had been established. On her return home, Florence Nightingale opened a training school for nurses.

A 19th-century painting of Florence Nightingale in Selimiye Barracks

The Bosphorus Trip

One of the great pleasures of a visit to Istanbul is a cruise up the Bosphorus. It is relaxing and offers a great vantage point from which to view the city's famous landmarks. You can go on a pre-arranged guided tour or take one of the small boats that tout for passengers at Eminönü. But the best way to travel is on the official trip run by Istanbul Şehir Hatlari (SH, see p399). The SH ferry makes a round-trip to the upper Bosphorus once or twice daily, stopping at six piers along the way, including a leisurely stop at Anadolu Kavağı for lunch. You can return to Eminönü on the same boat or make your way back to the city by bus, dolmuş or taxi. The route shown here is the full Bosphorus Cruise.

Locator Map

Sadberk Hanım Museum
Housed in two yalıs (see p35), this private museum contains ethnographic displays and a private archaeology collection.

Fortress of Europe
Situated at the narrowest point on the Bosphorus, this fortress was built by Mehmet II in 1452 as a prelude to his invasion of Constantinople.

Dolmabahçe Palace
This opulent 19th-century Baroque palace is a symbol of Ottoman grandeur.

Bosphoris Bridge

Arnavutköy

Ortaköy

İnönü Stadium

Beşiktaş

İskele Mosqu

Kabataş

Üsküdar

Karaköy

View of the City
As the ferry departs, you have a view of many of the old monuments of Istanbul, including Süleymaniye Mosque.

Eminönü

Leander's Tower

Harem

Saiy

Büyükde

Ceng

Black Sea

ISTANBUL

Rumeli
Kavağı

Anadolu
Kavağı

Anadolu Kavağı
The last stop on the trip brings you to this village and a ruined 14th-century Byzantine fortress, the Genoese Castle.

Huber
Köşkü

Beykoz

iköy

Paşabahçe

tinye

Çubuklu

Kanlıca

Fatih Sultan
Mehmet Bridge

Fortress of
Asia

illi

Beykoz
Beykoz is the largest fishing village along the Asian shore. Situated in the village square is this fountain dating from 1746.

Yeniköy
Handsome 19th-century *yalıs* line the waterfront of this ancient village. It was invaded by Cossacks who crossed the Black Sea in 1624.

0 kilometres   2

0 miles   1

Fortress of Asia
Fifty years older than the Fortress of Europe, this fortress was built by Sultan Beyazıt I just before the failed Ottoman siege of Constantinople in 1396–7.

Key

━━ Motorway

━━ Main road

═══ Other road

For additional map symbols *see back flap*

The Bosphorus suspension bridge between Ortaköy and Beylerbeyi

㉗ Ortaköy

Map 3 F2. 🚌 25E, 40, 41.

Crouched at the foot of the Bosphorus Bridge, the suburb of Ortaköy has retained a village feel. Life centres on İskele Meydanı, the quayside square, which was once busy with fishermen unloading the day's catch. Nowadays, though, Ortaköy is better known for its lively Sunday market, which crowds out the square and surrounding streets, and its shops selling the varied wares of local artisans. It is also the location for a thriving bar and café scene, which in the summer is the hub of Istanbul's nightlife (see pp136–7).

Mecidiye Mosque (better known as Ortaköy Cami), Ortaköy's most impressive landmark, sits on the waterfront. It was built in 1853 by Nikoğos Balyan, who was also responsible for Dolmabahçe Palace (see pp126–7).

Ortaköy's fashionable waterfront square and ferry landing

㉘ Bosphorus Bridge
Boğaziçi Köprüsü

Ortaköy and Beylerbeyi. **Map** 3 F2. 🚌 200, 202 (double deckers from Taksim).

Spanning the Bosphorus between the districts of Ortaköy and Beylerbeyi, this was the first bridge to be built across the straits that divide Istanbul. Construction began in 1970, and the bridge was inaugurated on 29 October 1973, to coincide with the 50th anniversary of the founding of the Turkish Republic (see p62). It is 1,074 m (3,524 ft) long, and is the world's ninth longest suspension bridge. It reaches 64 m (210 ft) above the water.

The Bosphorus is especially popular in summer, when cool breezes waft off the water.

㉙ Beylerbeyi Palace
Beylerbeyi Sarayı

Abdullah Ağa Cad, Beylerbeyi Mahallesi, Asian side. **Tel** (0216) 321 93 20. 🚌 15 (from Üsküdar), 10 (from Beşiktaş). 🇩 from Üsküdar. **Open** 9:30am–6pm Tue–Wed & Fri–Sun. 🎫🎥📷🏛

Designed in the Baroque style of the late Ottoman period, Beylerbeyi Palace was built between 1861 and 1865 by members of the Balyan family under the orders of Sultan Abdül Aziz. A previous palace had stood here, and the gardens were already laid out by Murat IV in 1639. As the Ottoman empire withered, palaces proliferated in a flourish of grandeur and showmanship. Abdül Aziz had Beylerbeyi built as a pleasure palace to entertain dignitaries and royalty. The Empress Eugénie of France (wife of Napoleon III) was a guest at the palace in 1869 on her way to the opening of the Suez Canal. The Duke and Duchess of Windsor also visited Beylerbeyi. The fountains, baths and colonnades were meant to impress, as were the lovely frescoes of Ottoman warships.

To keep himself distracted, Aziz also had a zoo built on the site and, apparently, delighted in the flocks of ostriches and several Bengal tigers. The zoo is no longer there, but parts of the palace have been refurbished and restored to some of their former elegance.

Third-but-last of the line of sultans, the autocratic Abdül Hamit II spent six years as a prisoner in an anteroom of the palace and died there, virtually forgotten, after being deposed in 1909.

There are superb views of the palace from the Bosphorus, from where the two prominent bathing pavilions – one for the Harem and the other for the *selamlık* (the men's quarters), can be seen.

The most attractive room is the reception hall, which has a pool and fountain.

Ornate landing at the top of the stairs in Beylerbeyi Palace

㉚ Fortress of Asia
Anadolu Hisarı

Riyaziyeci Sokak (on the harbour front), Asian side. **Tel** (0212) 263 53 05.

The fortress of Asia was built around 1398 by Mehmet II's grandfather, Sultan Yildirim

The Fortress of Europe, built by Mehmet the Conqueror to enable him to capture Constantinople

Beyazıt I (1389–1402). It was the Sultan's trump card in his attempt to defend Constantinople from the haughty Venetians, who walked a tightrope between consolidating their territorial ambitions and trying to avoid conflicts that might threaten the riches of their lucrative Ottoman trade. In spite of the fortress as a deterrent, a low-level war took place, lasting from 1463 to 1497.

The Fortress of Asia is closed to the public, but the neighbourhood is one of Istanbul's most charming and least affected by modern life.

🚩 Sakıp Sabancı Museum

Sakıp Sabancı Müzesi

İstinye Cad 22, Emirgab 34467. **Tel** (0212) 277 22 00. 🚌 40, 41 from Taksim Sq; any bus to Istinye or Sarıyer. **Open** 10am–6pm Tue, Thu, Fri, Sun; 10am–10pm Wed, Sat. 🗐 📷 🔓 🖥 🖥 🔤 **muze.sabanciuniv.edu**

With a superb view over the Bosphorus, the Sakıp Sabancı Museum, is also known as the Horse Mansion (Altı Köşk). Exhibitions comprise over 400 years of Ottoman calligraphy and other Koranic and secular art treasures. The collection of paintings is exquisite, with works by Ottoman court painters and European artists enthralled with Turkey. A Picasso exhibition in 2005 made this museum the first in Turkey to host a major solo exhibition of a Western artist. The museum continues to host must-see exhibitions.

🚩 Fortress of Europe

Rumeli Hisarı

Yahya Kemal Cad 42, European side. **Tel** (0212) 263 53 05. 🚌 40 and 41 (from Taksim Square). **Open** 9am–5pm Thu–Tue. 🖼

This fortress was built by Mehmet the Conqueror in 1452 as his first step in the conquest of Constantinople *(see p58)*. Situated at the narrowest point of the Bosphorus, the fortress controlled a major Byzantine supply route. Across the straits is Anadolu Hisarı, the Fortress of Asia, which was built in the 14th century by Beyazıt I.

The Fortress of Europe's layout was planned by Mehmet himself. While his grand vizier *(see pp60–61)* and two other viziers were each responsible for the building of one of the three great towers, the sultan took charge of the walls. Local buildings were torn down to provide the stones and other building materials. One thousand masons laboured on the walls alone. It was completed in four months – a considerable feat, given the steep terrain.

The new fortress was garrisoned by a force of Janissaries *(see pp60–61)*, whose troops trained their cannons on the straits to prevent the passage of foreign ships. After they had sunk a Venetian vessel, this approach to Constantinople was cut off. Following the conquest of the city, the fortress lost its importance as a military base and was used as a prison, particularly for out-of-favour foreign envoys and prisoners of war. The structure was restored only in 1953.

Today it is in excellent condition and is a pleasant place for an afternoon outing. Some open-air theatre performances are staged here during the Istanbul Festival of Arts and Culture *(see p39)*.

Birds of the Bosphorus

In September and October, thousands of white storks and birds of prey fly over the Bosphorus on their way from their breeding grounds in eastern Europe to wintering regions in Africa. Large birds usually prefer to cross narrow straits like the Bosphorus rather than over an expanse of open water such as the Mediterranean. Among birds of prey on this route you can see the lesser spotted eagle and the honey buzzard. The birds also cross the straits in spring on their way to Europe but, before the breeding season, they are fewer in number.

The white stork, which migrates over the straits

SHOPPING IN ISTANBUL

Istanbul's shops and markets, crowded and noisy at most times of the day and year, sell a colourful mixture of goods from all over the world. The city's most famous shopping centre is the massive Grand Bazaar. Turkey is a centre of textile production, and Istanbul has a wealth of carpet and fashion shops. If you prefer to do all your shopping under one roof, head for one of the city's modern shopping malls. Wherever you shop, be wary of imitations of famous brand products – even if they appear to be of a high standard and the salesman maintains that they are authentic. Be prepared to bargain where required: it is an important part of a shopping trip.

General Information

Most shops trade from 9am to 8pm Monday to Saturday, and markets open at 8am. Large shops and department stores open later in the morning. The Grand Bazaar and Spice Bazaar are open from 8:30am to 8pm. Malls are open from 10am to 10pm seven days a week. Details on payment, VAT exemption, buying antiques and sending purchases home appear on pp362–3.

Carpets and Kilims

In the Grand Bazaar (see pp108–9), **Şişko Osman** has a good range of carpets, and **Galeri Şirvan** sells Anatolian tribal *kilims* (rugs).

Award-winning **Bereket Halicilik** is the most reliable seller of antique carpets. **Hazal Halı**, in Ortaköy, stocks a fine collection of kilims.

Fabrics

In addition to carpets and kilims, colourful fabrics in traditional designs from all over Turkey and Central Asia are widely sold. **Sivaslı Yazmacısı** sells village textiles, headscarves and embroidered cloths.

Leather

Turkish leatherwear, while not always of the best quality hides, is durable, of good craftsman-ship and reasonably priced.

The Grand Bazaar is full of shops selling leather goods. **Meb Deri**, for example, offers a good range of fashion handbags and accessories, and **Desa** has an extensive range of both classic and fashionable designs.

Jewellery

The Grand Bazaar is the best place to find gold jewellery – it is sold by weight, with only a modest sum added for craftsmanship. The daily price of gold is displayed in the shop windows. Other shops in the same area sell silver jewellery, and pieces inlaid with precious stones. **Urart** stocks collections of unique gold and silver jewellery inspired by the designs of ancient civilizations. **Antikart** specializes in restored antique silver jewellery.

Pottery, Metal and Glassware

Shops in the Grand Bazaar are stocked with traditional ceramics, including pieces decorated with exquisite

How to Bargain

In up-market shops in Istanbul, bargaining is rare. However, in the Grand Bazaar and the shops located in or around the old city (Sultanahmet and Beyazıt) haggling is a must, otherwise you may be cheated. Bazaar shopkeepers, known for their abrasive insistence, expect you to bargain. Take your time and decide where to buy after visiting a few shops selling similar goods. The procedure is as follows:

- You will often be invited inside and offered a cup of tea. Feel free to accept, as this is the customary introduction to any kind of exchange and will not oblige you to buy.
- Do not feel pressurized if the shopkeeper turns the shop upside down to show you his stock – this is normal practice and most salesmen are proud of their goods.
- If you are seriously interested in any item, be brave enough to offer half the price you are asked.

Haggling over the price of a carpet

- Take no notice if the shop-keeper looks offended and refuses, but raise the price slightly, aiming to pay about 70–75 per cent of the original offer. If that price is really unacceptable to the owner he will stop bar-gaining over the item and turn your attention to other merchandise in the shop.

Brightly decorated candle lanterns in the Grand Bazaar

blue-and-white İznik designs *(see p165)*. Other types of pottery come from Kütahya, which makes use of a free style of decoration, and Çanakkale, which features more modern designs. For a modern piece of Kütahya ware, visit **Mudo Pera** which stocks pieces by master potter, Sıtkı Usta. Most museum shops also sell a good range of pottery.

The Grand Bazaar and the Cavalry Bazaar are centres of the copper and brass trade and offer a huge selection.

For glassware, **Paşabahçe**, the largest glass manufacturer in Turkey, offers the best range, and some exquisite, delicate pieces with gilded decoration.

Handicrafts

Ideal gifts and souvenirs include embroidered hats, waistcoats and slippers, inlaid jewellery boxes, meerschaum pipes, prayer beads, alabaster ornaments, blue-eye charms to ward off the evil eye and *nargiles* (bubble pipes). At the Istanbul Crafts Centre you can see calligraphers at work. **Rölyef** in Beyoğlu, the Book Bazaar and **Sofa** sell antique and reproduction calligraphy, as well as *ebru* (marbled paintings) and reproductions of Ottoman miniatures.

Bookshops

Books written in English on architecture, history, religion and travel, as well as popular and classic fiction, can be found at **Galeri Kayseri** in the heart of Sultanahmet and at **Robinson Crusoe** in Beyoğlu.

Food, Drink, Herbs and Spices

The Spice Bazaar *(see p102)*, also known as the Egyptian Bazaar, is the place to buy nuts, dried fruits, herbs and spices, jams, various herbal teas, and even exotic delicacies such as caviar. The Galatasaray Fish Market is excellent.

International names alongside Turkish shops in Akmerkez

Shopping Malls

Istanbul's modern shopping malls contain cinemas, "food courts", cafés and hundreds of shops. The most popular are **Akmerkez** in Etiler, **Galleria**, next to the yacht marina in Ataköy, and **Kanyon**, which features 160 local and global brands. Seasonal sales take place mainly in clothes shops, but also in department stores and some speciality shops.

DIRECTORY

Carpets and Kilims

Bereket Halıcılık
Peykhane Cad,
Sultanahmet.
Map 5 D4.
Tel (0212) 517 46 77.

Galeri Şirvan
52–54 Halıcılar Cad,
Grand Bazaar.
Map 4 C4.
Tel (0212) 520 62 24.

Hazal Halı
27–9 Mecidiye Köprüsü
Sok, Ortaköy.
Map 3 F3.
Tel (0212) 261 72 33.

Şişko Osman
49 Halıcılar Cad,
Grand Bazaar.
Map 4 C4.
Tel (0212) 528 35 48.

Fabrics

Sivaslı Yazmacısı
57 Yağlıkçılar Sok,
Grand Bazaar.
Map 4 C4.
Tel (0212) 526 77 48.

Leather

Desa
140 İstiklâl Cad, Beyoğlu.
Map 1 A4.
Tel (0212) 243 37 86.

Meb Deri
14/2 Abdi İspekci Cad,
Nişantası.
Map 1 C1.
Tel (0212) 576 26 10.

Jewellery

Antikart
209 İstiklâl Cad,
32 Atlas Kuyumcular
Çarşısı, Beyoğlu.
Map 1 A4.
Tel (0212) 252 44 82.

Urart
18 Abdi İpekçi Cad,
Nişantaşı. **Map** 1 C1.
Tel (0212) 246 71 94.

Pottery, Metal and Glassware

Mudo Pera
401 İstiklâl Cad, Beyoğlu.
Map 1 A5.
Tel (0212) 251 86 82.

Paşabahçe
314 İstiklâl Cad,
Beyoğlu. **Map** 1 A5.
Tel (0212) 244 05 44.

Handicrafts

Rölyef
16 Emir Nevruz Sok,
Beyoğlu. **Map** 1 A4.
Tel (0212) 244 04 94.

Sofa
85 Nuruosmaniye Cad,
Cağaloğlu. **Map** 5 D4.
Tel (0212) 520 28 50.

Bookshops

Galeri Kayseri
58 Divanyolu Cad,
Sultanahmet. **Map** 5 D4.
Tel (0212) 512 04 56.

Pandora Bookshop
Büyükparmakkapi Sokak
3, off İstiklâl Cad, Beyoğlu.
Map 1 A5.
Tel (0212) 243 35 03.

Robinson Crusoe
389 İstiklâl Cad, Beyoğlu.
Map 1 A5.
Tel (0212) 293 69 68.

Food, Drink, Herbs and Spices

Antre Gourmet
40A Akarsu Cad,
Cihangir. **Map** 5 D1.
Tel (0212) 292 89 72.

Kurukahveci Mehmet Efendi
66 Tahmis Cad,
Eminönü.
Map 5 D1.
Tel (0212) 511 42 62.

Şekerci Hacı Bekir
83 Hamidiye Cad,
Eminönü. **Map** 5 D3.
Tel (0212) 522 06 66.

Shopping Malls

Akmerkez
Nispetiye Cad, Etiler.
Tel (0212) 282 01 70.

Galleria
Sahil Yolu, Ataköy.
Tel (0212) 559 95 60.

Kanyon
185 Büyükdere Cad,
Levent.
Tel (0212) 353 53 00.

ENTERTAINMENT IN ISTANBUL

Istanbul offers a great variety of leisure pursuits, ranging from arts festivals and folk music to belly dancing and nightclubs. The most important cultural event is the series of festivals organized by the Istanbul Foundation for Culture and the Arts between March and November. Throughout the year, traditional Turkish music, opera, ballet, Western classical music and plays are performed at Cemal Reşit Rey Concert Hall (CRR) and some other venues around the city. Beyoğlu is the main centre for entertainment

of all kinds. This area also has the highest concentration of cinemas in the city, and numerous lively bars and cafés. Though Konya *(see pp254–5)* is the home of the religious dervish order, productions of the mystical whirling dervish dance are staged at the Mevlevi Monastery in Beyoğlu once a month. Ortaköy, on the European shore of the Bosphorus, is another very popular venue for dining, music and dancing. For a trip to the beach on a hot day, the Princes' Islands *(see p162)* are best.

Entertainment Guides

A bi-monthly magazine in English, *The Guide* lists cultural events and activities in the city. Entertainment information and contact numbers are available in the English *Turkish Daily News*, as well as Turkish Airlines' in-flight magazine and the Turkish daily newspaper *Hürriyet*.

Entertainment guides available in Istanbul

Festivals

Five major annual festivals (theatre, film, music and dance, jazz, and a biennial fine arts exposition) are organized by the Istanbul Foundation for Culture and the Arts. All tickets can be obtained via telephone from the **Istanbul Festival Committee** or at the individual venues themselves.

Istanbul also hosts the Yapı Kredi Arts, Akbank Jazz, and Efes Pilsen Blues festivals in autumn each year.

During festivals a special bus service runs between show venues and the city centre.

Western Classical Music and Dance

The **Cemal Reşit Rey Concert Hall (CRR)** stages Western classical music concerts and hosts music and dance groups.

Concerts are also held at smaller venues across the city. Contact the Sultanahmet Tourist Office *(see p83)* for details.

Laser disc screenings of opera, ballet and classical music performances are held most days at 2pm and 6pm at the **Aksanat Cultural and Arts Centre**. It also sometimes stages live plays and music recitals.

Booking Tickets

Most concert, theatre, arts and sports tickets can be booked by phone through Biletix (tel: 0216 556 98 00). You can also go to the website at www. biletix.com for more information about ticket availability; the website also shows point of sale outlets.

Rock and Jazz

An increasing number of Istanbul's clubs and bars plays good live music. **Hayal Kahvesi** is a bar dedicated to jazz, rock and blues and has an outdoor summer venue in Çubuklu. The **Q Club**, in the grounds of the Çırağan Palace Hotel Kempinski, is an exclusive

jazz bar. The **Rock House Café** in Ortaköy has live bands on some weeknights. Other venues are **Babylon** and **Yeni Melek** (jazz and Turkish pop).

Traditional Turkish Music and Dance

Traditional Turkish music performed at the CRR includes Ottoman classical, mystical Sufi and Turkish folk music. Summer recitals of Turkish music are organized in the Basilica Cistern *(see p90)*, which has wonderful acoustics. The Sultanahmet Tourist Office can provide more information.

Fasıl is a popular form of traditional music that is best enjoyed live in *meyhanes* (taverns) such as **Ece**, **Kallavi 20** and **Hasır**. It is performed on the *kanun* (zither), as well as *tambur* and *ud* (both similar to the lute). **Galata Tower** restaurant is an alternative venue for Turkish folk music and

Folk dancing at the Kervansaray venue

dance, while belly dancing is a nightclub attraction in Beyoğlu.

Other places featuring top performers of traditional art are **Kervansaray, Orient House** and **Manzara**.

Nightclubs

A top nightclub is the **Sortie Bar Restaurant**, a bar-restaurant complex popular with celebrities and located in the centre of town. Its large outdoor space is a must for hot summer nights. Avoid seedy-looking clubs in the Beyoğlu district. These have been known to coerce unsuspecting clients into paying extortionate bills for entry and drinks.

Cinemas and Theatre

The latest foreign films are on circuit at the same time as in the rest of Europe, albeit with

Classical concert in the church of Haghia Eirene *(see p76)*

Turkish subtitles. **Alkazar** and **Beyoğlu** show mainly art-house films. The first show is half-price. Many cinemas offer half-price tickets on Wednesdays, and students with a valid student card are entitled to discounts.

Theatres stage local and international plays, but only in Turkish. The theatre season runs from September to June.

Sports

Main five-star hotels have good swimming pools and welcome non-residents for a fee. Turks are fanatical about football: **Beşiktaş, Fenerbahçe** and **Galatasaray** are the league players.

Horse races take place at **Veli Efendi** racecourse on weekends and Wednesdays.

Children

Yıldız Park *(see p125)* has much to offer children, as does **Miniatürk**, with over 100 miniature replicas of Turkey's famous cultural landmarks.

Late-night Transport

The last late-night buses and dolmuşes leave the Taksim area at midnight, but taxis are available all night. For more information *see pp396–9.*

DIRECTORY

Istanbul Festival Committee

Tel (0216) 454 15 55.
W iksv.org

Classical Music and Dance

Aksanat Cultural and Arts Centre
İstiklal Cad 16,
Taksim. **Map** 7 D4.
Tel (0212) 252 35 00.

CRR
Gümüş Sok, Harbiye.
Map 1 C1.
Tel (0212) 232 98 30.

Rock and Jazz

Babylon
Sehbender Sok 3, Asmali-
mescit, Tünel, Beyoğlu.
Tel (0212) 292 73 68.

Hayal Kahvesi (Beyoğlu)
Büyükparmak Kapı Sok
19, Beyoğlu. **Map** 1 B4.
Tel (0212) 244 25 28.

Q Club
Çırağan Palace Hotel
Kempinski; A Blok,
Beşiktaş. **Map** 3 D3.
Tel (0212) 236 24 89.

Rock House Café
Dereboyu Cad 36–8,
Ortaköy. **Map** 3 F2.
Tel (0212) 227 60 10.

Yeni Melek
Gazeteci Erol Dernek
Sokak 13, Beyoğlu.
Tel (0212) 244 97 00.

Traditional Turkish Music and Dance

Ece
Tramvay Cad 104,
Kuruçeşme.
Tel (0212) 265 96 00.

Galata Tower
Büyükhendek Cad,
Galata. **Map** 1 A1.
Tel (0212) 213 81 80.

Hasır
Beykoz Korusu,
Beykoz.
Tel (0216) 322 29 01.

Kallavi
Kallavi Sok 20,
Beyoğlu. **Map** 1 A4.
Tel (0212) 251 10 10.

Kervansaray
Cumhuriyet Cad 30,
Harbiye. **Map** 1 C2.
Tel (0212) 247 16 30.

Manzara
Conrad Hotel,
Yıldız Cad, Beşiktaş.
Map 2 C3.
Tel (0212) 227 30 00.

Orient House
Tiyatro Cad 27, Beyazıt.
Map 4 C4.
Tel (0212) 517 61 63.

Nightclubs

Majesty
Muallim Naci Cad 10/2,
Salhane Sok, Ortaköy.
Map 3 F3.
Tel (0212) 236 57 57.

Sortie Bar Restaurant
Muallim Naci Cad 54,
Ortaköy. **Map** 3 F3.
Tel (0212) 327 85 85.

Cinemas

Alkazar
İstiklal Cad 179, Beyoğlu.
Map 1 B4.
Tel (0212) 293 24 66.

Beyoğlu
İstiklal Cad 140, Halep-
Pasajı, Beyoğlu.
Map 1 B4.
Tel (0212) 251 32 40.

Sports

Beşiktaş FC
Spor Cad 92, Beşiktaş.
Map 2 A4.
Tel (0212) 227 87 80.

Fenerbahçe FC
Kızıltoprak, Kadıköy.
Tel (0216) 345 09 40.

Galatasaray FC
Hasnun Galip Sok 7,
Galatasaray.
Map 1 B4.
Tel (0212) 251 57 07.

Veli Efendi Hipodromu
Osmaniye, Bakırköy.
Tel (0212) 444 08 55.

Children

Miniatürk
Imrahar Cad, Sütlüce.
Tel (0212) 222 28 82.

STREET FINDER

The map references that are given throughout this section refer to the maps on the following pages. Some small streets with references may not be named on the map. References are also given for hotels *(see pp330– 32)*, restaurants *(see pp346– 9)*, shops *(see pp134–5)* and entertainment venues *(see pp136–7)*.

The map provided below shows the area covered by the six maps, and the key lists the symbols that are used. The first figure of the reference tells you which map page to turn to; the letter and number indicate the grid reference. The map on the inside back cover shows public transport routes.

Key to Street Finder

- ▢ Major sight
- ▢ Place of interest
- ▢ Other building
- ⛴ Ferry boarding point
- ⛴ Sea bus boarding point
- 🚉 Railway station
- Ⓜ Metro station
- 🚊 Tram stop
- 🚡 Cable car station
- 🚌 Main bus terminus

- 🚟 Funicular/Tünel station
- Ⓓ Dolmuş terminus
- 🛈 Tourist information
- ➕ Hospital
- 🚔 Police station
- ♨ Turkish baths
- Ⓒ Mosque
- ✡ Synagogue
- ✝ Church
- — Railway line

- — Tram line
- ▬ Motorway
-    Pedestrian-only street
- — City wall

Scale of Maps 1–6

0 metres   250

0 yards   250

Street Finder Index

In Turkish, Ç, Ğ, İ, Ö, Ş and Ü are listed as separate letters in the alphabet, coming after C, G, I, O, S and U, respectively. In this book, however, Ç is treated as C for the purposes of alphabetization and so on with the other letters. Hence Çiçek follows Cibinlik as if both names began with C. Following standard Turkish practice we have abbreviated Sokak to Sok, Caddesi to Cad and Çıkmazı to Çık.

TURKEY REGION BY REGION

Turkey at a Glance

Turkey occupies the rugged Anatolian Plateau, an arid upland region that is encircled by the mighty Taurus and Pontic mountain systems. The country's unrivalled wealth of historic sights includes Istanbul – the capital of three empires, as well as the ruins of classical sites such as Ephesus, Hierapolis and Aphrodisias. In the interior of the country are the unique cave cities and churches of Cappadocia. The eastern provinces of Turkey are less frequently visited, but offer such spectacular attractions as Lake Van, Armenian churches and the enigmatic stone heads at the summit of Mount Nemrut.

Istanbul's skyline is defined by the silhouettes of great mosques such as Süleymaniye Mosque (see pp104–105), built by the architect Sinan in the 16th century.

War Memorials on the Gallipoli Peninsula (see pp172–3) salute the bravery of the soldiers who fought and died here in World War I.

0 kilometres 50

0 miles 50

Edirne

Keşan

ISTANBUL
(see pp64–149)

Bolu

THRACE AND THE SEA OF MARMARA
(see pp154–73)

Bursa

Balıkesir

Eskişehir

Anka

Ayvalık

Kütahya

THE AEGEAN
(see pp174–207)

ANKARA AND WESTERN ANATOLIA
(see pp240–63)

İzmir

Çeşme

Dinar

Aydın

Denizli

Bodrum

MEDITERRANEAN TURKEY
(see pp209–39)

Antalya

Alan

Marmaris

Kaş

Anam

The Castle of St Peter (see pp200–1) guards the harbour at Bodrum. The castle was built by the Knights of St John in the 15th century, using stones taken from the ruins of the celebrated Mausoleum of Halicarnassus.

◄ Marmaris Castle and harbour on the Datça Peninsula

The Mevlâna Museum (see pp256–7) is a place of pilgrimage that contains the tombs of important Mevlevi Dervish mystics. Nearby is the Selimiye Mosque, an emblem of Konya.

Haghia Sophia, a Byzantine church in the historic port of Trabzon *(see pp274–5)* was rebuilt in the mid-13th century on the site of a Roman temple. The church, now a museum, was restored from 1957 to 1963, and features superb frescoes and mosaic floors.

Mount Ağrı (Ararat), said to be where Noah's Ark came to rest after the biblical flood, looms over the eastern Anatolian town of Doğubayazıt. İshak Paşa Sarayı *(see p319)*, an 18th-century palace, lies outside the town.

ebolu

Bafra

Samsun

The BLACK SEA
(see pp264–79)

Hopa

Artvin

Trabzon

Amasya

Gümüşhane

Kars

CAPPADOCIA AND
CENTRAL ANATOLIA
(see pp280–303)

Sivas

Erzincan

Erzurum

Kırşehir

EASTERN ANATOLIA
(see pp304–23)

Ağrı

evşehir

Kayseri

Niğde

Malatya

Tatvan

Van

Kahramanmaraş

Diyarbakır

Hakkâri

ersin
(İçel)

Adana

Gaziantep

Şanlıurfa

Mardin

Silifke

İskenderun

Samandağı

Cappadocia's many churches, cave dwellings, monasteries and underground cities *(see p285)* were carved out of hardened volcanic ash deposited many thousands of years ago.

Sabancı Central Mosque in Adana *(see pp234–5)* is one of the largest mosques in the Islamic world. The Ottoman-era clocktower is an older landmark of this fast-growing southern city.

THRACE AND THE SEA OF MARMARA

Standing at a natural crossroads, Istanbul makes a good base for excursions into the neighbouring areas of Thrace and the Sea of Marmara. Whether you want to see great Islamic architecture, immerse yourself in a busy bazaar, relax on an island or catch a glimpse of Turkey's rich birdlife, you will find a choice of destinations within easy reach of the city.

On public holidays and at weekends nearby resorts are crowded with Istanbul residents taking a break from the noisy city. For longer breaks, they head for the Mediterranean or Aegean, so summer is a good, quiet time to explore the Thrace and Marmara regions.

The country around Istanbul varies immensely from lush forests to open plains and, beyond them, impressive mountains. The Princes' Islands, where pine forests and monasteries can be toured by a pleasant ride in a horse-drawn carriage, are also just a short boat trip away from the city. A little further away, the lakeside town of İznik is world famous for its ceramics. This art form, which reached its zenith in the 16th and 17th centuries, is one of the wonders of Ottoman art, and original pieces are highly prized.

To the northwest, near the Greek border, is Edirne, a former Ottoman capital. It is visited today for its mosques, especially the Selimiye with its towering minarets. Edirne also stages Kırkpınar grease-wrestling matches every June when enthusiastic crowds flock to enjoy the contest and the accompanying folk festival.

South of the Sea of Marmara is the pretty spa town of Bursa. Originally a Greek city, it was founded in 183 BC. The first Ottoman capital, it has some fine architecture and also maintains the tradition of the Karagöz shadow puppet theatre. Near the mouth of the straits of the Dardanelles lie the ruins of the legendary city of Troy, dating from about 3600 BC. North of the Dardanelles are cemeteries commemorating the thousands of soldiers killed in the battles fought over the Gallipoli Peninsula during World War I.

Boats in Burgaz Harbour on the Princes' Islands, a short ferry ride from Istanbul

◀ The vast Selimiye Mosque, a prominent landmark in Edirne

Exploring Thrace and the Sea of Marmara

Istanbul is the jewel of the Thrace and Marmara region, but places like Edirne and Bursa – and others within a radius of about 250 km (150 miles) – each have their own history and importance, with some fine museums and mosques. Şile, located on the Black Sea coast, is a day's outing from Istanbul, as is the quaint hamlet of Polonezköy. Bird parks, the superb tiles of İznik, along with the spas and ski slopes around Bursa give the Marmara area the edge for variety. A visit to the World War I battlefields and cemeteries of the Gallipoli Peninsula is a moving experience.

French war cemetery, Gallipoli Peninsula

Sights at a Glance

1. *Edirne pp158–9*
2. Princes' Islands
3. Polonezköy
4. Şile
5. İznik
6. Uludağ National Park
7. *Bursa pp166–7*
8. Bird Paradise National Park
9. *Gallipoli Peninsula pp172–3*

0 kilometres 30

0 miles 15

Bird Paradise National Park – an area rich in protected wildlife

Getting Around

The Trans European Motorway (TEM) system means that a six-lane superhighway bypasses the hub of Istanbul using the Fatih Sultan Mehmet Bridge over the Bosphorus. On this toll road, the Istanbul to Ankara journey takes about 3 hours. Car ferries (no reservations required) commute frequently between Gebze and Yalova. A sea bus service (advance booking essential) does the Yenikapı (central Istanbul) to Bandırma run in a few hours. From Istanbul, local and intercity trains depart from Sirkeci Station on the European side and Haydarpaşa Station on the Asian side. Ferries depart from the Eminönü ferry piers in Istanbul to four of the Princes' Islands and from Kabataş, near the Dolmabahçe Palace, to the islands on the south coast of the Sea of Marmara, as well as from Bostanci on the Asian side.

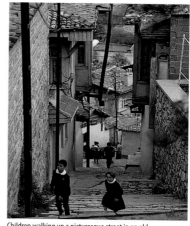

Children walking up a picturesque street in an old quarter of Bursa

Key

- Motorway
- Major road
- Minor road
- Scenic route
- Main railway
- Minor railway
- International border

● Edirne

Standing on the river Tunca near the border with Greece, Edirne is a provincial university town that is home to one of Turkey's star attractions, the Selimiye Mosque *(see pp160–61)*. As this huge monument attests, Edirne was historically of great importance. It dates back to AD 125, when the Emperor Hadrian joined two small towns to form Hadrianopolis, or Adrianople. For nearly a century, from 1361 when Murat I took the city until Constantinople was conquered in 1453 *(see p58)*, Edirne was the Ottoman capital. The town has one other claim to fame – the annual grease-wrestling championships in June.

Entrance arch, Mosque of the Three Balconies

common afflictions. The colonnaded inner mosque courtyard, unlike most later examples, covers three times the area of the mosque itself. Inside, the weight of the impressive dome is supported on sweeping pendentives.

◖ Mosque of the Three Balconies
üç Şerefeli Camii
Hükümet Cad. **Open** daily. ⊠
Until the fall of Constantinople, this was the grandest building of the early Ottoman state. It was finished in 1447 and takes its name from the three balconies which adorn its southeastern minaret – at the time the tallest in existence. In an unusual touch, the other three minarets

of the mosque are each of a different design and height. Unlike its predecessors in Bursa *(see pp166–7)*, the mosque has an open courtyard, a feature that set a precedent for the great imperial mosques of Istanbul. The interior plan was also innovative. With minimal obstructions, both the *mihrab* and *minbar* can be seen from almost every corner of the prayer hall.

◖ Old Mosque
Eski Cami
Talat Paşa Asfaltı. **Open** daily. ⊠
The oldest of Edirne's major mosques, this is a smaller version of the Great Mosque in Bursa *(see p168)*. The eldest son of Beyazıt I, Süleyman, began the mosque in 1403, but it was his youngest son, Mehmet I, who completed it in 1414.

A perfect square, the mosque is divided by four massive piers into nine domed sections. On either side of the prayer hall entrance there are massive

Entrance to Beyazıt II Mosque viewed from its inner courtyard

◖ Beyazıt II Mosque
Beyazıt II Külliyesi
Yeni Maharet Cad. **Open** daily.
Health Museum: **Tel** (0284) 212 09 22.
Open 9:30am–5:30pm daily. 🏛 ♿
Beyazıt II Mosque stands in a peaceful location on the northern bank of the Tunca River, 1.5 km (1 mile) from the city centre. It was built in 1484–8, soon after Beyazıt II succeeded Mehmet the Conqueror *(see p58)* as sultan.

The mosque and its courtyards are open to the public. Of the surrounding buildings in the complex, the old hospital, which incorporated an asylum, has been converted into the **Health Museum**. Disturbed patients were treated in this asylum – a model facility for its time – with water, music and flower therapies. The Turkish writer Evliya Çelebi (1611–84) reported that singers and instrumentalists would play soothing music here three times a week. Overuse of hashish was one of the most

Grease-Wrestling

The Kırkpınar Grease-Wrestling Championships take place annually in June, on the island of Sarayiçi in the Tunca River. The event is famed throughout Turkey and accompanied by a week-long carnival. Before competing, the wrestlers don knee-length leather shorts *(kıspet)* and grease themselves from head to foot in diluted olive oil. The master of ceremonies, the *cazgır*, then invites the competitors to take part in a high-stepping, arm-flinging parade across the field, accompanied by music played on a deep-toned drum *(davul)* and a single-reed oboe *(zurna)*. Wrestling bouts can last up to two hours and involve long periods of frozen, silent concentration interspersed by attempts to throw down the opponent.

Wrestlers performing a ceremonial ritual before the contest

Arabic inscriptions proclaiming "Allah" and "Mohammed".

🏛 Rüstem Paşa Caravanserai
Rüstem Paşa Kervansarayı
İki Kapılı Han Cad 57.
Tel (0284) 212 61 19.

Sinan *(see p105)* designed this caravanserai for Süleyman's most powerful grand vizier, Rüstem Paşa, in 1560–61. It was constructed in two distinct parts. The larger courtyard, or han *(see pp28–9)*, which is now the Rüstem Paşa Kervansaray Hotel, was built for the merchants of Edirne, while the smaller courtyard, now a student hostel, was an inn for other travellers.

A short walk away, on the other side of Saraçlar Caddesi, is the **Semiz Ali Paşa Bazaar**. This is also the work of Sinan, and dates from 1589. It consists of a long, narrow street of vaulted shops.

🏛 Museum of Turkish and Islamic Arts
Türk ve İslam Eserleri Müzesi
Kadir Paşa Mektep Sok.
Tel (0284) 225 11 20. **Open** 8:30am–noon & 1:30–5:30pm Tue–Sun. 🖼

Edirne's small collection of Turkish and Islamic works of art is attractively located in the *medrese (see p36)* of the Selimiye Mosque.

The museum's first room is devoted to the local sport of grease-wrestling. It includes enlarged reproductions of miniatures depicting 600 years of the sport. These show the wrestling stars resplendent in their leather shorts, their skin glistening with olive oil.

Other objects on display include the original doors of the Beyazıt II Mosque. There are also military exhibits. Among them are some beautiful 18th-century Ottoman shields, with woven silk exteriors, and paintings of military subjects.

The tranquil 15th century Muradiye Mosque

VISITORS' CHECKLIST

Practical Information
🗺 150,000.
ℹ Hürriyet Meydanı 17, (0284) 213 92 08. 🏢 Mon, Wed, Sat.
🤼 Grease-Wrestling (Jun).

Transport
✈ 🚌 Ayşekadın, (0284) 235 26 73. 🚍 E-5 exit at Highway Maintenance Depot, (0284) 226 00 20. 🄳 in front of tourist office (Hürriyet Meydanı 17).

🄲 Muradiye Mosque
Muradiye Camii
Küçükpazar Cad. **Open** daily. 🖼

What is today a tranquil mosque was first built as a *zaviye* (dervish hospice) in 1421 by Murat II, who dreamed that the great dervish leader Celaleddin Rumi *(see pp256, 259)* asked him to build a hospice in Edirne. Only later was it converted into a mosque. Its interior is notable for its massive inscriptions, similar to those in the Old Mosque, and for some fine early 15th-century İznik tiles *(see p165)*. It may be locked outside prayer times.

Edirne City Centre
① Beyazıt II Mosque
② Mosque of the Three Balconies
③ Old Mosque
④ Rüstem Paş Caravanserai
⑤ Selimiye Mosque
⑥ Museum of Turkish and Islamic Arts
⑦ Muradiye Mosque

| 0 metres | 750 |
| 0 yards | 750 |

Edirne: Selimiye Mosque
Selimiye Camii

The Selimiye is the greatest of all the Ottoman mosque complexes, the apogee of an art form and the culmination of a life's ambition for its architect, Sinan *(see p105)*. Built on a slight hill, the mosque is a prominent landmark. Its complex includes a *medrese (see p36)*, housing the Museum of Turkish and Islamic Arts, a school and the Kavaflar Arasta, a covered bazaar.

Selim II commissioned the mosque. It was begun in 1569 and completed in 1575, a year after his death. The dome was Sinan's proudest achievement. In his memoirs, he wrote: "With the help of Allah and the favour of Sultan Selim Khan, I have succeeded in building a cupola six cubits wider and four cubits deeper than that of Haghia Sophia." In fact, the dome is comparable in diameter and slightly shallower than the building Sinan had so longed to surpass.

★ **Minarets**
The mosque's four slender minarets tower to a height of 84 m (275 ft). Each one has three balconies. The two northern minarets contain three intertwining staircases, each one leading to a different balcony.

Ablutions Fountain
Intricate, pierced carving decorates the top of the 16-sided open *şadırvan* (ablutions fountain), which stands in the centre of the courtyard. The absence of a canopy helps to retain the uncluttered aspect.

KEY

① **Above the Courtyard Portals** are striking arches that were built using alternating red and honey-coloured slabs of stone. This echoes the decoration of the magnificent arches running around the mosque courtyard itself.

② **The columns** supporting the arches of the courtyard are made of old marble, plundered from Byzantine architecture.

③ **The *müezzin mahfili*** still retains original, intricate 16th-century paintwork on its underside. Beneath it is a small fountain.

④ **Mihrab**, cut from Marmara marble.

★ **Dome**
The 43 m (141 ft) dome dominates the interior of the mosque. Not even the florid paintwork – the original 16th-century decoration underwent restoration in the 19th century – detracts from its effect.

VISITORS' CHECKLIST

Practical Information
Mimar Sinan Cad, Edirne.
Tel (0284) 213 97 35.
Open daily. **Closed** prayer times.
🏛 donation.

★ **Minbar**
Many experts claim that the Selimiye's *minbar*, with its conical tiled cap, is the finest in Turkey. Its lace-like side panels are exquisitely carved.

The Interior
The mosque is the supreme achievement of Islamic architecture. Its octagonal plan allows for a reduction in the size of the buttresses supporting the dome. This permitted extra windows to be incorporated, making the interior exceptionally light.

Entrance from
Kavaflar Arasta

Sultan's Loge
The imperial loge is supported on green marble columns. They are connected by pointed arches, whose surrounds are adorned with floral İznik tiles *(see p165)*. Unusually, its ornately decorated *mihrab* contains a shuttered window, which opened on to countryside when the mosque was built.

Main entrance

Burgazada, one of the relaxed and picturesque Princes' Islands

❷ Princes' Islands

Kızıl Adalar

🗺 17,200. 🚢 from Eminönü or sea bus from Kabataş (European side), sea bus from Kadıköy (Asian side) or from Bostancı (further Asian side). ℹ️ Town Hall, (0216) 382 70 71 and (0216) 382 78 56.

The pine-forested Princes' Islands provide a welcome break from the bustle of the city and are just a short ferry ride southeast of Istanbul. Most ferries call in turn at the four largest of the nine islands: **Kınalıada, Burgazada, Heybeliada** and **Büyükada**.

Easily visited on a day trip, the islands take their name from a royal palace built by Justin II on Büyükada, then known as Prinkipo (Island of the Prince) in 569. In Byzantine times the islands became infamous as a place of exile for royalty, and also as the site of several monasteries.

In the latter half of the 19th century, with the inauguration of a regular steamboat service

Visitors strolling along a street in the village of Büyükada

from Istanbul, many wealthy foreigners settled on the islands. One who found the tolerant attitude to foreigners and generous morality attractive was Leon Trotsky, who lived in one of Büyükada's finest mansions from 1929 to 1933. Zia Gökalp *(see p314)*, a key figure in the rise of Turkish nationalism, lived here during the waning years of the Ottoman era.

Büyükada is the largest of the Princes' Islands, and it attracts many visitors because of its lovely sandy beaches, outdoor summer culture and the Art Nouveau style of the wooden dwellings that have given the island much of its lingering Ottoman atmosphere. Büyükada and Heybeliada shun any form of motorized transport in favour of horse-drawn carriages or donkeys. At the top of Büyükada's wooded southern hill stands the Monastery of St George, built on Byzantine foundations.

Heybeliada, the second largest island, houses the imposing former Naval High School (Deniz Harp Okulu), built in 1942. Less touristy than Büyükada, this island offers quieter pleasures such as lovely, tiny beaches and walks in pine groves. The island's northern hill is the stunning location of the

Door to the Monastery of St George, Büyükada

Greek Orthodox School of Theology, which was built in 1841. Its library, famous among Orthodox scholars, is open and worth a visit.

The smaller islands of Kınalıada and Burgazada are less developed and therefore more peaceful.

❸ Polonezköy

🗺 800. 🚌 221 from Taksim or 101 from Beşiktaş to Beykoz, then dolmuş. 🎪 Cherry festival (first two weeks of Jun).

Polonezköy still reflects clear signs of the Polish roots of its founders, who came here in 1842 fleeing Russian oppression. United by politics, Poles fought in Abdül Mecid I's army against Russia in the Crimean War (1853–56). Exempted from taxes for their efforts in the war, they settled in their namesake village. Unlike many people who came to Istanbul principally for trade, Poles came here in search of freedom and some of them converted to Islam. Polonezköy's old-world charm and culinary traditions are still there, but it has become very popular for a day's outing or a weekend break. Turks make up most of its current population.

There are excellent walks in the surrounding countryside and, even though villas and spas have sprung up, there are still several authentic restaurants serving Polish specialities, including the wild boar for which the town was once well known.

The surrounding beech forest, which also offers pleasant walks, has become a conservation area protected from further development.

❹ Şile

🗺 5,000. 🚌 from Üsküdar.

The quintessential Black Sea holiday village, Şile has several fine, sandy beaches and a large, black-and-white striped lighthouse high on a clifftop. In ancient times, the village, then known as Kalpe, was a port used by ships sailing eastward from the Bosphorus. Şile's lighthouse, the largest in Turkey, was built by the French for Sultan Abdül Aziz in 1858–9. Visiting it after dusk on a warm evening makes a pleasant outing. Apart from tourism, Şile is known for producing cotton, as well as a cool, loose-weave cotton cloth, known as *şile bezi*, which is sold in local shops.

❺ İznik

See pp164–5.

❻ Uludağ National Park

Uludağ Milli Parkı

Tel (0224) 283 21 97. 🚌 City bus marked "Teleferik" from Koza Park, then cable car to look-out point at Sarıalan. 🚌 to Sarıalan, then dolmuş. **Open** daily. 🚗 only for vehicles.

One of a number of Turkish mountains to claim the title of Mount Olympus, Uludağ, at 2,540 m (8,340 ft), was believed by the Bithynians (of northwestern Asia Minor) to be the abode of the gods. In the Byzantine era, it was home to several monastic orders. After the Ottoman conquest of Bursa, Muslim dervishes (*p259*) moved into the abandoned monasteries. Nowadays, however, no traces of Uludağ's former religious communities remain.

Spring and summer are the best times for visiting Uludağ National Park, as its alpine heights remain relatively cool, offering a welcome escape from the heat of the lower areas. Visitors will find plenty of good opportunities for peaceful walking and picnicking.

The park includes about 670 sq km (258 sq miles) of woodland. As you ascend, the deciduous beech, oak and hazel gradually give way to juniper and aspen, and finally to dwarf junipers. In springtime, the slopes are blanketed with hyacinths and crocuses.

The main tourist season in Uludağ starts in November, when it becomes Turkey's most fashionable and accessible ski resort, with a reliable cable car service and a goods election of hotels.

Osman Gazi (*see p58*) is supposed to have founded seven villages for his seven sons and their brides here. **Cumalıkızık**, on the lower slopes of Uludağ, is the most perfectly preserved of the five surviving villages and it is registered as a national monument. Among its houses are many 750-year-old half-timbered buildings.

❼ Bursa

See pp166–71.

Spoonbill wading in the lake at Bird Paradise National Park

❽ Bird Paradise National Park

Kuşcenneti Milli Parkı

Tel (0266) 735 54 22. 🅳 from the old bus station in Bandırma. **Open** sunrise to sunset daily. 🚗 📷

An estimated 255 species of birds visit Bird Paradise National Park at the edge of Kuş Gölü, the lake formerly known as Manyas Gölü. Located on the great migratory paths between Europe and Asia, the park is a happy combination of plant cover, reed beds and a lake that supports at least 20 species of fish. The park will delight amateur and professional birdwatchers alike, and a good field guide and some mosquito repellent will enhance the experience.

At the entrance to the park, there is a small museum with displays about various birds. Binoculars are provided at the desk and visitors make their way to an observation tower.

Two main groups of birds visit the lake: those that come here to breed (March–July), and those that pass by during migration, either heading south (November) or north (April–May). Among the birds that breed around the lake are the endangered Dalmatian pelican, the great crested grebe, cormorants, herons, bitterns and spoonbills. Over 3 million birds fly across the area on their migratory routes – storks, cranes, pelicans and birds of prey like sparrowhawks and spotted eagles. April and May are the best months to enjoy this area. Close to the main park area, there is a restaurant that serves fresh trout, and it is a good spot to break for lunch.

Uludağ National Park, a popular ski resort in winter

❺ İznik

🏠 20,122. 🚌 Yeni Mahalle, Yakup Sok. (0224) 757 25 83. 🛈 Belediye Hizmet Binası, Kılıçaslan Cad 97, (0224) 757 19 33, (0224) 757 14 54. 🛒 Wed. 🎭 İznik Flower and Summer Festival (1st or 2nd week of May); Liberation Day (28 Nov).

A charming lakeside town, İznik gives little clue now of its former glory as a capital of the Byzantine Empire. Its most important legacy, however, dates from the 16th century, when its kilns produced the finest ceramics ever made in the Ottoman world.

The town first reached prominence in AD 325, when it was known as Nicaea. In that year Emperor Constantine *(see p53)* chose it as the location of the first Ecumenical Council of the Christian Church. The meeting produced the Nicene Creed, a statement of doctrine on the nature of Christ in relation to God.

The Seljuks *(see p56)* took Nicaea in 1081 and renamed it İznik. It was recaptured in 1097, during the First Crusade, on behalf of Emperor Alexius I Comnenus. After the Crusader capture of Constantinople in 1204 *(see p57)*, the city served as the capital of the "Empire of Nicaea" for 50 years. In 1331, Orhan Gazi captured İznik and incorporated it into the Ottoman empire.

Grand domed portico fronting the Archaeological Museum

İznik still retains its original layout. Surrounded by the town walls, its two main streets are in the form of a cross, with minor streets running out from them on a grid plan. The walls still more or less delineate the town's boundaries. They were built in 300 BC by the Greek Lysimachus, then ruler of the town, but were frequently repaired by the Byzantines and, later, the Ottomans. Extending for some 3 km (2 miles), the walls are punctuated by huge gateways. The main one, Istanbul Gate (İstanbul Kapısı), marks İznik's northern limit. It is decorated with a carved relief of fighting horsemen and is flanked by Byzantine towers.

Istanbul Gate from within the town walls

One of the town's oldest surviving monuments, the ruined church of **Haghia Sophia**, stands at the intersection of the main streets, Atatürk Caddesi and Kılıçaslan Caddesi. An earlier version of the church was the principal place of worship in Byzantine Nicaea. The current building was erected after an earthquake in 1065. The remains of a fine mosaic floor, and also of a Deësis (a fresco depicting Christ, the Virgin and John the Baptist), are protected from damage behind glass screens. Just off the eastern end of Kılıçaslan Caddesi, the 14th-century **Green Mosque** (Yeşil Camii) is named after the tiles covering its minaret. Unfortunately, the original tiles have been replaced by modern copies of inferior quality. Opposite the mosque, the Kitchen of Lady Nilüfer (Nilüfer Hatun İmareti), one of İznik's loveliest buildings, now houses the town's **Archaeological Museum**. This *imaret* was set up in 1388 by Nilüfer Hatun, wife of Orhan Gazi, and served as a hospice for wandering dervishes. Entered through a spacious five-domed portico, the central domed area is flanked by two more domed rooms. The museum has displays of Roman antiquities and glass, as well as some examples of Seljuk and Ottoman tiles.

🏛 **Haghia Sophia**
Atatürk Cad. **Tel** (0224) 757 10 27.
Open 9am–noon & 1–5:30pm daily. 🎫

Green Mosque
Müze Sok. **Open** daily (except prayer times).

🏛 **Archaeological Museum**
Müze Sok. **Tel** (0224) 757 10 27. **Open** 9am–noon & 1–5:30pm daily. 🎫

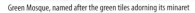
Green Mosque, named after the green tiles adorning its minaret

İznik Ceramics

İznik was one of two major centres (the other being Kütahya) where fine, painted and glazed pottery was fashioned during the Ottoman period. Pottery vessels, plates, and flat and shaped tiles were produced at İznik from the 15th to the 17th century. The last major commission was for 21,043 tiles of some 50 different designs for the Sultanahmet Mosque in Istanbul, completed in 1616. Early İznik pottery is brilliant blue and white. The potteries reached their peak in the 16th century when the famous "tomato red" colour was fully developed. Today visitors can see it sparkle on the superb tilework of the 1561 Rüstem Paşa Mosque *(see p102)* in Istanbul. This period of İznik greatness in ceramic art coincided with the great period of design at the Nakkaşhane design studio in the Topkapı Palace *(see pp72–5)*.

Chinese porcelain, which was imported into Turkey from the 14th century and of which there is a large collection in Topkapı Palace, often inspired the designs used for İznik pottery. During the 16th century, İznik potters produced imitations of pieces of Chinese porcelain, such as this copy of a Ming dish.

Rock and wave border pattern

Damascus ware was the name erroneously given to ceramics produced at İznik during the first half of the 16th century. They had fantastic floral designs in the new colours of turquoise, sage green and manganese. When such tiles were discovered at Damascus, the similar İznik pots were wrongly assumed to have been made there.

Cobalt blue and white was the striking combination of colours used in early İznik pottery (produced between c.1470–1520). The designs used were a mixture of Chinese and Arabesque, as seen on this tiled panel on the wall of the Circumcision Chamber in Topkapı Palace. Floral patterns and animal motifs were both popular at this time.

Armenian bole, an iron-rich red colour, began to be used around 1550, as seen in this 16th-century tankard. New, realistic tulip and other floral designs were also introduced, and İznik ware enjoyed its heyday, which lasted until around 1630.

Wall tiles were not made in any quantity until the reign of Süleyman the Magnificent (1520–66). Süleyman used İznik tiles to refurbish the Dome of the Rock in Jerusalem. Some of the best examples are seen in Istanbul's mosques, notably in the Süleymaniye *(see pp104–5)*, Rüstem Paşa Mosque and, here, in this example from the Blue Mosque *(pp92–3)*.

Miniature depicting potters

❼ Bursa

The city of Bursa – known to Turks as *yeşil Bursa* ("green Bursa") – has tranquil parks and leafy suburbs set on the lower slopes of Mount Uludağ *(see p163)*. This disguises the vibrant commercial heart of the city, which is today made prosperous by automobiles, food and textiles, as it was by the silk trade in the 15th and 16th centuries. The Romans developed the potential of Bursa's mineral springs, and there are estimated to be about 3,000 thermal baths in the city today. In 1326 Bursa became the first capital of the Ottoman Empire after it succumbed to Osman *(see p58)*.

View over the rooftops of the city of Bursa

Bursa has been a provincial capital since 1841 and, despite its commercial centre, it has retained its pious dignity. No city in Turkey has more mosques and tombs. Paradoxically, it is also the home of the satirical shadow-puppet genre known as Karagöz *(see p30)*.

◀ Yıldırım Beyazıt Mosque
Yıldırım Beyazıt Camii
Yıldırım Cad.
Open daily (except prayer times).

This mosque is named after Beyazıt I, whose nickname was "Yıldırım", meaning "thunderbolt". This referred to the speed with which he reacted to his enemies. Built in 1389, just after Beyazıt became sultan, the mosque at first doubled as a lodge for Sufi dervishes *(see p259)*. It has a lovely portico with five domed bays.

Inside, the prayer hall and interior court (a covered "courtyard" in Bursa mosques, which prefigures the open ones preferred by later Ottoman architects) are divided by an impressive, gravity-defying arch. This rises from two *mihrab*-like niches. The walls of the prayer hall itself are adorned with several attractive pieces of calligraphic design *(see pp32–3)*.

🔹 Green Tomb
Yeşil Türbe
Yeşil Cad. **Open** daily. 🔸 donation.

The tomb of Mehmet I, which stands elevated among tall cypress trees, is one of the city's most prominent landmarks. It was built between 1414 and 1421.

The tomb is much closer to the Seljuk style of architecture than classical Ottoman. Its exterior is covered in green tiles – mainly 19th-century replacements for the original faïence. A few older tiles survive around the entrance portal. The interior, entered through a pair of superbly carved wooden doors,

is simply dazzling. The space is small and the ornamentation, covering a relatively large surface area, is breathtaking in its depth of colour and detail. The *mihrab* has especially intricate tile panels, including a representation of a mosque lamp hanging from a gold chain between two candles.

The sultan's magnificent sarcophagus is covered in exquisite tiles and adorned by a long Koranic inscription. Nearby sarcophagi contain the remains of his sons, daughters and nursemaid.

◀ Green Mosque
Yeşil Camii
Yeşil Cad. **Open** daily (except prayer times).

Bursa's most famous monument was commissioned by Mehmet I in 1412, but it remained unfinished at his death in 1421 and still lacks a portico. Nevertheless, it is the finest Ottoman mosque built prior to the conquest of Constantinople *(see p58)*.

The main portal is tall and elegant, with an intricately carved canopy. It opens into the entrance hall. Beyond this is an interior court with a carved fountain at its centre. A flight of three steps leads up from here into the prayer hall. On either side of the steps are niches for worshippers to leave their shoes. Above the entrance to the court is the sultan's loge *(see p37)*, resplendent in richly patterned tiles created using the *cuerda seca* technique. They are in beautiful greens, blues and yellows, with threads

The distinctive and prominent Green Tomb of Sultan Mehmet I

of gold that were added after firing. The tiling of the prayer hall was carried out by Ali Ibn İlyas Ali, who learned his art in Samarkand. This was the first time that tiles were used extensively in an Ottoman mosque, and it set a precedent for the later widespread use of İznik tiles *(see p165)*. The tiles covering the walls of the prayer hall, which is well lit by floor-level windows, are simple, green and hexagonal. Against this plain backdrop, the effect of the *mihrab* is especially glorious. Predominantly turquoise, deep blue and white, with touches of gold,

the *mihrab*'s tiles depict flowers, leaves, arabesques and geometric patterns. The mosque's exterior was also once clad in tiles, but these have disappeared over time.

🏛 Museum of Turkish and Islamic Arts

Türk ve İslam Eserleri Müzesi
Yeşil Cad. **Tel** (0224) 327 76 79.
Open 8am–noon, 1–5pm Mon–Fri.

This interesting museum is housed in a fine Ottoman-era building, once the *medrese (see p36)* associated with the Green Mosque. The façade of the building is quite striking. A colonnade surrounds its courtyard on three sides. The cells leading off from this courtyard are now exhibition galleries. Exhibits date from the 12th to the 20th centuries, and include Seljuk and Ottoman ceramics, elaborately deco-rated Korans and beautiful cere-monial costumes.

Façade of the Museum of Turkish and Islamic Arts

🏛 Bursa City Museum

Bursa Kent Müzesi
Atatürk Cad 8. **Tel** (0224) 220 26 26.
Open 9:30am–5:30pm Tue–Sun. ♿

The former Justice courts have been restored as a lively museum that traces local life over many years. Displays show how culinary skills, handicrafts, costumes, archaeological artifacts and city planning moulded urban spirit. Bursa city fathers, Atatürk and the local *commedia dell arte* puppet genre of Karagöz *(see p30)* have first-rate exhibits.

Bursa City Centre

① Yıldırım Beyazıt Mosque
② Green Tomb
③ Green Mosque
④ Museum of Turkish and Islamic Arts
⑤ Bursa City Museum
⑥ Tophane Citadel
⑦ Tombs of Osman and Orhan Gazi
⑧ Alaeddin Mosque
⑨ Muradiye Mosque
⑩ Archaelogical Museum

Key

▪ Street-by-Street area *see pp168–9*

0 metres 750
0 yards 750

ANKARA CAD
KIBRIS ŞEHİTLER CAD
ÇEKİRGE
⑩ Archaeological Museum
Kültür Parkı
STADYUM CAD
CEKİRGE CAD
HAMZABEY CAD
⑨ Muradiye Mosque
ALTIPARMAK CAD
SAKARYA CAD
İZVZİ ÇAKMAK CAD
MURADİYE
KAPICA CAD
MASTALARYURDU CAD
ORTAPAZAR CAD
DEMİRKAPI CAD
ORHANELİ CAD
Alaeddin Mosque ⑧
TOPHANE
Bursa City Museum ⑤
ALACAHIRKA CAD
⑦ Osman Gazi Tomb
⑥ Tophane Citadel
CUMHURIYET CAD
UZUN ÇARŞI CAD
Çakır Aia Hamamı
İNEBEY CAD
MAKSEM CAD
Great Mosque
ATATÜRK CAD
PINARBAŞI CAD
HAŞİM İŞCAN CAD
HAŞİM İŞCAN CAD
İNÖNÜ CAD
NAMAZGAH CAD
Airport 20 km (12 miles) ✈
ANKARA, İSTANBUL
① Yıldırım Beyazıt Mosque
Museum of Anatolian Carriages
İNCIRLI CAD
Museum of Turkish and Islamic Art ④
YEŞİL CAD
③ Green Mosque
② Green Tomb
YEŞİL
Gök Dere
PEÇIÇLIK CAD

Bursa: The Market Area

Bursa's central market area is a warren of streets and Ottoman *hans* (warehouses). The area emphasizes the more colourful and traditional aspects of this busy industrial city and is a good place to experience the bustle of inner-city life. Here too you can buy the local fabrics for which the city is famous, particularly hand-made lace, towelling and silk. The silkworm was introduced to the Byzantine empire in the 6th century and for centuries there was a brisk trade in silk cocoons in Koza Han. Today, as well as silk products, you can also find hand-made, camelskin Karagöz puppets *(see p30)*.

★ Covered Bazaar
The great bazaar, built by Mehmet I in the 15th century, consists of a long hall with domed bays, with an adjoining high, vaulted hall. The Bedesten is home to jewellers' shops.

★ Great Mosque (Ulu Camii)
A three-tiered ablutions fountain stands beneath the central dome of this monumental mosque, which was erected in 1396–9.

Şengül Hamamı Turkish baths

Bey Han (also called Emir Han) was built as part of the Orhan Gazi Mosque complex, to provide revenue for the mosque's upkeep.

Cafés

K O Z A   P A R K I

A T A T Ü R K   C A

Umur Bey Hamamı, built by Murat II (1421–51), is one of the world's oldest Turkish baths. It now houses workshops.

Koza Park
The gardens in front of Koza Han, with their fountains, benches and shaded café tables, are a popular meeting place for locals and visitors throughout the day.

★ Koza Han
This is the most attractive and fascinating building in the market area. It was built in 1491 by Beyazıt II, and was central to the silk trade.

Geyve Han is also known as İvaz Paşa Han.

Fidan Han dates from around 1470, when it was built by a grand vizier of Mehmet the Conqueror.

İçkoza Han

BORSA SOK

UZUN ÇARŞI CAD

ÇÖMEK SOK

BELEDİYE CAD

0 metres   40
0 yards   40

Flower Market
The numerous bunches of flowers for sale in the streets around the town hall make a picturesque sight in the midst of Bursa's bustling market area.

The Belediye, Bursa's town hall, is a Swiss chalet-style, half-timbered building that forms a surprising landmark in the centre of the city.

Orhan Gazi Mosque
Built in 1339, just 13 years after the Ottoman conquest of Bursa, this mosque is the oldest of the city's imperial mosques.

Key
— Suggested route

For additional map symbols *see back flap*

Exploring Bursa

Tophane, the most ancient part of Bursa, is distinguished by its clocktower, which stands on top of a hill. This area was formerly the site of the citadel and is bounded by what remains of the original Byzantine walls. It is also known as Hisar, which means "fortress" in Turkish. If you continue westwards for 2 km (1 mile), crossing the Cılımboz River, you come to the historic district of Muradiye. Çekirge (or "cricket") is Bursa's most westerly area. The origin of this name is not known, but the cool, leafy character of this suburb gives Bursa the tag of *yeşil*, or "green", by which it is known in Turkey.

Tophane

Tophane's northern limit is marked by the best-preserved section of the citadel walls, built on an outcrop of rock. At the top is a pleasant park, filled with cafés, which also contains the imposing clocktower and the tombs of Osman and Orhan Gazi, the founders of the Ottoman dynasty.

🏛 Tophane Citadel
Hisar
Osman Gazi Cad. **Open** daily. ♿
The Citadel walls can be viewed from a set of steps leading uphill from the intersection of Cemal Nadir Caddesi and Atatürk Caddesi. These steps end at the tea gardens above. The citadel fell into Ottoman hands when Orhan Gazi's troops broke through its walls. Later, he built a wooden palace inside the citadel and had the old Byzantine ramparts re-fortified. Until this era the walls had delineated the entire circumference of the ancient city. However, Orhan encouraged Bursa's expansion and developed the present-day commercial heart of the city further to the east.

⚰ Tombs of Osman and Orhan Gazi
Osman & Orhan Gazi Türbeleri
Ulu Cami Cad. **Open** daily. 🎁 donation.
Osman Gazi began the process of Ottoman expansion in the 13th century (*see p56*) and attempted to capture Bursa. But it was his son, Orhan, who took the city just before Osman Gazi died. Orhan brought his father's body to be buried in the baptistry of a converted church and he himself was later buried in the nave. The tombs that can be seen today date from 1868.

⚰ Alaeddin Mosque
Alaeddin Camii
Alaeddin Mahallesi. **Open** daily. 📷
The Alaeddin Mosque is the oldest in Bursa: it was built in 1335, only nine years after the city was conquered in 1326. It is in the form of a simple domed square, fronted by a portico of four Byzantine columns with capitals. The mosque was commissioned by Alaeddin Bey, brother of and vizier to Orhan Gazi.

Muradiye

Muradiye is a leafy, residential district of Bursa. Close to the Muradiye Mosque, the Hüsnü Züber House is a fine example of a traditional Turkish home. It is no longer open to the public but the fine architecture can be seen from the outside. To the north is a park; among the attractions are a boating lake and the Archaeological Museum.

Tomb of Osman Gazi, the first great Ottoman leader

⚰ Muradiye Mosque
Muradiye Külliyesi
Murat II Cad. **Open** daily. 🎁 donation.

This mosque complex was built by Murat II, the father of Mehmet the Conqueror (*see p58*), in 1447. The mosque itself is preceded by a graceful domed portico. Its wooden door is finely carved and the interior decorated with early İznik tiles (*see p165*). The *medrese* (*see p36*), next to the mosque, now serves as a dispensary. It is a perfectly square building, with cells surrounding a central garden courtyard. Its *dershane*, or main classroom, is richly tiled and adorned with an ornate brick façade.

The mosque garden, with its cypresses, well-tended flower beds and fountains, is one of Bursa's most tranquil retreats. Murat II was the last of the Ottoman sultans to be buried in Bursa and his mausoleum stands in the garden beside the mosque. The other 11 tombs in the garden are a reminder of the Ottoman code of succession, which recognized a future sultan as the strongest (or most cunning) male relative, even if not always the most

Popular café in the park above the ancient citadel walls in Tophane

Interior of Muradiye Mosque, showing the decorative *mihrab*

suitable to rule. Competing male relatives could expect to be put to death or spend most of their lives in enforced solitary confinement, known as "the cage". This did not, however, prevent the ruling offspring from having an emotive memorial built for a deposed brother. Selim II ("the Sot"), for example, had an elaborate octagonal mausoleum built in Bursa for his older brother, Mustafa.

🏛 Archaeological Museum

Arkeoloji Müzesi
Resat Oyal, Kültür Parkı. **Tel** (0224) 234 49 18. **Open** 8am–noon & 1–5pm Tue–Sun. 🔲 🖵

Finds dating from the 3rd millennium BC up to the Ottoman conquest of Bursa in 1326 are collected in this museum. The ceremonial armour accessories are the most interesting items, with the Roman glass a close second. There are a number of Roman statues and bronzes, as well as Byzantine religious objects and coins. The labelling of objects has been improved.

🏛 Bursa Museum of Anatolian Carriages

Bursa Anadolu Arabaları Müzesi
Umurbey Mah, Kapıcı Cad, Yıldırım. **Tel** (0224) 329 39 41. **Open** 10am–5pm Tue–Sun. 🖵 ♿ (the museum is mostly on one floor). 🖼

The discovery of a 2,600-year-old carriage made of iron and wood stimulated interest in the city's non-motorized transport heritage. This museum traces the wheeled history of *kupa* (war chariots), ox carts, gun mountings, hay ricks, pleasure carriages and horse-drawn railway rolling stock. Artistic motifs painted on carriages were a craftsman's early trademark.

The museum skilfully highlights carriage-making as a precision engineering trade. Bursa is modern Turkey's "motown" and a local automotive producer sponsored the research and reconstruction, applying modern spare-parts cataloguing techniques to latter-day wagons. Housed in a former silk-making factory, the museum is enhanced by beautiful gardens and mature trees. A bookshop sells mainly books and posters of the various wagons.

The art of carriage-making, Bursa Museum of Anatolian Carriages

Çekirge

The Çekirge neighbourhood offers some of the most prominent and best developed natural mineral springs *(kaplıca)* in Turkey. In the 6th century, Emperor Justinian *(see p53)* built a bath house here; his wife, Theodora, arrived later with a retinue of about 4,000 to take the waters.

Today, Çekirge is the city's most attractive residential area, still known for its therapeutic hot springs and having excellent spa accommodation. Located above the city, there are wonderful alpine vistas and cool breezes.

🌊 New Spa

Yeni Kaplıca-Karamustafa
Kaynarca Termal Otel and Baths, Kükürtlü Mah, Osmangazi. **Tel** (0224) 236 69 68. **Open** 5am–11pm daily (separate spas for men and women).

Contrarily, the New Spa baths have a substantial pedigree and were rebuilt in 1522 by Rüstem Paşa, grand vizier to Süleyman the Magnificent. Two steamy thermal water sources, Kaynarca and Karamustafa, feed the therapeutic pools and treatment centres, all set in expansive tropical gardens.

Karamustafa has been restored as an aqua culture residential complex. Kaynarca is only for women, with professional spa staff, private baths and social facilities. Visitors unfamiliar with Turkey's spa heritage will be warmly welcomed here.

🛏 Çelik Palas Hotel

Çelik Palas Otel Çekirge Cad 79. **Tel** (0224) 233 38 00.

This five-star hotel is a famous local icon. Built in 1933, it is the city's oldest and most prestigious spa hotel. Atatürk *(see p62)* frequented its baths, which are open to both sexes.

🌊 Old Spa

Eski Kaplıca
Kervansaray Termal Oteli, Çekirge Meydanı **Tel** (0224) 233 93 00. **Open** 8am–10:30pm daily.

The Old Spa baths were established by Sultan Murat I in the late 14th century and renovated in 1512 during the reign of Beyazıt II. The spa contains radium and is for men only. The women's section focuses more on cosmetic, not thermal, treatments.

Attractive, tranquil interior of the Old Spa baths

⓿ Gallipoli Peninsula

Gelibolu Yarımadası

Washed by the Aegean Sea to the west, the Gallipoli Peninsula is bordered to the east by the Dardanelles, a strategic waterway giving access to the Sea of Marmara, the Bosphorus and the Black Sea. In ancient times, this deep channel was called the Hellespont. Today, the peninsula is an unspoiled area of farmland and pine forest, with some lovely stretches of sandy beach. However, it was also the scene of one of the bloodiest campaigns of World War I, in which more than 500,000 Allied (Australian, British, French, Indian and New Zealand) and Turkish soldiers laid down their lives. The region has three museums, and is dotted with cemeteries and monuments. In 1973, the Gallipoli National Historic Park was created in recognition of the area's great historical significance.

Suvla Bay
On 7 August 1915, British troops landed here in an attempt to break the stalemate further south.

★ Kabatepe Information Centre
The centre is also a museum, with letters, photographs, shrapnel and other memorabilia relating to the Gallipoli campaign.

French Cemetery
A sombre obelisk and rows of striking black crosses honour the French troops who fell during the Anglo-French landing at Cape Helles on 25 April 1915.

KEY

① **The Çanakkale Şehitleri Abidesi** commemorates fallen Turkish soldiers.

② **At Y Beach**, ambiguous signals led to an unauthorized withdrawal on both sides.

0 kilometres   5
0 miles   2

For hotels and restaurants in this area see pp330–39 and pp346–61

Reconstructed Trenches

At some points, the Allied and Turkish trenches were no more than a few metres apart.

Kumköy

anafarta

Yalova

lipolo efields

Bigali

atürk atue

Chunuk Bair

etcik orial

Kilye Bay

abat idos)

ürk um

Çanakkale

Kilitibahir

The Narrows

Kepez

Dardanelles (Çanakkale Boğazı)

550

★ Chunuk Bair
Various monuments honour the 28,000 men who died here on 6–9 August 1915.

★ Mehmetcik Memorial
This memorial was unveiled in 1985. Atatürk's eulogy unites the fallen sons of Turkey (Mehmetcik) with the Allied dead ("Johnnies").

The Gallipoli Campaign 1915–16

After the start of World War I, Allied leaders developed a plan to seize the Dardanelles. This would give them control of Constantinople and diminish the threat of Russia gaining control of the strategic waterway. A naval assault was repulsed by Turkish shore batteries and minefields, so the order was given to land troops to secure the straits. At dawn on 25 April 1915 British and French troops landed at the tip of the Gallipoli Peninsula. Further north, a large force of ANZACs (Australia and New Zealand Army Corps) came ashore but met dogged opposition from the Turkish defenders. A second landing at Suvla Bay failed to win any new ground. Many soldiers died from disease, drowning or the appalling conditions of trench warfare. After nine months, the Allied force withdrew.

British troops landing under fire at Cape Helles

Key
▬ Major road
═ Other road
═ Minor road

For additional map symbols see back flap

Exploring the Agean

Around 26 million people – roughly a third of Turkey's population – inhabit the Aegean region. Here, incomes are generally higher and the lifestyle more westernized than elsewhere in the country. Tourists are attracted to this area for its beaches, nightlife and yachting, but there are many other worthwhile sights from the green and fertile Menderes River Valley to the Roman city of Ephesus near Selçuk. Visitors can explore the countryside in day-trips from Marmaris to Knidos on the scenic Datça Peninsula.

Sights at a Glance

❶ Çanakkale
❷ Troy
❸ Behram Kale (Assos)
❹ Ayvalık
❺ *Bergama (Pergamum) pp180–81*
❻ Foça
❼ *İzmir pp182–3*
❽ Çeşme
❾ Selçuk
❿ *Ephesus pp186–7*
⓫ Kuşadası
⓬ Aydın
⓭ Menderes River Valley
⓮ *Hierapolis pp190–91*
⓯ *Aphrodisias pp192–3*
⓰ Denizli
⓱ Priene
⓲ Miletus
⓳ Didyma
⓴ Lake Bafa
㉑ Altınkum
㉒ Labranda
㉓ Milas (Mylasa)
㉔ Güllük
㉕ *Bodrum pp198–9*
㉗ *Marmaris pp204–5*

Tours

㉖ *Bodrum Peninsula Tour pp202–3*
㉘ *Datça Peninsula Tour pp206–7*

0 kilometres   50
0 miles   25

Temple of Trajan, Bergama (Pergamum)

For additional map symbols *see back flap*

Getting Around

The Aegean region is well served by good roads and public transport. Dolmuşes ply the routes to the smaller towns and villages. İzmir and Bodrum both have airports with frequent connections to Istanbul. İzmir is also served by rail, with connections to the city's Adnan Menderes Airport. Ferry services link İzmir, Marmaris and Bodrum with ports in Greece.

Bursa

Susurluk

565

Kepsut

Umarlar Dağı

Balıkesir

Dursunbey

230

Tavşanlı

555

Bigadiç

240

Sındırgı

Alaçam Dağları

Emet

240

Demirci

240

Simav

Gediz

595

hisar

Gördes

585

Selendi

Gediz Çayı

Afyon

Uşak

Gölü Marmara

Demirköprü Barajı

Kula

300

Salihli

Alaşehir

Eşme

Çivril

Dağları

Sarıgöl

Adıgüzel Barajı

Ödemiş

310

585

Buldan

Aydın Dağları

Nysa

Nazilli

Saraköy

14 HIERAPOLIS

DIN

320

13

Akçay

320

Dinar

MENDERES RIVER VALLEY

16 DENİZLİ

Çine

15 APHRODİSİAS

Kemer Barajı

Tavas

550

Kale

BRANDA

agina

Yatağan

330

Stratonikeia

Muğla

S

Fethiye

400

MARMARIS

27

NSULA

400

İçmeler

Pamukkale's travertine terraces, near Hierapolis

Key

═══ Motorway
═══ Dual carriageway
━━━ Major road
═══ Minor road
━━━ Scenic route
╍╍╍ Main railway
──── Minor railway

Bodrum's marina and Castle of St Peter

Çanakkale, a historic crossing point between Asia and Europe

❶ Çanakkale

🏙 81,000. 🚢 from Eceabat or Kilitbahir. 🚌 Atatürk Cad. 🛈 İskele Meydanı 67, (0286) 217 11 87. 🎪 Fri. 🎭 Navy Days (13–18 Mar), ANZAC Days (24–25 Apr), Sardine Festival (30–31 Jun – Gelibolu).

Çanakkale occupies the narrowest point of the straits called the Dardanelles, which are 1,200 m (3,937 ft) wide at this point. In 450 BC, the Persian King Xerxes built a bridge of boats here to land his troops in Thrace, and the final battles of the Peloponnesian War took place in these waters around 400 BC.

During his campaign to take Constantinople in 1453, Mehmet II (the Conqueror) built two fortresses to secure the straits: Kilitbahir (on the European side) and Çimenlik (in Çanakkale harbour). Today, ferry services link Çanakkale with Kilitbahir and Eceabat on the other side. Çanakkale makes the most convenient base for tours of the Gallipoli battlefields (see pp172–3) across the straits.

The town has an attractive harbour, a naval museum and the landmark clock in the main square. Çanakkale means "pottery castle" and the town was once a centre for the production of high-quality kaolin for a flourishing ceramics industry. Today this type of clay is imported, but the vitreous enamel ware (see p364) made in Çanakkale remains one of Turkey's top export earners.

Environs
A few kilometres south of the town is the **Archaeological Museum**, which though small should not be missed.

🏛 **Archaeological Museum**
Arkeoloji Müzesi
Barbaros Mahallesi, Yüzüncü Yıl Cad.
Tel (0286) 217 67 40. **Open** 8am–noon, 1–5pm Tue–Sun. 🚫

❷ Troy

🛈 İskele Meydanı 67, Çanakkale, (0286) 217 11 87. 🚌 from Çanakkale, then taxi. 🎭 Troy Festival (based in Çanakkale but includes Troy and environs, 10–18 Aug).

Few areas of Turkey have been as thoroughly excavated as Troy (Truva in Turkish). Nine different strata have yielded pieces of a history that runs from around 4000 BC until about AD 300. Troy was the pivot of Homer's *Iliad* and was where the decade-long Trojan War (13th century BC) was fought.

The site is known as **Hisarlık**, or "castle kingdom" in Turkish. The stonework and walls are impressive. Visible today are a defence wall, two sanctuaries (probably dating from the 8th century BC), houses from various periods and a Roman theatre. The site called the Pillar House at the southern gate may have been the palace of King Priam.

Reconstruction of the Trojan Horse

The site is well marked with 12 information points and some ongoing excavations. The most visible attraction is a large wooden Trojan Horse, a reconstruction of the device used by the Greeks to deceive and ultimately vanquish the Trojans, and a universal symbol of treachery today. In August each year, Turkish school-children release a white dove from the Trojan Horse to celebrate peace.

🏠 **Hisarlık**
5 km (3 miles) from main E87 road. 🚌 from Çanakkale every 30/40 minutes. **Open** 8am–7:30pm (5pm in winter) daily. 🚫 🅿 🏪

Schliemann's Search for Ancient Troy

The German-born Heinrich Schliemann – regarded by many as an unscrupulous plunderer and by others as an archaeological pioneer – nurtured a lifelong ambition to discover Homer's Troy. In 1873, three years after starting excavations at Hisarlık, he stumbled upon what he claimed to be King Priam's hoard of gold and silver jewellery. The over-eager explorer damaged the site, but his valuable find demonstrated that Greek civilization started 1,000 years earlier than previously believed. Part of the hoard, which was on display in a Berlin museum, vanished after World War II. It reappeared in the Pushkin Museum in Russia in 1996. Its return, authenticity and origins are still controversial.

Heinrich Schliemann's wife, wearing "Priam's" jewellery

Humpbacked Ottoman bridge on the outskirts of Behram Kale

❸ Behram Kale (Assos)

🏙 3,000. 🚌 to Ayvacık, 19 km (12 miles) N, then dolmuş. 🅳 from Edremit or Çanakkale.

Nestled on the shores of the Gulf of Edremit and sheltered by the Greek island of Lesbos, 10 km (6 miles) offshore, it is easy to see why Assos enjoyed the reputation of the most beautiful place in Asia Minor. Ancient Assos reached the pinnacle of its glory when Plato's protégé, Aristotle, founded a school of philosophy here in 340 BC. In the 2nd century BC, the town included not only the present citadel, with the remaining Doric columns of the Temple of Athena (built in the 6th century BC), but also the village of Behram Kale, 238 m (781 ft) below.

St Paul is reputed to have passed through Assos on his third biblical journey, and the town is referred to in the Acts of the Apostles. After the fall of the Byzantine empire, the town's commercial fortunes declined, but today this charming and cultured retreat attracts many artists and scholars, who leave the bustle of the city and find a source of inspiration here.

As you come into the town, note the fine Ottoman bridge dating from the 14th century. There is also a mosque and a fort from this time, all built by Sultan Murat I. Residents of Assos favour houses with archways and overhanging balconies, and there is bougainvillea everywhere.

❹ Ayvalık

🏙 30,000. 🚌 1.5 km (1 mile) N of town centre. 🛈 Opposite the yacht harbour, (0266) 312 21 22. 🛍 Thu. 🖥 🛍

Ayvalık takes its name from *ayva*, the Turkish word for quince, but the fruit is only available in season (January and February). Of the many villages along the Aegean coast peopled by Greeks until 1923 (*see p62*), Ayvalık is the one that has most retained the flavour of a bygone age. There are many stone houses, and the town's mosques betray their Greek Orthodox origins. A Greek church and a few Greek-speakers remain.

Ayvalık's appeal stems from its cobbled streets and leisurely lifestyle. The beach at Sarımsaklı and peninsula of Alibey (also known by its Greek name of Cunda) are within reach by road, but the ferry journey is more restful.

❺ Bergama (Pergamum)

See pp180–81.

❻ Foça

🏙 14,000. 🛈 Atatürk Bulvarı 1 (entrance to Foça), (0232) 812 55 34. 🚌 from İzmir to Foça turn off on main E87. 🅳 from junction of E87. 🎭 Tourism & Culture Festival (Aug–Sep).

Phocaea, ancient Foça, was probably settled around 1000 BC and was part of the Ionian League (*see p194*). Around 500 BC the Phocaeans were famed as mariners, sending vessels powered by 50 oars-men into the Aegean, Mediterranean and Black Sea. There is a small theatre dating from antiquity at the entrance to the town. Near the centre of town, you will find a stone tomb known as **Taş Küle**. There is also a restored Genoese **fortress**. But apart from a few *hamams* (Turkish baths), this is the extent of Old Foça.

Environs

23 km (14 miles) up the coast is the town of Yenifoça (New Foça), with good campsites and beaches. The military presence in the area may have helped keep it off the tourist trail. Apart from summer weekends and holidays, it is an ideal place to escape the crowds. The area is known for its monk seal conservation programme, but they are seldom seen.

Boats, old houses and up-market cafés in Foça's harbour

➎ Bergama (Pergamum)

Perched on a hilltop above the modern town of Bergama, the great acropolis of Pergamum is one of the most dramatic sights in Turkey. Originally settled by the Aeolian Greeks in the 8th century BC, it was ruled for a time by one of Alexander the Great's generals. The city prospered under the Pergamene dynasty founded by Eumenes I, who ruled from 263 to 241 BC, when this was one of the ancient world's main centres of learning. The last ruler of this dynasty, Attalus III, bequeathed the kingdom to Rome in 133 BC, and Pergamum became capital of the Roman province of Asia. The great physician Galen was born here in AD 129, and established a famous medical centre, the Asclepieum.

★ **Temple of Trajan**
Built of white marble, it was completed during Hadrian II's reign (AD 125–138).

City Walls
Eumenes II (197–159 BC) extended the city walls until they reached a length of about 4 km (3 miles), enclosing the entire hilltop.

Plan of Pergamum

Arsenal
Palace
Gate
Heroon
Temple of Trajan
Altar of Zeus
Theatre
Upper Agora
Temple of Dionysus
East Baths
Terrace
Upper Gymnasium
Acropolis
Wall Course
Wall Course
Temenos of Demeter
Lower Agora
Ulu Cami
Selinus
Bergama Town
To Archaeological Museum & Asclepieum

Key
- Building
- Road
- Ancient Road

0 metres   400
0 yards   400

0 metres   500
0 yards   500

Library Ruins
Reputedly containing 200,000 parchment scrolls, many works from Pergamum went to its rival library in Alexandria as part of Mark Anthony's wedding gift to Cleopatra in 41 BC.

VISITORS' CHECKLIST

Practical Information
Tel (0232) 631 28 83.
Open 8:30am–5pm (winter), 8am–7pm (summer) daily.
There is much uphill walking, as the Acropolis and Asclepieum are 8 km (5 miles) apart. Allow a full day to tour the site.

Transport
from Izmir.

★ Altar of Zeus
One of Pergamum's largest temples, the first stone reliefs of the building were found in the 1870s. The altar was rebuilt in Berlin's Pergamum Museum.

KEY

① **Temple of Dionysus**

② **Arsenal**

③ **King's Palace**

④ **Temple of Athena**

⑤ **The Heroon** was a shrine built to honour the kings of Pergamum.

⑥ **The Upper Agora** (marketplace) lay immediately below the Altar of Zeus. From here, a ramp led up to to the main city gate.

⑦ **Theatre Terrace**

★ Theatre
Constructed in the 3rd century BC, the theatre has 80 rows of seats and an estimated capacity of 10,000. The seats were constructed of andesite, and the royal box in the lower section of marble.

⊘ İzmir

The most western-leaning of Turkish cities, İzmir's position at the head of the Gulf of İzmir (İzmir Körfezi) has given it a trading edge that has lasted from the 3rd century AD to today. For centuries, it was known as Smyrna, a name possibly derived from the myrrh trees that grow here. The city's origins are believed to date back to 8500 BC, based on finds from the Teşılova Mound. Until 1922, the city had a large Christian population, including thousands of Greek Orthodox, most of whom fled during the turmoil of the War of Independence *(see p62)*. As Turkey's third largest city and the regional headquarters of NATO, İzmir has a multicultural sophistication.

The Governor's Palace, in the centre of the city

Exploring Izmir

İzmir's broad boulevards are balanced by leafy pedestrian precincts. Buses, ferries and a Metro make it easy to get around, or horse-drawn carriages will do for the more sedate tourist. Be sure to explore the old wharf area (İskele), now restored as a stylish shipping pier.

🏛 Archaeology Museum

Halil Paşa Cad, Bahri Baba Park İçi. **Tel** (0232) 489 07 96/483 72 54. **Open** 8:30am–4:30pm Tue–Sun. 📷 with permission.

The main displays consist of artifacts from the Teşılova Mound, which was settled from about 3000 to 300 BC. The Byzantine glassware is especially eye-catching, but the highlight is the Treasury (*Hazine*). It is kept locked and the guard may need to be summoned, but the gold jewellery dating from the 6th–3rd centuries BC offers ample proof of ancient artistic talent. The Roman and Byzantine imperial silver and gold coins are well displayed.

🏛 Ethnographic Museum

Next to the Archaeology Museum. **Open** 8:30am–4:30pm Tue–Sun. 📷

Housed in a former French hospital, built in 1831, the museum highlights local crafts and skills – from quilting and felt-making to weapons and woodblock printing. Bridal costumes, glassware, an oven used to fire blue beads (*mavi boncuk*) and a replica of İzmir's first apothecary shop. The museum remains open during renovation work.

🕌 Konak Clock Tower

Saat Kulesi
Konak Square. 🚌 any bus marked "Konak".

Built in 1901, the clock tower is the symbol of İzmir. It was one of 58 built in Ottoman times to encourage Turks to adopt European timekeeping habits. İzmir's is one of the finest of these monuments. Its ornate decorative style offers a strong contrast to the exquisite simplicity of the tiny Konak Mosque (Konak Camii) that nestles beside it.

🏬 Kızlarağası Han

Look for signs off the N end of Fevzi Paşa Cad. **Open** 8am–9pm Mon–Sat.

This typical Ottoman trading complex (*see pp28–9*) has been restored, with the courtyard turned into a café. There are craft and furniture restoration workshops on the upper floor. This is a good place to purchase handicrafts and copper.

⛪ St Polycarp Church

Necatibey Sok 2. **Tel** (0232) 484 84 36. **Open** to groups only, 9am–noon & 3–5pm daily.

The patron saint of İzmir, St Polycarp was a Christian martyr who gave us the adage, "The spirit indeed is willing, but the flesh is weak." This is the oldest Roman Catholic church in İzmir and the seat of the Catholic archbishop. Permission to build a chapel to St Polycarp was granted in 1620 by Süleyman the Magnificent (*see p56*). To the right of the altarpiece is a self-portrait of Raymond Peré, designer of the Konak Clock Tower.

The Konak mosque, adorned with ceramic tiles from Kütahya

Corinthian columns in the Agora, the city market in Roman times

0 metres 400
0 yards 400

Alsancak terminal
600 metres (650 yards)

1381
İF ÇINAR BUL
1379
LOZAN MEYD

JEVRES BEY BUL MONTRÖ MEYD

Kültürpark

ŞAIR EŞREF BUL
HÜRRİYET BUL
REFIK SAYDAM BUL

Airport 20km (12 miles)
Bus terminal 8km (5 miles)

GAZI BUL
DOKUZ EYLÜL MEYD
MÜRSELPAŞA BUL

1369
KAYA
VZİPAŞA BUL
GAZILER CAD
Basmane Train Station

OTELIER SOK

AKINCİ
ANAFARTALAR CAD
967
945

⑥ Agora

HACI ALIEFENDI CAD

⑦ Velvet Castle

🏛 Agora
Tel (0232) 483 46 96.
Open 8:30am–noon & 1–5:30pm Tue–Sun.

The present remains of the Agora, the central market of the Roman city of Smyrna, date from about the 2nd century AD, when it was rebuilt by the Emperor Marcus Aurelius following an earthquake in AD 178. There are several Corinthian columns with well-preserved capitols still standing, and enough arches, as well as part of a basilica (city hall), to give the flavour of a Roman town. It was used until the Byzantine period.

🏛 Velvet Castle
Kadifekale
from Konak Clock Tower marked "Kale", then on foot.

Also known as Mount Pagos, the Velvet Castle was built on Hellenistic foundations. Originally it had 40 towers, with numerous additions made by the Romans, Genoese and Ottomans over the centuries.
The castle is a good spot for an afternoon's outing, and offers unsurpassed vistas over İzmir Bay.

Dario Moreno Street, with the Asansör in the background

Asansör
Open 7am–late.
Tel (0232) 261 26 26 (restaurant).

The Asansör is a working 19th-century elevator in the Karataş district. From its roof-top restaurant, there are fine views over the city.
Leafy Dario Moreno Street (Dario Moreno Sokağı) lies in a restored section of İzmir's old Jewish quarter. The street is named after a 1960s singer who was fond of the city.

Sights at a Glance

① Archaeology Museum
② Ethnographic Museum
③ Konak Clock Tower
④ Kızlarağası Han
⑤ St Polycarp Church
⑥ Agora
⑦ Velvet Castle

The Velvet Castle (Kadifekale), İzmir's ancient citadel

❽ Çeşme

🏛 21,120. 🚢 from Brindisi, Bari, Venice and Chios. 🚌 1 km (0.5 mile) S of ferry dock. 🅳 for local sights. ℹ️ İskele Meydanı 8, (0232) 712 66 53. 🛍 Wed and Sun; Sat (Alaçatı). 🎭 İzmir International Arts Festival (10 Jun–10 Jul).

The town's main feature is the 14th-century Genoese Castle of St Peter, a powerful symbol of Italian Renaissance mercantilism. Sultan Beyazıt II (1481–1512) fortified the castle to counter attacks by both pirates and the Knights of St John, who operated from bases on the island of Rhodes and at Bodrum (see pp200–1). The castle contains a **museum** with nautical exhibits. The hotel next to the harbour was formerly a kervansaray (see pp28–9).

Unlike other more popular resorts, Çeşme is dedicated to promenading, yachting and the simpler pleasures of life. There are several fine restaurants, and the cosmopolitan, tolerant atmosphere attracts world-class performers, who come here for the month-long İzmir International Arts Festival.

The long peninsula around Çeşme is serviced by a fast, six-lane highway from İzmir. However, you can still take the old road, stopping at beaches in Ilıca or spending an afternoon at Alaçatı, the kite- and windsurfing capital of Turkey, where wind energy supplies a quarter of the town's power requirements.

🏛 Museum
Çeşme Castle. **Open** 9am–noon & 1–5:30pm Tue–Sun. 🎫

Çeşme waterfront, with the Castle of St Peter above the town

❾ Selçuk

🏛 35,000. 🚆 from İzmir or Denizli. 🚌 Atatürk Cad. ℹ️ Agora Çarşısı 35 (0232) 892 63 28. 🆆 selcuk.gov.tr. 🛍 Sat. 🐪 Camel Wrestling (3rd and 4th week in Jan).

Visitors often bypass Selçuk on their way to Ephesus, but it deserves a stopover. The town is dominated by a 6th-century Byzantine citadel (Ayasoluk Hill) with 15 well-preserved towers. Nearby are the remains of a Byzantine church and a Seljuk mosque. You enter the citadel through a Byzantine gate. At the foot of the hill is the Basilica of St John, built by the Emperor Justinian (see p54) in the 6th century on the site of an earlier shrine. It is believed to contain the tomb of St John the Evangelist, who spent his later years at Ephesus during the 1st century. Restoration has brought back some of the basilica's former glory, and there are some fine frescoes in the chapel.

The **Ephesus Museum** is one of Turkey's best. Marble and bronze statues and frescoes are beautifully displayed, and exhibits include a sculpture of Artemis, jewels and numerous artifacts thought to have come from the nearby Artemision, the ancient Temple of Artemis (one of the Seven Wonders of the Ancient World). Today, the waterlogged ruins of the Artemision are home to storks who nest on the columns.

The İsa Bey Mosque, an ornate 14th-century Seljuk mosque, is located near the museum. It is not always open to visitors but the exterior calligraphy and inlaid tilework are worth a visit.

🏛 Ephesus Museum
Behind Tourism Information Office. **Tel** (0232) 892 60 10. **Open** 8:30am–noon & 12:30–5pm daily. 🎫

Environs
The former Greek village of Şirince, 8 km (5 miles) east of Selçuk, has a peaceful air that is welcoming after the bustle of Ephesus.

At Çamlık is the **Open-Air Steam Train Exhibition**, a museum run by Turkish State Railways. There are more than 24 steam locomotives and other railway vehicles on display at the site.

🏛 Open-Air Steam Train Exhibition
Çamlık, 12 km (7 miles) S of Selçuk on the E87. 🎫

❿ Ephesus

See pp186–7.

Byzantine gateway in Selçuk, at the foot of Ayasoluk Hill

⓫ Kuşadası

🏙 50,000. 🚢 from Samos (Apr–
Oct). 🚌 from Selçuk, Söke and İzmir.
🚏 1 km (0.5 mile) S of town centre
on Söke road. ℹ️ Liman Cad 13,
(0256) 614 11 03. 🛍 Wed.

Kuşadası is a frequent port
of call for luxury cruise liners.
Only Bodrum and Istanbul
can match it for fast-paced,
hedonistic nightlife.

The town's name, meaning
"bird island", is taken from an
islet, known as Pigeon Island,
tacked onto the mainland by
a causeway. A 14th-century
Genoese fort reveals the town's
commercial origins.

Environs

Dilek Peninsula National Park
protects the last of Turkey's
wild horses and rare Anatolian
cheetahs. The military presence
has ensured that the area has
been left undisturbed. Hike
to the summit of Samsun Dağı
(ancient Mount Mycale) for
fine views of the peninsula.

🏞 Dilek Peninsula
National Park

Dilek Yarımadası Milli Parkı 18 km
(11 miles) W of Söke. 🚌 from Kuşadası
or Söke. **Tel** (0256) 646 10 79. **Open**
8am–6pm daily. 🚗 extra for vehicles.

Camel wrestling, a popular event in Aydın

⓬ Aydın

🏙 150,000. 🚌 700 m (0.5 mile) S of
town centre. 🚉 from İzmir and
Denizli. ℹ️ Adnan Menderes Mah-
Denizli Bul 2, (0256) 211 28 42. 🛍 Tue.
🐪 Camel Wrestling (Sep–Mar), Fig
Festival (1st week in Sep), Chestnut
Festival (Dec).

Known in Roman times
as Tralles, Aydın's tranquil
appearance stems from long
periods of prosperity. It was
known variously as Caesarea
and Güzelhisar before falling
under Ottoman rule in the
late 14th century. Frequent
earthquakes have meant that
there are few ruins to be seen,
and the region is still subject
to tremors.

The region is famous for its
figs (*incir*), black olives, cereals,
and cotton, and Aydın is a
leading exporter of snails and
salmon. In the 1920s,
Atatürk (*see p62*)
targeted the region as
the focus of a new state-
owned cotton industry.
Today, raw cotton and
ready-to-wear clothing
remain Turkey's biggest
export commodities.

Suffering badly
in the War of Indep-
endence (*see p62*),
nowadays Aydın is more
peaceful, with a **museum** and
several distinctive mosques.

🏛 Museum

W of gardens. **Tel** (0256) 225 22 59.
Open 9am–noon, 1:30–5pm Tue–Sun.
📷 🖼 🅿️

⓭ Menderes River Valley

One of Turkey's main grain-
growing regions, and a major
producer of fruit and cotton,
the Menderes Valley is made up
of the Büyük Menderes (Great
Meander) and Küçük Menderes
(Lesser Meander) rivers, with a
wide alluvial plain in between.
The S-shaped bends formed
by the slow-moving Büyük
Menderes below Aydın have
given us the word "meander".

Nysa, a Seleucid foundation
dating from around 280 BC,
presents a lovely sight as you
approach from Sultanhisar (just
to the south). There is a theatre
overlooking a tributary of
the Büyük Menderes, and a
gymnasium, library, agora and
council house. The whole city
is built in and over a ravine
(although the bridge is in poor
condition). Its claim to fame
was as a sanctuary to Pluto,
god of the underworld.

At **Tire**, north of Aydın, lie
the remains of a number of
kervansarays (*see pp28–9*) dating
from the 14th and 15th centuries.
In the wake of the capture of
Constantinople in 1453,
Mehmet II (*see p58*) ordered
the removal of the inhabitants
of Tire, as part of the effort to
repopulate the capital. There is a
dramatic domed bazaar building
here and a lively bazaar is still
held each week on Tuesdays.

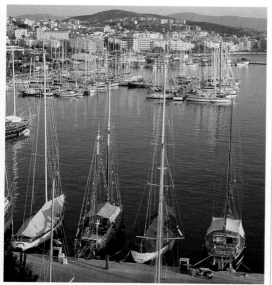

The yacht marina at Kuşadası, one of the largest on the Aegean coast

⑩ Ephesus

Ephesus is one of the greatest ruined cities in the western world. A Greek city was first built here in about 1000 BC and it soon rose to fame as a centre for the worship of Cybele, the Anatolian Mother Goddess. The city we see today was founded in the 4th century BC by Alexander the Great's successor, Lysimachus. But it was under the Romans that Ephesus became the chief port on the Aegean. Most of the surviving structures date from this period. As the harbour silted up the city declined, but played an important role in the spread of Christianity. Two great Councils of the early Church were held here in AD 431 and 449. It is said that the Virgin Mary spent her last days nearby and that St John the Evangelist came from the island of Patmos to look after her.

Restored Mural
Murals in the houses opposite the Temple of Hadrian indicate that these were the homes of wealthy people.

★ Library of Celsus
Built in AD 114–117 by Consul Gaius Julius Aquila for his father, the library was damaged first by the Goths and then by an earthquake in 1000. The statues occupying the niches in front are Sophia (wisdom), Arete (virtue), Ennoia (intellect) and Episteme (knowledge).

The House of Mary

According to the Bible, the crucified Jesus asked St John the Evangelist to look after his mother, Mary. John brought Mary with him to Ephesus in AD 37, and she spent the last years of her life here in a modest stone house. The house of the Blessed Virgin is located at Meryemana, 6 km (4 miles) from the centre of Ephesus. The shrine, known as the Meryemana Kultur Parkı, is revered by both Christians and Muslims, and pilgrims of both faiths visit the shrine, especially on 15 August every year.

The house of the Blessed Virgin

| 0 metres | 200 |
| 0 yards | 200 |

For hotels and restaurants in this area see pp330–39 and pp346–61

★ Theatre
Carved into the flank of Mt Pion during the Hellenistic period, the theatre was later renovated by the Romans.

★ Temple of Hadrian
Built to honour a visit by Hadrian in AD 123, the relief marble work on the façade portrays mythical gods and goddesses.

Gate of Hercules
The gate at the entrance to Curetes Street takes its name from two reliefs showing Hercules draped in a lion skin. Originally a two-storey structure, and believed to date from the 4th century AD, it had a large central arch with winged victories on the upper corners of the archway. Curetes Street was lined by statues of civic notables.

KEY

① **Temple of Domitian**

② **Private houses** featured murals and mosaics.

③ **The brothel** was adorned with a statue of Priapus, the Greek god of fertility.

④ **The Commercial Agora** was the main marketplace of the city.

⑤ **The *skene*** (stage building) featured elaborate ornamentation.

⑥ **Marble Street** was paved with blocks of marble.

⑦ **The Odeon** (meeting hall) was built in AD 150.

⑧ **Colonnaded Street** Lined with Ionic and Corinthian columns, the street runs from the Baths of Varius to the Temple of Domitian.

⑨ **Baths of Varius**

Spectacular travertine pools at Pamukkale ▶

★ **Tetrapylon**
One of the jewels of Aphrodisias, this 2nd-century gateway was reconstructed with four groups of Corinthian columns.

VISITORS' CHECKLIST

Practical Information
Between Aydın and Denizli, 40 km (24 miles) S of E87 highway to Geyre.
Tel (0256) 448 80 86 (museum).
Open 8am–5pm daily.

Sculptures
Works produced by the city's famous school of sculpture were exported as far afield as North Africa and Rome. Some are exhibited in the museum.

★ **Temple of Aphrodite**
Completed in the 1st century AD, the temple was the heart of Aphrodisias. It was later converted for Christian worship, with walls and colonnades dismantled and reused to enlarge and modify the building.

Plan of Aphrodisias

0 metres 50
0 yards 50

North Temenos Complex
Temple of Aphrodite
Odeon
Tetrapylon
Museum
• Agora
Sebasteion
Portico of Tiberius
Large Basilica
Theatre
Theatre Baths

Key
■ Building

The Atatürk Ethnography Museum in Denizli

⓰ Denizli

🏠 275,000. 🛈 554/1 Sokak 5, (0258) 264 39 71.

Denizli is often thought of as a tourist backwater, but the town has little need to pander to visitors. It is a thriving agricultural centre, a centre for carpet production and one of Turkey's major textile towns, continuing a prosperous trade begun as far back as Roman times. Today, Aegean cotton fibres fetch more on world markets than many other spun cottons.

Denizli, literally translated as "with sea", takes its name from the many springs that feed the River Lycus. In pre-Roman times, another city linked with water, Hydrela, was located here. Denizli is a good base for touring the ancient sites of Hierapolis and Pamukkale *(see pp190–91)*, the latter being about 22 km (16 miles) away.

The town was conquered by the Seljuks in the 11th century and came under Ottoman rule in 1428. At some point in between, when Denizli was known as Ladik, it seems that the inhabitants of nearby Laodiceia moved here after their own city was ravaged by one of the many earthquakes that have marked this region.

The **Atatürk Ethnography Museum** has some interesting local folk art and decorative artifacts on display. Denizli's Great Mosque (Ulu Camii) is also worth a visit.

🏛 **Atatürk Ethnography Museum**
Kayalık Cad, Saraylar Mah 459 Sok 10.
Tel (0258) 262 00 66. **Open** 8am–5pm Tue–Sun (to 7pm summer).

The Temple of Athena at Priene, a superb example of Ionian architecture

⑰ Priene

D from Söke or Milas to Güllübahçe.
Open 8am–7pm (5pm in winter)
daily. 🖼

The ancient city of Priene has
a breathtaking setting between
the Büyük Menderes River and
Mount Mykale. Like Miletus and
Ephesus (see pp186–7), it was a
member of the Ionian League, a
group of 12 city-states believed
to have been settled by Greek
colonists before 1000 BC.

Laid out by the architect
Hippodamos of Miletus in
about 450 BC, Priene is in a
good state of preservation.
The Temple of Athena, built in
the 4th century BC in honour
of the city's patron goddess,
is considered one of the great
achievements of Ionian
architecture. The work was
supervised and financed by
Alexander the Great (see pp52–3)
when he occupied the city.
Because of Priene's strong Greek
ties, it was not viewed with
favour by the Romans. Its
importance declined and by
Byzantine times it had
been abandoned. This
neglect has meant
that Priene is one of the
most intact Hellenistic
settlements to be
seen. The theatre, dating
from the 3rd century BC,
could seat 5,000 people.
The bou leuterion

(council chamber) could hold
640 delegates. There is also
a stadium, complete with
starting blocks for athletes,
and sanctuaries to Demeter
and Kore. The lower gymnasium
walls are adorned with
schoolboy graffiti from over
2,000 years ago!

⑱ Miletus

D from Söke or Milas. Directions: take
the road that descends to Didyma,
turn W at the village of Akköy, 7km
(4 miles) from the main road. 🖼

Although less impressive than
Priene, Miletus was more
renowned for its art, politics and
trade than many other Greek
cities. Known as Milet today,
it was once the principal port
of the Ionian League, and
flourished as a centre for art

Ilyas Bey Mosque, built in the 15th century at Miletus

and industry. In Roman times
it supplied wool and textile dyes
to the wool trade in Ankara
(see p244). One of its sons, the
scientist and mathematician
Thales – known as one of the
Seven Sages of Antiquity –
correctly forecast a total eclipse
of the sun in 580 BC.

The Persians took control of
the Ionian cities in the mid-6th
century BC. Miletus led a revolt
against Persian rule in 500–494
BC, but in 479 BC succumbed
to the tyrannical Persian
king, Darius. It was rebuilt
by the Romans.

Of the surviving buildings, the
finest is the 15,000-seat theatre,
dating from AD 100. Over the
centuries, Greeks, Romans
and Byzantines all made
alterations to the structure.
The bouleuterion (council
chamber) was built in 175–164
BC during the reign of the
Seleucid king, Antiochus IV
Ephiphanes. The well-preserved
Baths of Faustina date from AD
43, and were named for the
wife of Emperor Marcus
Aurelius. The complex
includes a palaestra
(gymnasium), and there
is a stadium nearby.
The Baths of Faustina
was a model for the
development of the
Turkish bath, or hamam
(see p81). It is also worth
strolling around the

stadium, nymphaeum (reservoir) and shrine of Apollo Delphinius (built in 500 BC).

Incongruously, a mosque reposes amid the ruins of ancient Miletus. The İlyas Bey (or Balat) Mosque was built in 1403 by İlyas Bey, emir (ruler) of the Beylik of Menteşe. It celebrated his return from exile at the court of the Mongol ruler Timur, also known as Tamerlane (see p57), after Timur's invasion of Anatolia in 1402. The mosque is built of brick and both white and coloured marble that was taken from Roman Miletus. There is splendidly detailed carving on the marble window grilles, screen and prayer niche (mihrab), and the use of coloured marble on the façade is impressive. The dome measures 14 m (45 ft) in diameter and was the largest built during the Beylik period (see p57). İlyas Bey died the year after the mosque was completed and is buried in the adjacent tomb (dated 1404). The mosque is a beautiful early forerunner of the Ottoman külliye (see p36), a building style that flourished during the 16th century. The külliye combined social welfare and residential functions with facilities for Islamic worship.

The Temple of Apollo in Didyma, with its ornate carved columns

⑰ Didyma

🚍 from Söke or Milas to Yenihisar. 🚌 from Bodrum twice a week in summer (check first). 🛈 Kaymakamlık Binası, (0256) 811 37 25. **Open** 9am–7pm (5pm in winter) daily. 🏞

The prime reason to visit Didyma (modern Didim) is for the Temple of Apollo, built in the 7th century BC to honour the god of prophecy and oracles. By 500 BC, the shrine at Didyma was one of the leading oracles of the Greek world. It even had a sacred spring. Branchid priests, who were reputedly connected to the great oracle at Delphi, were in charge of the shrine. Marble from nearby Lake Bafa (see p196) was used to build the temple. A carved relief of the head of

Head of Medusa, Didyma

Medusa, with its serpentine curls, has become almost synonymous with Didyma.

The well below the Medusa head was the place where arriving pilgrims would purify themselves before approaching the oracle. It is now roped off to prevent accidents.

In its heyday, the Temple of Apollo featured 108 Ionic columns. Only three are still intact. However, the surviving stumps are still impressive.

The Temple of Apollo was destroyed by Persians in the mid-6th century BC, but was restored around 350 BC by Alexander the Great. With the coming of Christianity, the temple was converted into a church and Didyma became a bishopric. In 1493, an earthquake destroyed the temple and Didyma was abandoned. The Ottomans renamed it Yenihisar (new castle) in the 18th century.

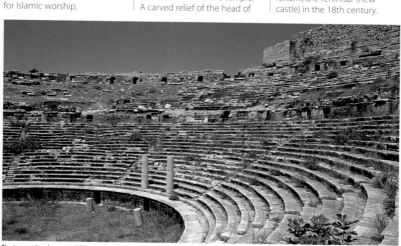

The impressive theatre at Miletus, capable of seating 15,000 in Roman times

⑳ Lake Bafa

25 km (16 miles) W of Söke. ■ via
Söke or Milas. 🎭 ◻ ♨ ⬆ Ⓓ 🏃

Considered one of the most
picturesque landscapes in
Turkey, the Lake Bafa area is
the setting for several classical
gems, with the peaks of Mount
Latmos as a backdrop. Rising
to 1,500 m (4,915 ft), the
mountain is aptly known as
Beş Parmak (five fingers).

In ancient times, Lake Bafa
was an arm of the sea. When silt
eventually closed the gulf, the
port of **Herakleia**, near the
eastern shore of the lake, was left
landlocked. The same process
was responsible for the decline of
Miletus and Priene *(see pp194–5)*.
Lake Bafa is brackish and
supports many species of fish.

Herakleia, also known as
Herakleia-under-Latmos,
occupies a dramatic setting
at the lakeside. Its fortifications,
towers and well-preserved
Temple of Athena are tangible
vestiges of its former status.
In such settings, legends are
fostered: a young shepherd,
unrequited love and eternal
sleep are part of local lore.
A shrine to the shepherd-hero,
Endymion, can be visited near
the lake. There are some
difficult-to-reach monasteries
high up the mountain.

Herakleia

10 km (6 miles) from Camiçi (by car
on track). 🚤 from Lake Bafa.

Environs

Euromos, located to the
southeast of Lake Bafa, wholly
deserves its reputation as having
one of the best preserved

Lake Bafa, an arm of the Aegean in ancient times

temples in Turkey. Euromos
was, in fact, an amalgamation
of several cities, including
Herakleia, owing allegiance to
Milas *(see p197)*. In time, rivalries
emerged between them, and
Euromos (meaning "strong" in
Greek) turned out to be
politically fickle. Like many cities
of ancient Caria, it opted to ally
itself with Rome and Rhodes,
not Greece.

🏛 Euromos

12 km (7 miles) NW of Milas. Ⓓ from
Selimiya to Milas. **Open** 8am–7pm
(5pm in winter).

㉑ Altınkum

4 km (3 miles) S of Didyma. 🅰 2,300.
Ⓓ via Priene and Miletus.

The protected sandy bay of
Altınkum offers a relaxing spot
to unwind, especially after a day
spent tramping around classical
ruins. Most day trips to Priene,
Miletus and Didyma *(see pp194–
5)* end up here. In fact, locals
generally refer to the area

as Didyma, or Didim (on bus
schedules, for example). Like
many idyllic retreats that have
experienced rapid growth,
Didyma's success has spilled over
to nearby towns. Charter groups
and tours flock to Altınkum and
it can be very busy in summer.
This was one of Turkey's original
camping venues. As it grew,
pensions opened, and Turkish
families began to flock here for
sun and sand. There is not much
else here – for anything more,
you will have to go to Yenihisar
(ancient Didyma). Few people
know how to enjoy themselves
as much as Turks, and Altınkum
finds them in full holiday mode.

㉒ Labranda

15 km (9 miles) N of Milas on
unsurfaced track (by car, taxi, or on
foot from Milas). **Open** 8am–7:30pm
(5pm in winter).

Getting to Labranda is certainly
worth the effort for those who
persevere. This Carian sanctuary
nestles high on the mountains
above Milas, at an impressive
elevation of 610 m (2,000 ft),
giving good views of the
surrounding area. From early
times, it fell under the jurisdiction
of Milas (Mylasa). The remains
of the sacred way leading there
are one of the sights to note.

Despite being damaged by
several fires and earthquakes,
the remains of a stadium have
been uncovered by Swedish
archaeologists. Baths and a
fountain house (which may
have been a water storage

The popular beach at Altınkum

depot) date from about the 1st century BC and the area still boasts an abundant source of spring water. The most interesting buildings are three androns (banqueting halls), the second built by Mausolus (see p198), who ruled from nearby Milas.

The chamber tombs and sarcophagi, although pillaged, are unusual and reveal much about ancient burial practices.

㉓ Milas (Mylasa)

🏠 42,000. ✈ 13 km (8 miles) SW of town, (0252) 523 01 01. 🚌 Intercity buses to Bodrum. ℹ at airport, (0252) 523 00 66. 🛍 Tue.

The origins of Milas are uncertain and the many theories are largely unsubstantiated. What is clear is that its most noteworthy and prosperous period was when it was capital of Caria and the administrative seat for the Persian satrap (subordinate ruler), Mausolus. Like most Carian cities, Milas was ruled in turn by the Persians, Alexander the Great, the Romans and the Byzantines before finally falling under Ottoman control in 1425.

The remains of the ancient city lie within the present town centre. The first thing you notice is the two-storey **Gümüşkesen** (silver money-bag) **Mausoleum**, a structure of uncertain age. The lower floor is the actual tomb, with an aperture in the roof to provide sustenance to the deceased. The town's most intact monument is the handsome Baltılı (Axe) Gate.

As an administrative seat, Milas issued regulatory decrees, notably concerning money. Inscriptions dating from the 3rd century AD list detailed regulations that ban illegal conversions from imperial (Roman) to local money and black-market money dealings.

Save some time for modern Milas, which has some charming timber houses with lattice-work shutters. The town

The Gümüşkesen Mausoleum, a Carian monument in Milas

is justly famed for its carpets, characterized by soft neutral and beige tones.

Environs
Yatağan, site of a thermal power station and known for its environmental pollution, has little to offer, but two interesting sights are located in the area. **Stratonikeia** was founded in 295 BC. It was apparently named after the wife of Seleucas I, king of Syria. The ruins to be seen – an agora (market-place), a rather unkempt Hellenistic theatre with seating for 10,000 and the Temple of Sarapis – are in the village of Eskihisar on the 330 road, south of the city.

The town's small museum houses mainly Roman finds but includes a Mycenaean mug from about 1000 BC.

Lagina is located northwest of Yatağan and is best known for its association with the cult of Hecate, the Greek goddess

Local carpet in Milas

of darkness and sorcery. The gate of the temple precinct dates from between 125 and 80 BC. The Temple of Hecate would have stood here but the site has not yielded major finds.

🏛 **Stratonikeia**
20 km (12 miles) W of Milas. Own transport. 🚌 on main Yatağan–Milas road. 🅿

🏛 **Lagina**
15 km (9 miles) N of Yatağan. Own transport essential.

㉔ Güllük

🏠 5,600. 🚌 from Milas, 28 km (17 miles) SE of Güllük, then 8 km (5 miles) to town.

This is a lovely bay and harbour with a genuine nautical atmosphere and lots of accommodation. The real reason for coming to Güllük is to see the site of ancient **Iasus**, with its elaborate wall, 810 m (2,658 ft) long, built during the 5th century AD.

The fortunes of Iasus were tied to fishing. Bronze Age finds from here bear detailed inscriptions that have shed new light on the lifestyles of the ancients. Legends of boys frolicking with dolphins also originated here.

Almost opposite Güllük on the main 330 road is the site of Cindya. To the south is the ancient Barbylia (modern Varvil Bay), a town that grew wealthy by trading in salt.

🏛 **Iasus**
🚤 by boat from Güllük to Kıyıkışlacık. 18 km (11 miles) from main Milas road.

The large ruined theatre at Stratonikeia

㉕ Bodrum

Bodrum is the modern name for the ancient Dorian city of Halicarnassus, location of the famous Mausoleum built by Mausolus (375–53 BC), ruler of ancient Caria, who made the city his capital. The city walls, also built by Mausolus, were almost destroyed during Alexander the Great's siege in the 4th century BC. Herodotus, the father of written history, was born here in 484 BC, as was Dionysius, the great rhetoric teacher of the 1st century BC. Modern Bodrum was the first Turkish town to experience a tourist boom, its major sight being the 15th-century Castle of St Peter *(see pp200–1)*, now a museum of nautical archaeology.

The busy harbour, attracting cruising yachts of all sizes

Exploring Bodrum

Bodrum is subtly divided by the Castle of St Peter into a bustling, vehicle-free eastern sector with beaches and a quieter western hub which borders the yacht harbour. Dolmuşes make transport easy. Those marked "Şehir İçi" (inner city) stop at all major points. Boat trips to nearby beaches are also available from the harbour.

Halikarnas Disco

Cumhuriyet Cad, No 178.
Open Apr–Sep. **Tel** (0252) 316 80 00.
ⓦ halikarnas.com.tr

Located at the water's edge with a view of the Castle of St Peter, open-air Halikarnas is one of the most famous nightclubs in Turkey and an emblem of hedonistic nightlife. With a capacity of 5,000, Halikarnas offers a spectacular laser light show and the best DJs. The open-air cabaret, revue and musical acts feature top performers. Smart dress is required.

🏛 Zeki Müren Museum

Zeki Müren Sanat Müzesi
Zeki Müren Cad 11. **Tel** (0252) 313 19 39. **Open** Tue–Sun. 📷

Zeki Müren (1931–96) was one of Turkey's most accomplished and beloved singers and composers, with a career that spanned 45 years. He was fondly known as "The Sun of Art" and, although considered the Turkish Liberace, only the glitzy attire was comparable. Müren was a professional musician, actor and his unpretentious home is preserved as a delightful museum. His extravagant

The famous open-air Halikarnas nightclub

costumes are in the limelight along with record albums, radiograms and other musical and personal memorabilia.

Rooms and furnishings seem to be anticipating his arrival, for example the 1950s' Cadillac reposing on the front lawn.

The museum is an inspiring memory to an outstanding Turkish cultural idol, who died in 1996 during a live performance. Thousands attended his funeral.

🛁 Bodrum Hamam

Cevat Şakir Cad, Fabrika Sok (opposite the bus station).
Open 6am–midnight daily.
Tel (0252) 313 41 29.
ⓦ hamam.com. 📷

Linked to the Çemberlitaş Baths in Istanbul, the Bodrum Hamam is housed in a lovely old stone building. Service is highly professional, emphasizing cleanliness and an authentic Turkish bath experience. Masseurs are well-trained and you are bound to feel like a "new penny" when you exit. The owners claim a 500-year lineage. The hamam runs a shuttle that will collect and return you, suitably pampered.

🏛 Old Dockyard (Tersane) and Arsenal Point

W of the marina entrance at the end of Neyzen Tevfik Cad.
Open dawn to dusk. 📷

The ancient dockyard on the end of Arsenal Point is part of the effort to restore Bodrum's walls. Its position, opposite the Castle of St Peter, overlooks the main harbour. The dockyard was built in the 18th century, when the Ottoman sultans made an attempt to revive the empire's naval strength. Attractions include a cistern, an Ottoman Tower on the west side of the harbour, a graveyard, fortification to protect the shipyard and a grand tomb built in 1729 to commemorate Cafer Paşa, who was a naval hero and prominent city patron.

The scant remains of the great Mausoleum

Mausoleum

Turgut Reis Cad (corner of Hamam Sok). **Open** 8am–noon & 1:30–5pm Tue–Sun.

The colossal Mausoleum of Halicarnassus was one of the Seven Wonders of the Ancient World. Named for Mausolus, ruler of Caria, and intended as his tomb, work on the structure began in 355 BC and was completed by his widow, Artemisia, the only woman to rule Caria. It measured 41 m (134 ft) in height, with a podium, a colonnade of 36 columns and a pyramid, resplendently topped by a horse-drawn chariot statue.

The tomb stood for about 1,500 years but had fallen into ruin by 1402, when the Knights of St John arrived and used many of the stones to construct the Castle of St Peter.

As you enter, don't miss the authentic reconstruction models to the left.

Antique Theatre

Kıbrıs Şehitler Cad (N of the Mausoleum). **Open** dawn to dusk.

Little remains of the ancient city of Halicarnassus, but the theatre on the south slopes of the Göktepe district is one of the more intact sites. Excavations began here in 1973 and restoration still goes on. Dating from the 4th century BC, the theatre consists of a stage building, an orchestra and rows of seating. It was probably used

The Myndos Gate, the western portal of the city in ancient times

more for gladiatorial fights than for theatrical performances. The unusual balustrades in the orchestra may have been put there to protect spectators!

Myndos Gate

Cafer Paşa Cad. **Open** dawn to dusk.

The Myndos Gate was the western exit from ancient Halicarnassus and originally featured two monumental towers made of andesite blocks. The gate and most of the city walls were demolished by Alexander the Great and his army in 334 BC. The structure was restored in 1998.

Bodrum City Centre

① Halikarnas Disco
② Zeki Müren Museum
③ Bodrum Hamam
④ Castle of St Peter
　(see pp200–1)
⑤ Old Dockyard and Arsenal Point
⑥ Mausoleum
⑦ Antique Theatre

For keys to symbols *see back flap*

Castle of St Peter

Bodrum's most distinctive landmark is its castle, begun in 1406 by the Knights of St John *(see p231)*. Its five towers represented the languages of its formidable inhabitants. When Süleyman the Magnificent conquered Rhodes in 1523, both Bodrum and Rhodes came under Ottoman rule and the knights left for Malta. Neglected for centuries, the castle became a prison in 1895 and was damaged by shells from a French warship during World War I. In the early 1960s, it was used to store artifacts found by local sponge divers. This led to a fruitful Turkish-American partnership to restore the castle and put on display the spectacular undersea treasures found around Turkey. The innovative reconstructions of ancient shipwrecks and their cargoes have brought the museum international acclaim.

German Tower
This tower is on the walkway around the battlements.

★ **Glass Shipwreck Hall**
A steel frame supports the original timbers of a Fatimid-Byzantine ship thought to have sunk in 1025. The glass shards and ingots, among other finds, make this a time capsule of the era.

KEY

① **The Commander's Tower** forms the inner entrance to the castle and details some World War I history.

② **Castle moat**

③ **Land-facing battlements**

④ **The Glass Hall** displays Mycenaean beads and Damascus glass, including some items dating from the 15th century BC. Syrian glass ingots, used in the production of glass items, date from the 14th century BC.

⑤ **Spanish (or Snake) Tower**

⑥ **Gatineau Tower**

⑦ **French Tower**

⑧ **Italian Tower**

⑨ **Carian Princess Hall**

⑩ **5th-century BC shipwreck**

⑪ **Chapel and Eastern Roman Shipwreck**

Outer entrance

★ **Amphora Exhibit**
Earthenware jars and pots were used to transport oil, wine and dry foods in ancient times. Pointed bases allowed for upright storage in layers.

View of the Castle Across the Harbour
Medieval engineers ensured that the castle was virtually immune to attack. It even had secure water supplies.

English Tower
Also known as the Lion Tower, it was one of England's first foreign projects funded by taxpayers.

★ Late Bronze-Age Shipwrecks
Ancient nautical life and trade are captured in this life-size replica of a ship that sank off Kaş (see p218) in the 14th century BC.

Diver recovering amphorae from the floor of the Mediterranean

Diving for Treasure

Many underwater treasures were located accidentally by sponge divers who risked their health and endurance working at depths of 40–50 m (131–164 ft). Some of the museum's priceless displays are the result of more than 20,000 dives and painstaking scientific research by experts and restorers. The partnership between the museum and the Institute of Nautical Archaeology has made Bodrum a showpiece of historical treasures beautifully preserved in their last port of call.

㉖ Bodrum Peninsula Tour

The Bodrum Peninsula was originally peopled by the Lelegians, migrants from mainland Greece who maintained historic ties to the Carians. There were eight Lelegian cities, dating from as early as the 4th or 5th century BC. Myndos was the most prominent, but Pedasa offers the most to see.

Today, the Bodrum Peninsula is renowned as a holiday paradise. Its secluded bays are ideal for yachting, watersports and getting away from it all. The windmills to be seen on the hills were once used to grind grain. The terrain varies from lush coniferous forests to rocky cliffs and sandy coasts. The coastline claimed many ancient ships and some of their treasures are displayed in Bodrum's Castle of St Peter *(see pp200–1)*.

⑥ Yalıkavak
Formerly an important sponge-fishing port, Yalıkavak is an ideal spot for a meal. Local delicacies include sea beans and stuffed marrow flowers.

⑤ Gümüşlük (Myndos)
Gümüşlük occupies the site of ancient Myndos, founded by King Mausolus *(see pp198–9)* in about 350 BC. The remains of a sunken city lie offshore.

④ Kadıkalesi
The town takes its name from *kadı*, (Arabic for "judge"), after a former resident. The old Greek church (now awaiting restoration) on the hill is the most intact Greek building in the area. Tangerine groves are a beautiful sight, either in blossom or bearing fruit, and there are superb views of the nearby islets.

③ Turgut Reis
The town is named after a famous Ottoman admiral and naval hero. The rich alluvial soil is perfect for growing figs, which abound in this area.

Aegean Sea

Bahçe

Yakaköy

Gürece

Akçaalam

Bağla

Cıfit

Akyarlar

Bağla Bay

Key

▬ Tour route

═ Other road

Küçük Tavşan Island

0 kilometres 5

0 miles 2.5

Gölköy

Yulk Gölköy

Torba

stafa Paşa ower

330

Bodrum

Gümbet

İç Island

Karaada Island

⑦ **Göl Türkbükü**
Two neighbouring towns, Gölköy and Türkbükü, amalgamated their names in 1999. Watersports are a speciality here. The area is a hideaway for celebrities.

① **Pedasa**
Though difficult to reach, Pedasa is worth the journey. The ruins cover about 2.5 sq km (1 sq mile), and show a typical Lelegian town. Extensive research and restoration is being done on the site, which includes the remains of a citadel, main gate, rampart walls and castle keep.

② **Ortakent**
This inland village boasts the imposing 17th-century Mustafa Paşa Tower, a rare example of local architecture. It is one of the easiest sights to reach on the peninsula, and has abundant water and lovely orchards.

Tips for Drivers

Tour length: 100–120 km (63–75 miles), with paved roads and two-way traffic most of the way. The tour can be done by dolmuß, but it is then more difficult to see the ancient sites.
🅳 Turgut Reis, (0252) 382 39 33. Turgut Reis is the only major town, with a number of petrol stations and amenities.
When to go: Any time of year.

㉗ Marmaris

Like most of the resorts along the Aegean coast, it is difficult to envisage Marmaris as the quaint fishing village it used to be. The stretch of beach, now lined with hotels, extended to the main street until the 1990s. Marmaris was extensively damaged by an earthquake in 1957, which destroyed most of the old town. Today the rebuilt (and greatly expanded) town is a top holiday destination.

Ancient inscriptions indicate that Marmaris was once the Dorian city of Physcus, attached to the city of Lindos and part of the island state of Rhodes. Süleyman the Magnificent *(see pp60–61)* assembled a mighty fleet here in 1522 to prepare for his conquest of Rhodes, at which time he regained possession of the Datça Peninsula *(see pp206–7)* and had Marmaris Castle rebuilt.

Exploring Marmaris

Few places can compete with Marmaris' exclusive setting in a sheltered bay rimmed with oleanders, liquidambar trees and pine forests. All major attractions are located within a few metres of the seafront and can be reached on foot. The harbour and quay extend along a beach walkway that runs the length of the town.

Netsel Marina
Tel (0252) 412 27 08 and 412 14 39.
ⓦ netselmarina.com

Turkey's largest and most luxurious marina has it all – parking, top-class restaurants, entertainment, bars, excellent shops and plenty of service facilities such as banks, ATMs and travel agents. All major currencies and credit cards are accepted for mooring, refuelling and other marina services. Among several yacht brokerage firms here, **Gino Marine** will organize luxury charter cruises for a view of Marmaris from the water. There is berthing for over 750 yachts up to 40 m (130 ft) in length.

The Netsel call sign on VHF channel 06 is "Port Marmaris". Marmaris is a safe anchorage, with no underwater currents, sandbanks or rocks, and can be approached night and day in most weather conditions.

Gino Marine
Tel (0252) 412 06 76.
ⓦ ginogroup.com

Bar Street
Hacı Mustafa Sokağı.

Most tourist towns have their bars and pubs concentrated on a couple of streets. Those in Marmaris occupy much of Hacı Mustafa Sokağı. Despite the noise, it is always worth strolling along the street to observe those who want to be observed. Some of the bars have been nicely done up and, decibels aside, this is not an unattractive area. There are also a number of hotels and pensions in the area, but visitors in search of rest and relaxation would do better to look elsewhere.

Restored Greek houses in the Old Quarter near the harbour

🏠 Greek Revival Houses in Old Quarter
Tepe Mahallesi.

The Old Quarter around the Castle is by far the most charming part of Marmaris. Many houses that were either abandoned or derelict have been restored to their original appearance. Most belong to professional people who seem to be accustomed to strangers peeking into a shady courtyard or admiring a handsome brass knocker. Karaca Restaurant, just outside the entrance to the Castle, has a well-preserved interior. From the top terrace of the restaurant, you will get a wonderful view of the town and its numerous delightful "barbecue" chimneys. See if you can spot the one and only remaining original Greek chimney from here. As you wander the cool and shady lanes above the bustle of the harbour, you could find yourself wishing that some of Turkey's other coastal resorts had retained the same quaint neighbourhood appeal as this corner of Marmaris.

Netsel Marina, offering a complete service to touring yachts

For hotels and restaurants in this area see pp330–39 and pp346–61

The Castle, incorporating a nautical museum

🏛 Castle and Museum

Tel (0252) 412 14 59. Open 8am–noon & 1–5pm Tue–Sun. 📷

The original castle was rebuilt by Süleyman the Magnificent in 1522 after his successful campaign against Rhodes. Today, the restored structure is a museum housing a small collection of nautical items. There are also inscriptions and sculptures displayed in the courtyard. More engaging for most visitors, however, will be the panoramic view of the harbour and old renovated Greek houses.

🛍 Bazaar

Entrance from Kordon Caddesi and the street beside the tourist office.

You may find a unique item among the tourist bric-a-brac offered up for sale in the bazaar, among the leather goods, jewellery, herbs, spices and teas. A delicious local speciality is Marmaris honey, which is produced along the scenic Datça Peninsula *(see pp206–7)*. Both pine *(çam)* or flower *(çiçek)* honey are fragrant, thick and dark.

Marmaris honey

VISITORS' CHECKLIST

Practical Information

🏔 35,000. ℹ İskele Meydanı (central harbour), (0252) 412 10 35. 🗓 Thu. ⛵ Yacht Race Week (Oct/Nov every year).

Transport

🚢 from Rhodes. ✈ Dalaman, 120 km (75 miles) E of town, (0252) 792 52 91. 🚌 NE of town centre on Muğla road.

By the end of October the last of the honey and fresh summer produce will have been sold.

Environs

A number of large holiday villages are located in **İçmeler**, about 6 km (4 miles) around the bay from Marmaris. Transport to and from Marmaris is easy, as dolmuşes make the trip on a regular basis. İçmeler lacks the quaint atmosphere of an old Turkish town, as do many parts of Marmaris, but visitors (particularly families) prefer the more up-to-date facilities and much cleaner beaches here.

Marmaris Town Centre

① Netsel Marina
② Bar Street
③ Greek Revival Houses in Old Quarter
④ Castle and Museumi
⑤ Bazaar

❽ Datça Peninsula Tour

The narrow finger of the Datça Peninsula, pointing westward from Marmaris, lies at the place where the Mediterranean and the Aegean meet. Locals claim that the air is rich in oxygen, thanks to the prevailing wind *(meltem)* and the mixing of salinity levels and current patterns in the sea. The route along the peninsula follows narrow and twisting roads, affording glimpses of the sea through pine-clad gullies. At the western tip, about 35 km (21 miles) west of Datça, lie the ruins of Knidos, one of the most prosperous port cities of antiquity. In its heyday it was home to an eminent medical school. Here, you can lunch on seafood, and swim in the sheltered bay.

⑤ **Knidos**
This port was the site of a shrine of Aphrodite, dating from about 360 BC. The remains of a theatre, agora, houses and a round temple are visible today.

Gulf of Gökova

Murdalabük
Reşadiye
Yazıköy
④
Çeşmeköy
③
Eski Datça
②
⑤

Datça Gulf

Sömbeki island

0 kilometres 5
0 miles 2.5

④ **Yazıköy**
The western half of the peninsula consists of rugged, pine-clad mountains dotted with olive and almond groves. The village of Yazıköy, at the end of the paved portion of the road, lies deep in the olive-growing region.

③ **Palamut Bükü**
This bay can also be reached by boat from Datça, and offers a long, tranquil pebble beach lapped by brisk, clear water. Palamut Bükü is a good spot for lunch, with several simple but good fish restaurants.

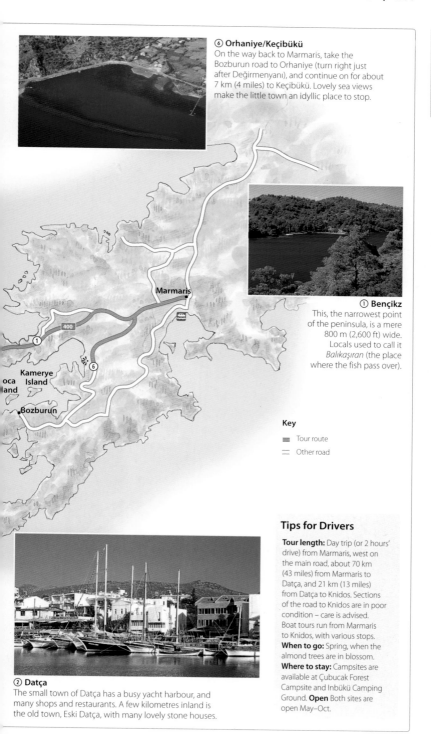

⑥ Orhaniye/Keçibükü

On the way back to Marmaris, take the Bozburun road to Orhaniye (turn right just after Değirmenyanı), and continue on for about 7 km (4 miles) to Keçibükü. Lovely sea views make the little town an idyllic place to stop.

① Bençikz

This, the narrowest point of the peninsula, is a mere 800 m (2,600 ft) wide. Locals used to call it *Balıkaşıran* (the place where the fish pass over).

Key

▬ Tour route

═ Other road

Tips for Drivers

Tour length: Day trip (or 2 hours' drive) from Marmaris, west on the main road, about 70 km (43 miles) from Marmaris to Datça, and 21 km (13 miles) from Datça to Knidos. Sections of the road to Knidos are in poor condition – care is advised. Boat tours run from Marmaris to Knidos, with various stops. **When to go:** Spring, when the almond trees are in blossom. **Where to stay:** Campsites are available at Çubucak Forest Campsite and Inbükü Camping Ground. **Open** Both sites are open May–Oct.

② Datça

The small town of Datça has a busy yacht harbour, and many shops and restaurants. A few kilometres inland is the old town, Eski Datça, with many lovely stone houses.

Exploring the Western Mediterranean Coast

Separated from the dry Anatolian plateau by the Taurus Mountains, the Mediterranean coast of Turkey is dominated by plunging cliffs and headlands interspersed with fertile alluvial flood plains, and fringed in places with fine sandy beaches. Throughout the region, the many civilizations that have shaped Turkey left their mark on cities, harbours, roads and rivers. To leave your own footprints, venture along the Lycian Way from Fethiye to Antalya, which is rated as one of the world's top treks, or take the "Blue Voyage" on a traditional *gület* (wooden yacht).

Butterfly Valley, near Ölü Deniz

Hiking in Saklıkent Gorge

Getting Around

Antalya's Bayındır International Airport has direct access to many European destinations. From here, fast main roads run east and west, parallel to the coast. In many places, two-lane roads snake around steep, rocky gorges. Views are dramatic but care is required. With only a few exceptions, all the main sights and attractions are easily accessible by both bus and dolmuş.

For additional map symbols *see back flap*

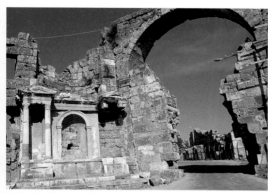

The Vespasian Monument, a Roman fountain in Side

Sights at a Glance

The picturesque yacht harbour at Antalya

Key

 Dual carriageway

— Major road

=== Minor road

— Scenic route

△ Summit

Exploring the Eastern Mediterranean Coast

The Mediterranean coastline east of Alanya is much less populous (and visited) than the western portion, but offers sights every bit as diverse. These include the bird-watcher's paradise of the Göksu Delta, several Armenian and Crusader castles, and the important Hittite site of Karatepe. The region also has a decidedly Middle Eastern flavour: the further east you go, the more lively and colourful the bazaars become and the foods tingle with stronger spices. This influence is most apparent in the southeast, around İskenderun and Antakya. Turkey's fourth largest city, Adana, is the main centre in the area. It has a subtropical climate, which receives rainfall mainly during the autumn and winter months.

Remnants of the Temple of Zeus, Silifke

Castle on an island off Kızkalesi (ancient Korykos)

Key

━━ Motorway

━━ Dual carriageway

━ Major road

═══ Minor road

━ Scenic route

╍╍ Main railway

── Minor railway

▬▬ International border

△ Summit

For additional map symbols *see back flap*

Sights at a Glance

Mosaic in the Antakya Archaeological Museum

Getting Around

From Mersin to Gaziantep a motorway system is in place, with the hub at Ceyhan, but this is the only section of the Mediterranean coast that is served by fast-track highways. Venturing off the east–west axis of the coastal road, the roads are picturesque and generally passable, but winding and narrow. The Taurus mountain range runs the length of the coast; respect the mountains and remember that, in winter, minor roads may be blocked by snow and tyre chains are essential if you plan to drive over the mountain passes.

Lake Köyceğiz, a haven for water birds

❶ Köyceğiz

30 km (19 miles) N of Dalyan.
🏛 8,600. **Tel** (0252) 262 47 03.

Independent Menteşe clans
governed this area even after
the beginning of Ottoman
rule in 1424. By the late 1830s,
when the English archaeologist
Charles Fellows visited the area,
the power of the family had
declined, however. The family
konak (manor house) has been
restored. Another manor, once
the centre of a cotton estate
belonging to the *khedive*
(viceroy) of Egypt, is now the
Dalaman state farm. Many
people in Köyceğiz village are
distant descendants of African
slaves brought here to work on
cotton plantations. A plantation
of *liquidambar orientalis*, the tree
used to produce church incense,
survives as a reminder of a once-
important local industry.

The reed-fringed lake of
Köyceğiz, 10 m (33 ft) deep
in places, is home to many
water birds, including the
rare Smyrna kingfisher.

❷ Caunos

6 km (4 miles) from Dalyan. **Tel** (0252)
284 20 44. **Open** Apr–Oct: 8:30am–
7pm; Nov–Mar: 8:30am–5pm. 📷

The ancient city of Caunos
bordered the kingdoms of Lycia
and Caria. Although a Carian
foundation, its culture shared
aspects of both states. The local
tombs are Lycian *(see p219)* in
style, but were in fact carved by
the Carians. Like Xanthos, capital
of Lycia, Caunos resisted the
Persian general, Harpagus,
during the 6th century BC,

for which many citizens of
Caunos were slaughtered in
a final sally. The city was
re-established and Hellenized,
especially by the Carian ruler,
Mausolus *(see pp198–9)*. Caunos
welcomed Alexander the Great,
but after his death came under
the rule of Rhodes.
It won independence
from Rome, but after
supporting Mithridates
against the Romans,
the city was punished
by return to Rhodian
rule. Caunos was
known both for
its figs and malarial
mosquitoes. It was
a major seaport until the
harbour silted up.

At the site are defensive walls
built in the 4th century BC,
a theatre dating from the 2nd
century BC, a temple to Apollo
and a Roman bath. There is
a Doric temple and an agora
(marketplace) with a
nymphaeum (fountain) thought
to have been built to honour
Emperor Vespasian.

❸ Dalyan

13 km (8 miles) from the main D400
road. 🏛 8,250. ✈ Dalaman, 25 km
(16 miles) E of Dalyan, (0252) 792 52
91. 🚌 Ortaca, 13 km (8 miles) NE of
Dalyan. 🚗 entry road to Dalyan,
(0252) 284 24 58. 🛈 (0252) 284 42 35.
🐢 Caretta (turtle) Festival (end Aug–
early Sep). 🛒 Sat.

This bustling resort takes its
name from the Dalyan River
(Dalyan Çayı), meaning "fishing
weir", which flows through
the town. Although the town
is a fast-growing tourist centre,
fishing has long been the
mainstay of the local economy.
Over the years, the town
replaced ancient Caunos as a
fishery when the latter's harbour
became choked by silt. A weir
built on the river, together with a
fish-processing plant, means that
you can enjoy the delicious local
red roe caviar, which comes in
a pot sealed with beeswax.
Local fish is available at
waterside eateries.
The threatened
loggerhead turtle
(see p215) has
become a symbol
of Dalyan, drawing
increasing numbers of visitors
to the area. This came about
in 1986, when conservationists
managed to persuade civic
authorities to protect the
turtles' breeding ground from
development. Since then,
local people have adopted the
loggerhead turtle as a motif
for the town. The Turtle Statue
(Kaplumbağa Heykeli) on
Cumhuriyet Meydanı is a

Turtle Statue in Dalyan

The resort town of Dalyan, by the tranquil Dalyan River

tangible symbol of Dalyan's passion for conservation.

On the eastern bank of the Dalyan River are two rows of tombs cut into the cliffs. Constructed for the citizens of Caunos, the tombs are mainly of the house type and date from the 4th century BC (see p219), with Ionic columns and triangular pediments. Most have a small chamber with three stone benches to accommodate the dead. The surviving inscriptions are mainly in Latin, for the tombs were reused during Roman times. They are fenced off and must be viewed from some distance away. The rock tombs can be reached by river-boat tours, which depart from the Dalyan Sea Co-operative.

Environs

A short distance upriver from Dalyan (about 10 minutes by boat) lie the **mud baths** of Ilıca. With a constant temperature of 40°C (104°F), they are reputed to be beneficial for rheumatism and gynaecological disorders, and are certainly relaxing. Beyond Ilıca, at Sultaniye Kaplıcaları, on the shores of Lake Köyceğiz, a domed building lined with marble surrounds a natural pool where water wells up at 39–41°C (102–106°F). Locals report that, after the Adana earthquake of 1998, the water at the bathhouse gave off a plume of sulphur gas and that the water changed colour and appeared gassy.

Turtle Beach (İztuzu Plajı), which partly bars the mouth of the Dalyan River, has for

Yachts moored in Göcek's harbour

centuries been a refuge for breeding loggerhead turtles and is now a protected area. The beach is closed to tourists at night so that the young turtles are not attracted by the bright lights, which would lead them away from the life-giving sea.

As staying on the beach after dark is forbidden, you are unlikely to catch a glimpse of the turtles, but you may see blue crabs. The best way to get to the beach is to take one of the frequent, co-operative run boat-taxis from the river bank near the centre of Dalyan. Alternatively, there are full-day tours to the beach that take in both Caunos and the mud baths at Ilıca.

🔵 **Mud Baths**
Çamurlu Kaplıcası
Tel (0252) 284 20 35.
Open daily. 🏧 💻

❌ **Turtle Beach**
İztuzu Plajı
12 km (7.5 miles) from town centre.
🚤 from Dalyan (40 min): depart before 10:30am, return between 3pm and sunset. 🏧 for car park only.

❹ Göcek

23 km (14 miles) E of Dalaman.
🚤 1 km (0.5 mile) from town centre.
ℹ️ Club Marina *(private yacht club)*, (0252) 645 18 00; municipal yacht club, (0252) 645 19 38.

Near the pass of the same name, and just south of the main D400 road, Göcek is now a major yachting centre. Popularized by Prince Charles and former Turkish president, Turgut Özal, the town has a remarkable concentration of up-market facilities, including a luxury hotel and several striking waterside housing developments. The public marinas have berths for about 350 boats, with a further 200 berths available in a secluded private marina. Near the tip of the peninsula can be seen the ruins of the Roman town of Lydae, with two mausolea and a fort.

Loggerhead Turtles

The loggerhead turtle *(Caretta caretta)* has become closely associated with Dalyan, where soft sand and a tranquil south-facing beach provide an ideal nesting ground.

Loggerhead turtles can mate several times in a season. Between May and September, the females arrive *en masse* to drag themselves up onto the beaches where they themselves hatched. There they laboriously dig a pit and lay their eggs above the tide line. The sand keeps the eggs at an even temperature until they are ready to hatch.

Loggerhead turtle *(Caretta caretta)*

Kayaköy, once the prosperous Gre... ...n 1923

❺ Fethiye

🏠 81,000. ✈ Dalaman, 50 ...
miles) NW of town. 🚌 2 k... ...
of town centre. ⛴ from Rho... ...
(summer only). 🛈 İskele Karşıs... ...
(0252) 614 15 27 and 612 19 75.
🏪 Tue & Fri.

A medium-sized market town and agricultural centre, Fethiye fringes a sheltered bay with a large harbour, making it a good place for scuba diving and boating. In addition to having many upscale holiday resorts, Fethiye has a splendid farmers' market every Friday that attracts crowds of locals as well as visitors.

Modern Fethiye stands on the ruins of the Lycian city of Telmessus. Earthquakes in 1856 and 1957 levelled most of the ... ...nich included ... ..., but a Roman ... ...arbour ... ...the cliffs above ...t are several ...ombs (see p219), som... ...4th century BC. Charles Texier, a 19th-century French explorer, carved his initials on one of these tombs.

Fethiye Museum displays artifacts from the half-flooded ruins of Letoön (see p218), including stelae, which scholars used in their efforts to decode the Lycian language.

🏛 Fethiye Museum
Fethiye Müzesi
Off Atatürk Cad. **Tel** (0252) 614 11 50.
Open Jun–Sep: 8am–7pm daily;
Oct–May: 8am– 5pm Tue–Sun. 🅿

❻ Kayaköy

10 km (6 miles) SW of Fethiye.
🚍 from Fethiye or Ölü Deniz. **Open**
Apr–Oct: 8:30am–6:30pm daily;
Nov–Mar: 8:30am–5pm daily. 🅿

Derelict Kayaköy, formerly known as Karmylassos, then Levissi, was a thriving Greek town until it was abandoned in the 1923 exchange of populations (see p62). About 400 roofless houses stand on the hillside overlooking a fertile plain. The Orthodox church of Panayia Pyrgiotissa has been restored and is the main focus of movement for peace and international reconciliation.

Now a UNESCO World Heritage site, Kayaköy and its ruins have been preserved as an historic settlement. The town inspired the novel *Birds Without Wings*, which focuses on the rise of Turkish patriotism after the disintegration of ·
the Ottoman Empire.

❼ Ölü Deniz

20 km (12 miles) S of Fethiye.
🏠 1,200. 🚍 from Fethiye.
🛈 Tourism Co-operative, (0252) 617
04 38, (0252) 617 01 45.

Made famous in the 1970s by visitors from Britain, the inviting beach and lagoon at Ölü Deniz (which means dead sea – because of the calm water) now adorn many posters promoting

Lycian tombs cut into the cliffs above Fethiye

Turkish travel. The land behind the restaurant-fringed beach is lined with hotels, pensions and camp sites. The lagoon itself is part of a national park, open dawn to dusk, with a small entry fee. The adjoining mountain, Baba Dağı, is the jump-off point for paragliders. Ölü Deniz also marks the start of the Lycian Way, Turkey's first long-distance walking route, which ends just short of Antalya.

❽ Saklıkent Gorge

30 km (18 miles) E of Fethiye. **D** from Fethiye and then on foot. 🚌 summer only. 🚻 ♿ 🍴 Tlos: **Open** 8:30am–8:30pm daily. 🚻

Saklıkent Gorge cuts into the rugged flank of the 3,016 m (9,895 ft) Gömbe Akdağı, and delivers a rushing stream of pure limestone-filtered water. From the restaurants at the base of the gorge, which specialize in local trout, you can walk for a few hundred metres into the gorge on platforms built over the torrent. To walk further up the canyon you need to join a guided walk, led by one of the guides offering their services at the entrance. Bougainville Travel of Kaş *(see p375)* organizes abseiling trips into the gorge. These involve scrambling over rocks to cross the waterfalls that tumble down the walls.

The beautiful lagoon and beach at Ölü Deniz

If you enter by road and footpath, along the flank of Akdağı, there is quite a steep descent, but this brings you to the trout farms. At Saklıkent, 7 km (4.5 miles) from the main D400 road, consider a meal at one of the trout restaurants, which have low tables placed over the water. Enjoy the cool air before you return to sea level – when the temperature is 40°C (104°F) at the coast, Saklıkent is refreshing.

Also in the area is the ruined city of Tlos, one of the oldest and most important Lycian cities. Hittite records from the 14th century BC refer to a settlement called Tlawa, which was probably

Tlos. Built on a hill, with a commanding view over the valley of the Eşen River (Eşen Çayı) – known in ancient times as the Xanthos – the main Lycian/Roman remains consist of tombs hewn from rock, as well as a stadium, gymnasium and palaestra, and baths. In Byzantine times, Tlos was a bishopric, and the churches at the site were most probably former temples. The acropolis was used until the 19th century, when it was the stronghold of a pirate known as Kanlı Ali Ağa (Bloody Ali).

Agencies in Fethiye and Kaş offer tours of both Saklıkent Gorge and Tlos.

Catwalk built over the water in Saklıkent Gorge

Butterfly Valley

From Ölü Deniz, it is a short boat ride to Butterfly Valley (Kelebek Vadisi), a flat-bottomed valley enclosed by towering cliffs. The valley was named for the migratory *Euplagia quadripunctaria*, commonly known as the Jersey Tiger, a spectacular red, black and white tiger moth that colonizes the valley by the thousand during the summer. Other species are present year-round, with some unique to the area. A 20-minute trek leads to a waterfall from the mill stream at Faralya, which cascades into the valley, providing damp conditions for the butterflies and supporting a variety of plants. No permanent buildings are allowed on or behind the beach, but a wooden bar-restaurant supplies beer and food to those wishing to camp. Alternative access is by steep path from Faralya, the village perched 600 m (1,968 ft) above, but this route is not recommended since the path is dangerous.

Euplagia quadripunctaria

Tombs cut into the rock at Pınara

❾ Pınara

50 km (31 miles) E of Fethiye.
Open 8:30am–dusk daily.

One of the most important cities of ancient Lycia, Pınara, whose name means "round", is situated on and around a huge circular plug of rock above the village of Minare, some 5 km (3 miles) west of the main D400 road. The entrance is about 3 km (2 miles) along an unpaved track that is passable by car.

The rock face is honey-combed with tombs, mainly square holes, which must have been sealed after use. The acropolis is approached by steps carved into the rock. A well-preserved theatre is cut into the hillside below, with baths nearby. The agora (marketplace) lies just above the ticket office.

Visitors strolling through the picturesque streets of Kalkan

❿ Kalkan

9,000. at junction with main coast road. Thu.

The village of Kalkan has been permanently inhabited only since the eradication of malaria-bearing mosquitoes in the 1950s. In earlier times, the local people avoided the pests by migrating in summer to the *yayla* (summer pasture) of Bezirgan, above the village. The core of stone, Greek-style houses built around the harbour is today surrounded by tiered ranks of modern villas on the hills. Good accommodation and a choice of restaurants make it an ideal base for the ancient Lycian cities of Xanthos, Letoön and Patara.

Xanthos (now Kınık), the ancient capital of the Lycian League (*see p219*), is 30 minutes by bus west of Kalkan, just before the bridge spanning the Eşen River. The site is extensive and spectacular, and includes superb examples of Lycian tombs. A bilingual Greek-Lycian pillar found at the site helped researchers to decipher the Lycian language.

Letoön, site of the temples of Leto, Artemis and Apollo, was a cult centre favoured by Alexander the Great. Letoön and Xanthos are both UNESCO World Heritage sites and reflect the way Hellenistic and Lycian cultures influenced each other.

Patara was once the major port of the Lycian League. Damaged by severe earth-quakes in AD 141 and AD 240, its harbour silted up.

⓫ Kaş

8,500. Dalaman, 155 km (96 miles) NW of town, or Bayındır Intl Airport (Antalya), (0242) 330 36 00, 210 km (130 miles) NE of town. Atatürk Cad. 5 Cumhuriyet Meydanı, (0242) 836 12 38. Fri. Kaş/Lycia Festival (Sep).

Kaş was built adjoining a long, narrow peninsula, over the ancient port city of Antiphellos (port of Phellos), and was noted for its cork oaks. In 1839, it was so tiny and impoverished that the English archaeologist Charles Fellows (who excavated the nearby Lycian site of Xanthos) had to cross to the island of Castellorizo to buy chickens to eat. Today, the situation is reversed: the islanders buy their chickens at Kaş market on Fridays. The harbours are filled with scuba-diving boats and yachts making trips to the Blue Cave and the sunken city at Kekova (*see p220*), with hotels and pensions along the waterfront. Uzun Çarşı, the shopping street, has many unusual and

"Hand of Fatma" door knocker, Kaş

original handicraft and antique shops.

A 5th-century BC Lycian sarcophagus is at the top of the street.

The tourism information office in the main square can provide information on the annual Kaş/Lycia Festival, which makes good use of the tiny Hellenistic theatre located on the peninsula road just west of the town.

Fishing boats and touring yachts in the harbour at Kaş

Lycian Tombs

Ancient Lycia, a federation of 19 independent cities, lay in the mountainous area between modern Fethiye and Antalya. Burials must have had an important role in the beliefs of the Lycians, for they cut hundreds of tombs into cliff faces and crags that can be seen throughout the area. They were probably copies of domestic architecture, intended as houses for the dead. Most have carved doors, beam ends, pitched roofs and prominent lintels – typical of construction in wood. During the 4th century BC, the rulers of Xanthos (modern Kınık) produced some of the most remarkable tombs, combining Greek and Persian styles. One of the most famous of these, the Nereid Monument, is now in the British Museum in London.

The doorway of a house tomb often featured a sliding slab.

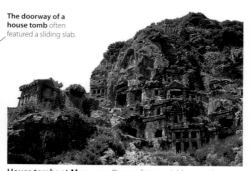

The house tomb of one to three storeys, shown here at Tlos, was carved into solid rock. A sliding slab door opened into an inner chamber. Some tombs had exterior porticoes with carvings.

House tombs at Myra, near Demre, feature richly carved façades. The elaborate reliefs on some of the tombs still bear traces of paint applied by the original builders.

Rock cut away to make a roof space

Sarcophagus placed atop the pillar base

The freestanding temple tomb had a temple façade and a portico, from which a door led to a grave chamber with benches for the dead.

Partly hollow base topped by a stepped lid

Pillar tombs (on a stepped base or built directly on rock) are the oldest Lycian tombs. These are found only at Xanthos, the chief city of Lycia, and Apollonia. This example is from Xanthos.

Prominent lid ridge

"Beam ends" used to open the lid of the sarcophagus

Stepped base

Sarcophagus tombs had a stepped base, a lower grave chamber (called a hyposorion), a flat plate for the coffin and a lid. The pitched, rounded lid symbolized a house roof, and had a prominent ridge. From 500 BC to AD 300, elaborate "saddlebacked" sarcophagus tombs were produced.

Varnished charter vessels and quaint fishing boats share the little harbour at Üçağız

⑫ Üçağız, Simena and Kekova Island

38 km (24 miles) E of Kaş. 🚗 2,800. 🚌 from Demre or Kaş.

The picturesque waterfront village of Üçağız ("Three Mouths") is a 19 km (12 mile) drive south of the D400, just east of Kaş. Dolmuşes will drop you at the main road, but no scheduled transport leads directly to the village.

Built on the site of (and using stones from) the Lycian town of Teimiussa, houses, restaurants and pensions front a sheltered bay with three openings to the sea. There are some signs of subsidence, probably as a result of an earthquake that took place in about AD 530. Submerged saddleback tombs *(see p219)* can be seen at the Lycian site

of Aperlae and the village of Kale (ancient Simena) nearby, where a castle built in around 1440 surrounds a tiny theatre cut into the rock. A pleasant stroll along the coast via the marked Lycian Way leads to its rarely visited twin.

Above Demre, an asphalt road provides a shortcut to Üçağız. Daily boat tours call in to the pretty bay enclosed by Kekova Island (Kekova Adası).

⑬ Demre (Myra)

🚗 19,200. 🚌 100 m (100 yards) from main square. 🛈

The small market town of Demre would have little appeal to visitors were it not for its claims to be home to the original Santa Claus, St Nicholas, and the proximity of the superb ancient site of Myra.

St Nicholas legends originated in Mediterranean Patara (his birthplace), but the Church of St Nicholas is the most charming reason to linger in Demre. This petite Byzantine church is spiritually and architecturally heavenly and some long-concealed frescoes are being brushed back into life.

The ancient city of Myra and the port of Andriake, 3 km (2 miles) southwest of Demre, date from around the 5th century BC, and grew rich on coastal trade, supplying incense to Egypt and Constantinople.

The most popular parts of Myra are the theatre and two cliffs carved with spectacular house tombs. When Charles Fellows visited the site in 1840, the paint on the tombs was still visible and letters of the inscriptions were picked out in red and blue. The oldest part of Myra was on the acropolis hill, with a 5th-century BC defensive wall. Myra's water supply ran in channels cut into the wall of the Demre gorge and the frigid sulphur springs at Andriake provided therapeutic baths and healing drinking waters.

The Real Santa Claus

Nicholas, the 4th-century Bishop of Myra, was famed for his unfailing generosity and piety. He was beatified, and legend established him as the patron of fishermen and children, and the town as a place of pilgrimage. (He is also the patron saint of bakers, brewers and brides.) There are two statues of St Nicholas (Noel Baba in Turkish) in Demre: one is a gift from the Russian Orthodox Church, and is mounted on a revolving pedestal.

The saint's myrrh-impregnated bones were buried on his church's premises. Although this church was destroyed by the Arabs in 809, the bones survived and were moved to Bari, Italy, in 1087. The church at Demre was rebuilt by a Russian prince in the 19th century. Demre is also the headquarters of the St Nicholas Foundation.

Statue of St Nicholas in Demre

Carved mask relief from the theatre at Myra

⑭ Finike

🏔 25,000. 🅸 Halk Kütüphane,
(0242) 855 39 92. 🚌 off D400
highway. 🚢 Sat.

Finike is a market town located
at the foot of the Gülmez Dağları,
a long spur of the Taurus
Mountains, and on the banks
of the Karasu (Black Water) River.

In ancient times, Finike was
known as Phoenicus. The original
harbour, once noted for its export
of the timber that was used
in building the Ottoman fleet,
is now buried under silt, and
a modern yacht harbour has
replaced it. In Byzantine times,
the surrounding mountains
were a source of cedar of
Lebanon (used in shipbuilding),
but the tree is rarely found in
these parts today.

Finike has since prospered
through the export of citrus fruit
and other produce. Its fertile
orchards brim with orange and
lemon trees, and the town's
logo is an orange.

Not much is known about
the early history of **Olympos**,
although it was an influential
member of the Lycian League.
The site is reached by a narrow
road through a gorge with a
seasonally dry river bed. The
ruined city occupies a charming
setting adjoining a 4 km-long
(3 mile) beach. To the south is
an extensive necropolis,
including unique square tombs
with sliding doors. A theatre,
baths and landing stages also
occupy the south bank. The
northern side has an acropolis,
more tombs, a temple dating
from the time of Emperor Marcus
Aurelius and a Byzantine bathhouse. The whole site is starred
with anemones in spring;
kingfishers whirr over the stream
and ducks nest in the reeds.

Fronting the same beach as
Olympos but reached from the
main road by a different valley,
low-key Çıralı boasts more than
100 pensions and hotels
nestling in the shade of citrus
orchards. Turtle-nesting beach
apart, the main point of interest
here is the Chimaera. Set at an
altitude of 300 m (984 ft), are
two outcrops of volcanic rock,
where escaping natural gas is

Escaping natural gas burning near Olympos

permanently alight. The flame is
known as Yanartaş (burning
stone). In ancient times, the fire
was guided upwards to light a
beacon to warn ships of impend-
ing danger. There is also a
Byzantine church here, probably
once a temple of Vulcan.

According to myth, this
mountain is where the hero
Bellerophon, mounted on the
winged horse, Pegasus, killed
the three-headed Chimaera
by pouring molten lead into
the monster's mouth.

🏛 Olympos
11 km (7 miles) E of main D400 road.
🅳 from café on D400, or taxi. 🍴
Open Apr–Oct: 9am–7pm daily; Nov–
Mar: 8am–5pm daily. 🎫

⑮ Phaselis

40 km (24 miles) SW of Antalya.
Open daily. 🎫 🖥

Decked with flowers in spring,
the ruined city of Phaselis is
a popular stopping place for
cruise yachts.

The Lycian port city was sold to
Greek settlers from Rhodes by a
local shepherd in the 7th century
BC. They built an extensive town
with three harbours around
an acropolis on a headland. The
canny Phaselians, noted for their
skill in trade and commerce,
invited Alexander the Great
to winter here in 333 BC, even
presenting him with a golden
crown in return for valuable
protection. Phaselis became
a pirate stronghold before it
was absorbed into the Roman
province of Lycia-Pamphylia in
AD 43. It survived Arab raiding,
only to be eclipsed by Antalya
in Seljuk times.

Most of the ruins date from
the Roman era. They include
a theatre, two sets of baths,
an agora, an aqueduct leading
from Mount Olympos and
a marble gateway erected
in honour of Emperor Hadrian.

The north harbour at Phaselis, with Mt Olympos in the background

⑯ Antalya

Antalya's population has increased to more than one million since the tourism boom began in the late 1980s. Mountains, beaches and the seaside setting are the obvious magnets, and the city is now one of Turkey's premier resort areas. Antalya (ancient Attaleia) was founded by Attalus II, a king of Pergamum, in 159 BC. The city prospered during the Roman, Byzantine and Seljuk eras before coming under Ottoman rule in 1390. The most important remains are the Roman city walls and imposing Hadrian's Gate.

Roman marble sculpture from the Antalya Archaeological Museum

The attractive old harbour, showing remnants of the city walls

Exploring Antalya

Antalya's broad, palm-lined boulevards and interesting Old Town (Kaleiçi) make it a pleasant place to explore. The beaches, parks, excellent shops and lively cultural scene make it a focal point of the Mediterranean coast.

Antalya has one speciality not found anywhere else in Turkey – *hibeş*, a hot, spicy sesame-paste dip.

Minicity Antalya

Arapsu Mahallesi, Konyaaltı. **Tel** (0242) 229 45 45. **Open** 8am–7pm daily (Nov–Apr: from 9am). 🎫 🖥 🏠 ♿

A Mediterranean theme pervades here, with diminutive beaches and sail boats as well as miniature replicas of many of Turkey's historic sights. Replicas of the Gallipoli graves are particularly moving.

Antalya's Beaches

For visitors staying in the Old Town of Kaleiçi the most convenient beach is the small, pebbly Mermerli beach, located at the foot of the cliffs just south of the harbour. Owned by the Mermerli restaurant, a fee is charged to

access it. Konyaaltı beach, a long shingle strip backed by cafés and hotels is easily reached from the city centre on the nostalgic tram. Get off at the last stop (Archaeological Museum) and walk down the hill. Some 10 km (6 miles) east of the city, and reached from the centre by bus, is sandy Lara Beach. Both Konyaaltı and Lara beaches have sun loungers for hire.

🏛 Antalya Archaeological Museum

Konyaaltı Cad 1, Konyaaltı. **Tel** (0242) 238 56 88. **Open** Apr–Oct: 9am–7pm Tue–Sun; Nov–Mar: 8am–5pm Tue–Sun. 🎫 🖥 🏠 🎥 with prior permission.

The museum, perched on the cliffs 2 km (1.25 miles) west of the city centre, is the true jewel of Antalya. It houses a unique collection of Roman marble sculptures dating from the 2nd century AD, many of them from nearby Perge (*see p224*). The statues are beautifully lit and superbly displayed.

Displays also include Bronze-Age urn burials, silver found in Phrygian tumulus burials, relics of St Nicholas (*see p224*) and a collection of early Byzantine church silver. There is also an ethnography section. If your time in Antalya is limited, save it for this – one of the handful of Turkish museums that is truly outstanding. The Sarcophagi Hall and Gallery of the Gods are also recommended viewing. Don't miss the sarcophagus of a dog called Stephanos.

Antalya's Harbours

Limanılar

Marina (Kaleiçi): Selsuk Mah. **Tel** (0242) 248 45 30. Harbour (Port Akdeniz): Büyük Liman Mevkii. **Tel** (0242) 259 13 80. **Open** 8am–5pm Tue–Sun. 🏊

The picturesque Old Harbour in Kaleiçi is used mainly for gulet (*see p210*) tours to Rat Island or the waterfalls at Lara. The waterfront is lined with restaurants and is a pleasant place to stroll. The harbour has won an award for its attractive setting, plan and use of resources. The city's main harbour is 10 km (6 miles) west of the centre and is used mainly by commercial and private yachts, as well as cruise ships. It is also the site of Antalya's fish market.

🕌 Fluted Minaret

Yivli Minare

A 13th-century minaret dating from the reign of Seljuk Sultan Alaeddin Keykubad (*see p254*), this has become the symbol of Antalya. The red bricks were once decorated with turquoise tiles. The adjoining mosque is still used, and just above is the Fine Arts Gallery.

The Fluted Minaret

Hadrian's Gate, with the deep wheel ruts clearly visible

🏛 Clock Tower
Saat Kulesi
Cumhuriyet Cad

This local landmark was built in 1244 and marked the upper limit of the Old Town. Its sombre appearance indicates that the tower was once part of the city's defensive system.

🏛 Hadrian's Gate
Üçkapılar
Atatürk Cad.

Built to honour the visit of Emperor Hadrian in AD 130, Hadrian's Gate consists of three arched gateways fronted by four Corinthian columns.

For years, the structure was encased in the Seljuk city wall and was uncovered only in the 1950s. Restoration work has been carried out and the pavement between the arches stripped back to the Roman level, showing clearly the wheel ruts cut into the stone.

🏛 Truncated Minaret
Kesik Minare
Hesapçı Sok.

The Truncated Minaret is the landmark decapitated tower next to the ruins of what has been, variously, a Greek temple, the Church of St Peter and a mosque. The tower was badly damaged by fire in 1851. Various architectural styles, especially on the capitals, give clues to its past. You cannot go inside, as railings surround the site, but it is worth a look.

🌳 Karaalioğlu Park and Hıdırlık Tower

Located on the southeastern side of the harbour, the park has a variety of mature exotic trees in which wild ring-necked parakeets nest. It also has tea gardens with fabulous views over the Gulf of Antalya, Mount Tahtalı and the distant Beydağlar Mountains.

VISITORS' CHECKLIST

Practical Information
🗺 1,130,000. 🛈 Cumhuriyet Cad, (0242) 241 17 47.
🎭 Aspendos Festival (2nd week Jun–1st week Jul), Golden Orange Film Festival (1st week Oct).

Transport
✈ JCF Airports, 12 km (8 miles) E of city, (0242) 330 36 00. 🚌 4 km (2.5 miles) N of city centre, (0242) 331 12 50. 🚎 from Işıklar Cad to Konyaaltı Cad. 🚍 Doğu Garajı.

Tea garden beside a reflecting pool in Karaalioğlu Park

The circular Hıdırlık tower dates from the 2nd century BC, and was probably a lighthouse in Roman times. Locals linger here to watch the setting sun.

Antalya City Centre

① Konyaaltı and Mermerli beaches
② Archaeological Museum
③ Old Harbour
④ Fluted Minaret
⑤ Clock Tower
⑥ Hadrian's Gate
⑦ Truncated Minaret
⑧ Karaalioğlu Park

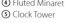

Bus station 5 km (3 miles)
Airport 12 km (8 miles)

Muratpaşa
Doğu Garajı
Ismetpaşa
Kalekapisi
Minicity Antalya
Archaeological Museum ②
Barbaros
Meslek Lisesi
Selekler
Clock Tower ⑤
Üçkapılar
Fluted Minaret ④
Hadrian's Gate ⑥
Müze
KONYA ALTI CAD
Atatürk Park
Old Harbour ③
Konyaaltı beach ①
Mermerli beach ①
Hıdırlık Tower
Truncated Minaret ⑦
Karaalioğlu Park ⑧
Belediye
Mediterranean Sea
Antalyaspor Stadium
Işıklar

FEHRETTIN ALTAY CAD
100 YIL BULVARI
GÜLLÜK CAD
MILLI EGEMENLIK CAD
KAZIM ÖZALP CAD
ALI ÇETINKAYA CAD
TEOMAN PAŞA CAD
TURGUT CAD
PAMIR CAD
CUMHURIYET CAD
HESAPÇI SOK
ATATÜRK CAD
ALI FUAT CEBESOY CAD
ANK CAD
TINAZ TAPE CAD
19 MAYIS CAD
FEVZI ÇAKMAK CAD
IŞIKLAR CAD

0 metres   600
0 yards   600

⑰ Termessos

35 km (22 miles) NW of Antalya;
9 km (6 miles) off the main road.
Open 9am–5pm daily.

Termessos was built by the Solymians in a strategic position on the shipping route to the Aegean. The Greek historian Arrian (around AD 95–180) said of the location that "the two cliffs make a sort of natural gateway so that quite a small force can, by holding the high ground, prevent an enemy from getting through". The city's formidable natural defences convinced Alexander the Great not to attempt to take the city during the 4th century BC.

The main buildings visible today are a theatre, the defensive walls below the gymnasium, the gymnasium itself, the temples of Hadrian and Zeus, an odeon (for musical performances), cisterns in the agora, the stoas (covered walk) of Attalos and Osbaras, and the temple of Artemis. A large necropolis extends upwards as far as a modern fire-watch tower on the hill. You can walk from the gymnasium down to sea level along the old road, ending in a gorge.

Termessos lies in Güllük Dağ National Park, which includes an area for breeding wild goats and deer, and may be the last refuge of the Anatolian lynx. The area is also known for its butterflies.

The remains of the Hellenistic Gate at Perge

⑱ Perge

18 km (11 miles) NE of Antalya.
Open 9am–5:30pm daily.

Located on the Kestros River (modern-day Aksu), Perge was once a wealthy city. It declined in Byzantine times, and was abandoned in the 7th century. However, it still presents an impressive sight. The theatre is one of the most impressive remnants: its frieze of Neptune can be seen in the Archaeological Museum in Antalya (see p222). The huge stadium is largely intact. Much excavation and reconstruction work has been done here, with explanatory panels near most major buildings.

A pair of Hellenistic towers marks the entry to the city. The towers front a courtyard with a fountain. On the left, baths with under-floor heating systems face a colonnaded agora. A water channel leads from a second fountain on the acropolis hill into a channel down the main street, which cooled the air in summer. Plancia Magna, the city's benefactress, was buried outside the walls; a marble statue of her is in Antalya Archaeological Museum.

⑲ Selge

92 km (57 miles) NE of Antalya.
Open daily.

The village now occupying the site gives no idea of the former importance of Selge. Founded by Calchas of Argos (who also founded Perge), it was the first Pisidian city to mint coins, in the 5th century BC. Coins from Selge were used until the 5th century AD. The classical geographer Strabo cites olives, wine and medicinal plants as sources of revenue. Selge seldom features in classical histories, but we know from the Greek historian Polybius that, in 218 BC, when Selge was at war with the city of Pednelissos, it was able to field an army of 20,000 men. Selge was defeated in this war and had to pay tribute to its enemy. However, it regained prosperity and independence and flourished, especially in the 2nd century AD.

Visible today are a theatre, a stadium, a large temple to Zeus, a smaller one to Artemis, and a cistern. The site, with its spectacular mountain surroundings and cool air, is now part of the Köprülü Çayı National Park.

The theatre at Termessos, with seating for more than 4,000 people

⑳ Aspendos

Aspendos, located on the Eurymedon River (now the Köprülü River), was once the easternmost city of the kingdom of Pergamum (see pp180–81). In Roman times it became an important trading centre. Today, its main attraction is a beautifully preserved Roman theatre, built around AD 162 by the architect Zeno. The structure is enclosed by a stage building that once had a timber canopy. The theatre hosts the annual Aspendos Opera and Ballet Festival (usually mid-June–early July). Aspendos also has a remarkable aqueduct, and numerous remains.

VISITORS' CHECKLIST

Practical Information
50 km (31 miles) E of Antalya.
Open Apr–Oct: 9am–7pm daily;
Nov–Mar: 8am–5pm daily.
Closed early closing (4pm) for
festival performances (Jun). 🚻
🍴 in Belkis village. ♿ ground
level only.

Arched Gallery
Running right round the top of the theatre, the restored gallery provided patrons with an all-weather vantage point.

★ Theatre
The theatre, which can seat 12,000, was maintained by the Seljuks and traces of 13th-century paint still adorn the stage building.

Granite bedrock

Roof over the stage building

Dressing rooms

Covered passageway

Forty rows of marble seats divided into sections by staircases

Public entrance, used for festival performances today

★ Aqueduct
The aqueduct, built in around AD 100 by the architect Tiberius Claudius Italicus, incorporated a 1 km (0.5 mile) siphon system.

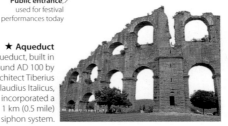

Stage Building
The stage building features carved niches intended to hold statues. Originally, the niches were separated by columns.

Lycian rock-cut tombs above Fethiye ▶

㉑ Side

The classical geographer Strabo tells us that Side (whose name means pomegranate) was settled by Greek colonists from Aeolia, near Smyrna (modern İzmir), in the 7th century BC. In the 2nd century BC, Side became a centre for pirates, who made large profits from slave trading. Under the Romans, it remained an important slave market. Excavations have shown that the city was burned by Arab raiders in the 7th century, but it revived under the Seljuks. During the 1920s, Side was settled by Muslims expelled from Crete in the Greet–Turkish population exchange *(see p62)*.

The partially reconstructed Temple of Apollo

The tranquil harbour, cradled by the remains of ancient breakwaters

Exploring Side
The busy resort of Side is an ideal place to take in ancient ruins, beaches and shopping without venturing too far afield. It is a haven for shoppers, with its leather, jewellery and souvenir stores and many bars and eateries in summer. Pedestrianization, the small pensions and quaint, family-run facilities have enabled the town to retain its "village" charm. Its monuments lend discipline and historic value to the narrow streets.

🚢 Harbour
Side occupies a peninsula that terminates in a small harbour. The remains of moles built in antiquity are visible in places offshore. From here, you can take a luxurious boat trip up the Manavgat River (Melas in ancient times), see a waterfall and stop for some lunch at a trout restaurant.

🏛 Temples of Apollo and Athena
At sunset, the marble columns and re-erected pediments of the temples of Apollo and Athena frame superb views of the Gulf of Antalya. Around the temples is a basilica, built later in a contrasting rough aggregate stone. The Medusa heads of the friezes date from the 2nd century AD.

🏛 Theatre
Open 8am–7pm daily. 🎫 at theatre, grants entrance to the whole site, reduction after 5pm.

Almost entirely freestanding, Side's large theatre was built on arches over Hellenistic foundations during the 2nd century AD. The lower seats are partially supported by the hillside, but the upper seats rest entirely on huge arches.

This was the largest theatre in Pamphylia, and could hold 17,000 spectators. There are 29 rows of seats above and

Waterfall on the Manavgat River, upstream from the town

Golfing in Belek
Between Side and Antalya lies the purpose-built golfing resort of Belek. Here, there are fourteen 18-hole courses, all beautifully landscaped through mature pine forests and offering considerable contrast, ranging from a links course to one set amid lakes and huge trees. The Belek courses operate in close partnership with excellent five-star hotels and have golf professionals who speak a variety of languages. The Mediterranean region's mild winter and early spring make this the most attractive time to visit. Several tournaments are held here each year.

Typical landscaped golf course

The large Roman theatre, built on Hellenistic foundations

29 below the main lateral aisle. Changes to the structure of the building permitted the orchestra pit to be flooded in order to enact naval dramas. The stage building had two storeys, decorated, as at Perge (see p224), with friezes of the story of Dionysus. These are currently being displayed in the nearby agora or museum garden while restoration work is carried out on them.

⬛ Vespasian Monument, Arch and Colonnaded Street

The arched gateway that marks the entrance to Side from its neighbour, Manavgat, blocks most vehicular traffic. Next to the arch is a fountain adorned with carved basins,

dedicated to the Emperor Vespasian. From here runs a colonnaded street lined with plain granite columns and the remains of Roman shops leading to the main street. A local tractor pulls an open bus, saving visitors the walk from the bus station.

⬛ Museum in Roman Bathhouse

Tel (0242) 753 10 06.
Open Apr–Oct: 9am–7pm daily; Nov–Mar: 8am–5pm daily.

The museum occupies a charming setting – the largest of Side's baths – and includes a number of superb marble sarcophagi, a trio of statues known as the Three Graces and another statue showing Hercules holding the golden apples of the Hesperides. There are also elegant portrait heads

The Vespasian Monument, with a carved pediment and inscription

and tiny carvings that include a house complete with dog peering around the door. The garden features a cupola with maze decoration and many friezes.

⬛ Aqueduct, Nymphaeum and City Walls

The Romans installed an impressive water-supply system. Outside the main gate was a nymphaeum (ornamental fountain), which was fed by a two-storey aqueduct running on arches for 30 km (19 miles) from the Melas (now the Manavgat) River. Clay pipes were used to distribute water to homes from the city cisterns.

Outside the massive Roman city walls are necropoli, with examples of temple tombs.

Side Town Centre

1. Harbour
2. Temples of Apollo and Athena
3. Theatre
4. Vespasian Monument, Arch and Colonnaded Street
5. Museum in Roman Bathhouse
6. Aqueduct, Nymphaeum and City Walls

0 metres 200
0 yards 200

For keys to symbols see back flap

The Red Tower, dominating the harbour at Alanya

❷ Alanya

🏔 110,000. 🚌 3 km (2 miles) W of city centre. ℹ️ Damlataş Cad 1 (near the cave), (0242) 513 12 40. 🛒 Wed & Fri. 🎽 International Triathlon (Sep). 🌐 sunsearch.info

The promontory and castle of Alanya are visible for miles and offer superb views of beaches and mountains. Now a large modern resort, in Roman times Alanya was called Coracesium, and was a stronghold of the pirates who menaced the grain fleets on their passage to Rome. After the defeat of the pirates in 65 BC, Coracesium became a thriving city. The Seljuk ruler, Alaeddin I Keykubad, made Alanya his winter residence and fortified it heavily.

A double line of defensive walls mount the promontory to enclose the Citadel (Kale), inside which is a Byzantine church. Punctuated by towers and gates, the walls are still in good condition. It takes about an hour to walk to the top, but there is an hourly bus service.

The harbour is commanded by the 35 m-high (115 ft) Red Tower (Kızılkule), a hexagonal structure built by Alaeddin Keykubad I in 1226 and now restored. The Red Tower protected Alanya's strategic dockyard, or *tersane*, which could accommodate five ships under construction at once. In Seljuk times, the plentiful local forests provided ample timber for shipbuilding and even for export. The garden of the museum has a collection of farming tools as well as items from Pamphylian sites in the area. A Phoenician inscription from the 6th century BC shows the development of lettering from its cuneiform origins.

Atatürk visited Alanya for a few days in 1935. The owner of the house where he stayed turned it into a museum. The ground floor has photographs and Atatürk memorabilia, and the upper floor displays the furniture of a typical Alanya house in Republican times.

There are several caves around the base of the cliffs, including a phosphorus cave, a pirate cave and a lovers' cave. The best known is the stalactite-hung **Damlataş Cave**, said to provide relief from asthma. The internal temperature registers a steady 23°C (73°F). Access is from the western beach, behind the Damlataş restaurant.

🏛 Museum
Hilmi Balcı Cad, Damlataş Cad. **Tel** (0242) 513 12 28 and 513 71 16. **Open** 8:30am–noon & 1–5pm Tue–Sun. 🗠

🗝 Damlataş Cave
Damlataş Mağarası
Open 6–10am for spa patients & 10am–7pm for the public. 🗠

Environs
Near Ehmedek, a village where local women sell silk and lace handicrafts, is a *bedesten* (trading hall) converted into a hotel, with high-arched rooms around a courtyard. There is a pool, a vaulted hall and cisterns below. Nearby is the restored 16th-century Süleymaniye Mosque and a 13th-century *türbe* (tomb).

❷ Anamur and Anemurium

110 km (68 miles) SE of Alanya. 🚌 on the coast road. ℹ️ at the bus station, (0324) 814 35 29.

The town of Anamur is bisected by the D400 coastal road, with the town centre to the north and the harbour to the south. There are good beaches and important turtle nesting sites here, and more to see at ancient Anemurium, located on a coastal headland – the southernmost tip of Turkey – west of the modern town.

Anemurium ("Place of the Winds"), first noted by the classical geographer Strabo (63 BC–AD 23), was founded in the 1st century AD, and thrived under the Byzantines. It was battered by an earthquake in around 580, and after the Arabs took Cyprus in 649, the vulnerable city was abandoned. It was never resettled, so many of the old Roman and Byzantine houses and tombs remain in good condition.

Environs
On the coast road 2 km (1 mile) east of Anamur lies **Mamure Castle**. Built over a Byzantine fort, it was occupied by the Crusaders. Rebuilt by Alaeddin Keykubad I, the castle was used by the Karamanoğlu dynasty and garrisoned by the Ottomans. Today, the fortress is often used as a film set.

🏯 Anemurium
Open 8am–7pm daily. 🗠

🏯 Mamure Castle
Mamure Kalesi. **Open** 8am–7:30pm daily. 🗠

The large baths complex at Anemurium

The Crusades in Turkey

Mediterranean Turkey is closely associated with the impact of the Crusades – the military campaigns mounted from the late 11th century onwards, in order to wrest the Holy Land from Muslim control.

The crusader armies marched through Anatolia to reach the Holy Land, capturing cities such as Edessa (Şanlıurfa) and Antioch (Antakya). The period reached its nadir with the sack of Constantinople by a crusader army in 1204 *(see p54)*. The military orders – the Knights Templar, Hospitaller Knights of St John and the Teutonic Order – were active all along the coast. The most prominent symbol of their presence is the Castle of St Peter at Bodrum *(see pp200–1)*.

Coastal Fortresses

Mamure Castle, near Anamur, is one of the best-preserved crusader castles on the southern coast of Turkey. The Ottomans expanded the castle and used it until 1921.

The 36 towers are still intact.

Crenellated walls

The castle is surrounded on three sides by the sea.

Shallow moat

Great Court

Death of Friedrich II
The Holy Roman Emperor drowned near Silifke in 1290. Silifke itself was held by the Knights of St John in 1211–66.

The Siege of Antioch 1095
Captured from the Seljuks during the First Crusade after a seven-month siege, Antioch (Antakya) became the seat of the Principality of Antioch, one of the three main Crusader kingdoms. It fell to the Mamelukes in 1284.

Insignia of the Templar order

The Capture of Rhodes
After taking Rhodes in 1310, the Knights of St John moved operations to Smyrna (now İzmir) in 1344. When Smyrna was lost to the Mongols, the knights moved down the coast to Bodrum.

The Knights Templar
The order was active in the Amanus Mountains and around Antioch (Antakya). The knights safeguarded the route into Syria.

The Knights of St John
The crests of English, French and German crusaders are carved into the walls of the Castle of St Peter at Bodrum.

Grand Master of the Teutonic Knights
The Teutonic Order held castles in Cilicia, in the Crusader-aligned Kingdom of Lesser Armenia (1198–1375).

Corinthian columns of the Temple of Zeus Olbia at Uzuncaburç

㉔ Silifke

🏠 105,000. 🚌 İnönü Cad. 𝒊 Göksu Mahallesi, Gürten Bozbey Cad 6, (0324) 714 11 51. **Closed** weekends. 🎭 Folklore and Culture Festival (3rd week in May).

Founded as Seleucia by one of Alexander the Great's generals, Silifke lies on an important route to Konya and the interior by way of the Göksu River valley. A temple of Jupiter, with its surviving columns topped by stork's nests, a Byzantine cistern and a Roman bridge can still be seen today. St Paul passed through here, and Thecla, his disciple, founded an underground church about 5 km (3 miles) east of Silifke. This is currently being restored. A Byzantine castle is accessible from the Konya road and,

9 km (6 miles) to the north, is a monument that points to where the Holy Roman Emperor Frederick Barbarossa drowned on 10 June 1190 while attempting to ford the deep Göksu River during the Third Crusade.

Silifke Museum, 1 km (0.5 mile) west of the town, houses the Gülnür hoard, a superb collection of 5,200 silver and gold coins dating from the reign of Alexander the Great.

🏛 Silifke Museum

Taşucu Cad. **Tel** (0324) 714 10 19. **Open** 8am–noon & 1–5pm Tue–Sun. 🎫

Environs

At **Uzuncaburç**, about 28 km (17 miles) north of Silifke, lie the remains of an impressive Roman city. Inhabited from Hittite times,

the city was called Olba by the Greeks and Diocaesarea by the Romans.

Beside the road are several temple tombs, complete with sarcophagi, which are worth a look. The centrepiece is the Temple of Zeus, with about 30 massive peristyle columns. However, the walls of the cella (which would have enclosed the statue of Zeus) were removed when the building was converted into a church. Other sights include a Greek theatre and two city gates. Also worth exploring are a Hellenistic tower, the necropolis and a pyramid-roofed mausoleum. Orchards surround the ruins today.

🏰 Uzuncaburç

Open Apr–Oct: 8am–8pm daily; Nov–Mar: 8am–5pm. 🎫 🎫 🎫

The romantic sea castle, off the coast near Kızkalesi

㉕ Kızkalesi

Kızkalesi is situated where the narrow coastal strip opens out onto the Çukurova plain. Its chief landmarks are two **castles**, one on the shore, and its sister, 200 m (656 ft) out to sea. Local fishermen will ferry you over to explore the ruins. The 12th-century castle on the shore was built on the ancient site of Korykos from the stones of Greek and Roman buildings preceding it.

In the early 19th century, a lighthouse marked the end of a mole leading from the sea castle, which lay on an island. Legend has it that a jealous father confined his daughter to this castle, but the fortress was more likely built for protection from the Mediterranean's fierce pirates.

Birds of the Göksu Delta

South of the main coast road near Silifke, where the Göksu River reaches the sea, 145 sq km (56 sq miles) have been designated as a region of outstanding environmental importance. The two lagoons are home to migrating and permanently residing water birds, including Dalmatian pelicans, pygmy cormorants, marbled

Nesting storks, Göksu Delta

and white-headed ducks, ospreys and terns. The marshlands provide food for wagtails, egrets, spoonbills and squacco, grey and purple heron. The best times to see the birds are at dawn and dusk in spring and autumn. Bird-watchers need their own transport to tour the delta, which is also an important nesting area for logger-head and green turtles.

Three km (2 miles) east of Kızkalesi are the ruins of **Elaiussa Sebaste**. The area around the theatre is under excavation by an Italian team. There is a Byzantine church and harbour buildings to the south of the road. The town must have been important in classical times, for no less than three aqueducts and numerous reservoirs were built to supply it with water. Four km (3 miles) further along the coast is Kanlıdivane ("Place of Blood"), a huge chasm 60 m (197 ft) deep, into which prisoners were thrown to their deaths. There are several churches and a Hellenistic tower around the chasm, which features carvings in niches in the side, and has become a haven for local wildlife. From this point onwards, the coast abounds in ancient ruins, although the population is sparse until you reach the holiday villages associated with Mersin.

The spectacular Selale Waterfall on the Tarsus River, outside Tarsus

🏰 **Castles**
Open 8am–7pm daily. 📷

🏰 **Elaiussa Sebaste**
Open 9am–6pm daily. 📷

㉖ Mersin (İçel)

🏙 1,327,000. 🚌 NE of city centre (service buses from train station). 🚉 İstiklal Cad NE of city centre, (0324) 238 16 48. 🚢 Near tourist office in the harbour area. ℹ️ İsmet İnönü Bul 5, (0324) 238 32 71. 🎭 Mersin Arts Festival (Sep).

Mersin is a harbour city with relatively few tourist attractions. The main reason to stay here is to catch a ferry to Northern Cyprus. Accommodation is plentiful and restaurants varied, with good fish and fast food. Mersin's **museum** contains local archaeological remains such as glass, earthenware and bronze items.

Mersin means "myrtle" in Turkish, referring to the shrub found all along the coast. The city's official name is İçel (the name of the province of which it is the capital).

Compared to other Turkish cities, Mersin is fairly young, and was first incorporated in 1852, with a cosmopolitan population of Turks, Greeks and Armenians. The Turkish government had plans to turn Mersin into a strategic port, but this never happened.

In 1989, the government initiated a housing scheme here for Kurds displaced by ethnic fighting in the eastern provinces. But the transition to city life has been hard for these people, and many remain jobless. Mersin has the transient feel of a port, which many believe stems from the city not having enjoyed the benefits of a structured Ottoman administration.

About 12 km (8 miles) west of Mersin lie the ruins of Pompeiopolis, where the remains of a harbour and a column-lined street that date from the 2nd century AD survive. In 1812, Captain Francis Beaufort described this street, the city gates, a substantial theatre and a "beautiful harbour with parallel sides and circular ends" as being on the whole so imposing that even "the most illiterate seaman in the ship could not behold it without emotion".

🏛 **Mersin Museum**
Republic Square, Halkevi Binası. **Tel** (0324) 231 96 18. **Open** 9am–noon & 1:30–4:30pm Tue–Sun. 📷

㉗ Tarsus

🏙 245,000. 🚌 Drop-off point at Cleopatra's Gate. 🚉 from Adana.

Although St Paul is referred to in the Bible as "the man from Tarsus", this does not mean that there is a lot to see in the town. The museum has moved to a cultural centre, near an excavated portion of the old city. Here, a section of Roman street, complete with stoas (covered walk-ways), has been exposed to a depth of 2–3 m (6.5–10 ft) below today's street level. In the back streets of the town is a covered well, named after St Paul, which is still a place of pilgrimage.

St Paul's well, Tarsus

Tarsus once controlled the Cilician Gates, a strategic pass through the Taurus Mountains into the Anatolian interior. The route is now bypassed by a motorway carrying oil tankers and other truck traffic to Ankara and beyond.

㉘ Adana

Adana is an important manufacturing centre, with its origins rooted in commerce and trade. The city lies on the Seyhan River, which is spanned by a Roman bridge. This bridge marks the lowest possible ford over the river, which bisected a crucial extension of the Silk Route through the Cilician Gates. The pass linked the coast with the interior of Anatolia. Adana was ruled by the Arabs, Seljuks, Armenians and Mamelukes until it came under Ottoman sovereignty in 1516. From 1918 until 1922 France held sway over Adana.

The Archaeological Museum, with local finds displayed outside

Exploring Adana

Adana's old quarter includes metal workshops, an 18th-century church and a clock tower. The Roman Stone Bridge, restful park and stunning Sabancı Central Mosque are all worth visiting, and the city makes a comfortable base if you are travelling further east.

Be sure to sample Adana's speciality kebab, which is made of highly spiced minced meat pressed onto a skewer and grilled. This is served with *şalgam*, a fiery blood-red drink made from red carrot pickles and turnip juice, or *aşlama*, a liquorice drink.

🏛 Ethnography Museum
Etnografya Müzesi
İnönü Cad (off Ziyapaşa Bulvarı). **Tel** (0322) 363 37 17. **Open** 8am–noon & 1–5pm Tue–Sun. 🚫

The museum is housed in a former church situated to

Colourful traditional *kilim* (rug) in the Ethnography Museum

the west of the old town, and includes a reconstruction of an old Adana house. There is a collection of ceremonial weaponry and firearms, while the displays of copper kitchenware illustrate a prominent local trade. Tents, carpets and textiles complete the display.

🏛 Archaeological Museum
Adana Müzesi
Fuzuli Sok 10. **Tel** (0322) 454 38 55. **Open** 8am–noon & 1–5pm Tue–Sun. 🚫 🚷

The museum contains objects from excavations of local late-Hittite sites, as well as Hellenistic and Roman remains from in and around the city. A highlight is the natural crystal figure of a Hittite god, Tarhunda, clad in a pointed hat, together with Eastern Anatolian Urartian belts from around 600 BC.

There is also a gold and silver ram-headed bracelet and a gold ring bearing the head of a woman. The fine Achilleus marble sarcophagus, from the 2nd century AD, has lively battle scenes; another sarcophagus is adorned with standing draped women. A Roman mosaic shows animals listening to lyre music.

🄲 Sabancı Central Mosque
Merkez Camii
Fuzuli Cad (near the Roman Stone Bridge). **Open** daily (except during prayer times). 🚫 donation.

Completed in 1998, this is Turkey's largest mosque and rivals most in the Middle East for sheer size. The principal dome is 54 m (177 ft) high. The architectural style of the mosque follows that of the Blue Mosque *(see p92)* in Istanbul and Edirne's Selimiye Mosque *(see p158)*. Only the Sabancı and Blue mosques feature the hallowed six minarets. All work on the mosque, down to state-of-the-art wireless acoustics, was carried out by Turkey's most prestigious craftsmen.

The massive Sabancı Central Mosque, with its six minarets

The Roman Stone Bridge, still in use after more than 18 centuries

🏛 Roman Stone Bridge
Taş Köprü

The graceful, 14-arch Roman Stone Bridge over the Seyhan River is 319 m (1,056 ft) long. Built in the 2nd century AD, during the reign of Emperor Hadrian, the bridge may be one of the oldest still used by vehicular traffic. It originally had 21 arches, but only 14 of these are visible and in use today. The bridge has been restored several times, first by Emperor Justinian in the 6th century and later under the Ottomans.

🕌 Great Mosque
Ulu Camii

Abidinpaşa Cad. **Open** daily (except during prayer times). 🛐 donation.

The Great Mosque was begun in 1507 by Halil Ramazanoğlu, scion of a powerful dynastic clan; however, it was not completed until 1541. Its octagonal minaret is a particularly striking feature. The bands of black and white stone used for the mosque are a typical feature of Syrian religious architecture. The impressive tomb of the Ramazanoğlu family, located

The Great Mosque, decorated with black and white marble

inside the mosque, is finished in beautiful tiles. A *medrese* (Koranic seminary) is located in the east wing of the building.

🕌 Covered Bazaar

Near the clock tower on Ali Münif Cad. **Open** dawn to dusk, daily.

Adana's medieval-looking clock tower was built in late Ottoman times. It overlooks the Covered Bazaar, where handicrafts, trinkets and food items are sold. Near the Covered Bazaar is the Çarşı Hamamı, a beautiful, domed Turkish bath with an exquisite marble interior. The baths are open to all.

Adana City Centre

① Ethnography Museum
② Archaeological Museum
③ Sabancı Central Mosque
④ Roman Stone Bridge
⑤ Great Mosque
⑥ Covered Bazaar I

㉙ Karatepe

Karatepe is a late Hittite fortress dating from the 9th century BC built on a hill beside the Seyhan River. It was discovered by the German archaeologist H T Bossert in 1946. When Bossert's team excavated the site, they found two entrances. Each was lined with relief carvings and featured an inscription in both ancient Phoenician and Hieroglyphic Hittite. As the Phoenician language had already been deciphered, this turned out to be a vital clue to the interpretation of the hieroglyphic form of the Hittite language, which was found to be close to Luwian, another ancient Anatolian language.

The pleasant hilltop site, next to a man-made lake, has several picnic areas and is well worth the 70 km (44 mile) drive from Adana. The site is open 8am–noon and 1–5pm daily, and there is an admission fee.

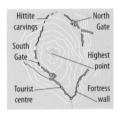

Hittite carvings — North Gate — South Gate — Highest point — Tourist centre — Fortress wall

Karatepe Fortress

Karatepe Hill juts into the waters of a lake created by the construction of the Aslantaş Dam. Water from the lake irrigates the fertile farmlands around Adana.

The Karatepe site is believed to have been the fortified residence of the Hittite king of Adana, Azatiwatas. Entry was through formal gateways, one of which is shown right. Each was lined with orthostats (carved relief panels). The gateways are now roofed to protect the ancient stonework.

Orthostat (relief panel)

Carved lion figure

The orthostats consist of carvings of sacrificial, hunting and feasting scenes. There are numerous figures of gods and sphinxes, interspersed with scenes of ordinary people, all done in a cheerful cartoon style.

Warrior figure

Relief carvings at Karatepe show influences from a number of cultures, including Assyria and ancient Egypt. Because of this, archaeologists believe the carvings were executed by foreign craftsmen recruited by King Azatiwatas to work on the site.

The remains of the theatre at Hierapolis (Castabala)

㉚ Hierapolis (Castabala)

22 km (14 miles) N of Osmaniye.
Open 8am–5pm daily. 🖼️

On the road leading to the Hittite site of Karatepe, take some time to see the ancient Roman city of Hierapolis (Castabala) – not to be confused with the other Hierapolis *(see pp190–91)*, near Denizli. Hierapolis (Castabala) was mentioned by the elder Pliny (AD 23–79) around AD 70. There is a colonnaded street, theatre, baths and a hill fortress.

㉛ Yakacık

22 km (14 miles) N of İskenderun.
ℹ️ in the town hall.
Open 8am–5pm daily. 🚻 🅿️ 🛏️

Yakacık (Ancient Payas) is the site of the Sokollu Mehmet Paşa complex. This is not well known, even though the local municipality, which runs the site with great enthusiasm, claims that many thousands of visitors come here each year. The complex features all the amenities beloved by Ottoman travellers – mosque, baths, caravanserai and theological college. The caravanserai was built in 1574 for Muslims making the *haj* (pilgrimage to Mecca). It was the brainchild

of Sokollu Mehmet Paşa, one of the most enlightened grand viziers ever to serve the Ottoman state. A Serb who rose to power from humble beginnings, Sokollu Mehmet Paşa served under three sultans between 1564 and 1579. It was under his initiative that Sultan Selim II (1524–74) seized Cyprus from the Venetians in 1571. However, Selim's fondness for the island's wine earned him the nickname of "the Sot" and proved to be his undoing, as he allegedly

slipped in the bath while inebriated and never regained consciousness.

㉜ İskenderun

🏙️ 166,000. 🚌 Atatürk Cad, (0326) 616 36 31. 🚆 İstasyon Cad, (0326) 614 00 49. ⛴️ İskele Cad, (0326) 613 54 00.
ℹ️ Atatürk Bulvarı 49/B, (0326) 614 16 20. 🎭 İskenderun Culture and Fine Arts Week (1st week in Jul).

The city of İskenderun (formerly Alexandretta) was originally founded to commemorate Alexander the Great's victory over Persian emperor Darius at the Battle of Issus in 332 BC *(see pp50–51)*. It was a major trading centre in Roman times, and is still an important port. The people of İskenderun are proud of their multicultural city and of its remaining Christian and Jewish communities. The surviving Armenian, Catholic, and Orthodox churches are hidden in the backstreets, along with mosques. None are particularly old, but all will welcome visitors on Sundays. The promenade, with its attractive French colonial architecture, is a favourite place for an evening stroll.

Massive Atatürk memorial statue on the promenade at İskenderun

For hotels and restaurants in this area see pp330–39 and pp346–61

❸ Antakya

Antakya was founded (as Antioch) by the Seleucids in 300 BC, and was their capital. Later, it became the third-largest city of the Roman Empire, and an important Christian centre. Antioch was devastated by earthquakes in the 6th century and fell into Arab hands in 638. Although recaptured by the Byzantines, its role was gradually displaced by the rise of Constantinople. In 1098, Antakya was captured by the Crusaders after a seven-month siege, and became capital of the Principality of Antioch. It passed to the Mamelukes in 1268 and the Ottomans in 1516, and eventually slipped into decline.

Exploring Antakya

Antakya is located on the Asi (Orontes) River. After World War I, it was part of French-ruled Syria Following a plebiscite in 1939, it became part of Turkey, together with the rest of Hatay Province. The city's mixed population, Arab cultural influence and vestiges of French colonial rule give Antakya a distinct character. You are likely to hear Arabic spoken, and many local dishes, such as *şam oruğu*, a wheaten ball filled with minced meat and walnuts, have Arabic origins. Quite different to mainstream Turkish cuisine, one of the real joys of a trip to Hatay is to sample delicious *hummus*, *muhammara* (a spicy dip made from hot peppers, walnuts and breadcrumbs) and the broad bean and tahini dip *bakla*. Antakya is also famous for its *künefe*, a wonderful cheese-based pastry dessert.

🏛 St Peter's Grotto

Open 9am–noon & 1:30–5:30pm (flexible for group tours) Tue–Sun.

This cave church is thought to have been founded by St Luke. It is named, however, after Peter, who was in the forefront of the early church movement from his headquarters in Antioch. Rebuilt by the Crusaders, it is partially floored with mosaic, and the remains of frescoes can be seen. A tiny spring in the church was used for baptisms. The church was repaired in the 19th century by Capuchin monks, who are now its custodians. A festival is held here annually on 29 June.

Near the church is a relief portrait carved into the hillside. This is thought by some to be

The Grotto where St Peter preached to the early Christians

Antakya City Centre

① St Peter's Grotto
② Bazaar
③ Archaeological Museum

YAVUZ SULTAN SELIM CAD
SÜREYYAHALEFOĞLU CAD
① St Peter's Grotto
Bus station
İSKENDERUN
4 Km
ABBDURAHMAN CAD
İSTİKLAL CAD
KANATLI CAD
ATATÜRK CAD
ASİ
PLIK CAD
GÜNGÖR CAD
UZUN ÇARŞI CAD
KURTULUŞ CAD
ULUS CAD
CUMHURİYET CAD
KEMAL PAŞA CAD
Archaeological Museum ③
② Bazaar
🅲 Habibi Neccar Camii
GÜNDÜZ CAD
SAMANDAG
ASİ
Greek Orthodox Church
🅣 Turkish Catholic Church
Antakya Park
HÜRRİYET CAD
RIHTIM CAD
OĞUZ CAD
ANKARTALAN CAD
VALİURGEN BUL
🆔
HARBİYE
HASTAHANE CAD

0 metres 750
0 yards 750

A cobbler at his work bench in the Bazaar

a representation of Charon, the boatman who conveyed the dead to Hades. However, the image is more likely to be that of a member of the Seleucid dynasty, founders of the city.

Three other churches operate in the city – the central Greek Orthodox Church, a Capuchin Catholic Church and the Korean Methodist church, the latter in the former French Embassy.

📖 Bazaar

Open 9am–9/10pm Mon–Sat.

A warren of streets to the east of the Roman Bridge houses Antakya's bazaar. Here, you can see *hans* (warehouses) dating from Ottoman times, in which skilled metalworkers are hard at work. Donkeys are a common sight in the streets around the bazaar, and the aroma of exotic foods fills the air. The shops in the bazaar are a good place to sample *künefe*, a pudding made of cream cheese and spun wheat, baked in a sweet sauce and served warm.

This is only one of the local specialities to be savoured in the city. Many restaurants are located in the bazaar.

Habibi Neccar Camii is a mosque converted from a Byzantine church, which itself succeeded a classical temple. The minaret was added in the 17th century. It is a place of pilgrimage in honour of a local saint, whose head is reputedly buried beneath it.

VISITORS' CHECKLIST

Practical Information
🗺 150,000. ℹ Şehit Mustafa Sevgi Cas 8/A, (0326) 216 60 98. 🏛 St Peter's Catholic Church Festival (29 Jun). 🛍 Mon–Sat.

Transport
🚌 Abdürrahman Melek Cad, NE of town centre, (0326) 214 91 97.

🏛 Archaeological Museum

Gündüz Cad 1. **Tel** (0326) 214 61 68. **Open** Apr–Oct: 9am–6:30pm Tue–Sun; Nov–Mar: 9am–5:30pm Tue–Sun. 📷

This museum was originally built by the French to store finds unearthed by foreign excavations when Hatay Province was part of the French protectorate of Syria. Today, the museum houses an impressive collection of Roman mosaics, surpassed only by the finds at Gaziantep recovered from Zeugma (*see p312*). The Antakya mosaics were found all over the province, though many come from the ancient pleasure gardens of Daphne (modern-day Harbiye). Executed in a lively, libertine style, the mosaics portray the deeds of Thetis, Orpheus, Dionysus, Hercules and other mythical figures.

Statue in the Archaeological Museum

The museum also has a coin collection, displays of palaeolithic objects and Hittite sculptures from Carchemish and other sites in northern Syria. The nearby park is a peaceful refuge from the city.

Environs

South of Antakya lies **Harbiye**, famed for its forests of cypress and laurel, and for its waterfalls and trout streams. In antiquity, the valley was known as Daphne, after the mythical "queen of the nymphs" pursued by Apollo, and was a popular resort. However, the ruins of the temple to Apollo and the ancient pleasure gardens have all disappeared. Reachable by dolmuş from Antakya, there are several good restaurants here, and local gift shops sell the popular laurel soap.

❸❹ Samandağ

25 km (15 miles) SW of Antakya. 🚐 local dolmuş from Antakya.

Southwest of Antakya lies Samandağ, a modest, largely Arabic-speaking resort town near the border, where you will feel that you have already entered Syria. There are a couple of hotels and seaside restaurants along the somewhat scruffy beach.

North of the town is the site of Seleucia ad Piera (modern-day Çevlik), founded as the port of Antioch in around 300 BC. This was the site of an important temple to Zeus, which still stands above the coast and affords grand views over the sea.

Because ancient Antioch lay at the junction of important trading routes, Seleucia ad Piera became a major port, but the danger posed by the region's periodic but devastating floods led Emperor Vespasian to commission a tunnel to divert floodwaters from the town. The **Titus Tunnel** (Titus ve Vespasianyus Tüneli), completed by Vespasian's son, Titus, is an impressive cutting running 1,380 m (4,527 ft) through solid rock. The tunnel is 7 m (23 ft) high and 6 m (20 ft) wide.

🏛 Titus Tunnel

25 km (16 miles) SE of Antakya. **Open** daily. 🌞 Only in summer.

The Titus Tunnel, a flood-control project built by the Romans

Exploring Ankara and Western Anatolia

Western Anatolia may seem somewhat bleak
and inhospitable, yet the vast steppes, remote
towns and salt lakes have much to offer the
visitor. This is also where Turkey's administrative
heart beats. Ankara, the efficient modern capital,
has excellent transport links to the rest of the
country and is a good starting point for tours
of the region. Southeast of the pious city
of Konya, former capital of the Seljuk
Sultanate of Rum, lies the Bronze Age
site of Çatalhöyük, widely regarded as
the world's earliest urban settlement.

Houses painted in pastel shades, Afyon

Sights at a Glance
1. Ankara pp244–51
2. Konya pp254–7
3. Çatalhöyük
4. Beyşehir
5. Eğirdir
6. Afyon
7. Sivrihisar
8. Şeyitgazi Valley
9. Eskişehir
10. Kütahya pp262–3
11. Çavdarhisar

Sunset at tranquil Lake Eğirdir

Key
- Motorway
- Dual carriageway
- Major road
- Minor road
- Scenic route
- Main railway
- Minor railway
- △ Summit

For additional map symbols *see back flap*

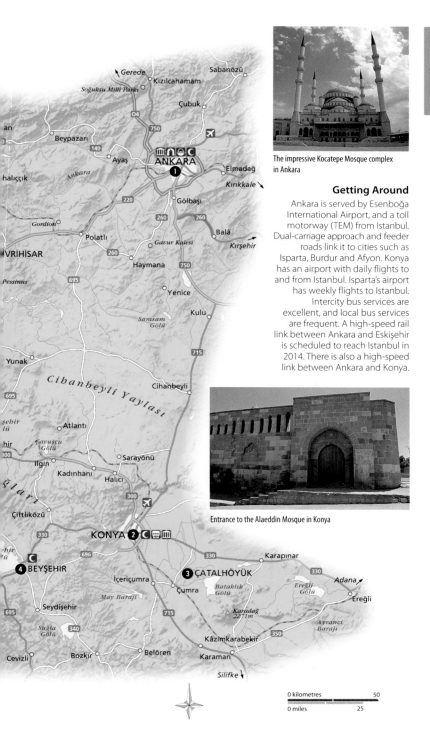

The impressive Kocatepe Mosque complex in Ankara

Getting Around

Ankara is served by Esenboğa International Airport, and a toll motorway (TEM) from Istanbul. Dual-carriage approach and feeder roads link it to cities such as Isparta, Burdur and Afyon. Konya has an airport with daily flights to and from Istanbul. Isparta's airport has weekly flights to Istanbul. Intercity bus services are excellent, and local bus services are frequent. A high-speed rail link between Ankara and Eskişehir is scheduled to reach Istanbul in 2014. There is also a high-speed link between Ankara and Konya.

Entrance to the Alaeddin Mosque in Konya

0 kilometres 50

0 miles 25

❶ Ankara

Ankara, the modern capital of the Turkish Republic, occupies a strategic location on the east–west route across the Anatolian steppe. Believed to have been the site of a Hittite city, there is evidence of Phrygian settlement here in 1200 BC, when it was known as Ancyra. The city was occupied by the Lydians and Persians before its absorption into the Roman Empire in 24 BC. Annexed by the Seljuks in 1073, the city played a military and commercial role until Byzantine times. At this time, wool from the Angora (Ankara) goat became a major export. When Atatürk chose Ankara as the new capital in 1923, land values boomed and developments spread out across the surrounding hills.

View of Ankara, a modern capital with attractive, wide boulevards

Exploring Ankara

A metro system, state theatres and good museums combine with lush parks and good shopping in the Ulus/Hisar district to ensure a pleasant visit. Buses and dolmuşes cover the main routes in the city.

🏛 Roman Baths

Hamamları
Çankırı Cad, Ulus. **Tel** (0312) 310 72 80.
🚌 Ulus. **Open** 8:30am–5:30pm daily. 🎫

Very little remains to be seen of these 3rd-century Roman baths. With the trademark features of *frigidarium* (cold room), *tepidarium* (warm room) and *caldarium* (hot room), these baths were built to honour Asclepius, the Greek god of medicine.

🏛 Temple of Augustus and Rome

Augustus Tapınağı
Ulus. 🚌 Ulus. **Open** daily.
This temple was built in about 20 BC by King Pylamenes of

Galatia to honour a visit by the great Roman emperor, Augustus. The inscription on the outer walls is one of the few surviving testaments to authenticate Augustus's accomplishments. The temple became a Byzantine church in the 4th century AD.

Adjoining the temple are the mosque (dating from 1425) and tomb of **Hacı Bayram Veli** (1352–1429), founder of the Bayrami religious sect. The fine Seljuk wooden interior, in particular, is worth seeing. Some renovation work was done in the 17th century by the famous architect Mimar Sinan (*see p105*).

Nearby is the **Column of Julian**, reaching 15 m (49 ft) and dating from AD 362. The column commemorates a visit by this Roman emperor.

🎫 Hacı Bayram Veli

🚌 Ulus. **Open** daily (except during prayer times). 🎫 donation appreciated.

🏛 Column of Julian

Jülyanüs Direği. 🚌 Ulus.

A typical shop selling old carpets in the Hisar area

🏛 Museum of the War of Independence

Kurtuluş Savaşı Müzesi
Cumhuriyet Bulvarı, Ulus.
Tel (0312) 310 71 40.
🚌 Ulus. **Open** 9am–noon & 1–5pm Tue–Sun.
🎫 (students, soldiers and teachers free).

Ankara City Centre

① Roman Baths
② Temple of Augustus and Rome
③ Museum of the War of Independence
④ Republic Museum
⑤ Bazaars and Markets
⑥ Ethnography Museum
⑦ Museum of Anatolian Civilizations (*see pp246–7*)
⑧ Çengelhan Rahmi M. Koç Museum
⑨ Citadel
⑩ Youth Park
⑪ Locomotive Museum
⑫ Atatürk Mausoleum
⑬ Kocatepe Mosque
⑭ Atatürk Boulevard
⑮ Kavaklidere
⑯ Turkish Grand National Assembly

The attractive museum building once served as the Grand National Assembly. A collection of photographs, ephemera and documents records the events that led up to the founding of the Republic (1919–23). Although captions are in Turkish, the exhibits are self-explanatory.

🏛 Republic Museum

Cumhuriyet Müzesi
Cumhuriyet Meydanı. **Tel** (0312) 310 53 61. 🚌 Ulus. 🚇 Ulus. **Open** 8:45am–4:30pm Tue–Sun. 🎫 (students, soldiers and teachers free).

The displays in the museum celebrate the advances and achievements that the Turkish Republic has made since its inception in 1923. Most of the labels are in Turkish.

Bazaars and Markets

🚌 Ulus. **Open** 9:30am–5:30pm daily.
The most interesting and "authentic" shopping districts are in the Ulus/Hisar area. The streets to look for are Salman Sokak, Konya Sokak and Çıkrıkçılar Sokak. Markets cater to tourists and sell a wide range of jewellery, carpets, herbal remedies, spices, iron and copper trinkets, as well as various textiles. Also look out for the Bakırcılar Çarşısı (Copperworkers' Bazaar) on Salman Sokak.

Local flea markets and produce markets are held in most districts at least once a week. One of the best takes place on Saturdays on Konya Sokak in the Ulus area.

🏛 Ethnography Museum

Ethnografya Müzesi
Talat Paşa Bulvarı. **Tel** (0312) 310 30 07. 🚌 Ulus. **Open** 8:30am–12:30pm & 1:30–5:30pm Tue–Sun. 🎫 🚌

Set in a pretty, white marble kiosk (summerhouse), with beautiful Ottoman interiors, and carpets and mosque woodwork dating from Seljuk times onwards, the museum offers

a charming record of Turkish costume and handicrafts through the years.

🏛 Çengelhan Rahmi M. Koç Museum

Çengelhan Rahmi M. Koç Müzesi
Sutepe Mah, Depo Sokak 1, Altındağ, Ankara. **Tel** (0312) 309 68 00. **Open** 10am–5pm Tue–Thu, 10am–7pm Sat & Sun. 🎫 🏛 🚻 ♿ 🌐 rmk-museum.org.tr

A sister museum to the Rahmi Koç Industrial Museum in Istanbul, the Ankara site is opposite the entrance to Ankara Castle in a restored 16th century *kervansaray*.

Eclectic exhibits range from toys, bicycles, prams and scientific instruments to air, rail and sea transport. Early motor cars include a 1918 Model T Ford. A replica of the Nile river boat from the film "African Queen" is among the 1,200 items on display. The museum café is pleasant but try the Brasserie on the ground floor for gourmet fare.

🏛 Turkish Grand National Assembly

T.B.M.M. (Türkiye Büyük Millet Meclesi
Ismet Inönü Bul. **Tel** (0312) 420 67 42. 🚌 Bakanlıklar. **Closed** to the public.

This impressive complex, housing the legislature, is of a pre-World War II, German design. Visitors wishing to see the General Assembly Meeting Hall of the TGNA must call (0312) 420 68 87 to make an appointment.

Triangular fountain outside the Turkish Grand National Assembly

Museum of Anatolian Civilizations
Anadolu Medeniyetleri Müzesi

Turkey's most outstanding museum occupies two renovated Ottoman-era buildings and is situated in the Atpazarı (horse market) district of the city, below the citadel. The museum displays the achievements of Anatolia's many diverse cultures. Exhibits range from simple Paleolithic stone tools to clay tablets inscribed in Assyrian cuneiform and exquisite Hellenistic and Roman sculptures. The displays are laid out in chronological order, and include a statuette of the Mother Goddess from Çatalhöyük (see p258), Bronze Age treasures from the royal tombs at Alacahöyük (see p298) and superb Hittite sculptures and orthostat reliefs.

★ Serving Table
Found at Gordion (see p251), this 8th century BC folding wooden table is an outstanding example of Phrygian craftsmanship.

Lecture theatre

Urartian Lion Statuette
Unearthed at Kayalıdere, this small bronze lion shows the skill of the Urartian craftsmen.

Museum Entrance
The main displays are housed in the Mahmut Paşa Bedesten, a bazaar warehouse built in the 15th century.

Terracotta Cooking Pot
Neolithic peoples favoured the use of terracotta. This small pot and stand, found at Çatalhöyük (see p258), dates from approximately the 6th millennium BC.

Gallery Guide

The museum is undergoing refurbishment and reorganization, so the layout may differ from the floorplan shown. While the work is being carried out some sections of the museum may be closed.

★ **Sphinx Relief**
This well-preserved Neo-Hittite stone relief, dating from the 9th century BC, was found at Carchemish.

VISITORS' CHECKLIST

Practical Information
Saraçlar Sokak (below the Citadel).
Tel (0312) 324 31 60. **Open** Apr–Oct: 8:30am–7pm daily; Nov–Mar: 8:30am–5:30pm.

Transport
Ulus.

Ground floor

Interior
The uncluttered layout of the interior provides the perfect setting for the vast range of historic collections.

Golden Bowl with Studs
This early-Bronze Age bowl from Alacahöyük dates from the 3rd millennium BC.

★ **Roman Head**
The spread of classical Greek and Roman civilization gave rise to more realistic works of art, such as this marble head.

Lower floor

Key

- Urartian Period
- Phrygian Period
- Hittite Period
- Assyrian Colonies
- Early Bronze Age
- Chalcolithic and Neolithic
- Paleolithic
- Classical Period

Artifacts displayed in the museum gardens

Exploring Ankara

Visitors travelling to Ankara will notice the striking contrasts between the modern city centre and the old town. Wide, tree-lined boulevards, green parks, smart embassies, government buildings and universities make up the new administrative centre, while parts of the old town – particularly a number of streets around the citadel – are remarkably simple and traditional. Atatürk's striking mausoleum dominates the modern part of this capital city, symbolizing a fusion of ancient and modern concepts.

Aerial view of Ankara's Youth Park

🏰 Citadel
Hisar
Hisarparkı Cad. 🚌 Hisar. **Open** daily.

The Hisar, or Byzantine citadel, dominates the northern end of Ankara. The walls enclose a ramshackle collection of wooden houses, with some passable restaurants, several carpet shops and junkyards filled with antiques and collectables. Salman Sokak, or "Copper Alley", lives up to its nickname, with plenty of old and new copper pieces on offer. You will find bargains and bric-a-brac here, but few real treasures.

Youth Park
Gençlik Parkı
Atatürk Bulvarı. 🚌 Opera or Ulus. 🚇 Ulus. **Open** dawn to dusk daily.

The Youth Park just south of Ulus is Ankara's liveliest and most popular area for urban recreation. Now extensively renovated, the park has a small lake with fountains. There are also a few pleasant cafés, where tea is served in a *samovar* (double-tiered pot) at tables overlooking the lake. There is

also a funfair *(luna park)*, a sports stadium, tennis courts and a swimming pool.

The lovely Korean Garden, on the other side of Cumhuriyet Bulvarı, commemorates the oft-forgotten combat role played by Turkish soldiers during the Korean War (1950–54). The 45 m-high (148 ft) Parachute Tower here was once popular with daredevils willing to pay for leaping from its heights.

🚂 Turkish Railways Open-Air Steam Locomotive Museum
Açık Hava Buharlı Lokomotif Müzesi
Ankara Gar Sahası, Celâl Bayar Bulvarı üzeri. **Tel** (0312) 309 05 15. **Open** 9am–6pm daily. 🚻

This impressive open-air museum close to the Ankara Railway Station is bound to appeal to a broad audience, and not simply those visitors interested in steam traction. It should not be confused with the Turkish Railways (TCDD) Museum, which

is located inside the station. Atatürk's personal railway carriage, a gift from Adolf Hitler, can be seen adjacent to the main station concourse. The open-air collection of steam-driven giants, located across the railway tracks to the left, includes a number of old German models which were used during the invasion of Russia in World War II.

If the museum is closed, ask one of the railway personnel in the station building to arrange for someone to open it.

Guard at the Atatürk Mausoleum

🏛 Atatürk Mausoleum
Anıtkabir
Anıt Cad, Anıttepe. **Tel** (0312) 231 79 75. 🚌 Anıttepe. 🚇 Tandoğan. **Open** Feb–mid-May: 9am–4:30pm; mid-May–Oct: 9am–7pm; Nov–Jan: 9am–4pm. Sound and light show (summer).

Ankara's most imposing site commands a hill to the west of the city. Construction of this monument, begun in 1944, was completed in 1953. Twenty four stone lions flank the pathway leading to the mausoleum. To one side of the central courtyard, bronze doors open into the marble-lined hall and cenotaph, where visiting heads of state and vast numbers of ordinary Turks still come to pay their respects to Turkey's supreme leader. İsmet İnönü, second President of the Republic, is entombed opposite. A hall nearby houses some splendid vintage cars used by Atatürk, and visitors can also admire a display of personal possessions and gifts presented to Atatürk by fellow heads of state over the years.

Vintage steam engine at the Open-Air Steam Locomotive Museum

Kocatepe Mosque

Kocatepe Camii
Olgunlar Sok. Kocatepe. Kızılay.
Open daily (except during prayer times). donations appreciated.

Kocatepe Mosque is a landmark in Ankara. One of the world's largest mosques, it is a four-minaret replica of the Blue Mosque *(see pp92–3)* in Istanbul. Underneath it is a western-style shopping centre called Beğendik, as well as a large car park.

Atatürk Boulevard

Atatürk Bulvarı
Ankara's premier boulevard links the old city with the Presidential Palace and the official government buildings. Along the way is the original home of the Red Crescent (Kızılay), the Islamic equivalent of the Red Cross, as well as Turkey's first department store, Gima.

Kavaklıdere and Çankaya

Ankara's up-market shopping areas cater for the diplomatic corps and government elite. The best can be found south of Kızılay in the suburbs of Kavaklıdere and Çankaya, where many foreign embassies are located. Going south on Tunalı Hilmi Caddesi, parallel to Atatürk Bulvarı, you reach Kuğulu Park and Cinnah Caddesi. Both streets are studded with designer boutiques. Karum, opposite the park, is an exclusive shopping centre. Do not expect bargains here.

Atakule

Atatürk Bulvarı terminates in Çankaya Caddesi. A short stroll down this lively street will take

Chandelier inside the Kocatepe Mosque

you to the impressive Atakule tower and shopping complex. In good weather, the restaurant at the top of the 125-m high (410 ft) tower affords excellent views over the city.

Presidential Palace

Cumhurbaşkanlığı Köşkü
Çankaya Cad. **Tel** (0312) 470 11 00.
Çankaya. **Open** 1–5pm Sun & national holidays only. no entrance fee, but passport or identity card required.

Set in a formal garden, the residence is not open to the public, but visitors can view Atatürk's house, which is now a museum, within the grounds. The father of the Turkish republic moved here in 1921 and this is where he planned the direction his country would take in years to come. The house has a slightly sombre atmosphere. The ground floor is decorated in a classic Ottoman fashion, while upstairs provides visitors with a glimpse of Atatürk's lifestyle and personal tastes.

Sign at Atatürk Farm

Atatürk Farm and Zoo

Atatürk Orman Çiftliği
Çiftlik Cad. **Tel** (0312) 211 01 70.
Gazi. **Open** 9am–5pm Tue–Thu & Sat & Sun.

Ankara's many parks were established in the early years of the republic, since Atatürk believed that parks and natural recreation areas were part of his country's heritage.

His farm on the outskirts of Ankara is one such peaceful retreat and is a good destination for those with children.

Apart from a replica of Atatürk's boyhood home in Salonika (modern Thessaloniki), there are large leafy grounds and orchards to explore and enjoy.

Much of the produce that can be sampled at the farm, such as ice cream, yoghurt, and meat rolls, are made on site. There is also a beer brewery.

The farm grounds adjoin the railway line. It is most convenient to take the suburban train to Gazi Station and make your way from there.

The vast central courtyard and stark simplicity of Atatürk's mausoleum, housing his plain sarcophagus

Ankara: Further Afield

Life in the Turkish capital is enhanced by a number of green belts situated around the outskirts of the city. Here, the focus is on outdoor and leisure activities. These are made possible by the proximity of forests, ski centres, thermal spas and some attractive picnic areas. Most forest areas and parks are open from dawn to dusk; a guardian or ranger is generally in attendance and a small fee will be charged for vehicles. Taking your own vehicle is recommended for maximum enjoyment; the centres are clearly marked off the main roads. Note that camping is restricted to designated areas only. Most of the attractions listed here are day outings from Ankara, but if you want to "take the waters" at a spa, plan to spend a few days.

A pleasant outdoor swimming pool at Kızılcahamam

The town of Kızılcahamam, with the blue spa building on the left

🎿 Apple Mountain
Elma Dağı
23 km (14 miles) E of Ankara on the Sivas road. 🚗

Located at an altitude of 1,855 m (6,085 ft), this is the nearest ski centre to Ankara. On snowy weekends the slopes are crowded with locals skiing, skating and tobogganing. Although the season here is limited and the runs short and busy, Apple Mountain makes a good place to practise before heading eastwards to try the more challenging runs at Palandöken (*see p323*).

🌲 Soğuksu National Park
Soğuksu Milli Parkı
82 km (51 miles) N of Ankara. **Tel** (0312) 736 11 15 (national park office). 🚗

If you like walking and trekking in a beautiful and safe forest area, this is the ideal place to go. The forest park, situated at an altitude of 975 m (3,200 ft), has

picnic places and well-marked hiking trails, and offers a relaxing retreat from the city.

The region's many natural hot mineral springs have been developed to create spa resorts. One of the best of these is **Kızılcahamam**. Of all the thermal spas scattered around

Shady forest footpath in the Soğuksu National Park

Ankara, it is also the most suited to tourists. There are comfortable hotels and other facilities for visitors who want to stay for a few days. Some treatments involve not only bathing in, but also drinking, the mineral-rich waters, which contain bicarbonate, chloride, sodium and carbon dioxide.

🎿 Bolu
137 km (85 miles) NE of Ankara. Take toll motorway (E89) from Ankara to Istanbul, or highway (no toll) E80.
ℹ️ (0374) 212 22 54.

The Bolu area is known for its deciduous forests and a steep mountain pass, which affords splendid views. It also produces a delicious ewe's milk cheese. At Kartalkaya, 42 km (26 miles) east of the town of Bolu, one of Turkey's best ski centres is open from December to March.

🎿 Gölbaşı Lake and Çubuk Dam
25 km (16 miles) S of Ankara along the E90 towards Konya and 12 km (7.5 miles) N of Ankara on the D180 towards Çorum respectively.

Gölbaşı and the Çubuk Dam are popular with Turkish families for day outings, weekend picnics and informal waterside lunches. Both locations also offer excellent lakeside restaurants.

♨️ Haymana Hot Springs
Haymana Kaplıca
60 km (38 miles) S of Ankara. **Tel** contact hotels directly for bookings. 🎪 Hot Springs Festival (3rd week in Jun).

Haymana is one of six thermal spas within easy reach of Ankara, and its history extends as far back as Roman times. It is worth coming here for the

Municipal water fountain in the centre of Haymana

relaxing atmosphere and to experience the feeling of physical well-being after a good soak. At Haymana, the waters emerge at 45°C (113°F) and you can smell the calcium, magnesium, sodium and bicarbonate. There are several good hotels here, providing a wide range of facilities.

🔲 Infidel's Castle

42 km (26 miles) NE of Haymana **Open** daily.

A sight worth visiting in this region is the **Infidel's Castle** (Gavur Kalesi). Strategically perched on a sheer cliff, it consists of an underground cult tomb with two adjoining tomb chambers, and was discovered in 1930. Gavur Kalesi depicts two gods standing opposite a sitting goddess. There are also remnants of a burial chamber 2 m (6.5 ft) underground.

Polatlı and Gordion

70 km (43 miles) W of Ankara. 🔲 from Ankara to Polatı, then taxi. 🚌 intercity bus between Ankara and Afyon, getting off at Polatı. Take a taxi or one of the infrequent dolmuşes from there.

The village of Yassıhöyük stands on the site of Gordion, the capital of ancient Phrygia, dating from around the 8th century BC. There are several sights worth seeing here, and you can easily tour the site in the course of a day trip from Ankara. If you wish to stay over, however, the nearby town of **Polatlı**, some 18 km (11 miles) to the southeast is well supplied with hotels and some good restaurants.

Gordion was famous as the seat of the legendary King Midas, whose touch was said to have turned everything to gold. Legend has it that this power turned on Midas when he touched his daughter, as well as his food and drink. The problem was solved only when the god Dionysus took pity on him and granted him a cure. It is thought that Midas took his own life in 695 BC after a crushing military defeat.

Phrygia reached its zenith in the middle of the 8th century BC, but Gordion was made famous again by Alexander the Great *(see pp50–51)*. In 333 BC, after wintering in Lycia, Alexander led his army northward from Sagalassos to Gordion. Here, he came upon and cut the Gordion knot *(see p51)*, fulfilling a prophecy that whoever loosed the bond would become the ruler of the known world.

Today, little remains of the palace, but about 80 burial mounds of Phygrian kings have been excavated in the Gordion area over the past 40 years. The most interesting of these is the **Midas Tomb** (Midas Tümülüsü), which lies within the grounds of the **Gordion Museum** (Gordion Müzesi). The large mound is thought to cover the chamber in which the king was buried, and is 50 m (164 ft) in height. When archaeologists opened

Phrygian mosaic, Gordion Museum

the tomb they found the skeleton of a man of around 60 years of age, who is now believed to be another king from the same dynasty.

The acropolis has also been excavated, and shows layers of civilization from the Bronze Age to Greek and Roman times. Although the acropolis gives an idea of the size and extent of the historic settlements in the region, most of the mosaics found there have been moved and are now kept in the museum. In other places, simple roof structures have been erected to protect excavated mosaics from the elements.

The Gordion Museum was established in 1963, and has been nominated for several awards over the years. It displays Bronze Age, Hittite, Hellenistic, Greek and Roman finds, but its displays concentrate on the Phrygian period, and feature many superbly crafted artifacts. The exhibits include ceramics, woodwork and several bronze vessels found in the Midas Tomb, as well as musical instruments and more.

🔲 Midas Tomb
Open 8am–5pm daily. 🖼

🏛 Gordion Museum
9 km (5 miles) N of the town.
Tel (0312) 638 21 88.
Open 8:30am–5:30pm Tue–Sun.

Entrance to the burial mound said to house the tomb of King Midas

Sufi dervishes performing a mystic dance as part of the Sama worship ceremony, Konya ▶

❷ Street-by-Street: Konya

Konya is set on a high, bleak plain in the middle of
the Anatolian steppe. Known throughout Turkey for
its pious inhabitants and strong Islamic leanings, this
ancient city has an increasingly modern and prosperous
appearance. Konya has been inhabited since Hittite
times. It was known as Iconium to the Romans and
Byzantines. The city's heyday was in the 12th century,
when it was the capital of the Seljuk Sultanate of Rum.

At the heart of the city lies the circular Alaeddin Park
(Alaeddin Parkı), a low hill dominated by the Alaeddin
Mosque, Konya's largest. It was finished in 1220 by
Alaeddin Keykubad I (1219–36), the greatest and
most prolific builder of the Seljuk sultans.

Villa of Sultan Kılıç Arslan
A concrete arch covers the remains
of this Seljuk landmark. Nearby are
tea gardens.

★ Konya Fairground
Fairs are now held elsewhere,
so the shady gardens are
a cool, restful retreat.

ALAEDDIN BULVARI

The Seminary of the Slender
Minaret, now housing the Museum
of Wood and Stone Carving, is
named for its elegant tiled minaret.

Ottoman House
Gracious three-storey
houses with projecting
balconies are typical of
middle-class homes
built during the late
Ottoman period.

0 metres		80
0 yards		80

★ Karatay Museum
Housed in the Great Karatay Seminary, a 13th-century Seljuk theological school, the Karatay Museum has a superb collection of ceramics and tiles.

★ Alaeddin Mosque
The mosque is set in beautiful wooded surroundings on a site that has been used since prehistoric times.

Tiled mihrab
The *mihrab* in the Alaeddin Mosque is adorned with some of the finest Seljuk tilework.

Car Park

Key
— Suggested route

Mevlâna Museum

Mevlâna Müzesi

The city of Konya has close links with the life and work of Celaleddin Rumi, or Mevlâna, the 13th-century founder of the Mevlevi dervish sect – better known as the "whirling" dervishes *(see p259)*. Rumi developed a philosophy of spiritual union and universal love, and is regarded as one of the Islamic world's greatest mystics. He settled in Seljuk-ruled Konya and is believed to have died here in 1273.

The entrance to the museum, with the famous green-tiled dome

The museum is an enlargement of the original dervish lodge *(tekke)*. It contains the tomb of Rumi, the ceremonial hall *(semahane)*, and displays of memorabilia and manuscripts. There are also galleries for spectators and musicians.

Entrance

Hürrem Sultan Mausoleum

Cemetery

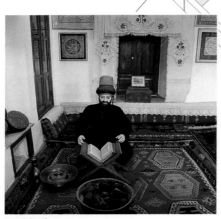

★ **Ablutions Fountain**
Used in the dervish cleansing ritual, the ablutions fountain *(şadırvan)* is pleasantly cooling on hot days.

Dervish Life
Life-like mannequins clad in authentic dress illustrate the spiritual aspects of the daily life of an initiate in the lodge.

Mother-of-Pearl Case
This case is said to contain the
beard of the Prophet Mohammed.

**Prominent
female** members
of the Mevlâna
order are buried
in this graveyard.

Verandah

★ **Semahane** (Ceremonial Hall)
Once the setting for the whirling ceremony,
the Semahane now houses museum displays.

Musical Instruments
Instruments used by the dervishes
include this *ud*, finely worked in ivory
with a mother-of-pearl fretboard.

★ **Mevlâna's Tomb**
Gilded calligraphy adorns the
walls around the sarcophagus.
The tombs of Rumi's father and
other dervish leaders are nearby.

Key

- Dervish Lodge
- Administrative Offices
- Dervish Assembly Chamber
- Monumental Fountain
- Recitation Room
- Mescid-Chapel Mosque
- Semahane (Ceremonial Hall)
- Tombs of Çelebi

❸ Çatalhöyük

60 km (36 miles) S of Konya. Own transport or taxi recommended. Turn left to Çumra, from the Karaman/Mersin road. **W catalhoyuk.com**

Dating from as early as 7000 BC, Çatalhöyük is one of the world's earliest urban settlements. It was originally discovered and excavated by James Mellaart in 1958. Research under the leadership of Ian Hodder resumed in 1993. The site is on the UNESCO World Heritage list.

It is thought that roughly 10,000 people lived here in flat-roofed square houses with rooftop entrances and high windows. The city was the focus of a culture that produced an array of mural decoration, decorative textiles and pottery.

Visitors can enter the site only when accompanied by an official museum guide. The **Çatalhöyük Museum** displays the latest finds, and there are "virtual reality" exhibits in houses and shrines. Artifacts displayed in the museum are repro-ductions; the originals are either in museums in Konya or the superb Museum of Anatolian Civilizations (*see pp246–7*) in Ankara.

Bronze bowl found at Çatalhöyük

▥ Çatalhöyük Museum
Tel (0332) 452 56 21.
Open 9am–5pm daily.

Eğirdir Lake, a tranquil haven for naturalists

❹ Beyşehir

▲ 67,872. **▦** frequent buses from Konya, or intercity buses to Burdur.

Beyşehir is the largest of the fresh-water lakes in what is known as Turkey's Lake District, and the third largest in the country. Its shallow waters contain carp, perch and pike. The town of the same name, at the southeastern corner of the lake, features an unusualcombined weir and bridge.

One of the main reasons for coming to Beyşehir is to see the **Eşrefoğlu Mosque** (Eşrefoğlu Camii), dating from 1297. The wooden interior, with its 48 wooden columns and *mihrab* (prayer niche) decorated with cut tiles, is among the finest examples of this type of architecture remaining from the Beylik period (*see p57*).

▣ Eşrefoğlu Mosque
Beside the bus station, NW after crossing the weir-bridge. **Open** prayer times, but a guardian will let visitors in at other times. **▨** donation.

❺ Eğirdir

▲ 40,817. **▣** daily to Istanbul via Afyon, (0246) 311 46 94. **▦** (0246) 311 40 36. **ℹ** 2 Sahil Yolu, (0246) 311 43 88. **▤** Thu. **▨** Apple Festival (Sep).

Ringed by mountains rising to 3,000 m (9,842 ft), Eğirdir Lake makes a good base for walkers, birders and flower enthusiasts. In May, the hills display many flowering bulbs, orchids and become a stop-over for migrating birds. Eğirdir makes an ideal base for exploring the northern sections of the St Paul trail, Turkey's second longest long-distance walk.

Environs
Antiocheia-in-Pisidia is famous as the place where St Paul first preached to the Gentiles. The ruins of the city include the basilica of St Paul, a synagogue, Roman theatre, baths and a superb aqueduct.

Davraz Ski Centre is oper-ational from December to April. There are two hotels at the centre itself, and more accom-modation in Çobanisa village, some 7 km (4 miles) below.

Davraz Ski Centre
W davrazkayakmerkezi.com for the most up-to-date information.

The unusual wooden interior of the Eşrefoğlu Mosque

For hotels and restaurants in this area see pp330–39 and pp346–61

The Whirling Dervishes

The Mevlevi order, better known as the Whirling Dervishes, was founded by the Sufi mystic, Celaleddin Rumi, also called Mevlâna. He believed that music and dance represented a means to induce an ecstatic state of universal love and offered a way to liberate the individual from the anxiety and pain of daily life. His greatest work, the six-volume *Mesnevi*, consists of 25,000 poems that were read in the *tekkes* (lodges) of the order. Central to the practice of the dervishes is the *sema*, or whirling ceremony. This consists of several parts, each with its own meaning. Love is the central theme of the mystical cycle of the *sema*, which symbolizes the sharing of God's love among earthly beings. For man, the dance is a spiritual ascent to divine love. The *sema* combines both spiritual and intellectual elements, emphasizing self-realization and the ultimate goal, which is perfect union with God.

Conical headdress

Black cloak

Clothing Clothing worn for the *sema* has symbolic meaning. The headdress, for example, stands for the tomb of the ego.

Ney — Ud — Duvar — Cymbals

Musical accompaniment is highly symbolic: the ney (reed flute) represents the breath of God.

The Sema Ritual

The sema consists of five parts, the first three of which are prayers, greetings, and musical improvizations. The ritual then moves into four salutes (selams): truth through knowledge, the splendour of creation, total submission before God and coming to terms with destiny.

Whirling is the climax of the *sema*. Its *selams* (salutes) represent stages during the rapture of submission to God.

The wide white skirt symbolizes the ego's shroud.

The movement concludes with a bow, signifying the return to a state of subservience.

The dervishes greet one another and salute the soul, which is "enslaved" by shapes and bodies.

The dervishes extend their arms, to allow divine energy to enter the right palm, move through the body, and pass out through the left palm into the earth.

Verses from the Koran are read after the dance, including a prayer for the peace of all souls.

Cobbled street in the old quarter of Afyon

❻ Afyon

🗺 186,000. 🚌 İsmet İnönü Cad, (0272) 212 09 63. 🚍 (0272) 213 00 22. 🚺 Cumhüriyet Meydanı, Hükümet Konağı Yanı, (0272) 213 54 47.

The word Afyon means "opium", and it is difficult not to miss the fields of white and dark purple opium poppies if you visit the area in May. Opiates are extracted for medicinal purposes at a factory in nearby Bolvadın, using the special poppy straw method. The town museum has exhibits detailing various methods of opiate extraction.

Other local products are a white, soft marble, which is found in huge slabs along the roadsides and is used for everything from gravestones to kitchen basins. Afyon Kaymağı, a rich clotted cream, is typically served on small metal trays and eaten with honey for breakfast.

Towering over the town is a 225 m (738 ft) crag that can be reached by climbing 700 steps. The Hittites and Byzantines may have used its commanding position for a fortress, but exact dates are speculative.

The Seljuks left the greatest mark on Afyon's history. The major Seljuk building is the **Great Mosque** (Ulu Camii), completed in 1272. It features a geometric wooden ceiling and 40 wooden columns, some with traces of paint on the intricately carved capitals.

The **Archaeological Museum** contains a collection of largely Roman artifacts, which were excavated from around Isparta, Uşak, Burdur and Kütahya.

Afyon was Atatürk's headquarters for the final stages of Turkey's War of Independence (see p62), which reached a climax with the victory over the advancing Greek army at Dumlupınar on 26 August 1922. The **Victory Museum** (Zafer Müzesi), known more for its classical Anatolian architecture than for its contents, recalls the heady days of national liberation. Most of the top Republican commanders stayed in this building during the campaign. There is also a war memorial at nearby Dumlupınar.

ⓒ Great Mosque
Ulu Camii
Open during prayer, or ask the guardian on duty to let you in. 🐾 donation.

🏛 Afyon Archaeological Museum
Kurtuluş Cad 96. **Tel** (0272) 215 11 91. **Open** 8:30am–noon & 1:30–5:30pm Tue–Sun. 🐾

🏛 Victory Museum
Zafer Müzesi
In front of the Governor's Building. **Tel** (0272) 212 09 16. **Open** 9am–noon & 1–5pm Tue–Sun.

❼ Sivrihisar

🗺 32,600. 🚌 along the E90 from Polatlı, then dolmuş to the town.

Sivrihisar is the ancient town of Justinianopolis, built by Emperor Justinian (see p53) to guard the western route to Ancyra (ancient Ankara). The modern town is spread out at the foot of a crag, on which lie the remains of the original Byzantine fortress. The Great Mosque (Ulu Camii), built in 1247, is an excellent example of a Seljuk mosque. Some of its 67 wooden pillars have intricately carved and painted capitals. A warren of pretty Ottoman houses surrounds the mosque, and the Sivrihisar area is famous for fine hand-woven kilims.

Environs
14 km (9 miles) to the south of Sivrihisar lie the ancient ruins of **Pessinus**, near the modern village of Ballıhisar (honey castle). During the 3rd century BC, Pessinus was an important Phrygian cult centre but was abandoned in around AD 500 or 600. Sights include the scant remains of a temple of Cybele, the Anatolian mother goddess. However, nothing is left of the stadium and theatre. At one time, it is believed that there were over 360 springs here, and the remains of hydraulic works can still be seen. The site is open to the public and access is free, if not easy.

The "forest of columns" in the Great Mosque in Sivrihisar

The Tomb of King Midas (left), cut from solid rock

❽ Şeyitgazi Valley

🚹 32,600. 🚌 or on foot.

The village of Şeyitgazi is named after Şeyyid Battal Gazi, an Arab commander and martyr *(şehit)*, and "warrior of the faith", who died during the siege of Afyon in about AD 750. His large tomb, and that of the Byzantine princess who fell in love with him, are housed in a beautiful *tekke* (monastery complex), built by Hacı Bektaş Veli *(see p297)* about 10 km (6 miles) to the northwest of the town centre.

The main attraction of the valley is the monumental tomb (5th or 6th century BC) of King Midas at Midasşehir, or Yazılıkaya. The tomb lies 65 km (40 miles) south of Eskişehir in a marvellous, open-air setting. The site is open from dawn to dusk and you can wander freely here and in the small museum.

Aslantaş, 35 km (22 miles) north of Afyon, was a major Phrygian cult centre. There are other Phrygian sites at Kümbet and Aslankaya, but the roads here are unpaved and there are few visitors.

❾ Eskişehir

🚹 872,650. 🚃 from Istanbul and Ankara, (0222) 231 13 65. 🚌 (0222) 225 80 94. 🛈 Valilik Binası, ground floor, (0222) 230 17 52. 🎭 International Yunus Emre Culture and Fine Arts Week (6–10 May), Meerschaum Festival (3rd week Sep). 🎪 most days.

Commanding the main road from Istanbul to Ankara, Eskişehir (ancient Dorylaeum) has prospered from trade for

centuries, but has also been ravaged by passing armies. It was badly damaged during the War of Independence and has few historical monuments. Today, it is a major railway junction, as well as the home base of the Turkish air force.

Eskişehir is also a mining centre, with supplies of borax, chrome and manganese, as well as meerschaum (or "sea foam"), a soft, porous, heat-resistant, light white clay used to make elaborate carved tobacco pipes *(see p364)*, which are popular among visitors to Turkey. The **Meerschaum Museum** (Lületaşı Müzesi) has displays of historic pipes and old photos of the mines. You can watch carvers at work on Sakarya Caddesi, and purchase pipes and other decorative items made from meerschaum.

Meerschaum pipe

🏛 **Meerschaum Museum**
Lületaşı Müzesi
İki Eylül Cad. **Tel** (0222) 233 05 82.
Open 10am–5pm daily. 🎟

❿ Kütahya

See pp262–3.

⓫ Çavdarhisar (Aezani)

60 km (37 miles) SW of Kütahya. 🚌 infrequent dolmuş to and from Kütahya. **Open** 9am–noon & 1–5pm daily. 🎟

The Phrygian site at Aezani (today's Çavdarhisar) does not feature on most tourists' itineraries, but a visit here will be highly rewarding.

Aezani reached its zenith in the 2nd century AD, when it was transformed from a minor settlement into a large, thriving city and sanctuary of Zeus, ruler of the gods. At this time, the legend of Zeus's birth in the nearby cave at Steunos reinforced the belief in pagan culture, even though such cult worship was at that time being challenged elsewhere by early Christian communities. Today, the cave can be reached only with a four-wheel-drive vehicle. The most impressive remains are of the Temple of Zeus, built during the reign of Emperor Hadrian (AD 117–138). There is a crypt under- neath the temple that is believed to have been the seat of the cult of Cybele, the mother goddess of Anatolia.

The scattered remains of a theatre, municipal gymnasium and stadium are visible today. These were envisaged on a scale that would rival cities like Ephesus or Pergamum. However, Aezani's influence had begun to wane by the 3rd century AD. In 1970, an earthquake demolished much of the site. Some fine mosaics of Phrygian gods can be seen in the ruins of the bathhouse and gymnasium.

Remains of the well-preserved Temple of Zeus at Aezani

⑩ Kütahya

Kütahya's earliest inhabitants were the Phrygians in the 7th century BC. Alexander the Great called the city Kotaeon and used it as his headquarters as he advanced on Gordion (*see p251*) in 332 BC. The Byzantines later occupied the fortress on the acropolis hill until it fell to the Seljuks. Kütahya's golden age was under Sultan Selim I (the Grim; 1512–20), when ceramic craftsmen from Persia were settled here. In 1833, the breakaway ruler of Egypt, Paşa Muhammad Ali, occupied Kütahya. In 1922, Greek forces were routed near here, marking a turning point in the War of Independence (*see p62*). Today, this is a peaceful and devout town and most shops shut during prayer times on Fridays. The numerous splendid period houses hint at untapped tourist potential.

The double-walled fortress, built by the Ottomans

The Dumlupınar monument, honouring Turkish war dead

Exploring Kütahya

Almost all of the town's sites can be seen on foot. Allow at least an afternoon to see the scores of mansions and townhouses.

Between the 15th and the 17th centuries, Kütahya was the rival of İznik (*see pp164–5*) in the painting and glazing of tiles and ceramics. By the early 20th century, the local ceramic industry had all but vanished. Now, Kütahya is again the focus of a revival of this skilled art. The town is acclaimed for beautiful hand-painted ceramic items, and workshops are found in many of the back streets.

The Dumlupınar monument, 50 km (31 miles) south of the town, is also worth visiting. It commemorates the soldiers who fell in the decisive battle of the War of Independence.

▣ Kossuth House Museum

Kossuth Evi Müzesi
Macar Sokak (off Gediz Cad).
Tel (0274) 223 62 14. **Open** 9am–1pm & 2–6pm Tue–Sun. ▨ ▨ ▭

This house/museum complex was the home of Hungarian freedom fighter, Lajos Kossuth (1802–94), who sought refuge in Turkey after leading an unsuccessful revolt to free his homeland from the rule of the Hapsburgs in 1848. Kossuth and his family stayed here as the guests of the Ottoman government in 1850–51, and the 19th-century stone-and-wood house where they lived has changed remarkably little since that time.

The statue of Kossuth in the rose garden was erected in 1982, and Hungarians renew friendship ties here annually on 5 April. The house is also referred to as "the House of the Hungarian Patriot".

▣ Fortress

Kale
Proceed up Gediz Cad from the Kossuth House Museum.

The ruined fortress resembles many other Ottoman-period citadels. Not much is known about its history, but the Kütahya-born historian and traveller, Evliya Çelebi (1811–82), wrote that it had 70 towers. One of the few remaining ones has been extensively restored. Most people come here for the delightful revolving restaurant, **Döner Gazino**, at the top.

Döner Gazino
Open dawn to dusk daily.

▣ Kütahya Tile Museum

Kütahya Çini Müzesi
Gediz Cad. **Tel** (0274) 223 69 90.
Open 9am–1pm & 2–6pm Tue–Sun. ▨ ▨

Since 1999, the Tile Museum has been housed in a restored 15th-century soup kitchen (*imaret*) located behind the Great Mosque (Ulu Camii). This is one of Turkey's most attractive small museums. The displays focus on tiles, vases, ewers and decorative porcelainware produced in the town from the 14th century to the present, and are arranged around a typical ornamental pool (*şadırvan*).

▣ Great Mosque

Ulu Camii
End of Cumhuriyet Cad, Börekciler Mahallesi. **Open** daily, except at prayer times. ▨ donation.

This is the biggest mosque in Kütahya, but not the oldest.

Restored mosque soup kitchen, now housing the Kütahya Tile Museum

Building started under Sultan Yıldırım Beyazıt early in the 15th century, but it was not finished until the time of Mehmet II (1451–81). Many of the marble columns come from Aezani (see p261). The Sakahanesi (watersellers' square) near the mosque is a popular local gathering place.

🅱 Bazaars

Open 9am–6pm Mon–Sat.
Kütahya's bazaars occupy two buildings. The Grand Market (Büyük Bedesten) was built in the 14th century and stands on Çemberciler Caddesi. The 15th-century Small Market (Küçük Bedesten) is just next to it on Kavafiye Sokak (Shoemaker's Street). Don't miss the vaulted ceilings. Today, the bazaars sell chiefly vegetables and second-hand

Spices and pulses for sale outside the Grand Market

Interior of the Great Mosque showing the women's balcony

goods. More specialized traders overflow into the surrounding streets.

🏛 Kütahya Archaeology Museum

Kütahya Arkeoloji Müzesi
Gediz Cad, Börekciler Mahallesi.
Tel (0274) 224 07 85. **Open** 8am–noon & 1–5pm Tue–Sun. 📷

Adjoining the Great Mosque, the museum is housed in the mosque's former seminary, the Vacidiye Medresesi, built in 1314 by a local ruling clan. The museum was restored in 1999, and its centrepiece is a stunningly beautiful Amazon tomb dating from the 2nd century AD, found at Aezani

VISITORS' CHECKLIST

Practical Information
🗺 250,000. ℹ Hükümet, (0274) 223 62 13. 🎪 Dumlupınar Fair, Turkey's largest handicraft fair (last three weeks of Jul); Culture and Tourism Fair (mid Jul for three days). 🛒 Wed and Sat on Belediye Sok (central area). Local market (Thu) along Gediz Cad.

Transport
🚃 İstasyon Cad, (0274) 223 61 21. 🚌 Atatürk Bulvarı, (0274) 224 33 00.

in 1990. The displays also include fossils, Phrygian terracotta toys, Roman glass and sculptures and delicate earthenware figurines.

🏚 Historic Kütahya Manor Houses

Tarihi Kütahya Konakları
The town's spacious period houses date mainly from the 18th and 19th centuries. All are derelict and so only the exteriors can be seen. They usually have three storeys, projecting balconies and front and back entrances. Look near the Ulu Camii on Ahi Erbasan Sokak (in Gazi Kemal Mahallesi) and Germiyan Sokak for typical examples.

Kutahya Town Centre

① Kossuth House Museum
② Fortress
③ Kütahya Tile Museum
④ Great Mosque
⑤ Bazaars
⑥ Kütahya Archaeology Museum
⑦ Historic Kütahya Manor Houses

Exploring the Black Sea

With its mild, damp climate, the Black Sea region is suitable to visit all year round. The best time to go is in springtime, when the mountain valleys are carpeted with wild flowers. The high peaks of the coastal mountains are known for their luxuriant pine forests, alpine lakes and racing rivers which descend to the coastal plain. In the extreme northeast, the Kaçkar range is the highest of the Pontic mountain chain, which defines the region. These mountainous areas receive heavy snowfalls in winter. Safranbolu and Sumela Monastery are the outstanding sights of the region. There are many villages where locals still practise Ottoman-era crafts: Devrek, for example, is renowned for its decorative wooden canes.

Picturesque Amasra, built on a rocky promontory

0 kilometres 50

0 miles 25

Sights at a Glance

1. Amasra
2. *Safranbolu pp272–3*
3. Kastamonu
4. Samsun
5. *Trabzon pp274–5*
6. *Sumela Monastery p276*
7. Zigana
8. Gümüşhane
9. Bayburt
10. Uzungöl
11. Rize
12. Hemşin Valley
13. Hopa
14. Artvin
15. Yusufeli

Government House at Safranbolu

For additional map symbols *see back flap*

Getting Around

Renting a car, or even a four-wheel-drive vehicle, is probably the best way to see the Black Sea coast. This option offers the flexibility to explore minor roads and lanes. Take the central highway only when necessary, or risk missing much of what the region has to offer. Samsun and Trabzon are both served by nonstop flights from Istanbul and Ankara. Intercity buses run daily, or more frequently, to the major centres. Otherwise, visitors must rely on local minibuses, erratic dolmuşes or foot. Take walking shoes and rain gear in any season. Don't expect to find the same sophisticated, scheduled transport as in other parts of Turkey. But if you are adventurous and flexible, a Black Sea journey will be highly rewarding.

Breathtaking Sumela Monastery

Haghia Sophia, a well preserved Byzantine church in Trabzon

Key

▬▬ Motorway

▬▬ Dual carriageway

▬▬ Major road

= = = Minor road

▬▬ Scenic route

⎯⎯ Minor railway

▬▬ International border

The small harbour at Amasra, with its Roman bridge and watch tower

❶ Amasra

🏙 8,200. 🚌 Atatürk Meydanı. ℹ️ Büyük Liman Cad, (0378) 315 12 19.

The picturesque and tranquil town of Amasra is located about 15 km (9 miles) from Bartın. In the 6th century BC, Amasra was called Sesamus, and its inhabitants were known as Megara. By the 9th century, Amasra was of sufficient importance to be designated a bishopric. It was destroyed by Arab raiders, and then rebuilt in the 12th century by the Genoese.

They recognized the trading advantages that Amasra could give them and rented the castle and harbour from the Byzantines. The two fortresses built by the Genoese during the 14th century can still be seen today. One overlooks the main harbour and the other – no more than the remains of a small tower – sits at the harbour mouth. Amasra came under Ottoman rule in 1460.

Interesting places to see in the town include the **Fatih Mosque**, a former Byzantine church, and the 19th-century **İskele Mosque**. Some portions of the Byzantine city walls are still standing, as is a Roman bridge in the harbour.

Carved wooden implements, Amasra

🅲 Fatih Mosque
In the town centre. **Open** daily (except during prayer times).

🅲 İskele Mosque
On the harbour. **Open** daily (except during prayer times).

❷ Safranbolu

See pp272–3.

❸ Kastamonu

🏙 60,000. 🚌 10 min walk N of town centre. ℹ️ Nasrullah Meydanı, (0366) 212 01 62. 🛒 Wed & Sat. 🎭 Atatürk Hat Festival (23–30 Aug), Garlic Festival (1st week Sep). 🔆 near Daday at Çömlekciler.

Kastamonu is well known for outdoor activities as well as for crafts. The pastures of nearby Daday offer some of the very finest trail riding in all of Turkey. The local women are famed for hand-printed tablecloths and upholstery fabrics made from cotton and flax. Other specialities of the area include colourful knitted wool socks and fruit jams.

During the 11th century, Kastamonu was controlled by the powerful Comnene family, rulers of Trabzon (see pp274–5).

Indeed, the town's name probably comes from Castra Comneni (Latin for "camp of the Comnenes").

The town fell under Ottoman rule in 1459. During this era, the region around Kastamonu produced rice, iron, cotton fabrics and mohair, mostly for export. Kastamonu Castle was built by the Byzantines in the 12th century and was kept in good repair by the Seljuks and Ottomans. Today, its remains serve as a fire tower and lookout point.

Displays at the Kastamonu **Ethnographic Museum** include Byzantine and Greek mementos and 17th-century agricultural tools. There is a library on the first floor and a coin display. The building itself is of historic importance, for it was here on 25 August 1925 that Atatürk delivered a famous speech forbidding the wearing of the fez (the old-fashioned conical felt hat).

The **Archaeology Museum** displays finds from Byzantine and Ottoman times, and has a room that commemorates Atatürk's 1925 visit to the town.

The town's main mosques are the Atabey Mosque (uphill, behind the Aşir Efendi Han shopping centre), with its 40 wooden pillars and stone door, and the İbni Meccar Mosque, built in 1353 by

Mahmut Bey Mosque, containing a beautiful wooden interior

the Çandaroğulları family. This lovely mosque in stone and wood is also known as *Eli güzel* ("beautiful hand").

🏛 Ethnographic Museum
Hepkebirler Mah, Sakarya Cad. **Tel** (0366) 214 01 49. **Open** 9am–noon & 1–5:30pm Tue–Sun. 🅿

🏛 Archaeology Museum
İsfendiyarbey Mahallesi, Cumhuriyet Cad 6. **Tel** (0366) 214 10 70. **Open** 9am–noon & 1–5:30pm Tue–Sun. 🅿

Environs
The Mahmut Bey Mosque is located some 17 km (10 miles) northwest of Kastamonu in the village of Kasaba. For a small donation, the local *imam* (Muslim priest) will open the mosque. Inside the well-preserved building are some beautiful paintings and fine calligraphy.

Cide, Abana and İnebolu are all easy day trips from Kastamonu. Cide is a pretty, unspoiled fishing village, and Abana is renowned for its fish restaurants and good, clean swimming. İnebolu has some well-preserved houses.

About 63 km (39 miles) south of Kastamonu is **Ilgaz Mountain National Park**, reachable by dolmuş or your own transport. Visitors to the park can see bears, foxes and deer. There is also a deer breeding and research station. This area offers excellent skiing from November until March. A culinary speciality here is whole lamb, cooked *tandır* style (in a wood-fired clay oven) for four to five hours until the meat falls off the bone. The dish is traditionally eaten with the fingers.

🪂 Ilgaz Mountain National Park
Tel (0336) 212 58 71. **Open** all year. 🚗 for vehicles.

➍ Samsun

🏙 355,000. 🛈 Yaşar Doğu Spor Salonu, (0362) 431 12 28. 🚌 from Ankara to Atatürk Bulvarı, (0362) 445 15 82. 🚌 Yeni Garajlar 1, (0362) 238 11 70. ✈ direct from Ankara or Istanbul; 8 km (5 miles) from Samsun on the Amasya road. 🚢 from Istanbul (30 hrs). 🎭 Samsun Fair (Jul), Akdağı Annual Summer Migration Festival "Hıdrellez" (Jun or Jul depending on weather). 🛍 Sat.

Apart from producing a popular cigarette brand, Samsun also holds a proud place in Turkish hearts as the place where Atatürk came after his escape from Istanbul on 19 May 1919, to draw up plans for a Turkish republic. Today, this anniversary is celebrated as a national holiday, Youth and Sports Day.

Samsun has two museums devoted to the revered memory of Atatürk and his legacy. The **Gazi Museum** occupies a former hotel where he stayed in 1919 and the **Atatürk Museum** has displays of his clothing, various personal items and a collection of photographs.

The **Archaeological and Ethnographic Museum** is a treasure-trove of antiquities from the surrounding villages. It has Bronze Age artifacts as well as ceramics, bronze and brass implements, glass and mosaics dating from the Hittite, Hellenic, Roman and Byzantine eras. There is also some beautiful gold and silver jewellery, as well as several fine hand-written books and hand-woven kilims.

About 80 km (50 miles) southwest of Samsun in the **Havza** district are a number of thermal springs (*kaplıca*) that are popular.

🏛 Gazi Museum
Tel (0362) 431 75 35. **Open** 9am–noon & 1–5:30pm Tue–Sun. 🅿

🏛 Atatürk Museum
Tel (0362) 435 75 35. **Open** 9am–noon & 1–5:30pm. 🅿

🏛 Archaeological and Ethnographic Museum
Cumhuriyet Meydanı. **Tel** (0362) 431 68 28. **Open** 9am–noon & 1–5:30pm Tue–Sun. 🅿

Men's section at a thermal spring in the Havza area

Environs
Near Bafra, about 40 km (25 miles) northwest of Samsun, excavations at a site called İkiztepe (twin hills) have revealed early Hittite bronze finds. The bronze items have been removed, but the site is open and there is no entrance fee. Hittite copper and bronze artifacts have also been uncovered at Dündartepe, 3 km (2 miles) outside Samsun, where excavations continue.

Atatürk and aides, Atatürk Museum

View over the rooftops of UNESCO World Heritage-designated Safranbolu ▶

❷ Street-by-Street: Safranbolu

Safranbolu's market area, a warren of narrow streets and merchant shops, has many restored Ottoman dwellings *(see p35)*. Because of its important architectural heritage, Safranbolu has been declared a World Heritage Site. In Ottoman times, the town lay on a major trade route. Its many handsome three-storey stone-and-timber *konaks* (mansions) were erected by wealthy merchants and craftsmen. In summer they lived in the cool Bağlar district, and in winter they moved down to the more sheltered Çarşı (bazaar) quarter around the Kazdağlıoğlu Mosque.

Köprülü Mehmet Paşa Mosque
The mosque, located near the massive Cinci Hanı, opened for worship in 1661.

★ **Cinci Hanı**
The 350-year-old Cinci Hanı, a refuge for travelling merchants and now a hotel, gives a good idea of the scale of commerce centuries ago.

The Covered Way was formerly used by cobblers and shoemakers.

Cinci Hamamı is a 17th-century Turkish bath still in use today.

Kastamonu ← **CİNİ HANI**

ŞEKERCİLER SOKAKA

YUKARI ÇARŞI SOKAK

Kiranköy ↙

0 metres 40
0 yards 40

★ **Kazdağlıoğlu Mosque**
Located in the main square, the mosque was built in 1779.

Key

— Suggested route

Sundial
An interesting sundial occupies the shady courtyard of the Köprülü Mehmet Paşa Mosque.

VISITORS' CHECKLIST

Practical Information
🏙 23,500.
Tel (0370) 712 38 63.
ℹ Arasta Çarşısı 7. 🛍 Sat.
ⓦ **safranbolu.gov.tr**

Transport
🚌 10 km (6 miles) SW of town centre in Karabük. 🚉 in Karabük.

Shoemakers' Street
The name of this street recalls a local craft. During World War I the town made boots for the Ottoman army.

KUNDURACILAR SOKAK

Grain Market ↑

ESKI HAMAM SOKAK

CEBICI SOKAK

Macunlar Mansion
The upper storey of Macunlar Mansion shows typical wooden shutters and stencilled wall decorations made with natural dyes.

ARASTA SOKAK

M ÜTEÜSOSOKAK

The Tourism Information Office
A restored original Ottoman house, built in the style that Safranbolu is famous for, houses the tourist office, located in the Arasta (market) area.

Market Street
Restored *konaks* line the narrow Arasta Sokak (Market Street). Some of these old houses have been turned into atmospheric guest houses, complete with authentic decor and furniture.

❺ Trabzon

The earliest evidence of civilization in Trabzon dates from 7000 BC. Established as a Greek colony (with Amasra and Sinop), the town benefited from its position on the busy trade route between the Black Sea and the Mediterranean. It grew quickly and was a focal point for the Pontic kings.

Trabzon Castle, established in the 5th century BC

At the beginning of the 13th century, the Comnene dynasty established a Byzantine state with its capital at Trabzon. During the Comnene era, the city gained a reputation as a beautiful, sophisticated cultural centre. The Genoese and the Venetians came here to trade, as Trabzon was the terminus of a northern branch of the Silk Route. In 1461, Trabzon fell under Ottoman rule.

🏛 Church and Museum of Haghia Sophia

Aya Sophia Müzesi
Follow İnönü Cad. **Tel** (0462) 223 30 43. **Open** 8am–noon & 1–5:30pm Tue–Sun (8:30am–noon & 1–5pm Tue–Sun in winter).

This restored 13th-century Byzantine church, situated just a few kilometres from the city centre, is by far the most impressive sight in Trabzon. It was originally built by the Comnene emperor, Manuel VII Palaeologus. In 1577, it reverted to a mosque and, after serving as an ammunition depot and also as a hospital, became a museum in 1957. The interior frescoes depicting scenes from the Old Testament are among the finest in Turkey. The patterned mosaics date from Byzantine times, and you can still see the original coloured marble covering of the floor. Restoration work on the old frescoes is intermittent.

🔼 St Anne's Church

Küçük Ayvasıl Kilisesi
Kahraman Maraş Cad.

An Armenian church built in the 9th century, St Anne's has a beautiful exterior and the entrance is adorned with crucifixes and angels. With advance notice to the Tourism office, groups are allowed inside to view the interior. Another Armenian church, St Basil's (Büyük Ayvasil), is also located nearby.

🏰 Trabzon Castle

Trabzon Kalesi
İç Kale Sok.

The castle is located on the flat-topped hill (*trapezus* in Greek) that gave Trabzon its name. Today, only a small portion of the castle walls remain, but the area originally had three distinct wards, each with its own mosque. The only one still standing is the Fatih Camii in the Ortahisar (middle castle) section. Before it became a mosque, this was the principal church of the Comnene dynasty and its dome was topped with gold. Sadly, the gold, like the mosaics and frescoes inside, is long gone.

🏰 Zağnos Bridge and Tower

Zağnos Köprüsü ve Kale Kule
Zağnos Cad.

Built in 1467, the Zağnos Bridge crosses the Kuzgun ravine. In Ottoman times, the bridge provided access to charitable institutions. The Zağnos Tower was formerly a much-feared prison. Today, there is little reminder of its grim past, and visitors can tour the site and enjoy a meal at the tower restaurant.

🕌 Gülbahar Mosque and Tomb

Gülbahar Hatun Camii
Tanjant Yolu.
Open except during prayer times.

Built in 1514 by Sultan Selim the Grim in memory of his mother, Gülbahar, this is one of the few mosques in the city that was not originally a church. Gülbahar was noted for her charity work, and the mosque was built as part of an *imaret*, an Ottoman social welfare institution consisting of a soup kitchen and hostel for students and the poor. The main place of worship was the black-and-white stone section, with its five cupolas. The mosque is all that remains of the complex. Just to the east is Gülbahar's octagonal tomb.

Fresco in Haghia Sophia, showing Jesus turning water into wine at Galilee

St Eugenius Church, turned into a mosque in 1461

🏛 St Eugenius Church

Yeni Cuma Camii
Follow signs from Fatih Hamami on Kasım Sok. **Open** 9am–5pm.

In the 14th century, this was the Church of St Eugenius, named for the martyred 5th-century archbishop of Carthage. In Ottoman times, the church became a mosque.

🏛 Trabzon Museum

Uzun Sok, Zeytinlik Cad 10.
Tel (0462) 322 38 22. **Open** 9am–noon & 1–5:30pm Tue–Sun. 🖼

Trabzon Museum occupies a mansion built in the late 19th century for a Greek banker. The finely restored house is decorated in Baroque style and contains displays of local archaeology and ethnography.

Environs

A few kilometres outside the centre of the city is **Atatürk's Villa**, an ornate three-storey mansion where Atatürk stayed several times after 1924. It was here that he made his will in 1937, the year before his death. The house was built in 1903, and is a typical example of upper-class Crimean architecture. The city of Trabzon presented it to Atatürk, and he left it to his sister, Makbule Atakan, at his death. The interior has been left almost undisturbed.

🏛 Atatürk's Villa

Atatürk Köşkü
Soğuksu Cad, 4 km (2.4 miles) SW of city centre. **Tel** (0462) 231 00 28.
Open 8:30am–4:30pm daily.
📷 on inquiry at the entrance. 🖼

VISITORS' CHECKLIST

Practical Information
🏠 228,000. ℹ İskenderpaşa Mahallesi, Ali Naki Effendi Sok 1/A, (0462) 326 47 60. 🎭 Hıdrellez Summer Migration Festival (6 May). 🛒 daily.

Transport
✈ 8 km (5 miles) from city centre, (0462) 325 9952.
🚌 Değirmendere, 3 km (2 miles) from city centre, (0462) 325 23 43.
🚢 from Istanbul and Rize.

Atatürk's Villa, a handsome early 20th-century mansion

Trabzon City Centre

1. Church and Museum of Haghia Sophia
2. Mosque of the Three Balconies
3. Trabzon Castle
4. Zağnos Bridge and Tower
5. Gülbahar Mosque and Tomb
6. St Eugenius Church
7. Trabzon Museum

❻ Sumela Monastery

Sümela Manastırı

Sumela Monastery sits high up on the cliffs of Mt Mela, southeast of Trabzon. It was founded in the 4th century by two Greek monks, Barnabas and Sophronius, who were guided to the site by an icon of a "black" image of the Virgin, allegedly painted by St Luke. After their deaths, Sumela became a place of pilgrimage. It was decorated with frescoes, and its treasures included priceless manuscripts and silver plates. The monastery was rebuilt several times – the ruins seen by today's visitors date largely from the 19th century.

In the Ottoman era, Sumela enjoyed the protection of the sultans, but it was abandoned and badly damaged during the War of Independence. Extensive restoration work has been carried out to preserve the monastery.

VISITORS' CHECKLIST

Practical Information
55 km (34 miles) SE of Trabzon in Altındere National Park. **Tel** (0462) 230 19 66 (lower entrance) and (0462) 531 10 64 (upper entrance). **Open** May–Oct: 8am–6pm daily; Nov–Apr: 9am–3pm daily.

★ Frescoes
Though badly damaged by vandals, lovely fresco panels cover the walls of the church.

Restoration
A fire in the 1920s left many of the monastery buildings roofless and exposed to the elements. Restoration work involves rebuilding the roof trusses and adding tiles.

★ Living Quarters
The cells used by the Greek Orthodox monks are ranged along the five-storey outside building overlooking the Altındere valley.

Forest Path
A 1 km (0.5 mile) path winds through pine forest to the often mist-shrouded monastery. It takes 30 minutes to make the ascent.

❼ Zigana

🎭 Kadırga Festival: migration to high pastures and nomadic origins (usually held in spring and summer).

After visiting the Sumela Monastery, travellers can return to Trabzon or continue further southwest to reach the spectacular alpine area known as Zigana and situated in the Kalkanlı Mountains. There is some skiing here, but only day trips are possible as there are no hotels.

Fog and snow cover the Zigana area for about seven months of the year, and it is usually damp here. Heavy winter snowfalls make access difficult and even dangerous.

To get to Zigana, you can drive through the 1,500 m (4,291 ft) mountain tunnel, the longest in Turkey.

A more challenging, but much more scenic route runs parallel to the main 885 road through Hamsiköy village. It is worth stopping here to sample the excellent local cuisine. The speciality is a nourishing, creamy rice pudding.

❽ Gümüşhane

🏛 37,500. ℹ Valilik Binası, Kat 4, (0456) 213 10 07.

Gümüşhane (silver works) takes its name from the rich deposits of silver ore found here. In the late 16th century, silver was more valuable than gold. However, by the late 19th century, the silver industry had declined.

Before World War I, the area was a focus of conflict between the Russians and the Ottomans,

A ruined Byzantine church in the old section of Gümüşhane

The Çoruh River, running through the fortress town of Bayburt

for Gümüşhane occupied a strategic position on the trade route between Anatolia and Persia (Iran).

Here, visitors can explore the surrounding castles, and several mosques. The most interesting of these is the Süleymaniye (or Küçük) Camii. There are also eight *hamams* (Turkish baths), which cater for men and women.

Gümüşhane is renowned for its rosehip (*kuşburun*) syrup and sweet cherry jam (*kiraz reçeli*).

Wild poppy near Bayburt

❾ Bayburt

🏛 38,000. ℹ Hükümet Binası, Kat 4, (0458) 211 44 29. 🚌 Mon. 🎭 Dedekorkut Cultural Festival (2nd week in Jul).

Situated on the Çoruh River, Bayburt is the capital of the smallest of Turkey's 78 provinces. Bayburt Castle was probably built in Byzantine times, but there is evidence of an older fortress on the site.

The castle has a violent history. It had to be rebuilt by the Byzantine Emperor Justinian and was repaired by both Seljuks and Ottomans following various attacks. At its peak,

there were 300 houses within the complex. Provision for daily needs included a bakery and flour mill. The community even produced its own paint.

Today, visitors can see a theological school, a mosque, *hamams* and kitchens, as well as a dervish lodge.

The eastern corner contains the remains of a church built between the 8th and 14th centuries.

On the hills at the southern edge of the city stand the twin mausoleums of Şehit (martyr) Osman and his sister. Osman Park, beside the river, is a good place to relax and enjoy a glass of tea.

About 20 km (12 miles) northwest of Bayburt are the remains of underground cities dating from Byzantine times. These are usually open to visitors. For details, inquire at the tea garden at the entrance or at the tourism office in the town centre.

Outside Bayburt, on the way to Aşkale and Erzurum, travellers must negotiate a spectacular mountain pass which rises to the dizzying height of 2,302 m (7,552 ft).

Village on the shores of Uzungöl (Long Lake)

❿ Uzungöl

🚌 tour bus from Trabzon or dolmuş from Of (90 min); dolmuşes are less frequent in the winter months.

For mountain scenery, few places in Turkey compare with this alpine lake, which was carved out during the Ice Ages. At an altitude of over 1,000 m (3,280 ft), Uzungöl (Long Lake) is a hidden gem surrounded by lush greenery and remote meadows.

At weekends, Uzungöl is popular with local people, who journey here by dolmuş from the coastal village, Of, but there is not much to do besides camping, hiking in the nearby hills, fishing and relaxing. The village has a few basic hotels, and the local lake trout is excellent.

⓫ Rize

🏚 72,000. 🚌 0.8 km (0.5 mile) west of town. 👔 Valilik Binası, A Blok, Kat 5, (0464) 213 04 07. 🛍 Russian bazaar daily. 🎭 Tea Festival (3rd week Jun).

In ancient times, Rize was ruled by the Pontic kings (see p302) and was known as Rhizus. The name means rice, although the town is now better known for its tea.

Rize was strongly fortified by the Byzantines in the 6th century and later became part of the Comnene empire. Like Trabzon, it came under Ottoman control in 1461.

In Ottoman times, many people left Rize to seek work in Russia. There they learned the art of bread- and pastry-making, which they brought back with them when they returned.

Today, many of Turkey's master pastry chefs and bakers come from Rize.

Visitors will notice many locals clad in the versatile *Rize bezi*, a light cloth made of silk, cotton or wool, in black and purple. It is mainly used as a head covering for women, but also doubles as a useful rain bonnet and a handy receptacle when the local women go out to gather tea leaves.

The small **Rize Museum** is not outstanding, but has some displays of local life and lore.

🏛 **Rize Museum**
Piri Çelebi Mahellesi, PTT Arkası.
Tel (0464) 214 02 35. **Open** 9am–noon & 1–5:30pm Tue–Sun. 🎫

⓬ Hemşin Valley

42 km (26 miles) E of Rize.

East of Rize, the road turns off to the Hemşin Valley. About 20 km (12 miles) further east a second turning goes to Çamlıhemşin. The road rises steeply and the air is filled with the smell of boxwood trees. This area lies deep within the Kaçkar Mountains (Kaçkar Dağları), at an altitude of 3,932 m (12,900 ft).

Continue on the same road signposted to Ayder, famous for its hot springs. The local inhabitants, the Hemşin, were once Christian Armenians who converted to Islam. They delight in their seasonal festivals, folklore traditions, and distinctive ethnic costumes. A staple food of the valley is *mıhlama* (corn bread), that is served hot from the baking pan. Sometimes, *lor* (white, unsalted cheese) is served alongside *mıhlama* as a breakfast dish.

There are two castles near Çamlıhemşin. One is Kale-i Bala, above the village of Hisarcık Köyü, dating from 200 BC. Further up the valley is the lonely Zilkalesi (Bell Castle) with eight ramparts overlooking the valley of the Storm River (Fırtına Çayı).

Corn bread, Hemşin Valley

Turkish Tea

Turkey's first tea plants were brought from Japan in 1878, but the industry did not take off until the 1930s. The moist climate of the Black Sea coast provides superb growing conditions. Rize is the centre of the Turkish tea industry, and the home of the country's Tea Institute (Çay Enstitüsü).

To sample the best tea, look for *tomurcuk* (the flowering bud of the tea bush). Leaves from other parts of the plant are not as flavourful. Turks prefer the black tea sold in local markets; green tea is exported. Specialized fragrant teas are also produced, again mostly for export.

Glasses, spoons, sugar and some good company are all part of enjoying Turkish tea, which is brewed in a double boiler. The leaves are scalded before brewing to impart an earthy, smoky flavour.

Turkish tea served in a typical "tulip" glass

Roads and driving in general are a challenge in the Hemşin Valley's short summer season. A four-wheel-drive vehicle is recommended, as local dolmuş transport can be daily, not hourly.

Because of the vertical valleys, local people have devised an ingenious transport solution: the *vargel*, a cable car on a pulley system. It is powered by electricity (or people power, if no electricity is available). It is a quaint solution, which offers a bird's eye view of the isolated gorges.

Russian dolls for sale in Hopa, near the Georgian border

⑬ Hopa

🚆 on W bank of river.

Hopa is the last main town before the frontier with Georgia. It is a garrison town, and there is a strong military presence. Hopa was a major port in ancient times, and is still the main seaport (after Trabzon) on the eastern Black Sea coast. Today, the town is dominated by the boat-building industry and a large thermal power station.

⑭ Artvin

🏔 25,000. 🛈 Katliotopark Binası, Kat 3, (0466) 212 30 71. 🎭 Kafkasör Festival (Jun). 🌐 artvin.gov.tr

Artvin receives more rain than any other place in Turkey, so everything grows wonderfully here. The people of Artvin are known for their many festivals, which feature traditional dancing, games, music, food and costumes. The major annual celebration is the Kafkasör (Caucasian)

Bulls fighting at the Kafkasör Festival in Artvin

Festival in June, featuring the spectacle of fighting bulls.

Around Artvin are a number of beautiful villages. Şavşat, about 55 km (34 miles) to the east on the road to Ardahan, is a lovely alpine hamlet. The road goes on to Veliköy and, 19 km (11 miles) further on, reaches the **Karagöl-Sahara National Park**, which has extensive forests and lakes.

Environs

The natural beauty of the north-eastern reaches of the Çoruh Valley around Artvin had once only been visited by more adventurous travellers. Conservation groups, like TEMA Tours, offer visitors rustic accommodation and ecological tours that support the dwindling lifestyles of the region. For more details see www.biyotematur.com

🏞 **Karagöl-Sahara National Park**
Tel (0466) 531 21 37. **Open** May–Oct: daily. 🚗 for cars only. 🚻

⑮ Yusufeli

68 km (42 miles) S of Artvin or 150 km (93 miles) NE of Bayburt (difficult route). 🏔 4,000.

Yusufeli is a nature-lover's paradise, with some of the most rugged scenery in Turkey. As it is a designated conservation area, hunting is strictly controlled and many wild species are protected.

Yusufeli is becoming well known for whitewater rafting *(see p372)* on the challenging Çoruh River. The best time to go is in spring when the wild flowers are in bloom. There are outstanding opportunities for photography, particularly around the deep, icy lakes.

Around Yusufeli, there are many Georgian and Armenian churches and out-of-the-way castles. Dört Kilise (Four Churches) is a few kilometres southwest of the town, while İşhan is a superb 11th-century church in the mountains east of Yusufeli off the main road (signposted to Olur). A track leads to the church.

The churning waters of the spectacular Çoruh River

Exploring Cappadocia and Central Anatolia

The majestic jewel of Central Anatolia is the Cappadocia region, a bewitching landscape of spectacularly eroded tuff (hardened volcanic ash). Mount Erciyes (Erciyes Dağı), an extinct volcano, looms over this haunting panorama. Volcanic deposits have made this a fertile area for agriculture, with grapes, apricots, cherries, sugar beets and chickpeas grown locally.

The main Hittite sites in Asia Minor are found at Boğazkale and Alacahöyük. Often neglected, Kayseri is a treasure-trove of Seljuk history and should not be missed. The Pontic kings *(see p52)* once ruled in Amasya, an unspoiled town in the valley of the Yeşilırmak River. The region's varied sights complement the country crafts, such as carpet weaving and the beautiful decorative pottery produced around Avanos.

Uçhisar village, overlooked by cave dwellings

Hot-air balloon drifting over the eroded tuff landscape

Sights at a Glance

The King's Gate at Boğazkale, in Hattuşaş National Park

Key

— Major road

═ Dual carriageway

═ Minor road

— Scenic route

⊢ Main railway

— Minor railway

△ Summit

Getting Around

Kayseri and Nevşehir are both served by intercity buses, as well as regular flights to and from Istanbul and a few other Turkish cities. Most of the main sights are a 40–60-minute drive on good paved roads from these centres. Minibuses and dolmuşes run frequently between major tourist attractions, but renting your own vehicle will give you the greatest flexibility. Some sights (even the underground cities) involve quite a bit of walking. Coach tours from centres throughout Turkey serve the region.

The Blue Seminary (Gök Medresesi) in Amasya

Rock Formations of Cappadocia

The landscape of Cappadocia was created around 30 million years ago, when erupting volcanoes blanketed the region with ash. The ash solidified into an easily eroded material called tuff, overlain in places by layers of hard volcanic rock. Over time, the tuff was worn away, creating distinctive formations, including the capped-cone "fairy chimneys" near Ürgüp. Cappadocia covers a relatively small area – around 300 sq km (116 sq miles). It has become a popular area for tourists, and the area around Nevşehir, together with nearby Ürgüp and Göreme *(see pp286–7)*, offer the best opportunities to see the bewitching natural formations for which the region is celebrated.

Locator Map
☐ Tuff formation

Cavities below the hard layer are turned into dwellings.

Erosion and Weathering

Cappadocia's extraordinary landscape is partly the result of erosion by water, wind and changes in temperature. Rainfall and rivers wear down the tuff and, like the wind, carry away loose material. In winter, extreme temperature changes cause the rocks to expand and contract and eventually to disintegrate.

Mushroom Shape
This "mushroom" rock, an unusual example of erosion, is located near Gülşehir.

Fairy Chimneys

The extraordinary formations pictured below are called "fairy chimneys" because early inhabitants of Cappadocia believed that they were the chimneys of fairies, who lived under the ground. Some of them reach heights of up to 40 m (130 ft).

Complete erosion wears away the protective caps and creates the conical shapes found in the Göreme Valley.

Elongated Shape These columns are capped with layers of slightly harder material.

Pedestal Shape Created when a lump of basalt rests atop a tuff column.

Cone Shape Erosion thins tuff beneath the basalt cap, which then falls off.

Eroded Tuff Field

In the triangle defined by Nevşehir, Ürgüp and Avanos, the tuff layer was originally up to 100 m (328 ft) thick. As the older tuff continues to erode, younger cones are formed. This process has been taking place for around 10 million years.

Lava flows harden into a protective layer over the tuff.

Erosion widens cracks and fissures, separating sections from the main body and allowing for the development of strange shapes.

Underground cities

Cracks in the tuff layers allowed people to hollow out dwellings and churches.

Protective caps give a tubular shape to the eroded formation.

Volcanoes of Anatolia

Snowcapped Mount Erciyes, 20 km (13 miles) southwest of Kayseri

Volcanic activity in Central Anatolia is a product of the region's position *(see pp22–3)* at the boundaries of two of the tectonic plates that make up the Earth's crust. Mount Erciyes is the largest in a chain of extinct volcanoes created by the collision of the heavy Arabian with the lighter Anatolian Plate. The collision pushed magma to the surface, building up immense pressure and eventually causing Mounts Erciyes, Hasan and others to erupt, spewing forth enormous amounts of rock and lava that greatly altered the landscape of Central Anatolia. The Hittites *(see pp48–9)* worshipped snow-covered Mount Erciyes. They called it "Harkassos" (White Mountain).

Underground Cities

The softness of the tuff made it easy to excavate in order to create dwellings. In some places, as at Derinkuyu (above), whole cities were constructed underground. These settlements had living quarters, stables, wells, ventilation systems, churches and storage rooms.

❶ Nevşehir

As the capital of Cappadocia, Nevşehir makes a very good starting point for touring the region. Known as Nyssa in antiquity, the town has the Kurşunlu Mosque and *medrese (see p36)*, dating from 1725, as well as a castle and a good museum. The surrounding tuff formations and troglodyte (underground) cities are the most popular attractions, but visitors are likely to leave the Nevşehir area with strong memories of sunflowers, chickpeas, donkeys and sugar beets, as well as apricots drying on rooftops. Christianity has a long history in the Nevşehir region, with monks and hermits inhabiting Cappadocia as early as the 4th century.

Passageway in Derinkuyu, showing "millstone" door

Zelve

10 km (6.2 miles) NE of Nevşehir.
Open Apr–Oct: 8am–7pm daily; Nov–Mar: 8am–5pm daily.

A secluded monastic retreat, Zelve lies in a series of deep valleys and is dotted with rooms and caves on many levels. Metal walkways and stairs lead to less accessible chapels and hideaways which hold a few frescoes. In 1950 an earthquake shook the Çavuşin/Zelve area, and the cave dwellings remain somewhat unkempt today. The nature of the site will appeal to the fit and adventurous. Many of the caves and rooms are only accessed by clambering through dark holes and tunnels, so bring a torch and spare batteries.

Two small churches lie on the valley floor: the Üzümlü Kilise (Grape Church) and the Balık Kilise (Fish Church), both featuring ornate carvings. The latter is an Ottoman mosque, but with a stone steeple.

Derinkuyu

30 km (18.6 miles) S of Nevşehir.
Open Apr–Oct: 8am–7pm daily; Nov–Mar: 8am–5pm daily.

There are believed to be about 36 underground cities in this region, but only a few have been excavated. Of these, Derinkuyu (deep well) is the biggest, most popular and best lit. It is thought to have been home to around 20,000 people. The eight-level complex is 60 m (197 ft) deep. A long "transit" tunnel was supposed to have linked Derinkuyu with a similar "ant hill" settlement at Kaymaklı, about 10 km (6 miles) away. At peak times (11am–3pm) the tunnels can get somewhat uncomfortably crowded – anyone who tries to backtrack will be very unpopular.

The first levels include a stable, wine-press and a large vault. Deeper down, there are living quarters, a kitchen and a church. The heavy millstones recessed into the walls were, in fact, doors that could be rolled into place to seal off strategic areas of the settlement. Huge ventilation shafts still function, but damp is a problem. Living here for any extended period of time could not have been easy.

Ürgüp

12 km (7 miles) E of Nevşehir.
18,000. Parkı İçi, (0384) 341 40 59. Wine/grape Festival (end Sep, early Oct).

Ürgüp is now so synonymous with the troglodyte cities built during Byzantine times that it is easy to overlook the town's

Spread over three valleys and with many fairy chimneys, Zelve was inhabited until 1952

House in Ürgüp dating from the period of Greek habitation

VISITORS' CHECKLIST

Practical Information
75,800. *i* in front of the State Hospital, (0384) 212 95 73. Cappadocia Mountain Biking Festival (1st week Jul).

Transport
Kapadokya, (0384) 421 44 50. Gülşehir Cad, Nevtur, (0384) 213 11 71 and 213 12 29. Göreme Tur, (0384) 213 55 37 and 213 47 09.

Roman and Seljuk history. Ürgüp's ancient name was Assiana, and it was known as Başhisar under the Seljuks. Seljuk influence can be seen in the 13th-century remains of the Kadıkalesi (castle) and the Altıkapı Tomb. Near the Nükrettin Mausoleum is a library named after Tasinağa, a 19th-century town squire. Until 1923, when Turkey became a republic, the town had a large Greek population.

Ürgüp's **museum** contains ceramics and statues from prehistoric to Byzantine times, as well as displays of textiles, costumes, weapons and books.

Ürgüp is a convenient base to tour Cappadocia. There are plenty of pensions and hotels, yet the town has retained its village charm. This area has always been well known for its farm produce, particularly for grapes. Ürgüp-labelled wine is refreshing and light. In general, the white wines are more authentic and interesting than the reds.

Several local spots offer impromptu entertainment in the evenings.

🏛 Museum
Kayser Cad 39. **Tel** (0384) 341 40 82. **Open** 8am–noon, 1–5pm Tue–Sun.

Avanos
16 km (10 miles) NE of Nevşehir. 14,500. *i* Atatürk Cad, (0384) 511 43 60.

Watered by the Kızılırmak (Red River), Avanos is a pretty, leafy town noted for its pottery and ceramics. Carpet-weaving and tapestry-making are equally important local skills.

In Roman times, Avanos was called Venessa. It fell under Ottoman suzerainty in 1466 along with Nevşehir. Today it is a typical country town, albeit with a lack of grand mosques or *medreses*. In the town centre is the Yeraltı (Ulu) Mosque, dating from the 15th century, and the Alaeddin Mosque, built by the Seljuks.

Ceramics and wine are the town's lifeblood. Visitors can purchase many serviceable pottery items, while exquisite porcelain designs are the stock in trade of places like Kaya Seramik Evi. These pieces are thrown by hand, then painted and glazed. The intricate designs are painstakingly reproduced from the İznik originals *(see p165)*.

About 5 km (3 miles) east of Avanos is Sarıhan, a Seljuk *han* or caravanserai *(see p28)* built in 1238 on the classic square plan. The repaired *han* gives a good idea of the accommodation facilities, as well as stables and a small mosque, available to

Shaping a jug in a pottery workshop in Avanos

traders making the long trek along the Silk Route *(see pp28–9)*. It also hosts atmospheric whirling dervish shows.

Kaymaklı
20 km (12 miles) S of Nevşehir. **Open** Apr–Oct: 8am–7pm daily; Nov–Mar: 6am–5pm daily.

Discovered in 1964, Kaymaklı is the second most important underground city in the region. It is believed to have housed thousands of people from the 6th to 9th centuries. Although five levels are open to visitors, experts believe Kaymaklı has eight levels. The underground area is thought to cover an area of about 2.5 sq km (1 sq mile).

Being smaller and less crowded than many of the region's other underground cities, the rooms and their various functions seem more convincing. It is advisable to arrive there early.

Göreme
10 km (6 miles) NE of Nevşehir. 1,100. *i* Next to the bus station, (0384) 271 25 58.

At the heart of northern Cappadocia's fairytale landscape, the small village of Göreme is extremely popular with backpackers and other tourists. There are dozens of pensions and hotels here (many with cave rooms) and restaurants to suit all budgets. It is also a good place from which to arrange tours of the region and to take part in outdoor activities ranging from walking the valleys to hot air ballooning. The main attraction is the village's open-air museum *(see pp288–9)*.

❷ Göreme Open-Air Museum

The Göreme Valley holds the greatest concentration of rock-cut chapels and monasteries in Cappadocia. Dating largely from the 9th century onwards, the valley's 30 or more churches were built out of the soft volcanic tuff. Many of the churches feature superb Byzantine frescoes depicting scenes from the Old and New Testaments, and particularly the life of Christ and deeds of the saints. The cultural importance of the valley has been recognized by the Turkish government and they have restored and preserved the many caves to create the Göreme Open-Air Museum. UNESCO has declared the Göreme Valley a World Heritage Site. A 2006 excavation of tombs uncovered human skeletons.

Tokalı Church
The Tokalı Church, located near the entrance to the museum, contains some of the most beautiful frescoes in the Göreme Valley.

★ Kızlar Monastery
Monks lived and worked in this hollowed-out formation. Ladders or scaffolding were probably used to reach the upper levels.

Camel Tours
Portions of the Göreme Valley and surrounding area can be viewed from atop a camel on guided tours.

★ **Karanlık Church**
A pillared church, built around a small courtyard, the Karanlık Church contains frescoes depicting the ascension of Christ.

VISITORS' CHECKLIST

Practical Information
15 km (9 miles) E of Nevşehir.
Tel (0384) 271 21 67.
Open Apr–Oct: 8am–7pm;
Nov–Mar: 8am–5pm.
🎟 extra fee for Tokalı Church
and Karanlık Church. 🖥 📷

Transport
✈ Nevşehir Kapadokya
Havalimanı (30 km/19 miles from
Nevşehir) (0384) 421 44 55.

Yılanlı Church
The barrel-vaulted church has painted panels devoted to a number of saints.

Entrances to Monks' Cells
The southern end of the valley is honeycombed with the tiny cells once occupied by monks.

KEY

① **The walking route** starts at the car park near the entrance.

② **Çarıklı Church**

③ **Katherina Church**

④ **Dining Hall**

⑤ **Barbara Church** takes its name from a fresco on the west wall, which is thought to depict St Barbara. A seated figure of Christ occupies the central apse. Saints Georgius and Theodorus are depicted killing the dragon.

★ **Elmalı Church**
Noted for the sophistication of its frescoes, the church dates from the 11th century.

The Church of Constantine and Helen, in Mustafapaşa

❸ Mustafapaşa

6 km (4 miles) S of Ürgüp. 🏔 3,800.

Formerly known as Sinasos, Mustafapaşa is a perfectly preserved Greek village, whose inhabitants left during the exchange of populations between Greece and Turkey in 1923. The houses have a wealth of carved stonework, wall paintings and reminders of the former inhabitants' lifestyles. Although some houses are neglected, the balconies and sculptured windows are sure to delight. The large, 18th-century Church of Constantine and Helen contains some faded frescoes and draws pilgrims from Greece. Of note are the monastery of St Nicholas and the Church of St Basil, the latter located outside the village.

Several pensions and a few hotels have been restored to their former Greek appearance.

❹ Kayseri

See pp294–5.

❺ Bünyan

35 km (22 miles) E of Kayseri. 🏔 5,780. 🎭 Yoghurt Festival (18 May).

Bünyan lies east of Kayseri, off the main highway to Sivas. This is a good place for a relaxed outing for a few hours or an afternoon, and often features on sightseeing tours to the region.

The economic mainstay of the town is handicrafts, mainly the carpets handwoven by the women. You can see them at work on the looms and learn about the designs and the amount of work involved. A particular feature of carpets from Bünyan is the use of thin, high-tensile mercerized cotton to make bedspreads, floor rugs, and prayer mats. This ensures that the finished carpet always lies flat.

❻ Mount Erciyes

Erciyes Dağı

Mount Erciyes, at a height of 3,916 m (12,848 ft), is Cappadocia's dominant natural landmark. Locals regard this extinct volcano with respect because of its role in shaping the landscape when it buried the area in volcanic dust and ash millions of years ago. The residual tuff – fine-grained, compressed volcanic ash – is the area's major geological feature *(see pp284–5)*. The calcium in the tuff enriches the soil, encouraging the growth of trees and vines.

Between the two peaks (Greater and Lesser Erciyes) are two lovely moraine lakes, Cora and Sarı. Mount Erciyes is also a ski centre *(see p372)* with a chair-lift and a lodge. The season runs from November to May. Hiking is possible in summer, but you will need a guide and proper gear.

❼ Soğanlı

38 km (24 miles) S of Ürgüp. 🏔 4,650. **Open** 8:30am–5:30pm daily. 🎭

The main attraction of the Soğanlı Valley is that it is quiet and undisturbed. It is possible, even, to think of this valley as a microcosm of the whole

Pigeon coops cut into the rocks at Soğanlı, marked with white rings to attract the birds

◀ Preparations for evening festivities in the Cappadocian town of Göreme

Göreme Valley. There are six interesting churches to visit here, though it is thought that more than 100 flourished at one time. All six are in good condition and can be seen on foot during the course of a day trip.

The delicate, pastel tones of Soğanlı's frescoes differ from the harsher hues to be seen in the churches at Göreme, where ongoing restoration has produced stronger colours.

The distinctive, colourful cloth dolls sold throughout Cappadocia are produced by Soğanlı's handicraft industry.

8 Niğde

🏙 115,000. 🚌 Adana Yolu, 1.5 km (1 mile) east of the city centre. 🚉 end of İstasyon Cad, 1 km (0.5 mile) from town centre, (0388) 232 35 41.
ℹ Belediye Sarayı, (0388) 232 33 93.
🛍 Women's Handicraft Market (Sat).
🎭 Tepecuması Folklore and Country Festival (27 May).

Known in Hittite times as Nahita, Niğde survived 10th-century Arab raids better than its neighbours. Its position on a major trade route to the Mediterranean appealed to the enterprising Seljuks, and so Niğde flourished as a regional capital until the time of the Mongol invasions (see p57).

The Seljuks filled the town with fine architecture, notably the Alaeddin Mosque (1223), distinguished by its superb stonework, ornate portal and typical squat minaret, and the Great Mosque (Ulu Camii), which was built around 1335. There is also a Seljuk tomb, the Hüdavend Hatun Türbe, featuring the octagonal forms typical of Seljuk architecture.

Niğde's bazaar (bedesten), with its fine clock tower, is a vestige of the town's heyday. The museum has sections on ethnography and Asian civilizations, and displays the mummified remains of a nun from the Ihlara Valley (see p296).

Do try and taste Niğde's deliciously creamy ewe's milk cheese, which comes "packaged" in a woolly sheepskin. Such local cheeses are called *tulum peyniri*.

Environs
There are several interesting places near Niğde. The best are **Bor**, a carpet-weaving centre that lies 15 km (9 miles) to the southwest, and **Kemerhisar**, which is 20 km (12 miles) to the south. This Hittite site dates from about 1200 BC. At the site, you can see the arches of an aqueduct and a mineral spring.

The Byzantine monastery church at **Eski Gümüş** was restored in the early 1990s and is one of the best-kept secrets in Turkey. The frescoes here are outstanding.

If you are a mountaineer, the **Aladağlar Mountains** offer some excellent climbing and include Demirkazık, the highest peak in the region. To reach the summit, the best starting point is the village of the same name, which lies 65 km (40 miles) east of Niğde. Northeast of Niğde is **Sultansazlığı Bird Sanctuary**, which is considered to be Turkey's most important bird sanctuary after Lake Manyas (Kuşcenneti; see p161). With a total area of 172 sq km (66 sq miles), the

A narrow gorge in the spectacular Aladağlar Mountains, near Niğde

White-headed duck

marshes are regarded as some of the largest and most important wetlands in Europe and the Middle East. The area is protected by the Ramsar Convention, an agreement signed in Iran in 1971 to conserve wetlands and their resources. The reserve is a haven for around 300 species of bird, including ducks, flamingoes, terns, cranes, egrets and plovers. Partridges, swordbeaks, whimbrels and pelicans all come here to breed. The best bird-watching spot is the lookout at Ovaçiftlik.

🦆 **Sultansazlığı Bird Sanctuary**
70 km (44 miles) SW of Kayseri.
Tel (0352) 658 55 49. **Open** Mar–Dec: 5am–midnight daily. 🅿

🏛 **Eski Gümüş**
9 km (6 miles) NE of Niğde. **Tel** (0388) 232 33 90. **Open** Apr–Oct: 8am–7pm daily; Nov–Mar: 8am–5pm daily. 🅿

The Sultansazlığı Bird Sanctuary, a bird-watcher's paradise

For hotels and restaurants in this area see pp330–39 and pp346–61

❹ Kayseri

Dominated by Mount Erciyes, Kayseri has been fought over by Persians, Arabs, Mongols and Ottomans. Its most prosperous era was undoubtedly under the Romans – when it was known as Eusebeia/Mazaka and then Caesarea – but it also flourished under the Seljuks. At the junction of five roads, the city was a key point on the Roman road system, and the Romans established an imperial munitions factory here. By the 4th century Kayseri was a focal point of Christian life and faith. Its most famous cleric (and bishop) was St Basil the Great (around AD 329–379), who defended church doctrine against heretical movements.

Entrance to the Twin-Turreted Theology Complex

Exploring Kayseri

Kayseri was once a prominent centre of education, and has many religious institutions, tombs and mosques to visit. Agriculture, textiles and manufacturing are all crucial to the local economy, but it has preserved traditional crafts such as carpet making. In addition the best *sucuk* (salami) in Turkey comes from here and the 20 varieties of *pastırma* (cured beef) are also a regional speciality.

◖ Twin-Turreted Theology Complex
Çifte Medresesi
Sinan Park. **Tel** (0352) 231 35 65.
Open 8am–5pm Wed–Sun.

The complex consists of two adjoining theological centres, the Gıyasiye Medresesi and the Şifahiye Medresesi. The Seljuks placed great emphasis on learning – this extended to anatomy and medicine. This was the first Seljuk academy of medicine and is now called the Gevher Nesibe Medical History Museum. Here you can learn more about Seljuk medical practices. There is an operating theatre and accommodation for psychiatric patients.

The architectural scheme incorporates arches, vaulted antechambers (*eyvan*) and an open courtyard.

🕌 Three Bazaars
Behind the Ulu Camii. **Closed** Sun.
Kayseri's three bazaars offer a contrast to the city's wealth of tombs and mausoleums. The Covered Bazaar (Kapılı Çarşı) dates from 1859, but the other two, the Bedesten and Vizir Han, date from the 15th and 16th centuries respectively.

There are few places that capture the keen spirit of age-old trading better than the bazaars of Kayseri. All three are still patronized by local people and traders, who barter and haggle in a lively atmosphere. Many of the local specialities, such as textiles and carpets, can be bought in the bazaars.

🏰 Citadel
Kale
The north wall and ramparts of the Citadel were built by the Emperor Justinian in the 6th century. However, little of the outer fortifications can be seen today. The black basalt structure originally had 195 bastions, and it is still an imposing sight – albeit as a shopping centre today.

🏛 Güpgüpoğlu Stately Home
Güpgüpoğlu Konağı
Tennuri Sok, Cumhuriyet Mahallesi.
Tel (0352) 222 95 16. **Open** 8am–5pm Tue–Sun. 🖼

A family home built between 1417 and 1419, the house has been carefully preserved and restored to its former glory, with each room highlighting specific aspects of Ottoman life. There are guest rooms, a bridal chamber, meeting areas for family gatherings and men's and women's quarters. Notable features are the built-in cupboards (*yüklük*) for storing mattresses, and the kitchen area, which consists of a pantry and a large main kitchen (*tokana*).

◖ Hunat Hatun Mosque Complex
Hunat Hatun Camii ve Medresesi
Behind tourism information office.
Open 9am–5:30pm daily.

This *külliye* (religious and educational institution adjoining a mosque) was one of the first mosque precincts the Seljuks built in Anatolia, although the minaret was erected in 1726. The complex has a mosque, training centre and *hamam* (Turkish bath) for

The 13th-century Citadel, now a busy shopping centre

For hotels and restaurants in this area see pp330–39 and pp346–61

Owner of a typical *pastırma* (cured beef) shop in Kayseri

men and women, and also includes the substantial mausoleum of Mahperi Huand Hatun, wife of Alaeddin I Keykubad *(see p254)*. Her inscription on the east door dates back to 1238.

🏛 Octagonal Tomb
Döner Kümbet
Talas Cad.

There are many grand tombs to be found all around Anatolia, but the elegance and pure simplicity of the Döner Kümbet makes it one of the most impressive. The tomb was constructed around 1250 as the final resting place of Şah Cihan Hatun, who was a Seljuk princess.

The Octagonal Tomb

🏛 Archaeology Museum
Arkeoloji Müzesi
Gültepe Mah. Kışla Cad 2.
Tel (0352) 222 21 49/232 48 12.
Open 8am–5pm Tue–Sun. 🖼

The museum consists of two large halls and a pleasant garden. The displays run in chronological sequence from the Bronze Age to the Byzantine period. By far the most valuable and interesting items to be seen are the series of cuneiform tablets documenting the commercial transactions of the Assyrian trading colony which flourished here during the late Hittite era *(see pp28–9)*.

VISITORS' CHECKLIST

Practical Information
🗺 1,050,000.
ℹ Cumhuriyet Meydanı, Sivas Cad (0352) 222 39 03 and 222 03 63. 🎭 Culture and Art Week (1st week Apr), Pastırma Festival (15 Sep).

Transport
🚌 Osman Kavuncu Cad, (0352) 327 45 00. 🚃 North end of Atatürk Bulvarı, 1 km (0.5 mile) from city centre, (0352) 231 13 13. ✈ Erkilet, (0352) 337 52 44.

Environs

Kültepe, formerly known as Kanesh or Kanış, and now Karum, is one of the most important Bronze Age sites in Turkey. In the second millennium BC, Kültepe was the foremost Assyrian trading colony. Most of the objects found here can now be seen in the museum in Kayseri or in the Museum of Anatolian Civilizations in Ankara *(see pp246–7)*.

Kültepe
21 km (13 miles) NE of Kayseri on the Sivas highway.
Open 8am–5pm daily. 🖼

Kayseri City Centre

① Twin-Turreted Theology Complex
② Three Bazaars
③ Citadel
④ Güpgüpoğlu Stately Home
⑤ Hunat Hatun Mosque Complex
⑥ Octagonal Tomb
⑦ Archaeology Museum

0 metres 400
0 yards 400

For keys to symbols *see back flap*

❾ Güzelyurt

28 km (17 miles) SE of Aksaray.
🚐 4,380. 🚌 infrequent from
Aksaray or Ihlara Valley.

Güzelyurt means "beautiful
country" and is an apt des-
cription of this charming
and friendly town, which is
surrounded by citrus groves.
This is a popular area for
horseback riding and mountain
biking. The latter is a restful
alternative to driving.

It is estimated that there
were over 50 Greek Orthodox
churches here once, though
only a few endure today.
The church of St Gregory of
Nazianzus, one of the four
founders of the Greek Orthodox
church, has been converted
into a mosque. It was first built
in AD 385, but the current
church dates from 1896.

A government protection
order is in force in Güzelyurt, so
all restoration and construction
work must conform to official
guidelines. Local stone must be
used and the buildings must
be appropriate to the town.

The valley 4 km (2 miles) to
the northeast of the town, also
known as the Monastery Valley,
has an abundance of rock-
carved churches.

❿ Ihlara Valley

To many people, the Ihlara
Valley is more compelling than
the rock churches and dwellings
in the region. The setting is
dramatic, with the Melendez
River winding along the
canyon floor.

The main part of the valley lies
between the village of Selime to
the north and the town of Ihlara
to the south. You could spend
an entire day exploring the
15 km-long (9 mile) canyon.

Of the 60 or so original
churches in the valley, which was
known as Peristrema in Greek
times, only about 10 can be seen
and some of the interior frescoes
are in less than pristine condition.

Most of the churches in the
valley date from the 11th century.
Their unusual names signify
their use or a peculiar feature:
Hyacinth, Black Deer, Crooked
Stone and Dovecote. Many of the
interior frescoes depict scenes
from the lives of the saints, the
lives of the ascetic monks, or
punishments for wrongdoing.

It was once thought that a
medical school, where the art
of mummification was taught
and practised, was located
between the villages of
Belisırma and Yaprakhisar.

The Eğri (Leaning) Minaret, built by
the Seljuks in the 13th century

⓫ Aksaray

🚐 236,000. 🚌 0.5 km (0.3 mile) from
main square. 🅸 Taşpazar Mahallesi,
Kadıoğlu Sok 1, (0382) 213 24 74 and
212 46 88.

In Roman times, Aksaray was
known as Archelais, after
Archelaus II, the last king of
Cappadocia. By 20 BC, the
kingdom had been reduced
to a virtual protectorate of
Rome and the king enjoyed
only token status.

From the south, Aksaray is
overlooked by the twin peaks of
Mount Hasan (Hasan Dağı), an
extinct volcano known as "little

The spectacular Ihlara Valley, one of Central Anatolia's best hiking areas sister" to Mount Erciyes. Aksaray is close to the eastern end of the Tuz Gölü (Salt Lake). In Ottoman times, the lake brought prosperity to Aksaray as it was the main source of salt for almost the whole of Anatolia.

Aksaray might appear to be a sleepy base for tourists, but spare some time to view the fine Seljuk building styles and architecture, with vestiges of the original ochre-coloured sandstone. Worth seeing are the Great Mosque (1314), with its beautifully carved *minbar* (pulpit), and the **Zinciriye Medresesi**, a 14th-century Koranic school, that now serves as the museum.

Aksaray has its own leaning tower, the Eğri (Leaning) Minaret, on Nevşehir Caddesi. The minaret is part of the Kızıl (Red) Minare Mosque, which was built in 1236 during the reign of the great Seljuk Sultan Alaeddin I Keykubat (*see p254*). The mosque was built on sand, which has shifted over time, causing the minaret to lean.

🏛 Zinciriye Medresesi
Muhsin Çelebi Sokak. **Tel** (0382) 213 16 67. **Open** 8am–noon & 1–5pm daily. 🅿

⑫ Kırşehir

160 km (100 miles) SE of Ankara. 🅰 83,450. ℹ Terme Cad, Ulucan I Apartman, Kat 1, (0386) 213 14 16.

In Byzantine times, Kırşehir was known as Mokyssos. It prospered under the Seljuks, who renamed it Gülşehir, or Rose Town. One of the finest of the city's Seljuk buildings is the Cacabey Mosque, built in 1272 as an astrological observatory and theological college. The Alaeddin Mosque, built in 1230, and the Ahi Evran Mosque are also located in Kırşehir. The latter contains the tomb of Ahi Evran, founder of a *tarikât* (religious brotherhood) whose members helped to spread the message of Islam to the Christian communities of Anatolia.

Gravestone at Hacı Bektaş

Various artifacts from Kalehöyük, an important Hittite archaeological site 55 km (34 miles) to the north-west of Kırşehir, are on display in the excellent **Archaeology Museum**. Kalehöyük is one of the many Hittite centres that are being excavated in the area. The museum has more than 3,300 artifacts on display, including coins, ethnographic items and archaeological materials.

Another prime reason for visiting the area is a Japanese arboretum, the **Mikasonmiya Memorial Garden** (Mikasonmiya Anı Bahçesi). One of the largest and most pleasant parks in Turkey, it is planted with some 16,500 trees, made up of 33 different species.

🏛 Archaeology Museum
Ahi Evren Cad 10. **Tel** (0386) 213 33 91. **Open** 8am–5pm daily. 🅿

🌳 Mikasonmiya Memorial Garden
ℹ Contact the Kırşehir tourist office, (0386) 213 1416, for opening hours.

⑬ Hacı Bektaş

🅰 9,348. ℹ Opposite the Museum, (0384) 441 36 87. 🅿 🅿 Hacı Bektaş Veli Commemoration Festival (16–18 Aug).

The mystic and spiritual philosopher Hacı Bektaş arrived in this area from Iran, via Mecca, in the late 13th century, and founded a centre of learning. His ideas were an offshoot of the Shi'ite sect of Islam, and rested on a belief in natural harmony that was bolstered by mysticism and divine love. The teachings of Hacı Bektaş offered an approachable and compassionate alternative to the main current of Islam. The Bektaşi doctrine, as set out in his book the *Malakat*, is based on both Islamic and Christian principles. This made it a popular belief. He attracted many devotees, most notably

Doorway into the tomb of Hacı Bektaş, in the third courtyard

among the Janissaries, who were the elite fighting force of the Ottoman sultans (*see p60*).

The **Hacı Bektaş Museum** (Pirevi, or "founder's house") is the chief attraction, along with the stunning wood carvings of the archaeological museum. Be sure you allow sufficient time to see the whole complex: there are tombs, courtyards, initiation cells, pools and a refectory (dining room) with authentic kitchen cauldrons. The tomb of Hacı Bektaş, in the third courtyard, has seven doors, and is particularly striking. Some of the inscriptions were done with natural dyes from the madder root, and later restored with oil-based paint.

Atatürk came through here in 1919 on his way from Sivas to Ankara; his visit is marked on 22 and 23 December each year. Admiration for the order did not prevent him banning all mystical sects and dervish lodges in 1925, because they were contrary to Turkey's secular state dogma.

The symbol of the order is the rose and blond onyx that is found in the area. It is known as Hacı Bektaş stone.

🏛 Hacı Bektaş Museum
Nevşehir Cad. **Tel** (0384) 441 30 22. **Open** 8am–5pm Tue–Sun. 🅿

The 19th-century clock tower in the main square in Yozgat

⑭ Yozgat

🏙 80,000. 🛈 İl Özel İdare Hizmet Binası, Kat 3, (0354) 212 64 23. 🚌 (0354) 212 41 15. 🗓 Tue. 🎭 Summer Folklore and Culture Festival (10–15 Jun).

Research shows that there were settlements here as early as 3,000 BC. However, the tides of history barely affected Yozgat until it fell to the Ottomans in 1408 and the influential Çapanoğlu dynasty made the town their seat. The Çapanoğlus built or repaired many fine mosques, including the Ulu (Çapanoğlu) Camii. The **Yozgat Ethnographic Museum** is housed in a 19th-century *konak* (mansion), the Nizamoğulu Konağı.

In the centre of the town there is an interesting, though garish, clock tower built in 1897 by Ahmet Tevfikzade, the mayor of the town. Ask to see the mechanism if you are interested in timepieces.

🏛 **Yozgat Ethnographic Museum**
Emniyet Cad. **Tel** (0354) 212 27 73. **Open** 8am–5pm Tue–Sun.

Environs
Çamlık National Park, located about 5 km (3 miles) south of Yozgat, covers 8 sq km (3 sq miles) of woodland, and has abundant fauna and flora, picnic areas, mineral springs and a hotel.

🏞 **Çamlık National Park**
Tel (0354) 212 10 84. **Open** daily

⑮ Boğazkale

See pp300–1.

⑯ Alacahöyük

30 km (19 miles) SE of Çorum.

Located between Sungurlu and Çorum, Alacahöyük is the third and most important site (after Boğazkale and Yazılıkaya) in the Hattuşaş complex of Hittite sites in this region. Most of the artifacts found at the site are displayed in museums in Ankara *(see pp246–7)* and Çorum.

Excavations at Alacahöyük have yielded items ranging from the Chalcolithic period (5500 BC–3000 BC) up to the Phrygian period (750 BC–300 BC) – a staggering time span that makes the site one of Turkey's most important archaeological centres.

At the site itself, the Sphinx Gate is an imposing reminder of cult power, its half-man, half-animal statues displaying striking Egyptian influences. The royal

tombs can also be seen. The **Alacahöyük Museum** displays some of the earthenware pots that were used for burial rites.

🏛 **Alacahöyük Museum**
Tel (0364) 422 70 11. **Open** 8am–noon, 1–5pm Tue–Sun.

One of the carved sphinxes that guard the gate at Alacahöyük

⑰ Çorum

🛈 Yeni Hükümet Binası, A Blok, Kat 4, (0364) 213 85 02. 🎭 Hittite Festival (mid-Jun).

The town of Çorum dates from Roman times, when it was known as Niconia. The surrounding area is rich in Hittite history, making it likely that the site was inhabited as early as 1400 BC. Throughout Turkey, the name of Çorum is associated with roasted chickpeas *(leblebi)*, one of the many nuts that Turks munch compulsively. A particularly delicious local cheese is Kargi, made from cow's milk. Çorum makes a good base from which

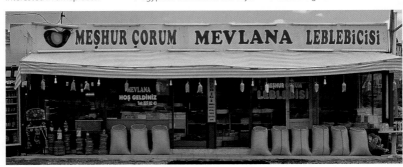

Shop in Çorum specializing in the famous local produce, chickpeas

to tour two major Hittite sights, Boğazkale *(see pp300–1)* and Alacahöyük. Both are located to the southwest of the town.

The **Çorum Museum** sprawls over several buildings. It is a serious and informative place with many artifacts and ethnographic displays, among them very good Hittite objects, as well as local *kilims* (rugs).

🏛 **Çorum Museum**
Town centre. **Tel** (0364) 213 15 68.
Open 8am–noon, 1–5pm Tue–Sun. ▨

⑱ Amasya

See pp302–3.

⑲ Tokat

🏙 121,000. ℹ Valilik Binası, Kat. 3, (0356) 214 37 53. 🚌 2 km (1 mile) from main square, (0356) 214 22 20. 🎉 Pinecone Festival (mid-Sep).

Tokat deserves a place on visitors' itineraries because there is a lot more to see here than ankle-high ruins. The Seljuks left the most to see, but the town is also known for resisting Ottoman rule. In protest at Ottoman authority, Turcoman tribesmen took to wearing distinctive red headgear, thus earning the name of Kızılbaşı (redheads), which became a term for "rebels".

The town flourished after Sultan Beyazıt I won control of trade routes to Erzincan. Trade caravans then began to use the Amasya–Tokat route, skirting Trabzon (Trebizond), to reach Bursa *(see pp166–71)*, the commercial jewel of the 15th and 16th centuries.

The Seljuks and Ottomans endowed Tokat with many fine buildings, especially the Blue Seminary (Gök Medrese) and two restored 19th-century Ottoman *konaks* (mansions): the Madımağın Celal'ın House and the Latifoğlu House. If time is limited, Tokat's interesting **Archaeological Museum** is the place to go.

Tokat has a proud 300-year tradition of hand-printed textiles *(yazmacılık)*. The craft

The Heavenly Seminary in Sivas, showing filigree stonework

still thrives in the Gazi Emir Han near the business hub of Sulu Sokak. The town is also renowned for copper-working and ceramics in bold primary colours.

Specialities include *pekmez*, a delicious drink made from concentrated grape juice, and the full-bodied, fruity Karaman red wine.

🏛 **Archaeological Museum**
Gaziosmanpaşa Bulvarı 143.
Tel (0356) 214 15 09.
Open 8am– noon & 1–5pm Tue–Sun.

Environs

The ruined city of Sebastopolis is located 68 km (42 miles) southwest of Tokat. The modern name, Sulusaray (watery palace), comes from the thermal springs, which bubble water at 50°C. Interesting finds here include a city wall, bath chambers and a temple.

Shop selling hand-printed textiles in Tokat

⑳ Sivas

🏙 318,000. ℹ Atatürk Kültür Merkezi, (0346) 223 92 99. 🚆 İstasyon Cad, (0346) 221 10 91. 🚌 3 km (2 miles) SE of main square, (0346) 226 15 90. 🎉 Nevruz (21 Mar).
🅦 sivas.gov.tr

Situated at an altitude of 1,275 m (4,183 ft), Sivas is the highest city in Central Anatolia. Known as Sebasteia in Roman times, its position on a caravan route made it an important trade centre.

Sivas boasts the cream of Seljuk architecture, with tiles, intricately etched stonework, star mosaics, honeycombed decorative motifs and bold blue hues all in evidence. The Heavenly Seminary (Gök Medresesi), built in the 1200s, and Twin Minaret Seminary (Çifte Minareli Medresesi), with its outstanding carved details, should not be missed. The Darüşşifası (Medical Hospice) housed a hospital. The Bürüciye Medresesi (1271) has a quiet courtyard and some excellent tilework.

The Sivas Congress (to consolidate Atatürk's plans to free Turkey from foreign domination) was held in a schoolroom here in 1919. The room is preserved in the **Ethnography Museum**. Local artisans are known for long-stemmed wooden pipes, penknives and bone-handled knives.

🏛 **Ethnography Museum**
Istasyon Cad. **Tel** (0346) 221 04 46.
Open 8am–5pm Tue–Sun. ▨

⓯ Boğazkale

Hattuşaş National Park

Boğazkale is the modern name for the ancient Hittite capital city of Hattuşaş, built around 1600 BC on a strategic site occupied since the third millennium BC. An Assyrian trading colony was also active here early in the second millennium BC. A UNESCO World Heritage site, it is one of the most important ancient sites to be found in Anatolia. The many thousands of clay and bronze tablets discovered here have provided scholars with a wealth of information about the ancient Hittite civilization.

The city occupies an extensive site bordered on three sides by steep ravines. Sections of the walls, including the impressive Lion's and King's gates, are still standing. The builders adapted the fortifications in masterly fashion to take advantage of topographical features.

Bronze Plaque
This plaque found at Boğazkale records a treaty between the Hittite king, Tudhaliyas IV, and another ruler.

Entry to excavation site

★ Lion's Gate (Aslanlıkapı)
The Lion's Gate takes its name from the two lion statues that guarded the city over 3,000 years ago. The lions here are only replicas – the originals are now in the Museum of Anatolian Civilizations in Ankara (see pp246–7).

Hittite Civilization

A people of Indo-European origin, the Hittites arrived in Anatolia from the Caucasus region around 2000 BC. Over the next few centuries, they built up a powerful state, with a capital at Hattuşaş (now known as Boğazkale). At its height, the Hittite kingdom controlled much of Anatolia, rivalling both Egypt and Babylon. Hittite art reached its peak between 1450 and 1200 BC, and Hittite artisans were renowned as superb carvers and metalworkers.

One of the twelve gods in stone relief at Yazılıkaya, near Boğazkale

| 0 metres | 550 |
| 0 yards | 550 |

★ **Great Temple (Büyük Mabet)**
One of the best preserved Hittite temples, the
Great Temple was built around 1400 BC, and
was dedicated to the storm god, Teshub. The
temple complex contains ritual chambers,
administrative areas and storage rooms.

VISITORS' CHECKLIST

Practical Information
Part of Çorum Museum, within
Hattuşaş National Park.
Tel (0364) 452 20 06.
Open 8am–5pm daily.
Admission includes entry to
the Yazılıkaya site nearby.

The Citadel (Büyükkale)
The walled citadel was the seat of
government at Hattuşaş. A monumental
staircase led up to three courts, one
of which contained the living quarters
of the royal household.

Rough stone
blocks

Battlements, probably
made of mud bricks

Corbelled archway

KEY

① **The Sphinx Gate** (Yerkapı)
is built into an artificial hill, and
incorporates a tunnel 70 m
(230 ft) in length.

② **Yenice Citadel**

③ **Modern village of Boğazköy**

④ **Sarı Citadel**

⑤ **King's Gate**

★ **Reconstruction of the King's Gate**
*The King's Gate (Kral Kapı) was named after the regal-
looking Hittite war god on the stone relief guarding
the entrance. The city wall is built with huge, roughly
worked stone blocks, and totals about 7 km (5 miles)
in length. The height of the stone portion was about
6 m (20 ft). Like the other structures in the city, this
would have been overlaid with sun-dried brick.*

⑱ Amasya

Lying in a secluded valley of the Yeşilırmak River, Amasya has seen the passage of nine civilizations, from the Hittites to Ottomans. Its most prosperous era was as royal capital of the Roman kingdom of Pontus, when it was called Amaseia; the tombs cut into the cliffs above the town contain the graves of the Pontic kings. However, a glance at Amasya's many fine Ottoman buildings will confirm that the four centuries of Ottoman rule were equally illustrious. In the 15th century, Amasya was second only to Bursa in cultural and trading importance. By the 1800s, the city excelled as the empire's leading centre for Islamic education.

The carved portal of the Teaching Hospital Complex

Exploring Amasya

Its dramatic location and air of tranquillity aside, Amasya is known for the tasty apples grown on the surrounding farms and for colourful hand-knitted socks. All main sights are conveniently accessible on foot. The citadel is the only exception, but it can be reached by car.

The Citadel, perched dramatically on a hilltop

🅲 Great Lord's Seminary

Büyük Ağa Medresesi
Zubediye Hanım Sok.
Closed during lessons.

The wonderful airy symmetry and octagonal plan of this complex, also known as the Kapıağası, are its outstanding features. It was built in 1488 by Hüseyin Agha, a private consort of Sultan Beyazıt II. The vaulted porticoes and domed rooms are now used by Koranic students, who adhere to exactly the same rigorous discipline as their predecessors did two or three centuries ago.

🅷 Citadel

Kale
Can be reached by 2-hour climb from the front, or by a road from behind.

The original Hittite fortress was reinforced by the Pontic king, Mithradates *(see p52)*. He built eight layers of walls, with 41 towers, to protect a self-sustaining complex with a palace, cisterns, storage areas, powder magazine and cemetery. From the Citadel there are stupendous views of the nearby Rock Tombs.

🅡 Rock Tombs

Kral Kaya Mezarları
Entrance under the railway line off Hazeranlar Sok. **Open** 8am–5pm (7pm in summer).

The tombs of the Pontic kings date from 333 BC to 44 BC, covering the Hellenistic and Roman periods. The Mirror Cave (Aynalı Mağrası), about 1 km (0.5 mile) from the main tombs, has a coloured painting showing the Virgin Mary and the Apostles.

🏛 Teaching Hospital Complex

Daruşşifa/Bimarhane Medresesi
Atatürk Cad. **Open** 9am–6pm daily.

The outer walls of the original asylum date from 1308. The complex served as a medical research centre, a school for interns and a hospice for mental patients. Music and speech therapy were used to calm disturbed patients. The carved front portal is wonderfully detailed and represents a rare architectural remnant of the Ilhanid Persian empire of the 13th century. The building houses a café and the offices of the local Music and Fine Arts Directorate.

🏛 Hazeranlar Mansion

Hazeranlar Konağı
Hattuniye Mahallesi. **Tel** (0358) 218 40 18. **Open** 8am–noon, 1–4:45pm.

This restored mansion dates from 1865. It was built by a local treasury officer, Hasan Talat Efendi, in memory of his sister, Hazeran Hanım (Lady Hazeran). The layout, typical of the time, features separate areas for men and women. The carpets, from the late Ottoman period, are particularly fine.

The tombs of the Pontic kings, carved into the limestone cliffs

For hotels and restaurants in this area see pp330–39 and pp346–61

Konaks (mansion houses) along the Yeşilırmak River

C Sultan Beyazıt Mosque and Theological College

Sultan Beyazıt II Külliyesi
Mustafa Kemal Paşa Cad.
Closed during prayer times.
🅿️ donation.

This was Amasya's primary theological complex, eclipsing all other places of religious learning. It was a product of the prosperity and social stability that prevailed under Sultan Beyazıt II (1481–1512). In that era, Muslim principles and obedience to the state were instilled at an early age. The wonderful domes and portals are inspirational in themselves, and the oak trees in the garden are said to be as old as the mosque itself.

🏛 Archaeology and Ethnography Museum

Arkeoloji ve Etnografik Müzesi
Mustafa Kemal Paşa Cad 91.
Tel (0358) 218 45 13.
Open 8am–5pm Tue–Sun. 🅿️

The museum has been improved and modernized, and so the concept of space is much enhanced. Notable among its exhibits is the bronze statue of the Hittite storm god, as well as a collection of Roman coins minted in the town.

The museum is best known for its collection of mummies, which were found in Anatolia and date from the Ilhanid period (around the 14th century). Previously housed in a dank tomb adjacent to the museum, these now have much more prominence in their display cases.

The Sultan Beyazıt Mosque, completed in 1486, with its famous rose garden

VISITORS' CHECKLIST

Practical Information
🅰️ 92,000. 🅸 Atatürk Cad, Pirinç Mah (opposite Bimarhane), (0358) 218 50 02.

Transport
🚉 2 km (1 mile) W of town centre, (0358) 218 12 39.
🚌 2 km (1 mile) NE of town centre, (0358) 218 80 12.

C Blue Seminary

Gök Medresesi
Mustafa Kemal Paşa Cad (Torumtay Sok). **Open** contact a guardian to let you in. **Closed** during prayer time.
🅿️ donation.

A theological complex dating from 1267, the Blue Seminary is typical of 13th-century Seljuk architecture. It was formerly used as a mosque and Koranic school, and takes its name from the turquoise/ blue tiles and glazed bricks used in its construction. The elaborately carved wooden doors contrasted with the austere interior and are now housed in the Archaeology and Ethno-graphic Museum.

Adjoining the complex is the Torumtay Türbe, a square tomb built in 1279 in memory of the Emir Torumtay, Seljuk governor of the province and founder of the seminary.

Amasya City Centre

① Great Lord's Seminary
② Citadel
③ Rock Tombs
④ Teaching Hospital Complex
⑤ Hazeranlar Mansion
⑥ Sultan Beyazıt Mosque and Theological College
⑦ Archaeology and Ethnography Museum
⑧ Blue Seminary

For keys to symbols *see back flap*

Exploring Eastern Anatolia

From the baking plains of Upper Mesopotamia to the icy heights of Mount Ağrı (Ararat), this vast region of Turkey is relatively undeveloped and unspoiled, making it a natural target for the more adventurous traveller. It is a land of frontiers, from cold and lonely Kars – a short step away from Armenia – through the Turkish-Iranian border town of Doğubayazıt, to the bustling bazaar city of Şanlıurfa close to Syria. Many peoples have lived in and fought over this land. Visitors can see Armenian churches and Kurdish castles, Arab houses, Syrian Orthodox monasteries and both Seljuk and Ottoman mosques vying with ruins from the Urartian and Roman eras. Late spring and early autumn are the best seasons to visit.

The citadel at Şanlıurfa

Stone head on Mount Nemrut

Sights at a Glance

0 kilometres 80

0 miles 40

Key

⚍ Motorway
⚍ Dual carriageway
▬ Major road
▭ Minor road
▬ Scenic route
⚎ Main railway
⎯ Minor railway
▬ International border
▲ Summit

Seljuk tombs at Erzurum

Getting Around

Comfortable intercity coaches connect all the major cities in the region, and are reasonably priced. For rural areas or out-of-the-way sites, the best option is a locally hired taxi. Rental cars are available in major cities such as Gaziantep, Şanlıurfa and Van, as well as in smaller tourist towns such as Mardin. Non-stop flights from Istanbul and Ankara serve Şanlıurfa, Mardin, Erzincan and Kars. Rail travel between Erzurum and Kars, and Malatya and Tatvan, on Lake Van, is slow but scenically rewarding.

The island of Akdamar, in Lake Van

The Atatürk Dam, centrepiece of the GAP (Southeast Anatolian Project)

❶ Kâhta

43 km (27 miles) E of Adıyaman.
🛈 Kâhta Kaymakamlik, (0416) 725
50 05 (all year); (0416) 725 50 07
(summer only). 🎭 International
Kâhta Kommagene Festival (last week
in Jun).

Although it is located close to
the lake created by the monumental **Atatürk Dam** (Atatürk
Barajı), Kâhta's main attraction
is its proximity to Mount
Nemrut (Nemrut Dağı), located
70 km (44 miles) northeast.

Environs
The Atatürk Dam, part of the
GAP project, has intruded into
the Euphrates basin's ancient
past. Building of this and other
dams has flooded important
historic treasures and sites.

The town of **Adıyaman** is
slightly further away from
Mount Nemrut (about a half-
hour drive west of Kâhta), and
makes an alternative base.

An attractive place to visit is
the lush, green village of Karadut
(Black Mulberry), set in dramatic
mountain scenery 12 km
(7 miles) below the summit.

Adıyaman
🛈 Atatürk Bul 184, (0416) 216 10 08.

❷ Mount Nemrut

Nemrut Dağı

See p310.

❸ Malatya

🗺 740,000. ✈ 4 km (2.5 miles) W of
city centre, off Turgut Özal Bul, (0422)
238 47 68. 🚌 2 km (1 mile) W of city
centre, (0422) 212 40 40. 🚉 23 km
(14 miles) W of city centre. 🛈 Valilik
Binası, (0422) 323 30 25/29 42.
🛒 daily. 🎭 Cherry Festival (18 Jun);
Apricot Festival (3rd week Jul).

Malatya is famous for its
apricots, grown in the vast
surrounding orchards. It was
also the birthplace of two
Turkish presidents: İsmet İnönü,
Atatürk's right-hand man during
the War of Independence; and
Turgut Özal, an economist who
served first as Prime Minister,
and then President, from the
mid-1980s *(see p63)*.

Malatya is a pleasant and
fairly prosperous town with a
university and a military base,

Apricot vendor in Malatya's Apricot Bazaar

but makes a less convenient
base than Kâhta for trips to
Mount Nemrut.

The town's most interesting
sights are its bazaars. The **Apricot
Bazaar** specializes in locally
grown and dried apricots. Trading
takes place after the harvest,
and during the Apricot Festival in
July. Around the central mosque
is the **Copper Bazaar**, a group
of copper-beating workshops
where you can buy hand-made
trays, pots and vases.

Aslantepe, a Hittite site
located 4 km (3 miles) northeast
of Malatya was flooded as a
result of the GAP project. Dating
back to the 4th millenium BC
this artificial settlement mound,
which has been excavated by
Italian teams since the 1960's,
is now an open-air museum.
Complete with walkways and
informative sign boards, it
gives valuable insights into the
Chacolithic, Hittite, Roman and
Medieval periods and is set in
delightful apricot orchards.

Finds from Aslantepe are on
display in the **Malatya
Archaeological Museum**. Items
including Hittite stone god
statues, cuneiform seals, bone
idols and early bronze swords
were transferred to the museum.
There are over 15,500 items
spanning most historic periods.
The Neolithic sculptures from
8000 BC are particularly impressive, as are the obsidian knives.

Local carpets and *kilims* (rugs) have distinctive features, such as the rectangular "tower bastion" motif. The *yedi dağ çiçeği* (seven-point flower) motif can be found on *kilims*. Carpets generally have simpler designs in strong, primary colours, with borders featuring stylized flowers, rams, medallions or dragons. Small hand-loomed carpets and goat-hair rugs are also found in and around Malatya.

Apricot Bazaar
New Malatya Quarter. **Open** Mon–Sat.

Copper Bazaar
New Malatya Quarter. Adjoining the Apricot Bazaar. **Open** Mon–Sat.

▥ Aslantepe
4 km NE of Malatya.
Tel (0422) 321 30 06. **Open** 8am–5pm Tue–Sun. ▨

▥ Malatya Archaeological Museum
Dernek Mahallesi, Kanal Boyu. **Tel** (0422) 321 30 06. **Open** 8am–5pm Tue–Sun. ▨

Environs
Eski Malatya, the old part of town, lies about 12 km (7.5 miles) north of the modern centre. A little village of 2,000 inhabitants has developed inside these walls, once an important Roman and then Byzantine stronghold. The 17th-century Silahtar Mustafa Paşa Caravanserai had been restored, but is now sadly neglected and visitors have to wander around among chickens and donkeys.

The much-restored **Great Mosque** (Ulu Camii) is built around a tiny courtyard, its graceful interior divided into separate summer and winter areas. The winter area is supported by massive pillars and enclosed by thick walls, while the summer section has a beautifully carved wooden pulpit, and amazing herring-bone brick vaulting decorated with scattered turquoise tiles.

🄲 Great Mosque
Ulu Camii
Opposite the bus station. **Open** daily (except during prayer times).

❹ Kahramanmaraş

🄼 326,000. 🚌 W of main highway on Azerbaycan Bulvarı, (0344) 235 30 06. 🚆 Cumhuriyet Cad, (0344) 235 00 75. 🄸 Valilik Bahçesi, (0344) 223 03 55.

Copper tea pot from Malatya

Like many other Turkish towns, Kahramanmaraş has a deceptive air of calm and tranquillity that conceals a turbulent past. The first part of its name (meaning "heroic") was added by Atatürk in recognition of the town's successful expulsion of French and British troops in 1920.

It is, however, often just called "Maraş", after its particularly famous product, Maraş Dondurması – a delicious type of ice cream containing gum arabic that is pounded or whipped

The pleasant park below the citadel at Kahramanmaraş

into glutinous form. It is sold all over Turkey by costumed vendors. Locally, it is sold by the metre and cut with a knife. You can also buy it served in a cone.

The town's citadel, probably used as defence against Arab raiders in the 7th century, is now a popular tea garden and park. Two mosques, the Great Mosque and the Hatuniye Camii, date from the 15th- and 16th-century Beylik period. Their interiors feature fine wooden carvings.

The local **Archaeological and Ethnographic Museum** displays Hittite statues, ceremonial costumes, *kilims* and textile items from various eras.

▥ Archaeological and Ethnographic Museum
Azerbaycan Bul. **Tel** (0344) 223 44 88. **Open** 8am–noon & 1–5pm Tue–Sun. ▨

The 17th-century Silahtar Mustafa Paşa Caravanserai in Eski Malatya

➋ Mount Nemrut

Nemrut Dağı

The huge stone heads on the summit of Mount Nemrut (Nemrut Dağı) were built by King Antiochus I Epiphanes, who ruled the Commagene kingdom between 64 and 38 BC. To glorify his rule, the king had three enormous terraces (east, west and north) cut into the mountaintop. Colossal statues of himself and the major gods (both Greek and Persian) of the kingdom were placed on the terraces, and the summit became a sanctuary where the king was worshipped. Today's visitors can still see the remains of the east and west terraces (not much is left of the north terrace), which also feature large, detailed stone reliefs.

The enigmatic site was discovered in 1881 by a German engineer, Karl Sester, but was not fully documented until the 1990s.

VISITORS' CHECKLIST

Practical Information
70 km (44 miles) from Kâhta,
84 km (52 miles) from Adıyaman
in Nemrut Dağı National Park.
Tel (0416) 725 50 07.
Open May–Oct: 8am–7pm daily.
Closed Nov–Apr. 🏛

★ **East Terrace**
The site affords superb views of the surrounding region. Behind the sanctuary rises a 50 m (165 ft) high mound rumoured to contain the tumulus of King Antiochus

Eagle
Lion
Tyche
Zeus
Apollo
Heracles
Eagle
Lion

Reconstruction
This artists' impression depicts the East Terrace as it probably looked in the 1st century BC. The limestone figures were 8–10 m (26–33 ft) in height.

Head of Antiochus
The re-erected head of King Antiochus stands near the tumbled one of Tyche, Commagene goddess of fortune.

❺ Gaziantep

🗺 1,400,000. 🚉 İstasyon Cad, (0342) 323 31 96. ✈ Sazgan, 18 km (11 miles) from city centre, (0342) 582 11 11. 🚌 5 km (3 miles) North of city centre, (0342) 328 92 46. 🛈 Yüzyıl Atatürk Kültür Parkı, (0342) 230 59 69. 🎉 Pistachio Festival (1st week in Sep).

Named Ayntap, or pure spring, by the Byzantines, Gaziantep's modern prefix of *gazi* (war hero) derives from heroic resistance to French and English invaders in 1920. The site has been occupied for 8,000 years and was a strategic defence hub in Hittite times (1200–700BC). The city sprawls around an imposing castle (*kale*) perched atop a partly man-made mound. On the approach to the castle is the Panorama Museum (open daily), which gives a vivid insight into the Turks' defence of the city from the invading French in 1920. After decades of economic decline the city has boomed, not least because of its proximity to the Southeast Anatolian Project *(see p23)*.

Just below the citadel is a bazaar, where craftsmen produce and sell copperware and furniture inlaid with mother-of-pearl, a craft for which the town is famous.

Stroll around the old town to see traditional architecture adapted for regional life, like the *hayat*, or summer courtyard, seen in the **Hasan Süzer Ethnographic Museum**. The central **Gaziantep Archaeological Museum** is worth a visit to see Hittite and Roman statuary as well as Assyrian, Babylonian and Urartian artifacts.

The jewel of the city's museums is the state-of-the-art **Gaziantep Zeugma Mosaic Museum**. Spread over three floors, it is the world's largest mosaic museum, housing more than 3,500 sq m of largely 2nd- and 3rd-century mosaics rescued from the floodwaters of a dam on the nearby Euphrates. The mosaics once adorned the villas of the wealthy citizens of Zeugma, a frontier city that controlled trade along an arm of the silk route. Of particular note are the statue of Mars and the gypsy girl mosaic, which is a regional idol and symbol of the Zeugma excavations. Also housed in the museum are superb reconstructions of courtyard villas complete with mosaic floors, frescoes and columns and the remains of a Roman bath house.

Gaziantep is an important agricultural and industrial centre, and olives, grapes and pistachio nuts are grown around the city. The city's distinctive cuisine is famed throughout the country, particularly sweet pastries such as pistachio-filled *baklava*. To find out more about the city's cuisine it is worth visiting **Emine Göğüş Culinary Museum** in the bazaar quarter below the castle.

Gypsy girl mosaic, Gaziantep Zeugma Mosaic Museum

Statue of Mars, Gaziantep Zeugma Mosaic Museum

🏛 **Hasan Süzer Ethnography Museum**
Eyüboğlu Mah, Hanifioğlu Sok 64. **Tel** (0342) 230 47 21. **Open** 8:30am–noon & 1–4:30pm Tue–Sun. 📷

🏛 **Gaziantep Archaeological Museum**
İstasyon Cad. **Tel** (0342) 324 8809. **Open** 8:30am– noon & 1–6pm Tue–Sun. 📷

🏛 **Gaziantep Zeugma Mosaic Museum**
Konukoğlu Bulvarı. **Tel** (0342) 325 27 27. **Open** Apr–Oct: 9am–5pm Tue–Sun; Nov–Mar: 9am–5:30pm Tue–Sun. 📷

🏛 **Emine Göğüş Culinary Museum**
Hasırcı Sok. **Tel** (0342) 220 08 88. **Open** 9am–6pm daily. 📷

Gaziantep's bazaars, colourful and brimming with local goods

❻ Şanlıurfa

🏙 765,000. 🚌 5 km (3 miles) N of city centre, (0482) 412 1549.
✈ 6 km (4 miles) S of city centre, (0414) 313 78 23. ℹ Atatürk Bul, Vilayet Binası, Kat 3, (0414) 312 53 32.

The city of Şanlıurfa is one of the most interesting and colourful in the region. First settled by the Hurri peoples around 5,500 years ago, it was occupied by a succession of peoples, such as the Hittites, Assyrians, Greeks and Romans.

Alexander the Great named it Edessa, and the Ottomans renamed it Urfa. The city acquired the prefix *şanlı* (glorious) through the role it played in resistance to the French in 1920.

During Şanlıurfa's long Christian history it was used as a centre of the Nestorian movement, and later became the capital of a crusader state (1097–1144). Churches, now mosques, in the old town include the Selahattin Eyubi Camii, once the church of St John. Many Armenians lived in Urfa until 1920.

Most visitors, however, come here to see the Gölbaşı (lakeside) area at the foot of the citadel. This pleasantly landscaped garden contains the Pool of Abraham, said to be the site where the biblical prophet was saved from the vengeful Assyrian king, Nimrod (Nemrut). A small cave nearby is said to be the birthplace of Abraham. The stone covered bazaar, or Kapalı Çarşı, is an Ottoman structure, with designated rows

People playing games and relaxing in Gümrük Hanı, a lovely courtyard in Sanlıurfa's bazaar

of streets devoted to particular trades. Traditional crafts and skills predominate, and it is a good place to shop for locally produced cloth. Don't miss the Gümrük Hanı in the bazaar. This beautifully shady Ottoman-era courtyard building is full of locals drinking tea and coffee, and playing endless games of backgammon.

Local specialities include *çiğ köfte* (raw meatballs), once believed to be a dish prepared for Hittite kings; and *lahmacun* (a flat, pizza-like bread topped with spicy meat).

It is worth noting, however, that stomach bugs are not uncommon here so be wary.

Environs

Set on a rounded hilltop some 15 km (9 miles) northeast of Şanlıurafa, **Göbekli Tepe** is

Beehive-shaped hosues in Harran

one of the most exciting sights in Turkey. A temple complex of immense significance, its discovery in 1995 challenged traditional concepts that mankind was only able to produce monumental buildings after the transition had been made from a hunter-gatherer to a settled society. Some of the monolithic, anthropomorphic T-shaped stones here are 5 m (16 ft) tall and the earliest pre-date Stonehenge by nearly 8,000 years. Arranged in circles in chambers hollowed from the hilltop, most of the stones are decorated with raised relief carvings of foxes, wild boars, snakes and lions. Raised walkways allow visitors to examine the temple complex, though there are no set opening hours or admission fee.

It is worth making the 45-km (28-mile) trip southeast of Şanlıurfa to see the curious beehive houses of **Harran**, once an important city but which was destroyed by the Mongols in the 13th century. Most of the inhabitants of this austerely beautiful place are Arabs, and some still live among the ruins of old Harran in "beehive"-shaped houses made from mud-plastered stone. Substantial remains include the citadel and Ulu Camii, a massive (though now ruined) mosque denoted by a square minaret.

The Pool of Abraham in Şanlıurfa

For hotels and restaurants in this area see pp330–39 and pp346–61

❼ Mardin

🏙 88,000. ℹ Valilik Binası, (0482) 212 18 52, (0482) 212 37 76. 🎏 Kite Festival (third week Jun).

Superbly situated atop a limestone crag overlooking the Mesopotamian plain, Mardin is justly famed for its beautiful vernacular architecture. Many of its superb stone houses have been converted into boutique hotels and, after Gaziantep, it is the arguably most tourist-friendly city in southeast Turkey. The city was captured by Muslims in about 640 AD and ruled by various Arab and Kurdish states until the 11th century. Some exceptional theological buildings, like the Zinciriye Medresesi and the Kasımiye Medresesi, date from the 14th and 15th centuries respectively.

The unusual terrace-style dwellings and narrow, labyrinth-like streets invoke the style and form of their Arab heritage. A city landmark is the **Mardin Museum**, whose archaeological section displays works from 4000 BC until the 7th century BC.

The Ulu Camii, a 12th-century Syrian-style mosque, built by an Artukid chieftain, is another city symbol. It rises in stately contrast to the animated, ethnic bazaar that surrounds it. In the bazaar, look for the artisanal silver *tekari* (jewellery), for which Mardin is famous.

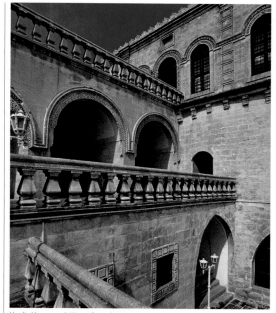

Mardin Museum, which was formerly the Syrian Catholic Patriarchate

A state-of-the-art ethnography museum housed in a beautifully restored period stone building, **Sakip Sabancı City Museum** is the place to find out about the traditional way of life in Mardin. Exhibits range from audiovisual presentations on metal-working and fabric printing to superb photographs of the town's myriad mosques and churches. Temporary exhibitions are also held at the museum.

🏛 **Mardin Museum**
Cumhuriyet Meydani, Latifiye Mah, Mardin. **Open** 9am–6pm Tue–Sun. 📷

🏛 **Sakip Sabancı City Museum**
Gül Mahallesi Eski Hükümet Cad, Mardin. **Tel** (0482) 212 93 96.
Open 8am–5pm Tue–Sun. 📷

Environs

Mardin, and the Tör Abdin plateau east of it, has long been a stronghold of the Syrian Orthodox Church. **Deyr-az-Zaferan**, known as the Saffron Monastery due to the colour of the yellowish stones it is built with, is the showcase of a much persecuted minority, and is beautifully set in a peaceful valley below dramatic bluffs some 6 km (4 miles) southeast of Mardin. A guide accompanies visitors around the picturesque stone-built monastery dating back to the 5th century and still in operation. There is a also a café, and one guest room is available for overnight stays.

🏛 **Deyr-az-Zaferan**
6 km (4 miles) SE of Mardin.
Open 8am–noon, 1–5pm daily. 📷

Traditional stone houses in Mardin

⑧ Diyarbakır

Southeastern Turkey's liveliest city, Diyarbakır is situated on the edge of a high bank dropping down to the Tigris River. Its 6 km (4 miles) of black basalt walls encircle an old centre of cobbled streets and alleys, mosques, churches and mansions.

As the unofficial capital of Turkey's Kurdish-dominated southeast, political feelings can run high here. However, the inhabitants are generally warm and open to visitors, and justly proud of their atmospheric but economically deprived home city.

Diyarbakır is renowned for the gigantic watermelons sold in its markets. Watered by the Tigris River and fertilized with pigeon droppings, these can reach weights of up to 50 kg (112 lbs).

Vendor offering one of the region's famous watermelons

Exploring Diyarbakır
Most of the city's sights are concentrated in the central area and can be seen on foot. Walking alone around the walls is not recommended.

🔒 Diyarbakir's Churches
Diyarbakır'ın Kilise
Church of the Virgin Mary. **Open** daily; services 8am–noon Sun. Church of St George. **Open** admission via caretaker.

The city's oldest church is the Syrian Orthodox Church of the Virgin Mary (Meryaman Kilise), possibly dating back to the 4th century. Restored to its former splendour, the Armenian Apostolic Church of St George (St Giargos Kilesesi) is reckoned to be one of the largest churches in the Middle East.

🏛 Hasan Paşa Hanı
Gazi Cad. **Open** Mon–Sat.
Located opposite the Great Mosque (Ulu Camii), and built by governor Verizade Hasan Paşa, this 16th-century *han (see pp28–9)* is still used by traders, and has some decent jewellery, carpet and antique outlets. The black basalt façade is dignified by a bold white limestone frieze.

🕌 Great Mosque
Ulu Camii
Gazi Cad. **Open** daily.
Closed during prayer times.
A fairly plain building with a basilica-plan style, the Great Mosque is the most significant building in Diyarbakır, and is regarded as one of the holiest places in the Islamic world. It was

The Great Mosque, originally built by the Arabs in the 7th century

built on the site of a church around AD 639 after the Arabs captured the city. In 1091–92, the Seljuk ruler Malik Şah remodelled the building, using the revered Great Ummayad Mosque in Damascus as a model.

The interior is spacious and austere, while the courtyard buildings are built from black basalt with bands of white limestone, faced with blind arches supported by Roman columns interspersed with Seljuk friezes. The mosque faces a Roman *stoa* (portico), topped by a library.

🏛 Ziya Gökalp Museum
Ziya Gökalp Müzesi
Ziya Gökalp Bul. **Tel** (0412) 228 13 26.
Open 8:30am–noon & 1–5pm Tue–Sun.
Ziya Gökalp, one of the chief ideologues of Turkish nationalism during the period of the Young Turks *(see p61)*, was born in Diyarbakır. His house is now a museum.

🕌 Kasım Padişah Mosque
Dört Ayaklı Camii
Yeni Kapı Cad. **Open** daily.
Closed during prayer times.
🔲 donation.
This was the last of the great mosques built under the reign of the Akkoyunlu (White Sheep) Turkomans. It is unusual for its free-standing minaret supported by four 2 m (6.5 ft) high basalt pillars carved from a single block of stone, known as the Dört Ayaklı Minare (four-legged minaret). It is said that your wish will be granted if you walk seven times around its pillars.

🕌 Behram Paşa Mosque
Behram Paşa Camii
Melik Ahmet Cad. **Open** daily.
Closed during prayer times.
🔲 donation.
Built in 1572 on the orders of the governor, Behram Paşa, this centrally located mosque is the city's largest. The black basalt exterior is enlivened by white stone banding, and the interior is light and graceful. The central ceiling has a calligraphic frieze of inlaid mother-of-pearl.

Black-and-white banding on the Behram Paşa Camii

The impressive walls surrounding the old city

VISITORS' CHECKLIST

Practical Information
835,000. Dağ Kapısı Burçu Giriş Bölümü, (0412) 228 17 06. Watermelon Festival (Sep); Nevruz (21 Mar); Hıdrellez Festival celebrating spring migration (6 May, depending on weather).

Transport
Kaplaner, 3 km (2 miles) SW of city centre, (0412) 233 27 19.
1 km (0.5 mile) W of city centre, (0412) 221 87 87/87 86.

City Walls
Diyarbakır'ın Kalesi

The black walls encircling the city – said to be visible from space – were originally built by the Romans (who captured Diyarbakır from the Sassanids in the 3rd century AD), since the city lacked natural defences. The Byzantines added to the structure, but what can be seen today is mainly the work of Seljuks, who captured the city in 1088.

Constructed from blocks of black basalt, the walls are pierced by four major gates (Harput, Yenikapı, Mardin and Urfa) and studded with 72 towers. The walls are 12 m (39 ft) high and more than 5 km (3 miles) in length. It is possible to walk along the top for much of the way.

The most impressive views are from the southern walls, looking down over the Tigris River winding its way towards Iraq. The Tower of the Seven Brothers (Yedi Kardeş Burçu), located between the Mardin and Urfa gates and built in 1208, provides a particularly good vantage point.

Environs
The **Atatürk Villa** was given to the founder of the Turkish Republic in 1937 by the citizens of Diyarbakır. On display are period photographs and personal effects. It is situated a few kilometres south of the city, off the road to Mardin, and has expansive views of the Tigris and the Dicle Köprüsü (Tigris Bridge). Built in 1065 on the site of an older structure, the bridge spans the river in 10 arches.

Atatürk Villa
Atatürk Köşkü

Open 8:30am–noon & 1:30–5pm daily.

Diyarbakır City Centre

① Hasan Paşa Hanı
② Great Mosque
③ Ziya Gökalp Museum
④ Kasım Padişah Mosque
⑤ Behram Paşa Mosque
⑥ City Walls

Bus station 1.5km (1 mile)
ZIYA GÖKALP BUL
UNIVERSITE YOLU
ALI EMIRI CAD
KIBRIS CAD
Dağ Kapısı
Hazreti Süleyman Camii
Çifte Kapısı
INÖNÜ CAD
Nebi Camii
IZZET PAŞA CAD
Oğrun Kapısı
İskender Paşa Camii
Saray Kapısı
Airport 3 km (2 miles)
Train station 500 metres (550 yards)
Ziya Gökalp Museum ③
Great Mosque ② ① Hasan Paşa Hanı
GAZI
Urfa Kapısı
Safa Camii
MELIK AHMET CAD
Surp Giargos Kilisesi
Keldani Kilisesi
Fatih Paşa Camii
Behram Paşa Mosque ⑤
④ Kasım Padişah Mosque
YENI KAPI CAD
Yeni Kapı
Meryamana Kilisesi
GAZI CAD
City Walls ⑥
TURISTIK CAD
Mardin Kapısı
Yedi Kardeş Burçu
Atatürk Villa

0 metres   250
0 yards   250

For keys to symbols *see back flap*

9 Lake Van

548,000. ✈ 6 km (4 miles) S of city centre, (0432) 216 10 19. 🚌 Ipek Yolu, NW of town centre. 🚂 to Tatvan, (0432) 223 41 38. ⛴ 5 km (3 miles) from town centre. ℹ Cumhuriyet Cad 105, (0432) 216 20 18.

The startlingly blue waters of Lake Van (Van Gölü) mirror the surrounding peaks, the highest of which soars to a dizzying 4,058 m (13,313 ft). The lake is seven times larger than Lake Geneva and may be up to 400 m (1,312 ft) deep. The lake has a salinity level well above that of sea water. It is so alkaline that locals need not use soap for washing. It is lovely for swimming.

The Van basin was once the centre of the Urartian civilization (contemporaries and foes of the Assyrians). The remnants of their fortified capital straddle the imposing **Rock of Van**, located close to the eastern shore of the lake. This spectacular rock outcrop, sheer on its southern side, was once the premier settlement of the Kingdom of Urartu. The most obvious remains left by this remarkable civilization are their cuneiform inscriptions, seen most obviously on the entrance to the Tomb of Argishti, which is reached by steps from near the top of the rock. The remains of an Ottoman mosque now crown the rock, while at its feet spread the remanants of old Van, a walled settlement completely destroyed in World War I. A few

The Rock of Van, with an ancient Urartian citadel at the summit

kilometres away is the modern city of Van. Although the centre lacks historical interest, it has plenty of decent restaurants. Try the famed Van breakfast, which includes clotted cream and honey, plus fried eggs and strips of lamb. The region is also proud of its local champion breed of cat, with one blue eye and one amber. Out of character for a cat, this breed enjoys water.

🏛 Rock of Van
Van Kalesi. **Open** 8:30am–7:30pm daily. 📷

Environs
Çavuştepe, 35 km (22 miles) southeast of Van, is another Urartian site, with a palace, sacrificial altar and inscriptions. It is best visited en route to the stark and hauntingly beautiful 17th-century castle at Hoşap, 60 km (37 miles) from Van on the same road.

The high point of a visit to the Lake Van area is the exquisite 10th-century Armenian **Church of the Holy Cross** (Akdamar Kilise), on a small island a few kilometres from the southern shore of the lake. Beautifully restored, the exterior boasts a remarkable series of bas-relief carvings and friezes showing biblical scenes. Cruciform in plan, and just 15 x 12 m (49 x 39 ft) in size, the church is topped by a conical roof.

Its classical beauty makes this church one of the most photographed buildings in eastern Anatolia. The frescoes that adorn the interior walls and cupola are unique in their artistic merit. Following the restoration of the church, services have been held, attracting many worshippers from both the Armenian community in Istanbul and from Armenia itself.

On the lake's north-western shore is the crescent-shaped crater lake on Nemrut Dağı (not the mountain with the statues near Kâhta) and the Seljuk cemetery and *kümbet* (domed tombs) at Ahlat. Both are worth a visit and can be accessed from Tatvan.

The local cheese, *otlu peynir*, is a real delicacy. A whole-milk cheese flecked with nutritious and flavoursome mountain herbs, it is now rarely found outside the Van area.

🏛 Church of the Holy Cross
40 km (25 miles) SW of Van. ⛴ from Gevaş. **Open** 8:30am–7:30pm daily. 📷

Frieze on the wall of the Church of the Holy Cross

◀ Collosal statues on the Eastern terrace of Mount Nemrut

⑩ Doğubayazıt

🏠 73,000. 🚌 Belediye Cad, W of town centre.

Situated on the main road between Turkey and Iran, Doğubayazıt is a half-hour drive from the border. It is a typically untidy frontier town, with a large military base on its eastern outskirts, and few visitors spend more than a night here. Mount Ağrı (Ararat), Turkey's highest mountain, rises 5,165 m (16,945 ft) above the landscape. Although said to be the resting place of Noah's Ark, little evidence has ever been found to support this claim. Access is difficult and prospective climbers need to obtain permission from the Ministry of Culture and Tourism in Ankara (*see p375*) in advance.

The impressive **İshak Paşa Sarayı** lies 8 km (5 miles) southeast of Doğubayazıt. The fortress-like palace was constructed from honey-coloured sandstone by an Ottoman governor in the late 18th century, although the variety of building styles (Ottoman, Persian, Armenian/Georgian and Seljuk) makes it difficult to attach an exact date. In Ottoman times, the palace lay on an important caravan route, explaining why such an opulent structure was erected in this lonely and remote part of the country.

The lavish arrangement of 366 rooms includes a harem with 14 bedrooms, *selamlık* (men's quarters) and a small but beautiful mosque whose interior has been badly damaged over the years. Ottoman and Russian troops occupied **İshak Paşa Sarayı** at various times and showed little regard for its historic importance.

Nearby attractions, best visited on a dolmuş tour from Doğubayazıt, are the sulphur springs at Diyadin, and the Meteor Çukuru (meteor crater), just before the Iranian border.

🏛 İshak Paşa Sarayı
Open 9am–noon & 1–5:30pm Tue–Sun. 🎫

İshak Paşa Sarayı, on a hillside southeast of Doğubayazıt

⑪ Kars

🏠 131,000. 🛫 2 km (1 mile) SE of town centre, (0474) 223 14 45.
🚌 off Cumhuriyet Cad, (0474) 223 43 99/43 98. 🚕 (0474) 223 06 74.
ℹ Cumhuriyet Mah, Lise Sokak 15, (0474) 212 68 17.

Remote but strategically very important, Kars is set on a grassy plain that is backed by distant peaks. The word *kar* means "snow" in Turkish and winters here are long and cold, while the spring and autumn rains turn streets to mud. The brief summer season is hot, dry and dusty.

Founded in the 10th century by the Armenian King Abas I, Kars was once a metropolis of around 100,000 inhabitants. In 1064, it was captured by the Seljuks, and subsequently came under Georgian and Ottoman rule. It was held by the Russians from 1878 to 1919, and the grid plan and numerous run-down Neo-Classical houses are significant reminders of their presence here.

The citadel (Kars Kalesi) was built by the Ottomans, as was the 15th-century Taş Köprü (stone bridge) over the River Kars. The 10th-century Armenian Church of the Apostles is today a mosque.

The small **Archaeological Museum**, just east of the town centre, is surprisingly good, particularly its displays of *kilims* (rugs) and carpets.

Kars is known for its huge wheels of Kaşar, a classic cow's milk cheese. One of the city's gourmet secrets is its Gruyère that is produced by one cheese-maker using authentic Swiss techniques.

🏛 Archaeological Museum
Cumhuriyet Cad 365. **Tel** (0474) 212 14 30. **Open** 8am–noon & 1–5pm Tue–Sun.

Environs
Most visitors visit Kars to see Ani (*see pp320–21*), a visually dramatic, ruined 11th-century Armenian city 43 km (27 miles) away to the east, on the border with Armenia.

The citadel at Kars, overlooking a Turkish bath

⑫ Ani

The ruined city of Ani, on the border with Armenia, is one of the most evocative historical sites in Turkey. Set on a windswept, grassy plateau along the Barley River (Arpa Çayı), the site contains important remnants of Armenian architecture, including the city walls protecting its northern border, parts of which are still intact.

In 961, Ani became the capital of the Bagratid kings of Armenia. It reached its apogee under King Gagik I (990–1020), when it was known as "the city of a thousand and one churches". Sacked by the Turks in 1064, Ani eventually recovered, only to be razed by an earthquake in 1319.

Located on the sensitive Turkish-Armenian border, parts of the site are off-limits to visitors – stick to the marked trail. Photography is also restricted so avoid pointing your camera across the border.

★ Church of St Gregory (of Abugramentz)
This twelve-sided rotunda is one of three churches dedicated to St Gregory.

View from Menücehir Mosque
This bridge, now ruined, spanned the Barley River (Arpa Çayı) in a single arch 30 m (32 yards) in length. The river demarcates the border between Turkey and Armenia.

Citadel
The Citadel is the oldest part of Ani and housed most of its residents until 961, when the Bagratids moved their capital here from Kars. It contains the ruined palace of the Bagratid kings.

KEY

① Maiden's Castle

② City Walls

③ Church of St Gregory (of Gagik)

④ Ruined Bridge

★ City Walls
Double walls protect the northern side of the city. Built of rubble, they are faced with basalt blocks.

VISITORS' CHECKLIST

Practical Information
44 km (27 miles) E of Kars.
Open 8am–5pm daily
(heavy snow in winter may restrict access).
🎫 Tickets available from Ani entrance.

Church of the Redeemer
This partially collapsed church was built in 1036 as a domed rotunda to house a fragment of the True Cross.

A Conical Roof once rested on the cylindrical drum.

The Roof is made of stone shingles.

★ Ani Cathedral
The Cathedral at Ani is still intact, although the drum has collapsed. Founded by King Smbat II in the late 10th century, it became the Fethiye Mosque in 1064, but was returned to Christian worship in 1124.

High Windows illuminated the interior of the cathedral.

Four Columns supported the drum.

The West Entrance was used by the citizens of Ani.

The Apse is lined with semi-circular niches.

The South Entrance, reserved for the king, was one of three entrances.

⑬ Erzurum

Sprawling across a vast plain at an altitude of almost 2,000 m (6,560 ft) and ringed by mountains, Erzurum is Turkey's coldest city. It is also by far the most developed city in the region. Because it was located astride the main caravan route from India to Europe, and controlled the passage between the Caucasus and Anatolia, Erzurum was fought over and ruled by many peoples – Byzantines, Sassanids, Arabs, Armenians, Seljuk Turks, Mongols and Ottomans. Its most famous sights date from Seljuk times. Like Kars, the city was in Russian hands for over 40 years. In 1919, Atatürk's Nationalists met here to map out the frontiers of modern Turkey.

The ornate entrance portal of the Yakutiye Seminary

Exploring Erzurum

Erzurum has a university and a large garrison population. It also hosts a rough-and-ready horse-back competition (*cirit*), which involves throwing a spear at a target.

🏛 Archaeological Museum
Arkeoloji Müzesi
Paşalar Cad 11. **Tel** (0442) 233 04 14.
Open 8am–5pm Tue–Sun.

Exhibits here range from Urartian metalwork and pottery to the jewellery and glassware of the Hellenistic and Roman eras.

Ⓒ Lala Mustafa Paşa Mosque
Cumhuriyet Caddesi. **Open** daily.
This charming Ottoman mosque, built in 1562, conforms to a typical square-plan design, with columns and cupolas around a courtyard with a fountain. Original tile work adorns the interior.

Ⓒ Yakutiye Seminary
Yakutiye Medrese
Cumhuriyet Cad. **Open** 8am–noon & 1–5pm Tue–Sun.

Built in 1310 by Hoca Yakut, governor of the İlhan Mongols, this ornate Koranic school is regarded as the city's most beautiful building. The carved stone-work around the entrance is very appealing and the short minaret features an elaborate lattice of brick and turquoise tiles. The building houses the Ethnography Museum.

🏰 Citadel
Kale
N of Çifte Minareli Medresesi.
Open 8am–noon & 1–5pm daily (7pm in summer).

The citadel was built in the 5th century, during the reign of Byzantine Emperor Theodosius. It was restored in 1555 by Sultan Süleyman I (the Magnificent) and served as the eastern base of the Janissaries (*see p60*). Inside is a ruined clocktower and also a mosque. There are fine views over the city from the walls.

Ⓒ Twin Minaret Seminary
Çifte Minareli Medresesi
Cumhuriyet Cad.
Open 8am–5pm daily.

The two minarets that flank the portal of the Çifte Minareli Medresesi have become the

Erzurum City Centre

① Archaeological Museum
② Lala Mustafa Paşa Mosque
③ Yakutiye Seminary
④ Citadel
⑤ Twin Minaret Seminary
⑥ Three Tombs

VISITORS' CHECKLIST

Practical Information
🏘 485,000. ℹ Cemal Gürsel Caddesi 9, (0442) 233 71 99 and 235 09 25. 🎭 Atatürk Congress and Festival (23 Jul).
🎪 most days.

Transport
✈ 10 km (6 miles) NE of city centre, (0442) 327 28 35. 🚌 3 km (2 miles) NW of city centre.
🚆 1 km (0.5 mile) N of city centre.

symbols of Erzurum. They are thought to have been built in 1253 on the authority of Hunat Hatun, daughter of Seljuk Sultan Alaeddin Keykubad II. At the rear of the complex is the 12-sided cylinder tomb that contains her remains.

The gorge of the Euphrates (Firat) near Kemaliye

Twin Minaret Seminary

🕌 Three Tombs
Üç Kümbet
S of Twin Minaret Seminary.
Open daily.

Built by the Seljuks, the oldest of these conical mausoleums dates from the early 12th century. It is distinguished by the use of contrasting light and dark stone and by its truncated cone.

Environs
Erzurum has a reliable ski season that runs from November to May. Palandöken Ski Centre *(see p388)*, situated 8 km (5 miles) southwest of the city centre, has four hotels and six ski lifts serving 30 km (19 miles) of piste.

⓮ Erzincan
🏘 280,118. ℹ Atatürk Mah, Bariş Manço Parkı içi, Kültür Sitesi, (0446) 214 30 79 or 223 06 71.

Erzincan's history has been marked by earthquakes, notably in 1939 and 1992. It was once considered one of Turkey's most impressive cities, but rebuilding work over the years has left it with few historic attractions.

Erzincan's specialities include decorative copperware and *tulum peynir*, a cheese made from raw milk, and sold encased in a sheep skin.

Environs
Altıntepe (Golden Hill), a Urartian site 27 km (17 miles) east of Erzincan, dates from around 700 BC. Many of the objects found here are now on display in Ankara's Museum of Anatolian Civilizations *(see p246–7)*. One of the best of these is a bronze cauldron with handles in the shape of bulls' heads.

The little town of **Kemaliye** (formerly known as Eğin) lies in the Munzur Mountains not far from Erzincan. Founded in the 11th century, Kemaliye's pebbled streets, wild streams and trim wooden buildings offer a charming snapshot of life in Ottoman times. The Village Life Museum in Ocakköyü, near Kemaliye, is the only private ethnographic museum in Turkey.

🏛 Village Life Museum
Köy Müzesi
Ocakköyü. **Tel** (0446) 754 40 65.
Open 9am–noon & 1–5pm Tue–Sun.

⓯ Divriği
🏘 18,000. 🚌 S of town centre, on road to Elazığ. 🚆 from Sivas, Erzincan or Malatya.

After the Seljuk victory at Manzikert (Malazgirt) in 1071 *(see p56)*, Divriği became the seat of the Mengüçek state and was ruled by the Mengüç family from 1142 to 1252. Among many fine buildings they left behind is the *külliye* (mosque-hospital complex), the best example of 13th-century Seljuk stonecarving in Turkey, and now a UNESCO World Heritage Site. The ornate portals of the **Ulu Camii**, or Great Mosque (built around 1229) and the adjoining *daruşşifa* (hospital) – easy to spot as you come into town – display exceptionally rich decoration.

Carving detail, Divriği

🕌 Ulu Camii
Open during prayer times daily.

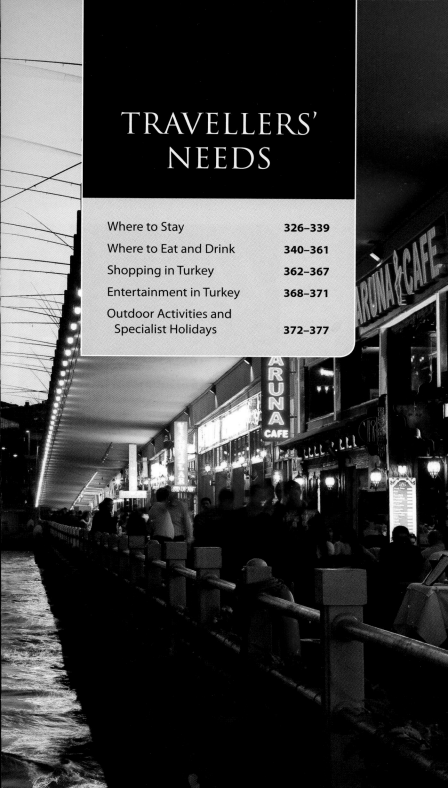

TRAVELLERS'
NEEDS

WHERE TO STAY

Whether you wish to stay in an Ottoman sultan's opulent palace, a quaint yalı (traditional wooden house) on the Bosphorus or a comfortable family home, it is fairly easy to find the accommodation of your choice in Turkey. The country's hotels and guesthouses cater for a wide range of budgets and, in general, these are found clustered around the main sightseeing areas: in Sultanahmet and Taksim in Istanbul for instance. Some of the old towns, notably Safranbolu *(see pp272–3)*, offer accommodation in restored mansions and family homes around the historic town centre. The choice of hotels in Turkey's eastern provinces is more restricted, though accommodation options in all price ranges are steadily improving. The hotel listings provided on pp330–39 will help visitors to find accommodation that will suit their budget.

Choosing a Hotel

Many hotels in Turkey are rated by the Ministry of Tourism according to a star system – from one to five – with five stars representing the most luxurious. However, try not to make a choice exclusively on the basis of star ratings – the comfort and service levels may vary regardless of such ratings based on technical criteria.

Most hotels can be easily reached by public transport from the airport, bus or train station. With advance notice, many hotels will also ferry guests to and from the airport.

A lot of hotels in resort areas close from late October to March or April. Check when booking or on the hotel's website. Most hotels also have direct reservation pages on their websites.

Summer is hot and humid in the southern coastal areas, so it is worth paying extra for an air-conditioned room. Water shortages are not uncommon, and in cheaper hotels reliant on solar heating hot water may run out at busy times.

The impressive lobby of the Zorlu Grand Hotel, Trabzon *(see p338)*

In Turkey you may come across the term Special Class hotels. These are generally considered to be establishments that comply with strict standards of hospitality and service. So even if it is listed as a *pansiyon* (pension), the comfort levels, decor and food will be first rate. It is advisable to book well in advance at these establishments.

Luxury Hotels

Upmarket international hotel chains are well represented in Istanbul, Ankara, İzmir and other large cities. Almost all five-star hotels offer fine views over the city or the Bosphorus, in the case of Istanbul.

Luxury hotels also typically have pools, fitness and health facilities, *hamams* (Turkish baths) and conference facilities. Resort hotels and holiday villages feature nightly entertainment, such as traditional music and dancing. Most hotels will gladly arrange city or boating tours, as well as day trips to local attractions. Visitors can also organize these trips personally to get reasonably lower rates.

A good reference point for plush properties is **The Luxury Hotels of Turkey**, an organization that offers an exclusive selection of luxury establishments – the Turkish counterpart of "World's Leading Hotels".

Holiday Villages

The coastal areas of Turkey have numerous holiday villages and self-contained resorts that offer a full range of holiday options for visitors, usually with access to their private stretch of beach. Staying in a holiday village can be very economical, especially for families with children, as the activities on offer are included in the price of the holiday.

Most holiday villages offer programmes for children, as well as babysitting services and nightly entertainment.

The Baylo Suites' garden terrace boasts superb views of the Goldern Horn and Süleymaniye Mosque *(see p331)*

◄ Restaurants and cafés under the Galata Bridge which spans the Golden Horn, Istanbul

Beautifully decorated suite at the Museum Hotel in Uçhisar *(see p339)*

Budget Hotels

There is a wide range of inexpensive accommodation in Turkey, from hotels and motels to family-run pensions (*pansiyons*). Some of the budget hotels are not rated by the Ministry of Tourism but by the local municipality, whose standards depend on the region. Therefore, when choosing one of these hotels, take care not to make a decision solely on the basis of what you see in the newly renovated lobby; it is always best to see if the carpet runs past the first stairs. Most budget hotels provide only minimal services, which could mean communal rather than private washing facilities. A far better option than a one-star hotel is a *pansiyon*. The vast majority of these are family-run establishments offering friendly, good-value accommodation. Most have comfortable rooms with air-conditioning, television and en-suite facilities.

Boutique Hotels

Boutique hotels are usually historic buildings that have been restored and transformed into quaint hotels full of character. Or, they may have outstanding features such as unique architecture, innovative design, artistic value, an exceptional view or an excellent location. Facilities may vary from the grand and luxurious to the more basic.

In Istanbul, most such hotels are found in the older quarters, and give guests a chance to experience closely the lifestyle of the late-Ottoman era. Cappadocia is another region where some outstanding boutique hotels can be found clustered together.

The **Association of Small Hotels** pulls together a refined group of boutique hotels, and offers booking facilities online.

What to Expect

In the popular regions, front desk staff can be expected to speak English, but this is less likely when staying in more remote areas. The average rooms may not be very spacious, especially for those travelling with family. Single occupancy rooms can be difficult to find, and travellers requiring a single room usually end up paying for single occupancy in a double or twin room. A double bed is usually queen-sized. King-sized beds are rare, except at international five-star hotels, and in some boutique hotels. A triple room is usually a double room with enough space for a cot, a roll-out or a divan. Quads are almost unheard of,

but many hotels offer connecting rooms or family suites that can accommodate four people.

Most multi-storey hotels have lifts but this will not be the case in older buildings converted into boutique hotels. Facilities for wheelchair users and other disabled guests are also only found in the more expensive hotels.

Noise can be quite a problem in downtown areas, even in the luxury hotels, so be sure to ask for a quiet room when you make your reservation.

All hotels must provide floors or sections where smoking is forbidden – all public areas are non-smoking by law.

The price of the room usually includes breakfast and this will be either a set Turkish breakfast that includes fresh bread, butter, jam, soft white cheese, tomatoes, cucumbers and black olives, or a self-service buffet with more choice. Coastal hotels and holiday villages offer half board, with an evening meal thrown in. This is usually another buffet spread.

Internet access is widespread. Most of the hotels across the country offer high speed Wi-Fi either for free or for an additional charge.

Yeşil Ev, a boutique hotel, Istanbul *(see p331)*

The elegant reception area at the Ferahi Evler Butik Otel, Ayvalik *(see p333)*

Prices and Discounts

Hotel prices are quoted per room, not per person in Turkish lira, euros or US dollars. Bargaining when booking a room is perfectly acceptable, and discounts are often available if you pay in cash or book ahead online. Luxury hotels may also offer a discount to business travellers; ask for the corporate rate. In general, your success in bargaining will depend on how busy the hotel is at the time. Expect to pay premium prices during religious or national holidays, when virtually all accommodation is booked. Check individual hotel websites to find their latest discounts and promotions – hotels usually offer their best rates on the Internet.

Booking a Room

It is always a good idea to book early, especially in Istanbul or other popular destinations, and during high season between May and October. Telephone and e-mail bookings are both accepted. If you haven't prebooked accommodation, or you have changed your itinerary to get off the beaten track, visit any of the tourist information offices to inquire about available places to stay. Tourist offices can also give you advice on approximate prices. Don't be shy about looking around, seeing rooms and comparing prices.

If travelling with an organized tour group, your agent should handle all the arrangements.

Checking Out and Paying

Guests are expected to check out by noon, but on request most hotels will agree to hold luggage for collection later.

Except for the very remote or low-cost establishments, most hotels listed in this guide accept major international credit cards. Travellers' cheques however are almost obsolete.

Value-added tax (VAT) is known as KDV in Turkish *(see p384)* and is generally included in the price of a room. When registering at a hotel, you may be asked for your credit card, which will then be swiped through an authorization machine. Sign the transaction form and the card is then re-submitted for payment when your account is settled.

Tips for the staff are always appreciated. A few dollars should suffice for junior personnel, while a little more is good for the front desk if they have done something special. Remember that phone calls and mini-bar drinks are additional charges that can increase the overall bill substantially.

Children

In most hotels, children up to the age of six years can stay in their parents' room at no extra charge. Many hotels also offer up to 50 per cent discount for 12–15 year-olds sharing a room with their parents. Some smaller boutique-style hotels may not take children under 12 years so check when booking. Cots for babies are willingly provided even by mid-range hotels. Children's menus are usually available in family resort areas and holiday villages. In Turkey, children generally eat when their parents do and they also tend to stay up late, particularly during the hot summer months.

Hostels

Hostels are a budget option worth exploring. Turkey has a growing number of decent hostels welcoming travellers of all ages. Membership to these establishments is not required. Hostels are usually clustered in Istanbul's Old Town and other popular destinations, including the smaller resort towns such as Çanakkale and Fethiye. They generally offer basic comforts in shared dormitories, however, many also have private rooms with or without private facilities. The majority of hostels have a good range of amenities, including free Wi-Fi and breakfast. Some also organize local tours and excursions. **Hostel World** is an international booking portal with a good listing of Turkish hostels.

The major advantages of using a hostel are that you are guaranteed to meet like-minded travellers.

Luxurious room at the Hilton Bursa, with views of Bursa City and the Uludağ Mountains *(see p332)*

Camping and Caravanning

Caravanning and camping holidays are becoming increasingly popular and many new areas are being developed into well-equipped, highly organized camping grounds that provide ample space for tents or trailers, as well as for washing or other facilities.

However, visitors should note that camping is only allowed in designated areas, so be sure to check with the **Turkish Camping and Caravanning Association**, who will be able to provide a comprehensive list of approved sites.

Parking a caravan or pitching a tent on any deserted beach, or simply pulling over to the side of the road in a caravan is strongly discouraged.

In some parts of the country, cosy, furnished bungalows may be available for self-catered holidays in a natural environment.

Self-catering

Most major cities and coastal resorts in Turkey have plenty of apartments for short-term rental. Pensions, too, often include cooking facilities, but these are usually shared with other guests. For tax reasons, Istanbul and Ankara apart, many self-catering apartments do not advertise openly, and word of mouth is the best way to locate these places. Some travel agents have lists of apartments that they own and maintain. These are available for self-catering holidays.

A quaint, old-fashioned pension in the back streets of Selçuk

Recommended Hotels

The hotel listings in this book offer a selection of places to stay throughout the country across a range of budgets. Divided into eight geographical areas corresponding to the chapters in this guide, the entries are then organized by town and price. The accommodation options have been selected for their excellent facilities and value for money and cover a diverse array of places to stay from no-frills budget options to luxury properties that take hospitality standards to a high level.

Choose from historic hotels that exude the charm of a bygone era or opt for strikingly designed modern hotels that offer all the latest conveniences and amenities. To enjoy the comforts of home, try a family-run pension (pansiyon).

Boutique hotels are usually smaller establishments that offer a unique stay. Amenities may be limited in some, but the experience and warm staff more than make up for the missing extravagances found in the larger chain hotels. These establishments often only have a handful of rooms, so it's worth booking in advance.

Entries highlighted as DK Choice offer something extra special. They may be nestled within beautiful surroundings, be historically important buildings, have a noteworthy sustainable outlook, offer exceptional service, or may be incredibly charming. Whatever the reason, it is a guarantee of a memorable stay.

Brightly Coloured façade of the Kybele Hotel, Istanbul (see p330)

Where to Stay

Istanbul

Seraglio Point

Gulhane Park Hotel ₺
Modern **Map** 5 E3
Nöbethane Cad 1, 34112 Sirkeci
Tel *(0212) 519 68 68*
Ⓦ gulhaneparkhotel.com.tr
Overlooking the Topkapı Palace
gardens; facilities include a gym
and *hamam*.

Romantic Mansion Istanbul ₺₺
Apartment **Map** 5 E3
*Nobethane Cad, Tayahatun Sok 28,
Sirkeci, 34112*
Tel *(0212) 638 96 35*
Ⓦ romanticmansion.com
Three elegant two-bed apart-
ments in a charming building.

Sultanahmet

Akdeniz Hotel Guest House ₺
Budget **Map** 5 D4
*Divanyolu Cad, Haci Tahsin Bey
Sok 7, 34410*
Tel *(0212) 520 20 99*
Ⓦ istanbulakdenizhotel.com
A modest hotel up a flight of stairs
with clean, comfortable rooms.

Arden City Hotel ₺
Modern **Map** 5 E4
Yerebatan Cad 2–6, 34110
Tel *(0212) 526 15 32*
Ⓦ hotelarden.com
Contemporary rooms in a superb
location. Excellent service.

Hippodrome Hotel ₺
Boutique **Map** 5 E4
Mimar Mehmet Ağa Cad 38, 34400
Tel *(0212) 517 68 89*
Ⓦ hippodromehotel.com
A wide range of rooms to choose
from including an apartment that
can accommodate six adults.

The bright yellow building of the Ottoman
Hotel Imperial sits infront of Haghia Sophia

Hotel Sultanahmet ₺
Budget **Map** 5 D4
Divanyolu Cad 20, 34110
Tel *(0212) 527 02 39*
Ⓦ hotelsultanahmet.com
Inexpensive hotel with good views,
great location and friendly service.
Enjoy delicious food and wine at
the lovely terrace restaurant.

Spectra ₺
Boutique **Map** 5 D5
Şehit Mehmetpaşa Yokuşu 2, 34400
Tel *(0212) 516 35 46*
Ⓦ hotelspectra.com
A converted Ottoman house with
all basic amenities at good prices.
No-frills, comfortable rooms;
most with views of Hippodrome
Square and the Blue Mosque.

Sultan Hostel ₺
Hostel **Map** 5 E5
Akbıyık Cad 17, 34122
Tel *(0212) 516 92 60*
Ⓦ sultanhostel.com
A backpacker's haven. Helpful
staff, neat dormitories and private
rooms. Close to all the main sights;
and there is a pub downstairs.

Aren Suites ₺₺
Boutique **Map** 5 D5
*Küçükayasofya Cad,
Gelinlik Sok 13, 34122*
Tel *(0212) 517 31 26*
Ⓦ arensuites.com
Rooms are stylish and kept
meticulously clean. The terrace
and many of the rooms overlook
the Sea of Marmara.

Aruna ₺₺
Boutique **Map** 5 E5
*Cankurtaran Mah, Ahirkapi Sok 74,
34122*
Tel *(0212) 458 54 88*
Ⓦ arunahotel.com
Inviting hotel with sauna and
hamam. Suites have private
Jacuzzis. Good breakfast spread.

Ayasofya Konakları ₺₺
Boutique **Map** 5 E4
Soğukçeşme Sok, 34400
Tel *(0212) 513 36 00*
Ⓦ ayasofyakonaklari.com
A leafy cobbled street leads to
nine wooden 19th-century Otto-
man mansions with basic rooms.
Relax at the pretty courtyard café.

Blue House–Mavi Ev ₺₺
Boutique **Map** 5 E4
Dalbasti Sok 14, 34110
Tel *(0212) 638 90 10*
Ⓦ bluehouse.com.tr
Family-run hotel with tasteful
rooms. The suites have great
views of the Sea of Marmara.

Price Guide
Prices are based on one night's stay in
high season for a standard double room,
inclusive of service charges and taxes.

₺	under ₺100
₺₺	₺100 to ₺200
₺₺₺	over ₺200

Deluxe Golden Horn Hotel ₺₺
Boutique **Map** 5 D4
Binbirdirek Meydanı Sok 1, 34400
Tel *(0212) 518 17 17*
Ⓦ goldenhornhotel.com
The ambience at this hotel is
reminiscent of the Orient Express
era. Ornately decorated lobby.

Dersaadet ₺₺
Boutique **Map** 5 D5
*Küçük Ayasofya Cad, Kapıağası Sok 5,
34400*
Tel *(0212) 458 07 60*
Ⓦ dersaadethotel.com
Impressive red wooden Ottoman
mansion near the Blue Mosque.
The traditionally decorated
rooms have Turkish carpets.

Hotel Nomade ₺₺
Boutique **Map** 5 E4
Ticarethane Sok 15, 34410
Tel *(0212) 513 81 72*
Ⓦ hotelnomade.com
Well appointed rooms with a
cosy atmosphere. Enjoy breakfast
or drinks on the terrace.

DK Choice

The Kybele Hotel ₺₺
Boutique **Map** 5 E4
Yerebatan Cad 23, 34410
Tel *(0212) 511 77 66*
Ⓦ kybelehotel.com
Although decorated with
4,000 coloured-glass lamps,
rich fabric and wallpaper, this
wooden town house never
feels kitch or over-done.
The relaxing ambience and
friendly staff ensure a good stay.

Ottoman Hotel Imperial ₺₺
Boutique **Map** 5 E4
Caferiye Sok 6/1, 34400
Tel *(0212) 513 61 51*
Ⓦ ottomanhotelimperial.com
Sheer opulence; some rooms
have private *hamams* and close-
up views of Haghia Sophia.

Pierre Loti Hotel ₺₺
Modern **Map** 5 D4
Piyer Loti Cad 1, 34400
Tel *(0212) 518 57 00*
Ⓦ pierrelotihotel.com
Comfortable and hassle-free stay.
Excellent spa and *hamam*
facilities on site.

Sura Hotel ₺₺
Boutique   Map 5 E4
Ticarethane Sok 45, 34400
Tel *(0212) 513 66 66*
W surahotels.com
Strikingly designed hotel. Each
floor has a different colour theme.
Rooms come with rain showers.

DK Choice

White House Hotel ₺₺
Boutique   Map 5 D4
Çatalçeşme Sok 21, 34110
Tel *(0212) 526 00 19*
W istanbulwhitehouse.com
Gorgeous golden colours
make this lovely hotel stand
out. The rooms are elegant and
well-decorated. Enjoy breakfast
on the terrace, with views
of the Bosphorus. Free Wi-Fi.

Four Seasons Sultanahmet ₺₺₺
Historic   Map 5 E4
Tevkifhane Sok 1, 34110
Tel *(0212) 402 30 00*
W fourseasons.com/istanbul
Top-notch hotel in an old Ottoman
prison. Herb-scented courtyard.

**Hagia Sophia Hotel Istanbul
Old City**
Modern   Map 5 E4
Yerebatan Cad 13, 34110
Tel *444 93 32*
W cphagiasophia.com
A surprisingly sleek option
in the heart of the Old City with
an English-style pub.

Yeşil Ev ₺₺₺
Boutique   Map 5 E4
Kabasakal Cad 5, 34122
Tel *(0212) 517 67 85*
W yesilev.com.tr
Velvet curtains and oil paintings
adorn the pretty rooms at Yeşil Ev.
In the summer, breakfast is served
in the garden.

The Bazaar Quarter

Beyazit Hostel ₺
Hostel   Map 4 C4
*Gedikpaşa Cad, Hattat Sok 19,
Beyazıt, 34126*
Tel *(0212) 517 11 31*
W beyazithostel.com
Comfortable hostel near the Grand
Bazaar. Rooms all have private
bathrooms. Beautiful roof terrace.

Antik Cisterna ₺₺
Historic   Map 4 B4
Sekbanbaşı Sok 10, 34130
Tel *(0212) 638 58 58*
W antikhotel.com
An extraordinary hotel with an
old cistern dating back to 450–
500 AD in the basement that is
used as a restaurant.

Beyoğlu

DK Choice

#Bunk ₺
Budget   Map 1 A4
Balik Sok 7, 34435
Tel *(0212) 244 88 08*
W bunkhostels.com
Launched by an international
group of friends, #Bunk is
a unique establishment offering
low-cost accommodation
with a seriously cool design.
They also sell their own brand
of quirky t-shirts.

Chill Out Hostel and Cafe ₺
Budget   Map 1 A5
Balyoz Sok 3, 34445
Tel *(0212) 249 47 84*
W chillouthostelistanbul.com
No curfew, friendly staff and a
choice of private rooms or dorms.
Close to the entertainment spots.

Adahan Istanbul ₺₺
Historic   Map 1 A5
General Yazgan Sok 14, 34430
Tel *(0212) 243 85 81*
W adahanistanbul.com
Sensitively restored building in
the heart of the European Quarter.
More of a home than a hotel.

Galata Flats ₺₺
Apartments   Map 1 A5
Tünel Meydani 84, 34430
Tel *(0212) 244 26 76*
W galataflats.com
Comfortable apartments that are
serviced daily. The larger ones
have terraces and balconies.

Galateia Residence ₺₺
Apartments   Map 1 A5
*Sahkulu Bostan Sok 9-11, Tunel,
34425*
Tel *(0212) 245 30 32*
W galateiaresidence.com
A wide range of large, well-
designed apartments with easy
transport links to entertainment
and nightlife.

Palazzo Donizetti ₺₺
Historic   Map 1 A5
Asmalimescit Sok 55, 34400
Tel *(0212) 249 51 51*
W palazzodonizetti.com
Similar to a European château,
Palazzo Donizetti is all about
elegance and luxury.

Sub Hotel ₺₺
Boutique   Map 1 B5
Necatibey Cad 91, Karaköy, 34435
Tel *(0212) 243 00 05*
W subistanbul.com
An ultra-stylish hotel with well-
appointed rooms. Free Wi-Fi.

Many coloured-glass lamps adorn the ceiling
of this double room at The Kybele Hotel

DK Choice

Baylo Suites ₺₺₺
Apartments   Map 5 D1
Galata Kulesi Sok 24, 34420
Tel *(0212) 245 98 60/61*
W baylosuites.com
Four individually decorated
apartments inside a historic
19th-century Galata building,
lovingly restored by a mother-
daughter team. Energy saving
systems have been installed
throughout the building. Wonderful views from the terrace.

Georges Hotel Galata ₺₺₺
Boutique   Map 1 A5
Serdar-ı Ekrem Cad 24, 34425
Tel *(0212) 244 24 23*
W georges.com
Set in a grand old town house,
Georges Hotel Galata offers first-
rate services and stunning views.

The Marmara Taksim ₺₺₺
Modern   Map 1 B3
Taksim Meydani, 34437
Tel *(0212) 251 46 96*
W taksim.themarmarahotels.com
Landmark hotel towering over
much of the modern city. Great
views from the gym and pool area.

Pera Palace Hotel Jumeirah ₺₺₺
Historic   Map 1 A5
Meşrutiyet Cad 52, Tepebaşı, 34430
Tel *(0212) 377 40 00*
W jumeirah.com
The elegant suites here are named
after famous guests such as
Agatha Christie and Hemmingway.

Witt Istanbul Suites ₺₺₺
Boutique   Map 1 B5
Defterdar Yokusu 26, Cihangir, 34433
Tel *(0212) 293 15 00*
W wittistanbul.com
A choice of enormous rooms
with retro design touches.

For more information on types of hotels *see p329*

Luxurious Turkish *hammam* at the Hilton Bursa Convention Center & Spa, Bursa

Further Afield

Kariye Hotel   ₺
Boutique
Kariye Camii Sok 6, Edirnekapi, 34080
Tel *(0212) 534 84 14*
🆆 kariyeotel.com
Tastefully restored 19th-century mansion close to the famous Chora Church, near the city walls.

Khalkedon Hotel   ₺
Budget
Moda Cad, Tellaizade Sok 2, Kadikoy, 34710
Tel *(0216) 700 13 40*
🆆 khalkedonhotelistanbul.com
Clean and comfortable rooms. Close to the ferries to Europe.

Çırağan Palace Kempinski   ₺₺₺
Historic
Çırağan Cad, Beşiktaş, 34349
Tel *(0212) 258 33 77*
🆆 kempinski.com
The only hotel in Istanbul set in a royal Ottoman palace. Waterside terrace and heated infinity pool.

DK Choice

The Edition   ₺₺₺
Luxury
Büyükdere Cad 136, 34330
Tel *(0212) 317 77 00*
🆆 editionhotels.com
Enter a private world of luxury in the heart of Istanbul's busy business district. There is a stunning full-floor penthouse and a top-notch restaurant. Good transport connections to the main tourist sites.

Hilton Istanbul   ₺₺₺
Modern
Cumhuriyet Cad, Harbiye, 34367
Tel *(0212) 315 60 00*
🆆 placeshilton.com
The Hilton group's first step outside the USA – hence the footprint-shaped swimming pool. All rooms have private balconies.

DK Choice

Sumahan on the Water   ₺₺₺
Historic
Kuleli Cad 51, 34684
Tel *(0216) 422 80 00*
🆆 sumahan.com
A multi-award winning gem in a converted distillery. Every room boasts superb sea views and some open onto a lawn terrace. Unwind at the fully equipped spa or grab a bite at the excellent on-site restaurant.

The House Hotel Bosphorus ₺₺₺
Boutique
Salhane Sok 1, Ortaköy, 34347
Tel *(0212) 327 77 87*
🆆 thehousehotel.com
Celebrities' favourite; close to the city's most exclusive night spots.

Thrace and the Sea of Marmara

BURSA: Boyugüzel Termal Otel ₺
Budget
Asker Hastanesi Karşısı Çekirge, 16090
Tel *(0224) 239 99 99*
🆆 boyuguzel.com
Tasteful rooms, a modest spa and Turkish bath in the city centre.

DK Choice

BURSA: Kitap Evi Hotel   ₺
Boutique
Kavaklı Mah, Burç Üstü 21, 16040
Tel *(0224) 225 41 60*
🆆 kitapevi.com.tr
Choose from 13 comfortable rooms at this delightful place. The rooms are all charming and uniquely decorated. There is an elegant restaurant on site that opens out onto a beautiful garden.

BURSA: Almira Hotel   ₺₺
Budget
Ulubatlı Hasan Bulv 5, 16200
Tel *(0224) 250 20 20*
🆆 almira.com.tr
Sparkling clean rooms at Almira with friendly and attentive staff.

BURSA: Marigold Thermal Spa Hotel ₺₺
Boutique
1 Murat Cad 47, Çekirge, Osmangazi, 16070
Tel *444 40 00*
🆆 marigold.com.tr
A thermal therapy hotel on a hilltop. Rooms are large with comfortable beds.

BURSA: Hilton Bursa Convention Center & Spa ₺₺₺
Modern
Yeni Yalova Cad 347, 16210
Tel *(0224) 500 05 05*
🆆 bursa.hilton.com
A 35-floor tower hotel boasting an ultra-smart spa. Good gym facilities and excellent service.

EDIRNE: Edirne Palace Hotel ₺
Boutique
Sabuni Mah, Vavlı Cami Sok 4, 22030
Tel *(0284) 214 74 74*
🆆 hoteledirnepalace.com
Very close to the Selimiye Mosque, Edirne Palace offers well-equipped rooms and tasty Turkish breakfast.

EDIRNE: Otel Şimşek   ₺
Budget
Trakya Üniversitesi Tıp Fakültesi Karşısı, 22000
Tel *(0284) 236 60 00*
🆆 hotelsimsek.com.tr
Located just across from the university campus; playground for kids and a simple fitness centre.

EDIRNE: Taş Odalar Hotel   ₺
Historic
Selimiye Camii Arkası Merkez, 22000
Tel *(0284) 212 35 29*
🆆 tasodalar.com
A 15th-century mansion converted into a lovely hotel; Ottoman sultan Mehmet II was born here.

EDIRNE: Edirne Antik Hotel ₺₺
Boutique
Marif Cad 6, Kaleiçi, 22030
Tel *(0284) 225 15 55*
🆆 edirneantikhotel.com
Charming hotel in the historic centre; small restaurant on-site.

EDIRNE: RYS Hotel   ₺₺
Modern
I Murat Mah, Talatpaşa Cad 82/A Merkez, 22030
Tel *(0284) 213 07 97*
🆆 ryshotel.com
Smart hotel with a great spa and modern Turkish bath and Jacuzzi.

İZNIK: Cem Otel ₺
Budget
Mustafa Kemal Paşa Mah, Göl Sahili
Cad 34, 16860
Tel *(0224) 757 16 87*
🅦 cemotel.com
Simple rooms, some with lake
views. The on-site restaurant has
superb food.

İZNIK: İznik Otel ₺
Budget
Selçuk Mah, Göl Sahil Yolu 22, Liman
Karşısı, 16860
Tel *(0224) 757 22 55*
🅦 iznikotel.com
A no-frills hotel set beside İznik
Lake. Basic rooms, with air
conditioning and free Wi-Fi.

The Aegean

ASSOS: Nazlihan Hotel ₺
Budget
Behramkale Köyü Antik İskele Mevkii
Ayvacık, 17860, Çanakkale
Tel *(0286) 721 73 85*
🅦 assosedengroup.com
Idyllic location on the ancient
harbour. Spacious, well-furnished
rooms in the wing.

ASSOS: Assosyal Butik Otel ₺₺
Budget
Alan Meydani, 8 Behramkale, 17860,
Çanakkale
Tel *(0286) 721 70 46*
🅦 assosyalotel.com
A small but beautifully maintained
hotel offering great views of
Edremit Bay.

AYVALIK: Butik Sızma Han ₺₺
Boutique
Gümrük Cad 2, Sok 49, 10400
Tel *(0266) 312 77 00*
🅦 butiksizmahan.com
Set in a former olive oil press, this
hotel has a lovely waterfront
location and comfortable rooms.

AYVALIK:
Ferahi Evler Butik Otel ₺₺
Boutique
Sakarya Mah, Atatürk Bulv 20,
Sok 1,3,5, 10400
Tel *(0266) 312 33 55*
🅦 ferahievler.com
A small waterfront hotel with
traditional decor and volcanic
stone walls. Close to Lesbos ferries.

BERGAMA: Hera Hotel ₺
Boutique
Talatpaşa Mah, Tabak Köprü Cad 21,
35700
Tel *(0232) 631 06 34*
🅦 hotelhera.com
Two historic buildings have been
converted to house ten rooms
named after Greek deities.

DK Choice

BODRUM:
El Vino Bodrum ₺₺
Boutique
Omurça Mah, Pamili Sok 14,
48400
Tel *(0252) 313 87 70*
🅦 elvinobodrum.com
A small but charming hotel
overlooking Bodrum Castle,
with spacious, tasteful rooms.
The garden level rooms have a
private patio; most others have
balconies. Relax at the pool or
in the garden, or see spectacular
sunsets from the rooftop.
Excellent and efficient service.

BODRUM:
The Marmara Bodrum ₺₺
Boutique
Yokusbaşı Mah, Suluhasan Cad 18,
48400
Tel *(0252) 999 10 10*
🅦 bodrum.themarmarahotels.com
The rooms boast breathtaking
views of the city and the castle.
There is an art gallery in the lobby.

BODRUM:
Vogue Hotel Bodrum ₺₺
Luxury
Bodrum, Milas, Torba, 48400
Tel *(0252) 337 10 70*
🅦 voguehotel.net
An upmarket hotel with smart
rooms, suites and villas.

BODRUM PENINSULA:
Casa dell'Arte ₺₺₺
Luxury
İnönü Cad 66 Torba, Muğla, 48400
Tel *(0252) 367 18 48*
🅦 casadellartebodrum.com
Ideal for art enthusiasts, with art-
works exhibited in the rooms and
throughout the hotel. Or choose
to stay on a luxurious yacht.

The pretty, tranquil pool area at the El Vino
hotel in Bodrum

BODRUM PENINSULA:
Divan Bodrum Palmira Hotel ₺₺₺
Boutique
Kelesharim Cad 6, Göltürkbükü, 48483
Tel *(0252) 377 56 01*
🅦 divan.com.tr
Upscale place with landscaped
gardens. Complimentary fresh
fruit in all the elegant rooms.

BODRUM PENINSULA:
Kempinski Hotel
Barbaros Bay ₺₺₺
Luxury
Kizilagac Köyü, Gerenkuyu Mevkii,
Yaliciftlik, 48400
Tel *(0252) 311 03 03*
🅦 kempinski.com
Plush hotel with private beach
and a variety of watersports.
Luxurious spa on site.

ÇANAKKALE: Akol Hotel ₺
Modern
Cevat Paşa Mah, Kordon Boyu,
Kayserili Ahmet Paşa Cad, 17100
Tel *(0286) 217 94 56*
🅦 hotelakol.com
Located in the city centre, this
hotel mainly caters to bus tour
groups. Good on-site restaurant.

ÇANAKKALE: Çanak Otel ₺
Budget
Cumhuriyet Meydanı Dibek Sok,
17100
Tel *(0286) 214 15 82*
🅦 canakhotel.com
Popular with backpackers and
students. Small but neat rooms.
Great loaction.

ÇANAKKALE:
Grand Anzac Hotel ₺
Budget
Kemalpaşa Mah, Kemalyeri Sok 11,
17100
Tel *(0286) 217 77 77*
🅦 grandanzachotel.com
Centrally located, with decent
rooms and friendly staff. Street
facing rooms can be noisy.

ÇANAKKALE: Helen Otel ₺
Budget
Kemalpaşa Mah, Cumhuriyet
Meydanı 57, 17100
Tel *(0286) 212 18 18*
🅦 helenhotel.com
Modern hotel with clean, simple
and well-appointed rooms.
Good restaurant on site.

ÇEŞME: Albano Hotel ₺
Budget
Açık Hava Tiyatrosu Karşısı Çevre
Yolu, 35930
Tel *(0232) 712 82 02*
🅦 cesmealbanohotel.com
Half board lodging option with
comfortable rooms but small
showers. Varied breakfast spread.
Close to the city centre.

**ÇEŞME: Grand Hotel
Ontur Çeşme** ₺₺
Modern
*Cumhuriyet Mah, 4330/3 Sok 63/A,
Dalyan, 35280*
Tel *(0232) 724 00 11*
🔲 onturhotels.com/onturcesme
Beachside hotel offering spacious
rooms with balconies.

**ÇEŞME: Ilıca Hotel Spa &
Wellness Resort** ₺₺
Luxury
Boyalık Mevkii Ilıca, 35937
Tel *(0232) 723 31 31*
🔲 ilicahotel.com
Plush rooms and a beautiful
location on a pristine beach.

CUNDA ISLAND: Taş Konak ₺₺
Boutique
*Mithat Paşa Mah, Şafak Sok 15,
Alibey, Ayvalik, 10400*
Tel *(0266) 327 26 33*
🔲 taskonak.com.tr
Situated on a cobbled street lined
with historic homes, this place has
lovely rooms, some with sea views.

**CUNDA ISLAND:
Yund Antik Cunda Konakları** ₺₺
Boutique
*Namık Kemal Mah, Hayat Cad 27,
Alibey Adası, Ayvalik, 10405*
Tel *(0266) 327 30 60*
🔲 yundantik.com
Elegant hotel with immaculate
rooms. Closed Nov–Mar.

DATÇA: Han Royal Villa Datça ₺
Boutique
*İskele Mah, Pir Sultan Abdal Sok 7,
Datça, Muğla, 48900*
Tel *(0252) 712 29 52*
🔲 hanroyalhotels.com/datca
Family-run establishment close to
a public beach with pristine waters.

İZMIR: Key Hotel ₺₺
Historic
Mimar Kemalettin Cad 1, Konak, 35260
Tel *(0232) 482 11 11*
🔲 keyhotel.com
An old building on the waterfront.
Smart rooms, a wellness centre
and restaurant.

İZMIR: Met Boutique Hotel ₺₺
Boutique
Gazi Bulv 124, Çankaya, 35210
Tel *(0232) 483 01 11*
🔲 metotel.com
Stylish hotel with comfortable
beds in the business district.

İZMIR: Mövenpick Hotel ₺₺
Modern
Cumhuriyet Bul 138, 35210
Tel *(0232) 488 14 14*
🔲 moevenpick-izmir.com
Award-winning hotel geared
towards corporate travellers.
Stylish, contemporary rooms.

İZMIR: Swissotel Büyük Efes ₺₺₺
Luxury
*Gaziosmanpaşa Bulv 1, Alsancak,
35210*
Tel *(0232) 414 00 00*
🔲 swissotel.com/izmir
An opulent landmark of İzmir with
a huge garden and excellent spa.

KUŞADASI: Club Caravanserai ₺
Historic
Atatürk Bulv 2, 09400
Tel *(0256) 614 41 15*
🔲 kusadasihotelcaravanserail.com
Built in 1618, this former
caravanserai offers basic rooms
around a spacious courtyard.

KUŞADASI: Hotel Carina ₺
Budget
Yılancıburnu Mevkii 1, 09400
Tel *(0256) 612 40 21*
🔲 hotelcarina.com.tr
Pretty gardens and an outdoor
pool charm guests. Some rooms
have balconies with sea views.

**KUŞADASI: Alkoçlar
Adakule Hotel** ₺₺
Modern
Bayraklıdere Mevkii, 09400
Tel *(0256) 618 11 43*
🔲 kusadasiadakulehotel.com
A private beach, an outdoor pool
and an aqua park ensure a fun stay.

**KUŞADASI: Charisma Deluxe
Hotel** ₺₺
Luxury
Akyar Mevkii 5, 09400
Tel *(0256) 618 32 66*
🔲 charismahotel.com
Breathtaking infinity pool with
sweeping views of the Aegean
Sea. Rooms all have Jacuzzis.

**KUŞADASI:
Efe Boutique Hotel** ₺₺
Boutique
Güvercinada Cad 37, 09400
Tel *(0256) 614 36 60*
🔲 efeboutiquehotel.com
Comfortable rooms, most with
balconies. Can be slightly noisy.

A luxurious superior room with a spacious
sitting area at the Key Hotel, İzmir

**KUŞADASI: Korumar
Hotel DeLuxe** ₺₺
Luxury
Gazi Beğendi Mevkii PK 18, 09400
Tel *(0256) 618 15 30*
🔲 korumar.com.tr
Great sea views, two private
beaches, pools and a spa – one of
the best five-star hotels in town.

KUŞADASI: Kısmet Hotel ₺₺₺
Luxury
Gazi Beğendi Bulv 1, 09400
Tel *(0256) 618 12 90*
🔲 kismet.com.tr
Views of the Aegean Sea from all
the rooms at Kısmet. Private
beach area and an outdoor pool.

MARMARIS: D-Hotel Maris ₺₺₺
Luxury
*Datça Yolu, Hisaronu Mevkii,
PO Box 119, 48700*
Tel *(0252) 441 20 00*
🔲 dhotel.com.tr
A romantic getaway inside a
natural reservation. Refined
service. Summer only.

**MARMARIS:
Martı Hemithea Hotel** ₺₺₺
Boutique
*Martı Marina & Yacht Club, Orhaniye
Köyü Keçibükü Mevkii, 48700*
Tel *(0252) 487 10 55*
🔲 martihemitheahotel.com
Beautifully decorated hotel with
a yacht marina and classy rooms.
Sample delicious food at the
Mistral Restaurant.

**PAMUKKALE: Spa Hotel
Colossea Thermal** ₺₺
Luxury
*Fatih Mah 112, Sok 4, Pamukkale
Mevkii Karahayıt, Denizli, 20290*
Tel *(0258) 271 41 56*
🔲 colossaehotel.com
One of the best establishments
in town, with vast gardens, huge
pools, and excellent spa and
thermal services.

PAMUKKALE: Venus Hotel ₺₺
Pension
*Pamuk Mah, Hasan Tahsin Cad 16,
20280*
Tel *(0258) 272 21 52*
🔲 venushotel.net
A friendly, family-run place with
bright, tastefully decorated
rooms. Relax on the large patio
or in the beautiful gardens.

SELÇUK: Ephesus Suites ₺
Budget
*İsabey Mah, Anton Kallinger Cad
1056, 35920*
Tel *(0232) 892 63 12*
🔲 ephesussuites.com
Four basic but comfortable rooms.
Close to the main sites. Delicious
breakfast served in the garden.

SELÇUK:
Güllü Konakları ₺₺
Boutique
Şirince Köyü 44, 35920
Tel *(0232) 898 31 31*
W gullukonak.com
Elegant hotel in a charming
village, 20 minutes from Ephesus.
Lovely public spaces.

Mediterranean Turkey

ADANA: Hotel Seyhan ₺
Budget
*Turhan Cemal Beriker Bulv 20/A,
01120*
Tel *(0322) 455 30 00*
W otelseyhan.com.tr
Sleek hotel, located a short
distance from the major sights.

ADANA: Riva Reşat Bey
Boutique & Business Hotel ₺
Boutique
*Reşatbey Mah, Adalet Cad 20,
Seyhan, 01170*
Tel *(0322) 401 00 00*
W adanariva.com
Eco-friendly hotel with unique
architecture and modern decor.

ADANA:
Adana Hilton SA Hotel ₺₺
Luxury
*Sinanpaşa Mah, Hacı Sabancı Bulv 1,
01220*
Tel *(0322) 355 50 00*
W hilton.com.tr
Spacious rooms and an attractive
lobby at this riverside hotel. Good
on-site restaurant and bar.

ADRASSAN:
Ottoman Palace Hotel ₺
Budget
*Deniz Mah, Çavuşköy Beldesi
Kumluca Antalya, 07100*
Tel *(0242) 883 14 62*
W jonnyturk.com
Run by a hospitable couple who
also organize walks on the Lycian
Way. Excellent service.

ALANYA: Hotel Villa Turka ₺
Boutique
*Tophane Mah Kargı Sok 7, Alanya,
Antalya, 07400*
Tel *(0242) 530 54 76 41*
W hotelvillaturka.com
Stylish and homely Ottoman-
period hotel perched above the
sea within the walls of the citadel.

ALANYA: Gold Island Hotel ₺₺₺
Modern
Fuğla Mah, Gölcük Cad 27, 07400
Tel *(0242) 510 03 00*
W goldhotels.com.tr
Hotel on a peninsula surrounded
by beaches. Courteous staff.

The indoor pool area at the Adana Hilton
SA Hotel, Adana

ANTAKYA: The Liwan Hotel ₺
Boutique
Silahlı Kuvvetler Cad 5, 31070
Tel *(0326) 215 77 77*
W theliwanhotel.com
Charmingly converted from a
1920s building, this hotel has
elegant rooms. Great breakfasts
and a good central location.

ANTAKYA: Savon Hotel ₺₺
Boutique
Kurtuluş Cad 192, 31070
Tel *(0326) 214 63 55*
W savonhotel.com.tr
A soap factory converted into a
fine hotel. Most rooms are large
and luxurious. The hotel lobby
has plush sofas and a grand piano.

ANTALYA: Ninova Pension ₺
Pension
*Barbaros Mah, Hamit Efendi
Sok 9, Kaleiçi, 07100*
Tel *(0242) 248 61 14*
W ninovapension.net
This establishment in the Old
Town has been converted from
an old, traditional house. Quiet
rooms and a lovely garden.

ANTALYA: Hotel Villa Perla ₺
Boutique
*Barbaros Mah, Hesapçı Sok 26,
Kaleiçi, 07100*
Tel *(0242) 248 97 93*
W villaperla.com
A small Ottoman-period hotel
with a handful of rooms set
around a courtyard and pool.

ANTALYA: Rixos Downtown ₺₺
Luxury
*Sakip Sabancı Bulv, Konyaaltı Sahili,
07050*
Tel *(0242) 249 49 49*
W rixos.com
On the clifftop near the famous
Konyaaltı beach, this hotel has
large, well-appointed rooms;
good for business travellers.

BELEK: Cornelia Diamond
Golf Resort & Spa ₺₺₺
Luxury
İskele Mevkii, 07500
Tel *(0242) 710 16 00*
W corneliaresort.com
An all-inclusive golf resort on
the Mediterraean with several
restaurants and bars. Spacious,
elegant rooms.

BELEK: Maxx Royal Belek
Golf & Spa ₺₺₺
Luxury
İskele Mevkii, 07505
Tel *(0242) 710 27 00*
W maxxroyal.com
Exclusive deluxe 18-hole golf
resort with an aqua park; also has
a spa, private beach and pools.

BELEK: Susesi Luxury Resort ₺₺₺
Luxury
İskele Mevkii, 07506
Tel *(0242) 710 24 00*
W susesihotel.com
A large resort right on the beach
with well-manicured gardens.

DALYAN: Midas Pension ₺
Pension
Maraş Cad, Kaunos Sok 32, 48840
Tel *(0252) 284 21 95*
W midasdalyan.com
Small place right by the river,
with wonderful views.

FETHIYE: Alesta Yacht Hotel ₺
Budget
Yat Limanı Karşısı 17, 48300
Tel *(0252) 601 00 00*
W alestayachthotel.com
Just across from the yacht
harbour with a rooftop restaurant
and beautiful rooms. The staff
offers personalized service.

FETHIYE: Yacht Boutique Hotel ₺
Boutique
*1 Karagözler Mevki Fevzi Çakmak
Cad, 48300*
Tel *(0252) 614 15 30*
W yachthotelturkey.com
A city-centre hotel with modern
rooms decorated in warm colours.

GÖCEK: Dalya Life ₺
Boutique
*Şerefler Köyü, Tersakan Mah 37, PK
36, Dalaman, 48770*
Tel *(0252) 791 10 40*
W gocekotel.com
Off-the-beaten-track bungalows
and suites surrounded by a pine
forest. Organic food available.

GÖCEK: Yonca Resort ₺
Budget
Cumhuriyet Mah, 48310
Tel *(0252) 645 22 55*
W yoncaresort.com
Run by a welcoming couple, this
peaceful gem has pleasant rooms.

For more information on types of hotels *see p329*

GÖCEK: Göcek Lykia Resort ₺₺
Modern
Cumhuriyet Cad 109, Sok 3, 48310
Tel *(0252) 645 28 28*
Ⓦ goceklykiaresort.com
Very close to the harbour with a
garden and pool. Good service.

KALKAN: Allegra Hotel ₺
Boutique
Zeytinlik Cad, 07960
Tel *(0242) 844 24 36*
Ⓦ allegrahotel.com
Charming small sized hotel set on
a mountain slope. Simple rooms
with balconies. Infinity pool on site.

KALKAN: Ekinhan Hotel ₺
Boutique
Kalamar Yolu, 07960
Tel *(0242) 844 10 50*
Ⓦ ekinhan.net
Exotic flowers and olive trees fill
the garden of this tranquil hotel.

KALKAN: White House ₺₺
Boutique
Menteşe Mah, 5 Nolu Sok, 07960
Tel *(0242) 844 37 38*
Ⓦ whitehousekalkan.com
Superbly restored old Greek
house mixes period charm with
all mod-cons. Very welcoming
Anglo-Turkish hosts.

KAŞ: Aqua Princess Hotel ₺
Budget
Hükümet Cad 71, 07580
Tel *(0242) 836 20 26*
Ⓦ aquaprincess.com
Small hotel with a resort feel set
on a quiet beach. Half board
option is available.

KAŞ: Gardenia ₺₺
Boutique
*Küçük Çakil, Hükümet Cad 41, Kaş,
07580*
Tel *(0242) 836 23 68*
Ⓦ gardeniahotel-kas.com
Stylish hotel above a small beach
with views to the Greek island of
Meis. Very friendly owners. Child-
ren under 12 are not encouraged.

DK Choice

KAŞ: Lukka Exclusive Hotel ₺₺
Boutique
*Çukurbağ Yarımadası Oteller
Bölgesi Bülent Kalkavan Sok 16,
07580*
Tel *(0242) 836 14 20*
Ⓦ lukkahotel.com
A beautiful cliffside location
makes Lukka one of the most
romantic sunset spots in the
area. There is a private beach
down the steps and an infinity
pool with wonderful views. The
classy rooms either look out over
the sea or the pretty garden.

The large resort of Rixos Sungate set on the
coast right by the beach, Kemer

KAŞ: Doria Hotel Yacht Club ₺₺₺
Boutique
*Uğur Mumcu Cad, Bucak Denizi
Acisu Mevkii, 07580*
Tel *(0242) 836 42 04*
Ⓦ doriahotekas.com
Set on a peaceful Blue Flag beach;
impressive architecture. Some
rooms have Jacuzzis.

KEMER: Rixos Sungate ₺₺₺
Luxury
Çifteçeşmeler Mevkii, Beldibi 3, 07985
Tel *(0242) 824 00 00*
Ⓦ rixos.com
Offering all-inclusive vacations
and the deluxe amenities
associated with the Rixos hotel
chain. Service may be downsized
in the winter.

**KEMER:
Vogue Hotel Avangarde** ₺₺₺
Luxury
*Esentepe Mah, Ahu Ünal Aysal Cad 1,
Goynuk, 07070*
Tel *(0242) 813 60 00*
Ⓦ voguehotel.net
A resort town west of Antalya
with spacious, elegant rooms.
Beautiful location.

LARA: Mardan Palace ₺₺₺
Luxury
Kundu Koyu, Oteller Mevkii, 07110
Tel *(0242) 310 41 00*
Ⓦ mardanpalace.com.tr
Gold and marble opulence at
every corner in this hotel out
on Lara Beach, east of the city.

**ÖLÜ DENIZ:
Morina Hotel** ₺
Budget
Belceğiz, Fethiye, 48340
Tel *(0252) 617 02 55*
Ⓦ morinahotel.com
Set in an attractive olive grove,
close to Ölü Deniz lagoon. Choose
from a variety of basic rooms.

**ÖLÜ DENIZ:
Oyster Residences** ₺₺
Boutique
*Belceğiz Mevkii 1, Sok Ölü Deniz
Fethiye, 48340*
Tel *(0252) 617 07 65*
Ⓦ oysterresidences.com
Beautifully decorated hotel set in
lush gardens in the heart of a
lively resort. Close to the beach.

**SIDE: Crystal Queen
Luxury Resort & Spa** ₺₺
Luxury
*Bilgeşik Mevkii Side Kumköy Yolu
Side, 07600*
Tel *(0242) 753 47 83*
Ⓦ crystalhotels.com.tr
Part of the Crystal Resort hotel
chain, this deluxe property is ideal
for an all-inclusive beach vacation.

Ankara and Western Anatolia

AFYON: İkbal Thermal Hotel ₺
Modern
İzmir Karayolu 9 km, 03000
Tel *(0272) 252 56 00*
Ⓦ ikbal.com.tr
Ikbal offers simple, chic rooms
with marble bathrooms. Some
rooms have balconies. Great spa.
Near the coastline.

**AFYON: Güral Afyon Wellness
& Convention** ₺₺
Modern
İzmir Karayolu 7 km, 03000
Tel *(0272) 220 22 22*
Ⓦ guralafyon.com
Unwind at the immaculately kept
pool and enjoy warm Turkish
hospitality at this large hotel.

ANKARA: Alba Hotel ₺
Budget
Yüksel Cad 19, Kızılay, 06000
Tel *(0312) 419 10 20*
Ⓦ albaankara.com
Well-kept rooms and friendly
service. Close to the city centre.

ANKARA: And Butik Hotel ₺
Boutique
*İçkale Mah Istek Sok 3, Altındağ,
06680*
Tel *(0312) 310 23 04*
Ⓦ andbutikhotel.com
Located in the heart of the city,
with bright modern rooms. Breakfast is available for an extra charge.

ANKARA: No 19 ₺
Boutique
Birlik Mah 457, Sok 19, 06000
Tel *(0312) 495 00 00*
Ⓦ no19hotel.com
Sleek, minimalist hotel in a trendy
neighbourhood. The spa is owned
by top model Adriana Karambeau.

**ANKARA: Sonno Boutique
Rooms & Suites** ₺
Boutique
Tunus Cad 52, Çankaya, 06000
Tel *(0312) 466 27 27*
w sonnohotel.com
An elegant landmark building
with French country-style decor.

DK Choice

ANKARA: Divan Çukurhan ₺₺
Boutique
*Ankara Kalesi Necatibey Mah,
Depo Sok 3, Ulus, 06240*
Tel *(0312) 306 64 00*
w divan.com.tr/TR
Located close to Ankara Castle
and the Museum of Anatolian
Civilizations, this superb period
hotel is the pride of the wealthy
Koç family. Rooms are individ-
ually decorated and have high
quality furnishings. Great
attention to detail.

ANKARA: Rixos Grand Hotel ₺₺
Business
*Atatürk Bulvarı, No. 183 Kavaklıdere
06680*
Tel *(0312) 410 55 00*
w rixos.com
Located opposite the parliment
house. Spacious, modern rooms.

**ANKARA: Sheraton Hotel &
Convention Centre** ₺₺
Modern
Noktalı Sok, Kavaklıdere, 06700
Tel *(0312) 457 60 00*
w sheratonankara.com
Striking cylindrical architecture.
Some rooms offer stunning views.

ANKARA: JW Marriot Hotel ₺₺₺
Luxury
*Kızılırmak Mah, Muhsin Yazıcıoğlu
Cad 1, Söğütözü, 06520*
Tel *(0312) 248 88 88*
w jwmarriottankara.com
Expect all the plush frills from this
top-notch establishment.

**ÇAVDARHISAR: Anemon
Çavdarhisar Hotel** ₺
Boutique
*Cereller Mah, Başaran Ulusoy Sok 22,
Kütahya, 47500*
Tel *(0274) 351 22 88*
w anemonhotels.com
The only hotel in an agricultural
town near Aizanoi. Comfortable
rooms and attractive lobby.

ESKİŞEHIR: Abacı Konak Hotel ₺
Boutique
*Akarbaşı Mah, Türkmen Hoca Sok 29,
Odunpazarı, 26000*
Tel *(0222) 333 03 33*
w abaciotel.com
Traditional family rooms in the
historic market district of Eskişehir.

ISPARTA: Barida Hotels ₺₺₺
Modern
102 Cad 81, 32040
Tel *(0246) 500 25 25*
w baridahotels.com
Hospitable and friendly hotel
that aims to cater for every need.
There's even a pillow menu. The
view from the roof top is superb.

KONYA: Hilton Garden Inn ₺
Modern
*Aziziye Mah, Kışlaönü Sok 4, Karatay,
42020*
Tel *(0332) 221 60 00*
w hilton.com.tr
Comfortable place adjacent to the
Museum of Whirling Dervishes.

KONYA: Paşapark Hotel ₺
Modern
*Şems-i Tebrizi Mah, Sultan Veled
Cad 3, Karatay, 42030*
Tel *(0332) 305 00 00*
w pasapark.com.tr
Smart hotel with traditional
touches. Bathrooms have hydro-
massage shower heads.

KONYA: Selçuk Hotel ₺
Budget
*Mevlana Cad, Mashar Babalık Sok 4,
Karatay, 42050*
Tel *(0332) 353 25 25*
w otelselcuk.com.tr
Pleasant hotel owned by farmers.
The delicious breakfast buffet
only uses local produce.

**KONYA: Dedeman Konya
Hotel Convention Center** ₺₺
Modern
*Isparta Beyşehir Yolu Yeni Sille Cad,
Özalan Mah, Selçuklu, 42080*
Tel *(0332) 221 66 00*
w dedeman.com
Though outside the city centre,
this large stylish hotel has all the
usual amenities and good service.
Great spa.

KÜTAHYA: Hilton Garden Inn ₺
Modern
Servi Mah, Atatürk Bulv 21, 43030
Tel *(0274) 229 55 55*
w kutahya.hgi.com
Centrally located, good value
chain hotel offering comfortable
rooms, a cooked-to-order
breakfast and a fitness centre.

The Black Sea

AYDER PLATEAU: Bukla Oberj ₺
Pension
Ayder Yaylası, Çamlıhemşin, 53750
Tel *(0464) 657 20 55*
w oberj.com
Set across a waterfall with a huge
spruce forest in the backdrop.
Popular with hikers.

**AYDER PLATEAU:
Naura Otel** ₺
Pension
*Ayder Yaylası Turizm Merkezi, Rize,
Çamlıhemşin, 53780*
Tel *(0464) 657 20 35*
w naturaotel.com
Simple en-suite rooms and family
rooms with bunk beds.

**BOLU:
Büyük Abant Hotel** ₺₺
Modern
14800 Bolu
Tel *(0374) 224 50 33*
w buyukabantoteli.com
Located besides Abant lake.
Heated indoor pool and sauna.

DK Choice

BOLU: Kartal Hotel ₺₺
Ski lodge
Kartalkaya Mevkii PK 5, 14200
Tel *(0374) 234 50 05*
w kartalotel.com
This upmarket ski resort has
direct access to the south-facing
slopes of Mount Bolu. Heated
indoor pool and a large and
comfortable lobby. Range of
accommodation available from
basic rooms to spacious suites.
Higher prices on weekends.

HOPE: Heyamo Hotel ₺
Budget
Cumhuriyet Cad 44, 08600
Tel *(0466) 351 23 15*
w otelheyamo.com
A charming waterfront hotel
located on a bustling street.

**MAÇAHEL:
Maçahel Konukevi** ₺
Guesthouse
Camili Köyü, Maçahel Borçka, 08400
Tel *(0466) 485 24 04*
w macahelkonukevi.com
Eco-friendly place. Some rooms
have bunk beds. Good value.

The sleek, contemporary bar at Rixos
Grand Ankara, Ankara

For more information on types of hotels *see p329*

MAÇKA: Coşandere Tesisleri Ƀ
Pension
Sümela Yolu 5 km, De Coşandere
Köyü Turistik Tesisleri, 61750
Tel *(0462) 531 11 90*
☒ cosandere.com
Basic, en-suite rooms overlooking
the picturesque Coşandere river.

RIZE: Dedeman Hotel Ƀ
Modern
Ali Paşa Köyü, 53100
Tel *(0464) 223 44 44*
☒ dedeman.com
Set on a rocky cliff on the Black
Sea. Most rooms have sea views.
Decent buffet dinners.

SAFRANBOLU: Mehveş
Hanım Konağı Ƀ
Boutique
Hacıhalil Mah, Mescit Sok Numara
30, Karabük, 78600
Tel *(0370) 712 87 87*
☒ mehveshanimkonagi.com.tr
No-frills hotel with antique
furniture. Close to the city centre.

DK Choice

SAFRANBOLU: Gülevi ƀƀ
Boutique
Hükümet Sokak 46, TR - 78600
Tel *(0370) 725 46 45*
☒ canbulat.com.tr
A UNESCO Heritage Site, Gulevi
was converted from an 18th-
century mansion. Delicate wood
carvings adorn the walls, and
all rooms have fireplaces
and window shutters. Sleek,
modern bathrooms.

SAMSUN:
Venn Boutique Hotel ƀƀ
Boutique
Cumhuriyet Mah, Adnan Menderes
Bulv 325, Atakum, 55200
Tel *(0362) 407 00 01*
☒ vennbutikotel.com
A range of spacious rooms and
lovely terrace views at Venn
Boutique. Delicious breakfast.

SINOP: Zinos Hotel Ƀ
Budget
Ada Mah, Enver Bahadır Yolu 69,
Karakum, 57000
Tel *(0368) 260 56 00*
☒ zinoshotel.com.tr
This hotel has two sections:
country and business. Rooms are
either homely or modern in style.

TRABZON: Taş Konak Hotel Ƀ
Boutique
Esentepe Mah, Y Selim Bulv 89, 61100
Tel *(0462) 325 77 11*
☒ taskonakbutikotel.com.tr
Converted from a historic house,
this stylish choice has cosy
rooms; some with sea views.

TRABZON: Zorlu Grand Hotel ƀƀ
Luxury
Maraş Cad 9, 61110
Tel *(0462) 326 84 00*
☒ zorlugrand.com
This hotel has comfortable rooms
and offers a great breakfast buffet.
The impressive lobby has a
stunning glass ceiling.

Cappadocia and Central Anatolia

AMASYA: Lalehan Hotel Ƀ
Boutique
Pirinçci Mah, Mehmet Paşa Sok 31,
05000
Tel *(0358) 212 77 77*
☒ lalehanotel.com
Clean, well-appointed rooms,
some have balconies overlooking
the river. Near the Pontic tombs.

GÖREME: Kookaburra Pension Ƀ
Guesthouse
Orta Mah, Konak Sok 10, 50180
Nevsehir
Tel *(0384) 271 25 49*
☒ kookaburramotel.com
Long-established, friendly place.
Popular with backpackers.

GÖREME: Melek Cave Hotel Ƀ
Budget
Gaferli Mah, Ünler Sok 28, 50180
Tel *(0384) 271 22 33*
☒ melekcave.com
Inexpensive, cheerful village hotel
offering a choice of Ottoman-era
and cave rooms. Lovely garden.

GÖREME: Cappadocia
Cave Suites ƀƀ
Boutique
Gaferli Mah, Ünlü Sok19, 50180
Tel *(0384) 271 28 00*
☒ cappadociacavesuites.com
Decent sized cave rooms but
the fairy chimney rooms are
smaller. The restaurant uses
local produce.

GÖREME: Anatolian Houses ƀƀƀ
Boutique
Gaferli Mah, Nevşehir, 50180
Tel *(0384) 271 24 63*
☒ anatolianhouses.com.tr
The best conversion of a series
of rock-cut cave dwellings in the
village. Lovely courtyard and spa/
Turkish bath complex.

KAYSERI: Bent Hotel Ƀ
Budget
Gevher Nesibe Mah, Atatürk Bulv 40,
Kocasinan, 38020
Tel *(0352) 221 24 00*
☒ benthotel.com
Located in the historic centre of
the city. Rooms are decorated
with warm colours.

Selection of tasty savory and sweet treats
served in the Zorlu Grand lobby, Trabzon

KAYSERI: Ibis Hotel Ƀ
Modern
Yenipervane Mah, Kocasinan Bulv
163, 38110
Tel *(0352) 207 30 30*
☒ ibis.com
A delightful hotel with a lovely
garden. Close to the airport.

KAYSERI: Novotel Ƀ
Modern
Yeni Pervane Mah, Kocasinan Bulv
163, Kocasinan, 38110
Tel *(0352) 207 30 00*
☒ novotel.com
A typical Novotel. Some rooms
have views of Mt Erciyes.

DK Choice

MUSTAFAPAŞA:
Cappadocia Estates ƀƀ
Boutique
Şahin Bey Cad, Vezir Sok 12, 50420
Tel *(0384) 535 50 20*
☒ cappadociaestates.com
An elegant little gem converted
from registered historical
properties. Exquisitely decorated
with antiques, custom-made
furniture and original works of
art. Spacious cave rooms with
high ceilings and tall windows.

MUSTAFAPAŞA: Gül Konakları ƀƀ
Historic
Sümer Cad, Ürgüp, 50401
Tel *(0384) 353 54 86*
☒ gulkonaklari.dinler.com
Restored stone-built house with
cave rooms and a Turkish bath.

NEVŞEHIR:
Dedeman Cappadocia
Convention Centre ƀƀ
Modern
Ürgüp Yolu, 2 km, 50200
Tel *(0384) 213 99 00*
☒ dedeman.com
One of the biggest hotels in town
with several hundred rooms.

ORTAHISAR: Cave de Luxe 🏠🏠
Historic
Tahir Bey Sok 14, Ortahisar/Ürgüp, 50400
Tel *(0384) 343 33 93*
W www.cavedeulxe.com
Rustic Turkish hamlet in a secluded spot. Hearty breakfast.

UÇHISAR:
Argos in Cappadocia 🏠🏠🏠
Boutique
Uçhisar, 50240
Tel *(0384) 219 31 30*
W argosincappadocia.com
Located on a sloped hillside, this charming hotel offers great views of Uçhisar Castle.

UÇHISAR: Museum Hotel 🏠🏠🏠
Boutique
Tekelli Mah 1, 50240
Tel *(0384) 219 22 20*
W museum-hotel.com
Cappadocia's oldest cave hotel is a registered museum, so is full of interesting artifacts. Rooms feature whirlpool baths. Great views.

ÜRGÜP: Ürgüp Esbelli Ev 🏠🏠
Boutique
Dolay Sok 8, 50400
Tel *(0384) 341 33 95*
W esbelli.com
One of the first, and still one of the best, period boutique hotels in Cappadocia. Lovely cave rooms and great breakfasts.

Eastern Anatolia

DIYARBAKIR: Büyük Kervansaray Diyarbakır 🏠🏠
Boutique
Sur İçi Gazi Cad, Deliler Han, 21200
Tel *(0412) 228 96 06*
W kervansarayotel.com.tr
Well-established hotel beautifully fashioned from a caravanserai. Small but well-appointed rooms.

DIYARBAKIR: Dedeman Diyarbakır Hotel 🏠🏠
Modern
Elazığ Cad, Büyükşehir Belediyesi Yanı, 21400
Tel *(0412) 229 00 00*
W dedeman.com
Next to one of the biggest malls in town, this is a large hotel with many rooms and good facilities.

DOĞUBEYAZIT: Simer Hotel 🏠
Budget
İran Transit Yolu, 3 km, Doğubeyazıt, Ağrı, 04400
Tel *(0472) 312 48 48*
W simerotel.com
A modest hotel east of town on the road to Iran. Stunning views of Mt Ararat.

ERZURUM: Grand Hitit Hotel 🏠
Budget
Mehmet Akif Ersoy Mah 26, Sok, 25200
Tel *(0442) 233 50 01*
W grandhitithotel.com.tr
Centrally located, with a large lobby and fuctional rooms.

ERZURUM: Dedeman Palandöken Ski Lodge Hotel 🏠🏠
Boutique
PK 115, 25000
Tel *(0442) 317 05 00*
W dedeman.com
This small hotel has direct access to the ski slopes and a dedicated room to store ski equipment.

GAZIANTEP:
The Anatolian Hotel 🏠
Modern
Mücahitler Mah, Gazimuhtarpaşa Bulv 50, Şehitkamil, 27010
Tel *(0342) 211 40 40*
W theanatolianhotel.com
Hotel with clean and comfortable rooms and a wellness club in an upmarket neighbourhood.

GAZIANTEP:
Zeynep Hanım Konağı 🏠
Boutique
Bey Mah, Atatürk Bulv, Eski Sinema Sok 17, 27010
Tel *(0342) 232 02 07*
W zeynephanimkonagi.com
Charming pension set in a historic building with lots of character. Rustic and traditional.

KAHTA: Zeus Hotel 🏠
Modern
M Kemal Cad 20, Adiyaman
Tel *(0416) 725 56 94*
W zeushotel.com.tr
Modest hotel with friendly staff, lovely gardens and a fine pool. Located at the foot of Mt Nemrut.

The Cave de Luxe hotel nestled into the rock formations of Cappadocia, Ortahisar

KARS: Kar's Hotel 🏠🏠
Historic
Yusufpaşa Mah, Halitpaşa Cad 31, 36100
Tel *(0474) 212 16 16*
W karsotel.com
Stately old Russian mansion now converted into an elegant hotel. Breakfasts feature local produce.

MARDIN:
Antik Tatlı Dede Konağı 🏠
Boutique
Ulucami Mah 104, Sok 27, 47100
Tel *(0482) 213 27 20*
W tatlidede.com.tr
Delightful hotel near the Ulu Camii. The spacious rooms have barrel vaulted ceilings and decorative carvings.

MARDIN: Erdoba Elegance Hotel Convention Centre 🏠🏠
Business
Midyat Yolu, 3 km, 47100
Tel *(0482) 212 15 00*
W erdobaelegance.com
A good choice for larger groups and conventions. Fine service.

DK Choice

MIDYAT:
Kasr-ı Nehroz Hotel 🏠🏠
Boutique
Işıklar Mah 219, Sok 14, 47500
Tel *(0482) 464 25 25*
W hotelnehroz.com
A wonderful find in the historical centre of Midyat, this hotel is in a lovingly and tastefully converted honey-coloured mansion house where no expense has been spared. Combines period-charm with modern conveniences.

ŞANLIURFA: Dedeman Hotel 🏠🏠
Modern
Atatürk Mah, Hastane Cad, 63100
Tel *(0414) 318 25 00*
W dedeman.com
Part of the Dedeman chain with pleasant rooms, a spa and gym.

ŞANLIURFA: Manici Otel 🏠🏠
Boutique
Balıklıgöl Civarı Şurkav Alışveriş Merkezi 68, 63200
Tel *(0414) 215 99 11*
W maniciurfa.com
Spacious, elegant rooms featuring painted furniture. The Cave of Abraham is a short walk away.

VAN: Ada Palas Hotel 🏠
Modern
Şerefiye Mah, Cumhuriyet Cad, 65100
Tel *(0432) 216 27 16*
This spotless place is the best budget option in Van. Front rooms may get some street noise. Very friendly.

For more information on types of hotels *see p329*

WHERE TO EAT AND DRINK

Restaurants in Turkey range from the informal *lokanta* and kebab houses, found on every street corner, to upscale gourmet restaurants. In Istanbul, and in most major tourist centres, the restaurants cover a wide variety of cuisines, from French to Korean. Restaurants on the Mediterranean and Aegean coasts specialize in seafood dishes, and Cappadocia is famous for its wines and traditional cuisine. A range of interesting local dishes can be found along the Black Sea coast and in the interior of Anatolia. Every region presents its own culinary specialities: you can sample thick, clotted cream in Afyon, spicy meatballs in Tekirdağ, chewy ice cream in Kahramanmaraş and whole-milk yogurt in distant Erzurum. As you move further away from Istanbul, vegetarian restaurants become somewhat scarce.

Where to Look

The smartest and most expensive restaurants are usually located in upmarket neighbourhoods of major cities, often as part of renowned international hotel chains. The main roads and central business districts of most towns have a selection of fast-food eateries, cafés and inexpensive restaurants where the locals go to eat – most of these towns also have a number of cafés, patisseries and pudding shops which specialize in *muhallebi* (traditional sweet milk puddings). In the interiors, most restaurants focus on regional food and the menu caters to locals more than tourists. However, coastal resorts cater to all ages and tastes, and offer a wide variety of dishes from across the world.

The sumptuous Beyti restaurant in Florya, Istanbul *(see p349)*

Types of Restaurant

The most common type of restaurant in Turkey is the traditional *lokanta*. These

Slicing meat from a revolving grill for a döner kebab

establishments serve a variety of dishes, often listed on a board near the entrance. They offer *hazır yemek* (ready to be served food), usually consisting of hot meat and vegetable dishes that are displayed in a *bain marie*, or steam table. Other dishes on the menu may be *sulu yemek* (stews) and *ızgara* (grilled meat and kebabs).

Equally popular eating joints include the *kebapçı* or *ocakbaşı* (kebab house). Most kebab houses also serve the popular *lahmacun*, a thin dough base topped with fried onions, minced meat and tomato sauce – this dish is the Turkish version of a pizza. Some also serve *pide*, a flat-bread base with various toppings such as eggs, cheese and cured meat. If you have had too much to drink you may need a bowl of *işkembe* (tripe soup), the traditional Turkish cure for a hangover, before going to bed. *İşkembe* restaurants stay open until the early hours of the morning.

Fish restaurants are sometimes concentrated along the same street, creating a lively atmosphere and making the street seem like one large restaurant. The meals here typically consist of a selection of *mezes* (appetizers) *(see p344)*, followed by the catch of the day, which might include *palamut* (bonito), *lüfer* (bluefish), *kalkan* (turbot), *kılıç balığı* (swordfish) and *levrek* (sea bass). Also popular are Black Sea *hamsi* (a kind of anchovy) and deep fried *barbun* (red mullet). Wild-caught fish is much more expensive than farmed fish, the latter of which is widely available in many restaurants that do not specialize in fish. The most common varieties of farmed sea fish are a type of bream known as *çipura* and levrek (sea bass). *Alabalık* (trout) is also popular from fish farms by rivers. Fish is served grilled or fried, and is usually accompanied by salad and *rakı (see p345)*, an anise-flavoured spirit.

A trout restaurant on the river at Saklıkent

Meyhanes are also quite popular in Turkey – they are similar to taverns, serving alcohol and *mezes*, and often have live music.

International culinary influences are encouraging local chefs to be more adventurous and innovative. Wealthier Turks frequent the foreign restaurants found in a number of Istanbul neighbourhoods, while global icons such as Starbucks and Gloria Jean's have become part of everyday life in major cities and coastal resorts.

Opening Hours

Turks eat when they are hungry, without looking at the clock, and will simply drop in at the most convenient place around. Restaurants and kebab houses open at about 11am and stay open for business until the last customer leaves in the evening.

During Ramadan Muslims fast from sunrise to sunset. Hence restaurants in rural Turkey remain closed during the day, or they may serve only a special *iftar* (fast-breaking) menu in the evening. There are no firm guidelines on opening hours. Restaurants in many of the tourist resorts grind to a halt by the end of October, to re-open in March or April when the weather improves.

What to Expect

In Turkey, a meal is always an occasion and, for special meals, it is best to book ahead. In large centres vegetarians can enjoy variety, but the options become scarcer as you travel further east.

When choosing a place to eat, remember that many of the cheaper restaurants and kebab houses do not serve alcohol. Alcoholic drinks are generally expensive due to high taxes – this can double the cost of the overall bill. The more conservative places may have a separate section for families or women. These are designated by a sign with the words *aile salonu* (family room), and single men do not enter.

Turks are proud of their hospitality and service. Good service is always found in the upmarket restaurants with well-trained, professional waiters and kitchen staff, and the same level of attentive service is also present at cheaper eateries. It is natural for Turks to call a waiter by saying, *bakar mısınız* (service, please).

Service Charges and Paying

All major credit cards are widely accepted, except in the cheaper restaurants, kebab houses, local *bufes* (snack kiosks) and some *lokantas*. Value-added tax (KDV in Turkish) is always included in the bill, but the policy on service varies. Some restaurants may add a service charge of 10 per cent or more while others leave it to the discretion of the customer. Some restaurants charge a *kuver* (cover) of a few liras per person for sitting down,

which usually includes bread and water. Always check the bill and make sure you are being charged only for the things you ordered and received.

Recommended Restaurants

The restaurants recommended on the following pages have been carefully selected for their quality food, good value and decent service. They range from understated local cafés to glitzy restaurants serving international dishes. Divided into eight geographical areas corresponding to the chapters in this guide, the entries are then organized by town.

The listings cover the various types of restaurant in Turkey *including lokantas, kebab restaurants and meyhanes (see opposite)*. Restaurants listed as regional will serve specialty dishes of the area, usually cooked with locally sourced ingredients. Look out for South East Anatolia cuisine – a vibrant mix of Kurdish, Arabian, Syrian and Turkish flavours, advertised in restaurants as *"Güney Doğu Anadolu Mutfağı"*. Black Sea fare is also worth sampling, usually made up of Black Sea fish (mainly anchovy), corn and corn flour, collard greens, milk, cream, butter and cheese.

Restaurants labelled as DK Choice offer something extra special. This may be their superb location, inviting or romantic ambience, sensational cuisine, or impeccable service.

Waterside restaurant on Bird Island, near the Aegean resort of Kuşadası

The Flavours of Turkey

The wide range of climatic zones across Turkey make it one of the few countries that can grow all its own food. Tea is cultivated in the mountains by the Black Sea and bananas in the sultry south. The Anatolian plain in between is criss-crossed by wheat fields and rich grasslands on which cattle graze, providing top quality meat and dairy produce. Fruit and vegetables flourish everywhere and fish abound in the salty seas that lap the nation's shores. Freshness is the hallmark of this varied cuisine, drawn from the many cultures that were subject to nearly five centuries of Ottoman rule.

Pomegranates

A stall in the Egyptian Bazaar, one of Istanbul's oldest markets

The Anatolian Steppe

The steppe stretching from Central Asia to Anatolia is one of the oldest inhabited regions of the world. Dishes from this vast area are as varied as the different ethnic groups that live here, but are mainly traditional and simple. To fit in with a mainly nomadic way of life, food generally needed to be quick and easy to prepare. Turkey's most famous culinary staples – yogurt, flat bread and the kebab – originate in this region.

The common use of fruits, such as pomegranates, figs and apricots, in Turkish savoury dishes stems from Persian influences, filtering down with the tribes that came from the north of the steppe. From the Middle East, further south, nomads introduced the occasional fiery blast of chilli. Its use was once an essential aid to preserving meat in the searing desert heat.

Ottoman Cuisine

It was in the vast, steamy kitchens of the Topkapı Palace in Istanbul that a repertoire of

Lamb şiş kebab

Chicken şiş kebab

Stuffed aubergine (eggplant)

Chilli sauce

Prawn (shrimp) kebab

Lamb cutlet

Doner kebab

A selection of typical Turkish kebabs

Local Dishes and Specialities

Fish has been caught and consumed in abundance in Turkey since Greek times and is usually prepared very simply. Since ancient times the Bosphorus has been known for its excellent fishing and in the winter months especially, there is a bounty of oil-rich fish, such as bluefish, bream, bonito tuna, sea bass, mullet and mackerel, waiting to be reeled in. The Black Sea in the North is also provided with a steady supply of juicy mussels and *hamsi*, a type of anchovy. Sweets are also popular and eaten throughout the day, not just after a meal. They are sold in shops, on stalls and by street vendors. Turkey is renowned for its *baklava*, sweet pastries coated with syrup and often filled with nuts.

Turkish Delight

Midye dolması Mussels are stuffed with a spiced rice mixture, steamed and served with a squirt of lemon juice.

A splendid array of fruit, vegetables and dried goods in the Egyptian Bazaar

Bazaar Culture

A visit to the food markets in Turkey, especially Istanbul's Egyptian Bazaar (*see p102*) is a must. A cornucopia of fine ingredients is brought here daily from farms that surround the city. Apricots, watermelons, cherries and figs sit alongside staple vegetables, such as peppers, onions, aubergines and tomatoes. Fine cuts of lamb and beef, cheeses, pickles, herbs, spices and honey-drenched pastries and puddings are also on offer.

mouth watering dishes to rival the celebrated cuisines of France and China grew up. At the height of the Ottoman Empire, in the 16th and 17th centuries, legions of kitchen staff slaved away on the Sultan's behalf. Court cooks usually specialized in particular dishes. Some prepared soups, while others just grilled meats or fish, or dreamed up combinations of vegetables, or baked breads, or made puddings and sherbets. As Ottoman rule expanded to North Africa, the Balkans and parts of southern Russia, influences from these far-flung places crept into the Turkish imperial kitchens. Complex dishes of finely seasoned stuffed meats and vegetables, often with such fanciful names as "lady's lips", "Vizier's fingers" and the "fainting Imam", appeared. This imperial

tradition lives on in many of Turkey's restaurants, where dishes such as *karnıyarık* (halved aubergines (eggplant) stuffed with minced lamb, pine nuts and dried fruit) and *hünkar begendili köfte* (meatballs served with a smooth purée of smoked aubergine and cheese) grace the menu.

Fresh catch from the Bosphorus on a fish stall in Karaköy

Know Your Fish

The profusion of different species in the waters around Turkey makes the country a paradise for fish lovers:

Barbun Red mullet

Çipura Sea bream

Dilbalığı Sole

Hamsi Anchovy

Kalamar Squid

Kalkan Turbot

Kefal Grey mullet

Kılıç Swordfish

Levrek Sea bass

Lüfer Bluefish

Midye Mussels

Palamut Bonito tuna

Uskumru Mackerel

İmam bayıldı Aubergines, stuffed with tomatoes, garlic and onions, are baked in the oven until meltingly soft.

Levrek pilakisi This stew is made by simmering sea bass fillets with potatoes, carrots, tomatoes, onions and garlic.

Kadayıf Rounds of vermicelli are stuffed with nuts and doused with honey to make a sumptuous dessert.

Mezes

As in many southern European countries, a Turkish meal begins with a selection of appetizing starters known as *mezes*, which are placed in the middle of the table for sharing. In a basic *meyhane* restaurant, you may be offered olives, cheese and slices of melon, but in a grander establishment the choice will be enormous. Mainly consisting of cold vegetables and salads of various kinds, *mezes* can also include a number of hot dishes, such as *börek* (cheese pastries), fried mussels and squid. *Mezes* are eaten with bread and traditionally washed down with *rakı* (a clear, anise-flavoured spirit).

Humus with *pide* bread

Zeytinyağlı enginar
(artichokes cooked in olive oil)

Çoban salatası
(tomato, red onion and cucumber salad)

Ayşe Fasulye
(green beans with tomato sauce)

Kavun ile beyaz peynir
(melon with a creamy, feta-like cheese)

Yalacı yaprak dolması
(stuffed vine leaves)

Tarama (a dip made with cod's roe, garlic and olive oil)

Turkish Breads

Bread is the cornerstone of every meal in Turkey and comes in a wide range of shapes and styles. Besides *ekmek* (crusty white loaves) the other most common types of Turkish bread are *yufka* and *pide*. *Yufka*, the typical bread of nomadic communities, is made from thinly rolled sheets of dough which are cooked on a griddle, and dried to help preserve them. They can then be heated up and served to accompany any main meal as required. *Pide* is the type of flat bread that is usually served with *mezes* and kebabs in restaurants. It consists of a flattened circle or oval of dough, sometimes brushed with beaten egg and sprinkled with sesame seeds or black cumin, that is baked in an oven. It is a staple during many religious festivals. In the month of Ramadan, no meal is considered complete without *pide*. Another popular bread is *simit*, a crisp, ring-shaped savoury loaf that comes covered in sesame seeds.

A delivery of freshly baked *simit* loaves

What to Drink in Turkey

The most common drink in Turkey is tea (çay), which is normally served black in small, tulip-shaped glasses. It will be offered to you wherever you go: in shops and bazaars, and even in banks and offices. Breakfast is usually accompanied by tea, whereas small cups of strong Turkish coffee (kahve) are drunk mid-morning and also at the end of meals. Cold drinks include a variety of fresh fruit juices, such as orange and cherry, and refreshing syrup-based sherbets. Although Turkey does produce its own wine and beer, the most popular alcoholic drink is rakı, which is usually served to accompany mezes.

Soft drinkseller

Soft Drinks

Bottled mineral water (su) is sold in corner shops and served in restaurants everywhere. If you're feeling adventurous, you might like to try a glass of ayran, salty

Vişne suyu   Ayran

liquid yoghurt. Boza is made from bulgur wheat and is another local drink to sample. There is always a variety of refreshing, cold fruit and vegetable juices available. They include cherry juice (vişne suyu), turnip juice (şalgam suyu) and şıra, a juice made from fermented grapes.

Coffee and Tea

Turkish coffee is dark, strong and served in tiny cups, with the grounds left in the bottom. It is ordered according to the amount of sugar required: az (little), orta (medium) or şekerli (a lot). Insist on Turkish coffee, or the waiter may assume you want Nescafé. Tea (çay) is served with sugar but without milk, and it comes in a small, tulip-shaped glass. Also popular is apple (elma) flavour tea, but there are also rosehip (kuşburnu) and a delicious mint (nane) variety.

Traditional samovar for tea

Alcoholic Drinks

Turkey's national alcoholic drink is rakı, a clear, anise-flavoured spirit that turns cloudy when water is added and is drunk with fish and mezes. The Turkish wine industry has yet to realize its full potential. Kavaklıdere and Doluca, the best-known brands, are overpriced for table wines. Villa Doluca is preferable. Sevilen offers several interesting wines, such as Majestic, and an outstanding Merlot. All alcohol is heavily taxed, making simple table wine a luxury. The locally brewed Efes Pilsen beer, also widely available on draught, is quite drinkable but note that alcohol may not be served in some cheaper restaurants and kebab houses.

Rakı   Beer   Red wine   White wine

Turkish coffee is a very strong drink and an acquired taste for most people.

Sahlep is a winter drink made from orchid root.

Apple tea   Limeflower tea

Where to Eat and Drink

Istanbul
Seraglio Point

Bizim Mutfak　　　　　₺
Lokanta　　　　　**Map** 5 D3
*Şeyhülislam Hayri Efendi Cad 2,
Eminönü, 34110*
Tel (0212) 522 78 46
Locals flock to this modern
dining establishment to enjoy
a wide variety of soups, meats,
vegetarian delights and desserts.

Şehzade Erzurum Cağ Kebabi　₺
Kebab　　　　　**Map** 5 E3
Hocapaşa Sok 3A, Sirkeci, 34400
Tel (0212) 520 33 61
Unpretentious eatery that serves
a delicious, succulent marinated
lamb kebab on warm *lavash*
(flatbread). A must for meat lovers.

Can Oba　　　　　₺₺
Turkish　　　　　**Map** 5 E3
Hocapaşa Sok 10, Sirkeci, 34400
Tel (0212) 522 12 15
This restaurant presents
imaginatively prepared dishes
that make sure there is always
a crowd.

DK Choice

Imbat　　　　　₺₺
Regional　　　　　**Map** 5 E3
*Hudavendigar Cad 34, Sirkeci,
34410*
Tel (0212) 520 71 91
A very popular restaurant atop
the Orient Express Hotel. The
lamb is highly recommended,
and the menu also caters to
vegetarians. Attentive staff
ensure a pleasant dining
experience. Reserve ahead to
secure a coveted Bosphorus-
facing spot on the terrace.

Paşazade　　　　　₺₺
Turkish　　　　　**Map** 5 E3
İbn-i Kemal Sok 5A, Sirkeci, 34110
Tel (0212) 513 37 50
Authentic Turkish fare that is hard
to find elsewhere. The menu
features tasty *mahmudiye* (a fruity
chicken dish).

Balıkçı Sabahattin　　　₺₺₺
Seafood　　　　　**Map** 5 E4
*Seyit Hasan Kuyu Sok 1,
Cankurtaran – Eminönü*
Tel (0212) 458 18 24
Housed in a restored wooden
mansion near the Armada
hotel, this old Istanbul favourite
specializes in seafood. In summer
the crowd of diners spills out
onto garden tables.

Karakol　　　　　₺₺₺
Turkish　　　　　**Map** 5 F3
*Inside Topkapi Palace grounds, next
to Aya Irene*
Tel (0212) 514 94 94
Housed next to the 6th-century
church Haghia Iren, Karakol
presents Turkish cuisine at its
best. Outdoor dining; but in
winter, patrons can sit inside the
restored sentry-post building.

Sultanahmet

Fes Café　　　　　₺
Café　　　　　**Map** 5 D6
*Ali Baba Türbe Sok 25,
Nuruosmaniye, 34200*
Tel (0212) 526 30 71
An unusually glamorous café in
the streets around the bazaar.
Fruit sherbets, tasty coffees and
modest lunch options in cool
retro surroundings.

DK Choice

Tarihi Sultanahmet Koftecisi　₺
Kebab　　　　　**Map** 5 D4
Divanyolu Cad 12, 34400
Tel (0212) 520 05 66
One of the best places to
come for kebabs. The juicy *kofta*
(meatballs) have garnered many
famous admirers over the
years – find their written reviews
framed on the walls. Eat *kofta*
with *piyaz* (bean salad), and
follow it up with *semolina helva*
for dessert.

Fuego Restaurant　　　₺₺
International　　　　**Map** 5 E4
Incili Cavus Sok 15A, 34110
Tel (0212) 531 36 97
Sample a range of dishes
from pizzas and fresh pastas
to delectable kebabs and
mouthwatering desserts.

Beautifully cooked lamb cutlets at Karakol
served outdoors in summer

Price Guide
Prices categories include a thrre-course
meal for one (excluding alcohol), and all
extra charges including service and tax.

₺　　　under ₺35
₺₺　　₺35 to ₺50
₺₺₺　over ₺50

Sultanahmet Fish House　₺₺
Regional　　　　　**Map** 5 D6
*Prof Kasim Ismail Gurkan Cad 14,
34400*
Tel (0212) 527 44 45
Great place for fish and seasonal
specials including salt-baked
sea bass. Wide range of *mezes*
and there are also a number of
kebab choices.

DK Choice

Giritli Restaurant　　　₺₺₺
Cretan Meyhane　　　**Map** 5 E5
*Keresteci Hakkı Sok, Cankurtaran,
34122*
Tel (0212) 458 22 70
A Cretan restaurant hidden
in a lovely courtyard down
an alley. There is a good value
all-you-can-eat menu, which
includes limitless alcoholic
drinks and about 20 differernt
kinds of *meze*. Octopus and
fresh fish have featured on
the seasonal menu.

Seasons Restaurant　　₺₺₺
International　　　　**Map** 5 E4
*Four Seasons Hotel, Tevkifhane Sok 1,
Cankurturan*
Tel (0212) 402 31 50
In a converted late-Ottoman
prison, this popular restaurant
offers everything from sushi and
antipasti to classic Turkish fare.

The Bazaar Quarter

Can Restaurant　　　₺
Lokanta　　　　　**Map** 4 C4
Sorguclu Han 19–26, Kapalicarsi
Tel (0212) 511 91 53
Workers and shoppers from the
Bazaar come here to get their
fill of hearty home-style cooking.
The delicious meat broth
thickened with egg is worth
the trip.

Gaziantep Burç Ocakbaşi　₺
Kebab　　　　　**Map** 4 C4
Parçacilar Sok 12, Kapalicarsi
Tel (0212) 527 15 16
This delightful bazaar restaurant
serves meat dishes from the
southeastern region of Turkey,
famed for its flavourful kebabs.
Stuffed and dried vegetables are
a delicious alternative.

The spacious dining area and one of the counters displaying tasty treats at Nar Lokanta

Havuzlu   ₺₺
Lokanta   **Map** 4 C4
Gani Çelebi Sok 3, Grand Bazaar, 36420
Tel (0212) 527 33 46
A rare dining option in the Grand Bazaar, Havuzlu is a pleasant restaurant serving freshly cooked local food. Try the soups.

Daruzziyafe   ₺₺₺
Kebab   **Map** 4 B3
Şifahane Sok 6, Süleymaniye, 36420
Tel (0212) 511 84 14
Located in the grounds of the restored Süleymaniye mosque, this large, airy restaurant mostly caters to tour groups. Do not miss the *keşkul* (milk pudding).

DK Choice

Nar Lokanta   ₺₺₺
Lokanta   **Map** 5 D4
Armaggan store 5th Floor, Nuruosmaniye Cad 65
Tel (0212) 522 28 00
An excellent choice tucked away in the Grand Bazaar, Nar makes a point of only using seasonal ingredients – from which they manage to fashion 50 dishes daily. Step into the glamorous dining room inside and take your pick from an open buffet of vegetable specials. There is also an extensive list of Turkish wines.

Beyoğlu

Café Grand Boulevard   ₺
Café   **Map** 1 A4
Hazzo Pulo Pasaji, Hengecidi Sok 116, Istiklal Cad, 34433
Tel (0212) 293 34 46
Great spot to drink tea and play backgammon in the pleasant courtyard of Hazzopulo Pasaj. Perfect place to take a break from sight seeing.

DK Choice

Canim Cigerim   ₺
Kebab   **Map** 1 A5
Minare Sok 1, 34430
Tel (0212) 252 60 60
Famous for its skewers of liver, this inexpensive and welcoming restaurant is popular with locals and tourists alike. Get succulent meat pieces wrapped up with onions and greens. Try the mouthwatering *kunefe* (sweet cheese pastry) for dessert.

Cuppa   ₺
Café   **Map** 1 B4
Yeni Yuva Sok, Cihangir 22, 34433
Tel (0212) 249 57 23
The go-to destination for Cihangir's smoothie lovers. Also serves quick healthy bites. The Nutella French toast is delicious.

Datli Maya   ₺
Lokanta   **Map** 1 B5
Türgücü Cad 59/A, Cihangir
Tel (0212) 292 90 56
Exuberant chef Dilara Erbay leads this restaurant featuring a menu of creatively re-imagined Turkish street food staples.

Fasuli   ₺
Lokanta   **Map** 5 E1
Kilicalipasa CD 6, Topĥane, 34425
Tel (0212) 243 65 80
Famous for the Black Sea-style beans after which it is named, the menu at Fasuli also features corn bread, *mihlama* (fondue) and salads.

Furreyya   ₺
Seafood   **Map** 1 A5
Serdari Ekrem Sok 2B
Tel (0212) 252 48 53
This miniature restaurant, a stone's throw from the Galata Tower, serves tasty fish soups, wraps and sandwiches.

Lale Işkembecesi   ₺
Turkish   **Map** 1 A4
Tarlabaşı Bulvarı 13, 34437
Tel (0212) 252 69 69
Open 24/7, this restaurant is one of the oldest in the city. It is popular with late-night diners for its *işkembe*, a tripe soup that is known locally as a hangover cure.

Namli   ₺
Lokanta   **Map** 5 E1
Rıhtım Cad, Katotopark Altı, Karaköy
Tel (0212) 293 68 80
A delightful deli with a lot of variety; they stock several different kinds of *salgam suyu* (pickled turnip juice) as well as a wide range of cheeses.

Van Kahvalti Evi   ₺
Kurdish   **Map** 1 B5
Defterdar Yokusu No 52A
Tel (0212) 293 64 37
This hip Kurdish breakfast joint offers a lot of regional specialties. There can be a wait to get in but the food is worth it.

49 Cukurcuma   ₺₺
International   **Map** 1 A4
Turnacıbaşı Sok 49, 34433
Tel (0212) 249 00 48
Scrumptious pizza and excellent Turkish wines from the island of Bozcaada are available at this cool café with exposed-brick decor. Friendly service.

Ara Kafe   ₺₺
Turkish   **Map** 1 A4
Tosbağ Sok 8, 34433
Tel (0212) 245 41 05
The photos on the wall and the decor here bring a slice of old-world Istanbul to guests. No alcohol but indulge in milky Indian teas and home-made lemonades.

Culinary Institute   ₺₺
Fusion   **Map** 1 A4
Meşrutiyet Cad 59, Asmalı Mescit, 34437
Tel (0212) 251 22 14
Feast on persimmon martinis, dried aubergine (eggplant) stuffed kebabs and bean and rice dishes in the dining room of this cookery school.

Ficcin   ₺₺
Meyhane   **Map** 1 A4
Kallavi Sok 7/1–13/1
Tel (0212) 293 37 86
This Circassian-influenced *meze* place comprises a series of eateries lining the same street. Don't miss the *cerkez tavuk* (a garlicky chicken and walnut dish) or the signature meat pie.

For more information on types of restaurants *see p340*

The entrance to Akdeniz Hatay Sofrasi, Istanbul

Helvetia   ₺₺
Lokanta   **Map** 1 A5
Asmalı Mescit Mh, Gen Yazgan Sok 12
Tel (0212) 245 87 80
Good place for vegetarians
though there are a number of
choices for meat lovers as well.
After eating, enjoy an aromatic
herbal tea.

Jash   ₺₺
Meyhane   **Map** 1 B4
Pürletaş Mah, Cihangir Cad 9
Tel (0212) 244 30 42
Armenian *mezes* are served in
this cozy *meyhane*. When the
musicians move in with their
accordians, things can get a
bit raucous.

DK Choice

Kahve 6   ₺₺
Breakfast   **Map** 1 B5
Anahtar Sok 13, Cihangir
Tel (0212) 293 08 49
A great place for breakfast,
Kahve 6 offers poached eggs
with spinach and garlic sauce
and "life-saver simit" – a seeded
bread ring with all the essential
Turkish breakfast jams, cheeses
and olives. A trendy Cihangir
hang-out with creative versions
of old favourites.

Karaköy Lokantası   ₺₺
Lokanta   **Map** 5 E1
Kemankes Cad 37 , Karaköy, 34425
Tel (0212) 292 44 55
Beautiful tiled interiors at this
hip *lokanta*. Popular lunch choice
for business people in the area.
Order *mezes* or try the chicken
and lemon pasta served with
dried mint and paprika.

Kiva   ₺₺
Kebab   **Map** 5 D1
Galata Kulesi Meydanı 4
Tel (0212) 292 00 37
Huge range of Anatolian dishes
to try at this vibrant restaurant.
Excellent beef casseroles and a
choice of rice items on the menu.

Klemuri   ₺₺
Meyhane   **Map** 1 B4
Büyükparmakkapi 2, 34400
Tel (0212) 292 32 72
A friendly *meyhane*. The seasonal
menu focuses on Black Sea
cuisine. Vegan and vegetarian
options available.

Lokanta Maya   ₺₺
Lokanta   **Map** 5 E1
Kemankes Cad 35A
Tel (0212) 252 68 84
The chef at this charming restau-
rant creates a well presented
menu of daily specials.

Mekan   ₺₺
Meyhane   **Map** 1 A4
Eski Çiçekçi Sok 3, 34250
Tel (0212) 252 60 52
An Armenian *meyhane* just off
Istiklal Caddesi offering *mezes* such
as *topik* – made with chickpeas,
currants and cinnamon.

Zencefil   ₺₺
Lokanta   **Map** 1 B3
Şht Muhtar Mh, Kurabiye Sok 8, 34430
Tel (0212) 243 82 34
A very pretty vegetarian café set
in a glasshouse building. A calm
oasis away from the noise and
traffic of Taksim's busier end.

Diners relaxing in the gently lit interiors at
Lokanta Maya

Ca'd'oro Salt Restaurant
and Café   ₺₺₺
International   **Map** 5 D1
SALT Galata, Bankalar Cad, 34420
Tel (0212) 243 82 92
Choose from a small café menu
of pizzas and sandwiches, or go
to the upstairs restaurant for
Italian food with a Turkish twist.

Çok Çok Thai   ₺₺₺
Thai   **Map** 1 A4
Mesrutiyet Cad 51, 34420
Tel (0212) 292 64 96
Upmarket restaurant with a
hip ambience and friendly staff.
The honey grilled salmon with
mung bean salad is a winner.

La Mouette   ₺₺₺
Turkish   **Map** 1 A5
Tomtom Kaptan Sok 18, 34433
Tel (0212) 292 44 67
Smart restaurant with an
impressive *degustation* menu –
sample a gamut of creative and
witty dishes. Superb city views.

Leb-I derya   ₺₺₺
International   **Map** 1 A5
Richmond Otel Kat 6, İstiklal Cad 227
Tel (0212) 243 43 75
Sample a modern take on
traditional Turkish cuisine on the
top floor of the refined Richmond
Hotel. Good breakfast buffet.

Munferit   ₺₺₺
Mediterranean   **Map** 1 A4
Yeni Çarşı Cad 19, Galatasaray, 34425
Tel (0212) 252 50 67
Cutting edge interiors and great
food combine at Munferit. Ideal
for some after-dinner dancing.

Ninja   ₺₺₺
Japanese   **Map** 1 C4
Inonu Cad 43, Gümüşsuyu, 34398
Tel (0212) 237 23 28
Ninja serves grills as well as
noodles and sushi. Smaller
booths for private parties.

Further Afield

Asude   ₺
Lokanta
*Perihan Abla Sok 4, Kuzguncuk,
Üsküdar*
Tel (0216) 334 44 14
Crowded family-run lunch spot
with a few revolving specials.
Home-made Turkish ravioli is the
speciality on Mondays.

Kanaat   ₺
Lokanta
Selmanipak Cad 9, Üsküdar
Tel (0216) 341 54 44
A good choice in Üsküdar, Kanaat
has a wide range of olive oil dishes
and meat lunch specials. Delicious
milky pudding for dessert.

Pierre Loti Coffee House ₺
Café
Gümüşsuyu Balmumcu Sok 1, Eyüp
Tel (0212) 581 26 96
Named after the French novelist,
Pierre Loti, this is a modest tea
spot, famous for its spectacular
views up the Golden Horn.

DK Choice

Akdeniz Hatay Sofrası ₺₺
Kebab
Ahmediye Cad 44, Fatih, 34091
Tel (0212) 444 72 47
This restaurant is a showcase
of the Antakya region's
flavourful cuisine. Try the sour
minced meat, chickpea and
pomegranate soup or the
home-made bread cooked
in an infusion of cheese and
herbs. Call ahead to sample
the special salt-baked chicken.

DK Choice

Çiya Kebap ₺₺
Kebab
*Güneşli Bahçe Sok 48/B, Caferağa,
Kadıköy*
Tel (0216) 330 31 90
A humble trio of kebab houses
make up Çiya, all located along
the same Kadıköy street. Gorge
on creative variations of kebabs,
and be sure to try the *alinazik
kebab* – made from chargrill-
smoked and spiced aubergine
(eggplant) purée. An immense
range of candied nuts and
fruits on offer.

Incir Altı ₺₺
Meyhane
Arabacılar Sok 4, Beylerbeyi, 34398
Tel (0216) 557 66 86
A beautiful walled garden
surrounds this lovely restaurant.
Classic Istanbul *mezes* on the
menu. The grilled octopus and
fish in vine leaves are highlights.

Kosinitza ₺₺
Meyhane
Bereketli Sok 2, Kuzguncuk, Üsküdar
Tel (0216) 334 04 00
Surprise your tastebuds with an
interesting combination of
flavours – relish delicately spiced
fish stew or go for the usual plain
grilled offerings.

Suna'nin yeri Suna balik ₺₺
Meyhane
Kandilli İskele Cad 4, Kandilli
Tel (0216) 332 32 41
Unpretentious fish restaurant
offering delicious food. There is
no wine list, but ask the waiters
for their recommendations.

DK Choice

360 East ₺₺₺
Fusion
*Albay Faik 31, Sozdener Cad,
Kadıköy*
Tel (0216) 542 43 50
Take a boat ride to this sleek,
upmarket establishment that
is part of the 360 Istanbul chain.
It doubles up as a refined dining
space and a nightclub joint in
the fashionable neighbourhood
of Moda. The sea bass and the
lamb are cooked to perfection.
360 East also has wonderful
views and offers entertainment
in the form of international DJs
and world-class musicians.

Angel ₺₺₺
Meyhane
Salacak Sahil Yolu 46, Üsküdar, 34470
Tel (0216) 553 04 26
A smart *meyhane* which looks
out towards Seraglio Point. Fish
mezes are a big draw here, as well
as salt-baked John Dory, which is
wheeled to the table girded by
blue flames.

Beyti ₺₺₺
Kebab
Orman Sok 8, Florya, 34153
Tel (0212) 663 29 90
A pilgrimage site for meat-lovers,
Beyti also delights with its huge
portions. Do not miss the sizzling
mixed grill.

Lacivert ₺₺₺
Meyhane
Körfez Cad 57, Anadolu Hisarı, 34410
Tel (0216) 413 37 53
Practically under the second
Bosphorus bridge, Lacivert was
the locale for a set of 1970s
Turkish films. Good seafood.

Patrons sitting outside one of Çiya Kebap's
establishments on Kadıköy street

Beautiful sunset view from the funky
roof-top dining area at 360 East

Thrace and the Sea of Marmara

BURSA: Çırağan Restaurant ₺
Turkish/International
*Çekirge Cad, Süleyman Çelebi Parkı
No 155, 16150*
Tel (0224) 234 03 25
There is something to suit the
taste of all members of the family
here. The large bakery furnace
turns out traditional *pides*
(Turkish flatbread).

DK Choice

BURSA: Kebapçı İskender ₺
Kebab
*Tayyare Kültür Merkezi yanı,
Atatürk Cad 60, 16330*
Tel (0224) 221 10 76
A national favourite, İskender
kebab restaurants are found
all across Turkey, and this
place is where the dish
was born. İskender is döner
kebab served with a tomato
dressing and melted butter
on a single layer of diced *pide*
bread – heavenly.

BURSA: Şehir Lokantası ₺
Turkish
Tahtakale Mah, İnebey Cad, 16050
Tel (0224) 222 62 03
Since 1975, this established
restaurant has been serving
good traditional Turkish food.
Delicious stews on offer.

BURSA: Zeynel İnegöl Köftecisi ₺
Kebab
İzmir Yolu üzeri, 16500
Tel (0224) 618 03 16
Feast on *inegöl köfte*, a special
meatball made with minced
meat and red onions, cooked
on oak-wood grills.

For more information on types of restaurants *see p340*

Informal indoor and outdoor dining at Yelken Café, Ayvalik

BURSA: Darüzziyafe Bursa ₺₺
Turkish
Il Murat Cad 36, Muradiye Cami Karşısı, 16050
Tel (0224) 224 64 40
Located in a historic neighbourhood, this restaurant's specialties include *Yufkalı Darüzziyafe köfte* (meatballs). Good desserts.

BURSA: Uludağ Kebapçısı ₺₺
Kebab
Uluyol Şirin Sok 12, 16050
Tel (0224) 251 45 51
One of the oldest and most well-established kebab restaurants in Turkey, this place is also a city landmark. Simply delicious kebabs.

BURSA: Skylight Restaurant ₺₺₺
Mediterranean
Hilton Hotel, Yeni Yalova Cad 347, 16210
Tel (0224) 500 05 05
An elegant restaurant offering creative dishes based on fish, meat or vegetables. Gorgeous views of the city from its top floor location.

The tasteful, softly lit interior at Skylight Restaurant, Bursa

Key to Price Guide *see p346*

ÇANAKKALE: Cafe Du Port ₺₺
International
Yalı Cad 12, 17100
Tel (0286) 217 29 08
French toasts and omelette for breakfast, and freshly brewed Turkish tea and cakes in mid-afternoon. Good hearty food.

ÇANAKKALE: Rıhtim Restaurant ₺₺
Seafood
Eski Balıkhane Sok 7-9, 12100
Tel (0286) 212 53 67
Peaceful waterfront location with fantastic seafood. The daily catch is displayed on a counter by the entrance.

ECEABAT: Maydos Restaurant ₺
International
İsmetpaşa Paşa Mah, Kilitbahir Yolu, İstiklal Cad 105
Tel (0286) 814 14 54
This Australian-run restaurant in Maydos offers a very varied menu. Its location by the waterfront encourages outdoor dining on fair days. Also runs tours of the Gallipoli World War I battlefields.

ECEABAT: Liman Restaurant ₺₺
Seafood
İsmet Paşa Mah, İstiklal Cad 67, 17900
Tel (0286) 814 27 55
A low-key seafood restaurant with a coffee shop feel, especially on the outdoor terrace. The speciality is *paçanga* – a savoury phyllo roll, deep fried with pastrami and cheese.

EDIRNE: Sivrikaya Restaurant ₺
Turkish
Migros Kavşağı, Tren İstasyonu Cad, 22100
Tel (0284) 236 21 64
This restaurant partners a dairy farm known for its delicious dairy products, which are incorporated into the restaurant's menu.

EDIRNE: Hanedan Restaurant ₺₺
Turkish
Karaağaç Yolu üzeri, İki Köprü Arası, Tunca Köprüsü yanı, 22100
Tel (0284) 214 21 22
A renowned and large facility located on the Tunca river. Besides the *mezes*, they serve great fish and meat dishes.

EDIRNE: Poseidon Restaurant ₺₺
Seafood
Maarif Cad, Mithatpaşa Mah 6, 22100
Tel (0284) 212 02 10
Sea bream and sea bass can be found here, while deep-fried, delicate red mullet is on offer between July and October.

GELIBOLU: Gelibolu Osmanlı Mutfağı ₺
Turkish
Atatürk Cad 34, 17500, Çanakkale
Tel (0286) 566 12 25
Dishes once made to please the sultans are now enjoyed by all food lovers. Aubergine (eggplant) fillet or deep-fried dumplings dipped in honey syrup are favourites.

GELIBOLU: Gelibolu Restaurant ₺₺
Seafood
İskele Meydanı, Vapur İskelesi yanı, 17500
Tel (0286) 566 12 27
Conveniently located by the port, this eatery serves delicacies such as octopus, calamari, grilled fish and anchovies in Black Sea style.

İZNIK: Köfteci Yusuf ₺
Kebab
Selçuk Mah, Atatürk Cad 73, 16860
Tel (0224) 444 61 62
Inexpensive eatery rustling up delectable grilled meat, chicken and *Köfte* (meatballs) served with pepper, garlic and parsley paste.

İZNIK: Umut Restaurant ₺₺
Seafood
Göl Sahil Yolu 24, 16860
Tel (0224) 757 07 38
Situated on the lakefront, with an outdoor section shaded with vines. Expect to find freshwater fish dishes such as skewered catfish and carp.

The Aegean

ASSOS: Nazlıhan Restaurant ₺₺
Turkish
İskele Mevkii, Behramkale, 17860
Tel (0286) 721 73 85 86
The usual Turkish fare but the romantic setting – on the waterfront of the ancient harbour of Assos – makes it special.

Picturesque setting of Mimoza Restaurant, Bodrum Peninsula

AYVALIK: Avşar Büfe ₺
Fast Food
Barbaros Cad, 10400
Tel (0266) 312 98 21
One of the most well-known
sandwich kiosks in the country.
Food is served from a 1960s
style minibus.

AYVALIK: Paşalı Restaurant ₺
Turkish
Talatpaşa Cad 14, 14000
Tel (0266) 312 50 18
Relish hearty food at the centre
of Ayvalık's market district. Popular
for its soups.

DK Choice

AYVALIK: Yelken Café ₺₺
International
*Çamlık Mevkii İnönü Cad 14,
10400*
Tel (0266) 312 77 82
In an area full of touristy
restaurants, Yelken is a gem
and a local favourite. Located
on the waterfront, away from
the bustle of the town, this
casual restaurant rustles up
delicious Aegean, Italian and
seafood dishes cooked in
high-quality virgin olive oil.
Fine service.

AYVALIK: Şehir Klubü ₺₺₺
Seafood
Gazinolar Cad, Ayvalık Merkez, 10400
Tel (0266) 312 36 76
An elegant city-centre restaurant
on the waterfront. Try *karagöz* –
a kind of sea bream rarely
available elsewhere. Reservations
recommended on weekends.

BEHRAMKALE: Kale Restaurant ₺
Turkish
*Akropol Yolu, Behramkale Köyü,
Çanakkale*
Tel (0543) 317 49 69
Built against the ancient walls of
Assos, Kale serves *gözleme* (pastry
dish), *mantı* (Turkish ravioli) and
ayran (yogurt drink).

BERGAMA:
Kardeşler Restaurant ₺
Turkish
İzmir Yolu Üzeri, 35700
Tel (0232) 631 08 56
On the Izmir highway leading
to Bergama and its acropolis,
Kardeşler offers a daily buffet of
traditional food. Grilled meat and
chicken dishes are made to order.

BERGAMA:
Meydan Restaurant ₺
Turkish
Mustafa Yazıcı Cad 17/A, 35700
Tel (0232) 631 52 25
A short walk from the museum
this restaurant is a no-frills local
favourite. Offers daily cooked
dishes that change by the season.

BODRUM: Bodrum El
Vino Restaurant ₺₺
Regional/Seafood
Omurça Mah, Pamili Sok 14, 48400
Tel (0252) 313 87 70
Terrace restaurant in a peaceful
back street with delicious seafood
and awesome views overlooking
the town and Crusader castle.

BODRUM:
Meyhane Evgenia ₺₺
Regional/Seafood
Çarşı Sok, 48400
Tel (0533) 305 54 19
Informal, family-run restaurant
tucked away behind the fish
market. The *mezes* are all full of
flavour; ask the owners for their
recommendations – you won't
be disappointed.

BODRUM:
Marina Yacht Club ₺₺₺
Seafood/International
Neyzen Tevfik Cad, 48000
Tel (0252) 316 12 28
A restaurant and club in the
Marina with an all-day menu to
choose from. Good food and
cocktails. Fine jazz musicians
perform in the club section.
Great place to chill out with
friends and soak up the view.

BODRUM PENINSULA:
Bodrum Mantı & Cafe ₺₺
Turkish
*Bodrum Yarımadası, Götürkbükü,
Keleş Hanım Cad147, 48483*
Tel (0252) 377 51 00
A pretty Mediterranean type
restaurant famous for its *mantı*
(Turkish dumplings), which
come with a variety of toppings
and fillings; a wide choice of
omelettes is also available.

BODRUM PENINSULA:
Limon Cafe ₺₺
Café
*Bodrum Yarımadası, Yalı Mevkii 1,
48400*
Tel (0252) 394 40 44   **Closed** *winter*
A half-hour drive from Bodrum,
this café serves cakes and
lemonade in the afternoon – ask
for the ginger mint lemonade.

BODRUM PENINSULA:
Mimoza Restaurant ₺₺₺
Seafood
*Bodrum Yarımadası, Gümüşlük Köyü,
48970*
Tel (0252) 394 31 39   **Closed** *winter*
Elegant beach restaurant.
Highlights on the menu include
grilled octopus and clams, and
shrimps on grape leaves.

The wonderful view from the dining area at
Bodrum El Vino Restaurant, Bodrum

For more information on types of restaurants *see p340*

The exterior of İdaköy Çiftlik Evi, Edremit

ÇEŞME: İmren Lokantası ₺₺
Turkish
16 Eylül Mah, 3004 Sok 81, 35940
Tel (0232) 712 76 70
Sample classic kebabs and Turkish food at İmren Lokantası. The menu offers a lot of options including *mezes* and stews.

ÇEŞME: Ferdi Baba Restaurant ₺₺₺
Seafood
5464 Sok 3 Şifne, 35950
Tel (0232) 717 21 45 **Closed** winter
An excellent seafood restaurant. The sea bass in liquor and deep-fried fish are delicious; ask for the waiter's recommendations. Reservations required.

ÇEŞME: Maria'nın Bahçesi ₺₺₺
Seafood
Kemalpaşa Cad 1, 35937
Tel (0232) 716 05 76
The menu celebrates Aegean delicacies, clams, sea urchins, and fish cooked with fresh herbs. For the more conservative, they also have the usual fish dishes.

CUNDA ISLAND: Taş Kahve ₺
Regional
Sahil Boyu, Mevlana Cad 20, Alibey Adası, 10400
Tel (0266) 327 11 66
The Neo-Classical historic setting of this restaurant is like a movie set from the 1930s. They offer an excellent breakfast buffet and outdoor tables on the waterfront.

CUNDA ISLAND: Bay Nihat Restaurant ₺₺₺
Seafood
Sahil Boyu, Mevlana Cad, 10400 Alibey Adası Ayvalık
Tel (0266) 327 10 63
The most famous and expensive seafood restaurant in Cunda Island. Seafood *mezes* are made with local shellfish and fresh herbs. Go for the *kidonya* (a local clam cooked in white wine and spices).

DENIZLI: Kebapçı Halil ₺
Kebab
Eski Sarayköy Cad 357, Sok 11, Bayramyeri, 20100
Tel (0258) 261 13 57
A former butcher is the kebab chef at this restaurant. Their speciality is *denizli* kebab – made with lamb and slow-grilled on mastic gum tree wood.

DIDIM: Circus Restaurant ₺₺
Italian
Ataürk Bulv 221, 09270
Tel (0256) 813 74 14
Delightful, cozy place serving a varied menu of zesty dishes. The garlic prawn starter is a must. Attentive service.

DIDIM: Lush Café and Restaurant ₺₺
International
Çamlık Mah Sok 445, 09270
Tel (0256) 813 33 61
Best known for its steaks and friendly staff, this well-located eatery is a favourite with both tourists and locals alike.

The attractive interior with Chinese lamps at Fondragonpearl, Adana

EDREMIT: İdaköy Çiftlik Evi ₺₺
Regional
Çamlıbel Köyü, 10300
Tel (0535) 222 56 66
Seasonal delicacies include *mezes* made with local herbs cooked in home-made virgin olive oil. Reservations required.

FOÇA: İğdeli Cafe ₺
Café
Reha Midlii Cad 40, 35680
Tel (0232) 812 81 27
Sample Aegean coffee made with mastic gum or go for Mesopotamian-style coffee known as *dibek kahvesi*.

FOÇA: Celep Restaurant ₺₺₺
Seafood
Fevzipaşa Mah, Reha Midilli Cad 48, 35000
Tel (0232) 812 14 95
Located in one of the most pleasant northern Aegean towns, the daily catch at Celep is kept in a pool in the restaurant, and diners can choose a fish to be cooked.

İZMIR: Kır Çiçeği Restaurant ₺₺
Turkish
Kıbrıs Şehitleri Cad 83, Alsancak
Tel (0232) 464 30 90
Near the Hilton hotel, in the trendy Alsancak neighbourhood, this restaurant offers an amazing array of kebabs, *pides*, fresh salads and desserts.

İZMIR: Mezzaluna Restaurant ₺₺
Italian
Konak Pier, Atatük Cad 19, 35260
Tel (0232) 489 81 92
Housed inside a historic customs office designed by Gustave Eiffel, Mezzaluna is a good chain restaurant offering delicious and authentic Italian food. Try the gnocchi and veal carpaccio served with fresh arugula

İZMIR: Körfez Restaurant ₺₺₺
Seafood
Atatürk Cad 182/A 1, Kordon, 35200
Tel (0232) 421 01 90
Upscale, elegant and famous establishment. Sample the grouper, slowly cooked in a thick layer of salt. There is a great selection of starters and a wide range of desserts on offer too.

İZMIR: Rıhtım Restaurant ₺₺₺
Seafood
Konak Pier, Atatürk Cad, 35210
Tel (0232) 466 47 51
Located on the pier, inside the historic customs office. Upmarket restaurant with great breakfasts, omelettes and a good range of mains as well.

Key to Price Guide *see p346*

KARACASU:
Anatolia Restaurant ₺
Regional
Geyre Beldesi, Karacasu, 09385
Tel (0256) 448 81 38
Feels like an oasis with a lush garden filled with flowers. Waiters present beautifully prepared dishes in large trays. Very near to the ancient city of Aphrodisias.

KÜÇÜKKUYU ADATEPE KÖYÜ:
Dut Dibi Kahvesi ₺
Café
Adatepe Köyü, 17980
Tel (0286) 752 65 37
Situated in the centre of sleepy Adatepe village, this is a typical village café serving *mantı* (dumplings), *gözleme* (pastry dish), tea and *ayran* (yogurt drink). A casual and refreshing outdoor setting.

KUŞADASI:
Antepli Restaurant ₺₺
Kebab
Akyar Mevki Ege Vista Alış Veriş Merkezi 4/4, 09400
Tel (0256) 618 10 08
The chef at Antepli, located slightly away from the centre of Kuşadası, makes delicious pistachio kebabs, cooked on a skewer.

KUŞADASI:
Ayhan Usta Restaurant ₺₺
Turkish
Setur Marina, 09460
Tel (0256) 618 04 59
Amazing views of the marina and Aegean Sea accompany the great mix of seafood and succulent kebabs. Fresh *mezes* are prepared daily.

KUŞADASI:
Kazım Usta Restaurant ₺₺₺
Seafood
Liman Cad 4, 09400
Tel (0256) 514 12 26
Select scrumptious seafood from a refrigerated counter. The outdoor seating area is under a canopy of green vines.

PAMUKKALE: Ece Restaurant ₺
Turkish
Karahayıt Village, 20290
Tel (0258) 271 45 02
A short walk from most hotels in Pamukkale, this is a budget winner. Choose potato, spinach or cheese filling with home-made *gözleme* (pastry dish).

PAMUKKALE: Kayas Restaurant ₺
Kebab
Atatürk Cad 3, 20280
Tel (0258) 272 29 35
Centrally located restaurant with friendly staff and service. Go for *köftes* (meatballs) and shish kebab.

PAMUKKALE:
Yörük Evi Restaurant ₺
Turkish
Karahayıt Village, Atatürk Cad, 20180
Tel (0258) 271 42 43
Gözleme (pastry dish) is the main dish here, with a choice of fillings. They also have *sac kavurma* (diced lamb cooked on an iron plate).

SELÇUK: Petek Çöp Şiş ₺
Kebab
Atatürk Cad, Selçuk Devlet Hastanesi Karşısı, 35920
Tel 0 232 892 40 77
The local delicacy here is *çöp şiş* – small pieces of lean lamb grilled on tiny wood chops, served with grilled tomatoes, peppers and rice.

SELÇUK: Artemis Restaurant ₺₺
Regional
Şirince Village, 35920
Tel (0232) 898 32 40
Wine house producing grape and fruit wines. There is a cheese- and wine-tasting table in the garden.

TIRE: Kaplan Dağ Restaurant ₺
Regional
Kaplan Köy, 35900
Tel (0232) 512 66 52
Good vegetarian restaurant offering *keşkek* (a beaten wheat and meat dish served in traditional weddings).

Classy dining area at Spice Market Restaurant, Adana

TROY: Hisarlık Restaurant ₺
Turkish
Truva Sit Alanı Girişi, Tevfikiye Köyü, 17060, Çanakkale
Tel (0542) 243 93 59
Casual place with fresh Turkish food. The only eatery before the entrance of the ancient city of Troy. The owner is known to be the best tour guide for Troy.

Mediterranean Turkey

ADANA:
Spice Market Restaurant ₺₺
International
Hilton Hotel, Sinanpasa Mah, Haci Sabanci Bul, 1180
Tel (0322) 355 50 00
Enjoy fine views of the Seyhan river alongside the tasty Mediterranean cuisine. The chef's special is Adana kebab – grilled spiced mince meat.

ADANA: Yüzevler Kebap ₺₺
Kebab
Ziyapaşa Bulvarı Kurtuluş Mah, Yüzevler Apt 25, Seyhan, 01030
Tel (0322) 454 75 13
Savour mouthwatering *beyti* kebab (meat on a skewer) or go for the sizzling Adana-style kebab with garlic served in *pide* and with yogurt. Fine service.

ADANA:
Fondragonpearl Restaurant ₺₺₺
Chinese
Hilton Hotel, Sinanpasa Mah, Haci Sabanci Bul, 01180
Tel (0322) 355 50 00
Chic restaurant serving excellent Chinese food – the style here is mainly Cantonese. Do not miss the sweet and sour chicken.

Kazım Usta Restaurnat in Kuşadası, a haven for seafood lovers

For more information on types of restaurants *see p340*

**ALANYA: A La Turca
Restaurant** ₺₺₺
Kebab
*Gold City Hotel (Tourism Complex),
07400*
Tel (0242) 510 02 00
The excellent food at this restaurant attracts locals and tourists to the resort.

**ALANYA:
Harbour Restaurant** ₺₺₺
Seafood
Rıhtım Cad, İskele Meydanı, Kızıl Kule yanı, 07400
Tel (0242) 512 10 19
A local favourite, with a wide choice of seafood prepared by experienced chefs. Reservations are recommended, especially at weekends.

ANTAKYA: Anadolu Restaurant ₺
Regional
Hürriyet Cad 30/A, 31070
Tel (0326) 215 33 35
Try hummus, oregano or pepper salad with walnuts. The more adventurous can try *mumbar* – sheep intestines stuffed with rice, onions and herbs.

ANTAKYA: Sultan Sofrası ₺
Regional
İstiklal Cad 20/A, 31000
Tel (0326) 213 87 59
Very popular restaurant serving flavourful fare such as *kabak borani* – a zucchini dish with chick peas, diced veal, onion, garlic and peppermint. Or sample delicious *semirsek* (a savoury pastry).

ANTALYA: Castle Restaurant ₺₺
Turkish/International
Hıdırlık Kulesi Sokak 75, Kaleiçi, 07040
Tel (0242) 248 65 94
Located on the cliff-edge next to a Roman watch-tower, offering fantastic sunset views. The food mixes Turkish and international classics, all lovingly prepared.

**ANTALYA:
Stella's Manzara Restaurant** ₺₺
Mediterranean
Eski Lara Yolu, 40 07230
Tel (0242) 316 35 96
A former Italian trattoria turned into a glorious Mediterranean restaurant. Great service, menu and wine selection.

DK Choice

ANTALYA: 7 Mehmet ₺₺₺
Kebab/Seafood
Atatürk Kültür Parkı 201, 07200
Tel (0242) 238 52 00
Located west of the city centre, 7 Mehmet has been the most prominent local restaurant of Antalya for a number of generations. The daily *mezes* are exceptionally good, as is the tandoori lamb and the salad with avocado and plum. Both indoor and outdoor dining options are available. Great place for families.

**ANTALYA:
Seraser Restaurant** ₺₺₺
International
Tuzcular Mah, Karanlık Sok 18, 07100
Tel (0242) 247 60 15
Set in a historic building with indoor and outdoor seating, Seraser boasts exceptional service. Avocado salad, quail, mussels, beef carpaccio, salmon quartet and Rum Baba all stand out.

DALYAN: Saki ₺
Turkish
Gülpınar Mah. Geçit Sokak 21, 48840
Tel (0541) 284 52 12
Saki is a great value place in the heart of the town. Located on the river, it overlooks ancient Kaunos. There is no formal menu, but there are plenty of freshly prepared starters to choose from, as well as tender meat dishes.

DALYAN: Gel Gör Restaurant ₺₺
Seafood
Maraş Mahç, Dalko Çarşısı, 48840
Tel (0252) 284 50 09
A great place that benefits from its quiet location by the river, on the outskirts of town. Choose from a staggering menu of 50 types of starters and wild or farmed fish mains.

DALYAN: Ramazan Han ₺₺
Turkish/International
Maraş Cad, Çarşı İçi, 48840
Tel (0252) 284 41 83
A wide variety of starters, main courses and desserts feature on the menu here. Relish the *Incik* kebab (lamb with vegetables); a popular draw. There is a special menu for children.

FETHIYE: Alarga Restaurant ₺₺
Turkish/International
Yat Limanı 17, 48300
Tel (0252) 601 00 00
Located just opposite the marina, Alarga is one of the few restaurants with a clear view of the Fethiye gulf. Dig into the delicious swordfish kebab while enjoying beautiful sunset views.

DK Choice

**FETHIYE: Balıkçılar Hali
(Fish Market)** ₺₺
Seafood
Balıkçılar Hali 46, 48300
Tel (0252) 612 28 06
For a different dining experience head to this famous fish market that is in an atrium surrounded by restaurants. Buy the fish from the marble slab at the centre and have the fishermen clean and deliver it to a particular restaurant to be cooked to your liking. Usually there are 30 kinds of fish and 40 kinds of shellfish to choose from.

**FETHIYE: Ocakbaşı İskele
Restaurant** ₺₺
Kebab/Seafood
Fevzi Çakmak Cad, Karagözler, 48300
Tel (0252) 614 94 23
On the harbour, just in front of the ancient theatre by the marina, this is one of the best local restaurants for kebabs and seafood.

**GÖCEK:
Blue Restaurant & Bar** ₺₺
International
Turgut Özal Bulv, 48310
Tel (0252) 645 17 42
A trendy bar and restaurant frequented by yacht owners. Sample seafood, Turkish and international dishes, from pizzas and burgers to wholesome dinners.

Inviting, peaceful ambience of Stella's Manzara Restaurant, Antalya

The beautiful beach location of Buzz Grill & Beach Bar, Ölü Deniz

GÖCEK: Upper Deck   ₺₺
Seafood/International
Büngüş Koyu, Club Marina, 48310
Tel (0252) 645 14 56
Good food at a beautiful
waterfront location, with tables
set out on the jetty. There is also
a private beach for guests.
Extensive menu to choose from.

GÖCEK:
The Galley Restaurant   ₺₺₺
Turkish/International
Port Gocek Marina, 48310
Tel (0252) 645 25 35
Owned and run by famous
chef Uğur Vata, who also has
a restaurant in the UK. Delicious
food, a relaxed and informal
atmosphere and amazing views.

KALKAN: Agora Restaurant   ₺
Turkish/International
Hasan Altan Cad 3, 07960
Tel (0242) 844 37 16
One among the numerous
good restaurants here boasting
rooftop views. The slow-cooked
lamb served on an aubergine
(eggplant) base lives up to
its reputation.

KALKAN: Iso's Kitchen   ₺
Turkish
Süleyman Yıldız Cad 39, 07960
Tel (0242) 844 24 15
Excellent value for this expensive
resort. Standard Turkish fare
includes great starters and grills.
Set in an atmospheric old Greek
house with beautiful sea views
from the terrace.

KALKAN:
Aubergine Restaurant   ₺₺
International
Yalıboyu Mah 25–27, 07960
Tel (0242) 844 33 32
With a lovely harbourside
location and great ambience,
Aubergine offers a memorable

dining experience. Chef's specials
include wild boar and stuffed sea
bass. Excellent wine menu.

KAŞ: Bi Lokma   ₺
Turkish
Hükümet Cad 20, 07580
Tel (0242) 836 39 42
Bi Lokma means "one bite" in
Turkish. It is a small family-owned
restaurant serving tasty food and
refreshing lemonade.

KAŞ: Hayta Meyhane   ₺
Turkish
Zumrut Sok 5, Merkez, 07580
Tel (0242) 836 37 76
Low key *meyhane* in which
the starters and *raki* (aniseed-
flavoured aperitif) are as
important as the grilled mains.
Lovely old Greek house setting.

KAŞ: Mercan Restaurant   ₺₺
Seafood
Balıkçı Barınağı Marina, 07580
Tel (0242) 836 12 09
An exceptionally clean restaurant
with great sea views. Offers an
array of fresh fish and other
seafood dishes. Huge portions.

KAYAKÖY: Çin Bal Restaurant ₺₺
Turkish
Kayaköy, 48300
Tel (0252) 618 00 06
Choose your own piece of lamb
or fish and have it grilled over
charcoal. Dine at shady outdoor
tables in summer or inside with
the roaring log fire in winter.

KAYAKÖY: Levissi   ₺₺
Turkish
Kayaköy, 48300
Tel (0535) 275 01 73
Set in a restored period Greek
property at the foot of the ghost
town, this is an atmospheric
dining spot. Lovely terrace and a
log fire inside on cooler days.

MERSIN: 20. Cadde   ₺₺
International
*Adnan Menderes Bulvarı, Mersin
33200*
Tel (0324) 330 00 60
One of the chosen venues that
hosts meetings of Mersin's
Gourmet Club. Delicious *mezes*
can make a whole meal – stuffed
dried aubergine (eggplant) and
salads served with pomegranate
molasses are regional specialties.

MERSIN: Big Chef's   ₺₺
International
*Adnan Menderes Bulv, Mersin
Marinası, 33140*
Tel (0324) 330 02 30
A local chain that has become
incredibly popular with its trendy
decor, a varied menu and good
service. Fabulous choice of
home-made breads, as well as
olive oil and wines.

MERSIN:
İskele Marin Restaurant   ₺₺
Seafood
*Adnan Menderes Bulv, Mersin
Marinası, 33160*
Tel (0324) 330 00 55
An elegant seafront restaurant.
White grouper is a popular
main, while the semolina
pudding with ice cream makes
a fine ending to a delicious
Mediterranean meal.

ÖLÜ DENIZ:
Buzz Grill & Beach Bar   ₺₺
International
*Ölüdeniz Sahil Fethiye Muğla,
48300*
Tel (0252) 617 05 26
A renowned bar, arguably one
of the world's most attractive
dining establishments. Wraps,
paninis, margaritas, and ice
cream cocktails are available
and can all be enjoyed on the
outdoor rooftop deck.

For more information on types of restaurants *see p340*

ÖLÜ DENIZ:
Sultan Ahmet Restaurant ₺₺
Turkish/ International
Belceğiz Mah, 48340
An extensive menu on offer
that includes pizzas, kebabs,
fresh seafood and traditional
Turkish dishes such as *lavaş*
(puffy bread).

SAKLIKENT: Paradise Park ₺
Turkish/Italian
Fethiye Muğla, 48300
Tel (0252) 659 02 03
Tasty omelettes, salads, pastas
and pizzas are on the varied
menu here. Great base for
hikers and rafters.

SIDE: Ocakbaşı Restaurant ₺₺
Kebab
Zambak Sok 8, 07600
Tel (0242) 753 18 10
For finely prepared kebabs grilled
over charcoal right in front of
you, this is *the* place. It is right in
the heart of the old town and is
good value compared to Side's
often over-priced restaurants.

TARSUS: Şelale Restaurant ₺
Regional
Şelale Mevki, 33640
Tel (0324) 624 80 10
Just a short drive from the city
centre, this eatery enjoys lovely
views of Tarsus waterfall. Rich
local delicacies such as hummus
and *künefe* (a shredded wheat
dessert with unsalted cheese).

Ankara and Western Anatolia

AFYON: İkbal Lokantası ₺₺
Turkish
Uzun Çarşı 21, 3200
Tel (0272) 215 12 05
This venerable place is a local
institution famed for its grills,
home-produced spiced sausage
and desserts topped with the
local buffalo-milk clotted cream.

AFYON: Meşhur Aşçı
Bacaksız ₺₺
Kebab
Karaman Mah, Yeni Saraçlar Çarşısı 6
Tel (0272) 215 20 97
Late 19th-century restaurant that
specializes in kebabs and lamb
roasted to tender perfection in a
traditional tandoor oven.

ANKARA: Beykoz Restaurant ₺
Turkish
Hoşdere Cad 193/A, Y Ayrancı, 06550
Tel (0312) 442 68 68
The ideal restaurant for wholesome
Turkish food. Savour tripe soup,
cooked in broth with garlic and

dressed with vinegar and lemon.
The menu is seasonal but
includes a wide variety of
vegetables, stews and kebabs.

DK Choice

ANKARA:
Boğaziçi Lokantası ₺
Turkish
Ulus, Denizciler Cad 1/A, 06240
Tel (0312) 311 88 32
Since the 1950s this has been
the prime choice for Turkish
cuisine in Ankara. The restaurant
has a long menu, and each dish
is as good as the other. Try the
lamb shanks with aubergine
(eggplant), lamb chops or go
for Ankara *tava* with rice.

ANKARA: Çiftlik Merkez
Lokantası ₺
Turkish
Emniyet Mah, AOÇ, 06560
Tel (0312) 211 02 20
A locals' and expats' secret.
Some of the tasty specials
include chicken stuffed with
spicy rice, and aubergine (egg-
plant) purée with yogurt served
with seasoned ground meat.

ANKARA: Tavacı Recep Usta ₺
Southeast Anatolian
*Dikmen Vadisi Hoşdere Girişi 5, Kapı
Çankaya, 06540*
Tel (0312) 442 29 45
Welcoming eatery offering
such fare as stuffed lamb ribs
served in a bed of pilaf cooked
with onions – a rare dish to find.
The stuffed turkey is also
particularly well prepared.

ANKARA: Uludağ Kebapçısı ₺
Kebab
Altındağ, Denizciler Cad 54, 06240
Tel (0312) 309 04 00
Excellent döner kebabs in the
historic centre of Ankara.

The exterior of the Ottoman house where
Kınacızade Konağı is located, Ankara

Mushroom pilaf rice, slow roasted
lamb shanks and Turkish coffee
slowly cooked in a bed of hot
sand are specialties.

ANKARA: Çiçek Lokantası ₺₺
Turkish
2176 Sok, Söğütözü, 06510
Tel (0312) 284 08 88
Fresh meat and vegetable dishes
cooked in a traditional Ankara
wok-like pan. Both indoor and
outdoor dining available.

ANKARA: Gar Lokantası ₺₺
Turkish
*Filistin Sok 35, Gaziosmanpaşa,
06700*
Tel (0312) 447 29 96
Airy restaurant in a trendy and
upmarket neighbourhood.
Savour the lamb roast, rolled
cabbage leaves or monkfish.
Popular with locals.

ANKARA:
Kınacızade Konağı ₺₺
Turkish
Kale Mah Kalekapısı Sok 28, 06240
Tel (0312) 324 57 14
Tasty cuisine in a beautifully
restored Ottoman period
house. A great spot for breakfast,
lunch or dinner.

BEYŞEHIR:
Beyatik Restaurant ₺
Turkish
*Hacı Armağan Mah, Orman İşletmesi
karşısı, Vuslat Park yanı, 42700*
Tel (0332) 512 91 77
This spacious restaurant has
a large garden. Choose from
traditional dishes such as fried
carp, crayfish and other lake
products. Good selection of
desserts as well. Popular venue
for local events.

BEYŞEHIR:
Yusuf Ustanın Yeri ₺
Turkish
*Hacı Armağan Mah, Köprübaşı
Cad 53, 42700*
Tel (0332) 512 54 47
Simple, no-frills restaurant
offering a choice of stews and
home-made dishes. This place
remains one of the most
prominent dining establishments
in town. No alcohol is served.

ÇAVDARHISAR:
Aizonoi Restaurant ₺
Turkish
*Çavdarhisar Anemon Hotels, Cereller
Mah, Başaran Ulusoy Sok 22, 43710*
Tel (0274) 351 22 88
The only urban-style restaurant
in the Anemon hotel, near the
ancient city of Aizonoi. The menu
is simple and features soups,
salads and grills.

EĞIRDIR:
Derya Restaurant ₺
Turkish
Cami Mah 1, Sok 1, 32500
Tel (0246) 311 40 47
Spacious restaurant at a very picturesque location next to a beautiful lake with amazing mountain views. Don't miss the lake fish stews. Friendly, attentive service.

EĞIRDIR:
Pehlivan Restaurant ₺
Turkish
Yeşil Ada Mah Kilise Arkası 18
Tel (0246) 311 58 81
Set on a quiet northeast corner of the island, this simple place serves up delicious pancakes for lunch, and fish and meat grills in the evening. Generous portions. No alcohol.

ESKIŞEHIR:
Mezze Restaurant ₺
Seafood
Kızılcıklı Mahmut Pehlivan Cad, Nazım Hikmet Sok 2, 26060
Tel (0222) 230 30 09
A wide array of *mezes* to choose from and full fish dinners; the grilled fish is a must. Octopus and prawns are other house specialties. Service is good but it can get crowded so reserve in advance.

ESKIŞEHIR: 222 Park Club and Restaurants ₺₺
International
Hoşnudiye Mah, İsmet İnönü-1, Cad 103, 26130
Tel (0222) 320 11 11
Trendy complex of clubs and eateries, including an excellent grill restaurant, an American restaurant and a wine house. Attracts a younger crowd.

ESKIŞEHIR: Ada Cafe ₺₺
International
Kentpark, 26000
Tel (0222) 217 72 73
An elegant restaurant located on an island on the Porsuk river. Great food – from hearty breakfasts to wholesome dinners: a choice of crêpes, juicy steaks, schnitzel, kebabs and *mezes*.

ESKIŞEHIR:
Sempre Restaurant ₺₺
Italian
Gaffar Okkan Cad, Pehlivanlar Sok 11, 26120
Tel (0222) 221 04 31
A popular Italian restaurant attracting mainly university students and professors. It has a garden and, sometimes, live music on weekends during the spring and summer months.

A chef serving tasty Turkish food at Çiçek Lokantası, Ankara

GÖLBAŞI: Beykoz Gölbaşı ₺
Kebab
Haymana yolu 105, Karşıyaka Mah, 06830
Tel (0312) 484 44 46
This eatery acts as a tranquil escape destination for locals. The house speciality is *kuzu tandır* – lamb slow-cooked inside an earthenware pit in the ground.

GÖLBAŞI:
Şövalye Restaurant ₺
International
Karşıyaka Mah, Sahil Cad 392, Sok 3
Tel (0312) 484 27 64
Locals flock to this popular eatery in a peaceful riverside location. The recipes here have a French touch. Good selection of wines.

GÖLBAŞI: Chez Le Belge ₺₺₺
Belgian
Sahil Cad 24, 06830
Tel (0312) 484 14 78
Situated by Mogan Lake, this fine establishment has been in business since the 1980s. Crayfish dishes are its signature offering. Good wine selection.

ISPARTA:
Doğu Karadeniz Pide & Kebab ₺
Turkish/Regional
Ziraat Bankası yanı, Valilik Karşısı 1, 32100
Tel (0246) 212 15 19
Specializes in Black Sea-style *pides* and grills, enriched with butter. The best is *kavurmalı pide* for which *kavurma* (dried mutton) is stewed in its own juice for 12–14 hours.

ISPARTA: Özsüt ₺
Turkish
İstasyon Cad 23, Çağlar Ap, 32100
Mimar Sinan Cad 38, 32100
Tel (0246) 223 16 83
Part of a nationwide chain that originally served only desserts, this restaurant now offers a wide choice of soups, salads and grills in addition to delicious French- and Russian-style cakes.

ISPARTA:
Etopia Restaurant ₺₺
Turkish
İstanbul Cad, Toptancılar Sitesi 3, Blok 3, 32200
Tel (0246) 228 52 28
A meat lover's paradise. Specialties include meatballs with raisins, marinated T-bone steak and roast beef with puréed vegetables.

KONYA:
Cemo Etli Ekmek ₺
Turkish
Turkuaz İş Merkezi Selçuklu, 42060
Tel (0332) 249 66 66
Sample a Konya trademark, the *etli ekmek* – hand-chopped pieces of lamb or beef on a thin *pide* bread with tomatoes and onions. They also serve the usual grilled meat options.

KONYA: Hacı Şükrü ₺
Turkish
Devricedid Mah, Cem Sultan Cad 327/A, 42000
Tel (0332) 352 76 23
Visit Hacı Şükrü to try the *tandır kebabı* – the city's famous lamb tandoori cooked in an earthen pit for several hours. Traditionally the dish is eaten directly by hand but the restaurant does provide cutlery on request.

KONYA: Havzan Etli Ekmek ₺
Grill
Musalla Bağları Telgrafçı, Hamdibey Cad 8/A, 42060
Tel (0332) 236 14 14
Sample an interesting version of *etli ekmek* (Turkish-style pizza) laced with oregano or plain cheese. Also try the refreshing beet juice.

For more information on types of restaurants *see p340*

KONYA: Köşk Restaurant ₺
Regional
Akçeşme Mah, Topraklık Cad 66, 42100
Tel (0332) 352 85 47
Set in an historic 19th-century house, this restaurant has lots of local delicacies, including okra stew, which is a regional favourite. The honey and vinegar sherbet is delicious.

KONYA: Gül Bahçe ₺₺
Regional
Mevlana Külliyesi yanı, Karatay, 42010
Tel (0332) 353 07 68
Located next to the Mevlâna Museum, this restuarant serves excellent local Konya dishes. The grills, kebabs and oven-baked lamb are all tender and tasty. There are great views over the beautiful and peaceful Mevlana.

KÜTAHYA: Antepli Seyfi ₺
Regional
Cumhuriyet Cad 23, 43000
Tel (0274) 216 43 26
Gorge on aubergine (eggplant) and pistachio kebabs, *künefe* (a shredded wheat dessert with cheese), and *baklava* (sweet pastry), along with yogurt drinks and *şalgam suyu* (beet juice).

KÜTAHYA: Güral Sofrası ₺
Turkish
Perli Mah, Eskişehir Kütahya yolu, 43000
Tel (0274) 225 06 06
A wide selection of scrumptious Turkish dishes is available at this friendly restaurant owned and operated by the people behind the leading porcelain brand of Turkey. You can buy porcelain from the nearby shop.

KÜTAHYA: Ispartalılar Konağı ₺
Turkish
Pirler Mah, Germiyan Cad 58, 43000
Tel (0274) 216 19 75
Housed in a restored period dwelling, this atmospheric place serves up standard Turkish fare such as *tutmaç* (green lentil soup) and *cimcik* (local farfalle served with a yogurt dressing).

KÜTAHYA: Konağ ₺
Turkish
Kurşunlu Sok 13
Tel (0274) 223 88 44
Delightfully located in a converted Ottoman Turkish house, this great place features traditional favourites, including heart-warming stews and desserts such as figs stewed in milk. No alcohol.

The informal, simple interior of Koru Restaurant, Artvin

POLATLI: Kanca Lokantası ₺
Turkish
Cumhuriyet Mah, Bozkurt Cad, Ünal Ap 57, 06900
Tel (0312) 621 38 96
Relish wholesome Turkish home food. One of Turkey's most popular dishes, lima bean soup, is cooked beautifully here. This delicious soup, with tomato paste and veal, is served with rice pilaf.

POLATLI: Kebap 49 ₺
Kebab
Cumhuriyet Mah, Sümer Cad 48
Tel (0312) 623 69 70
A good choice for those going on a daily excursion to the ancient city of Gordion. Expect standard Turkish fare such as kebabs and *pides*; delicious food at reasonable prices.

The Black Sea

AMASRA: Canlı Balık ₺
Seafood
Küçük Liman Cad 8, 74300
Tel (0378) 315 26 06
Fresh flowers decorate tables at this elegant, waterfront restaurant. The salad made with 29 different herbs and vegetables is a popular draw. Interesting selection of desserts too – try the yogurt with honey and hazel nuts

AMASRA: Sahil Balık ₺₺
Seafood
Küçük Liman Cad15, 74300
Tel (0378) 315 34 65
The menu in the café area features omelettes, sandwiches and simple *mezes*, while the main restaurant offers a haven for seafood lovers with its extensive variety of dishes.

ARTVIN: Bizim Döner ve Köfte Salonu ₺
Kebab
İnönü Cad 77/C, 08000
Tel (0466) 212 15 51
Super kebabs and lamb specialties. Sometimes they also serve *baklava* (sweet pastry) or *kadayif* (a shredded wheat dessert). Lunch usually runs out by mid-afternoon, so come early.

ARTVIN: Koru Restaurant ₺
Regional
Koru Hotel Yeni Mah 19, Mayıs Cad, 08000
Tel (0466) 212 65 65
Sizzling grills and local delicacies such as *kuymak* (local fondue with cheese, butter and corn flour) and *silor* (a crispy *meze* made with phyllo, yogurt and butter) are on the menu here.

ÇAMLIHEMŞIN: Osmanlı Restaurant ₺
Regional
Ayder Yolu üzeri, Tarihi Köprü yanı Hoşdere Köyü Arderşen, 53400
Tel (0464) 752 42 23
En route to the Ayder plateau, this is mostly a seasonal restaurant serving hikers in summer. Delicious range of Black Sea dishes, as well as wonderfully cooked farm-raised trout.

ÇAMLIHEMŞIN: Yeşil Vadi Restaurant ₺
Regional
Merkez Mah, 53750
Tel (0464) 651 72 82
A spectacular location over the Fırtına river at the end of the valley. Sample traditional corn bread, *muhlama* (local fondue) and collard greens – the basis of their menu.

ÇAYELI: Hüsrev Lokantası ₺
Regional
Çayeli çıkışı, Hopa istikameti, Karayolu üzeri, 53200
Tel (0464 532 81 88
The restaurant advertises itself as the "master of beans". Serves a rich selection of Black Sea cusine. Ask for the cannellini bean soup prepared with diced beef, which this establishment is renowned for.

HOPA: Terzioğlu Restaurant ₺
Regionall
Sundura Mah, Rize Cad 27, 08600
Tel (0466) 351 51 11
Located in the Terzioğ lu Hotel close to the shore, this place is one of the few restaurants in Hopa. Come here to try the famous anchovy rice pilaf and sweet *laz böreği* (pastry with peppers). Great service.

KASTAMONU:
Münire Sultan Sofrası ₺
Regional
Hepkebirler Mah, Fevzi Efendi Cad, Münire Medresesi girişi, 37100
Tel (0366) 214 96 66
Housed inside a madrassa that was built in 1746, this restaurant serves delectable local fare. Order the *tirit* (bread rolls dipped in grape molasses) or savour the tasty broth with ground beef, garlic, yogurt and butter.

DK Choice

MAÇKA:
Coşandere Tesisleri ₺
Regional
Sümela Yolu Üzeri 5.km, Coşandere Köyü, 61750
Tel (0462) 531 11 90
A rustic restaurant on the way to Sumela Monastery by the Coşandere river. Don't let the simple interior of the venue dissuade you from dining here. The menu features delicious trout, rice pudding, *kuymak* (local fondue with cheese, butter and corn flour) and stuffed collard greens. There is a good selection of desserts on offer. They also organize local tours to the monastery and nearby uplands.

RIZE: Evvel Zaman Yöresel Yemek Lokantası ₺
Regional
Piri Çelebi Mah, Şeyh Cami Arkası Eski Rize Evi, 53100
Tel (0464) 212 21 88
A lovely restaurant set in a historic house at the centre of town, offering traditional Black Sea cuisine that includes *laz böreği* (pastry with peppers).

SAFRANBOLU:
Kadıoğlu Şehzade Sofrası ₺
Turkish
Arasta Sok 8, 78600
Tel (0370) 712 56 57
Excellent *pides* and soups are served in a traditional home. The town name comes from the rare plant of the region, saffron – used in the preparation of the exquisite *zerde* (rice pudding).

SAFRANBOLU:
Havuzlu Köşk ₺₺
Turkish
Dibekönü Cad 32, Bağlar, 78600
Tel (0370) 725 21 68
With tables placed around a small pool in the atrium, this intimate eatery has consistent service and focuses on traditional meat dishes.

Diners feasting on superb seafood in the restaurant at Sahil Balık, Amasra

SAFRANBOLU:
Taş Ev Sanat ve Şarap Evi ₺₺
International
Baba Sultan Mah, Hidirlik Yokusu 14, 78600
Tel (0370) 725 53 00
Popular wine bar and restaurant set in a historic stone house. It offers steaks, salads, pastas, and cheeses from Kars.

SAMSUN: Venn Café & Bistro ₺₺
International
Cumhuriyet Mah, Adnan Menderes Bulv 325, 55200
Tel (0362) 407 00 01
This place has a wide choice of international dishes. The service is attentive and the views are good. Look out for the weekly specials.

TRABZON: Bey Konağı ₺₺
Regional
Sahil Yolu Üzeri Bölge Trafiğe 300m Akyazı Beldes, 61195
Tel (0462) 273 25 14
Great place to sample Black Sea cuisine and seafood. Choose from a variety of anchovy dishes and vegetable specials made with collard greens.

TRABZON:
Galanima Restaurant ₺₺
Seafood/Grills
Adnan Kahveci Bulv 2, Sok 2, Söğütlü, 61300
Tel (0462) 248 71 27
Pleasant waterfront setting and courteous waiters ensure a good dining experience. Seasonal fish and grills on offer.

TRABZON:
Süleyman Restaurant ₺₺
Seafood/Kebab
Devlet Sahil Yolu Cad, Forum AVM, 61100
Tel (0462) 330 03 64
An upscale restaurant with a wide range of *mezes* and wines. There is occasional live music at the bar.

UZUNGÖL:
İnan Kardeşler Restaurant ₺
Regional
In the Uzungöl village, 61960
Tel (0462) 656 62 97
Rustic restaurant part of the İnan Kardeşler Hotel. Try the rare *benekli alabalık* (fried brown trout cooked with tomato and peppers).

YUSUFELI:
Hacıoğlu Cağ Döner Salonu ₺
Kebab
İnönü Cad, 08800
Tel (0466) 811 36 31
The *çağ* kebab – a döner kebab skewered over a charcoal fire is the only option here. Shepherd's salad or aubergine (eggplant) salad are good accompaniments to this dish.

YUSUFELI:
Yusufeli Saray Lokantası ₺
Turkish
Halitpaşa Cad 11, 08800
Tel (0466) 811 28 16
The restaurant is close to Çoruh River, the mecca of river rafters. Tasty, nourishing fare such as lentil soup, cannellini beans, rice pilaf and shepherd's salad.

The dining area at Coşandere Tesisleri, Maçka

For more information on types of restaurants *see p340*

Cappadocia and Central Anatolia

AMASYA: Ali Kaya Restaurant ₺
Kebab
Çakallar Mevkii, Amasya Merkez, 05100
Tel (0358) 218 13 16
Relish a mixed kebab platter while enjoying views of the river valley, mountains and the rock-cut tombs of the Pontic kings. Lamb and aubergine (eggplant) kebab is the signature dish.

AMASYA: Amasya Şehir Restaurant ₺₺
Kebab
Hatuniye Mah, H Teyfik Hafiz Sok 1, 05100
Tel (0358) 218 10 13
Do not miss the *baklali dolma* (rolled grape leaves stuffed with fava beans and wheat) here. On the banks of the Yeşil Irmak.

BOĞAZKALE: Aşıkoğlu Restaurant ₺
Turkish
Before the entrance of Hattuşaş city gate, 19310
Tel (0364) 452 20 04
Located near the capital city of the ancient Hittites, this is a spacious refectory-style cafeteria with self service. Phone ahead if you want to try the delicious grilled quail.

BELISIRMA: Belisirma ₺
Turkish
Ihlara Vadisi, Belisirma Köyü, 68570
Tel (0382) 457 30 57
No-frills restaurant with simple but tasty food. The menu has a choice of soups, grills and salads.

GÖREME: Dilbek ₺
Turkish
Meydan Nevşehir, 50180
Tel (0384) 271 22 09
This cave-set restaurant is the place to try *testi* kebab, a tasty meat and vegetable dish stewed in its own juices in a clay pot.

GÖREME: A'la Turca Restaurant ₺₺
Turkish/International
Gaferli Mah, Cevizler Sok 6, 50180
Tel (0384) 271 21 76
Delicious local *zülbiye* (chunks of lamb, pearl onions, tomato and garlic) and *calla* (veal, aubergine, tomato, pepper and garlic).

GÖREME: Cappadocian Cuisine ₺₺
Regional
Yani Uzundere Caddesi, Göreme, 50180
Tel (0536) 964 62 25
Home cooking at its best makes this *the* place to try local dishes at reasonable prices. You can watch the chef rustle up the dishes in her own kitchen.

GÜZELYURT: Karballa Restaurant ₺
Turkish
Karballa Hotel, Çarşı içi, Aksaray, 68100
Tel (0382) 451 21 03
The only proper restaurant in Güzelyurt, located in a former monastery with an impressive barrel-vaulted ceiling. Book ahead.

KAYSERI: Kaşıkla ₺
Turkish
Şeker Mah, Osman Kavuncu Bulv 370, Kocasinan, 38070
Tel (0352) 326 30 75
Feast on delicious *mantı* – the Turkish version of minced meat-filled ravioli, smothered in a rich, creamy yogurt and garlic sauce spiced up with sumac. They have grills and stews as alternatives.

KAYSERI: Beştepe Restaurant ₺₺
Turkish
Karacaoğlu Mah, Beştepeler Parkı, 38500 Melikgazi
Tel (0352) 347 18 18
This is a revolving restaurant with good views of the city and Mt Erciyes. The menu features local dishes with a focus on seafood. No alcohol.

KIRŞEHIR: Ahi Teras Restaurant ₺
Turkish
Terme Cad 8, 40000
Tel (0386) 214 14 24
Perfect combination of a bakery and restaurant. The café section of Ahi Teras offers *simit* (seeded bread ring) or *poğaça* (Balkan leavened bread).

UÇHISAR: Café Centrum ₺
International
Belediye Meydanı, 50200
Tel (0384) 219 31 17
Though it looks more like a teahouse, the food is surprisingly good. Try the vegetable and seafood pasta cooked in a traditional earthenware pot.

UÇHISAR: Elai Cappadocia ₺₺
International
Tekelli Mah, Eski Göreme Cad, 50240
Tel (0384) 219 31 81
A chic restaurant in sophisticated Uçhisar. The indoor section is a cave and the terrace offers superb views of the valley. The dishes are artfully prepared. Smart dress preferred for dinner.

ÜRGÜP: Dimrit Café & Restaurant ₺₺
Turkish
Yunak Mah, Teyfik Fikret Cad 40, 50400
Tel (0384) 341 85 85
Most main courses at Dimrit have a meat base but they also carry some seafood *mezes* and a fish of the day option. Lemon kebab and *testi* kebab (meat and vegetables cooked in a clay pot) are their specialties.

ÜRGÜP: Han Çırağan Restaurant ₺₺
Turkish/French
Cumhuriyet Meydanı 4, 50400
Tel (0384) 341 25 66
Owned and run by Francophiles settled in Cappadocia. Casual bar downstairs and a fine dining terrace space upstairs. Good cocktails.

DK Choice

ÜRGÜP: Old Greek House ₺₺
Turkish
Mustafapaşa Kasabası, 50420
Tel (0384) 353 53 06
A beautiful 19th-century Greek house with many preserved features. Original frescoes adorn the arches in the main courtyard shaded by grape vines. Enjoy authentic dishes cooked by the local village women. Seating is either at tables in the courtyard, or on cushions around low tables indoors. This is definitely the local favourite.

Low tables and cushions in one of the dining areas at the Old Greek House, Ürgüp

The elegant interior at Cerciş Murat Konağı, Mardin

ÜRGÜP: Şömine Restaurant ₺₺
Turkish
Cumhuriyet Meydanı 9, 50400
Tel (0384) 341 84 42
This is one of the most popular restaurants in Cappadocia. The menu features kebabs and other Turkish classics.

Eastern Anatolia

DIYARBAKIR:
Kaburgacı Selim Amca ₺₺
Turkish
Ali Emiri Cad 22/B Merkez
Tel (0412) 224 44 47
The original of a small chain with others in Mardin, Istanbul and Ankara, this place offers superb lamb ribs stuffed with piquant rice pilaf. No alcohol is served.

ERZURUM:
Güzelyurt Restaurant ₺
Turkish
Cumhuriyet Cad 42, 25100
Tel (0442) 234 50 01
Modern eatery, popular with local businessmen. Excellent *mezes*, kebabs and seafood. Good service.

GAZIANTEP: Imam Çağdaş ₺
Regional
Kale Cıvarı Uzun Çarşısı 49, 27100
Tel (0342) 231 26 78
A long established place that serves the city's best *lahmacun* (a thin, unleavened bread topped by spicy meat) and *baklava* (sweet pastry), as well as tender kebabs.

GAZIANTEP: Tahmis Kahvesi ₺
Café
Arasa Meydanı Elmacı Pazarı Şahinbey, 27000
Tel (0342) 232 89 77
Café serving traditional Turkish coffee. Try *menengiç* coffee, made with roasted pistachios and milk.

GAZIANTEP:
İncilipınar Antep Sofrası ₺₺
Regional
100 Yıl Kültür Parkı İçi, Ulu Cami yanı, 27100
Tel (0342) 234 26 57
Lovely place serving sour wheat balls in broth, *fındık lahmacun* (small, thin pizzas) and pistachio-filled *baklava* (sweet pastry).

KAHRAMANMARAŞ:
Küçük Ev Et Lokantası ₺
Turkish
İsmet Paşa Mah, Borsa Cad 11, 46000
Tel (0344) 223 25 55
Relish traditional stews with vegetables as well as kebabs. Simple setting and good service.

KAHRAMANMARAŞ:
Yaşar Pastanesi ₺
Ice cream
İsmet Paşa Mah, Trabzon Bulv, 27100
Tel (0344) 225 08 08
The original shop of the national chain Mado that popularized beaten ice cream made from goat's milk and roots of wild orchid.

KARS: Hanımeli Lokantası ₺
Regional
Orta Kapı Mah, Ordu Cad 65, 36100
Tel (0474) 212 61 31
Tasty vegetarian fare such as *manti* (Turkish ravioli) with caramelized onions and *bulgur* (wheat) pilaf with herbs.

KARS: Kars Kaz Evi ₺
Regional
Orta Kapı Mah, Şehit Polis Nuri Yıldız Sok 17, 36100
Tel (0474) 212 37 13
Come here for yogurt soup, goose roast and hot pickled vegetables. Book ahead.

MALATYA: Kaburga Sofrası ₺
Kebab
Cevatpaşa Mah, Karakavak, 44100
Tel (0422) 238 11 35
A no-frills city-centre eatery specializing in stuffed ribs, kebabs and meat dishes.

DK Choice

MARDIN:
Cerciş Murat Konağı ₺₺
Regional
Merkez 1, Cad 517, 47100
Tel (0482) 213 68 41
Housed in a beautifully restored mansion house, this is one of the best restaurants in Eastern Turkey. A trendsetter in excellent and unusual fare, this place offers distinctive dishes that will delight the tastebuds. Go for the set menu. Also on offer are unique Syrian Orthodox wines made from endemic Öküzgözü & Boğazakere grapes. Stunning views of the Mesopotamian Plain.

ŞANLIURFA:
Cevahir Konukevi Restaurant ₺
Regional
Büyükyol Cad, Selahaddin Eyyubi Cami Karşısı, 63000
Tel (0414) 215 93 77
Set in a historic building, Cevahir rustles up fiery Urfa dishes using Turkish hot pepper "Isot". Also organizes traditional folk evenings, which are a lot of fun.

ŞANLIURFA: Gülhan ₺
Regional
Atatürk Bulvarı, Urfa Merkez, 63200
Tel (0414) 313 33 18
This no-nonsense businessmen's establishment knocks out quality food at bargain prices – everything from hearty stews to soups and kebabs.

VAN: Sütçü Kenan ₺
Breakfast
Cumhuriyet Cad, Kahvaltıcılar Sok 7/A, 65100
Tel (0432) 216 84 99
Enjoy an elaborate breakfast buffet here. Also on offer is the famous Van honey as well as a selection of local cheeses, including some with herbs and some that have been smoked.

For more information on types of restaurants *see p340*

SHOPPING IN TURKEY

Even if you are not a shopper by nature, the varied and unusual selection of gifts found in Turkey's markets will easily tempt you. The grand shops and teeming streets of Istanbul are a world away from the ateliers and craft shops of smaller towns in rural areas. Outside Istanbul, you will also find bargaining *(see p130)* a less cut-throat pursuit. However, you are sure to encounter high-pressure sales pitches wherever you travel. The weekly market is a unique aspect of regional shopping. These markets are a holdover from the days of trading caravans, when shops as we know them did not exist. Traders still pay taxes to have a market stall, as they did 400 years ago. And the *zabıta* (municipal market police) still control weights, measures and prices.

Upmarket clothing boutique in Bodrum

Opening Hours

In large cities, shops are usually open from 9am to 7 or 8pm. But hours can be much extended in tourist and coastal areas, where many shops will stay open until midnight, seven days a week, particularly during the summer months, when the daytime heat discourages all but the most dedicated shoppers. Shopping malls are ubiquitous in most Turkish cities, and are usually open from 10am to 10pm.

In general, opening hours are much more flexible in rural areas. If you find a shop closed, you can ask where the owner is and it will not take long before someone tells him/her that there is a potential customer. Note that some shops may close during Muslim religious holidays.

How to Pay

Most shops that cater to tourists will be happy to accept foreign currency. If you can pay in cash, you can usually get a discount §on most goods. Exchange rates are often displayed in shops, and also appear in daily newspapers.

Credit cards are widely accepted for purchases (except in markets and smaller shops), and most vendors do not charge a commission. Visa, MasterCard and American Express are the most common, Diners Club less so. Vendors who accept credit cards may try to tell you that they will not be reimbursed for the transaction for several days, and ask you to pay a small compensatory commission. Resist this, and insist on paying without a commission. It is common for a vendor to ask you to go to the bank with him to draw the money out on your credit card. There is nothing wrong with this, but you will pay interest on your card for a cash advance. Note that very few shops in Turkey now accept travellers' cheques.

In rural markets, you will be expected to pay in cash. Some merchants will happily accept foreign currency.

Merchants in bazaars and markets expect customers to bargain. If you see something you want to buy, offer half the asking price. Increase the offer slightly if the merchant resists. He will then indicate whether he thinks that the bargaining should continue.

VAT Exemption

If you spend at least 118 TL in one shop, you can claim back the 18 per cent VAT (KDV in Turkey). VAT exemption is now widely available – look for the Tax Free Shopping logo displayed in the shop. The retailer gives you a Global Refund Cheque, which you should present to customs officials with your invoices and purchases for a cash refund when leaving Turkey.

Fresh herbs and spices, sold by weight at Kadıköy Market in Istanbul

Locally produced copper and brassware in the old quarter of Safranbolu

Buying Antiques

Before purchasing antique items, it is important to know what can and cannot be taken out of Turkey. The rule is that objects which are over 100 years old may be exported only with a certificate stating their age and granting permission to remove them from the country. Museums issue these certificates, as does the Culture Ministry in Ankara, who will also authenticate the correct age and value of an object, if necessary. The shopkeeper from whom you bought your goods will often know which museum will be authorizing your purchases for export. In theory, a seller should register with a museum all goods that are over 100 years old. In practice, sellers usually only seek permission after a particular item has been sold. In the past, antiques could be removed from Turkey without a certificate.

Although this has changed, the export of antiques is not forbidden, as some believe. If the relevant authorities permit your purchase to be exported, you can either take it with you or send it home, whether or not it is over 100 years old. Do take note, however, that taking antiques out of Turkey without proper permission

Ornate ceramic vase and saucer

is regarded as smuggling, and is a punishable offence.

Van cats and Kangal dogs are now also included in this category.

How to Send Purchases Home

If you have bought items from a reputable and trustworthy supplier, he will have an arrangement with an international courier company who can ship goods to your home address. Try to get your own copy of any shipping documents and an air waybill number. Do not use the post office (PTT) to send such items. Be aware that there are also some disreputable dealers, especially in carpets, who will either substitute an inferior item in place of the one you have bought or who will fail to send the goods. Beware of traders who advise you to ignore official rules.

Sizes and Measures

Turkey uses continental European sizes for clothes and shoes. Food and drink are sold in metric measures.

DIRECTORY

VAT Exemption

Global Refund
Tel (0212) 232 11 21.
W globalrefund.com

Antiques

Motif Handicrafts
Sirince Koyü, Selcuk, Izmir.
Tel (0232) 898 30 99.
W motiftr.com

Handicrafts and Gifts

Ceşni Turkish Handicrafts
Tunalı Hilmi Cad, Ertuğ Pasajı 88/44, Ankara.
Tel (0312) 426 57 87.

Gallery Anatolia
Hükümet Cad, Kaş.
Tel (0242) 836 19 54.
W gallery-anatolia.com

Robinson Crusoe Kitapevi
İstiklâl Cad 389, Beyoğlu, Istanbul. Tel (0212) 293 69 68. W rob389.com

Yörük Collection
Yerebatan Cad 35, Sultanahmet, Istanbul.
Tel (0212) 511 77 66.

Jewellery

Urart
Abdi Ipekçi Cad 18/1, Nişantaşıö, Istanbul.
Tel (0212) 246 71 94.
W urart.com.tr

Carpets/Kilims

Gallery Shirvan
Halıcılar Sok 50–54, Kapalıçarşı (Grand Bazaar) Istanbul.
Tel (0212) 522 49 86.

Istanbul Handicraft Center
Nuruosmaniye Cad 32, Istanbul. Tel (0212) 520 91 92. W istanbul handicraftcenter.com

Kaş and Carry
Liman Cad 10, Kaş.
Tel (0242) 836 16 62.
Fax (0242) 836 23 89.

Tribal Collections
Müze Yolu 24/C, Goreme, Nevşehir.
Tel (0384) 271 24 00.
W tribalcollections.net

Hand-worked Copperware

L'Orient
İçbedesten, Şerif Ağa Sok 22–23, Kapalıçarşı (Grand Bazaar), Istanbul.
Tel (0212) 520 70 46.

Linens

Özdilek
Yeni Yalova Yol, Bursa.
Tel (0224) 219 60 00.
W ozdilek.com.tr

Afyon
(on main highway junction of Ankara and Afyon road).
Tel (0272) 252 54 00.

Spices and Herbs

Ayfer Kaun
Mısır Çarşısı (Egyptian Bazaar) 7, Istanbul.
Tel (0212) 522 45 23.

Ucuzcular Kimya Sanayii
Mısır Çarşısı (Egyptian Bazaar) 51, Istanbul.
Tel (0212) 520 64 92.

What to Buy in Turkey

When it comes to shopping, nothing can compare with Istanbul's bustling bazaars, markets, shops and stalls. In contrast, the rural markets have an unhurried feel and unique products that often don't travel much beyond provincial boundaries, such as stout walking sticks made in Devrek (near Zonguldak), ceremonial pipes produced in Sivas and the angora goat-hair bedspreads and rugs made in Siirt. Markets are lively and colourful, and the best places to find handmade items that are produced in small quantities.

Pipes
Classic, beautifully crafted *nargiles* (water pipes) are still used by some Turkish men. They can make very attractive ornaments, even if you do not smoke.

Copper goblets

Copperware
Antique copperware can be very expensive. Newer items, however, are also available, at more affordable prices.

Antique copper water ewer

Box inlaid with mother-of-pearl

Box with painted scenes on bone inlay

Evil-eye pendants

Jewellery
Turkey produces stunning gold jewellery in original designs. Silver is also popular, and rings and necklaces are often set with precious stones. A simple blue glass eye *(boncuk)* is said to ward off evil.

Inlaid Wood
Jewellery boxes crafted from wood or bone, and then inlaid or painted, make unusual souvenirs. Backgammon players will be delighted at the delicate, inlaid rosewood backgammon *(tavla)* sets available in markets and shops around Turkey.

Ceramics
Ceramics are an important artistic tradition. The style varies according to the area of origin. İznik, Kütahya and Çanakkale are famous for ceramic production, but Avanos is also known for hand-painted pottery and porcelain.

Green jugs from Çanakkale

Blue and white decorated ceramic plate

Leather Goods

Shoes, handbags, briefcases and other leather accessories are good buys, as are jackets. For high-fashion, Istanbul is the place. Desa Deri is a good name all over Turkey. For acces- sories, look for the Matraş or Tergan brands.

Glassware

This elegant lamp is an example of the blue and white striped glassware called *çeşmibülbül*, which is made in the famous Paşabahçe works. The firm makes many utilitarian designs as well as an up-market range in fine lead crystal. Paşabahçe glassware makes a wonderful gift.

Çeşmibülbül lamp

Textiles

Hand-woven cloths, including *ikat* work (where the cotton is dyed as it is woven), and fine embroidery are just some of the range of textiles that can be bought. Turkey is also a leading producer of top-quality garments and knitwear. Bathrobes and towels are of high quality. Look for the Altınyıldız label for finest woollens and fabrics by the metre or yard.

Cotton *ikat* work

Embroidered scarves known as *oyalı*

Hand-printed *yazma* (shawls) from Tokat

Local Delicacies

Delicious sweets such as halva, Turkish delight and baklava are always popular. Many fragrant spices, as well as dried fruit and nuts are sold loose by weight in most markets and tourist shops throughout Turkey.

Halva

Nuts in honey

Turkish delight

Mulberries

Sunflower and pumpkin seeds

Apricots

Dried red peppers and aubergines

Chickpeas

Almonds

Pistachios

Turkish Carpets and Kilims

The ancient skill of weaving rugs has been handed down from generation to generation in Turkey. Rugs were originally made for warmth and decoration in the home, as dowry items for brides, or as donations to mosques. There are two main kinds of rug: carpets *(halı)*, which are knotted, and kilims, which are flat-woven with vertical (warp) and horizontal (weft) threads. Many foreign rugs are sold in Turkey but those of Turkish origin come in a particularly wide range of attractive colours. Most of the carpets and kilims offered for sale will be new or almost new; antique rugs are rarer and far more expensive.

A carpet may be machine-made or handmade. Fold the face of the rug back on itself: if you can see the base of the knots and the pile cannot be pulled out, it means that it is handmade.

Wool is the usual material for making a rug, although some carpets are made from silk.

Weaving a Carpet
Wool for rugs is washed, carded, spun and dyed before it is woven. Weaving is a cottage industry in Turkey; the women weave in winter, leaving the summer months for farming duties.

Carpet
This reproduction of a 16th-century Uşak carpet is known as a Bellini double entrance prayer rug.

Rug-making Areas of Western Turkey

The weaving industry in Turkey is concentrated into several areas of production, listed below. Rug designs are traditional to their tribal origins, resulting in a wide range of designs and enabling a skilled buyer to identify the area of origin.

Carpets

1. Hereke
2. Çanakkale
3. Ayvacık
4. Bergama
5. Yuntdağ
6. Balıkesir
7. Sındırgı
8. Milas
9. Antalya
10. Isparta

Kilims

11. Denizli
12. Uşak

Carpets and Kilims

13. Konya

Indigo

Madder

Camomile

Dyes
Before chemical dyes were introduced in 1863, plant extracts were used: madder roots for red; indigo for blue; and camomile and other plants for yellow.

The **"prayer design"** is inspired by a *mihrab*, the niche in a mosque that indicates the direction of Mecca *(see pp36–7)*.

The **tree of life** motif at the centre of the kilim is symbolic of immortality.

Buying a Rug

Before you buy a rug, look at it by itself on the floor, to see that it lies straight – without waves or lumps. Check that the pattern is balanced, the borders are of the same dimensions, and the ends are roughly the same width. The colours should be clear and not bleeding into one another. Bargaining is essential *(see p134)*, as the first price given is likely to be at least 30% higher than the seller really expects.

Buying a good-quality old rug at a reasonable price, however, is a job for an expert. The age of a rug is ascertained from its colour, the quality of the weaving and the design. Check the pile to make sure that the surface has not been painted and look for any repairs – they can easily be seen on the back of the rug. The restoration of an old carpet is acceptable but the repair should not be too visible. Make sure the rug has a small lead seal attached to it, proving that it may be exported, and ask the shop for a receipt.

Kilim

Kilims are usually made using the slit-weave technique by which a vertical slit marks a colour change.

The **width** of a rug is limited by the size of the loom. Most rugs are small because a large loom will not fit into a village house.

Kilim pieces are used to make a variety of smaller craft objects, also for sale in carpet shops.

Burdock motif

Chest motif

Motif from wolf track, crab or scorpion

Modern motif of a human figure

Motifs

The recurring motifs in rugs – some of them seemingly abstract, others more figurative – often have a surprising origin. For instance, many are derived from marks that nomads and villagers used for branding animals.

ENTERTAINMENT IN TURKEY

Almost every town and village in Turkey enjoys an annual celebration – be it grease wrestling, bull butting or simply an agricultural festival where farmers can show off their new tractors. Some of these events hark back to ancient seasonal rites, such as the Giresun Aksu Festival on the Black Sea in May. Even though most of these activities are aimed at locals, you are sure to be made welcome or even be a guest of honour. Spectator sports have

a very long history in Turkey. In classical times, the many amphitheatres of Anatolia hosted wrestling matches, circuses and risqué theatricals, which were entertainment as much as sport. Today, the average Turk identifies more with football (soccer) than any other type of sport. Visitors will soon notice the coloured banners and car horns blasting in support of favourite teams such as Beşiktaş, Galatasaray and Fenerbahçe.

Entertainment Guides

A number of magazines list events and entertainment in Istanbul and elsewhere in the country. Visitors to Istanbul and Bodrum should look for *The Guide*, while *The Gate* magazine is available for free at airports. Turkish Airlines also has its own publication, *Skylife*. *Jazz*, the quarterly Istanbul magazine, is a good source of information on various local jazz clubs, events and musicians.

Bodrum events guide

Art, Cinema, Theatre and Music Festivals

Turkey has a large cinema-going public. Most foreign films are shown in their original language with Turkish subtitles. The **Golden Orange Film Festival** is held annually in Antalya *(see pp222–3)*. Other items on the arts calendar are

the **International Opera and Ballet Festival** *(see p39)* held at Aspendos and the **Istanbul Biennial**, a multimedia arts festival that takes place on odd years (2015 and 2017). There is also an exciting series of Istanbul events that focus on theatre, classical music, film and jazz. Among these is the Istanbul Theatre Festival, held in May–June *(see p136)*.

Music festivals include the Akbank Jazz Festival, held in April and May in Istanbul, Ankara and other cities; the touring Efes Pilsen Blues Festival, held in the autumn; and the **Istanbul International Music Festival**, held each June.

Discos, Night Clubs and Belly Dancing

You will find huge, open-air discos in most summer resorts – Bodrum's Halikarnas *(see p198)* is the best known, with pillars and torchlight reminiscent of ancient times.

Despite a somewhat seedy reputation – especially in the back alleys of Istanbul – belly dancing *(see p27)* is outdoor family entertainment for Turks at seaside resorts in summer, and this is where you are likely to see the most authentic displays.

Special tourist floor shows at hotels and holiday villages in season frequently include folk dancing and traditional music. Folkloric whirling dervish performances are frequently staged but these are not the

Halikarnas disco in Bodrum

authentic troupe who perform during the Mevlâna Festival in Konya in December *(see p41)*.

Spectator Sports

Although football *(futbol)* is hugely popular, grease wrestling, or *yağlı güreş*, is Turkey's most time-honoured sport *(see p156)*. The main event is the four-day festival at **Kırkpınar**, near Edirne, in June. Wearing nothing but *kıspet* (black leather trousers soaked with olive oil), up to 1,000 men compete according to weight groups.

Camel wrestling *(see p41)* takes place every January and February. The biggest camel wrestling festivals are in Selçuk and around İzmir.

The Camel Classic Motor Racing series, which is held in the summer months, starts in Istanbul and follows a circuit that includes most of the western resort areas.

The major events on the horse racing calendar include the Gazi Race, held at the **Veli Efendi Hippodrome** in Istanbul at the end of June, and the

Borusan Istanbul Philharmonic Orchestra performing at the International Music Festival

Presidential Cup in Ankara at the end of October.

The Mediterranean coastal town of Alanya *(see p230)* is the venue for the **Alanya International Triathlon** (swimming, cycling and foot races) in October.

Theme Parks

Theme parks are growing in popularity in Turkey. **Minicity Antalya** *(see p222)* is a cross-cultural attraction that enchants visitors young and old, as does the original Istanbul version of a scale-model theme park, **Miniatürk**, which is located on the banks of the Golden Horn.

Some of the big holiday villages around Kemer or Alanya even have their own mini

theme parks tucked away within the hotel complex, but access to these is usually reserved for resident guests only.

At **Antalya Dolphin Parks**, the aquaparks, with their many slides, are popular with children of all ages.

Traditional Turkish Music and Dance

Traditional Turkish music is regularly performed at the Cemal Reşit Rey Concert Hall in Istanbul. In summer, recitals of Turkish music are occasionally organized in the Basilica Cistern *(see p90)*, which has wonderful acoustics. Traditional *Fasıl* music *(see pp26–7)* is best enjoyed

Folk dancers performing at Ephesus

live in *meyhanes* (taverns) such as Ece, Kallavi and Hasır in Istanbul. *Fasıl* is performed on instruments which include the violin, *kanun* (zither), *tambur* and *ud* (both similar to the lute).

Children

Children are welcome and will be fussed over almost everywhere. However, there are relatively few attractions that have been planned with children in mind. Beaches and theme parks are good bets, and holiday villages always have programmes for children. In Istanbul, there are large parks at Yıldız *(see pp128–9)* and Emirgan *(see p145)*. Also near Emirgan is Park Orman, with picnic areas, a pool, a giant walk-on chessboard and a theatre.

Miniature versions of Turkey's sights at Minicity Antalya

DIRECTORY

Art, Cinema, Theatre and Music Festivals

Ankara International Music Festival
Tel (0312) 427 23 53.
W ankarafestival.com

Ankara Theatre Festival
Tel (0312) 419 83 98.
W ankaratiyatro festivali.org

Aspendos International Opera & Ballet Festival
Ankara.
W aspendosfestival. gov.tr

Golden Orange Film Festival
Kültür Parkı İçi, Antalya.
Tel (0242) 238 54 44.
W altinportakal.org.tr

Istanbul International Music Festival
Tel (0212) 334 07 34.
W iksv.org

Istanbul Biennial
W biennialfoundation. org/biennials/istanbul-biennial/

Spectator Sports

Alanya International Triathlon
Alanya Municipality.
Tel (0242) 513 10 02.
W triathlon.org

Kırkpınar Grease-Wrestling
Edirne tourism office.
Tel (0284) 213 92 08.
W kirkpinar.org

Veli Efendi Hippodrome
Türkiye Jokey Kulübü, Osmaniye, Bakırköy, Istanbul.
Tel (0212) 543 70 96.
Tel (0212) 444 08 55.
W veliefendi.com

Theme Parks

Antalya Dolphin Parks
Several locations.
W antalyadolphinland. com

Miniatürk
Imrahor Cad, Sütlüceö, Istanbul.
Tel (0212) 222 28 22.
W miniaturk.com.tr

Minicity Antalya
Arapsu Mahallesi, Konyaaltı, Antalya.
Tel (0242) 229 45 45.
W minicity.antalya net.de

Music and Dance

Turkish music and dance are deeply rooted in history and tradition, having been influenced by Ottoman classics, mystical Sufi chants and Central Asian folk tunes, as well as jazz and pop. The result is a vibrant mosaic of old and new culture, an eclectic mixture of styles. In Turkey, visitors are treated to variety, from the meditational trance of Whirling dervishes and the merry twirling of folk dancers to the steady beat of Mehter bands, undulating rhythms of belly dancers and the stirring strains of *zurna* buskers. The country offers a musical and dance extravaganza second to none.

The *zurna* (shawm) is a member of the oboe family. Its characteristic, strident sound features strongly in Turkish folk music.

Traditional Instruments

Turkish instruments can be classified into three main groups. Stringed instruments include the *saz* and *ud*, winds the *kaval* and *ney*, and percussion the *davul* and *darbuka*.

11 strings

3 strings

Movable fret

Protective leather patch

Saz

Ud

Kaval   Ney

Saz **and** *ud* are the main string instruments. The saz is plucked. A piece of leather protects the belly of the ud from the strokes of the plectrum.

The woodwinds, *ney and kaval*, have ancient origins. The *ney* is made from reed, while the *kaval* is carved from the wood of the plum tree.

Stretched goatskin

Tupan stick

Percussion instruments originated with the Arabs. The body of the *darbuka* was traditionally ceramic, while the *davul* was metal.

Darbuka

Davul

Davul

A saz player entertains villagers in this 1950s photograph. Although tastes have changed, Turks remain proud of their musical traditions.

Sufi music uses the sounds of the ney, *ud* and *kanun* to interpret secular pieces based on the mode system and accompany poems that are chanted by a chorus. Through whirling motions, the dancers attain a trance-like state *(see p259)*.

The *Kılıç Kalkan*, or spoon dance, of the Black Sea region is performed to the rhythmic beating of two wooden spoons. Traditional folk dancing is an important part of Turkish culture, as are colourful regional costumes.

Low G clarinet

Bagpipes *(tulum)* made from goatskin

Belly dancing is popular in Turkey and remains a firm favourite with tourists. The sensuous rippling body movements, and gyrations of the hips, require impressive muscle control.

Arabesque and pop music are big business in Turkey, its heroes and heroines attaining cult status. Ibrahim Tatlıses is a much-loved performer of *arabesk*, Oriental-style music with lyrics that bemoan human hardship, while art-music trained Sezen Aksu is one of the top-selling pop stars.

Fasíl Music

Fasıl music is considered semi-classical and is performed in meyhane *(see p341) or concert halls. Its distinctive single harmony is similar to gypsy (*Çingene*) music, and both display a masterful control of traditional wind, string and percussion instruments. Fasıl music is intended to be listened to, but gypsy music is often accompanied by dancing.*

Mehter: Music of the Janissaries

Mehter performance

From 1299 until the dissolution of the Janissary corps in 1826, *mehter* music accompanied the armies of the Ottoman empire into battle, with a distinctive marching step to the rhythm of the words, "Gracious God is good. God is compassionate." Today the revived Mehter band performs at the Istanbul Military Museum *(see pp124–5)* and at Topkapı Palace.

OUTDOOR ACTIVITIES AND SPECIALIST HOLIDAYS

Turkey's geographical and climatic diversity presents almost limitless possibilities for outdoor enthusiasts. Anatolian winters are ideal for skiers and mountaineers, and the long, hot Mediterranean summers are perfect for yacht cruises, diving and windsurfing. Although spring and autumn are quite short, the temperate conditions are pleasant for walking and cycling. Turkey also has many options for themed holidays suitable for individuals or groups with particular interests, or those who prefer a more in-depth slant on historic events or sporting activities.

Walking and Trekking

Turkey's spectacular basalt and limestone mountain ranges provide ample opportunity for hiking. Since the opening of the first marked long-distance trek, the Lycian Way, in 1999 (see p206), marked walking trails have proliferated. The St Paul's Trail across the western Taurus, Abraham's Path in remote southeast Turkey and the Carian Way on the southern Aegean coast are just some of the routes. Non-marked hiking areas include the landscape of Cappadocia, with its celebrated "fairy chimneys" (see pp284–5).

Areas for good day walks include the mountains of Lycia on the Mediterranean coast, as well as the Turkish Lake District around Eğirdir (see p258). For more serious walking on unmarked trails, the Bolkar range and, in particular, the Aladağlar range (part of the Taurus Mountains), is superb as are the Kaçkar Mountains in the northwest. The highest peak in Turkey is Mount Ağrı (Ararat) (see pp318–19), near the eastern border with Armenia, rising to 5,165 m (16,945 ft). Adventure outfits like **Exodus, Mithra**

Travel and **World Expeditions** can organize guided treks. **Türkü Turizm** offers high-altitude trekking expeditions in the Kaçkar Mountains south of Rize (see p278). **Demavend Travel** is an excellent local outfit with treks on Ararat, the Kaçkar and the Aladağlar, as is **Middle Earth Travel**, with treks on the Lycian, St Paul and Carian trails among the routes on offer.

Mountaineering, Climbing and Canyoning

Turkey's mountain ranges offer fantastic opportunities for serious climbers. Deep snow in the Aladağlar and Kaçkar makes for great winter ski-mountaineering. **Bukla Tour** can organize treks and guides. **Bougainville** and **Get Wet** offer canyoning excursions.

Skiing

Turkey's most popular ski centre is Uludağ, near Bursa (see p163). It has many lifts and a range of runs. Kartal, between Istanbul and Ankara, offers newer facilities and less crowded runs. Near Isparta, the Davraz ski centre has reliable snow, two chairlifts, a couple of good hotels and more accommodation in Eğirdir. Erciyes, near Kayseri, has hotels, reliable snowfalls and long runs. Though remote, Palandöken (see p323) combines a long season with 45 km (28 miles) of piste well served by chairlifts and several very good hotels. **İçem Tour** will make bookings at most ski resorts.

The rapids of the Çoruh River are only for experienced rafters

Whitewater Rafting

In the northeast, the Çoruh River has Grade-5 rapids and is the ideal testing ground for serious rafters. Several overseas agencies offer trips. In contrast, day trips on the Köprülü River (between Antalya and Side), or the Dalaman river near Fethiye, are suitable for families and novices. Local agencies and hotels near to both rafting rivers offer day rafting packages on the rivers. **Adrift** offers Çoruh rafting tours; **Medraft** and others run day tours on the Köprülü River.

Paragliding

Few activities combine the serenity and high altitude scenery of paragliding. Babadağ Mountain, above the coastal resort of Olü Deniz (see p216)

The popular Palandöken ski resort near Erzurum

Paragliding above the Mediterranean coast near Ölü Deniz

and the mountain ridge above Kaş (see p218) both have the ideal updrafts, vistas and landing pads needed for this breathtaking sport. **Skysports** is an experienced and reputable company, offering expert tuition and equipment hire.

Horse Riding and Pony Trekking

Cappadocia's trails weave through valleys and uplands. **Bagana Ranch** near Antalya offers excellent accommodation, lessons and trail riding. In Istanbul, the **Klassis Golf and Country Club** has an indoor ring and jumping facilities. The best place for trail riding is the Equestrian Centre at Daday, a village near Kastamonu (see p268).

Sailing and Cruising Holidays

The Aegean and western Mediterranean coasts are perfect for cruises aboard comfortable gulets (traditional wooden sailing vessels). One- or two-week cruises (called "blue voyages") are an excuse to relax, swim and sunbathe, with occasional forays ashore for shopping or dining. Those with a historical bent can combine one of these cruises with visits to the many fascinating ancient sites along the coast, guided by an expert in Greek and Roman history. The chain of marinas, each about a day's sailing apart, also offer secure moorings and facilities for private yachts. **Arya Yachting** in Bodrum or the UK's

Alternative Travel Group offer cruises. **Westminster Classic Tours** have cruises with lectures and site visits. **Gino Group** in Marmaris rents and sells new and good-value reconditioned sailing yachts.

Diving

Marmaris, Bodrum, Fethiye Kaş and Alanya are all leading diving resorts, offering warm water and perfect conditions with splendid visibility. Here, qualified scuba instructors who are accredited to the Professional Association of Diving Instructors (PADI), offer tuition which takes novices as well as more experienced divers through an internationally recognized diving certificate course.

The **European Diving Centre** in Fethiye and **Ayışığı Diving** in Istanbul both offer high quality tuition and can be recommended.

Beaches

Turkey's Mediterranean, Aegean and Black Sea coasts have many beaches, offering a wide range of seaside pursuits.

Conditions are generally warm, though the Black Sea can be rough at times, with big waves. The Bodrum peninsula has ideal conditions for sailing and dinghy racing. Water-skiing, water parasailing and jet skiing are offered at major beachside hotels and resorts.

The best place near Istanbul for swimming and watersports such as water-skiing and windsurfing is the Princes' Islands (see p162).

Hotel-based Sports

Five-star hotels in the major resorts have good hard tennis courts. Most four- and five-star hotels also organize table tennis, billiards, archery, step dancing and aerobics; even some three-star hotels offer beach volleyball and excellent swimming pools.

Golf

The mild winter and early spring make golf a year-round sport in Turkey. There are more than 10 purpose-built courses at Belek, east of Antalya (see p228). **Pamfilya Travel Agency** can arrange tailor-made tours for amateurs or championship golfers. Near Istanbul, the **Kemer Golf and Country Club** has a championship course.

Diving school in Marmaris, offering courses at all skill levels

Historical and Cultural Tours

Given Turkey's wealth and variety of historic sites, it is no surprise that these are what attract most visitors to the country. Tourists who wish to visit ancient and classical sites can do so in the company of an expert in the field. The classical sites of the west and south, Ephesus *(see pp186–7)* and Pergamum *(see pp180–81)* in particular, draw large crowds of visitors, especially in the summer months. Others under excavation, such as Sagalassos and Aphrodisias *(see pp192–3)*, are also very impressive and may be less congested. Some sites, such as Patara and Xanthos *(see p218)* – whose chief tombs are on view in the British Museum – can be visited as part of a *gulet* tour *(see p373)*.

Istanbul deserves careful exploration, particularly its churches, mosques and museums. Since the major sites in Istanbul and around Göreme in Cappadocia are situated fairly close together, walking tours are an attractive option.

Much more recent history is movingly commemorated on the Gallipoli peninsula *(see pp172–3)*, site of some of the fiercest and most tragic battles of World War I.

The Traveller, **Andante Travels** and **Martin Randall** all offer tours of the classical sites, with Andante also covering much of the rest of the country. **Gallipoli and Troy Tours** operates tours to the Dardanelles and Gallipoli.

Memorial cemetery, Gallipoli

Wildlife Tours

Turkey's diverse habitats support many endemic plant species, especially of orchids and bulbs, with tulips being perhaps the best-known examples. This diversity, coupled with the country's pivotal position along migration routes between Europe, Asia and Africa, assures the presence of numerous bird species from three continents. In spring and autumn, over 200 species can be spotted in the course of a two-week holiday. DHKD, a local conservation group, records observations and works to preserve habitats such as wetlands. In-depth birding holidays are available from **Greentours**.

Marble head of Athena

The House of the Virgin Mary, near Ephesus *(see p186)*

Religious Tours

Modern-day pilgrims can follow in the footsteps of the Apostle Paul, whose faith led him from Tarsus to Ephesus and beyond. Visitors can tour the "Seven Churches" founded by Paul, and see the small house near Ephesus where the Virgin Mary is said to have spent her last days.

There are also quite a few Armenian and Greek Orthodox churches in Istanbul *(see p118)* that are still active. In southeastern Turkey, there are haunting Syrian Orthodox churches and monasteries.

Pacha Tours offer specialist itineraries for pilgrims who would like to trace the wanderings of St Paul.

A bird hide in the Göksu Delta, near Silifke

Rail Tours

Turkey's rail network *(see pp392–3)* is extensive and is being rapidly modernized. However, several antiquated lines, on which the trains retain old-fashioned couchettes and dining carriages, allow rail buffs to see the country in a relaxed and interesting way.

For rail buffs, there is an open-air rail museum at Çamlık, near Selçuk *(see p184)*, with well-marked displays and fine examples of vintage steam locomotives.

The most popular rail trips are from Istanbul to Kars, close to the Armenian border, and from Istanbul to Van in the southeast (which includes a ferry crossing of Lake Van). Both journeys take around three days, and are better undertaken in shorter hops. The Dutch company **SNP Reiswinkel** offers tours of the Istanbul–Kars route, with day breaks for exploration on foot.

Other Specialist Holidays

Several operators offer more specialized holidays that involve particular pursuits such as photography, or painting and sketching. **Kaş Eflatun Art Camp**, for example, runs weekly residential painting courses, while **Fotografevi** offers photographic tours.

Several companies use Turkey's relaxed atmosphere and natural beauty to offer breaks that include such activities as yoga, massage, tai chi and meditation. For details on active holidays, try **Exclusive Escapes**.

DIRECTORY

Ministry of Culture and Tourism

(For general information)
Atatürk Bul 29, Ankara.
Tel (0312) 309 08 50.
Fax (0312) 312 43 59.
w kulturturizm.gov.tr

Adventure Travel Companies

Bougainville
Çukurbağli Cad 10, Kaş.
Tel (0242) 836 37 37.
w bt-turkey.com

Demavend Travel
Esenbey Mah, Sefik Soyer
Meydani, Nigde.
Tel (0388) 232 73 63.
w demavendtravel.com

Exodus
Grange Mills, Weir Road,
London, SW12 ONE, UK.
Tel (44) 020 8772 3936 or
0845 869 8254.
w exodus.co.uk

Mithra Travel
Kılıçaslan Mah,
Hesapçı Sok 70.
Tel (0242) 248 77 47.
w mithratravel.com

Türkü Turizm
İnönü Cad 47,
Çamlihemşin, Rize.
Tel (0464) 651 72 30.
w turkutour.com

Walking and Trekking

Demavend Travel
(See Adventure Travel
Companies).

Exodus
(See Adventure Travel
Companies).

Middle Earth Travel
Karşı Bucak Cad, Göreme.
Tel (0384) 271 25 59.
w middleearthtravel.
com

Türkü Turizm
(See Adventure Travel
Companies).

World Expeditions
81 Craven Gardens,
London SW19 8LU, UK.
Tel (44) 20 8545 9030.
w worldexpeditions.
com

Mountaineering, Climbing and Canyoning

Bougainville
(See Adventure Travel
Companies.)

Bukla Tour
İstiklâl Cad, Postacilar Sok
1/2, Beyoğlu, Istanbul.
Tel (0212) 245 06 35.
w climbararat.com
w bukla.com

Get Wet
Eski Lara Yolu 198/1,
Şirinyalı, Antalya.
Tel (0242) 324 08 55.
w getwet.com.tr

Skiing

İcem Tour
Mimar Mehmet Aga Cad
34, Sultanahmet, Istanbul.
Tel (0212) 638 19 86.
w icemtour.com

Whitewater Rafting

Adrift
127 High St, Hungerford
RG17 0DL, UK.
Tel (44) 1488 711 52.
w adrift.co.uk

Medraft
Meydankavağı, Şehıtler
Cad, Antalya.
Tel (0242) 312 57 70.
w medraft.com.tr

Paragliding

Skysports
Carsi Cad, Tonoz Otel Alti,
Ölü Deniz, Fethiye, Muğla.
Tel (0252) 617 05 11.
w skysports-turkey.
com

Horse Riding and Pony Trekking

Bagana Ranch
Kemer, Antalya.
Tel (0242) 425 22 70.
w baganahorseclub.
com

Klassis Golf and Country Club
Seyman Köyü,
Altıntepe Mevkii, Silivri
(W of Istanbul).
Tel (0212) 710 13 13.
w klassisgolf.com.tr

Sailing and Cruising Holidays

Alternative Travel Group
69–71 Banbury Road,
Oxford OX2 6PE, UK.
Tel (44) 1865 315 678.
w atg-oxford.co.uk

Arya Yachting
Caferpaşa Cad 21/A,
Bodrum. **Tel** (0252) 316
15 80. w aryatours.com

Gino Group
Netsel Marina, Marmaris.
Tel (0252) 412 06 76.
w ginogroup.com

Westminster Classic Tours
108 Monkleigh Rd,
Morden SM4 4EP, UK.
Tel (44) 20 8286 7842.
w westminsterclassic
tours.com

Diving

Ayısığı Diving
Bağdat Cad, İçlaiye Apt
24/4, Kızıltoprak, Istanbul.
Tel (0216) 418 22 44.
w ayisigidiving.com

European Diving Centre
Fevzi Cakmak Cad 53,
Fethiye.
Tel (0252) 614 97 71.
w europeandiving
centre.com

Golf

Kemer Golf and Country Club
Göktürk Beldesi,
Kemerburgaz, Istanbul.
Tel (0212) 239 70 10.
w kg-cc.com

Pamfilya Travel Agency
İsıklar Cad 57/B, Antalya.
Tel (0242) 243 15 00.
w pamfilya.com

Historical and Cultural Tours

Andante Travels
The Old Barn, Old Road,
Alderbury, Salisbury
SP5 3AR, UK.
Tel (44) 1722 713 800.
w andantetravels.co.uk

Gallipoli and Troy Tours

Binbirdirek Mah,
Klodfarer Cad 3,
Istanbul.
Tel (0212) 516 53 00.
w gallipolianzac.com

Martin Randall
Barley Mow Passage,
Chiswick, London W4, UK.
Tel (44) 20 8742 3355.
w martinrandall.com

The Traveller
2 Bury Place, London
WC1A 2JL, UK.
Tel (44) 20 7269 2770.
w the-traveller.co.uk

Wildlife Tours

Greentours
Gauledge Lane,
Longnor, Buxton
SK17 0PA, UK.
Tel (44) 1298 83563.
w greentours.co.uk

Religious Tours

Pacha Tours
295 Madison Avenue,
New York, USA.
Tel (800) 722 4288 (US).
w pachatours.com

Rail Tours

SNP Reiswinkel
Molukkenstraat 7,
Nijmegen, Netherlands.
Tel (30) 024 327 70 00.
Fax (30) 024 327 70 99.

Other Specialist Holidays

Exclusive Escapes
Alexander House, 15
Princes Road,
Richmond,
TW10 6DQ, UK.
Tel (44) 20 8605 3500.
w exclusiveescapes.
co.uk

Fotografevi
Tütüncu Çikmazı 4,
Galatasaray, Beyoğlu,
Istanbul.
Tel (0212) 249 02 02.

Kaş Eflatun Art Camp
Çukurbag, Kaş,
Antalya.
Tel (0242) 839 54 29.
w kasartcamp.com

Spas and Hot Springs

Turkey's geophysical matrix, which occasionally causes earthquakes and tremors, has an unexpected upside seen in the geothermal springs on which the country seems to be floating. Over 1,000 thermal hot springs (and some icy cold ones) bubble from deep seismic fissures at high temperatures and under great pressure. Roman armies soothed battle wounds in the rich, therapeutic mineral pools. Turkish families have taken the waters for decades. Medical tourism in Turkey is on an upward curve and is marvellously rejuvenating.

Bathers in the rehabilitating calciferous pools at Pamukkale

Geothermal Spring Resorts

Turkey's most potent thermal springs have a high mineral content. There are springs all over the country but very few have accommodation facilities; these are among the best.

Reputed to have soothed the wounds of Agamemnon's Greek soldiers, **Balçova Thermal Hotel** was a pioneer in thermal tourism. The 70°C (158°F) geothermal springs have an exceptional mineral count.

Bursa is one of Turkey's most venerable spa cities. The **Yeni Kaplıca** complex is historic and hot, 85°C (185°F). The spa for men is a traditional 16th-century domed building. Mineral baths and treatments for families are also available.

Of the many geothermal areas north and west of Ankara, Kızılcahamam is best suited to accommodate visitors. Among these is the **Hotel Ab-ı Hayat**.

The mineral waters at **Yalova Thermal Hot Springs** bubble up at 65° C (149°F) from a deep volcanic source and are considered to be

the most remedial in Turkey. The cascading calciferous pools at Pamukkale *(see p190)* are very popular and a short distance away at Karahitit, the waters contain iron and the source is much hotter. **Pam Thermal Hotel** is one of the most professional and well-run of the thermal hotels.

Five-star Spas

Turkey's leading spa hotels are located in Istanbul, Ankara and near Bodrum. None has geothermal springs but all offer a sensual and invigorating experience.

The **Kempinski Hotel Barbaros Bay** is a renowned Six Senses Spa, the only in Turkey. Eastern traditions and remedies meet Aegean atmosphere at this fine spa.

One of the country's most spiritual spas is at **Hôtel Les Ottomans**, which adheres to oriental Feng Shui concepts.

Ankara's impressive **Swissôtel Amrita Spa and Wellness Centre** is huge and combines heavenly, healthy and wholesome treatments.

At the **Ritz Carlton's Laveda Spa**, staff are superbly trained

and the focus is on inner health and harmony. The healthy regime promotes relaxation and rejuvenation.

Hamams

The traditional Turkish bath, or *hamam (see p81)*, was an integral part of the Ottoman social structure, and scrubbing and massages were a ritual procedure. Top spa hotels all have *hamams*. Look for quality in the central stone – it should be transparent, smooth and highly polished. Bursa's **Çakır Hamam** is simple but friendly and dates from 1484. The historic Ottoman **Cağaloğlu Baths** in Istanbul are very popular. On the Aegean coast, **Bodrum Hamam** *(see p198)* has a hotel pick-up service. **Sefa Hamami** in Antalya is a restored 13th-century Seljuk bath, while the **Kelebek Hotel** is a cave hotel in Göreme with a splendid *hamam*.

Therapeutic Spas

Medical tourism is popular in Turkey and several spas concentrate on specific health problems. **Natur-Med Thermal Springs & Health Resort** offers treatments for, among others, chronic disease, weight loss and detoxification. Near Sivas *(see p299)* in the secluded hills are the **Kangal Fish Springs**, a healing centre for psoriasis. The hot springs contain selenium and support a type of fish that nibbles affected skin. Documented since Roman times, **Ayaş İçmece ve Kaplıcaları** is noted for cures and rehabilitation. There are two spas here sharing a thermal

The Turkish hamam at the luxury Hôtel Les Ottomans

Clients taking the healing waters of Natur-Med Thermal Spring

Set in a tranquil, rural location on the banks of the Meander River, **Umut Thermal Resort and Spa** is ideal. Standards are high and the atmosphere is clinical but friendly.

Located on the Meander River embankment, **Yenice Ilıcası Kamara İşletmesi** offers 15 basic rooms; however, clientele return regularly for its uncomplicated charm.

source. The waters are so hot and heavily mineralized that drinking and bathing are done under medical supervision.

Rural Spas

Ayder is a well-known Black Sea thermal centre, with hot springs ideal for physical therapy and rehabilitation. The facilities bask in pastoral high-altitude surroundings, with about 20 simple pensions.

A delightful spa village of small streams, gardens and rustic bridges forms the backdrop for the thermal waters of **Hamamayağı**. The healing spring contains radon in therapeutic quantities.

A remedial watering hole since the Phrygia era (800 BC), the **Hüdai** thermal waters relieve many of life's modern twinges.

Aqua Accessories

Beautiful spa and *hamam* products can be found in shops such as **Derviş Bath Accessories**, which has two outlets in Istanbul's Grand Bazaar, and **Abdullah Natural Products**.

Derviş Bath Accessories' products

TOURIST INFORMATION

Geothermal Spring resorts

Balçova Thermal Hotel
Vali Hüseyin Öğütcen Cad 2, Balçova, İzmir.
Tel (0232) 259 01 02.
Ⓦ balcovatermal.com

Hotel Ab-ı Hayat
Kazım Karabekir Cad, Kızılcahamam, 06890.
Tel (0312) 736 56 20.
Ⓦ ab-ihayat.com

Pam Thermal Hotel
Beytur Turizm İşletmeleri A. Ş., Karahayıt, Pamukkale.
Tel (0258) 271 41 40.
Ⓦ pamhotel.com

Yalova Thermal Hot Springs
Yalova Termal, 77400.
Tel (0226) 675 74 00.
Ⓦ yalovatermal.com

Yeni Kaplıca
Kükürtlü Mah, Yenikaplıca Cad 6, Osmangazi, Bursa.
Tel (0224) 236 69 68.

Five-star Spas

Hôtel Les Ottomans
Muallim Naci Cad 168, Kuruçeşme, Istanbul.
Tel (0212) 359 15 00.
Ⓦ lesottomans.com

Kempinski Hotel Barbaros Bay
Kızılağaç Köyü, Gerenkuyu Mevkii, Yalıçiftlik, Bodrum,
Tel (0252) 311 03 03. Ⓦ kempinski-bodrum.com

Ritz-Carlton
Süzer Plaza Elmadağ, 34367, Şişli, Istanbul.
Tel (0212) 334 44 44.
Ⓦ ritzcarlton.com

Swissôtel Amrita Spa and Wellness Centre
Yıldızevler Mah, Jose Marti Cad 2, Çankaya, Ankara.
Tel (0312) 409 36 66.
Ⓦ amritaspa.com

Hamams

Bodrum Hamam
Cevak Şakir Sok, Fabrika Sok 42, Bodrum.
Tel (0252) 313 41 29.
Ⓦ bodrumhamami.com.tr

Cağaloğlu Baths
Cağaloğlu, Istanbul.
Tel (0212) 522 24 24.
Ⓦ cagalogluhamami.com.tr

Çakır Hamamı
Atatürk Cad 101, Osmangazi, Bursa.
Tel (0224) 221 25 80.

Kelebek Hotel
Aydinli Mah, Yavuz Sok 1, Göreme.
Tel (0384) 271 25 31.

Sefa Hamami
Kokatepe Sokak Barbaros Mahallesi 32, Antalya.
Tel (0242) 241 23 21.
Ⓦ sefahamam.com

Therapeutic Spas

Ayas İçmece ve Kaplıcaları
İçmeler Mevkii Ayaş, Beypazarı, Ankara.
Tel (0312) 718 31 01.
Ⓦ ayasicmece.com.tr

Kangal Fish Springs
Kavak Köyü Mevkii, Kangal, Sivas.
Tel (0346) 469 11 51.
Ⓦ baliklikaplica.net

Natur-Med Health Resort
Davutlar, Kuşadası.
Tel (0256) 657 22 80.
Ⓦ natur-med.com.tr

Rural Spas

Ayder Turizm A.Ş.
Çamlihemşin, Rize.
Tel (0464) 657 20 37.
Ⓦ ayder.com.tr

Hamamayağı Tesisleri
Between Havza and Ladık.
Tel (0362) 782 00 01/02.

Hüdai Yeni Thermal Hotel
Sandıklı, Afyon.
Tel (272) 535 73 30.
Ⓦ hudai.sandikli.bel.tr

Umut Thermal Resort and Spa
Hasköy Tekke Köyü Yolu üzeri 9 km, Kokar Hamam Mevkii, Sarayköy, Denizli.
Tel (0258) 426 11 01.

Yenice Ilıcası Kamara İşletmesi
Yenicekent, Buldan, Denizli.
Tel (0258) 434 60 97.
Ⓦ umutthermal.com

Aqua Accessories

Abdullah Natural Products
Alibaba Türbe Sok 25, Nurosmaniye, Istanbul.
Tel (0212) 526 30 70.
Ⓦ abdulla.com

Derviş Bath Accessories
Kesiciler Cad 33–35 Kapalıçarşı, Istanbul.
Tel (0212) 514 45 25.
Ⓦ dervis.com

SURVIVAL GUIDE

PRACTICAL INFORMATION

Many first-time visitors to Turkey expect the country to be sedate and reserved, due to the influence of Islam, so the exuberant and lively character of Turkish life comes as a pleasant surprise. Observing a few local customs and learning some basic Turkish words or phrases will get you off to a good start. Always show respect for the laws of the country and for its religious differences, culture and class structure, even if you do not agree with the beliefs or politics. By and large, Turkish people are very friendly and all Turks will welcome any effort to appreciate their lifestyle and respect their traditions.

Visas and Passports

Visitors to Turkey must have a full passport with at least six months' validity. Citizens of the following countries require a visa paid for in cash at the point of entry into Turkey: UK and Ireland (£10), Australia and the USA (US$20) and Canada (US$60). Citizens of some countries must apply for a visa before arrival. Tourist visas are available electronically from www.evisa.gov.tr. Requirements change, so for up-to-date information, visit www.mfa.gov.tr or contact the Turkish consulate or embassy in your country.

Customs Information

Airports and main road entry points offer a full customs service, but customs hours at major ports are 8:30am–5:30pm on weekdays. Outside these hours, a fee must be paid for a customs official to carry out their inspections.

You can buy duty-free items at the airport upon entering the country. Visitors over 18 can bring in 1.5 kg (3 lb) of coffee, 120 ml (4 fl oz) of perfume, 1 litre or two 75 cl bottles (35 fl oz) of spirits and 200 cigarettes. There is no limit to how much currency you can bring in. The maximum when leaving is US$5,000 (or equivalent), but this is rarely enforced. You need a permit to export antiquities (see p363).

Turkey is strict regarding drugs; sniffer dogs are used at some airports. Contact the Turkish consulate or embassy in your country for more customs information.

Customs service emblem

Tourist Information

The sign for a tourist information office is a white "i" on a green background in a white box. There are tourist offices in most Turkish cities and resorts. They are usually open 9am–5pm Monday to Saturday, but some stay open later in summer; the one at Atatürk Airport is open 24 hours a day. In provincial areas the staff may speak only basic English. The Turkish tourist board in your own country will also be a good source of information.

Admission Fees and Opening Hours

Entry fees to major attractions in Turkey's main tourist areas (Istanbul, Cappadocia, the Western Mediterranean and the Aegean) are comparable to those in Europe. Lesser-known establishments are cheaper, as are sights in less touristy areas. Most museums close one day a week, often Monday, though closing days vary in Istanbul. Exhibits in the major museums are usually labelled in both Turkish and English, while less visited venues may have information in Turkish only. Museums tend to open from 9am to 5:30pm, sometimes with a lunch break. Archaeological sites usually operate from 9am to 7pm in summer and from 9am to 5pm in winter.

Most banks are open from 8:30am to 5pm Monday to Friday, and state banks close for lunch from noon to 1:30pm. Exchange offices (döviz) are usually open until 8 or 9pm (see p384).

Visitors on the steps leading up to Dolmabahçe Palace

Shops open from 9am to 7pm (see p362). Some close on Sundays, although shopping malls, supermarkets and small grocers are usually open seven days a week from 10am to 10pm.

Etiquette

Turks tend to dress smartly. In eastern areas of the country, conservative cities such as Konya and Kayseri, and devout areas of Istanbul, such as Fatih, many women cover their heads, arms and legs in public. Visitors are not expected to follow suit, but be aware that some Turks may be offended by exposed limbs. Public drunkenness is frowned upon, and men should avoid walking around shirtless away from the beach, even in resorts.

Make sure you always show respect for Atatürk, whose image you will see often.

Istanbul has a lively gay scene. Homosexual visitors are unlikely to experience problems, but it is best to avoid overt displays of physical affection.

Smoking is prohibited in all enclosed spaces, including public transport, restaurants and bars, and even water-pipe (nargile) cafés.

Visiting Mosques

Large mosques are open all day, closing after last prayers in the evening, while smaller ones open only for the five daily prayer times (namaz). Non-Muslims should not enter a mosque during prayers, the times of which are clearly displayed on a board outside or just inside the mosque. Prayer times are also signalled by the call to prayer (ezan) from a loudspeaker fixed to the minaret of the mosque.

Dress appropriately when visiting a mosque (see pp36–7). Everybody should cover their shoulders, and women should cover their heads, too; do not wear shorts or mini-skirts, and remove your shoes. Shawls to cover your head, arms and shoulders are provided by some mosques. Shoes are usually left on racks at the entrance, but you may prefer to carry them with you since theft is not unknown. Some mosques also provide elasticated plastic bags to slip over your shoes instead of asking you to remove them. Make as little noise as possible inside and show consideration for anyone who is praying there.

Language

Turks will appreciate any attempt to speak their difficult language, so try to learn a few words. Menus are printed in several languages in many restaurants and cafés, and in areas with lots of foreign visitors most shopkeepers can speak one other language.

Public Conveniences

Public toilets are thin on the ground in Turkish cities, but most mosques have facilities for both men and women. As with public toilets, there is usually an attendant and a small fee to pay on exit. Toilets are marked *Bay* for men and *Bayan* for women. The attendant may supply toilet paper, but it is a good idea to carry tissues with you.

If you are reluctant to use the squat toilets generally found in public and mosque facilities, you can ask to use the western-style toilets in most hotels, restaurants and cafés. Museums and major sights all have toilets, too, and outside the cities, motorway service areas have excellent, often free, washroom facilities.

Time

Turkey is 2 hours ahead of Greenwich Mean Time and British Summer Time. New York is 7 hours behind and Los Angeles is 10 hours behind.

Electricity

Turkey's electrical current is 220–240 volts AC. Plugs have two round pins, which fit most European two-pin plugs. Bring a universal adaptor for all other voltages.

Colourful display of fruit and vegetables at a market stall

Responsible Tourism

Environmental awareness is a fairly new concept in Turkey, though a few recycling bins grace the streets of Istanbul and other cities. Traditionally, recycling is carried out by the Roma community who, pulling handcarts fitted with giant sacks, scavenge through the waste bins left out on the street for collection. Plastics, paper, metal and glass are sold to private operators for recycling.

Some Turks help out by leaving recyclable materials next to, rather than in, the bins.

Electricity is expensive in Turkey, so many people use solar-energy systems for their hot-water needs. If you are serious about energy conservation, check that your proposed accommodation has such a system installed.

Personal Security and Health

For the sensible visitor, Turkey is probably safer to visit than many European countries. Unfortunately, however, high unemployment and the huge gap between rich and poor mean that petty theft and pickpocketing are on the rise in big cities. Health care is of a high standard, with a thriving private health sector alongside the state-run system, but it is essential to keep basic immunization up to date before you travel.

Police

There are a number of police forces in Turkey, from traffic wardens to rapid-response motorcycle units (Dolphin Police). The *Jandarma*, who are attached to the army, are responsible for policing rural areas. In towns, the *Emniyet Polisi* (Security Police) carry out law-enforcement duties. A special tourism police force *(Turizm Polisi)* operates in Istanbul and other tourist areas. The navy-blue uniformed *Zabıta* is a municipal police force that patrols bazaars and other areas of commerce.

It is obligatory to carry some form of identification with you in Turkey. The police and *Jandarma* carry out spot checks on cars, buses and trucks. A passport or driving licence is usually sufficient.

Police officers are very helpful, but should you need help, the first place to contact is your embassy. Most countries have missions in Ankara, and some have consulates in Istanbul *(see p381)*, İzmir or Antalya.

Badge of the Dolphin rapid-response unit

What to be Aware of

Petty crime is on the rise in Turkey. Visitors to Istanbul should be particularly vigilant, especially on the crowded public transport system, as pickpocketing is a growing problem. Bag-snatching is less common, but be wary.

Use a money belt, or wear your bag across your chest and walk on the inner part of the pavement. Do not leave valuables lying around in your hotel room. Whether you are male or female, avoid lonely areas, such as Istanbul's old city walls, especially at night. It is also best to avoid urban protests of any kind, particularly in areas such as Istanbul's Taksim Square *(see p115)*, because they can quickly spiral out of control.

If you are planning to visit remote areas, it is best to travel in a group. The ethnically Kurdish southeast has been unstable for many years, with protests and outbreaks of stone-throwing occurring from time to time. Visitors who wander into rural areas in this region may be viewed with suspicion by security forces.

The army, Atatürk and the Turkish flag are fundamental symbols of Turkish identity, and disrespect towards them is seen as an insult to the state. Always ask permission before taking photographs of any individuals, even in public places. Taking pictures of military installations is strictly forbidden.

In an Emergency

If your condition is life-threatening, you should be treated automatically, but it is a good idea to have your insurance details on you at all times in case your ability to pay is questioned. In Istanbul, the state-run **Taksim Ilkyardım Hastanesi** (Taksim Emergency Hospital) has a decent reputation; in provincial cities, it is best to use one of the many excellent private hospitals, several of which have an office staffed by at least one fluent English (and other languages) speaker.

Lost and Stolen Property

Turks will go to great lengths to return lost property. It is always worth returning to the last place your item was seen, or going to the tourism police. In Istanbul, property left on public transport can be reclaimed from the I.E.T.T. *(see p397)*.

If you have anything stolen in an area where there are tourism police, such as Istanbul, report the theft to them. Elsewhere, report it at a police station *(Emniyet Polis Merkezi)*, but bear in mind that most officers have either no, or only very basic, English language skills. To make an insurance claim, you will have to give (and sign) a statement. Contact your embassy or consulate for help *(see p381)*.

Security policeman   **Traffic policeman**   **Dolphin policeman**

Fire engine

Security Police *(Emniyet Polisi)* car

State ambulance

Hospitals and Pharmacies

The Turkish health system has both public and private hospitals. Private hospitals are generally better equipped and staffed, and less bureaucratic, than state hospitals. They may run their own ambulance services, and they are also more likely to have staff speaking a foreign language. Go to http://turkey.usembassy.gov/medical_information.html for a list of state and private hospitals.

Most non-prescription medications are available at reasonable prices from a pharmacy (*eczane*), and many types of antibiotics are available over the counter. Visitors are allowed to bring into the country sufficient quantities of medications as are required for the duration of their trip. Turkish pharmacists are professional and well trained; most are also qualified to give injections (*iğne*). If you need advice outside normal business hours, the name of the duty pharmacist (*nobetci eczane*) for that day is usually posted in a pharmacy window.

Condoms (*prezervatif*) are available in most pharmacies, even if not on display.

Minor Hazards

Before travelling to Turkey, be sure that your basic inoculations (diphtheria, polio, typhoid and tetanus) are up to date. Check with your doctor about hepatitis A and hepatitis B too.

Some visitors experience digestive upsets due to the amount of oil used in Turkish cooking. Try to eat lightly for the first few days, and keep alcohol intake to a minimum. Should you suffer from stomach troubles, remedies available include Lomotil, Ge-Oral (oral rehydration salts) and Buscopan. If you have serious and/or persistent stomach problems, it might be food poisoning and it is advisable to seek medical assistance.

Bottled water is safer to drink than tap water. Grilled meat is sometimes served lightly cooked. Ask for it well done (*iyi pişmiş*), and avoid foods that may have been sitting in the sun.

Mosquitoes can be an annoying problem along the Aegean and Mediterranean coasts, and even in big cities like Istanbul, so bring mosquito repellent from home. There is a very remote risk of contracting malaria in the Tigris and Euphrates river basins between April and July and you should consult a travel clinic for the latest advice. At the seaside, watch out for sea urchins (*deniz kestanesi*) clinging to the rocks. If you step on one, seek medical attention at once. In rocky terrain, look out for scorpions and snakes.

Rabies is prevalent in Turkey, so don't approach stray animals. If bitten, consult a doctor immediately. If you are hiking in remote areas, you may come across fierce shepherd dogs – don't come between the dog and its flock. More serious is a potentially fatal tick-borne disease, Crimean haemorrhagic fever. If you are hiking or camping, do not expose any bare flesh.

Travel and Health Insurance

Take out travel and medical insurance before leaving, and make sure repatriation cover is included. Turkey's state health system has few agreements with other countries, and private hospital costs are high. You have to pay for treatment and claim the money back on your insurance. Both state and private medical facilities accept major credit cards.

Banking and Currency

There is no limit to the amount of foreign currency you can bring into the country. After decades of high inflation, the Turkish lira *(Türk Lirası)* has stabilized, with inflation of around 6 per cent in 2013. A sign of this new-found confidence was the introduction in 2012 of the ₺ symbol to denote the currency. Note that although many goods and service prices are shown with the ₺ symbol or TRY, many places still use the "old" abbreviation for the *Türk Lirası*, TL. In large cities and the vast majority of coastal resorts it is easy to pay for everything using credit or debit cards, and to withdraw money from ATMs.

Cash dispenser with instructions in a range of languages

A branch of the Turkish bank Garanti in Istanbul

Banks and Bureaux de Change

Most private banks, such as **Garanti** are open 9am–5pm; some bigger branches have limited opening hours on Saturdays. State banks, such as **Ziraat**, close noon–1:30pm for lunch. Service can be slow, but they give the best exchange rate.

Even the smallest Turkish town will have at least one bank, generally found on the main shopping street. A number of foreign banks, such as Citibank and HSBC, can also be found in most cities.

Most banks offer an automated queuing system. Take a numbered ticket from the dispenser (for currency exchange there's usually a button marked *döviz*), and wait for your number to flash up on screen. Existing customers have priority, so you may wait a long time.

The İş Bankası at Istanbul's Atatürk Airport is open 24 hours a day. Several other Turkish banks also have outlets at airports, offering a full range of banking services, and there are plenty of ATM machines.

An alternative to banks are the numerous exchange offices *(döviz)*. One such office is **Bamka**

Döviz in Istanbul. *Döviz* are open for longer hours than banks, and usually on Saturdays too. However, be aware that their exchange rate is sometimes lower than in banks, and some charge commission.

ATMs

Automated Teller Machines (ATMs) accept most debit cards and some credit cards, such as MasterCard and Visa, allowing you to withdraw around £250 daily. There is an English-language screen prompt on every machine. It is worth remembering that using a debit or credit card at an ATM usually involves a fee.

Always exercise caution while using ATMs; be aware of anyone standing close to you and shield the numbered keypad when entering your PIN.

Traveller's Cheques and Credit Cards

Traveller's cheques are very difficult to cash, so visitors are advised not to bring them.

Credit cards such as **Visa**, **MasterCard** and **American Express** are accepted in most hotels, restaurants and shops. Many debit cards issued by international banks such as HSBC and Citibank are also accepted, but check that your card is valid internationally before you travel. Notify your bank before you leave, so they expect the card to be used in Turkey.

There is no fee for using credit cards, although many hotels offer discounts for cash payment. If you purchase an airline ticket from a travel agent, however, they will charge a commission of about 3 per cent of the fare.

If you need money in an emergency, try a money order *(havale)* service, such as Western Union, which works in conjunction with some banks and the Turkish Post Office (PTT, *see p387)*, providing a safe, speedy – but expensive – way to transfer money.

Value-added Tax

Value-added tax *(KDV* in Turkish) runs at 18 per cent and is included in all prices. If you need a receipt for purchases, ask for a *fiş*; if you need an invoice, ask for a *fatura*. For information on tax refunds, *see p362*.

DIRECTORY

Banks and Bureaux de Change

Bamka Döviz
Cumhuriyet Cad 23, Taksim, Istanbul. **Map** 1 C3.
Tel (0212) 253 70 00.

Garanti
Yeniçeriler Cad 25, Eminönü, Istanbul. **Map** 4 C4.
Tel (0212) 455 52 50.

Ziraat
Yeniçeriler Cad 55, Beyazıt, Istanbul. **Map** 4 C4. **Tel** (0212) 517 06 00.

Credit Cards

American Express
Tel (0212) 244 25 25.

MasterCard & Visa
Tel (0212) 225 00 80.

Currency

The currency in Turkey is known as the Turkish lira (or, more officially, as your credit card statement will show, TRY). A half-anchor symbol for the currency was introduced in 2012. The lira is divided into the kuruş, with 100 kuruş equalling 1 lira. The lowest denomination note is 5 lira, the highest 200 lira. Be aware that some Turkish people, out of habit, still talk in old, hyper-inflated lira terms, asking, for example, *bir milyon* (one million) for a glass of tea. Visitors are allowed to take up to US$5,000 out of Turkey in cash.

Banknotes

Turkish banknotes come in six denominations – 200 lira, 100 lira, 50 lira, 20 lira, 10 lira and 5 lira – each with its own colour. All notes show the face of Atatürk on the front, with another leading figure from Turkish history on the reverse.

₺200

₺100

₺50

₺20

₺10

₺5

Coins

Coins are in denominations of 5 kuruş, 10 kuruş, 25 kuruş, 50 kuruş and 1 lira (100 kuruş). All coins feature Atatürk on one side.

₺1

50 kuruş

25 kuruş

10 kuruş

5 kuruş

Communications and Media

Throughout the country, Türk Telekom monopolizes fixed-line telephone communications. Major Turkish cities enjoy easy access to high-speed broadband connections. Internet cafés abound, though their reign is being challenged by an ever-increasing number of places offering Wi-Fi and 3G technology.

Although slow, the postal service is pretty reliable. Post offices are clearly identified by the letters PTT. Many of them change foreign currency and offer a service for sending and receiving money (see p384). Making phone calls from countertop metered phones within a PTT building is fairly economical, too.

There are dozens of Turkish papers vying for readers' attention, ranging from the pro-Islamic to the staunchly secular – and all persuasions in-between. Satellite TV has revolutionized the country's once-staid, parochial broadcasting, and many foreign-language channels are available.

Making a call from a public telephone box in Istanbul

International and Local Telephone Calls

Istanbul has two area codes: 0212 for the European side and 0216 for the Asian side. To call a 0212 number from the Asian side, you must use the prefix 0212, and vice versa. To call another city in Turkey, use the appropriate area code, for example, 0224 for Bursa.

To make an international call from Turkey, dial 00 followed by the relevant country code (Australia: 61; Canada and the US: 1; New Zealand: 64; Republic of Ireland: 353; UK: 44). For international operator services, dial 115; for intercity services, 131.

Mobile Phones

Mobile (cell) phones are popular and essential items in modern Turkey. The market is dominated by three players: **Türkcell**, **Vodafone** and **Avea**.

Most visitors with a roaming facility can use their existing mobile phone as they would in their home country, since Turkey uses the standard 900 or 1800 MHz frequencies. North American phones, however, are not compatible with the Turkish system and will not work there.

Calls made using a locally bought SIM are cheaper than using your roaming facility. It is possible to buy a SIM locally, from the stands of the operators at both Istanbul airports and in most Turkish towns and cities. The big drawback is that the phone will be locked after two weeks. If you are staying longer, you can get around the problem by registering your phone with one of the main operators and paying a one-off import tax. Alternatively, buy a cheap second-hand phone in Turkey.

Türk Telekom Kontörlü Kart, one of several phonecards in Turkey

Public Telephones

Telephone calls can be made from public phone boxes, post offices (PTT), Türk Telekom (TT) centres or street kiosks using phonecards. The Alocart, with its scratch-off code, allows you to make calls from any landline in Turkey. The chipped Türk Telekom Kontörlü Kart comes in units of 5 lira, 10 lira and 25 lira. Both cards can be purchased from PTT and TT centres and, for an additional charge, from street sellers and kiosks. Many public phones also take credit cards.

Using a laptop computer in a designated Wi-Fi area

Internet Access

Internet cafés can be found in every Turkish town and city, although many are largely devoted to teenagers playing online games. They charge a very modest fee by the hour, but you can usually negotiate a half-hour rate for minimal usage. Most also offer hot and cold drinks and snacks at reasonable prices. Keyboards here naturally incorporate Turkish characters, which can make them very frustrating to use. Be particularly wary of the dotless "i" (ı), which, if typed in by mistake, renders Internet searches useless. The @ symbol is generally found on the Q key.

Many cafés in big cities and tourist resorts offer free wireless Internet connection. Wi-Fi is also found in most hotels and pensions, where it is usually free, although luxury establishments

An Internet café in Istanbul

sometimes charge a fee. Most hotels also have fixed terminals where you can check your emails.

A cheap way to make phone calls is by using VoIP (Voice over Internet Protocol). This system lets you make phone calls anywhere in the world from your own computer. The most popular one is Skype.

Postal services

There are post offices (PTT) in every city in Turkey and all major towns and resorts. Letters and postcards can be handed over the counter at a post office or mailed in letter boxes, which are yellow and labelled PTT. A sign indicates which slot you should put your letter in: *Şehiriçi* (local), *Yurtiçi* (domestic) and *Yurtdışı* (international).

Surface post is slow, so it is best to use air mail *(uçak ile)* when sending items abroad. Letters to Europe take around a week; allow twice as long for mail to other continents. A recorded delivery service (called APS) is available from post offices, with delivery in three days within Turkey.

If you want to send a parcel by surface mail, use registered *(kayıtlı)* post. To meet customs regulations, the contents of a package must be inspected at the post office, so take tape to seal your parcel at the counter.

Local courier companies such as **Yurtiçi Kargo** and **Aras Kargo** will deliver letters and parcels inland in a day or so at a comparable price, and they are much more efficient than the PTT. Both have websites in English, but don't expect staff

to speak it fluently. International players like **DHL** also have offices throughout Turkey, but they charge a little more for their services. Sending parcels abroad with courier companies is more expensive than using the PTT, but the service is more reliable and easier to track.

Newspapers and Magazines

Two daily English-language newspapers – *Today's Zaman* (www.todayszaman.com) and *Hürriyet Daily News* (www. hurriyetdailynews.com) – give a round-up of Turkish and foreign news. They are available in cities with large expat communities, such as Istanbul and Ankara, and in resort towns, but harder to find in provincial towns and cities. Broadly speaking, the two newspapers reflect the main division in the Turkish media: *Today's Zaman* is liberal Islamic in its outlook, while *Hürriyet Daily News* is nationalist and secular. Both papers can also be read online.

A range of foreign newspapers and magazines can be found in major tourist resorts and cities. For listings in Istanbul, try *Time Out Istanbul* or *The Guide Istanbul*.

Newspaper stand outside the Topkapı Palace

TV and Radio

Satellite TV has blossomed in Turkey, with dozens of Turkish and foreign channels competing for viewers. Widely available foreign news channels include BBC World News, Al Jazeera and CNN, with English-language entertainment provided by the likes of CNBCE, E2, BBC Entertainment and MTV. For foreign sports, look out for Eurosport, Premier League and SporMax. Most hotels receive global satellite television, but check in advance of booking if you particularly want foreign channels in your room. Large flat-screen TVs are to be found in many restaurants and bars, usually screening either local pop music or Turkish football.

The state-owned TRT (Türk Radyo ve Televizyon) runs six television channels and three radio stations. TRT2 television has news bulletins in English, French and German at 7pm and 10pm. TRT3 radio (FM 88.2) broadcasts news in English, French and German throughout the day (at 9am, noon, 5pm, 7pm and 9pm).

DIRECTORY

Mobile Phones

Avea
Tel 444 15 00.
W avea.com.tr

Türkcell
Tel 444 05 32.
W turkcell.com.tr

Vodafone
Tel (0542) 444 05 42.
W vodafone.com.tr

Postal Services

Aras Kargo
Tel 444 25 52.
W araskargo.com.tr

DHL
Tel 440 00 40.
W dhl.com.tr

Post Office (PTT)
W ptt.gov.tr

Yurtiçi Kargo
Tel 444 99 99.
W yurticikargo.com

TRAVEL INFORMATION

The easiest way to get to Turkey is by air. Turkish Airlines (THY) offers regular direct flights from many airports in Europe, North America and Asia. Several major European carriers, such as Lufthansa and KLM, also fly direct to Istanbul. Atatürk Airport, on the European side of the city, is still the most used Istanbul airport, but many airlines, especially the budget ones, use Sabiha Gökçen, on the Asian side of the city. There are also budget and charter flights from many European cities to resort destinations in the Aegean and Mediterranean. In addition, it is possible to reach Turkey overland, by coach or train, or by ferry.

The country's network of domestic flights is far-reaching, with Turkish Airlines and several private operators linking Istanbul and Ankara with many other Turkish destinations. Alternative internal travel options include a comprehensive intercity coach network and a rapidly improving rail network.

Green Travel

Although domestic flights are tempting in terms of the time saved reaching far-flung regions, Turkey's wonderful intercity bus network is a greener and cheaper alternative – as is the rail network with its fast-growing number of high-speed services.

In most large Turkish cities the main points of interest are often clustered together in the historic centre, so try to reach them on foot. In Istanbul, even the more remote sights can usually be reached easily enough by public transport. In Istanbul and many other conurbations, buses use natural gas, as do most taxis.

The weather in Turkey means it is very pleasant to spend time in the great outdoors, so environmentally aware visitors may wish to consider a walking, trekking or cycling holiday.

Arriving by Air

Many visitors arrive at either Istanbul's Atatürk Airport, on the European side of the city, or at Sabiha Gökçen, on the Asian side. For onward travel within Turkey, you can change to a domestic **Turkish Airlines** (THY) flight or use one of the several low-cost domestic carriers (see Directory).

Most major European carriers, including Lufthansa, KLM, Austrian Airlines and British Airways, have at least one daily flight to Istanbul. American Airlines, Qantas and other international carriers also serve the city, although not always with a direct flight.

In terms of budget airlines, easyJet and **Anadolujet**, a subsidiary of Turkish Airlines, connect the UK with Sabiha Gökçen Airport; the Turkish carrier **Pegasus Airlines** flies into both Istanbul airports from the UK and several European cities; while the German/Turkish carrier **Sunexpress** serves Sabiha Gökçen from many northern European countries. Aegean and Mediterranean resorts, notably Antalya and Bodrum, are served by UK charter airlines, such as Thomas Cook and Thomson.

May to October is peak season, but flights also fill up during school and religious holidays, including the annual Muslim pilgrimage to Mecca, the date of which varies with the lunar calendar.

Airports

Istanbul's **Atatürk Airport** (Atatürk Hava Limanı) lies 25 km (16 miles) west of the city centre, in Yeşilköy. Its huge international terminal (Dış Hatları) is a 15-minute walk from the domestic terminal (İç Hatları), linked by moving walkways and corridors. The international terminal has all the facilities you would expect including 24-hour banking, car-hire outlets, a tourist information office and a hotel-reservation desk. Allow at least 2 hours to check in for departures from busy Atatürk Airport.

Many domestic carriers, as well as international budget airlines, use **Sabiha Gökçen Airport**. Set in the suburbs on the Asian side of Istanbul, 32 km (20 miles) southeast of the city centre, it is less conveniently located but smaller and easier to navigate

Planes parked at Istanbul's Atatürk Airport

than Atatürk Airport, with all the usual facilities on offer.

Visitors flying to Ankara land at **Esenboğa Airport**, which is located 28 km (17 miles) from the city centre.

Buses operated by **Havataş** shuttle passengers from both Istanbul airports to the city centre, while the same service is provided by **Havaş** in Ankara and provincial cities (see p397).

Domestic Air Travel

Turkey is a vast country, and flying is the most convenient (if not the greenest) way to travel from Istanbul to eastern cities such as Erzurum, Trabzon and Van. Several carriers compete on the same routes, so prices are reasonable (from 70 TL) if booked early – between six and four weeks prior to departure. Tickets are available online or from high-street travel agencies at a slight premium.

It is possible to fly to several Turkish cities direct from both Istanbul airports, as well as from Ankara, İzmir and Antalya. Flights between other cities sometimes involve extended connection times in the hub airports of Istanbul or Ankara. Anadolujet and Sunexpress fly from Istanbul's Sabiha Gökçen. **Atlas Jet** and **Onur Air** use Atatürk Airport, while Pegasus Airlines and Turkish Airlines use both. Snacks and drinks are extras on all carriers except Turkish Airlines, and the baggage weight limit for budget airlines is usually 15 kg (33 lb).

Arriving by Rail

The Orient Express (see p80) no longer travels to Istanbul. The best overland route, which takes a couple of days, is from Munich via Budapest, Budapest and Bucharest. Information on train travel can be obtained from **The Man in Seat 61**, and bookings made through **European Rail Ltd**.

Istanbul has two main line stations. Trains from Europe arrive at **Sirkeci Station**, while those from Anatolia and Middle Eastern cities terminate at **Haydarpaşa**, which is linked

to the European side by ferry. For more information on rail travel, see pp392–3.

Arriving by Coach

Two leading Turkish coach companies, **Ulusoy** and **Varan**, operate direct services from several European cities to Istanbul, with tickets available online. Departure points for Ulusoy coaches include Munich and Frankfurt; Varan coaches depart from Budapest, Salzburg and Vienna.

Coaches arrive at Esenler coach station (see p391), 10 km (6 miles) northwest of Istanbul city centre. Esenler is also the main terminal for domestic connections. Coach companies usually operate a courtesy minibus from the terminal to the city centre.

A network of ferries links Turkey to Greece and Northern Cyprus

Arriving by Sea

There are no direct ferries from Italy, but it is possible to take a ferry from various Greek islands to Turkey. Routes include Samos to Kuşadası, Rhodes to Bodrum, Fethiye and Marmaris, Kos to Bodrum, and Lesbos to Ayvalık, though services are not always reliable. Ferries and high-speed catamarans (sea buses) also link Northern Cyprus to Turkey's southern Mediterranean coast. Winter crossings are infrequent.

The main cruise-ship docks in the country are at the Karaköy terminal, in central Istanbul, and at the Aegean resort of Kuşadası, gateway to the ancient city of Ephesus.

The **Feribot** website offers a wealth of useful information on sea travel.

DIRECTORY

Airports

Atatürk Airport
Tel (0212) 463 30 00.
ⓦ ataturkairport.com

Esenboğa Airport
Tel (0312) 590 40 00.
ⓦ esenbogaairport.com

Havaş
Tel (0212) 465 47 00 or 56 56.
ⓦ havas.com.tr

Havataş
Tel 444 26 56. ⓦ havatas.com

Sabiha Gökçen Airport
Tel (0216) 585 50 00.
ⓦ sgairport.com

Airlines

Anadolujet
Tel 444 25 38.
ⓦ anadolujet.com

Atlas Jet
Tel 444 33 87.
ⓦ atlasjet.com

Onur Air
Tel 444 66 87.
ⓦ onurair.com.tr

Pegasus Airlines
Tel 444 07 37.
ⓦ flypgs.com

Sunexpress
Tel 444 07 97.
ⓦ sunexpress.com

Turkish Airlines (THY)
Tel 444 08 49.
ⓦ turkishairlines.com

Arriving by Rail

European Rail Ltd
ⓦ raileurope.com

Haydarpaşa Station
Tel (0216) 336 04 75.

Sirkeci Station
Tel (0212) 527 00 50.

The Man in Seat 61
ⓦ seat61.com

Arriving by Coach

Ulusoy
Tel 444 18 88. ⓦ ulusoy.com.tr

Varan
Tel 444 89 99. ⓦ varan.com.tr

Arriving by Sea

Feribot
ⓦ feribot.net

Travelling by Bus and Dolmuş

Despite the proliferation of low-cost domestic flights in recent years, Turkey's intercity bus service remains arguably the best way to see the country. Travelling to a great number of destinations, buses are comfortable and often luxurious. In addition, bus travel is both cheaper and greener than air travel. There are also fewer hidden costs (for example, many provincial airports are way out of town, requiring a taxi into the city centre), and a bus ticket purchased near the departure date will likely be far cheaper than a last-minute flight. For a more informal travelling experience, and over shorter distances, a *dolmuş* (minibus) is the most cheerful, versatile and economical way to get around.

A fleet of modern, luxurious long-distance buses

Bus Travel

The profusion of coach and long-distance bus companies gives the impression that bus travel in Turkey is a highly competitive business. In fact, the entire industry operates on a franchise system: bus companies maintain relatively uniform fares based on petrol (gas) prices and the inflation rate. This system ensures that bus operators share revenue.

The leading intercity coach firms are **Kâmil Koç**, **Varan**, **Metro Turizm** and **Ulusoy**. They all run regular schedules with teams of well-trained drivers, comfortable vehicles and a steward who comes around at regular intervals to serve free hot or cold drinks and cakes or biscuits. Free water is available on request from the steward, who also supplies refreshing cologne. Some coaches are just three seats across, and all have on-board entertainment, such as films or television, with the

more expensive companies offering personal screens and headsets. Many companies also offer free Wi-Fi on board. Most buses stop for 30 or 40 minutes every 4 hours or so, with a shorter facilities stop in-between. Everything from a glass of tea to a full Turkish meal is available at most stops, and the quality of the food is surprisingly good, though prices are usually a little higher than the average high-street restaurant.

Journeys of more than 10 hours tend to be made overnight. As you move eastwards in Turkey, the intercity bus network becomes a little sparser, but these buses are often just as comfortable.

Although vehicles have tinted windows and air conditioning, it is best to sit on the side of the bus facing away from the sun in the hot summer months.

It is convention for passengers travelling alone to be

seated next to someone of the same sex, though this custom is often ignored in western Turkey. Consumption of alcohol and smoking are forbidden on board *(see p381)*. It is also worth noting that intercity buses do not have on-board toilets, hence the frequent rest stops.

Bus Tickets and Fares

When travelling by bus, it is advisable to book your tickets well in advance, particularly on weekends and during any school or religious holidays *(see p40)*, though on busy routes with several departures a day, you can usually just turn up at the bus station and find a seat. Bear in mind that certain bus operators have "hustlers" stationed at popular bus stations whose job is to take you to the ticket office of the company they work for. However, the bus company might not necessarily operate the most convenient departure times for you, so don't be persuaded to buy a ticket until you've seen what is available. Larger towns and cities often have several travel offices where you can pur-chase tickets and, usually, get a free shuttle to the bus station. Several firms have facilities for online booking and payment, with user-friendly websites in Turkish and English.

Despite fuel costs in Turkey being among the highest in the world, bus travel here remains very good value compared to most European countries. As a rule, a ticket from a standard bus company will cost about two-thirds of the price of an early-booking budget-airline ticket for the same route.

Travel offices in Marmaris selling long-distance bus tickets

Bus Stations

In most Turkish cities, the *otogar* (bus station) is located well away from the city centre. Typically, bus companies provide a free shuttle service from several central pick-up points to the *otogar*, and from there to the city centre at journey's end. In Istanbul, coach companies ferry passengers to and from their own terminals (close to the motorway) on the Asian and European sides of the city. In some cities, you will need to take a public minibus or, in the case of Antalya and Konya, the tram.

Istanbul's main intercity *otogar*, **Esenler**, is 10 km (6 miles) northwest of the city. It's a massive but rather drab affair, with more than 150 companies vying for business. There is also a bus terminal in **Harem**, on the Asian side. Some buses departing from Esenler stop at Harem before heading into Anatolia, but if that's where you're heading, boarding in Harem could save you tedious time stuck in Istanbul's notoriously congested traffic.

All major and most minor bus stations in Turkey have toilet facilities, which charge a small fee, shops selling everything from *lokum* (Turkish delight) and bottled water to newspapers, and amenities such as shoe-shines, restaurants, cafés and even hairdressers. Turkish bus stations are generally safe places to be, even at night, although you should take precautions against pickpockets.

Dolmuş and Minibus Travel

In Turkey, a *dolmuş* means two things: a shared taxi that follows a fixed route and departs when full (*see p396*), and a minibus, often cream-coloured (although in Istanbul they are sometimes blue), that follows fixed routes according to a schedule and is generally packed with passengers.

A *dolmuş* is a typically Turkish mode of transport

In most cities, *dolmuş* stops are indicated by a rectangular blue sign bearing a large "D" on a white or red panel. Destinations are shown on the front side of the vehicle, but be aware that these relate to districts rather than streets.

The best thing about travelling by *dolmuş* is that you can usually alight anywhere you like. Simply say *Müsait bir yer'de* ("at the next convenient point") or *İnecek var* ("somebody wants to get off"). The increased volume of traffic in some cities means that *dolmuşes* are no longer allowed to pull in wherever they like, though many still do.

Getting used to a city's *dolmuş* system is not easy. In practice, this mode of transport is most useful in tourist resorts, where the

Sign for a dolmuş stop

drivers know where visitors want to go and locals speak enough English to offer their help.

Minibuses, also confusingly referred to as *dolmuş* by many locals, serve smaller towns and villages, usually departing from, and returning to, a garage or depot in a larger provincial settlement. Unfortunately, many minibuses serving small towns in rural areas tend to cater to the needs of the villagers, departing the town/village early in the morning and returning in the late afternoon, which is usually not convenient to visitors planning a day trip in the country.

Dolmuş and Minibus Fares

Payment on *dolmuşes* and minibuses is by Turkish lira in cash. Tickets and electronic smart tickets are not accepted. Note that if you sit in the front, you will be responsible for passing fares and change to and fro between the passengers and the driver. Fares are low, so be sure to carry small change, as drivers get irate if presented with a 50 lira note for a 2 lira journey.

Fares on minibuses are cheaper pro-rata than inter-city bus fares, but the vehicles are often cramped and crowded, especially with villagers taking town-bought goods home.

DIRECTORY

Bus Travel

Kâmil Koç
Tel 444 05 62.
w kamilkoc.com.tr

Metro Turizm
Tel 444 34 55.
w metroturizm.com.tr

Ulusoy
Tel 444 18 88.
w ulusoy.com.tr

Varan
Tel 444 89 99.
w varan.com.tr

Bus Stations

Esenler
Bayrampasa, Istanbul.
Tel (0212) 658 05 05.
Open 5am–midnight daily.

Harem Station
Istanbul. Tel (0216) 333 37 63.
Open 5am–midnight daily.

Travelling by Train and Ferry

Turkey's once notoriously slow rail network is undergoing a major overhaul. A high-speed line now links Ankara with Konya and another links the capital to Eskişehir. The latter line is scheduled to reach Istanbul by 2015, thus linking Turkey's two major cities. More high-speed links are under construction. In the meantime, the old rail network provides a cheap and leisurely way to see the country. Most of Turkey's boat traffic is centred on Istanbul's busy waterways, and a number of ferries and high-speed catamarans cross the Sea of Marmara.

Haydarpaşa train station, on the Asian side of Istanbul

Train Travel

Turkey's national railway system is run by **Turkish State Railways** (Türkiye Cumhuriyeti Devlet Demiryolları, or TCDD). Owing to a massive project to bring the country's rail network up to date, visitors will have to find out the latest information about line closures and new routes before making their travel plans – and perhaps be prepared to travel from Ankara to Anatolian destinations rather than Istanbul owing to the uncertaintity over the future of **Haydarpaşa Station** (see p129).

Rail travel, like everything in Turkey, is split between Thrace (Europe) and Anatolia (Asia). Haydarpaşa Station, the main train station linking Istanbul with the rest of Anatolia, may be made redundant when the Istanbul Marmaray Project – a major overhaul of the city's infrastructure that includes a tunnel under the Bosphorus – is completed (scheduled for 2014, but after several delays this is by no means certain). Trains from Ankara are likely to terminate at Gebze, an Istanbul suburb, which will integrate

with the Marmaray Project/city centre transport network. **Sirkeci Station** (see p80), near the Galata Bridge, has traditionally been the terminus of European trains, though this too will be sidelined by the Marmaray Project.

Rail trips can be booked via the TCDD website. However, since it is quite tricky to use the site successfully, it may be better to use one of the many travel agencies endorsed to sell train tickets. If you want to purchase a sleeper ticket, you must do it from the station of departure, but note that you cannot book further ahead than two weeks. Credit cards are accepted at most intercity train stations.

Rail Routes

The Turkish State Railways network consists of both main and regional lines. A high-speed line links Ankara with Eskişehir, from where there's a standard train on to Istanbul; another links Ankara with Konya. Blue Trains (Mavi Trenler) are quicker than the standard Expresses (Ekspresler).

The most interesting routes for visitors are Ankara–Kars, on the Armenian frontier, which is a journey of almost 40 hours; and Ankara–Lake Van, which takes 36 hours. Because of the formidable barrier created by the Taurus Mountains, which separate Anatolia from the Mediterranean, there is no rail line along the southern Aegean and Mediterranean coasts. However, there is a service

A TCDD train travelling through the scenic Turkish countryside near Polatlı in Western Anatolia

from Eskişehir to the Eastern Mediterranean city of Adana, which takes about 12 hours.

Sleepers, Seats and Service

Most trains offer comfortable two-berth sleeping cars *(yataklı vagon)*. These have air conditioning and a basin; soap, a towel and bed linen are provided. There are squat toilets at either end of each sleeping car, and an attendant who will expect a small tip. There are also four- or six-berth couchettes, which are a little cheaper but less private since you will share the compartment with other passengers. On some routes bed linen is provided, while on others you will be expected to bring your own. Beds fold away in the daytime. The reclining Pullman seats are cheaper still, but for rock-bottom prices you can try an ordinary first- or second-class seat. Unless you are travelling as part of a group, however, a *yataklı vagon* makes the most sense, since it is the safest option – sleeping passengers make easy targets for thieves.

Many trains have a restaurant car *(büfe)* on board serving decent food and drinks. In remote areas, few stations have much in the way of facilities, so for long journeys it is wise to stock up before boarding.

Rail Tours

Making your own rail-travel bookings in Turkey can seem intimidating. However, there are several websites that take the language barrier out of the equation. One such site is www.neredennereye.com, which is useful for general travel and booking information.

A rail package tour through the Anatolian interior combines visits to the major tourist sights with bus and air travel to save time where necessary. The most popular route is Ankara to Kars. For more details on specialized rail tours, *see p374*.

If you are planning a longer trip to Turkey, consider a TCDD pass, which allows 30 days of unlimited rail travel. There are several different options, but the best one is probably the sleeping-car pass (500 lira). Cards can be purchased from most stations, but note that pass holders will still need to reserve their compartment in advance.

A high-speed catamaran sailing on the Bosphorus

Ferries

High-speed catamaran (sea bus) and ferry services are mostly limited to Istanbul and the Sea of Marmara. Operated by the **Istanbul Seabus Company (IDO)**, ferries link the European and Asian sides of the city, and run up and down the Bosphorus. Sea buses also travel to the Princes' and Marmara Islands, and across the Sea of Marmara to Güzelyalı (for Bursa), Yalova (for İznik), Bandırma (for Çanakkale) and Mudanya. Services are more frequent in the summer (mid-June to early September) and at weekends. For schedules, routes and fares, visit the IDO website.

Car ferries make the short hop across the Dardanelles, the strait joining the Sea of Marmara and the Aegean, useful if you are driving to Troy from Istanbul.

There are also ferries and sea buses to Girne, in Northern Cyprus, from Taşucu, Alanya and Mersin, and a thrice-weekly service linking Mersin and Famagusta.

DIRECTORY

Train Travel

Haydarpaşa Station
Haydarpaşa İstasyon Cad, Istanbul.
Tel (0216) 336 04 75.
Open 8am–6pm daily.

Sirkeci Station
Sirkeci İstasyon Cad, Sirkeci Istanbul.
Map 3 E3 (5 E1).
Tel (0212) 527 00 50/51.
Open 7am–midnight daily.

Turkish State Railways (TCDD)
Talat Paşa Bulvarı, 06330 Gar, Ankara.
Tel (0312) 309 05 15 or 444 82 33.
W **tcdd.gov.tr**
Online booking and information on rail routes, timetables, services, fares, authorized ticket agents, discounts and contact details.

Rail Tours

W **neredennereye.com**
Rail and ferry timetables and booking information. Also covers bus and air travel. Five languages.

Ferries

Akgunler Denizcilik
Galeria İş Merkezi Z/12, Taşucu.
Tel (0324) 741 40 33.
W **akgunler.com.tr**
Ferries and sea buses between Taşucu and Northern Cyprus.

Fergün Denizcilik
Girne Yeni Liman Yolu, Fergün Apt 1, Girne, Northern Cyprus.
Tel (0392) 815 18 70.
W **fergun.net**
Sea buses between Alanya and Northern Cyprus.

Istanbul Seabus Company (IDO)
Kennedy Cad, Yenikapı Hızlı Feribot İskelesi, Fatih, Istanbul.
Tel 444 44 36.
W **ido.com.tr**
Online booking and information on schedules and fares (English menu).

Travelling by Car and Bicycle

Most areas of Turkey can be reached quickly and efficiently by road, with motorways and/or six-lane highways linking most major centres. The drawbacks are the high cost of petrol and the alarmingly high accident rate. In addition, Turkey is a large country, and places that may appear close on a map can take much longer than expected to reach, especially if you venture off the beaten track. The major international car-rental firms are widely represented in Turkey, and there are also many local (usually cheaper) companies. Alternatively, you can bring your own vehicle or caravan.

The rugged terrain and long distances make cycling a strenuous way to see the country. However, cyclists have an inherent curiosity value, and they are certain to encounter helpful, friendly people during their journey.

The forecourt of a petrol station selling different types of fuel

The Bosphorus Bridge, one of two major road bridges in Istanbul

Car Rental

To rent a car, you need to present an international driving licence and your passport. To avoid having to pay a large deposit, use a credit card. Drivers must be over 18 years of age.

Be sure to read the small print on the rental contract; insurance cover usually excludes windscreen and tyre damage, or even theft. Keep your vehicle's documents (rhusat) with you at all times and do not leave them unattended in the car. Most international companies hire out vehicles with full tanks; many local firms with empty tanks. You return them the same way.

The easiest place to hire a car is at your arrival airport, but all major cities and most re- sorts will have several car-hire outlets. Most hotels can also arrange car rental for you.

Bringing your own Vehicle

If you drive your own vehicle into Turkey, you will need a valid driving licence and a Green Card to denote international insurance coverage. Documents such as proof of purchase or chassis number are not needed but can be useful. Cars can be brought into Turkey for a six-month period. The car's details will be entered in your passport so you cannot leave without it.

Fuel

Petrol (gas) is sold in leaded octanes of normal and super, and as unleaded (kurşunsuz). Many local vehicles run on otogaz (liquid petroleum gas), which is cheaper than regular petrol, but few hire cars have been converted to this form of fuel. Diesel (dizel) is becoming more common in hire cars, since it is much cheaper than petrol. Pay the extra for a diesel vehicle if you plan to drive a lot. Credit cards are accepted without commission (see p384).

Rules of the Road

When in Turkey, you must drive on the right, give way at junctions to traffic from the right, and wear a seatbelt. Distances are shown in kilometres, and road signs conform to the international standard. The police often stop cars to check identification; showing a passport or driving licence will usually suffice.

Look out for pedestrians, animals, tractors and vehicles without lights. Don't assume that you have the right of way. Drivers making a left turn may veer to the right and wait for traffic to pass. Turkish drivers often reverse on the motorway's hard shoulder if they have overshot their exit. On all major motorways and the Bosphorus Bridge, you will pay a fee, usually taking a ticket at the entry point and paying as you exit. Many toll motorways only accept pre-paid KGS (Kreditli Geçiş Systemi) smart cards – the larger hire car outlets should have them available and they are mandatory if you hire a vehicle at one of the two Istanbul airports.

Parking is a major problem in the cities. Street parking is possible, but in central areas there will be a charge. In open car parks, it is customary to leave your keys with the attendants so they can move your car if needed. Tow-away zones are indicated by a sign showing a breakdown van.

Emergencies

If you have an accident, call the police. Note that moving your vehicle is a crime and may negate your insurance. Heavy city traffic can slow the progress of ambulances, which tend to arrive less quickly than the police. Blood-group details are displayed on Turks' driving licences; in case of a serious accident, this is a sensible precaution.

On secondary roads, local people are usually very helpful if you break down or have a flat tyre. On the motorway around Istanbul, emergency telephones every few kilometres connect you to the police. A firm called **Tur Assist** handles recovery services. The **Touring and Automobile Association of Turkey (TTOK)**, known simply as Turing, can provide detailed advice on driving in Turkey, transit documents and assistance with breakdowns, accidents and insurance. Your consulate or embassy (see p381) can also be helpful in the event of a minor emergency.

Repairs

Most towns have a designated *sanayi area* (industrial zone) or a specialized *oto sanayi* (automotive repair zone) to handle repairs. For punctures, look out for *otolastikci* (tyre-repairer) signs at roadside establishments that are often little more than huts. If you bring your own vehicle, check whether spares for your model are available in Turkey.

Motorcycling and Cycling

Motorcycle enthusiasts usually ride overland through Europe to Turkey, or take a ferry from Greece (see p389). Outside major conurbations, Turkey's big, open spaces and relatively traffic-free roads are major attractions for bikers.

The same regulations that apply to bringing a car into the

Cycling is a fun and eco-friendly way to travel around Turkey

Roadside emergency telephone

country (see opposite) are valid for motorbikes. The risks associated with car travel in Turkey are magnified for motorcyclists, so ride carefully. Most resorts in Turkey have several outlets for motorcycle and scooter hire.

You can bring your own bicycle into Turkey without any customs formalities. It is wise to bring extra inner tubes and any spares that may be necessary, particularly for a long-distance cycle-tour, though most major towns have bike repair shops. It is also possible to rent bicycles, especially in coastal resorts and in Cappadocia (see Directory).

Getting Around

Road maps of Turkey are often inadequate, making it difficult to find your way on country roads or to out-of-the-way places. Route signage is also poor, so it is wise to purchase a good map in your home country prior to travelling. Rural roads make for great adventures, but the potholes can be a hazard. In addition, Turkish drivers may show very little consideration for cyclists. Villagers are generally very helpful, but the language barrier may prove insurmountable.

Mediterranean and Aegean coastal areas are the best for cycling, with exhilarating opportunities for freewheeling. Cappadocia is less well known for cycling, but it has accessible off-road trails and tracks, and the terrain is flatter than on coastal areas. Finding your way on unmarked routes will likely be your greatest challenge here.

Travel agents and tour operators can arrange cycling tours. The adventure company Bougainville (see p375) offers mountain-biking tours, both on the Western Mediterranean coast and in Cappadocia.

Getting Around Istanbul

The central areas of the city are well served by light railway, Metro and tram lines. Buses and *dolmuşes* provide city-wide transport, but roads and vehicles are very crowded at rush hour. Ferries and water taxis ply the Bosphorus and, to a lesser extent, the Golden Horn. The Marmaray Project, scheduled for completion in 2015, will link the European and Asian sides of the city by an underwater tunnel and create more than 7 0 km (43 miles) of suburban rail line, the city-centre sections of which will be underground. A third Bosphorus bridge is currently under construction.

Visitors strolling in front of the Blue Mosque (see pp82–3)

Walking

The creation of semi-pedestrianized areas, such as İstiklâl Caddesi and central Sultanahmet, and walking/jogging paths along sections of the Sea of Marmara and the Bosphorus has made it possible to walk with ease around some parts of Istanbul. Quieter backwaters, like Eyüp (see p124) and parts of Fatih (see p119), Fener and Balat have relatively little traffic, making them attractive destinations for a stroll.

Wherever you walk, bear in mind that traffic only stops at pedestrian crossings controlled by lights. On main roads, always use pedestrian overpasses and underpasses.

Istanbul, like any large city, has some unsavoury areas that are best avoided. The Tarlabaşı neighbourhood of Beyoğlu has a bad reputation, as do the parts around the Theodosian Walls. If you plan to walk in

places off the beaten track, seek local advice, take extra care and avoid walking in unfamiliar areas after dark.

Taxis

Taxis are ubiquitous in Istanbul. Operating day and night, they can be hailed in the street or found at taxi ranks. Hotel and restaurant staff can also phone for a taxi. Fares are cheap in comparison to other major European cities.

Cabs are bright yellow, with the word *taksi* on a sign on the roof. They take up to four passengers, and the fare is charged according to a meter. If you cross the Bosphorus Bridge, the toll will be added to the fare. Unless they have helped with your luggage, drivers will not expect a tip; simply round up the fare to the nearest convenient figure.

Most taxi drivers speak little or no English. They may not be familiar with routes to lesser-known sights either, so carry a map and have the name of your destination written down.

Dolmuşes

In Istanbul, *dolmuşes (see p391)* run throughout the day until mid-evening, and later on busy routes. Points of origin and final destinations are displayed in the front windows. Fares generally range between 3 lira and 6 lira.

The most useful *dolmuş* routes to the average visitor to Istanbul are on the Asian side of the Bosphorus. From Taksim, destinations include Aksaray, Beşiktaş, Kadıköy, Topkapı and Yedikule (for the Theodosian Walls). Vehicles depart from the Taksim end of Tarlabaşı Bulvarı and where İsmet İnönü Caddesi exits Taksim.

A *dolmuş* at a stop in Istanbul

Guided Tours

Several operators run special-interest tours of Istanbul, as well as general guided tours of the city and further afield. **Plan Tours** has a wide variety of offerings, including open-top bus tours of Istanbul, trips to Gallipoli, Troy and Bursa, Jewish heritage tours, and cruises along the Bosphorus. Reliable companies that organize city tours, including walking tours, are **Backpackers Travel**, **Fest Travel** and **Turista Travel**. For more companies providing trips outside Istanbul, see pp374–5.

A bright-yellow taxi on the streets of Istanbul

If you are approached by individuals offering their services as tour guides, ask to see their photo ID first, then tell them clearly what you want to see and agree a fee. If you do not wish to travel by public transport, you can negotiate a private tour with a taxi driver. This is best arranged through your hotel.

Travel Pass

Although you may see locals using a metal token mounted in a plastic holder, these have now been phased out and replaced by a credit-card style travel pass known as an Istanbulkart. The card is valid on the light rail, tram and metro systems, funiculars, suburban railway, all ferries and most city buses. Available outside Sabiha Gökçen airport, at the Havalimani (airport) stop on the light railway linking Atatürk Airport with the centre, and at many public transport offices across the city, the card costs a refundable 10 lira. Load it up at the point of purchase at a machine or kiosk and keep it topped up using the automatic machines outside major transport stops. Swipe the card across the screen at the turnstile machines at the entrance to the platforms for the light railway, tram, metro, suburban railway, funiculars and ferries, or next to the driver on buses. The fare is deducted automatically.

Travel Tokens

If you are not planning to use public transport very frequently you can purchase tokens (jeton)

Useful Bus Routes

12 Kadıköy – Üsküdar
22 Kabataş – Istinye
25/A Levent Metro – Rumeli Kavağı
28 Edirnekapı – Beşiktaş
28/T Topkapı – Beşiktaş
36/E Eminönü – Edirnekapı
40 Taksim – Sariyer
80T Taksim – Yedikule
830 Otogar – Taksim

Airport shuttle bus bearing the Havaş logo

valid for most forms of Istanbul transport from *Jetonmatik* automatic vending machines near many transpsort stops. However, you pay around a third more for each journey than if you use the Istanbulkart.

Buses

Inner-city buses are run by two companies. **I.E.T.T.** (Istanbul Omnibus Company) operates buses and environ-mentally friendly green ones (*yeşil motor*), while **Özel Halk** (a subsidiary of I.E.T.T.) has mainly green and light blue-and-green buses. Both accept the Istanbulkart and *jeton*, but cash payment is not permitted. If you cross either of the Bosphorus bridges, expect to pay double fare.

You queue and enter at the front of the bus and exit by the middle or rear doors. Push the button above the door or attached to the support poles to alert the driver that you wish to alight at the next stop. A list of stops is displayed on a board on the side of the bus or on a video screen. Bus shelters also have details of routes and stops. Most buses run from 6am until 10 or 11pm.

Metrobuses run in dedicated lanes, but the routes are of little interest to the vast majority of visitors.

Airport Transfers

A **Havataş** shuttle bus runs between Atatürk Airport and Taksim via Aksaray (for Sultan-ahmet) from 4am to 1am daily. The trip takes 30–40 minutes and costs 10 lira. There is also a Havataş bus from Sabiha Gökçen to Taksim, from 3:30am to 1am, which takes about an hour and costs 13 lira. Taxis charge about 40 TL to Taksim from Atatürk Airport and about 95 TL from Sabiha Gökçen.

For travellers on a budget, the cheapest option from Atatürk Airport is to take the light railway to Zeytinburnu, then change to the tram for Sultan-ahmet. For Taksim, continue to Kabataş, from where you can ride the funicular up to Taksim. From Sabiha Gökçen, take the E10 bus to Kadıköy, then a Turyol ferry (see p399) across the Bosphorus to Eminönü.

DIRECTORY

Guided Tours

Backpackers Travel
Yeni Akbıyık Caddesi 22, Sultanahmet, Istanbul.
Map 5 D4.
Tel (0212) 638 63 43.
W backpackerstravel.net

Fest Travel
Barbaros Bulvarı 44/20, Beşiktaş, Istanbul.
Map 2 C3.
Tel (0212) 216 10 36.
W festtravel.com.tr

Plan Tours
Cumhuriyet Cad 131/1, Elmadağ, Istanbul.
Map 1 C2.
Tel (0212) 234 77 77.
W plantours.com

Turista Travel
Divan Yolu Cad 16, Sultanahmet, Istanbul. **Map** 5 D4.
Tel (0212) 518 65 70.
W turistatravel.com

Buses

I.E.T.T.
Tel (0800) 211 60 68 or (0212) 245 07 20.
W iett.gov.tr

Özel Halk
Tel 444 18 71.
W iett.gov.tr

Airport Transfers

Havataş
Tel (0212) 465 56 56.
W havatas.net

A tram on Istanbul's modern tramway system

Tramway

Istanbul's tramway system is modern and efficient, if very crowded at peak times. The line runs from Zeytinburnu, where it connects with the light railway coming in from Atatürk Airport, through Aksaray and Sultanahmet. It then crosses the Galata Bridge to Kabataş.

Trams travel on the right-hand side of the street, so be sure to stand on the correct platform. To board a tram, buy a flat-fare token (*jeton*) from the machine (*jetonmatik*) near the platform. Tokens cost 3 lira. The Istanbulkart is also accepted on the tramway. To access the platform swipe the Istanbulkart or push the token into a slot. Trams are frequent, running every 5 minutes from 6am to 11:50pm.

The Nostalgic Tram (*Nostaljik Tramvay*) trundles along İstiklâl Caddesi from Tünel to Taksim Square. The trams are the original early 20th-century vehicles, taken out of service in 1966 but revived in 1989.

Light Railway and Metro

The light railway (*hafif metro*) runs from Atatürk Airport into the city centre, between 6am and 12:30am. The key stops are Zeytinburnu, for connecting to the tramway, and Esenler, for the intercity bus station. The last stop is Aksaray, which also links to the tramway, though this change involves a short walk over a bridge that may be difficult to cross with luggage.

The underground Metro is clean and well run, with air-conditioned cars. It runs from Şişhane, at the bottom of İstiklâl Caddesi, to the suburb of Hacıosman, between 6:15am and 12:30am. By 2015 the Metro network should cross the Golden Horn on a bridge and connect underground to Yenikapı.

Tokens (3 lira), purchased from *jetonmatiks* near the stations, operate the turnstiles for both the light railway and the Metro. The Istanbulkart is also valid.

Cable Cars and Funiculars

A cable car running from 8am to 10pm daily connects the shores of the Golden Horn in Eyüp with the Eyüp cemetery and tea gardens. There is also a cable car in Maçka Park, open from 8am to 8pm daily.

Tram, Light Rail and Metro Route Map

The Metro is an underground system that goes from Şişhane to Hacıosman. The tramway and light railway is mainly an electrified above-ground rail system.

Key

— Metro
— Suburban rail
≡≡ Lines under construction
— Light railway
— Tramway
— Nostalgic Tram
— Funicular

Inaugurated in 1875, the Tünel is an underground railway climbing steeply from Karaköy station, which is set back from the road just off the Galata Bridge, to Tünel Square in Beyoğlu. Here, it connects with the Nostalgic Tram on İstiklâl Caddesi. A token for the Tünel costs 4 lira. The Tünel closes at 10pm.

A modern funicular, open from 6am to midnight, links Taksim Square with the ferry terminal at Kabataş (3 lira).

Suburban Trains

Suburban trains (banliyö) run between Sirkeci and Halkalı (on the European side) along the coast of the Sea of Marmara. The service is slow, however, and the only useful stops for visitors are Yedikule (see p120) and Ataköy (for the Galleria shopping mall, see p135). On the Asian side, a line runs from Haydarpaşa to Gebze via Bostancı, one of the ferry piers for the Princes' Islands. It is likely that both lines will be transformed on completion of the Marmaray Project (see p396).

Suburban trains run from 6am until 11:30pm daily, and they accept the Istanbulkart and tokens (jeton).

For further information on the rail network, see the map inside the back cover.

Ferries, Sea Buses, Private Boats and Water Taxis

A great number of ferries (vapur) cross the Bosphorus and the Golden Horn. They are run by **Şehir Hatları (City Lines)**. The main ferry terminus on the European side is at Eminönü. Destinations include Haydarpaşa, Kadıköy and Üsküdar on the Asian shore. On the west side of the Galata Bridge is the pier for ferries sailing up the Golden Horn.

Another main terminus is Karaköy, situated opposite Eminönü; and from here ferries run to Haydarpaşa and Kadıköy. The international dock,

where cruise liners berth, is also located here.

There are ferries every 15 minutes or so from Eminönü to Kadıköy between 7am and 9pm, and from Eminönü to Üsküdar from 6am to 11:30pm. Comprehensive timetables are available online or from ticket booths at each ferry terminal.

A number of craft run by private companies such as **Dentur** and **Turyol** cross the Bosphorus and Golden Horn at various points and run up the Bosphorus. These routes are also served by İDO ferries, but private motor boats are more frequent, though slightly more expensive. Note that all motor boats accept only the Istanbulkart or tokens.

The modern, Swedish-built catamarans known as sea buses (deniz otobüsleri) are run by the **Istanbul Sea Bus Company** (İDO). Their interiors resemble aircraft cabins, with long rows of reclining seats, piped music and air conditioning. Sea buses are considerably faster and more comfortable than ferries, but they cost about three times as much. The most useful route is the one to the Princes' Islands (6–12 crossings daily).

There are 27 designated docks for water taxis across the city. To get a water taxi, either call a company such as **Deniz Taksi** or book online.

Buying Boat Tickets

For ferries and sea buses, buy a flat-fare token (jeton) from the booth at the pier. A ferry ticket costs 3 lira, while the sea bus to the Princes' Islands is 9 lira. You can use jetons for all local trips. Better still, use the Istanbulkart (see p397), which works out cheaper and makes boarding quicker. You cannot use the Istanbulkart for the Bosphorus trip; tickets cost 20 lira.

To enter the pier, put the jeton into the slot beside the turnstile, and then wait in the boarding hall for a boat.

Sign for the Metro

The Bosphorus Cruise

Istanbul Şehir Hatları runs daily excursions up the Bosphorus. They are very popular in the summer, especially at weekends, so arrive early to ensure that you get a deck seat with a view. The long Bosphorus Cruise costs 25 lira and is a 7-hour round trip. Light refreshments are served, with a lunch stop at the fishing village of Anadolu Kavağı. There is also a 2-hour version, going as far as the second Bosphorus bridge, costing 10 lira.

Alternatives to the official Bosphorus trip include the small private boats that also depart from Eminönü, just west of the Galata Bridge. However, they only offer the equivalent of Şehir Hatları's short cruise and are slightly more expensive. These only go halfway up the strait and do not stop on the way. You can also book a private cruise with a company such as **Hatsail Tourism**. For more on the Bosphorus cruise, see pp130–31.

DIRECTORY

Tramway

Istanbul Transportation Co
Tel (0212) 568 99 70 or 444 00 88.
[w] istanbul-ulasim.com.tr

Ferries, Sea Buses, Private Boats and Water Taxis

Deniz Taksi (Water taxis)
Tel (0212) 444 44 98.
[w] deniztaksi.com

Dentur
Tel (0212) 258 93 14 or (0216) 444 63 36.
[w] denturavrasya.com

Istanbul Sea Bus Company
Tel (0212) 444 44 36.
[w] ido.com.tr

Şehir Hatları (City Lines)
Tel 444 18 51.
[w] sehirhatlari.com.tr

Turyol
Tel (0212) 251 44 21.
[w] turyol.com

The Bosphorus Cruise

Hatsail Tourism
Tel (0212) 241 62 50/51.
[w] hatsail.com

General Index

Page (numbers) in **bold** type refer to
main entries

İznik tiles (cont.)
Prince's Mosque (Istanbul) 103
Rüstem Paşa Mosque (Istanbul) 100, **102**
Sokollu Mehmet Paşa Mosque (Istanbul) 96

J

Jandarma 382, 383
Janissaries 59, **60**, 61, 133
Jansen, Hermann 241
Jazz 136, 368
Jewellery
shopping for 134, 135, 363, 364
Jews 118, 237
John II Comnenus, Emperor 89
John the Evangelist, St 184, 186
Julian, Emperor 244
Justin II, Emperor 162
Justinian, Emperor 54–5
Basilica of St John (Selçuk) 184
Byzantine Great Palace (Istanbul) 96
Haghia Sophia (Istanbul) 86
SS Sergius and Bacchus (Istanbul) 96–7
Justinianopolis *see* Sivrihisar

K

Kaaba (Mecca) 37
Kabatepe Information Point (Gallipoli Peninsula) 172
Kaçkar Mountains National Park 27
Kadesh, Treaty of 77
Kadıkalesi 202
Kafkasör Culture and Arts Festival (Artvin) 39, 279
Kahramanmaraş 309
restaurants 361
Kâhta 308
hotels 339
Kale (Simena) 14, 220
Kalehöyük 297
Kalenderhane Mosque (Istanbul) 77, 103
Kalkan 14, **218**
hotels 336
restaurants 355
Kalkanlı Mountains 277
Kalpakçılar Başı Caddesi (Istanbul) 109
Kanlıdivane 233
Karaalioğlu Park (Antalya) 223
Karacasu
restaurants 353
Karagöl-Sahara National Park 279
Karagöz shadow puppet theatre 30, 155, 166, 167, 168
Karaman Mihrab (Archaeological Museum, Istanbul) 76
Karanlık Church (Göreme Open-Air Museum) 289
Karatay Museum (Konya) 15, 255
Karatepe 236
Karballa Hotel (Güzelyurt) 296
Karlowitz, Treaty of 60

Kars 319
hotels 339
restaurants 361
Kartalkaya 250
Kaş 14, **218**, 305, 306
events 40
hotels 336
restaurants 355
Kaş-Lycia Culture and Art Festival (Kaş) 40
Kasaba 269
Kasım Padişah Mosque (Diyarbakır) 314
Kastamonu 268–9
restaurants 359
Kavaklıdere area (Ankara) 249
Kayaköy 2–3, 14, **216**
restaurants 355
Kaymaklı 286, 287
Kayseri 281, 282, **294–5**
hotels 338
map 295
restaurants 361
Kazdağlıoğlu Mosque (Safranbolu) 272
Kebab houses 340
Keçibükü 207
Kekova Island 14, 220
Kemaliye 323
Kemer
hotels 336
Kemerhisar 293
Kervansarays 28–9
Kılıç Arslan II, Sultan 56
Villa of (Konya) 254
Kılıç Kalkan (spoon dance) 371
Kilims *see* Carpets and kilims
Kınalıada (Princes' Islands) 162
King's Gate (Boğazkale) 283, **301**
Kırkpınar Festival and Grease-Wrestling Championship (Edirne) 39, 368, 369
Kırşehir 297
restaurants 361
Kitchens (Topkapı Palace, Istanbul) 72
Kızılcahamam 250
Kızkalesi 232–3
Kızlar Monastery (Göreme Open-Air Museum) 288
Kızlarağası Han (İzmir) 29, 182
Knidos 206
Knights of St John 184, 198, 200, 231
Knights Templar 231
Koca Sinan Paşa
tomb 107
Kocatepe Mosque (Ankara) 243, **249**
Konak (mansion house) 35
Konak Clock Tower (İzmir) 182
Konak Mosque (İzmir) 182
Konya 15, 56, 57, 241, 242, **254–7**
events 41
hotels 337
restaurants 358
Street-by-Street map 254–5
Konya Fairground 254
Köprülü Mehmet Paşa Mosque (Safranbolu) 272
Köprülü National Park 224

Koran 32, 36, 37, 259
Korean War 248
Kösedağ 57
Kossuth House Museum (Kütahya) 262
Köyceğiz 14, 214–15
Koza Han (Bursa) 169
Koza Park (Bursa) 168
Küçükkuyu Adatepe Köyü
restaurants 353
Külliye (mosque complex) **36**, 195
Kültepe 47, **295**
Kümbet 261
Kurban Bayramı (Sugar Festival) 40
Kurds 63
Kürsü (throne in mosque) 37
Kurşunlu Mosque (Nevşehir) 286
Kurukahveci Mehmet Efendi (Istanbul) 100
Kuş Gölü lake 163
Kuşadası 13, 175, **185**
hotels 334
restaurants 353
Kuşcenneti National Park *see* Bird Paradise National Park
Kütahya 241, **262–3**
hotels 337
map 263
restaurants 358
tiles and ceramics 262

L

Labarna Hattushili I, King 48
Labour and Solidarity Day (national holiday) 41
Labranda 196–7
Lagina 197
Lake District 258
Lakes *see* by name
Lala Mustafa Paşa Mosque (Erzurum) 322
Landscape 24–5
Language 21, 62, 381
Hittite 236
Lara
hotels 336
The Last Judgment (fresco) (St Saviour in Chora, Istanbul) 123
Latifoğlu House (Tokat) 299
Latmos, Mount 196
Lausanne, Treaty of 62
Leander's Tower (Istanbul) 128
Leather goods
shopping for 134, 135, 365
Lelegians 202, 203
Leo VI (the Wise), Emperor 88
Lepanto, Battle of 59
Letoön 216, 218
Libraries
Library of Ahmet III (Topkapı Palace, Istanbul) 73
Library of Celsus (Ephesus) 20, **186**
Library of Mahmut I (Haghia Sophia, Istanbul) 88
Library Ruins, Bergama 181

Acknowledgments

Dorling Kindersley would like to thank the following people whose contributions and assistance have made the preparation of this book possible:

Main Contributor
Suzanne Swan graduated from Queen's University in Kingston, Ontario, Canada, and has lived in Turkey since 1990. She was contributing editor of *Antalya, the Guide* for two years and contributed to many articles and books on Turkey, including *Globetrotter Travel Guide to Turkey* and *Insight Guide to the Turkish Coast*. She is the Turkish correspondent for a trade publisher.

Contributors and Consultants
Dominic Whiting, a freelance writer-photographer, lived in Turkey for four years. He wrote *Footprints Turkey Handbook*, was a co-author of Time Out's *Istanbul City Guide*, and updated the *DK Eyewitness Guide to Istanbul*.
Dr Caroline Finkel is an Ottoman historian and academic researcher.
Dr Bianka Ralle has an MA in German Studies and worked in journalism as well as teaching and training programmes for developing countries. She was a consultant on Turkey for the Organization for Economic Cooperation and Development (OECD). Her doctoral thesis was on migration and modernization in Turkey.
Kate Clow was educated in the UK, but completed her MBA at Istanbul University in 1991 and stayed in Turkey. She has contributed to the *Rough Guide to Turkey*, *Top Treks of the World* and *Cornucopia Magazine*, and is the originator of the Lycian Way and St Paul Trail walks.
Terrance Duggan walked from Greece to Egypt in 1988–89, in the footsteps of Alexander the Great. A scholar and painter, he has written widely on Islamic and Turkish culture and art. His paintings of Seljuk and Ottoman designs have been exhibited in London, Istanbul and Italy.
Terry Richardson studied classics at Sheffield University, England. He has contributed to *Rough Guide to Turkey* and *Footprints Guide* and photographed for *Cornucopia Magazine* and *The Lycian Way*.
Nilüfer Tünay has a degree in Communication Technology, worked in the Turkish media sector and represented *Sea Trades Magazine* in Turkey. She is now retired.
Molly McNailly-Burke was Turkish correspondent for the *Irish Times* and a contributor to the *Insight* and *Columbus Guides*. She now lives in Hertfordshire, England.
Ronnie Askey-Doran edited a satirical broadsheet in Istanbul and now lives in her native Australia.
Christopher Gardner is a botanist and horticulturist who lives in England.
Rosie Ayliffe lived in Turkey for three years while working as a freelance writer in Istanbul. She was one of the authors of *Rough Guide to Turkey*, and contributed to the *Rough Guide to France*, *Time Out*'s London guides and the *DK Eyewitness Guide to Istanbul*.
Rose Baring is a travel writer who has spent many months exploring Istanbul. She was co-author of *Essential Istanbul* (AA) and *DK Eyewitness Guide to Istanbul*.

Barnaby Rogerson has travelled and lectured extensively in the eastern Mediterranean. With Rose Baring he co-wrote *Essential Istanbul* (AA) and contributed to other AA and Cadogan guides, as well as *DK Eyewitness Guide to Istanbul*.
Canan Silay was a journalist on the Turkish daily, *Hürriyet*, and then editor of *Istanbul, The Guide* for many years. She has contributed to several books on Turkey, including the Insight guides to Istanbul, Turkey and the Turkish coast.

Additional Contributors
Sean Fraser, Lisa Greenstein, Alfred LeMaitre.

Additional Photography
DK Studio/Steve Gorton, Nigel Hicks, Izzet Keriber, Dave King, Fatih Mehmet Akdan, Ian O'Leary, Clive Streeter.

Additional Cartography
Globetrotter Travel Maps; Haluk Inci, İki Nokta.

Revisions Team
Rudolf Abraham, Asad Ali, Emma Anacootee, Lale Aran, Jasneet Arora, Claire Baranowski, Kate Berens, Tarryn Berry, Marta Bescos, Sonal Bhatt, Hilary Bird, Nadia Bonomally, Leizel Brown, Jo Cowen, Lellyn Creamer, Neha Dhingra, Claudia Dos Santos, Emer FitzGerald, Karen Fitzpatrick, Anna Freiberger, Rhiannon Furbear, Camilla Gersh, Emily Hatchwell, Jennifer Hattam, Barbara Isenberg, Shobhna Iyer, Jacky Jackson, Nazlı Koca, Priya Kukadia, Simon Lewis, Irene Lyford, Alison McGill, Ian Midson, Jason Mitchell, Claire Naylor, George Nimmo, Catherine Palmi, Reetu Pandey, Susie Peachey, Helen Peters, Nicole Pope, Pure Content, Marisa Renzullo, Terry Richardson, Ellen Root, Sands Publishing Solutions, Gerhardt van Rooyen, Reinette van Rooyen, Conrad van Dyk, Ed Wright.

Proofreader and Indexer Pat Barton.
Publishing Manager Kate Poole
Managing Editor Helen Townsend
DTP Designer Jason Little

Cartographer
Casper Morris

Special Assistance
Dorling Kindersley would like to thank staff at museums, mosques, churches, government departments, shops, hotels, restaurants, transport services and other organizations in Turkey for their help.
Particular thanks are due to: Dr Oğuz Alpözen, Bodrum Museum; Ibrahim Baştutan; Emine Bilirgen, Topkapı Palace, Istanbul; Erol Çakır, İzmir Archaeology Museum; Süleyman Çakır; Sühelya Demirci, Sivas Museum; Hikmet Denizli; The Museum of Anatolian Civilisations, Ankara; Ercihan Düzgünoğlu, TÜRSAB, Istanbul; Veysel Ediz, Çorum Museum; Dr Donald Frey, Institute of Nautical Archaeology, Bodrum; Iclal and Muzaffer Guler; Ali Harmankaya, Side Museum; Kaili Kidner and Lars-Eric Möre, Göreme; Joanna March and Hülya Soylu, Turkish Tourist Office, London; Güney Paksoy, Yedikule and Rumeli Hisar Museums; Feyza Sürücü, Ministry of Tourism,

Ankara; Ertan Tezgör, Turkish Grand National Assembly, Ankara; Feridun Ülker, Presidential Palace, Ankara; Ürcel Üzerin, Bursa Archaeological Museum; Varan Turizm; Üsküdar Folklore and Tourism Society (ÜFTUD), Kırklareli region; Neco Yoksulabakan.

The following staff of provincial tourist offices were very helpful: Reşit Akgüneş, Diyarbakır; Nebahat Alkaya, Bodrum; Bülent Aslan, Amasya; Ayten Aydın, Dalyan; Mustafa Aydın, Kaş; Nurten Celikkaptan, İzmir; Polat Cengis, Çeşme; Ali Fuat Er, Amasya; Fadime Hanim, Sivas; Yaşar Gül, Kastamonu; Yücel Güneş, Nevşehir; Mehmet Hacıağaoğlu, Side; Hüsnü Küçükaslan, Tokat; Murat Keleş, Amasya; Mustafa Kurt, Amasya; Ferhat Malcan, Kaş; Halis Öğüt, Konya; Şentürk Özdemiş, Erzurum; Sare Özdemir, Safranbolu; Safiye Portal, Safranbolu; Kadir Savçı, Çanakkale; Cennet Tazegül, Kars; Ahmet Tazegül, Erzurum; Yüksel Unal, Samsun; Mevlut Uyumaz, Afyon; Erdal Uzun, Kütahya; Zübeyir Yılmaz, Antakya; İbrahim Yakup, Çorum; Garip Yıl, Osmaniye; Zeki Bey, Işak Paşa Saray, Doğubeyazıt.

Other associations and individuals whose assistance was invaluable: Faik Akın, Turkish Airlines, Istanbul; Çetin Akant, Pedasa/Bodrum; Baki Akpınar, Göreme; Ali Baba Rent a Car, Kaş; Dr Şakir Aktaş, Kaş; Ali Baysan, Foto Ali, Kaş; Ahmet Burcu, Istanbul; Ahmet Büyük Yilmaz, Director, Turkish State Mint; Hasan Dağlı, Kaş; Fatih Demirhan, Istanbul Ulaşim A.Ş.; Zafer Emeksiz, Payas/Yakacık Municipality; Ali and Nazife Gülşen, Kaş; Cengiz Güzelmeriç, Kaş; Prof. Dr Wilhelm Gernot, Würzburg University; Hülya Gürkan, Minitcity Antalya; Kamil Koç Otobüs İşletmeleri A.Ş., Bursa; Ahmet Karaşahin, Adana; Lars-Eric Möre, Kapadokya Balloons, Göreme; Kerim Mat, Alanya; Abdullah Muslu, Kaş; Myriam Hanim, St Polycarp Church, İzmir; Dr Munise Ozan, Kaş; Muhammed Özcan, Kaş; Aydın Özmen, Turkish Central Bank, Ankara; Cihat Şahin, Fethiye; Diler Şaşmaz, DHL, Antalya; Mustafa and Sultan Soylu, Kaş; Tahsin Bey Konak Hotel, Safranbolu; İsmail Tezer, Kayseri Governor's Office; Ömer Tosun, Ottoman House, Göreme; Tuğrul Bilen Unal, Turkish State Mint, Istanbul; Osman Uvuç, Kayseri Esnaf; Veysel Bey, İznik Municipality; Bayram Yıldırım, Bodrum; Özkan Yaşar, Kaş; Yenişehir Palas Hotel, Istanbul; Sevilay Yilmaz, İzmir Kültür ve Turizm Müdürlüğü; Hüsnü Züber, Bursa.

Photography Permissions

Dorling Kindersley would like to thank the following for their kind permission to photograph at their establishments: General Directorate of Monuments and Museums; Ministry of Culture; Ministry for Religious Affairs; İstanbul Valiliği İl Kültür Müdürlüğü; İstanbul Valiliği İl Müftülüğü; Milli Saraylar Daire Başkanlığı and Edirne Valiliği İl Müftülüğü.

Picture Credits

a - above; b - below/bottom; c - centre; f - far; l - left; r - right; t - top.

The publisher would like to thank the following individuals, companies, and picture libraries for their kind permission to reproduce their photographs:

360 Entertainment Group: Sashah Anton Khan 329tr; **4Corners Images:** SIME/ Schmid Reinhard 12tr. **A Turizm Yayinlari:** Topkapı Palace Museum 74cr, 88tr; Archaeological Museum 76bl, 77tr. **Advertising Archives:** 112tr; **Aisa Archivo Icongrafico, S.A., Barcelona:** 73bl, 75tl, 123tc; **Akdeniz Hatay Sofrasi:** 348tl;

AKG Photo: 62crb; Erich Lessing 1c, 51tl/bl; Haghia Sophia, Istanbul *Emperor Constantine IX Monomachus*, mosaic detail from south gallery 44; Musée du Louvre *The Abduction of Helena* by Guido Reni 47cr; National Museum of Archaeology, Naples *Battle of Alexander*, Roman mosaic from Pompeii 50–51; Bibliothèque Nationale, Paris from the *Djamil el Tawarik* 57crb; British Library, from the *Westminster Abbey Psalter* 57bl; Bibliothèque Nationale, Paris from *Avis directif pour faire la passage d'Outremer* by Jean Mielot (1455) 58bl; Topkapı Palace Museum *Map of the World* (detail) by Piri Reis (c.1513) 59tr; Erich Lessing/Künsthistorisches Museum, Vienna *Portrait of Süleyman the Magnificent* (c.1530), circle of Titian 59cr; Museo Civic Correr, Venice *The Battle of Lepanto*, Venetian 59br; **Alamy Images:** Art Directors & TRIP/Brian Gibbs 387tl; David Crossland 344br; Luis Dafos 312tr; Robert Harding World Imagery 304; Ali Kabas 343c; Justin Kase zsixz 383cla, 387bc; David Kilpatrick 394tr; Marshall Ikonography 116; Steven May 396cra; Hercules Milas 280; John Stark 342cla, 343tl; Peter Titmuss 395tc; **Ancient Art and Architecture Collection Ltd:** 55cr. **Ankara tourist attractions:** 248tr; **Aquila Photographics:** Hanne and Jens Eriksen 163tr; D. Robinson 25bl; Juan Martín Simón 293c. **Paul Artus** 21t; **Atlas Geographic:** Zafer Kizilkaya 32cl, 202bl, 206bl, 207tl/cr; **Tahsin Aydoğmus:** 55bl, 85cr, 86tr, 89bl, 92tr, 100tr, 123c/cr, 284cl, 285bl.

Baylo Suites: 326bl; **Ralf Bergmann:** 421cl; **Bridgeman Art Library, London:** British Library, detail from the *Catalan Atlas* (1375) 28cl; Yale Center for British Art, Paul Mellon Collection *Caravan at Mylasa* (1845) by Richard Dadd 29tr; Topkapı Palace Museum *Aristotle Teaching*, from *The Better Sentences and Most Precious Dictions* 56tr; Stapleton Collection *Osman I* by John Young 58cl; Topkapı Palace Museum *Süleyman the Magnificent at the Battle of Mohacs in 1526* (1588), by Lokman 58–9; Victoria and Albert Museum, London: 165cbl/cbr; © **The Trustees of the British Museum:** 165cla; **Reg Butler:** 21t; **Buzz Grill & Beach Bar:** 355tc.

Çalikoğlu Reklam Turizm Ve Tİcaret Ltd.: 137tc; **Cave De Luxe:** 339bc; **Cercis Murat Konagi:** 361tc; **Christel Clear Picture Library:** © Detlef Jens 40tl; **Cicek Lokantasi:** 357tr; **Manuel Çitak:** 113cr, 135tr; **Ciya Kebap:** 349bc; **Corbis:** 8-9; Dave Bartruff 187t; Gardel Bertrand/Hemis 324-5; Marc Dozier/Hemis 316-7; Neil Farrin/JAI 150-1; Gavin Hellier/Robert Harding World Imagery 208; Sierpinski Jacques/Hemis 82; Robert Landau 394cl; Ron Watts 226-7; **Sylvia Cordaiy Photo Library:** © Anthony Bloomfield 31cl; © James de Bounevialle 24tr; ğ Gable 23c, 219cr; p.s. L infoot 38bl; © Jonathan Smith 17c, 31tc, 38ca, 62bc, 217tr, 369tr; © Chris Taylor 23bl, 219cl; Julian Worker 24cl; **Cosandere Tesisleri:** 359br.

Dervis 377cra; C.M. **Dixon Photo Resources:** 76tr; **Dreamstime.com:** Annminina 64-5; Cobalt88; Richard Connors 98; Dbdella 312c; Sinan Durdu 154; Lukasz Frackowiak 15bc; Gecce33 264; Nadiia Gerbish 110; Pavel Losevsky 313bl; Maxfx 174; Nastya22 378-9; Rangpl 11tl; Rvc5pogod 10br, 14tl; Sailorr 12bl; Softdreams 380cra; Ali Riza Yildiz 240; Alexander Zotov 323cl.

Abbie Enock: 21br; **Mary Evans Picture Library:** 49tl, 49c, 50cl, 52c, 52bl, 53c, 53bc, 53br, 55br, 56c, 58br, 59tl, 60tc, 60bc, 61tc, 61bl, 61br, 62tr, 173b, 178bc, 231cl/cr/bl/cb/br.

Ferahi Evler Butik Otel: 328tl; **ffotograff:** © Nick Tapsell 152tr; **First Army Hq, Istanbul:** 129bl; **Fondragonpearl Restaurant:** Grayling 352bc; **Dr Donald Frey:** 201bc.

Chris Gardner: 24tl/cr/clb/br, 25tl/cr; **Gaziantep Archaelogical Museum:** 311tr; **Getty Images:** AFP 18; Eyes-WideOpen: 396br; John and Tina Reid 290-21; Stone/ Travelpix Ltd 14bc; Lucas Vallecillos 68; **Ara Güler:** Mosaics Museum 91c; Topkapı Palace Museum 75cr, 95tr, 165bl; 367tr: Şems/ Güner: 127tr.

Halikarnas Disco: 198bc; **Sonia Halliday Photographs:** Bibliothèque Nationale, Madrid 55tr; engraved by Thomas Allom, painted by Laura Lushington 75br; Topkapı Palace Museum 90br; **Robert Harding Picture Library:** J.H.C; Adam Woolfitt 23tr, 25cl, 37cl, 105tr, 155b; **Hilton Worldwide:** Adana Hilton SA Hotel 335tc, 353tr; Hilton Bursa Convention Centre & Spa 328bl, 332tl, 350bl; **Hotel Les Ottomans:** 376br; **Hulton Getty Images:** 26br, 27tl, 63tc; **The Hutchison Library:** © Robert Francis 31bl; © Jeremy Horner 30bl; © Joan Klatchko 190b, 237b; © Tony Souter 32b, 33bl, 138.

Idakoy Ciftlik Evi: 352tl; **iDO:** 389c, 393ca; **Istanbul Foundation for Culture and Arts:** Istanbul Music Festival/Bennu Gerede 368bl; **Istanbul Library:** 80b; **Istanbul Metropolitan Municipality:** 383tl; **Istanbul Museum of Modern Art:** Murat Germen 115tr.

Michael Jenner Photography: 187cr.

Ali Kabbas: 5c, 30tr, 33tc, 34b, 41b, 125tl; **Museum of Turkish and Islamic Arts, Istanbul, from** Hadiqat al-Su'ada (17th century), Baghdad 33br; **Gürol Kara:** 108cl; **Karakol:** 346bc; **İzzet Keribar:** 4–5, 20b, 21tr/c, 22cl, 24bl, 29b, 30cr/br, 32ba, 32–3, 35tr/bl, 48cl, 66bl/br; 78tr, 126tr, 132br, 137t, 153tl, 171c, 186tr, 197br, 209tr, 210bl, 222tr, 232bl, 259crb, 267t/b, 276cra/bc, 281b, 285cr, 298tr, 314–15, 340bl, 374c; **Key Hotel:** 334; **Kinacizade Konagi:** 356bc; **Kippa Nature Photo Agency:** H. Glader 25bra; J. van Holten; 25bc; E. Pott 25br; **Koru Restaurant:** 358tc; **Kybele Hotel:** 329bc.

Lokanta Maya: 348bc; **José Luczyc-Wyhowska:** 366cr, 367cl/cr/bl/blc/brc/br.

Magnum: Topkapı Palace Museum/Ara Güler 67c; **Mimoza:** 351tc; **Alberto Modiano:** 23br, 30cl, 161b; with approval of ÜFTUD (Üsküdar Folklore and Tourism Society, Kırklareli region) 31bcr; **Museum of Anatolian Civilizations, Ankara:** 45bl, 45cb, 46tc, 46cr, 46bl, 46br, 47tc, 47bl, 47br, 48bl, 48bc, 49bc, 49br, 51ca, 52tl, 52br, 53tc, 246tr/bc, 247tl/cr/c, 300tr; **Museum Hotel:** 327tl.

Nar Lokanta: 347tl; **Natural History Museum, London:** 217crb. **Natur-Med thermal Springs and health resort:** 377tl; **Network Photo-graphers:** Gerard Sioen/Rapho 5tr, 219c, 319tr.

Old Greek House: 360bl; **Dick Osseman:** 311cla, 311b; **Güngör Özsoy:** 4br, 161tl/tr, 305b.

Pera Museum: 113cb; **Photo Access Photographic Library:** Harvey Lloyd 26–7; **Photobank:** Adrian Baker 60bl; Jeanetta Baker 20t, 38cb, 194t, 195tr, 195b, 202cl, 374bl; Peter Baker 31tr, 178tl, 180tr, 181br, 186cl/bl, 196bl, 341br; **Pictures Colour Library Ltd.:** 28bl, 177cra, 228bl, 366cl;

Rixos Hotels: Rixos Grand, Ankara 337br; Rixos Sungate 336tc.

Safranbolu Tourism office: 300bl; **Sahil Balik:** 359tc; **Neil Setchfield:** 152bl, 198cl, 274bl, 362cla; **George Simpson:** 41cr; **Jeroen Snijders:** 19b, 120tr, 362br; **Jeff Spiby:** 215bc; **Stella's Manzara:** 354bl; 354bl; **Superstock:** J.D. Dallet/age fotostock 252-3; Funkystock/age fotostock 2-3; Photononstop 270-1.

Golkhan Tan: 26tl/cl/c/cr/r/bl/bc, 200clb, 201crb; **TAV Investment Holding Co:** 388br; **TCDD - Turkish State Railways:** 392cla, 392b; **Travel Ink:** Marc Dubin 27b, 191b, 196tr; Ken Gibson 175b; Simon Reddy 41t; **Trip Photographic Library:** 157tr; **Turkey Garantibank:** 384cla; **Turk Telekom:** 386tr.

El Vino: 333bc, 351br.

Andrew Wheeler: 35cl, 363tl; **Peter Wilson:** 74c, 89cl, 89tr, 93tl, 122cl.

Yelken Cafe: 350tl.

Zorlu Grand Hotel: 326cra; 338tr.

Front Endpaper
Alamy Images: Robert Harding World Imagery Rbr; Hercules Milas Rbc; **Corbis:** Gavin Hellier/Robert Harding World Imagery Rbl; Sierpinski Jacques/Hemis Lbl; **Dreamstime.com:** Richard Connors Lbr; Sinan Durdu Ltl; Gece33 Rtl; Nadiia Gerbish Lfbr; Maxfx Ltc; Ali Riza Yildiz Ltr; **Getty Images:** Lucas Vallecillos Lfbl.

Jacket
Front and spine - **Superstock:** Funkystock
All other images © Dorling Kindersley. For further information see www.DKimages.com.

Special Editions of DK Travel Guides

DK Travel Guides can be purchased in bulk quantities at discounted prices for use in promotions or as premiums. We are also able to offer special editions and personalized jackets, corporate imprints, and excerpts from all of our books, tailored specifically to meet your own needs.

To find out more, please contact:
in the United States **SpecialSales@dk.com**
in the UK **travelspecialsales@uk.dk.com**
in Canada DK Special Sales at **general@ tourmaline.ca**
in Australia **business.development@pearson. com.au**

Phrase Book

Pronunciation

Turkish uses a Roman alphabet. It has 29 letters: 8 vowels and 21 consonants. Letters that differ from the English alphabet are: **c**, pronounced "j" as in "jolly"; **ç**, pronounced "ch" as in "church"; **ğ**, which lengthens the preceding vowel and is not pronounced; **ı**, pronounced "uh"; **ö**, pronounced "ur" (like the sound in "further"); **ş**, pronounced "sh" as in "ship"; **ü**, pronounced "ew" as in "few".

In an Emergency

Help!	**İmdat!**	eem-**dat**
Stop!	**Dur!**	door
Call a doctor!	**Bir doktor çağrın!**	beer dok-**tor** chah-ruhn
Call an ambulance!	**Bir ambulans çağrın!**	beer am-boo-**lans** chah-ruhn
Call the police!	**Polis çağrın!**	po-**lees chah**-ruhn
Fire!	**Yangın!**	yan-**guhn**
Where is the nearest telephone?	**En yakın telefon nerede?**	en ya-**kuhn** teh-leh-**fon** neh-reh-deh
Where is the nearest hospital?	**En yakın hastane nerede?**	en ya-**kuhn** has-ta-**neh** neh-reh-deh

Communication Essentials

Yes	**Evet**	eh-**vet**
No	**Hayır**	h-**eye**-uhr
Thank you	**Teşekkür ederim**	teh-shek-**kewr** eh-deh-reem
Please	**Lütfen**	**lewt**-fen
Excuse me	**Affedersiniz**	af-feh-der-see-neez
Hello	**Merhaba**	**mer**-ha-ba
Goodbye	**Hoşça kalın**	hosh-**cha ka**-luhn
Good morning	**Günaydın**	gewn-**'eye'**-**duhn**
Good evening	**İyi akşamlar**	ee-**yee** ak-sham-**lar**
Morning	**Sabah**	sa-**bah**
Afternoon	**Öğleden sonra**	ur-leh-**den son**-ra
Evening	**Akşam**	ak-**sham**
Yesterday	**Dün**	dewn
Today	**Bugün**	**boo**-gewn
Tomorrow	**Yarın**	**ya**-ruhn
Here	**Burada**	**boo**-ra-da
There	**Şurada**	**shoo**-ra-da
Over there	**Orada**	**o**-ra-da
What?	**Ne?**	neh
When?	**Ne zaman?**	neh za-man
Why?	**Neden**	neh-**den**
Where?	**Nerede**	**neh**-reh-deh

Useful Phrases

How are you?	**Nasılsınız?**	**na**-suhl-suh-nuhz
I'm fine	**İyiyim**	ee-**yee**-yeem
Pleased to meet you	**Memnun oldum**	mem-**noon ol**-doom
See you soon	**Görüşmek üzere**	gur-rewsh-**mek ew**-zeh-reh
That's fine	**Tamam**	ta-**mam**
Where is/are …?	**… nerede?**	…neh-**reh**-deh
How far is it to …?	**… ne kadar uzakta?**	…**ney** ka-dar
I want to go to …	**… a/e gitmek istiyorum**	…a/eh geet-**mek** ees-**tee**-yo-room
Do you speak English?	**İngilizce biliyor musunuz?**	een-gee-**leez**-jeh bee-**lee**-yor moo-soo-nooz?
I don't understand	**Anlamıyorum**	an-**la**-muh-yo-room
Can you help me?	**Bana yardım edebilir misiniz?**	ba-**na** yar-**duhm** eh-deh-bee-**leer** mee-see-neez?

Useful Words

big	**büyük**	bew-**yewk**
small	**küçük**	kew-**chewk**
hot	**sıcak**	suh-**jak**
cold	**soğuk**	soh-**ook**
good/well	**iyi**	ee-**yee**
bad	**kötü**	kur-**tew**
enough	**yeter**	yeh-**ter**
open	**açık**	a-**chuhk**
closed	**kapalı**	ka-pa-**luh**
left	**sol**	sol

right	**sağ**	saa
straight on	**doğru**	doh-**roo**
near	**yakın**	ya-**kuhn**
far	**uzak**	oo-**zak**
up	**yukarı**	yoo-ka-**ruh**
down	**aşağı**	a-shah-**uh**
early	**erken**	er-**ken**
late	**geç**	gech
entrance	**giriş**	gee-**reesh**
exit	**çıkış**	chuh-**kuhsh**
toilets	**tuvaletler**	too-va-let-**ler**
push	**itiniz**	**ee**-tee-neez
pull	**çekiniz**	**cheh**-kee-neez
more	**daha fazla**	da-**ha faz**-la
less	**daha az**	da-**ha** az
very	**çok**	chok

Shopping

How much is this?	**Ne kadar?**	ney ka-**dar**
I would like …	**… istiyorum**	… ees-**tee**-yo-room
Do you have …?	**… var mı?**	…**var** muh?
Do you take credit cards?	**Kredi kartı kabul ediyor musunuz?**	kreh-dee **kar**-tuh ka-**bool** eh-dee-yor moo-soo-nooz?
What time do you open/ close?	**Saat kaçta açılıyor/ kapanıyor?**	Sa-**at** kach-**ta** a-chuh-**luh**-yor/ ka-pa-**nuh**-yor
this one	**bunu**	boo-**noo**
that one	**şunu**	shoo-**noo**
expensive	**pahalı**	pa-ha-**luh**
cheap	**ucuz**	oo-**jooz**
size (clothes)	**beden**	beh-**den**
size (shoes)	**numara**	noo-ma-**ra**
white	**beyaz**	bay-**yaz**
black	**siyah**	see-**yah**
red	**kırmızı**	kuhr-muh-**zuh**
yellow	**sarı**	sa-**ruh**
green	**yeşil**	yeh-**sheel**
blue	**mavi**	ma-**vee**
brown	**kahverengi**	kah-**veh**-ren-gee
shop	**dükkan**	dewk-**kan**
till	**kasa**	ka-**sa**
bargaining	**pazarlık**	pa-zar-**luhk**
That's my last offer	**Daha fazla veremem**	da-**ha faz**-la veh-**reh**-mem

Types of Shop

antiques shop	**antikacı**	an-tee-ka-**juh**
bakery	**fırın**	fuh-**ruhn**
bank	**banka**	**ban**-ka
book shop	**kitapçı**	kee-tap-**chuh**
butcher's	**kasap**	ka-**sap**
cake shop	**pastane**	pas-ta-**neh**
chemist's/ pharmacy	**eczane**	ej-za-**neh**
fishmonger's	**balıkçı**	ba-luhk-**chuh**
greengrocer's	**manav**	ma-**nav**
grocery	**bakkal**	bak-**kal**
hairdresser's (ladies)	**kuaför**	kwaf-**fur**
(mens)	**berber**	ber-**ber**
leather shop	**derici**	deh-ree-**jee**
market/bazaar	**çarşı/pazar**	char-**shuh**/pa-**zar**
newsstand	**gazeteci**	ga-zeh-teh-**jee**
post office	**postane**	pos-ta-**neh**
shoe shop	**ayakkabıcı**	'eye'-**yak**-ka-buh-juh
stationer's	**kırtasiyeci**	kuhr-**ta**-see-yeh-jee
supermarket	**süpermarket**	sew-per-mar-**ket**
tailor	**terzi**	ter-**zee**
travel agency	**seyahat acentesi**	say-ya-**hat** a-jen-teh-**see**

Sightseeing

castle	**hisar**	hee-**sar**
church	**kilise**	kee-**lee**-seh
island	**ada**	a-**da**
mosque	**cami**	**ja**-mee
museum	**müze**	**mew**-zeh
palace	**saray**	sar-**'eye'**
park	**park**	park
square	**meydan**	may-**dan**
theological college	**medrese**	med-**reh**-seh
tomb	**türbe**	tewr-**beh**
tourist information office	**turizm danışma bürosu**	too-**reezm** da-nuhsh-**mah** **bew**-ro-soo
tower	**kule**	koo-**leh**

town hall	**belediye sarayı**	*beh-leh-dee-yeh sar-eye-uh*
Turkish bath	**hamam**	*ha-mam*

Transport

airport	**havalimanı**	*ha-va-lee-ma-nuh*
bus/coach	**otobüs**	*o-to-bewss*
bus stop	**otobüs durağı**	*o-to-bewss doo-ra-uh*
coach station	**otogar**	*o-to-gar*
minibus	**dolmuş**	*dol-moosh*
fare	**ücret**	*ewj-ret*
ferry	**vapur**	*va-poor*
sea bus	**deniz otobüsü**	*deh-neez o-to-bew-sew*
station	**istasyon**	*ees-tas-yon*
taxi	**taksi**	*tak-see*
ticket	**bilet**	*bee-let*
ticket office	**bilet gişesi**	*bee-let gee-sheh-see*
timetable	**tarife**	*ta-ree-feh*

Staying in a Hotel

Do you have a vacant room?	**Boş odanız var mı?**	*bosh o-da-nuhz var muh?*
double room	**iki kişilik bir oda**	*ee-kee kee-shee-leek beer o-da*
room with a double bed	**çift kişilik yataklı bir oda**	*cheeft kee-shee-leek ya-tak-luh beer o-da*
twin room	**çift yataklı bir oda**	*cheeft ya-tak-luh beer o-da*
for one person	**tek kişilik**	*tek kee-shee-leek*
room with a bath	**banyolu bir oda**	*ban-yo-loo beer o-da*
shower	**duş**	*doosh*
porter	**komi**	*ko-mee*
key	**anahtar**	*a-nah-tar*
room service	**oda servisi**	*o-da ser-vee-see*
I have a reservation	**Rezervasyonum var**	*reh-zer-vas-yo-noom var*
Does the price include breakfast?	**Fiyata kahvaltı dahil mi?**	*fee-ya-ta kah-val-tuh da-heel mee?*

Eating Out

A table for ...please	**... kişilik bir masa lütfen**	*... kee-shee-leek beer ma-sa lewt-fen*
I want to reserve a table	**Bir masa ayırtmak istiyorum**	*beer ma-sa eye'-uhrt-mak ees-tee-yo-room*
The bill please	**Hesap lütfen**	*heh-sap lewt-fen*
I am a vegetarian	**Et yemiyorum**	*et yeh-mee-yo-room*
restaurant	**lokanta**	*lo-kan-ta*
waiter	**garson**	*gar-son*
menu	**yemek listesi**	*ye-meklees-teh-see*
fixed-price menu	**fiks menü**	*feeks meh-new*
wine list	**şarap listesi**	*sha-raplees-teh-see*
breakfast	**kahvaltı**	*kah-val-tuh*
lunch	**öğle yemeği**	*ur-leh-yeh-meh-ee*
dinner	**akşam yemeği**	*ak-sham yeh-meh-ee*
starter	**meze**	*meh-zeh*
main course	**ana yemek**	*a-na yeh-mek*
dish of the day	**günün yemeği**	*gewn-ewn yeh-meh-ee*
dessert	**tatlı**	*tat-luh*
rare	**az pişmiş**	*az peesh-meesh*
well done	**iyi pişmiş**	*ee-yee peesh-meesh*
glass	**bardak**	*bar-dak*
bottle	**şişe**	*shee-sheh*
knife	**bıçak**	*buh-chak*
fork	**çatal**	*cha-tal*
spoon	**kaşık**	*ka-shuhk*

Menu Decoder

badem	*ba-dem*	almond
bal	*bal*	honey
balık	*ba-luhk*	fish
bira	*bee-ra*	beer
bonfile	*bon-fee-leh*	fillet steak
buz	*booz*	ice
çay	*ch-'eye'*	tea
çilek	*chee-lek*	strawberry
çorba	*chor-ba*	soup
dana eti	*da-na eh-tee*	veal
dondurma	*don-door-ma*	ice cream
ekmek	*ek-mek*	bread
elma	*el-ma*	apple
et	*et*	meat
fasulye	*fa-sool-yeh*	beans
fırında	*fuh-ruhn-da*	roast
fıstık	*fuhs-tuhk*	pistachio nuts
gazoz	*ga-zoz*	fizzy drink
hurma	*hoor-ma*	dates
içki	*eech-kee*	alcohol
incir	*een-jeer*	figs
ızgara	*uhz-ga-ra*	charcoal grilled
kahve	*kah-veh*	coffee
kara biber	*ka-ra bee-ber*	black pepper
karışık	*ka-ruh-shuhk*	mixed
karpuz	*kar-pooz*	water melon
kavun	*ka-voon*	melon
kayısı	*k-'eye'-uh-suh*	apricots
kaymak	*k-'eye'-mak*	cream
kıyma	*kuhy-ma*	minced meat
kızartma	*kuh-zart-ma*	fried
köfte	*kurf-teh*	meatballs
kuru	*koo-roo*	dried
kuzu eti	*koo-zoo eh-tee*	lamb
lokum	*lo-koom*	Turkish delight
maden suyu	*ma-den soo-yoo*	mineral water (fizzy)
meyve suyu	*may-veh soo-yoo*	fruit juice
midye	*meed-yeh*	mussels
muz	*mooz*	banana
patlıcan	*pat-luh-jan*	aubergine
peynir	*pay-neer*	cheese
pilav	*pee-lav*	rice
piliç	*pee-leech*	roast chicken
şarap	*sha-rap*	wine
sebze	*seb-zeh*	vegetables
şeftali	*shef-ta-lee*	peach
şeker	*sheh-ker*	sugar
su	*soo*	water
süt	*sewt*	milk
sütlü	*sewt-lew*	with milk
tavuk	*ta-vook*	chicken
tereyağı	*teh-reh-yah-uh*	butter
tuz	*tooz*	salt
üzüm	*ew-zewm*	grapes
vişne	*veesh-neh*	sour cherry
yoğurt	*yoh-urt*	yoghurt
yumurta	*yoo-moor-ta*	egg
zeytin	*zay-teen*	olives
zeytinyağı	*zay-teen-yah-uh*	olive oil

Numbers

0	**sıfır**	*suh-fuhr*
1	**bir**	*beer*
2	**iki**	*ee-kee*
3	**üç**	*ewch*
4	**dört**	*durt*
5	**beş**	*besh*
6	**altı**	*al-tuh*
7	**yedi**	*yeh-dee*
8	**sekiz**	*seh-keez*
9	**dokuz**	*doh-kooz*
10	**on**	*on*
11	**on bir**	*on beer*
12	**on iki**	*on ee-kee*
13	**on üç**	*on ewch*
14	**on dört**	*on durt*
15	**on beş**	*on besh*
16	**on altı**	*on al-tuh*
17	**on yedi**	*on yeh-dee*
18	**on sekiz**	*on seh-keez*
19	**on dokuz**	*on doh-kooz*
20	**yirmi**	*yeer-mee*
21	**yirmi bir**	*yeer-mee beer*
30	**otuz**	*o-tooz*
40	**kırk**	*kuhrk*
50	**elli**	*eh-lee*
60	**altmış**	*alt-muhsh*
70	**yetmiş**	*yet-meesh*
80	**seksen**	*sek-sen*
90	**doksan**	*dok-san*
100	**yüz**	*yewz*
110	**yüz on**	*yewz on*
200	**iki yüz**	*ee-kee yewz*
1,000	**bin**	*been*
100,000	**yüz bin**	*yewz been*
1,000,000	**bir milyon**	*beer meel-yon*

Time

one minute	**bir dakika**	*beer da-kee-ka*
one hour	**bir saat**	*beer sa-at*
half an-hour	**yarım saat**	*ya-ruhm sa-at*
day	**gün**	*gewn*
week	**hafta**	*haf-ta*
month	**ay**	*'eye'*
year	**yıl**	*yuhl*
Sunday	**pazar**	*pa-zar*
Monday	**pazartesi**	*pa-zar-teh-see*
Tuesday	**salı**	*sa-luh*
Wednesday	**çarşamba**	*char-sham-ba*
Thursday	**perşembe**	*per-shem-beh*
Friday	**cuma**	*joo-ma*
Saturday	**cumartesi**	*joo-mar-teh-see*